AF528289

Chambers General Knowledge Companion

Chambers

General Knowledge

Companion

hachette
INDIA

First published in 2025 by Hachette India
(Registered name: Hachette Book Publishing India Pvt. Ltd)
An Hachette UK company
www.hachetteindia.com

1

ISBN 978-93-5731-688-0

Hachette Book Publishing India Pvt. Ltd
4th & 5th Floors, Corporate Centre,
Plot No. 94, Sector 44, Gurugram 122003, India

Typeset in Minion Pro 9/12 by MPS Limited, Noida
Printed and bound in India by Manipal Technologies Limited

CONTRIBUTORS

- **History:** Sufyan bin Uzayr
- **Geography:** Paromita Roy
- **Sciences (Physics, Chemistry, and Biology):** Anupama Manral, Sanjay Mukerji, Saubhik Ghosh
- **Information and Communication Technology:** Anupama Manral, Saubhik Ghosh
- **Space and Space Technology:** Bhavana Chopra Singhal
- **Transport:** Bhavana Chopra Singhal
- **Indian Economy:** Sanjay Mukerji
- **Indian Polity:** Sangita Sharma Phukan
- **Defence and Security:** Bhavana Chopra Singhal
- **International Organizations and Indices:** Bhavana Chopra Singhal
- **Environment and Wildlife:** Saubhik Ghosh
- **Arts and Culture:** Gopali Bandyopadhyay
- **Sports:** Bhavana Chopra Singhal
- **National Insignia:** Bhavana Chopra Singhal

CONTENTS

PREFACE

In a world driven by the power of information, being *au courant* and staying well-informed is no longer an option – it is an absolute necessity and a basic skill set. Whether one is a curious learner, a competitive exam aspirant, or a professional preparing for interviews, a strong foundation in general knowledge can unlock countless doors of opportunity. *Chambers General Knowledge Companion* has been designed with this very purpose: to be a trusted guide in mastering essential concepts across a wide array of subjects.

This book is not just a repository of facts, it's a comprehensive across-the-board refresher. From sciences to arts, history to space technology, and national insignia to global organizations, it meticulously weaves together the core elements of general knowledge. Whether one is brushing up on the Indian economy or exploring the wonders of wildlife conservation, the content has been carefully crafted to make learning accessible, enjoyable, and relevant.

This 'must-know' manual delves into each domain with a focus on clarity, relevance, and precision, ensuring that the information is not only comprehensive but also easy to absorb. It bridges the gap between fragmented facts and cohesive understanding, offering a robust reference that is as engaging as it is informative.

What sets this book apart is its reader-centric approach. The inclusion of images, charts, and fact files transforms static information into dynamic learning. The timelines and visual aids – using lexicographic principles – not only enhance memory retention but also connect the dots between seemingly unrelated events and concepts, giving readers a broader perspective.

In today's fast-paced world, time is a precious commodity. With this in mind, we've have ensured that the book is as concise as it is comprehensive. Each topic is presented with a methodical pinpointed approach, providing readers with just the right amount of detail to grasp the essentials. At the same time, it serves as a springboard for deeper exploration, should the reader wish to delve further into any subject.

This book has been written to meet the diverse needs of its readers and to be the one-volume essential reference that every reader in the segment needs. Students preparing for competitive exams will find it an invaluable resource for revision. Professionals appearing for interviews can rely on it for quick conceptual clarity. And lifelong learners will appreciate it as a handy reference to explore the fascinating tapestry of human knowledge.

Chambers General Knowledge Companion will not only equip its readers with a solid foundation of facts and concepts but also ignite a lifelong passion for learning. After all, knowledge is power!

Welcome aboard this journey of discovery and mastery. We hope this book will be your constant companion in your quest for knowledge and excellence.

Happy Reading, Happy Learning!

1 HISTORY – World and Indian

World History

FIRST CENTURY

The first century CE was a significant period in human history, marked by profound developments in various regions.

In 0 CE, the traditional date for the birth of Jesus Christ is placed, though the exact year is debated among scholars. Modern estimates suggest that Jesus may have been born between 6 and 4 BCE, based on historical and astronomical evidence. The story of Jesus' birth is central to Christian theology, marking the beginning of the New Testament era.

From 1 to 14 CE, Augustus, the first Roman Emperor, continues to rule the Roman Empire. Born Gaius Octavius Thurinus, he was later known as Gaius Julius Caesar Octavianus after his adoption by Julius Caesar. Augustus established the principate, a system of monarchy headed by an emperor holding power for life. This period is characterized by relative peace and stability, known as the Pax Romana, which lasted for over two centuries. Augustus implemented significant reforms in taxation, developed networks of roads, established a standing army and the Praetorian Guard, and rebuilt much of the city of Rome.

In 4 CE, Augustus adopts Tiberius Claudius Nero, his stepson from his marriage to Livia Drusilla, as his successor. This adoption was part of Augustus' broader strategy to ensure a stable succession. Tiberius, a capable military leader and administrator, had already distinguished himself in various military campaigns. His adoption and designation as heir were intended to secure the continuation of Augustus' policies and the stability of the empire.

By 6 CE, Judaea becomes a Roman province under direct Roman administration. This transition occurs after the deposition of Herod Archelaus, the ethnarch of Samaria, Judea, and Idumea, by Augustus. Judaea is then governed by Roman prefects and procurators. The change in administration leads to tensions and unrest among the Jewish population, who chafed under Roman rule and the

heavy taxes imposed by the empire. This period sees the rise of various Jewish sects and movements, including the Zealots, who advocated for armed resistance against Roman occupation.

In 9 CE, the Battle of the Teutoburg Forest marks a significant event in Roman history. Roman legions led by Publius Quinctilius Varus are ambushed and decisively defeated by Germanic tribes under the leadership of Arminius, a chieftain of the Cherusci who had previously served as an officer in the Roman auxiliary forces. The battle takes place in the dense forests of modern-day Germany, where the Roman legions, unfamiliar with the terrain and stretched out in a long column, are attacked on all sides. The defeat results in the annihilation of three Roman legions (the XVII, XVIII, and XIX) and significant auxiliary forces, amounting to a loss of about 15,000 to 20,000 soldiers.

The Battle of the Teutoburg Forest halts Roman expansion into Germania and has profound psychological and strategic implications for the Roman Empire. Augustus reportedly lamented the loss, exclaiming, 'Quintili Vare, legiones redde!' ('Quinctilius Varus, give me back my legions!'). The defeat forces Rome to consolidate its borders along the Rhine River and adopt a more defensive posture in its Germanic territories. The battle also elevates Arminius to the status of a national hero among the Germanic tribes, symbolizing resistance against Roman imperialism.

Between 14 and 37 CE, following the death of Emperor Augustus, Tiberius becomes the second Roman Emperor. Tiberius, born Tiberius Claudius Nero, is a capable and experienced military leader who had already proven himself in various campaigns before becoming emperor. His reign is marked by a continuation of Augustus' policies, but also by increasing reliance on the Praetorian Guard and a growing sense of mistrust and paranoia, particularly after the death of his son Drusus Julius Caesar in 23 CE. Tiberius eventually retreats to the island of Capri in 26 CE, leaving much of the day-to-day administration of the empire to his trusted advisor, Lucius Aelius Sejanus, who later falls from favour and is executed in 31 CE for plotting against Tiberius.

From 26 to 36 CE, Pontius Pilate serves as the Roman governor of Judaea. Pilate is known for his harsh administration and his lack of sensitivity to Jewish customs, which leads to significant unrest. His tenure is most famously marked by the trial and crucifixion of Jesus Christ, an event that takes place between 30 and 33 CE. The crucifixion of Jesus, considered by Christians to be the Son of God and the Messiah, becomes the cornerstone of Christianity. According to the New Testament, Jesus is arrested, tried, and sentenced to death by crucifixion under Pilate's governance. This event is seen as fulfilling Old Testament prophecies and becomes central to Christian belief in Jesus' resurrection and the promise of eternal life.

From 37 to 41 CE, Caligula, born Gaius Julius Caesar Augustus Germanicus, becomes the Roman Emperor following the death of Tiberius in 37 CE. Initially, Caligula's rule is welcomed with joy and optimism due to his family's legacy and his early acts of generosity. However, his reign quickly deteriorates into a period of extreme extravagance, cruelty, and erratic behaviour. Caligula's actions, such as declaring himself a god, engaging in lavish spending, and committing acts of violence and sexual misconduct, lead to widespread dissatisfaction among the Roman elite and the Praetorian Guard.

In 41 CE, Caligula is assassinated as part of a conspiracy involving the Praetorian Guard, senators, and courtiers. His assassination marks the end of his tumultuous and despotic rule. Following Caligula's death, his uncle Claudius, born Tiberius Claudius Drusus, is proclaimed Emperor by the Praetorian Guard. Claudius, who had been largely underestimated and considered an unlikely candidate for the throne due to his physical disabilities and scholarly interests, proves to be an effective and pragmatic ruler. His reign is marked by significant administrative reforms, the expansion of the Roman Empire through the conquest of Britain in 43 CE, and public works projects, including the construction of new aqueducts and roads.

Claudius' rule brings relative stability and continued prosperity to the Roman Empire, contrasting sharply with the chaotic and tyrannical reign of his predecessor, Caligula.

Between 41 and 54 CE, the Roman invasion of Britain begins under Emperor Claudius in 43 CE. This marks a significant expansion of Roman territory. Claudius, who had been seen as a relatively weak ruler, enhances his prestige through the successful campaign. Roman forces, led by General Aulus Plautius, defeat various British tribes, establishing Roman control over parts of the island and setting up the province of Britannia. Claudius' reign sees the construction of many important public works and administrative reforms.

Claudius dies in 54 CE, possibly poisoned by his wife Agrippina the Younger, who seeks to secure the throne for her son Nero. Nero becomes Emperor at the age of 16, with Agrippina initially holding significant influence over his rule. During Nero's reign from 54 to 68 CE, he becomes known for his artistic ambitions, extravagant lifestyle, and tyrannical behaviour. In 64 CE, the Great Fire of Rome occurs, destroying much of the city. Nero blames the Christians for the fire, leading to severe persecution. This event is a significant moment in the history of early Christianity. Nero's increasingly erratic and despotic rule leads to widespread discontent. In 68 CE, facing rebellion and loss of support from the Senate and the military, Nero commits suicide, ending the Julio-Claudian dynasty.

The year 69 CE is known as the Year of the Four Emperors, with a rapid succession of rulers: Galba, Otho, Vitellius, and Vespasian. This year of civil war and political chaos ultimately ends with Vespasian becoming Emperor. Vespasian establishes the Flavian dynasty and brings stability to the empire. Between 69 and 79 CE, during the First Jewish-Roman War, Roman forces led by Titus, Vespasian's son, destroy the Second Temple in Jerusalem in 70 CE. This event is a pivotal moment in Jewish history, leading to significant changes in Jewish religious practices and the dispersion of Jewish communities.

In 79 CE, Mount Vesuvius erupts, burying the cities of Pompeii and Herculaneum under ash and pumice. This catastrophic event preserves the cities, providing a unique archaeological record of Roman life.

From 79 to 81 CE, Titus becomes Roman Emperor following the death of Vespasian. Titus is known for completing the Colosseum and providing aid to those affected by the eruption of Mount Vesuvius. His short reign is marked by his popularity and effectiveness as a ruler. Domitian, Titus' brother, succeeds him as Emperor in 81 CE. Domitian's reign from 81 to 96 CE is characterized by a more autocratic style of governance and significant building projects. However, his increasing despotism and conflicts with the Senate lead to his assassination in 96 CE.

Nerva becomes Emperor in 96 CE, marking the beginning of the Nerva-Antonine dynasty. His brief reign from 96 to 98 CE is marked by efforts to restore senatorial authority and stabilize the empire after Domitian's autocratic rule. Upon Nerva's death in 98 CE, Trajan becomes Emperor. Trajan is one of the 'Five Good Emperors', known for his military conquests, including the expansion into Dacia (modern-day Romania), and significant public building projects.

During the first century CE, the Roman Empire experiences the Pax Romana (Roman Peace) period, which lasts until 180 CE. This era is characterized by relative stability, prosperity, and minimal expansion, although notable conquests include Britain and parts of the Middle East. Significant architectural works, such as the Colosseum, begin during this century, showcasing Roman engineering and cultural achievements. Roman law and culture spread throughout the empire, influencing various aspects of life in conquered territories.

The rise of Christianity is marked by Jesus Christ's teachings and crucifixion, leading to the formation of the Christian religion. His followers, the Apostles, spread his teachings throughout the Roman Empire, establishing early Christian communities. The First Jewish-Roman War (66–73 CE) results in the destruction of the Second

Temple in Jerusalem, leading to significant changes in Jewish religious practices and the diaspora of Jewish communities.

In Asia, the Han dynasty rules China, marked by significant cultural and scientific advancements. The brief interruption of the Han dynasty by Emperor Wang Mang's Xin dynasty (9–23 CE) is followed by the Eastern Han period. This era sees developments in areas such as astronomy, engineering, and the arts. The Silk Road facilitates trade and cultural exchange between China and other regions.

In South Asia, the Kushan Empire rises, playing a crucial role in the development of trade along the Silk Road and the spread of Buddhism. The Kushan Empire serves as a cultural bridge between the Indian subcontinent, Central Asia, and China.

In the Americas, early civilizations, such as the Moche in present-day Peru, begin to develop complex societies with significant architectural achievements, including pyramids and sophisticated irrigation systems. These early developments lay the foundation for the rich cultural traditions that will continue to evolve in the region.

The first century CE was a transformative period that shaped the future of civilizations across the globe. The rise of the Roman Empire, the spread of Christianity, significant cultural and scientific advancements in Asia, and early developments in the Americas all contributed to the rich tapestry of history during this century.

SECOND CENTURY

The second century CE was a period of relative stability and prosperity for many regions, particularly within the Roman Empire. Here is an extensive note detailing major events that occurred during this century, organized chronologically:

From 98 to 117 CE, Trajan rules as the Roman Emperor. His reign is marked by significant military campaigns and expansion, which enhance the wealth and power of the Roman Empire. In 106 CE, Trajan successfully conquers Dacia, located in modern-day Romania, after a series of battles against King Decebalus. The annexation of Dacia brings substantial wealth to the empire through the acquisition of gold mines. Trajan also leads successful campaigns in the East, including the annexation of the Nabataean Kingdom, which becomes the Roman province of Arabia Petraea, and the capture of the Parthian capital, Ctesiphon. Trajan's achievements in expanding the empire and his public building projects, such as Trajan's Forum, earn him a reputation as one of Rome's greatest emperors. In 117 CE,

Trajan dies while returning from a campaign, and his adopted son Hadrian becomes Emperor.

Between 117 and 138 CE, Hadrian rules as Emperor. Unlike his predecessor, Hadrian focuses on consolidating and fortifying the empire's borders rather than pursuing further expansion. One of his most famous constructions is Hadrian's Wall in Britain, built around 122 CE to protect the northern boundary of the Roman province of Britannia from Pictish tribes. Hadrian also commissions the rebuilding of the Pantheon in Rome and constructs the Temple of Venus and Roma. His reign is marked by relative peace and cultural flourishing, with Hadrian being a patron of the arts and architecture. He travels extensively throughout the empire, inspecting and improving its defences and fostering good relations with the provinces.

From 138 to 161 CE, Antoninus Pius becomes Emperor following Hadrian's death. Antoninus Pius' reign is notable for its internal stability and efficient governance. He is known for his administrative reforms and efforts to improve the legal system. Antoninus Pius continues the policies of his predecessors by maintaining the empire's borders and avoiding unnecessary military conflicts. His reign is a period of relative tranquillity and economic prosperity, earning him the reputation of a benevolent and capable ruler.

From 161 to 180 CE, Marcus Aurelius and Lucius Verus co-rule the Roman Empire, with Marcus Aurelius eventually becoming the sole emperor after Lucius Verus' death in 169 CE. Marcus Aurelius is known for his philosophical writings, particularly the *Meditations*, which reflect his Stoic beliefs. His reign, however, is marked by numerous military conflicts, including the Marcomannic Wars against Germanic tribes and the Parthian War in the East. Despite these challenges, Marcus Aurelius is remembered as a wise and just ruler who sought to maintain the stability and integrity of the empire.

In 180 CE, Commodus, the son of Marcus Aurelius, becomes Emperor. Commodus' reign is characterized by increasing autocracy and instability. His focus on personal luxury and the spectacle of gladiatorial games leads to neglect of the empire's administrative and military needs. Commodus' erratic behaviour and the resulting political turmoil eventually lead to his assassination in 192 CE, marking the end of the Antonine dynasty.

During the 2nd century CE, the Roman Empire experiences the height of the Pax Romana, a period of relative peace and stability that began under Augustus. The empire's extensive network of roads and sea routes facilitates trade and cultural exchange across its vast territories, contributing to economic prosperity and the spread of Roman law and culture. Significant architectural and engineering achievements, such as the construction of aqueducts, bridges, and monumental buildings, reflect the empire's advanced infrastructure and artistic accomplishments.

In the broader context of the ancient world, the second century CE also sees important developments in other regions. In China, the Han dynasty continues to rule, marked by scientific and cultural advancements. However, the dynasty faces internal challenges, including corruption and peasant uprisings, which eventually lead to its decline by the end of the century. The Kushan Empire in South Asia reaches its zenith during this period, playing a crucial role in the spread of Buddhism and facilitating trade along the Silk Road.

In summary, the second century CE is a transformative period characterized by the consolidation and fortification of the Roman Empire, significant cultural and architectural achievements, and relative peace and prosperity under a series of capable emperors. The events and developments of this century leave a lasting impact on the history and legacy of the Roman Empire and other civilizations across the globe.

The Antonine Plague, which scholars believe may have been smallpox, devastates the population from 165 to 180 CE, further weakening the empire's stability and economic productivity.

In 180 CE, Marcus Aurelius dies, and his son Commodus succeeds him as Emperor. Commodus' rule, lasting until 192 CE, is marked by his extravagant and erratic behaviour, which contrasts sharply with the philosophical and disciplined approach of his father. Commodus indulges in gladiatorial contests and lavish personal indulgences, leading to discontent among the Roman elite and the population at large. His reign initiates a period of decline characterized by corruption, political instability, and military setbacks.

Commodus' assassination in 192 CE triggers a brief period of civil war known as the Year of the Five Emperors (193 CE), culminating in the rise of Septimius Severus as Emperor. Septimius Severus, a capable military leader, restores stability to the empire and establishes the Severan dynasty, marking a transition from the Antonine period to a new era in Roman history.

Outside the Roman Empire, the second century CE witnesses significant developments across other regions:

- **China:** The Eastern Han dynasty continues to rule, achieving notable advancements in science, technology, and culture. The invention of paper by Cai Lun in 105 CE revolutionizes communication and record-keeping. However, internal strife, such as the Yellow Turban Rebellion in 184 CE, signals the beginning of the dynasty's decline.
- **South Asia:** The Kushan Empire reaches its zenith under Emperor Kanishka, who reigns from approximately 127 to 150 CE. Kanishka promotes Buddhism and facilitates the spread of Buddhist culture and art through the Gandhara region. The Kushans play a crucial role in facilitating trade along the Silk Road, connecting East and West.
- **Americas:** In Mesoamerica, the Teotihuacan civilization flourishes, evidenced by the construction of monumental architectural structures like the Pyramid of the Sun around 100 CE. Teotihuacan becomes a major urban centre and a hub of trade and cultural exchange in the pre-Columbian Americas.

Overall, the second century CE is a period of mixed fortunes: while the Roman

Empire experiences relative stability and cultural achievement under emperors like Antoninus Pius and Marcus Aurelius, challenges such as military conflicts and the Antonine Plague foreshadow the empire's eventual decline. Concurrently, developments in China, South Asia, and the Americas shape the broader landscape of global history, marking the century as a pivotal period of transformation and exchange across civilizations.

THIRD CENTURY

The Roman Empire experiences the Crisis of the Third Century, a period of severe military, political, and economic instability:

From 193 to 235 CE, the Severan dynasty rules the Roman Empire. Septimius Severus becomes Emperor in 193 CE after a brief civil war known as the Year of the Five Emperors. His reign focuses on military campaigns to secure the empire's frontiers and internal reforms to bolster the military's strength. After Septimius Severus' death in 211 CE, his sons Caracalla and Geta initially rule jointly. However, Caracalla murders Geta in 212 CE, becoming the sole emperor. Caracalla is notorious for instituting the Constitutio Antoniniana in 212 CE, which grants Roman citizenship to all free inhabitants of the empire in a bid to increase tax revenue. He is assassinated in 217 CE, leading to a period of instability characterized by short-lived emperors and continued internal strife.

From 235 to 284 CE, the Roman Empire plunges into the full throes of the Crisis of the Third Century. This period is marked by frequent changes of emperors, external invasions, internal rebellions, and economic decline. The empire faces significant threats from Germanic tribes, notably the Goths and Alamanni, as well as the powerful Sassanid Empire in the East. The internal turmoil culminates in the empire being briefly divided into three competing states:

- The Gallic Empire in the West, led by Postumus from 260 CE, encompassing Gaul, Britain, and parts of Hispania.
- The Palmyrene Empire in the East, ruled by Queen Zenobia from 267 CE, extending over Egypt, Syria, and parts of Asia Minor.
- The central Roman Empire, struggling to maintain control over its remaining territories in Italy and the Balkans.

In 260 CE, Emperor Valerian is captured by the Sassanid King Shapur I, a humiliating event that highlights the vulnerability of the Roman Empire to external threats. Valerian's capture and subsequent death in captivity exacerbate the empire's crisis, leading to further instability and challenges to central authority.

From 270 to 275 CE, Emperor Aurelian emerges as a pivotal figure in Roman history by restoring the empire's unity and stability. Aurelian undertakes successful military campaigns against both the

Palmyrene and Gallic Empires, reunifying the Roman territories under central authority. He also initiates significant administrative reforms and constructs the Aurelian Walls around Rome to fortify the city against external threats. Despite his efforts, Aurelian is assassinated in 275 CE, which plunges the empire once again into a period of uncertainty and internal conflict.

In 284 CE, Diocletian becomes Emperor and marks a turning point in Roman history. Diocletian's rise to power ushers in the beginning of the Tetrarchy, a system of rule by four emperors intended to stabilize the empire and manage its vast territories more effectively. Diocletian's reforms, including the division of imperial authority and the introduction of price controls and administrative reforms, aim to address the underlying issues that plagued the empire during the Crisis of the Third Century.

Overall, the third century CE is characterized by the profound challenges faced by the Roman Empire, including external invasions, internal rebellions, economic instability, and the fragmentation of political authority. The Crisis of the Third Century fundamentally alters the course of Roman history, setting the stage for reforms that will reshape the empire in the following centuries.

Diocletian's reign marks the end of the Crisis of the Third Century and the beginning of the Dominate period. Facing internal instability and external threats, Diocletian implements sweeping reforms to stabilize and strengthen the empire. Central to his reforms is the establishment of the Tetrarchy in 293 CE, dividing the empire into four regions, each governed by a co-emperor. This system, with two Augusti (senior emperors) and two Caesars (junior emperors), aimed to improve governance and defence against external invasions. Diocletian also restructured the administration, initiated economic reforms, and imposed price controls to address inflation. His efforts provided a brief period of stability after the tumultuous Crisis of the Third Century.

In 224 CE, Ardashir I establishes the Sassanid Empire after overthrowing the Parthians. The Sassanids quickly emerge as a formidable power in the Near East, frequently clashing with the Roman Empire. Under Shapur I (241–72 CE), the Sassanids achieve significant military successes, including the capture of Emperor Valerian in 260 CE, a major humiliation for Rome. The Sassanid Empire flourishes culturally and economically, becoming a centre of art, science, and trade in the region.

The Han dynasty, which had ruled China for centuries, collapses in 220 CE, leading to the Three Kingdoms period. This era is marked by the fragmentation

of China into three rival states: Wei, Shu, and Wu, each vying for supremacy. The period is characterized by intense military conflicts, political intrigue, and cultural development. The *Romance of the Three Kingdoms,* a later historical novel, romanticizes and popularizes the era, highlighting the struggles for power and alliances that defined this turbulent time.

In South Asia, the Kushan Empire declines during the third century CE, paving the way for the rise of the Gupta Empire towards the end of the century. The Gupta period (c. 320–550 CE) is often regarded as a golden age of Indian culture, marked by significant advancements in art, science, mathematics, and literature. The Gupta rulers patronize scholars and artists, fostering a flourishing intellectual and cultural environment that influences later Indian civilizations.

In the Americas, early civilizations continue to thrive. The Mayan civilization in Mesoamerica reaches its Classic Period during the third century CE, characterized by impressive achievements in architecture, astronomy, mathematics (including the concept of zero), and a complex writing system (glyphs). In the Andean region, the Moche civilization in present-day Peru continues its prosperous development, known for advanced irrigation systems, intricate ceramics, and skilled metalwork.

The third century CE was a period of significant instability and transformation, particularly within the Roman Empire during the Crisis of the Third Century. Despite these challenges, new powers like the Sassanid Empire emerged, while cultural and technological advancements continued across various regions. The era laid the foundation for future developments in governance, culture, and trade, shaping the course of history well beyond the third century CE.

FOURTH CENTURY

From 284 to 305 CE, the Roman Empire is governed by Emperor Diocletian, who undertakes substantial reforms to stabilize the empire following the Crisis of the Third Century. Diocletian institutes the Tetrarchy in 293 CE, dividing the empire into four regions, each ruled by a co-emperor (two Augusti and two Caesars), aiming to improve governance and defence against external threats. In 305 CE, Diocletian voluntarily abdicates, leading to a period of turmoil and power struggles known as the Tetrarchic Wars among his successors.

From 306 to 337 CE, Constantine the Great emerges as a dominant figure in Roman politics, eventually consolidating power to become the sole ruler of the Roman Empire. His reign is marked by several pivotal events:

- In 312 CE, Constantine achieves a decisive victory over Maxentius at the Battle of the Milvian Bridge, securing control over the Western Roman Empire. This battle is notable for Constantine's reported conversion to Christianity, influencing his subsequent policies.
- In 313 CE, Constantine issues the Edict of Milan, granting religious tolerance throughout the empire and effectively ending the persecution of Christians. This decree marks a significant turning point in Roman religious policy.
- In 324 CE, Constantine defeats his last remaining rival, Licinius, at the Battle of Chrysopolis, becoming the sole ruler of the entire Roman Empire.
- In 325 CE, Constantine convenes the First Council of Nicaea, a landmark event in Christian history. The council addresses theological disputes, particularly the Arian controversy, and leads to the formulation of the Nicene Creed, which establishes fundamental Christian doctrines.
- In 330 CE, Constantine establishes the new imperial capital at Byzantium, renaming it Constantinople (modern-day Istanbul). Constantinople becomes a flourishing centre of power, culture, and commerce, strategically located between Europe and Asia.

From 337 to 361 CE, Constantine's sons – Constantine II, Constantius II, and Constans – inherit different parts of the Roman Empire after his death. This division sparks power struggles and civil wars among the brothers, contributing to a period of instability. Constantius II ultimately emerges as the sole ruler and continues to govern until his death in 361 CE.

From 361 to 363 CE, Julian, known as Julian the Apostate, assumes the imperial throne. Julian attempts to revive paganism and reduce the influence of Christianity, reversing some of the policies of his predecessors. His short reign sees efforts to restore pagan religious practices and philosophical teachings. However, Julian dies in 363 CE during a campaign against the Sassanid Empire, and his death leads to the brief rule of Jovian, who reinstates Christianity as the state religion.

The fourth century CE is characterized by significant political, religious, and cultural transformations within the Roman Empire. The reign of Constantine the Great marks the triumph of Christianity and the establishment of Constantinople as a new imperial centre, while subsequent rulers grapple with internal divisions and external threats. The century sets the stage for further developments in the Byzantine Empire, Christian theology, and the evolution of European civilization.

From 364 to 375 CE, Valentinian I rules the Western Roman Empire, while his brother Valens rules the Eastern Roman Empire. Their reigns are characterized by military conflicts, including battles against Germanic tribes and the Goths. Valens suffers a major defeat and is killed at the Battle of Adrianople in 378 CE, a significant event that weakens the Eastern Roman Empire.

From 379 to 395 CE, Theodosius I, known as Theodosius the Great, becomes the last Emperor to rule over both the Eastern and Western Roman Empires. His reign is marked by the consolidation of Christianity as the state religion, including the banning of pagan practices. Theodosius convenes the Second Council of Constantinople in 381 CE, reaffirming the Nicene Creed and condemning Arianism. Upon his death in 395 CE, the Roman Empire is permanently divided into the Eastern Roman Empire (Byzantine Empire) and the Western Roman Empire.

In the Sassanid Empire, Shapur II rules from 309 to 379 CE, one of the longest reigns in Persian history. His rule is marked by military campaigns against the Romans and internal reforms that strengthen the empire. The Sassanid Empire becomes a significant cultural and economic power during this period, influencing trade and diplomacy across the Near East.

In China, the Jin dynasty continues until the early fourth century, followed by the Sixteen Kingdoms period (304–439 CE), characterized by fragmentation and warfare among various states. This period witnesses significant cultural and technological developments, including the spread of Buddhism in China, which becomes increasingly influential.

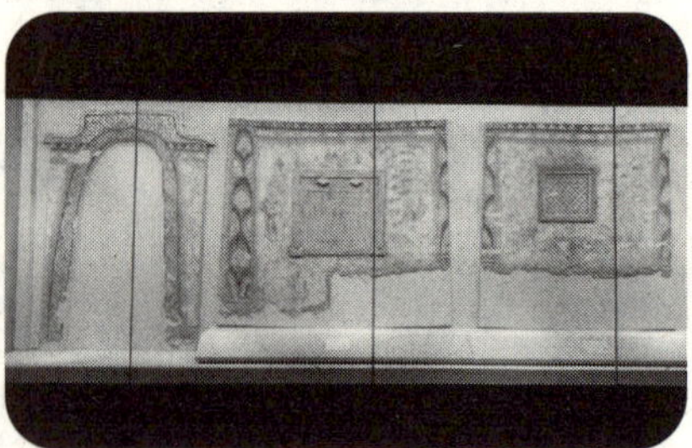

In South Asia, the Gupta Empire rises to prominence during the fourth century CE, marking a golden age of Indian culture, science, and art. Chandragupta I (r. 320–35 CE) and his successors, including Samudragupta (r. 335–75 CE) andChandragupta II (r. 375–415 CE), expand the empire through military conquests and patronize advancements in literature, astronomy, and mathematics. The Gupta period is renowned for its contributions to Hindu culture, including the development of the decimal system and the concept of zero.

In the Americas, early civilizations continue to thrive. The Mayan civilization in Mesoamerica reaches its Classic Period during the fourth century CE, characterized by the construction of impressive cities, pyramids, and temples. Advances in astronomy, mathematics (including the use of zero), and hieroglyphic writing further distinguish this period. In the Andean region, the Moche civilization in present-day Peru continues to flourish, known for their advanced art, architecture, and sophisticated irrigation systems.

The fourth century CE is a pivotal period marked by major transitions and significant events across various regions. In the Roman Empire, the establishment of Christianity as the state religion under Theodosius I and the subsequent division into Eastern and Western Empires shape the course of European history. The Sassanid Empire thrives under Shapur II, influencing politics and culture in the Near East. Meanwhile, in Asia and the Americas, cultural and technological advancements continue to flourish, setting the stage for future developments in these regions.

FIFTH CENTURY

The fifth century CE was marked by significant transitions and upheavals that reshaped the landscape of Europe and the Mediterranean. The century began with the Roman Empire divided into the Eastern Roman Empire, known as the Byzantine Empire, and the Western Roman Empire following the death of Emperor Theodosius I in 395 CE. This division set the stage for the dramatic events that would unfold over the next hundred years.

From 401 to 410 CE, the Visigoths, led by their king Alaric I, repeatedly invaded the territories of the Western Roman Empire. These invasions culminated in the sack of Rome in 410 CE, a significant event that not only symbolized the declining power and influence of the Roman Empire but also sent shockwaves throughout the ancient world. The sacking of Rome by the Visigoths was a profound psychological blow to the Roman populace and the wider world, highlighting the empire's inability to defend its own capital.

Meanwhile, from 429 to 439 CE, the Vandals, under the leadership of King Gaiseric, embarked on a major invasion of North Africa from their previous base in Spain. This campaign resulted in the rapid conquest of Roman territories in the region, including the critical city of Carthage in 439 CE. The establishment of the Vandal Kingdom in North Africa posed a significant threat to the Roman Empire's control of the Mediterranean, as the Vandals developed a formidable naval power that disrupted Roman shipping and trade routes.

The period from 434 to 453 CE was dominated by the fearsome incursions of the Huns, led by their notorious king Attila. Attila's campaigns spread devastation across the Roman Empire, threatening both the Eastern and Western Roman Empires. In 451 CE, a coalition of Roman and Germanic forces, led by the Roman general Flavius Aetius, confronted and defeated Attila at the Battle of the Catalaunian Plains, also known as the Battle of Châlons. This battle was one of the last major military victories for the Roman Empire and temporarily halted the advance of the Huns. However, Attila's death in 453 CE led to the rapid decline of the Hunnic Empire, which disintegrated without his unifying leadership.

In 455 CE, Rome experienced yet another catastrophic sack, this time at the hands of the Vandals under King Gaiseric. This second sack of Rome further underscored the vulnerability and weakening state of the Western Roman Empire. The inability to protect Rome, a city that had stood as the heart of the empire for centuries, highlighted the empire's continued decline and fragmentation.

The traditional date for the fall of the Western Roman Empire is 476 CE. In that year, Romulus Augustulus, the last Roman emperor of the West, was deposed by the Germanic chieftain Odoacer. Odoacer declared himself ruler of Italy, effectively ending the Western Roman Empire and marking the beginning of the Early Middle Ages in Western Europe. This event is often cited as the formal end of classical antiquity and the start of a new era in European history.

The fifth century CE thus stands out as a period of profound decline for the Western Roman Empire, beset by repeated invasions and internal turmoil. The rise of the Visigothic and Vandal kingdoms in Western Europe and North Africa, respectively, signalled a shift in power away from the Roman Empire. The invasions of Attila the Hun posed a significant threat but ultimately led to the fragmentation of the Hunnic Empire following his death. These events collectively marked a pivotal transition from the classical world of the Roman Empire to the medieval period, setting the stage for the development of new political, social, and cultural structures in Europe.

The fifth century CE was a period of significant transformation across various regions, characterized by the decline of some empires and the flourishing of others.

The Eastern Roman Empire, also known as the Byzantine Empire, experienced a period of consolidation and cultural achievement. From 408 to 450 CE, Emperor Theodosius II focused on fortifying the empire's defences, most notably overseeing the construction of the Theodosian Walls of Constantinople. These formidable walls provided enhanced protection for the capital and were instrumental in preserving the city's security for centuries. In 451 CE, the Council of Chalcedon was convened, defining the dual nature (both divine and human) of Jesus Christ. This council had a profound influence on Christian theology and led to significant theological debates and schisms within the church. Throughout the century, the Byzantine Empire continued to be a centre of culture, trade, and political stability in the Eastern Mediterranean, contrasting with the turmoil experienced by the Western Roman Empire.

In China, the collapse of the Eastern Jin dynasty in the early fifth century marked the beginning of the Northern and Southern Dynasties period, which lasted from 420 to 589 CE. This era was characterized by political fragmentation and regional conflicts, as various dynasties vied for control over different parts of China. Despite the political instability, there were significant cultural and technological advancements. The spread of Buddhism, which had been introduced to China earlier, continued to gain traction and influenced various aspects of Chinese culture, art, and philosophy.

South Asia saw the continued prosperity of the Gupta Empire, particularly under rulers like Kumaragupta I and Skandagupta. This period, often referred to as the golden age of Indian culture, science, and literature, was marked by remarkable achievements in various fields. However, in the late fifth century, the Gupta Empire began to face increasing pressure from Hunnic invasions. These invasions weakened the empire's influence in North

India, leading to its eventual decline and the rise of regional powers.

In the Americas, the Mayan civilization in Mesoamerica thrived during its Classic Period. This era was marked by the construction of impressive cities, significant advancements in astronomy, and the development of a complex writing system. The Mayans' achievements in mathematics and their sophisticated calendar system were particularly notable. Meanwhile, in the Andean region, the Moche civilization, known for its sophisticated art, architecture, and irrigation systems, began to decline. This decline may have been due to environmental changes and internal conflicts that disrupted their society.

The fifth century CE was thus a time of significant change and contrast across different regions. The decline of the Western Roman Empire, marked by repeated invasions and internal turmoil, stood in stark contrast to the relative stability and cultural achievements of the Byzantine Empire in the East. In Asia, political fragmentation in China coincided with cultural advancements, while South Asia experienced both the peak and subsequent decline of the Gupta Empire. In the Americas, Mesoamerican civilizations continued to advance, while the Andean region faced challenges that led to the decline of the Moche civilization. This century marked a pivotal transition from classical antiquity to the medieval era, with lasting impacts on global history and culture.

SIXTH CENTURY

The sixth century CE was a period of significant change and development across various regions. Here is an extensive note detailing major events that occurred during this century, organized chronologically:

From 527 to 565 CE, Emperor Justinian I reigns over the Byzantine Empire. His rule is marked by extensive reforms and military campaigns aimed at restoring the former glory of the Roman Empire. One of his most notable generals, Belisarius, reconquers the Vandal Kingdom in North Africa in 533–34 CE and then leads the Gothic War from 535 to 554 CE, resulting in the reconquest of Italy from the Ostrogoths. In 532 CE, Constantinople experiences the Nika Riots, which cause significant destruction and lead to the rebuilding of the Hagia Sophia, a masterpiece of Byzantine architecture. In 534 CE, Justinian's Code, or *Corpus Juris Civilis*, is published and becomes a foundational work for Western legal tradition. However, Justinian's reign also faces significant challenges, including the Plague of Justinian in 541–42 CE, which devastates the population.

In Western Europe, the early sixth century sees the Western Roman Empire remain fragmented into various Germanic kingdoms. These include the Ostrogoths in Italy, the Visigoths in Spain, and the Franks in Gaul. Clovis I of the Merovingian dynasty consolidates power over the Frankish tribes, converts to Christianity, and lays the foundation for what will become the Holy Roman Empire.

In South Asia, the Gupta Empire continues to decline, leading to political fragmentation and the rise of regional powers. The Chalukya dynasty rises in southern India, with Pulakeshin I establishing the dynasty around 543 CE. The Chalukyas become significant patrons of art and architecture.

China continues to experience the Northern and Southern Dynasties period until the reunification of China under the Sui dynasty. In 581 CE, Yang Jian, who becomes Emperor Wen, founds the Sui dynasty and begins efforts to reunify China. The Sui dynasty initiates major infrastructure projects, including the construction of the Grand Canal.

The sixth century CE is characterized by significant political and military activities, particularly in the Byzantine Empire under Justinian I, who seeks to restore the Roman Empire's former territories and influence. Western Europe sees the rise of the Frankish kingdom under Clovis I, while the British Isles experience continued Anglo-Saxon migration. In the Middle East, the Sassanid Empire remains a formidable power, engaging in conflicts with the Byzantine Empire. South Asia witnesses the decline of the Gupta Empire and the rise of the Chalukya dynasty. In China, the Northern and Southern Dynasties period ends with the rise of the Sui dynasty, which begins efforts to reunify China. The Americas see the continued development of the Mayan civilization and the emergence of new cultures in the Andean region. The century is marked by significant cultural, political, and technological advancements, shaping the future of various regions.

From 527 to 565 CE, Emperor Justinian I reigns over the Byzantine Empire. His rule is marked by extensive reforms and military campaigns aimed at restoring the former glory of the Roman Empire. One of his most notable generals, Belisarius, reconquers the Vandal Kingdom in North Africa in 533–34 CE and then leads the Gothic War from 535 to 554 CE, resulting in the reconquest of Italy from the Ostrogoths. In 532 CE, Constantinople experiences the Nika Riots, which cause significant destruction and lead to the rebuilding of the Hagia Sophia, a masterpiece of Byzantine architecture. In 534 CE, Justinian's Code, or *Corpus Juris Civilis,* is published and becomes a foundational work for Western legal tradition. However, Justinian's reign also faces significant challenges, including the Plague of Justinian in 541–42 CE, which devastates the population.

In Western Europe, the early sixth century sees the Western Roman Empire remain fragmented into various Germanic kingdoms. These include the Ostrogoths in Italy, the Visigoths in Spain, and the Franks in Gaul. Clovis I of the Merovingian dynasty consolidates power over the Frankish tribes, converts to Christianity, and lays the foundation for what will become the Holy Roman Empire.

In the British Isles, the Anglo-Saxon migration continues, with Germanic tribes such as the Angles, Saxons, and Jutes settling in England. This migration leads to the formation of several Anglo-Saxon kingdoms. During this time, the legendary figure King Arthur is said to have lived, though historical evidence for his existence is sparse.

The Middle East and Persia are dominated by the Sassanid Empire, which frequently clashes with the Byzantine Empire. Khosrow I, who rules from 531 to 579 CE, implements significant military, economic, and administrative reforms that help the Sassanid Empire reach its peak in terms of power and cultural development. The Sassanids engage in prolonged conflicts with the Byzantines, including the Byzantine-Sassanid War of 572–91 CE.

In South Asia, the Gupta Empire continues to decline, leading to political fragmentation and the rise of regional powers. The Chalukya dynasty rises in southern India, with Pulakeshin I establishing the dynasty around 543 CE. The Chalukyas become significant patrons of art and architecture.

China continues to experience the Northern and Southern Dynasties period until the reunification of China under the Sui dynasty. In 581 CE, Yang Jian, who becomes Emperor Wen, founds the Sui dynasty and begins efforts to reunify China. The Sui dynasty initiates major infrastructure projects, including the construction of the Grand Canal.

In the Americas, the Mayan civilization in Mesoamerica continues to thrive during its Classic Period. The Mayans build impressive cities, develop advanced astronomical knowledge, and create a complex writing system. In the Andean region, the Moche civilization begins to decline, while the Wari and Tiwanaku cultures start to rise, leading to the development of large urban centres and extensive trade networks.

The sixth century CE is characterized by significant political and military activities, particularly in the Byzantine Empire under Justinian I, who seeks to restore the Roman Empire's former territories and influence. Western Europe sees the rise of the Frankish kingdom under Clovis I, while the British Isles experience continued Anglo-Saxon migration. In the Middle East, the Sassanid Empire remains a formidable power, engaging in conflicts with the Byzantine Empire. South Asia witnesses the decline of the Gupta Empire and the rise of the Chalukya dynasty.

In China, the Northern and Southern Dynasties period ends with the rise of the Sui dynasty, which begins efforts to reunify China. The Americas see the continued development of the Mayan civilization and the emergence of new cultures in the Andean region. The century is marked by significant cultural, political, and technological advancements, shaping the future of various regions.

SEVENTH CENTURY

In China, the Sui dynasty, which had reunified the country in the late sixth century, faced internal strife and rebellion. The Sui dynasty was replaced by the Tang dynasty in 618 CE, founded by Emperor Gaozu. The Tang dynasty ushered in a period of prosperity, cultural flourishing, and territorial expansion. Under Emperor Taizong (r. 626–49 CE) and his successors, the Tang Empire expanded its influence into Central Asia, Korea, and the Indian subcontinent. The Tang dynasty also saw significant developments in literature, art, and technology.

In South Asia, the decline of the Gupta Empire led to political fragmentation and the rise of regional kingdoms. The Chalukya dynasty in southern India and the Harsha Empire in northern India were significant powers during this period. Harsha (r. 606–47 CE) managed to unify much of northern India and was known for his patronage of Buddhism and the arts.

In Japan, the Asuka period (538–710 CE) continued, characterized by significant cultural and political changes influenced by Chinese culture. The Taika Reform of 645 CE aimed to centralize and strengthen imperial power, adopting various aspects of Chinese administration and culture. Buddhism, which had been introduced in the mid-sixth century, continued to spread and gain influence.

In the Americas, the Mayan civilization in Mesoamerica continued to thrive during its Classic Period. The Mayans built impressive cities, developed advanced astronomical knowledge, and created a complex writing system. The city of Tikal reached its peak during this period, becoming a major political and cultural centre. In the Andean region, the Tiwanaku and Wari cultures continued to develop, leading to the establishment of large urban centres and extensive trade networks.

The seventh century CE was a period of profound transformation and significant events across various regions.

The Byzantine Empire continued to face challenges and transformations throughout the seventh century. Emperor Heraclius (r. 610–41 CE) led a series of military campaigns against the Sassanid Empire, culminating in a decisive victory in 627 CE at the Battle of Nineveh. This victory restored Byzantine control over the eastern provinces, but the empire soon faced a new threat from the rise of Islam. Following the death of Heraclius, the empire struggled with internal strife and external invasions. The themes system, a new military and administrative structure, was introduced to better defend the empire's territories.

The Sassanid Empire, weakened by the wars with Byzantium, faced internal decline and was ultimately conquered by the rapidly expanding Islamic Caliphate. The decisive battle of al-Qadisiyyah in 636 CE led to the fall of the Sassanid capital, Ctesiphon, and marked the end of the Sassanid Empire. The last Sassanid emperor, Yazdegerd III, was killed in 651 CE, signalling the complete collapse of the empire.

The rise of Islam in the Arabian Peninsula was one of the most significant events of the seventh century. The Prophet Muhammad, who began preaching in Mecca around 610 CE, united the Arabian tribes under the banner of Islam. Following his death in 632 CE, his successors, known as caliphs, continued to expand the Islamic state. The Rashidun Caliphate (632–61 CE) saw rapid territorial expansion, including the conquest of the Sassanid Empire and significant portions of the Byzantine Empire. The Umayyad Caliphate (661–750 CE) succeeded the Rashidun Caliphate and continued the expansion, establishing one of the largest empires in history.

In Western Europe, the Merovingian dynasty continued to rule the Frankish kingdom. However, the real power increasingly lay with the mayors of the palace, who acted as the kingdom's chief administrators. The most notable mayor of the palace was Pepin of Herstal, who consolidated power and laid the foundation for the future Carolingian dynasty. The British Isles saw the continued establishment and consolidation of Anglo-Saxon kingdoms, including Northumbria, Mercia, and Wessex. The spread of Christianity continued, with missionaries such as Augustine of Canterbury playing a key role in converting the Anglo-Saxons.

The seventh century CE was characterized by significant political and religious transformations. The rise of Islam and the expansion of the Islamic Caliphate dramatically reshaped the Middle East, North Africa, and beyond. The Byzantine Empire faced both triumph and adversity, while the Tang dynasty in China ushered in a golden age of cultural and economic prosperity. In Europe, the foundations were laid for future political developments, and in the Americas, advanced civilizations continued to thrive and evolve. This century laid the groundwork for many of the social, cultural, and political structures that would shape the subsequent history of these regions.

EIGHTH CENTURY

In the Byzantine Empire, the eighth century saw significant internal and external challenges. One of the most notable internal conflicts was the period of Iconoclasm, which began in 726 CE under Emperor Leo III. Iconoclasm involved the rejection and destruction of religious icons and images, leading to deep divisions within the church and society. The Iconoclastic Controversy created a rift between those who supported the veneration of icons and those who saw them as idolatrous. This period lasted until 787 CE when the Second Council of Nicaea, called by Empress Irene, restored the veneration of icons. The council reaffirmed the use of religious images and sought to heal the divisions within the church. Externally, the Byzantine Empire faced continued pressure from the expanding Islamic Caliphate. Despite these challenges, the Byzantines managed to defend their territories, notably repelling the Second Arab Siege of Constantinople in 717–18 CE. The successful defence of Constantinople against the Arab forces under the Umayyad Caliphate was a significant event, ensuring the survival of the Byzantine Empire and limiting the further expansion of Islamic forces into Europe.

The Islamic world saw significant expansion and cultural development during the eighth century. The Umayyad Caliphate, based in Damascus, continued its territorial conquests, extending Islamic rule into Spain in the west, where Muslim forces established the Emirate of Córdoba, and into Central Asia in the east, reaching as far as the Indus River and the borders of China. In 750 CE, the Umayyad Caliphate was overthrown by the Abbasid Caliphate, which established its capital in Baghdad. The Abbasid period is often considered a golden age of Islamic culture, marked by advancements in science, medicine, mathematics, and literature. The translation movement, centred in the House of Wisdom in Baghdad, played a crucial role in preserving and expanding knowledge from various cultures. Scholars translated works from Greek, Persian, Indian, and other sources into Arabic, fostering an environment of intellectual growth and cultural exchange. The Abbasids also promoted the arts, architecture, and the development of an extensive bureaucratic system that facilitated the administration of their vast empire.

In Western Europe, the eighth century was marked by the rise of the Carolingian dynasty. Charles Martel, the Mayor of the Palace of the Frankish Kingdom, halted the advance of Islamic forces into Western Europe at the Battle of Tours in 732 CE. His victory ensured the preservation of Christian rule in Western Europe and solidified the Carolingians' power. His grandson, Charlemagne, became King of the Franks in 768 CE and embarked on a series of military campaigns to expand and consolidate his empire. Charlemagne conquered the Lombard Kingdom in Italy, incorporated Bavaria into his realm, and launched campaigns against the Saxons in the east, which resulted in their eventual conversion to Christianity. By the end of the century, Charlemagne had established the Carolingian Empire, which would become a significant political and cultural force in medieval Europe. Charlemagne's reign also saw efforts to revive learning and culture, known as the Carolingian Renaissance. He established schools and promoted literacy and education, inviting scholars from across Europe to his court at Aachen. The copying and preservation of classical texts during this period had a lasting impact on European intellectual history.

In the British Isles, the eighth century was a time of continued consolidation and conflict among the Anglo-Saxon kingdoms. Kingdoms such as Mercia, Northumbria, and Wessex vied for dominance. The Viking Age began in the late eighth century, marked by the first recorded Viking raid on the monastery of Lindisfarne in 793 CE. This event signalled the beginning of increased Viking activity and raids throughout the British Isles and beyond. The Vikings, originating from Scandinavia, targeted monasteries and coastal settlements, exploiting their wealth and lack of defences. Despite these challenges, the Anglo-Saxon kingdoms continued to develop their political structures and cultural achievements. The period saw the consolidation of Christian institutions and the continued production of important literary works, such as the Anglo-Saxon Chronicle. Additionally, figures like Offa of Mercia emerged as powerful rulers, exerting influence over large parts of England and establishing trade links with continental Europe.

In East Asia, the Tang dynasty in China continued to flourish during the early part of the eighth century. The reign of Emperor Xuanzong (712–56 CE) is often considered a high point of Tang cultural and political achievement. Xuanzong's court became a centre of art, music, and literature, attracting poets like Li Bai and Du Fu, whose works became enduring classics of Chinese literature. However, the An Lushan Rebellion, which began in 755 CE, severely weakened the Tang dynasty, leading to a prolonged period of decline. The rebellion caused widespread destruction and loss of life, significantly impacting the stability and prosperity of the Tang Empire. The aftermath of the rebellion saw a reduction in central authority and an increase in the power of regional military governors, contributing to the fragmentation of the Tang state.

In Japan, the Nara period (710–94 CE) saw the establishment of a centralized state with its capital at Nara. This period was marked by the adoption of Chinese cultural and political models, including Buddhism, Confucianism, and administrative practices. The construction of significant Buddhist temples and the compilation of important historical records, such as the Kojiki and Nihon Shoki, were notable achievements of this era. The Nara period also saw the development of a sophisticated court culture and the establishment of a legal code based on Chinese models, which helped to centralize authority and enhance the power of the emperor.

In South Asia, the eighth century witnessed the rise of regional powers following the decline of the Gupta Empire. The Rashtrakuta dynasty emerged as a significant force in central and southern India, establishing their capital at Manyakheta. The Rashtrakutas were known for their military prowess and patronage of art and architecture, including the construction of the rock-cut temples at Ellora. The Chalukya dynasty also continued to exert influence in the Deccan region, engaging in conflicts with the Pallavas to the south and the Rashtrakutas to the north. This period saw significant developments in art, architecture, and literature, including the composition of important literary works in Sanskrit and regional languages. The spread of Hinduism and Buddhism continued to shape the cultural landscape of the Indian subcontinent.

In the Americas, the Mayan civilization in Mesoamerica continued to thrive, particularly in the northern Yucatán Peninsula. The city of Uxmal became an important centre of Mayan culture and political power during this period. The Mayans continued to develop their calendar system, astronomy, and hieroglyphic writing, producing significant architectural and artistic achievements. In the Andean region, the Wari and Tiwanaku cultures continued to develop, establishing large urban centres and extensive trade networks. These cultures contributed to the rich tapestry of pre-Columbian civilizations in South America, with significant advancements in agriculture, engineering, and social organization.

The eighth century CE was a period of significant transformation and development across the world. The Byzantine Empire faced internal religious conflicts and external threats, while the Islamic world experienced a golden age of cultural and scientific achievements under the Abbasid Caliphate. In Western Europe, the rise of the Carolingian dynasty and the beginning of the Viking Age shaped the political and cultural landscape. East Asia saw the flourishing and subsequent decline of the Tang dynasty, while Japan underwent significant cultural and political transformations. South Asia witnessed the rise of regional powers, and the Americas continued to see the development of advanced civilizations. This century laid the groundwork for many of the social, cultural, and political structures that would shape the subsequent history of these regions.

The eighth century CE was a period of profound change and development across various regions.

NINTH CENTURY

In the British Isles, the ninth century was a period of Viking invasions and the struggle for power among the Anglo-Saxon kingdoms. The Kingdom of Wessex, under the leadership of Alfred the Great (871–99 CE), emerged as a significant force in resisting Viking incursions. Alfred successfully defended his kingdom against the Great Heathen Army, a coalition of Viking forces, and initiated a series of military and administrative reforms. He also promoted learning and literacy, commissioning the compilation of the Anglo-Saxon Chronicle, a key historical record of the period. Alfred's efforts laid the foundations for the eventual unification of England.

In East Asia, the Tang dynasty in China continued to experience decline, marked by internal strife and rebellion. The Huang Chao Rebellion (874–84 CE) further weakened the Tang state, leading to widespread destruction and loss of life. Despite these challenges, the Tang dynasty managed to survive until its eventual collapse in 907 CE, giving way to the period of the Five Dynasties and Ten Kingdoms. This period was characterized by political fragmentation and regional conflicts. In Japan, the Heian period (794–1185 CE) continued, marked by the dominance of the imperial court and the flourishing of Japanese culture. The capital was moved to Heian-kyō (modern-day Kyoto), and this era saw significant developments in literature, art, and architecture, including the creation of classic works such as the *Tale of Genji* by Murasaki Shikibu.

In South Asia, the ninth century saw the continued rise of regional powers and the development of distinct cultural and political identities. The Rashtrakuta dynasty remained a dominant force in central and southern India, engaging in military campaigns and fostering cultural achievements. The Chola dynasty also began to rise in prominence in southern India, laying the groundwork for future expansion and the establishment of a powerful maritime empire. The Palas in Bengal and the Pratiharas in northern India were other significant regional powers during this period, contributing to the rich tapestry of medieval Indian history.

In the Americas, the Mayan civilization in Mesoamerica continued to thrive, particularly in the northern Yucatán Peninsula. The city of Chichen Itza emerged as a major political and cultural centre during this period. The Mayans continued to develop their calendar system, astronomy, and hieroglyphic writing, producing significant architectural and artistic achievements. In the Andean region, the Wari and Tiwanaku cultures continued to develop, establishing large urban centres and extensive trade networks. These cultures contributed to the rich tapestry of pre-Columbian civilizations in South America, with significant advancements in agriculture, engineering, and social organization.

The ninth century CE was a period of significant transformation and development across the world. The Byzantine Empire experienced a revival under the Macedonian dynasty, while the Islamic world saw continued cultural and scientific achievements despite political fragmentation. In Western Europe, the Carolingian Empire reached its zenith before facing division and Viking invasions. East Asia witnessed the decline of the Tang dynasty and the flourishing of Japanese culture during the Heian period. South Asia saw the rise of regional powers, and the Americas continued to see the development of advanced civilizations. This century laid the groundwork for many of the social, cultural, and political structures that would shape the subsequent history of these regions.

In the Byzantine Empire, the ninth century saw a resurgence of power and cultural revival. The empire gradually recovered from the turmoil of the previous centuries, particularly the Iconoclast Controversy, which ended with the restoration of the veneration of icons in 843 CE by Empress Theodora. This event, known as the Triumph of Orthodoxy, reaffirmed the importance of religious images in Byzantine worship and culture. The Macedonian dynasty, beginning with the reign of Basil I (867–86 CE), initiated a period of military and political resurgence. Under Basil I and his successors, the Byzantine Empire expanded its territories in the Balkans and the eastern Mediterranean, bolstering its position as a major power in the region. This period also saw a cultural and intellectual revival, known as the Macedonian Renaissance, characterized by a renewed interest in classical Greek learning and the flourishing of Byzantine art and literature.

The Islamic world continued to experience significant developments during the ninth century. The Abbasid Caliphate, with its capital in Baghdad, remained a centre of cultural and scientific achievement. The translation movement, centred in the House of Wisdom, continued to thrive, with scholars translating works from Greek, Persian, Indian, and other traditions into Arabic. This period saw notable advancements in mathematics, astronomy, medicine, and philosophy, with figures like Al-Kindi, Al-Razi, and Al-Farabi making significant contributions. However, the Abbasid Caliphate also faced political fragmentation and challenges to its authority. The rise of autonomous dynasties, such as the Tulunids in Egypt and the Samanids in Central Asia, indicated a decentralization of power. In 869 CE, a significant revolt known as the Zanj Rebellion broke out in southern Iraq, led by African slaves. The rebellion, which lasted for nearly 14 years, highlighted the social and economic tensions within the Abbasid state.

In Western Europe, the Carolingian Empire reached its zenith under Charlemagne, who was crowned Emperor of the Romans by Pope Leo III in 800 CE. Charlemagne's reign saw the consolidation of his empire, which covered much of Western and Central Europe, and the promotion of learning and culture through the Carolingian Renaissance. However, following Charlemagne's death in 814 CE, the empire faced internal divisions and external pressures. The Treaty of Verdun in 843 CE divided the Carolingian Empire among Charlemagne's grandsons, leading to the formation of distinct political entities that would eventually evolve into modern European states. The ninth century also witnessed increased Viking activity, with Norse seafarers conducting raids and establishing settlements across Europe. Notable Viking incursions included the sacking of Paris in 845 CE and the establishment of the Danelaw in England.

TENTH CENTURY

In the tenth century CE, profound changes shaped the political, cultural, and technological landscapes across diverse regions:

In the Byzantine Empire, the Macedonian dynasty, especially under Emperor Basil II (976–1025 CE), achieved a period of resurgence. Basil II, known as the Bulgar-Slayer, expanded Byzantine influence significantly through military campaigns against the Bulgars and other neighbouring peoples. His reign marked not only territorial expansion in the Balkans and Anatolia but also a cultural renaissance. Byzantine art, architecture, and literature flourished, reflecting the empire's renewed vigour and cultural richness.

Across the Islamic world, the tenth century was marked by the coexistence of several powerful states. The Abbasid Caliphate in Baghdad, under Caliph al-Muqtadir (908–32 CE), enjoyed a period of relative stability and cultural achievement. Baghdad remained a vibrant centre of learning and intellectual exchange, fostering advancements in literature, science, and philosophy that influenced both Islamic and European thought. Meanwhile, the Fatimid Caliphate, based in North Africa and Egypt, emerged as a formidable rival to the Abbasids. The Fatimids established Cairo as their capital and promoted Ismaili Shia Islam, shaping religious and political dynamics in the region.

In Western Europe, political structures were characterized by fragmentation and feudalism. The Holy Roman Empire, officially established in 962 CE under Otto I (Otto the Great), sought to centralize authority in Germany and parts of Italy. Otto I's reign marked a significant attempt to revive elements of Roman imperial authority, setting the stage for the evolving medieval political landscape. Viking raids continued to pose challenges across Europe, although Norse kingdoms such as Denmark, Norway, and Sweden began to consolidate their territories and establish more organized governance.

In England, the Anglo-Saxon kingdom saw notable developments under Æthelstan (924–39 CE), who successfully unified various Anglo-Saxon realms and asserted dominance over Viking-held territories. Æthelstan's reign laid the foundation for a more centralized monarchy and marked a period of cultural and administrative advancement. Meanwhile, in Ireland, Viking settlements and interactions with Gaelic kingdoms led to cultural exchange and political integration, influencing local governance and societal structures.

The tenth century CE stands as a pivotal era characterized by dynamic geopolitical shifts and cultural achievements. From the Byzantine Empire's cultural renaissance under Basil II to the flourishing intellectual centres of the Abbasid Caliphate and the evolving political landscapes of Western Europe and the British Isles, this century set the stage for the medieval period's complexities and transformations.

In China, the tenth century CE was marked by the transition from the turbulent Five Dynasties and Ten Kingdoms period to the stable and prosperous Song dynasty. The collapse of the Tang dynasty in 907 CE had plunged China into political fragmentation, with various regional powers vying for control. The subsequent Five Dynasties and Ten Kingdoms period saw rapid changes in leadership and constant warfare among competing states. However, in 960 CE, Zhao Kuangyin, founder of the Song dynasty, reunified much of China under his rule. The Song dynasty ushered in a period of economic growth, technological innovation, and cultural achievement. It is divided into two main periods: the Northern Song (960–1127 CE) and the Southern Song (1127–1279 CE), each contributing significantly to China's history.

In Japan, the tenth century continued the Heian period (794–1185 CE), characterized by the dominance of the imperial court centred in Kyoto. This era was a zenith of Japanese cultural development, known for its refinement in arts, literature, and courtly rituals. Murasaki Shikibu's monumental work, *The Tale of Genji*, stands as a pinnacle of Japanese literature from this period, offering insights into courtly life and societal norms.

South Asia witnessed the zenith of several powerful dynasties during the tenth century. The Chola dynasty, under the leadership of Rajaraja Chola I (985–1014 CE) and his son Rajendra Chola I (1012–44 CE), expanded their maritime empire across South India and exerted significant influence over trade routes in the Indian Ocean. Their rule saw remarkable achievements in temple architecture, administrative systems, and cultural patronage, making the Cholas one of the most illustrious dynasties in Indian history. Concurrently, northern India saw continued rivalry between the Pratihara dynasty, centred around Kannauj, and the Rashtrakuta dynasty, based in Deccan, contributing to regional diversity and cultural exchange.

In the Americas, Mesoamerican civilizations such as the Toltecs and the Maya flourished during the tenth century. The Toltecs, centred in Tula, expanded their influence in central Mexico, succeeding the earlier Teotihuacan culture and influencing subsequent Aztec civilizations. Meanwhile, the Maya city-states of the Yucatán Peninsula experienced a revival in architecture, arts, and intellectual achievements despite ongoing political fragmentation. In the Andean region, the decline of the Wari and Tiwanaku cultures allowed for the emergence of new polities, laying the groundwork for the rise of the Inca Empire in subsequent centuries.

Overall, the tenth century CE was a period of dynamic change and cultural achievement across diverse civilizations. From the consolidation of power in China under the Song dynasty to the cultural renaissance in Japan's Heian period and the flourishing empires of the Cholas in South Asia, this century set the stage for the medieval period's political, social, and cultural landscapes across the world.

ELEVENTH CENTURY

In the eleventh century CE, major civilizations across the world experienced significant political, cultural, and religious developments that shaped their histories. The Byzantine Empire, under the Macedonian dynasty, continued its cultural and military resurgence into the eleventh century. Emperor Basil II (976–1025 CE), known as the Bulgar-Slayer, expanded Byzantine territories significantly, reclaiming parts of the Balkans and Anatolia. His reign marked a peak of Byzantine power and influence, with the empire becoming a dominant force in the Eastern Mediterranean. The Macedonian Renaissance flourished during this period, characterized by a revival of classical Greek learning, art, and architecture. Byzantine art, particularly iconography and mosaic work, reached new heights, reflecting the empire's cultural vibrancy.

The Islamic world in the eleventh century was marked by both cultural achievements and political transformations. The Abbasid Caliphate in Baghdad continued to decline, with various regional powers asserting more autonomy. The Fatimid Caliphate in Egypt and North Africa thrived, promoting Ismaili Shia Islam and establishing Cairo as a centre of culture and learning. Meanwhile, the Seljuk Turks, originally from Central Asia, rose to prominence and captured Baghdad in 1055 CE, effectively ending Abbasid political authority. The Seljuks expanded their empire across Anatolia and into the Levant, becoming a significant military and political force in the Islamic world.

Western Europe in the eleventh century saw profound changes with the emergence of new political entities and cultural developments. The Holy Roman Empire, under the Salian dynasty, consolidated its authority over much of Central Europe. In 962 CE, Otto I was crowned Emperor by the Pope, establishing a close relationship between the Church and the Empire that would shape European politics for centuries. The Investiture Controversy, a struggle between the Church and secular rulers over the appointment of bishops, also began during this period, highlighting tensions between ecclesiastical and secular authority.

In the British Isles, the eleventh century was marked by Viking invasions and the consolidation of Anglo-Saxon rule. The Danish King Cnut the Great briefly ruled over England (1016–35 CE), Denmark, and Norway, creating a North Sea Empire. This period also saw the emergence of the Anglo-Norman dynasty after the Norman Conquest of England in 1066 CE, when William the Conqueror defeated Harold II at the Battle of Hastings. The Norman Conquest led to significant social and political changes in England, including the introduction of feudalism and the imposition of Norman culture and legal systems.

In China, the Five Dynasties and Ten Kingdoms period (907–60 CE) followed the collapse of the Tang dynasty, marked by political fragmentation and rivalry among regional powers. The Song dynasty emerged in 960 CE, reunifying much of China and ushering in a period of economic prosperity and cultural achievement. The Song dynasty developed advanced agricultural techniques, expanded trade networks, and made significant technological advancements, including the invention of gunpowder and the movable type printing press. The civil service examination system was also refined, promoting meritocracy and contributing to the efficient administration of the vast empire.

In Japan, the Heian period continued, characterized by the dominance of the imperial court in Kyoto and the flourishing of Japanese arts and literature. Aristocratic culture reached its zenith during this period, with the creation of classic literary works such as *The Tale of Genji* by Murasaki Shikibu and *The Pillow Book* by Sei Shonagon. The Fujiwara clan exerted significant influence over the imperial court, with their political power often overshadowing that of the emperors. The Heian period also saw the rise of powerful regional clans and the establishment of samurai as a distinct warrior class.

South Asia in the eleventh century saw the consolidation of several powerful dynasties. The Chola dynasty in southern India reached its zenith under Rajaraja Chola I (985–1014 CE) and his son Rajendra Chola I (1012–44 CE), establishing a maritime empire that dominated trade in the Indian Ocean. The Cholas built impressive temples, including the Brihadeeswara Temple, and promoted Tamil culture and literature. In northern India, the Pratihara dynasty and the Rashtrakutas continued to vie for supremacy, contributing to regional political diversity and cultural exchange. The Ghaznavid Empire, originating from present-day Afghanistan, expanded into the Indian subcontinent, leading to the spread of Islam and significant cultural interactions between Hindu and Muslim communities.

In East Asia, the eleventh century witnessed significant shifts in power and culture. The Tangut Empire, also known as Western Xia, began to decline, while the Song dynasty (960–1279 CE) rose to prominence in China. The Song dynasty is noted for continuing the economic prosperity and cultural achievements of its predecessors. This period saw remarkable advancements in arts, literature, and technology. Notable innovations included the invention of movable type printing and improvements in gunpowder weaponry. The civil service examination system was further refined, promoting meritocracy and enhancing the administration's efficiency. The Song dynasty also fostered a rich cultural environment, with significant contributions to poetry, painting, and philosophy.

In Japan, the late Heian period (794–1185 CE) was characterized by the dominance of the Fujiwara clan at the imperial court. This era is often regarded as a golden age of Japanese culture, known for its refined courtly traditions and literary achievements. The Fujiwara clan exerted considerable influence over the emperors, effectively controlling the government while promoting cultural and artistic endeavours. One of the most notable literary works from this period is *The Tale of Genji* by Murasaki Shikibu, which provides a detailed portrayal of court life and has been celebrated as a masterpiece of classical Japanese literature. The Heian period also saw the development of distinct Japanese art forms, including the yamato-e style of painting.

South Asia in the eleventh century experienced the consolidation of regional powers and the flourishing of Hindu and Buddhist cultural traditions. The Chola dynasty in southern India continued its dominance. Under leaders like Mahmud of Ghazni, the Ghaznavids conducted numerous raids into India, establishing a Muslim presence that contributed to cultural and religious syncretism. These interactions led to the blending of Persian, Central Asian, and Indian traditions in various aspects of culture, including art, architecture, and language.

In the Americas, Mesoamerican civilizations such as the Toltecs and the Maya continued to thrive. The Toltec Empire, centred in Tula, expanded its influence in central Mexico, succeeding the earlier Teotihuacan culture and laying the groundwork for subsequent Aztec civilizations. The Toltecs are noted for their impressive architectural and artistic achievements, including the construction of large pyramids and intricately carved statues. The Maya city-states of the Yucatán Peninsula experienced a resurgence during this period, marked by significant developments in architecture, arts, and intellectual achievements. Despite ongoing political fragmentation and warfare among the city-states, the Maya continued to advance their knowledge in astronomy, mathematics, and writing. The construction of grand cities like Chichen Itza and Uxmal exemplifies the architectural and cultural achievements of the Maya during the eleventh century.

The eleventh century CE was a period of dynamic change and cultural achievement across diverse civilizations. The Byzantine Empire, under the Macedonian dynasty, reached the height of its power with Emperor Basil II expanding Byzantine territories and fostering a cultural renaissance. The Seljuk Turks rose to prominence in the Islamic world, capturing Baghdad and establishing a significant military and political presence. Western Europe experienced profound changes with the Norman Conquest of England in 1066 CE, which led to the establishment of the Anglo-Norman dynasty and significant social and political transformations. This century laid the foundation for the medieval period's political, social, and cultural landscapes, with enduring impacts on the development of civilizations across the world.

TWELFTH CENTURY

In the twelfth century, Europe experienced a period known as the High Middle Ages, marked by significant economic growth, urbanization, and cultural flourishing.

Economically, advancements in agriculture such as the adoption of the heavy plough and the three-field system contributed to increased food production and population growth. This demographic expansion led to the growth of towns and cities, which became centres of trade, commerce, and intellectual activity. The establishment of guilds and the rise of a merchant class further stimulated economic development across the continent.

Culturally, the twelfth century witnessed the emergence and spread of Gothic art and architecture. Characterized by soaring cathedrals with pointed arches, ribbed vaults, and large stained glass windows, Gothic architecture symbolized the quest for spiritual elevation and the glorification of God. Structures like the Notre Dame Cathedral in Paris and Chartres Cathedral in France exemplified the technical and artistic achievements of the period, influencing architectural styles throughout Europe.

Politically and religiously, the Investiture Controversy was a central issue that shaped European politics and Church-state relations. Initiated by conflicts over the appointment of bishops and church officials, the controversy climaxed with the Concordat of Worms in 1122. This agreement, brokered between Pope

Calixtus II and Holy Roman Emperor Henry V, delineated the authority of secular rulers and the Church in appointing and investing bishops, resolving decades of tension and establishing a framework for future Church-state interactions.

The Crusades, launched by Pope Urban II in 1095, were pivotal events of the twelfth century that had profound political, economic, and cultural impacts on Europe and the Middle East. Initially motivated by religious fervour to reclaim Jerusalem and the Holy Land from Muslim control, the Crusades also served as a means to assert papal authority, divert internal conflicts, and expand European influence beyond its borders. The Crusader states established in the Levant, such as the Kingdom of Jerusalem, facilitated cultural exchanges between East and West and influenced European perceptions of the world.

In the Byzantine Empire, the Komnenos dynasty presided over a period of cultural and military revival. Emperors like Alexios I Komnenos (1081–1118) and Manuel I Komnenos (1143–80) strengthened Byzantine territories in Asia Minor and the Balkans, stabilizing the empire after earlier challenges. This era saw Byzantine art and literature flourish, with notable achievements in religious iconography, mosaic art, and theological writings that influenced Eastern European and Mediterranean cultures.

Across the Islamic world, the twelfth century witnessed the rise of powerful dynasties such as the Seljuks and the Ayyubids. The Seljuk Sultanate of Rum in Anatolia and the Ayyubid Sultanate in Egypt and Syria consolidated political power and fostered significant cultural and architectural achievements. Figures like the philosopher Averroes (Ibn Rushd) and theologian Al-Ghazali made enduring contributions to Islamic philosophy and theology, influencing debates on reason, faith, and governance within the Muslim world.

Overall, the twelfth century was a period of dynamic cultural interaction, economic expansion, and political evolution across Europe and the Islamic world. It set the stage for further developments in art, architecture, philosophy, and governance that would shape the medieval world and beyond.

In South Asia, the Chola dynasty in southern India continued to thrive, known for its maritime trade and temple construction. The Delhi Sultanate, established by Qutb al-Din Aibak after the Ghurid conquest of Delhi in 1206, marked the beginning of Muslim rule in northern India, leading to cultural syncretism between Hindu and Islamic traditions.

East Asia in the twelfth century was marked by the rise of the Song dynasty in China, known for its economic prosperity, technological innovations such as printing and gunpowder, and cultural achievements in poetry and landscape painting. In Japan, the Kamakura period began after the establishment of the Kamakura Shogunate in 1185, marking a shift towards feudalism and the dominance of the samurai warrior class.

In the Americas, Mesoamerican civilizations such as the Toltecs and the Mixtecs flourished, building upon the legacy of earlier cultures like the Maya. The Toltec capital at Tula became a centre of art, architecture, and trade in central Mexico, influencing subsequent Aztec civilization.

Overall, the twelfth century CE was a period of dynamic cultural exchange, technological innovation, and political consolidation across diverse civilizations, laying the groundwork for future developments in the medieval era and beyond.

THIRTEENTH CENTURY

In the Byzantine Empire, the thirteenth century began with the aftermath of the Fourth Crusade, which in 1204 resulted in the sacking of Constantinople and the establishment of the Latin Empire. This event marked a significant decline in Byzantine power and influence. The Latin Empire, established by Western European crusaders, ruled from Constantinople but struggled to maintain control over the former Byzantine territories. Meanwhile, the Byzantine Empire fragmented into successor states, notably the Empire of Nicaea, the Despotate of Epirus, and the Empire of Trebizond. The Empire of Nicaea, under the leadership of the Laskaris and later the Palaiologos dynasties, focused on recapturing Constantinople and restoring the Byzantine state. In 1261, Michael VIII Palaiologos successfully recaptured Constantinople from the Latin rulers, re-establishing the Byzantine Empire. However, the restored Byzantine state was significantly weakened and struggled to regain its former glory. The empire faced constant threats from both the West and the rising power of the Ottoman Turks in the East, leading to a period of decline that would eventually culminate in the fall of Constantinople in 1453.

The Islamic world in the thirteenth century was characterized by the rise and fall of powerful dynasties and the devastating impact of the Mongol invasions. The Abbasid Caliphate in Baghdad, which had already been in decline due to internal strife and the rise of regional powers, was finally destroyed in 1258 by the Mongols under Hulagu Khan. The sack of Baghdad marked a significant power vacuum in the region and the end of the Abbasid Caliphate as a political entity, though the Abbasid religious and cultural influence persisted. The Mamluk Sultanate, which emerged in Egypt, successfully resisted the Mongol advance at the Battle of Ain Jalut in 1260. This victory marked a turning point in Mongol expansion and established the Mamluks as a dominant military and political force in the Islamic world. The Mamluks, originally slave soldiers who seized power, established a strong state that became a cultural and economic centre. They fostered trade, particularly in the spice trade with Europe, and oversaw a flourishing of Islamic architecture and scholarship in cities like Cairo and Damascus.

In Western Europe, the thirteenth century was a period of significant political consolidation and cultural development. The Kingdom of France, under the reign of Philip II (1180–1223) and his successors, expanded its territories and centralized its administration. Philip II significantly weakened the English hold on French territories through military campaigns, reclaiming regions like Normandy. His reign marked the beginning of the transition from a feudal system to a more centralized monarchy. England experienced the reigns of King John (1199–1216) and Henry III (1216–72), marked by internal conflicts and the signing of the Magna Carta in 1215. The Magna Carta established important legal principles limiting the power of the monarchy and laid the groundwork for the development of constitutional law. The Holy Roman Empire saw the struggle for power between the Papacy and the emperors, culminating in the excommunication and deposition of Emperor Frederick II in 1245. Frederick II's reign was notable for his attempts to establish a centralized imperial authority and his conflicts with the Papacy, which resisted these efforts. The thirteenth century also witnessed the growth of towns and trade, the founding of universities, and significant achievements in art and architecture. Gothic architecture flourished, with cathedrals like Notre Dame in Paris and Chartres Cathedral exemplifying the era's artistic and architectural advancements. The establishment of universities in cities like Bologna, Paris, and Oxford fostered the growth of scholasticism and intellectual inquiry.

The British Isles in the thirteenth century experienced significant political and social changes. In England, the Magna Carta of 1215 established the principle that the king was subject to the law and protected the rights of nobles and, to some extent, commoners. This document, forced upon King John by rebellious barons, was a response to his heavy taxation and arbitrary rule. It laid the foundation for the development of parliamentary democracy and the legal system in England. Wales was gradually conquered by England, culminating in the annexation of the Principality of Wales under Edward I in 1284. Edward's campaigns against the Welsh princes, particularly Llywelyn ap Gruffudd, led to the incorporation of Wales into the English crown and the construction of imposing castles to assert English control. Scotland maintained its independence but faced English attempts at domination, leading to the Wars of Scottish Independence in the late thirteenth and early fourteenth centuries. The death of Alexander III in 1286 and the subsequent succession crisis provided an opportunity for Edward I to assert his authority over Scotland. This led to a series of conflicts, with figures like William Wallace and Robert the Bruce emerging as national heroes in the struggle for Scottish independence. The wars ultimately resulted in the recognition of Scotland's independence with the Treaty of Edinburgh-Northampton in 1328.

In East Asia, the thirteenth century witnessed significant political and cultural developments. The Song dynasty in China continued to experience economic prosperity and cultural achievements despite military pressures from the north. The Mongol Empire, under the leadership of Genghis Khan and his successors, expanded rapidly across Asia, eventually leading to the conquest of the Song dynasty. Kublai Khan, Genghis Khan's grandson, completed the conquest of China and established the Yuan dynasty in 1271. The Yuan dynasty integrated China into the vast Mongol Empire, promoting trade and cultural exchange across Eurasia through the Pax Mongolica. In Japan, the Kamakura Shogunate was established in 1192 by Minamoto no Yoritomo, marking the beginning of the feudal era in Japan. The shogunate successfully repelled two Mongol invasions in 1274 and 1281, reinforcing the samurai class's role as the dominant military force in Japan.

South Asia in the thirteenth century saw the consolidation of regional powers and the flourishing of Hindu and Buddhist cultural traditions. The Chola dynasty in southern India continued its maritime dominance and cultural patronage, building elaborate temples such as the Brihadeeswara Temple and expanding trade networks across Southeast Asia. The Chola navy controlled crucial maritime routes, facilitating cultural and commercial exchanges with Southeast Asia and beyond. In northern India, the Delhi Sultanate was established by Qutb-ud-din Aibak in 1206, marking the beginning of Muslim rule in India. The Sultanate expanded under rulers like Iltutmish and Alauddin Khilji, who implemented administrative and military reforms and promoted cultural and architectural achievements, such as the construction of the Qutub Minar and the Alai Darwaza.

In the Americas, Mesoamerican civilizations such as the Toltecs and the Maya continued to flourish. In the Andean region, the Inca civilization began to emerge, setting the stage for the establishment of the Inca Empire in the following century. The Inca developed advanced agricultural techniques, such as terrace farming, and established extensive trade networks across the Andes, laying the groundwork for their future expansion.

In East Asia, the Mongol Empire's rise was the most transformative event of the thirteenth century. Under Genghis Khan and his successors, the Mongols created the largest contiguous empire in history, stretching from Europe to Asia. Genghis Khan, originally named Temujin, unified the Mongol tribes and embarked on a series of military campaigns that expanded the empire's territory across Central Asia, the Middle East, and into Eastern Europe. His strategic brilliance and ruthless tactics ensured rapid conquests and the subjugation of numerous peoples. Following Genghis Khan's death in 1227, his descendants continued the expansion. Kublai Khan, Genghis Khan's grandson, played a pivotal role in the Mongol conquests in East Asia. He established the Yuan dynasty in China in 1271, becoming the first non-Han ruler to conquer all of China. The Yuan dynasty integrated China into the vast Mongol Empire, promoting trade and cultural exchange across Eurasia through the Pax Mongolica. This period of relative peace and stability facilitated the movement of goods, ideas, and people across the Silk Road, significantly influencing the cultures and economies of Europe and Asia.

South Asia in the thirteenth century saw the establishment of the Delhi Sultanate, beginning with the conquest of Delhi by the Ghurid general Qutb al-Din Aibak in 1206. The Delhi Sultanate marked the beginning of Muslim rule in India, which lasted until the arrival of the Mughals in the sixteenth century. The Sultanate was characterized by the rule of several dynasties, including the Mamluks, Khiljis, Tughlaqs, and Lodis. Qutb al-Din Aibak, originally a slave who rose to prominence under the Ghurid sultans, established the Mamluk dynasty, also known as the Slave dynasty. This period was marked by significant cultural and architectural achievements, including the construction of the Qutb Minar, the world's tallest brick minaret, and the development of Indo-Islamic culture. The Delhi Sultanate also saw the introduction of Persian art, culture, and administrative practices into the Indian subcontinent, laying the foundation for future cultural synthesis.

In the Americas, the thirteenth century was a period of growth and development for various civilizations. The Aztec civilization began to form, leading to the establishment of the Mexica people in the Valley of Mexico by the early fourteenth century. The Aztecs, originally a nomadic tribe, gradually settled in the fertile region around Lake Texcoco, where they would eventually establish the city of Tenochtitlan. The Maya civilization, although past its Classic period zenith, continued to flourish in the Yucatán Peninsula with significant urban centres such as Chichen Itza. Despite the decline of many central lowland cities, the Postclassic Maya maintained vibrant trade networks and produced remarkable architectural and artistic works. In the Andean region, the Inca civilization began to emerge, setting the stage for the establishment of the Inca Empire in the following century. The Incas, initially a small highland tribe, began to expand their territory under leaders like Manco Capac and his successors, developing advanced agricultural techniques and building the foundations of what would become a vast and sophisticated empire.

The thirteenth century CE was a period of dynamic change and cultural achievement across diverse civilizations. From the decline and resurgence of the Byzantine Empire to the Mongol conquests that reshaped Asia and the rise of powerful states in Europe and the Islamic world, this century laid the foundation for the medieval period's political, social, and cultural landscapes. The era also witnessed significant advancements in trade, technology, and the arts, contributing to the rich tapestry of global history. In Europe, the establishment of Gothic architecture reached its peak with the construction of grand cathedrals like Notre Dame and Chartres. The intellectual life of Europe was invigorated by the founding of universities in cities such as Bologna, Paris, and Oxford, fostering the growth of scholasticism and laying the groundwork for the Renaissance. In the Islamic world, despite the political upheavals caused by the Mongol invasions, cultural and scientific advancements continued, particularly in the Mamluk Sultanate and the remnants of the Abbasid Caliphate in Cairo. The interconnectedness brought about by the Mongol Empire facilitated the exchange of knowledge and technology across Eurasia, influencing developments in diverse fields such as astronomy, medicine, and engineering.

FOURTEENTH CENTURY

The fourteenth century CE was a period of significant upheaval and transformation across many regions of the world, marked by dramatic political, social, and cultural changes. Here is an overview of major events and developments during this century:

In Europe, the fourteenth century was a time of crisis and change. The century began with the Great Famine (1315–17), which caused widespread starvation and economic disruption. This was followed by the devastating Black Death (1347–51), a pandemic that killed an estimated one-third to one-half of Europe's population. The plague had profound social, economic, and cultural impacts, leading to labour shortages, social unrest, and shifts in power dynamics. Despite these challenges, the fourteenth century also saw the beginning of the Renaissance, particularly in Italy. This period marked a revival of interest in classical antiquity, humanism, and the arts. Key figures like Dante Alighieri, whose 'Divine Comedy' became a cornerstone of Italian literature, and Giotto di Bondone, a pioneering artist in realistic painting, emerged during this time.

In England, the fourteenth century was characterized by political turmoil and conflict. The Hundred Years' War between England and France began in 1337, driven by territorial disputes and claims to the French throne. The war saw significant battles such as the Battle of Crécy (1346) and the Battle of Poitiers (1356), where the English achieved notable victories due to their use of longbowmen. Domestically, England experienced the Peasants' Revolt in 1381, a major uprising triggered by economic hardship and oppressive taxation following the Black Death. The revolt highlighted the growing tensions between the ruling classes and the peasantry.

In France, the fourteenth century was marked by the struggles of the Hundred Years' War and internal conflicts. The war placed immense strain on the French monarchy and nobility, leading to significant political and military challenges. The Battle of Agincourt in 1415, although occurring slightly after the fourteenth century, was a pivotal event during this protracted conflict, showcasing the ongoing turmoil. France also faced internal crises, including the outbreak of the Jacquerie peasant revolt in 1358, driven by discontent with the heavy taxation and the devastation caused by the plague.

The Holy Roman Empire in the fourteenth century experienced political fragmentation and power struggles. The Empire was a complex and decentralized entity, with various princes, dukes, and bishops vying for control. The Golden Bull of 1356, issued by Emperor Charles IV, established a formal electoral process for choosing the Holy Roman Emperor, aiming to bring some stability to the political landscape. This decree recognized the autonomy of the prince-electors and laid the groundwork for the political structure of the Empire in the coming centuries.

In the Byzantine Empire, the fourteenth century was a period of decline and fragmentation. The empire faced numerous challenges, including internal strife, economic difficulties, and external threats. The civil war between John V Palaiologos and John VI Kantakouzenos weakened the empire, making it vulnerable to Ottoman expansion. By the end of the century, the Ottomans had established a significant foothold in the Balkans, posing an existential threat to the Byzantine state.

The Islamic world in the fourteenth century experienced significant political and cultural changes. The Mongol Empire, which had dominated much of Asia, fragmented into smaller khanates, including the Ilkhanate in Persia and the Chagatai Khanate in Central Asia. The Mamluk Sultanate in Egypt and Syria emerged as a dominant power, successfully repelling the Mongols and Crusaders and fostering a rich cultural and intellectual life in Cairo. The rise of the Ottoman Empire was another major development. Founded in the late thirteenth century by Osman I, the Ottomans expanded rapidly under leaders like Orhan and Murad I, establishing a powerful state that would eventually conquer Constantinople in 1453.

In South Asia, the fourteenth century saw the rise and fall of various dynasties and the establishment of significant states. The Delhi Sultanate continued to be a dominant power in northern India, with rulers like Alauddin Khilji and Muhammad bin Tughlaq undertaking ambitious military campaigns and administrative reforms. The Vijayanagara Empire was founded in southern India in 1336, becoming a significant cultural and political force in the region. The empire fostered the growth of Hindu culture and architecture, exemplified by the construction of grand temples and cities.

In East Asia, the fourteenth century was a period of transition and upheaval. The Yuan dynasty in China, established by the Mongols, faced internal rebellions and economic difficulties. The Red Turban Rebellion, which began in the 1350s, eventually led to the overthrow of the Yuan dynasty and the establishment of the Ming dynasty in 1368 by Zhu Yuanzhang, who became Emperor Hongwu. The Ming dynasty ushered in a period of stability, economic recovery, and cultural renaissance. In Japan, the fourteenth century was marked by the Kamakura and early Muromachi periods. The Kamakura shogunate faced challenges from the Mongol invasions in the late thirteenth century, which were successfully repelled. The Ashikaga shogunate was established in 1336, leading to a period of political instability known as the Nanboku-chō period, characterized by rival imperial courts and frequent conflicts among samurai clans.

In the Americas, the fourteenth century saw the continued development of pre-Columbian civilizations. The Aztecs, originally a nomadic tribe, began to establish themselves in the Valley of Mexico, founding the city of Tenochtitlan in 1325. This city would become the centre of the Aztec Empire, which would dominate Mesoamerica in the coming centuries. The Maya civilization, although past its Classic period zenith, continued to flourish in the Yucatán Peninsula with significant urban centres such as Mayapán. In the Andean region, the Inca civilization expanded its influence, laying the groundwork for the establishment of the Inca Empire in the fifteenth century. The Incas developed advanced agricultural techniques, impressive architectural achievements, and a complex administrative system that would enable them to control a vast territory.

The fourteenth century was a period of dynamic change and cultural achievement across diverse civilizations. From the crises and recovery in Europe to the rise of the Ottoman Empire and the transformation of East Asia, this century laid the foundation for significant developments in the medieval and early modern periods. The era also witnessed important advancements in trade, technology, and the arts, contributing to the rich tapestry of global history.

FIFTEENTH CENTURY

The fifteenth century CE was a pivotal period in world history, characterized by profound transformations in politics, culture, exploration, and technology across various regions. Here's an in-depth overview of the significant events and developments during this century:

In Europe, the fifteenth century was a time of significant political consolidation and cultural rebirth. The Renaissance, which began in Italy during the fourteenth century, reached its peak in the fifteenth century, spreading throughout Europe. This period saw remarkable advancements in art, literature, and science, driven by figures such as Leonardo da Vinci, Michelangelo, and Johannes Gutenberg, whose invention of the printing press around 1440 revolutionized the spread of knowledge.

Politically, the century witnessed the end of the Hundred Years' War between England and France in 1453, resulting in the expulsion of the English from most of France and the solidification of French national identity. England, in turn, experienced internal strife with the Wars of the Roses (1455–87), a series of civil wars for control of the throne between the houses of Lancaster and York. The conflict ended with the victory of Henry Tudor, who became Henry VII and founded the Tudor dynasty.

The Iberian Peninsula saw the completion of the Reconquista, the campaign by Christian states to reclaim territory from the Muslim Moors. In 1492, the Catholic Monarchs, Ferdinand of Aragon and Isabella of Castile, captured Granada, the last Muslim stronghold, unifying Spain under Christian rule. This same year, they sponsored Christopher Columbus's voyage, which led to the European discovery of the Americas and the beginning of Spanish colonial expansion.

The fall of Constantinople to the Ottoman Empire in 1453 marked a significant shift in the balance of power in the Eastern Mediterranean. Under Sultan Mehmed II, the Ottomans captured the Byzantine capital, transforming it into Istanbul and establishing it as the centre of a vast and expanding empire. The Ottomans continued to consolidate and expand their territories, becoming a dominant force in the region and a major player in European and Middle Eastern affairs.

In the Holy Roman Empire, the fifteenth century was a period of relative stability and gradual consolidation. The Habsburg dynasty began to rise to prominence, particularly with the election of Frederick III as Holy Roman Emperor in 1452. The Habsburgs would come to dominate the imperial throne for centuries. The empire also saw the growth of cities and trade, particularly in regions such as the Rhineland and northern Italy, which became centres of commerce and culture.

In Eastern Europe, the Grand Duchy of Moscow emerged as a significant power, gradually consolidating Russian territories under its control. Ivan III (Ivan the Great) expanded Muscovite territory and laid the foundations for a centralized Russian state. He also ended the dominance of the Golden Horde over Russia by refusing to pay tribute, marking the beginning of Russia's rise as a major power.

In China, the Ming dynasty continued to flourish, having overthrown the Mongol Yuan dynasty in the previous century. The fifteenth century saw the reign of the Yongle Emperor (1402–24), who moved the capital to Beijing and commissioned the construction of the Forbidden City. The Yongle Emperor also sponsored the voyages of the admiral Zheng He, who led large fleets on expeditions across the Indian Ocean, reaching as far as East Africa and the Middle East. These voyages demonstrated China's naval capabilities and facilitated trade and cultural exchanges, although they were eventually halted due to changing political priorities.

Japan in the fifteenth century experienced the turbulent Sengoku period, a time of civil war and social upheaval as powerful regional lords (daimyos) vied for control over the country. The Ashikaga shogunate, which had ruled Japan since the fourteenth century, gradually lost power and authority, leading to a fractured and decentralized political landscape. This era set the stage for the eventual unification of Japan under the Tokugawa shogunate in the early seventeenth century.

In South Asia, the fifteenth century witnessed the decline of the Delhi Sultanate and the rise of regional kingdoms and new empires. The Vijayanagara Empire in southern India reached its zenith, becoming a significant centre of Hindu culture, art, and architecture. In the east, the Sultanate of Bengal flourished as a wealthy and influential state. Meanwhile, the groundwork was being laid for the establishment of the Mughal Empire in the following century, which would come to dominate much of the Indian subcontinent.

In the Americas, the fifteenth century saw the continued development and expansion of indigenous civilizations. The Aztec Empire, centred in Tenochtitlan (modern-day Mexico City), became a dominant force in Mesoamerica through military conquest and alliances. The Inca Empire in the Andean region expanded rapidly under rulers like Pachacuti and his successors, creating an extensive and sophisticated state that stretched along the western coast of South America. Both empires developed advanced agricultural, architectural, and administrative systems, setting the stage for their encounters with European colonizers in the sixteenth century.

The fifteenth century was also a period of significant maritime exploration and the beginning of European colonial expansion. Portuguese explorers, such as Prince Henry the Navigator, initiated voyages along the west coast of Africa, seeking new trade routes and opportunities for expansion. By the end of the century, Portuguese navigators like Bartolomeu Dias and Vasco da Gama had reached the southern tip of Africa and established a sea route to India, opening up new possibilities for trade and colonization. Christopher Columbus's voyages, sponsored by Spain, led to the European discovery of the Americas in 1492, which would have profound and far-reaching consequences for global history.

The fifteenth century was a dynamic period of transformation, characterized by significant political shifts, cultural achievements, and the beginning of global exploration and exchange. The developments of this century laid the foundations for the modern era, shaping the political, social, and economic landscapes of the world for centuries to come.

SIXTEENTH CENTURY

The sixteenth century was a period of profound transformation and development in world history, marked by significant political, cultural, and technological changes across various regions. Here is an extensive overview of the major events and developments during this century:

In Europe, the sixteenth century was a time of dramatic change and upheaval. The Protestant Reformation, initiated by Martin Luther's 95 Theses in 1517, challenged the authority of the Roman Catholic Church and led to the establishment of Protestant denominations. This religious schism resulted in decades of conflict, including the Peasants' War in Germany (1524–25) and the Thirty Years' War (1618–48), profoundly affecting European society and politics.

The Catholic Church responded with the Counter-Reformation, spearheaded by the Council of Trent (1545–63), which sought to reform internal practices and reaffirm Catholic doctrine. The Society of Jesus (Jesuits), founded by Ignatius of Loyola in 1540, became a leading force in the Counter-Reformation, focusing on education, missionary work, and the reinforcement of Catholicism in Europe and abroad.

Politically, Europe saw the rise of powerful centralized states. In Spain, the union of Castile and Aragon under Ferdinand and Isabella, and the subsequent reign of their grandson, Charles V (1519–56), established Spain as a dominant European power. Charles V also became Holy Roman Emperor, ruling over a vast empire that included the Netherlands, Austria, and large parts of Italy and the Americas.

In France, the Valois dynasty faced religious turmoil with the French Wars of Religion (1562–98) between Catholics and Huguenots (French Protestants). The conflict ended with the Edict of Nantes in 1598, issued by Henry IV, which granted limited religious tolerance to the Huguenots and paved the way for the consolidation of royal power.

England experienced significant political and religious changes during the sixteenth century. Henry VIII's break with the Catholic Church and the establishment of the Church of England (Anglican Church) in 1534, as a result of the English Reformation, altered the religious landscape. His daughter, Elizabeth I (1558–1603), stabilized the nation and fostered a cultural renaissance, exemplified by the works of William Shakespeare and the flourishing of English literature and drama.

In Eastern Europe, the Ottoman Empire continued its expansion under Suleiman the Magnificent (1520–66), reaching its zenith in territorial extent and political power. The Ottomans captured key cities such as Belgrade (1521) and Rhodes (1522) and besieged Vienna in 1529. The empire's administrative and military systems became models of efficiency and organization, and its cultural achievements, including architecture and literature, flourished.

The Safavid Empire in Persia, under Shah Ismail I (1501–24) and his successors, established Shi'a Islam as the state religion, distinguishing Persia from its Sunni neighbours. The Safavids created a centralized state and a rich cultural heritage, including notable achievements in art, architecture, and textiles.

In South Asia, the Mughal Empire was founded by Babur in 1526, following his victory at the Battle of Panipat. His grandson, Akbar the Great (1556–1605), expanded the empire significantly and implemented policies of religious tolerance and administrative efficiency, fostering a period of economic prosperity and cultural flourishing. The Mughal Empire became known for its architectural achievements, including the construction of the Fatehpur Sikri and the development of Mughal painting.

In East Asia, the Ming dynasty in China continued to thrive, although it faced challenges such as internal corruption and external threats from the Mongols and Japanese pirates. The dynasty's maritime expeditions, led by Admiral Zheng He in the early fifteenth century, had been halted, and China adopted a more isolationist stance. Despite this, the Ming period was marked by significant cultural and technological advancements, including developments in ceramics, painting, and the production of literature.

Japan in the sixteenth century was marked by the Sengoku period (1467–1615), a time of civil war and social upheaval as powerful regional lords (daimyos) vied for control over the country. The century saw the rise of prominent figures such as Oda Nobunaga, who began the process of unifying Japan, and his successors, Toyotomi Hideyoshi and Tokugawa Ieyasu. The unification was completed in the early seventeenth century, leading to the establishment of the Tokugawa shogunate, which would rule Japan for over 250 years.

The sixteenth century was also a period of significant maritime exploration and the beginning of European colonial expansion. Portuguese explorers, such as Vasco da Gama, established sea routes to India and the Spice Islands, leading to the establishment of a Portuguese colonial empire in Asia, Africa, and South America. Spain, following Columbus's voyages, established colonies in the Caribbean, Central, and South America, leading to the conquest of the Aztec and Inca empires by Hernán Cortés and Francisco Pizarro, respectively. These conquests had profound and often devastating impacts on the indigenous populations and led to the establishment of the vast Spanish Empire in the New World.

In Africa, the transatlantic slave trade began to take shape in the sixteenth century, with European powers, particularly Portugal and Spain, establishing trading posts along the West African coast. This marked the beginning of a dark period in history, as millions of Africans were forcibly transported to the Americas to work on plantations, a practice that would continue for centuries and have lasting social and economic impacts on African societies.

The sixteenth century also witnessed significant technological and scientific advancements. The invention of the printing press by Johannes Gutenberg in the mid-fifteenth century revolutionized the spread of knowledge, making books more accessible and fostering the spread of new ideas. The Scientific Revolution began to take root, with figures such as Nicolaus Copernicus proposing the heliocentric model of the solar system, challenging long-held beliefs and laying the groundwork for modern astronomy.

In summary, the sixteenth century was a period of profound change and development across the world. From the rise of powerful empires and the spread of the Renaissance in Europe to the establishment of the Mughal Empire in India and the expansion of European colonialism, this century laid the foundations for the modern world. The era was marked by significant cultural, political, and technological advancements, as well as profound social and economic changes that would shape the course of history for centuries to come.

SEVENTEENTH CENTURY

The seventeenth century was a period of significant transformation and development, characterized by profound political, social, cultural, and scientific changes across the globe. Here is an extensive overview of the major events and developments during this century:

In Europe, the seventeenth century was marked by a series of major conflicts, political upheavals, and cultural transformations. The Thirty Years' War (1618–48), one of the most destructive conflicts in European history, devastated much of the continent. It began as a religious conflict between Catholic and Protestant states within the Holy Roman Empire but evolved into a broader political struggle involving many of the great powers of Europe. The Peace of Westphalia, which ended the war in 1648, redrew the

political map of Europe and established the principles of state sovereignty and non-intervention, laying the groundwork for the modern international system.

In England, the century saw the English Civil War (1642–51), which pitted the Royalists, supporters of King Charles I, against the Parliamentarians, led by Oliver Cromwell. The conflict led to the execution of Charles I in 1649 and the temporary establishment of the Commonwealth of England under Cromwell's rule. The monarchy was restored in 1660 with the accession of Charles II, but the Glorious Revolution of 1688 resulted in the overthrow of his brother, James II, and the establishment of a constitutional monarchy under William III and Mary II.

France emerged as a dominant European power under the reign of Louis XIV (1643–1715), known as the Sun King. Louis XIV centralized power built the lavish Palace of Versailles, and pursued an aggressive foreign policy to expand French territory and influence. His reign marked the height of absolute monarchy in France, with significant cultural achievements in art, literature, and architecture, known as the Classical Age of French culture.

The Dutch Republic experienced a Golden Age during the seventeenth century, becoming a leading economic and maritime power. The Dutch East India Company (VOC) played a crucial role in establishing a vast colonial empire in Asia, particularly in Indonesia. The period saw remarkable achievements in trade, science, and the arts, with figures such as Rembrandt and Vermeer contributing to a flourishing cultural scene.

In the Habsburg territories, the seventeenth century was marked by internal strife and external threats. The Austrian Habsburgs successfully defended their lands against the Ottoman Empire at the Battle of Vienna in 1683, marking the beginning of the decline of Ottoman power in Europe. The Spanish Habsburgs, however, faced decline and economic difficulties, exacerbated by costly wars and internal strife.

The Scandinavian countries of Sweden and Denmark–Norway were involved in several conflicts during the century, including the Thirty Years' War and the Northern Wars. Sweden, under the leadership of King Gustavus Adolphus, emerged as a major military power in Europe, achieving significant victories before his death in battle in 1632.

The seventeenth century was also a period of significant scientific advancements, known as the Scientific Revolution. Key figures such as Galileo Galilei, Johannes Kepler, and Isaac Newton made groundbreaking contributions to astronomy, physics, and mathematics. Galileo's support for the heliocentric model of the solar system challenged traditional views and laid the groundwork for modern astronomy. Kepler's laws of planetary motion provided a deeper understanding of the mechanics of the heavens, while Newton's laws of motion and universal gravitation, published in his seminal work *Principia Mathematica* in 1687, revolutionized the study of physics.

In East Asia, the Ming dynasty in China faced internal rebellion and external threats, leading to its collapse in 1644. The Qing dynasty, founded by the Manchus, succeeded the Ming and began to consolidate its control over China. The Qing dynasty expanded its territory significantly, incorporating Taiwan, Tibet, and parts of Central Asia into the Chinese empire. The seventeenth century also saw the flourishing of Chinese culture, with significant developments in literature, painting, and porcelain.

Japan underwent significant political and social changes during the seventeenth century. The Tokugawa shogunate, established by Tokugawa Ieyasu in 1603, brought about a period of relative peace and stability known as the Edo period.

The Tokugawa shogunate implemented strict social hierarchies, isolated Japan from most foreign influence through the sakoku (closed country) policy and fostered economic growth and cultural development.

In South Asia, the Mughal Empire reached its zenith under the rule of Emperor Shah Jahan (1628–58) and his son, Aurangzeb (1658–1707). Shah Jahan is renowned for commissioning the construction of the Taj Mahal, a masterpiece of Mughal architecture, as a mausoleum for his wife Mumtaz Mahal. Aurangzeb expanded the empire to its greatest territorial extent but faced increasing internal strife and resistance from regional powers, laying the groundwork for the empire's decline in the following century.

In Southeast Asia, European colonial powers continued to expand their influence. The Dutch East India Company (VOC) established dominance over the spice trade in the Indonesian archipelago, while the Spanish colonized the Philippines. The Portuguese maintained control over key trading ports, such as Goa and Macau, facilitating their presence in the region.

The Americas witnessed significant changes during the seventeenth century as European colonial powers expanded their territories. The English established successful colonies in North America, including Jamestown (1607) and Plymouth (1620), leading to the growth of the Thirteen Colonies. The French expanded their presence in Canada and the Mississippi River Valley, while the Spanish continued to consolidate their control over Central and South America.

The transatlantic slave trade grew significantly during this period, with millions of Africans forcibly transported to the Americas to work on plantations. This brutal system had devastating effects on African societies and contributed to the economic development of European colonies in the New World.

In Africa, the seventeenth century saw the rise of powerful states and empires, such as the Kingdom of Kongo, the Ashanti Empire, and the Oyo Empire. These states engaged in trade with European powers, exchanging goods such as gold, ivory, and slaves. The impact of the transatlantic slave trade on African societies was profound, leading to population displacement, social disruption, and economic changes.

In summary, the seventeenth century was a period of significant transformation and development across the globe. From the rise of powerful states and empires in Europe, Asia, and Africa to the profound cultural, scientific, and technological advancements of the Scientific Revolution, this century laid the foundations for the modern world. The era was marked by significant political upheavals, religious conflicts, and the expansion of European colonialism, shaping the course of history for centuries to come.

EIGHTEENTH CENTURY

The eighteenth century was a period of profound change across the world, marked by political revolutions, intellectual transformations, and significant social, economic, and cultural developments. Here's an extensive overview of the major events and trends during this century:

In Europe, the eighteenth century is often referred to as the Age of Enlightenment, a period characterized by intellectual and philosophical advancements. Thinkers such as Voltaire, John Locke, Jean-Jacques Rousseau, and Immanuel Kant emphasized reason, individualism, and scepticism of traditional authority. Their ideas laid the intellectual groundwork for political revolutions and reforms.

The century witnessed several significant political revolutions. The American Revolution (1775–83) resulted in the thirteen American colonies gaining independence from Great Britain and the establishment of the United States of America. The Declaration of Independence in 1776, written by Thomas Jefferson, articulated the colonies' demand for freedom and equality. The subsequent drafting of the U.S. Constitution in 1787 established a federal system of government and a framework for democratic governance.

The French Revolution (1789–99) was another major upheaval, profoundly impacting France and Europe as a whole. The revolution began with widespread discontent with the monarchy and the feudal system, leading to the fall of King Louis XVI and the establishment of the First French Republic. The revolution introduced radical social and political changes, including the abolition of feudal privileges, the rise of secularism, and the promotion of the principles of liberty, equality, and fraternity. The revolution also saw the rise of Napoleon Bonaparte, who would eventually become Emperor of

France and reshape the European political landscape.

In Britain, the century was marked by significant developments in political and economic spheres. The Union of England and Scotland in 1707 formed the Kingdom of Great Britain. The Industrial Revolution began in the latter half of the century, transforming Britain into the world's first industrialized nation. Innovations in technology, such as the steam engine, and the rise of factories revolutionized production processes and had far-reaching economic and social impacts.

In Eastern Europe, the Russian Empire under Peter the Great (reigned 1682–1725) and Catherine the Great (reigned 1762–96) underwent significant modernization and expansion. Peter the Great implemented extensive reforms to modernize the Russian military, government, and society, establishing St. Petersburg as a new, westernized capital. Catherine the Great continued these efforts, expanding Russian territory through wars with the Ottoman Empire and the partitioning of Poland.

The Ottoman Empire experienced both internal challenges and external pressures during the eighteenth century. The empire struggled with administrative inefficiencies, military defeats, and territorial losses to European powers. Despite these challenges, the Ottoman state remained a significant political and cultural force in the region.

In East Asia, the Qing dynasty in China reached the height of its power during the eighteenth century under emperors Kangxi, Yongzheng, and Qianlong. The Qing Empire expanded its borders significantly, incorporating Taiwan, Tibet, Xinjiang, and Mongolia. The period also saw flourishing arts and culture, with advancements in literature, painting, and porcelain. However, towards the end of the century, internal challenges and external pressures began to weaken the dynasty.

Japan remained under the Tokugawa shogunate, a period known as the Edo period, characterized by political stability, economic growth, and isolationist policies. The shogunate maintained strict social hierarchies and limited foreign contact, fostering a unique Japanese culture that included developments in arts, literature, and theatre, such as the kabuki and bunraku forms.

In South Asia, the Mughal Empire, which had been dominant in the previous centuries, began to decline due to internal strife, administrative inefficiencies, and external invasions. The decline of the Mughal Empire created a power vacuum that facilitated the rise of regional powers such as the Marathas, Sikhs, and the British East India Company. The Battle of Plassey in 1757 marked the beginning of British colonial dominance in India, which would eventually lead to the establishment of British rule over the Indian subcontinent.

In Africa, the eighteenth century was marked by the expansion of the Atlantic slave trade, which had devastating impacts on African societies. European powers established and expanded trading posts and colonies along the coast, engaging in the brutal trade of enslaved Africans to the

Americas. The consequences of the slave trade included significant population loss, social disruption, and economic changes in African communities.

In the Americas, European colonization continued to expand, with Spain, Portugal, Britain, France, and the Netherlands establishing and consolidating colonies. The Spanish and Portuguese empires in Latin America extracted vast wealth through mining and agriculture, relying heavily on enslaved labour. The British and French colonies in North America engaged in conflicts such as the French and Indian War (1754–63), which was part of the larger Seven Years' War, resulting in British dominance in North America.

The Haitian Revolution (1791–1804) was a significant event in the Caribbean, leading to the establishment of Haiti as the first independent black republic and the abolition of slavery. The revolution was led by enslaved Africans and free people of colour against French colonial rule, inspired by the principles of the French Revolution.

The eighteenth century also witnessed significant advancements in science and technology. The Enlightenment era's emphasis on reason and empirical observation led to scientific breakthroughs by figures such as Isaac Newton, who continued to influence physics and mathematics, and Carl Linnaeus, who developed the modern system of biological classification. The development of the steam engine by James Watt and others during the Industrial Revolution had profound impacts on transportation, manufacturing, and energy use.

Cultural developments in the eighteenth century included the flourishing of literature, music, and the arts. The period saw the rise of the novel as a literary form, with works by authors such as Daniel Defoe, Jonathan Swift, and Jane Austen. Classical music reached new heights with composers like Johann Sebastian Bach, Wolfgang Amadeus Mozart, and Ludwig van Beethoven, whose works remain central to Western musical tradition.

In summary, the eighteenth century was a period of significant transformation and development across the globe. Political revolutions, intellectual advancements, and cultural achievements reshaped societies and laid the foundations for the modern world. The century was marked by the rise and fall of empires, the spread of Enlightenment ideas, and significant social, economic, and technological changes that continue to influence contemporary history.

NINETEENTH CENTURY

The nineteenth century was a period of significant transformation, marked by industrialization, political revolutions, colonial expansion, and profound social and cultural changes. Here is an extensive overview of the major events and trends during this century:

In Europe, the century began with the aftermath of the French Revolution and the Napoleonic Wars. The Congress of Vienna in 1815 sought to restore stability and balance of power in Europe after the defeat of Napoleon. This period saw the rise of conservatism, as exemplified by the policies of Austrian Chancellor Klemens von Metternich, who aimed to suppress revolutionary movements and maintain the status quo. However, the century was also marked by numerous uprisings and revolutions, including the Revolutions of 1848, which spread across Europe and reflected widespread demands for political and social reforms.

The Industrial Revolution, which began in Britain in the late eighteenth century, continued to spread across Europe and North America throughout the nineteenth century. This period saw dramatic advancements in technology and industry, such as the development of the steam engine, the expansion of the railway network, and the rise of factories. These changes transformed economies, leading to increased production, urbanization, and significant social changes, including the rise of the working class and new labour movements.

In the United States, the nineteenth century was a period of territorial expansion and civil conflict. The concept of Manifest Destiny fuelled westward expansion, leading to the annexation of vast territories and conflicts with Indigenous peoples. The Mexican-American War (1846–48) resulted in the United States acquiring large parts of the present-day southwestern United States. The century was also marked by the Civil War (1861–65), fought between the Northern states (Union) and the Southern states (Confederacy) primarily over the issues of slavery and states' rights. The Union's victory led to the abolition of slavery and the eventual Reconstruction of the Southern states.

Latin America experienced a wave of independence movements in the early nineteenth century, leading to the liberation of most Spanish and Portuguese colonies. Figures like Simón Bolívar, José de San Martín, and Miguel Hidalgo played crucial roles in these struggles. The newly independent nations faced challenges in establishing stable governments and economies, often experiencing political instability and conflicts.

In Africa, the nineteenth century saw the intensification of European colonialism, known as the 'Scramble for Africa'. European powers, driven by economic interests and nationalist competition, carved up the continent into colonies. The Berlin Conference of 1884–85 formalized the division of Africa among European nations. This colonization had profound impacts on African societies, economies, and political structures, often leading to exploitation and resistance.

Asia also experienced significant changes during the nineteenth century. In China, the Qing dynasty faced internal rebellions, such as the Taiping Rebellion (1850–64), and external pressures from Western powers. The Opium Wars (1839–42 and 1856–60) resulted in significant territorial and economic concessions to Britain and other Western nations. Japan underwent a dramatic transformation with the Meiji Restoration in 1868, which ended centuries of feudal rule and initiated a period of rapid modernization and industrialization.

India, under British colonial rule, saw significant social, economic, and political changes. The British East India Company initially controlled large parts of India, but after the Indian Rebellion of 1857, the British Crown took direct control, marking the beginning of the British Raj. This period saw the introduction of Western education, legal systems, and infrastructure developments, alongside the exploitation of India's resources and people.

In the Ottoman Empire, the nineteenth century was a period of decline and attempts at reform. The Tanzimat reforms (1839–76) aimed to modernize the empire's administration, military, and economy, but the empire continued to lose territory and influence. Nationalist movements within the empire's diverse population further weakened its cohesion.

The nineteenth century also saw significant cultural and intellectual developments. The Romantic movement in literature and the arts emphasized emotion, nature, and individualism, reacting against the rationalism of the Enlightenment. Prominent figures included poets like William Wordsworth and Lord Byron, and composers like Ludwig van Beethoven and Franz Schubert. The latter part of the century saw the rise of Realism and Impressionism in art, with artists such as Gustave Courbet and Claude Monet.

Scientific advancements during the nineteenth century had profound impacts on society. Charles Darwin's theory of evolution by natural selection, published in *On the Origin of Species* in 1859, revolutionized biology and influenced many other fields. Advances in medicine, such as the development of vaccines and antiseptics, improved public health. The period also saw the rise of social sciences, with figures like Karl Marx and Sigmund Freud shaping the study of society and human behaviour.

Technological innovations transformed daily life and communication. The invention of the telegraph, telephone, and later the electric light bulb and internal combustion engine revolutionized industry and society. The expansion of railroads and steamships facilitated global trade and travel, shrinking distances and connecting people across continents.

In summary, the nineteenth century was a period of profound transformation marked by political revolutions, industrialization, colonial expansion, and significant social, cultural, and scientific developments. The changes of this century laid the foundations for the modern world, shaping the political, economic, and social structures that continue to influence contemporary history.

TWENTIETH CENTURY

The twentieth century was a period of extraordinary change and turbulence, marked by world wars, ideological conflicts, technological advancements, decolonization, and significant social transformations. Here's an extensive overview of the major events and trends of the century:

Early 1900s

The century began with the aftermath of the Industrial Revolution and the consolidation of empires. The early 1900s were characterized by relative peace in Europe, known as the Belle Époque, marked by technological and cultural advancements. This era saw significant progress in science, arts, and industry. Innovations such as the telephone, automobile, and cinema transformed daily life and communication. However, beneath this progress, tensions were brewing among the major powers due to militarism, alliances, imperialism, and nationalism.

1914–17

The outbreak of World War I in 1914 shattered the peace of the Belle Époque. This devastating conflict involved most of the world's great powers, divided into the Allies and the Central Powers. The war was characterized by trench warfare, chemical weapons, and massive casualties. Key battles such as the Battle of the Somme and the Battle of Verdun exemplified the war's brutality. The Russian Revolution of 1917 led to Russia's withdrawal from the war and the rise of the Soviet Union. The war ended in 1918 with the Treaty of Versailles, which imposed harsh penalties on Germany, including significant territorial losses, military restrictions, and reparations. This treaty redrew the map of Europe, creating new nations and setting the stage for future conflicts by fostering resentment in Germany.

1917–20s

The interwar period saw significant political and economic upheaval. The Russian Revolution of 1917 had profound effects, leading to the rise of the Soviet Union, the world's first communist state. The 1920s, known as the Roaring Twenties, were marked by economic prosperity, cultural dynamism, and technological innovation in many parts of the world, particularly in the United States and Western Europe. This era saw the rise of jazz, the flapper culture, and significant advancements in cinema and radio. However, this period of growth ended with the Great Depression of the 1930s, a severe

worldwide economic downturn that led to widespread unemployment, poverty, and political instability. The economic hardship contributed to the rise of totalitarian regimes, most notably Adolf Hitler's Nazi Germany and Benito Mussolini's Fascist Italy.

1939–45

World War II broke out in 1939, involving many of the same powers as the First World War, along with new participants. The conflict was characterized by massive military campaigns and significant global impact. Key events included the invasion of Poland by Germany, the Battle of Britain, the Eastern Front's brutal fighting between Germany and the Soviet Union, and the Pacific War between Japan and the Allies. The war saw horrific events such as the Holocaust, where six million Jews and millions of others were systematically murdered by Nazi Germany. Other atrocities included the Nanjing Massacre, and the widespread devastation caused by strategic bombings. The war ended in 1945 with the unconditional surrender of Germany in May and Japan in August, following the atomic bombings of Hiroshima and Nagasaki. The aftermath left much of Europe and Asia in ruins, and the United Nations was established in an effort to prevent future global conflicts.

1950–75

The post-war period saw the emergence of the United States and the Soviet Union as superpowers, leading to the Cold War, a prolonged period of geopolitical tension and ideological conflict between the capitalist West, led by the United States, and the communist East, led by the Soviet Union. This era was marked by a nuclear arms race, with both superpowers amassing vast arsenals of nuclear weapons, leading to the doctrine of mutually assured destruction. Numerous proxy wars occurred in regions such as Korea, Vietnam, and Afghanistan, where the superpowers supported opposing sides. Significant events included the Cuban Missile Crisis in 1962, which brought the world to the brink of nuclear war, and the Korean War (1950–53), which solidified the division of Korea into North and South. The Vietnam War (1955–75) was a protracted conflict that deeply divided American society and had profound effects on both Vietnam and the United States.

1957–69

The Cold War also spurred technological and scientific competition, leading to milestones such as the Space Race. The Soviet Union launched the first artificial satellite, Sputnik, in 1957, and in 1961, Yuri Gagarin became the first human to travel into space. The United States achieved a significant victory with the Apollo 11 mission in 1969, when astronauts Neil Armstrong and Buzz Aldrin became the first humans to land on the Moon.

1947–60

Decolonization was a major trend of the post-war period. Many African, Asian, and Caribbean nations gained independence from European colonial powers, often after prolonged struggles. India and Pakistan gained independence from Britain in 1947, followed by a wave of decolonization across Africa in the 1950s and 1960s. This period was marked by both peaceful transitions, as in Ghana, and violent struggles, as in Algeria and Vietnam. Newly independent states faced challenges such as political instability, economic development, and the legacy of colonial rule.

In the United States, the Civil Rights Movement of the 1950s and 1960s sought to end racial segregation and discrimination against African Americans, leading to significant legislative changes such as the Civil Rights Act of 1964 and the Voting Rights Act of 1965. The feminist movement also gained momentum, advocating for gender equality and women's rights, resulting in significant social and legal changes, including greater workplace equality and reproductive rights.

The twentieth century was also a period of rapid technological advancement and cultural change. The development of automobiles, aeroplanes, and telecommunications revolutionized transportation and communication. The invention of the computer and the rise of the internet transformed industries and societies, leading to the information age. Advances in medicine, such as the discovery of antibiotics, vaccines, and the development of modern surgical techniques, significantly improved public health and life expectancy.

Late Twentieth Century

The late twentieth century saw the end of the Cold War with the dissolution of the Soviet Union in 1991, leading to a unipolar world dominated by the United States. The period also saw significant economic changes, with the rise of globalization, the shift towards neoliberal economic policies, and the emergence of China as a major economic power. China's rapid industrialization and growth transformed it into a key player in global politics and economics.

Environmental issues gained prominence towards the end of the century, with growing awareness of climate change, pollution, and biodiversity loss. The establishment of environmental organizations and international agreements, such as the Kyoto Protocol, reflected increasing global concern for environmental sustainability.

The twentieth century was marked by significant political, social, and technological changes that transformed the world. The century witnessed devastating conflicts and ideological battles, but also remarkable advancements in science, technology, and human rights. The legacies of these changes continue to shape the contemporary world in profound ways.

TWENTY-FIRST CENTURY

The twenty-first century has been marked by rapid technological advancements, significant geopolitical shifts, and profound social changes. Here's an extensive overview of the major events and trends of the century so far.

Late Twentieth Century

The century began with the continuation of technological advancements that had gained momentum in the late twentieth century. The rise of the internet and digital technology has transformed every aspect of life, from communication and commerce to entertainment and education. The proliferation of smartphones, social media, and artificial intelligence has reshaped how people interact, consume information, and conduct business. Companies like Google, Apple, Facebook, and Amazon have become global powerhouses, driving innovation and economic growth. The development of cloud computing, big data analytics, and the Internet of Things (IoT) has further revolutionized industries and everyday life, enabling unprecedented connectivity and data-driven decision-making.

Early Twenty-First Century

The early twenty-first century was also marked by significant geopolitical events. The terrorist attacks on 11 September 2001, in the United States led to a global war on terror, resulting in the invasions of Afghanistan in 2001 and Iraq in 2003. These conflicts had far-reaching consequences, including prolonged military engagements, significant loss of life, and widespread instability in the Middle East. The rise of terrorist organizations like ISIS further complicated the geopolitical landscape, leading to international coalitions to combat terrorism and insurgency. The wars in Afghanistan and Iraq also sparked debates over foreign policy, human rights, and the balance between security and civil liberties.

2007–08

The global financial crisis of 2007–08 was another pivotal event, leading to severe economic downturns worldwide. The collapse of major financial institutions, the bursting of housing bubbles, and subsequent government bailouts highlighted systemic weaknesses in the global financial system. The crisis had lasting effects on economies, leading to austerity measures, increased unemployment, and a reevaluation of economic policies and regulations. In response to the crisis, governments and central banks implemented various monetary and fiscal measures to stabilize economies, such as stimulus packages, interest rate cuts, and quantitative easing. The crisis also prompted reforms in financial regulation, including the Dodd-

Frank Act in the United States, aimed at preventing future financial meltdowns.

Environmental issues have indeed gained increasing prominence in the twenty-first century, driven by the scientific consensus on climate change and its wide-ranging impacts. Efforts to mitigate climate change have become a global priority, culminating in significant agreements such as the Paris Agreement of 2015. This landmark accord aims to limit global warming to well below 2 degrees Celsius above pre-industrial levels, with efforts to pursue even more ambitious targets of 1.5 degrees Celsius. Despite these international commitments, challenges persist, exacerbated by visible effects like extreme weather events, rising sea levels, and disruptions to ecosystems and livelihoods worldwide. Debates over energy policies, the transition to renewable energy sources, and the role of industries in environmental sustainability remain contentious and urgent.

In the realm of social changes, the twenty-first century has witnessed notable strides in advancing human rights and social justice across various fronts. Movements advocating for LGBTQ+ rights have seen significant progress, with the legalization of same-sex marriage in numerous countries marking a milestone in equality legislation. The #MeToo movement, originating in 2006 but gaining widespread attention around 2017, has sparked a global reckoning against sexual harassment and assault, prompting shifts in workplace culture and legal reforms aimed at protecting victims and holding perpetrators accountable. Additionally, movements like Black Lives Matter (BLM) have mobilized global protests against systemic racism and police brutality, galvanized by high-profile incidents such as the killing of George Floyd in 2020. These movements have catalysed discussions on racial equity, police reform, and broader societal changes aimed at dismantling structural inequalities.

Economically, the twenty-first century has witnessed the ascent of emerging economies, particularly in Asia, reshaping global economic dynamics. China's rapid economic growth has positioned it as a formidable global player, challenging traditional Western dominance and influencing international trade, investment, and geopolitical strategies. India has also emerged as a significant economic powerhouse, contributing to the shift of the global economic centre towards Asia. These developments have spurred debates over economic policies, trade relations, and the distribution of global wealth and resources, reflecting a multipolar world order where emerging economies exert increasing influence on global affairs.

The twenty-first century has been defined by a complex interplay of environmental challenges, social movements for equality and justice, and shifts in global economic power dynamics. The ongoing efforts to address climate change, promote social inclusivity, and navigate the rise of emerging economies will continue to shape the trajectory of the century, influencing policies, cultures, and societies worldwide.

The twenty-first century has indeed been characterized by remarkable technological advancements that are reshaping industries and societies worldwide. Artificial intelligence (AI), machine learning, and automation have revolutionized various sectors, from manufacturing and finance to healthcare and transportation. These technologies offer unprecedented efficiencies and capabilities but also raise critical questions about job displacement, workforce reskilling, and the ethical implications of autonomous systems.

Biotechnology has also seen significant progress, particularly with the advent of CRISPR gene editing technology. This innovation holds promise for treating genetic disorders, developing personalized medicine, and advancing agricultural practices. However, ethical debates surrounding genetic manipulation, concerns over unintended consequences, and the need for robust regulatory frameworks continue to accompany these breakthroughs.

Late 2019–20

The COVID-19 pandemic, emerging in late 2019 and spreading globally in 2020, has profoundly impacted societies and economies worldwide. The pandemic caused widespread illness and death, overwhelmed healthcare systems, and led to unprecedented social and economic disruptions. Governments and industries mobilized swiftly to develop vaccines, demonstrating global scientific collaboration and the power of biomedical research. However, the pandemic also exposed vulnerabilities in healthcare infrastructures, disparities in access to healthcare, and the importance of global cooperation in responding to health emergencies.

In summary, the twenty-first century is unfolding against a backdrop of rapid technological innovation, complex geopolitical dynamics, and evolving social norms. The ongoing convergence of digital transformation, environmental challenges, public health crises, and social movements for justice and equality will continue to shape the global landscape in interconnected and profound ways. As societies adapt to these changes, the decisions made today will influence the trajectory of human development and well-being in the decades to come.

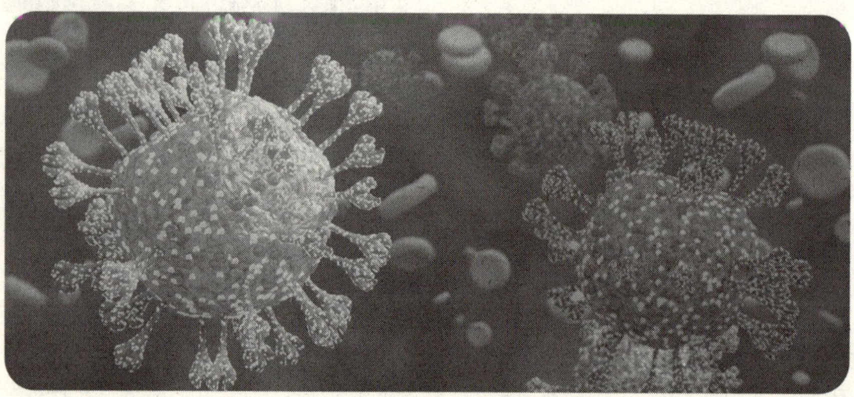

Indian History

FIRST MILLENNIUM BCE

The first millennium BCE was a dynamic period in Indian history, marked by the formation of the Mahajanapadas, the emergence of Buddhism and Jainism, and the rise of the Maurya Empire. Each of these developments played a crucial role in shaping the social, political, and religious landscape of ancient India.

The Mahajanapadas, which emerged around 600 BCE, represented the formation of sixteen large states or republics in northern India. These states were significant for their political organization and influence. The most prominent Mahajanapadas included Magadha, Kosala, Kuru, Panchala, and Vatsa. These states varied in their forms of government, with some being monarchies and others functioning as republics where governance was conducted through assemblies. The rise of the Mahajanapadas was facilitated by increased agricultural productivity, trade, and urbanization. This period saw the growth of cities and the development of more complex economic and administrative systems.

The emergence of Buddhism and Jainism in the sixth century BCE brought profound religious and philosophical changes to Indian society. Both religions challenged the existing Vedic traditions and introduced new ideas about spirituality, ethics, and social conduct.

Buddhism was founded by Siddhartha Gautama, who later became known as the Buddha. Siddhartha was born into a royal family in the Shakya clan but renounced his princely life to seek enlightenment. After years of meditation and asceticism, he attained enlightenment under the Bodhi tree in Bodh Gaya. The core teachings of Buddhism are encapsulated in the Four Noble Truths and the Eightfold Path. The Four Noble Truths outline the nature of suffering, its cause, its cessation, and the path to its cessation. The Eightfold Path provides a practical guide to ethical and mental development with the goal of attaining Nirvana, or liberation from the cycle of birth and rebirth. Buddhism emphasized non-violence, compassion, and the impermanence of all things. It rejected the caste system and rituals of the Vedic tradition, offering an inclusive path to spiritual liberation.

Jainism, founded by Mahavira, also emerged as a significant religious movement in the sixth century BCE. Mahavira, like Siddhartha, was born into a royal family but renounced worldly life to pursue spiritual awakening. Jainism's core teachings revolve around the principles of Ahimsa (non-violence), Satya (truth), Asteya (non-stealing), Brahmacharya (celibacy), and Aparigraha (non-attachment). Jainism places a strong emphasis on asceticism and self-discipline as means to achieve spiritual purity and liberation (moksha). The Jains practice strict non-violence, extending it to all living beings, which profoundly influences their diet, lifestyle, and occupation choices.

The rise of the Maurya Empire in 321 BCE marked the beginning of a new era of political unification and centralized governance in India. The founder of the Maurya Empire, Chandragupta Maurya, established control over the Magadha region and subsequently expanded his territory to include most of northern and central India. His rise to power was aided by the strategic counsel of his advisor, Chanakya (also known as Kautilya), who authored the Arthashastra, a treatise on statecraft, economic policy, and military strategy.

Chandragupta's successor, Bindusara, continued the expansionist policies, but it was under Ashoka the Great, the third Maurya emperor, that the empire reached its zenith. Ashoka's reign from 268 to 232 BCE is particularly notable for his conversion to Buddhism after the bloody Kalinga War. The war's immense human suffering deeply affected Ashoka, leading him to embrace Buddhism and promote its principles of non-violence and compassion.

Ashoka's efforts to spread Buddhism were unprecedented. He dispatched missionaries to various parts of India and abroad, including Sri Lanka, Central Asia, and Southeast Asia, facilitating the spread of Buddhism across Asia. He also erected numerous edicts and inscriptions on pillars and rocks throughout his empire, advocating for moral and ethical conduct based on Buddhist teachings. These inscriptions, known as the Ashokan Edicts, are among the earliest deciphered writings in Indian history and provide valuable insights into Ashoka's policies and the social and religious milieu of the time.

The Maurya Empire under Ashoka also saw significant administrative and economic developments. Ashoka established a centralized bureaucracy to govern the vast empire, with a network of officials overseeing various aspects of administration, justice, and revenue collection. The empire's economy flourished, with improvements in agriculture, trade, and infrastructure. Roads were built to connect distant regions, facilitating commerce and communication.

Despite its achievements, the Maurya Empire began to decline after Ashoka's death. Internal conflicts, succession disputes, and external invasions weakened the empire, leading to its eventual fragmentation. The last Maurya ruler, Brihadratha, was assassinated in 185 BCE, marking the end of the Maurya dynasty.

The first millennium BCE was thus a period of significant transformation in Indian history. The formation of the Mahajanapadas laid the groundwork for more complex political structures,

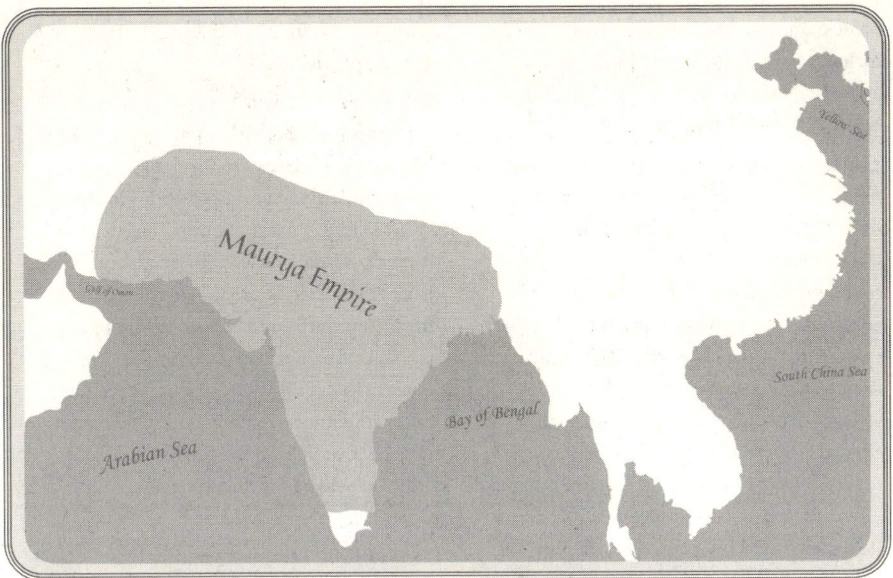

while the emergence of Buddhism and Jainism introduced new religious and philosophical ideas that challenged the existing social order. The rise and expansion of the Maurya Empire under Chandragupta and Ashoka represented a remarkable period of political unification, administrative innovation, and cultural flourishing. These developments collectively shaped the trajectory of Indian civilization, leaving a lasting legacy that influenced subsequent historical periods.

SECOND MILLENNIUM BCE

The second millennium BCE in India was a transformative period marked by significant cultural, social, and political changes. This era saw the arrival of the Indo-Aryans, the composition of the Vedas, and the development of early states and kingdoms, collectively shaping the trajectory of Indian civilization.

The Vedic Period, traditionally dated from around 1500 to 500 BCE, began with the migration of the Indo-Aryans into the Indian subcontinent. These people are believed to have originated from the steppes of Central Asia, bringing with them their language, customs, and religious beliefs. This migration marked the beginning of a new cultural era, characterized by the composition of the Vedas, the oldest and most revered scriptures of Hinduism.

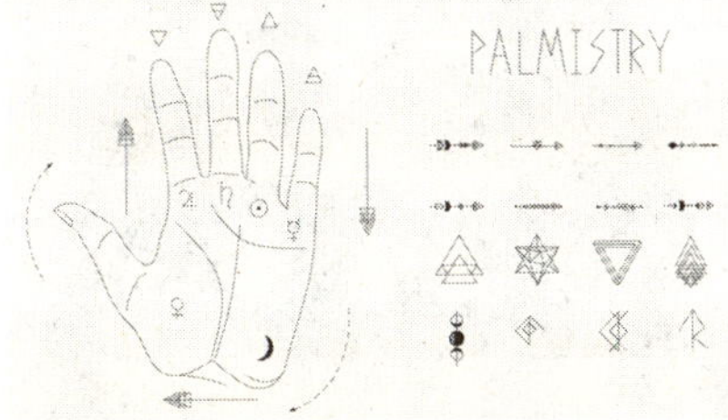

The Vedas consist of four primary texts: the Rigveda, the Samaveda, the Yajurveda, and the Atharvaveda. Composed in early Sanskrit, the Vedas are a collection of hymns, prayers, rituals, and philosophical discourses that form the foundation of Vedic religion and later Hindu practices. The Rigveda, the earliest of these texts, contains over a thousand hymns dedicated to various deities, reflecting the religious beliefs and practices of the early Indo-Aryans. The Samaveda is primarily a collection of melodies for chanting, while the Yajurveda contains prose mantras for rituals. The Atharvaveda includes hymns, spells, and incantations addressing more everyday concerns such as health and protection from harm.

The society described in the Vedas was predominantly pastoral and agrarian, with cattle playing a central role in the economy and social life. The early Vedic people lived in semi-nomadic communities, moving frequently in search of pastures for their herds. Over time, they began to settle in more permanent villages, leading to the development of agriculture and the establishment of more complex social structures. The Vedic society was organized into various tribes, each led by a chieftain (rajan) who was responsible for the protection and administration of the tribe. The chieftain was often supported by a council of elders (sabha) and a popular assembly (samiti), highlighting an early form of participatory governance.

Social stratification in Vedic society became more pronounced over time, eventually evolving into the varna system, a precursor to the caste system. The four primary varnas were the Brahmins (priests and scholars), the Kshatriyas (warriors and rulers), the Vaishyas (traders and agriculturists), and the Shudras (labourers and service providers). This division of society was based on occupation and duties, with the Brahmins holding the highest status due to their role in performing religious rituals and preserving sacred knowledge.

The religious beliefs of the Vedic people were polytheistic, with a pantheon of gods representing various natural and cosmic forces. Indra, the god of thunder and rain, was one of the most prominent deities, often depicted as a warrior god who protected the tribes from enemies. Other important deities included Agni, the god of fire, and Soma, associated with a sacred ritual drink. The Vedic rituals, or yajnas, involved elaborate ceremonies conducted by priests to invoke the blessings of the gods for prosperity, health, and victory in battles.

Around 1200 BCE, the Vedic culture transitioned into the Iron Age, marked by the use of iron tools and weapons, which significantly impacted agriculture, warfare, and settlement patterns. The introduction of iron technology facilitated the clearing of forests for agriculture, leading to the expansion of settlements and the establishment of larger and more permanent communities. This period also saw the rise of early states and kingdoms, laying the groundwork for more complex political structures.

By around 1000 BCE, the Vedic society had spread eastward into the fertile plains of the Ganga River, leading to the formation of numerous small kingdoms and tribal republics. These early states, known as Janapadas, were often in conflict with each other, competing for resources and territory. The consolidation of power in some regions gave rise to larger political entities, eventually leading to the formation of the Mahajanapadas by around 600 BCE.

The Mahajanapadas were sixteen large and powerful states that emerged in northern India, marking a significant shift from tribal and clan-based governance to more centralized political structures. Among the most prominent of these were Magadha, Kosala, Kuru, and Panchala. Each Mahajanapada had its own capital city, administrative machinery, and military forces. The period of the Mahajanapadas was characterized by increased urbanization, trade, and economic activity, setting the stage for the subsequent rise of great empires like the Maurya and Gupta dynasties.

The later part of the Vedic period also witnessed significant philosophical and religious developments. The composition of the Upanishads, a collection of philosophical texts, marked a shift from ritualistic practices to more introspective and speculative thought. The Upanishads explored concepts such as the nature of reality (Brahman), the self (Atman), and the relationship between the two, laying the foundation for later Hindu philosophy. This intellectual ferment also gave rise to new religious movements, including Buddhism and Jainism, which would profoundly influence Indian culture and society.

In summary, the second millennium BCE in India was a period of profound transformation, marked by the arrival of the Indo-Aryans, the composition of the Vedas, and the development of early states and kingdoms. The Vedic period laid the foundations for Indian civilization, with its religious, social, and political structures influencing subsequent historical developments. The transition to the Iron Age and the rise of the Mahajanapadas marked the beginning of a new era of urbanization, state formation, and intellectual growth, setting the stage for the rich and diverse history of ancient India.

THIRD MILLENNIUM BCE

The Indus Valley Civilization, also known as the Harappan Civilization, thrived from approximately 3300 to 1300 BCE in what is now Pakistan and northwest India. It stands as one of the world's earliest and most advanced urban cultures, contemporaneous with Mesopotamia and Ancient Egypt. Its discovery in the 1920s revolutionized our understanding of early human societies and revealed an intricate and sophisticated civilization.

Geographically, the Indus Valley Civilization covered a vast region, encompassing modern-day Pakistan and parts of northwest India, extending from the Arabian Sea in the south to the Himalayas in the north. Major urban centres included Harappa and Mohenjo-Daro, along with other significant sites like Dholavira, Kalibangan, Lothal, and Rakhigarhi. These cities were well-planned and exhibited a level of urban sophistication unparalleled at the time.

The hallmark of the Indus Valley Civilization was its advanced urban planning. Cities were laid out in a grid pattern, with streets intersecting at right angles, indicative of careful and deliberate urban design. Residential areas were segregated from commercial and administrative zones. The buildings were constructed using uniformly sized baked bricks, suggesting a standardized system of production and a high degree of organizational control. Multi-storied houses, often with private wells and bathrooms, were common, highlighting the emphasis on hygiene and public health.

One of the most remarkable aspects of the Indus Valley Civilization was its sophisticated drainage and sanitation system. The cities boasted an extensive network of covered drains and sewers, which ran alongside the streets and connected to larger channels, effectively managing wastewater. This advanced infrastructure ensured cleanliness and prevented the spread of diseases, underscoring the civilization's focus on public health and urban management.

The social organization of the Indus Valley Civilization remains a topic of scholarly debate, largely due to the undeciphered script of their writing system. However, archaeological evidence suggests a society that was both complex and highly organized. The standardized construction techniques, uniform weights and measures, and the widespread distribution of similar artefacts indicate a central authority or a cohesive political structure. Yet, unlike contemporary Mesopotamia or Egypt, there is no clear evidence of monumental architecture like palaces or temples, which complicates our understanding of their political and religious institutions.

Economically, the Indus Valley Civilization was diverse and dynamic. Agriculture formed the backbone of the economy, with evidence of the cultivation of wheat, barley, peas, and cotton. The discovery of granaries in Harappa and Mohenjo-Daro indicates the importance of grain storage and management. The civilization also engaged in extensive trade, both within the Indian subcontinent and with distant regions, including Mesopotamia, as evidenced by the discovery of Indus seals and artefacts in Mesopotamian sites. Trade goods likely included precious stones, metals, and crafted items such as pottery and beads.

Craftsmanship was highly developed in the Indus Valley Civilization. Artisans produced a wide range of goods, including pottery, jewellery, and tools. The pottery was often decorated with intricate designs, while beads made from carnelian, agate, and other semi-precious stones were highly valued.

The civilization is also known for its skill in metallurgy, with evidence of copper, bronze, lead, and tin being used to create various tools and ornaments. The famous 'Dancing Girl' statue from Mohenjo-Daro, a small bronze figure, exemplifies their artistic and metallurgical expertise.

Religious beliefs and practices of the Indus Valley people are not well understood due to the absence of decipherable written records. However, various artefacts provide clues. Seals depicting animals, human figures, and mythical creatures, as well as terracotta figurines, suggest a rich iconography and possibly a pantheon of deities. The 'Pashupati Seal', featuring a seated figure surrounded by animals, has been interpreted by some scholars as an early representation of the Hindu god Shiva. Additionally, the presence of large public baths, such as the Great Bath of Mohenjo-Daro, hints at ritualistic practices involving water, possibly for purification purposes.

The decline of the Indus Valley Civilization around 1900 BCE remains a subject of scholarly inquiry. Several theories have been proposed, including climate change, tectonic activity, and shifting river patterns, which may have led to agricultural decline and urban disintegration. There is also evidence of gradual abandonment of cities rather than sudden destruction, suggesting a complex process of decline over several centuries. The civilization's eventual disappearance did not, however, erase its legacy, as subsequent cultures in the Indian subcontinent inherited and adapted many of its technological and cultural advancements.

The Indus Valley Civilization's contributions to urban planning, architecture, and social organization had a lasting impact on the development of subsequent Indian civilizations. Its emphasis on hygiene, standardization, and trade connectivity reflects a sophisticated understanding of urban management and economic systems. The mystery surrounding its writing system and social structure continues to intrigue researchers, offering a tantalizing glimpse into one of humanity's earliest and most enigmatic civilizations.

In conclusion, the Indus Valley Civilization represents a pinnacle of ancient human achievement, characterized by its advanced urban planning, sophisticated craftsmanship, and complex social organization. While much remains to be discovered about their language, beliefs, and societal structures, the archaeological evidence paints a picture of a highly developed and interconnected society. The legacy of the Indus Valley Civilization endures as a testament to the ingenuity and resilience of early human societies, providing invaluable insights into the origins of urban life and culture in the Indian subcontinent.

FIRST MILLENNIUM CE

The first millennium CE was a transformative period in Indian history, marked by the rise and fall of several powerful dynasties, significant achievements in arts and sciences, and profound cultural advancements. The Gupta Empire, often referred to as the Golden Age of India, and the regional powers such as the Vakataka, Pallava, and Chalukya dynasties played crucial roles in shaping the subcontinent's historical and cultural landscape.

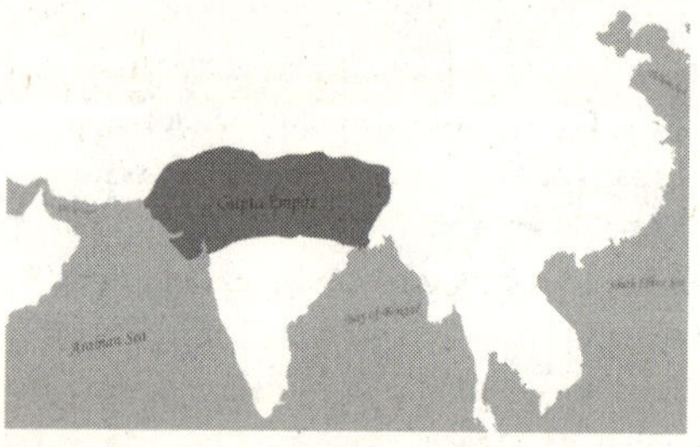

The Gupta Empire, which ruled from approximately 320 to 550 CE, is celebrated as a period of great cultural flourishing and intellectual achievement. Founded by Sri Gupta, the dynasty reached its zenith under rulers like Chandragupta I, Samudragupta, and Chandragupta II (Vikramaditya). The Gupta period is characterized by remarkable advancements in various fields, including literature, science, mathematics, astronomy, and the arts.

In literature, the Gupta era saw the composition of some of the most revered works in Sanskrit. Kalidasa, one of the greatest poets and dramatists of ancient India, wrote his masterpieces during this time. His works, such as 'Shakuntala', 'Meghaduta', and 'Raghuvamsha', are celebrated for their poetic beauty and profound themes. The period also witnessed the creation of important religious texts, such as the Puranas and Smritis, which codified Hindu religious practices and mythologies.

Scientific and mathematical achievements during the Gupta period were equally impressive. The mathematician Aryabhata, who lived during this era, made significant contributions to algebra, arithmetic, and astronomy. His seminal work, *Aryabhatiya* introduced the concept of zero as a number, the value of pi, and the approximation of the circumference of the Earth. Varahamihira, another prominent scholar, authored the *Brihat Samhita* an encyclopedic work covering various aspects of astronomy, astrology, and natural sciences.

The Gupta Empire also made notable advancements in medicine. The physician Sushruta, often referred to as the 'father of surgery', compiled the *Sushruta Samhita* a comprehensive text on surgery and medicine. This work detailed numerous surgical procedures, including cataract surgery, rhinoplasty (reconstruction of the nose), and the use of medicinal plants and herbs.

Art and architecture flourished under the Guptas, with significant developments in sculpture, painting, and temple construction. Gupta sculptures are renowned for their refined elegance, intricate details, and harmonious proportions. The Sarnath Buddha, a masterpiece of Gupta art, exemplifies the serene and meditative qualities of Buddhist iconography. Ajanta and Ellora caves, adorned with exquisite frescoes and rock-cut sculptures, are lasting legacies of Gupta artistry and religious devotion.

The Gupta period also saw the construction of numerous Hindu temples, characterized by their distinct architectural style. Temples such as the Dashavatara Temple in Deogarh and the Vishnu Temple in Tigawa showcase the Gupta architectural elements, including shikharas (tower-like structures), intricate carvings, and elaborate entranceways.

While the Gupta Empire dominated northern India, regional powers in central and southern India, such as the Vakataka, Pallava, and Chalukya dynasties, made significant cultural and architectural contributions.

The Vakataka dynasty, contemporaneous with the Guptas, ruled over parts of central and southern India. The Vakatakas are particularly noted for their patronage of the Ajanta caves, a UNESCO World Heritage Site. The Ajanta caves, a series of rock-cut Buddhist monasteries and temples, are renowned for their stunning murals and sculptures that depict scenes from the life of the Buddha and various Jataka tales. These caves represent the zenith of ancient Indian rock-cut architecture and painting.

The Pallava dynasty, which ruled from the fourth to the ninth century CE in southern India, is celebrated for its architectural innovations and contributions to Dravidian temple architecture. The Pallavas are credited with constructing some of the earliest stone temples in southern India, moving away from the earlier wooden structures. The Shore Temple and the Pancha Rathas at Mahabalipuram are exemplary of Pallava architectural prowess, showcasing intricate carvings and monolithic rock-cut structures. These temples not only served as religious centres but also as symbols of Pallava power and artistic achievement.

The Chalukya dynasty, ruling from the sixth to the twelfth century CE in central and southern India, further advanced Indian temple architecture. The Chalukyas are known for their distinctive architectural style, characterized by intricate sculptures, ornate pillars, and elaborate entranceways. The rock-cut temples at Badami and the structural temples at Aihole and Pattadakal are significant contributions of the Chalukyas to Indian architecture. The Virupaksha Temple at Pattadakal, a UNESCO World Heritage Site, exemplifies the grandeur and sophistication of Chalukya temple architecture, influencing subsequent temple construction in southern India.

The first millennium CE also witnessed the spread of Indian culture, religion, and trade beyond the subcontinent. Indian merchants, scholars, and monks travelled to Southeast Asia, Central Asia, and China, facilitating cultural exchanges and the spread of Buddhism and Hinduism. The influence of Indian art, architecture, and literature can be seen in the ancient temples and monuments of Cambodia, Indonesia, Thailand, and other parts of Southeast Asia.

In conclusion, the first millennium CE was a period of remarkable cultural, intellectual, and architectural achievements in Indian history. The Gupta Empire, often regarded as the Golden Age of India, laid the foundation for significant advancements in literature, science, mathematics, medicine, art, and architecture. Concurrently, regional powers such as the Vakataka, Pallava, and Chalukya dynasties made substantial contributions to cultural and architectural heritage. This era not only shaped the course of Indian civilization but also left a lasting impact on the broader cultural and historical landscape of Asia.

SECOND MILLENNIUM CE

The second millennium CE in India was characterized by the rise and fall of powerful empires and dynasties, significant architectural and cultural achievements, and dynamic socio-political changes. Among the most notable were the Chola Empire, the Delhi Sultanate, and the Vijayanagara Empire. Each of these entities left a profound impact on the Indian subcontinent, shaping its history, culture, and legacy.

The Chola Empire, which rose to prominence in the ninth century and lasted until the thirteenth century, was one of the most influential and powerful dynasties in southern India. The Cholas were renowned for their naval power, extensive trade networks, and magnificent temples. The empire reached its zenith under the rule of Rajaraja Chola I (985–1014 CE) and his son Rajendra Chola I (1014–44 CE), who expanded their territory beyond the Indian subcontinent to include parts of Southeast Asia.

One of the most significant contributions of the Chola Empire was its impressive naval strength. The Chola navy dominated the Bay of Bengal and the Indian Ocean, facilitating trade and cultural exchanges with Southeast Asia, China, and the Arabian Peninsula. The conquest of the Srivijaya kingdom in Sumatra and the establishment of Chola influence in the Malay Peninsula and the Maldives underscore the extent of their maritime prowess. These naval expeditions not only boosted the empire's wealth but also spread Indian culture, art, and religion across Southeast Asia.

The Cholas are also celebrated for their architectural achievements, particularly their temple construction. The Brihadeshwara Temple at Thanjavur, built by Rajaraja Chola I, is a UNESCO World Heritage Site and a testament to the architectural and engineering skills of the Cholas. This massive granite structure, with its towering vimana (temple tower), intricate carvings, and impressive frescoes, exemplifies the grandeur of Chola architecture. Other notable temples include the Airavateswara Temple at Darasuram and the Gangaikonda Cholapuram Temple, each showcasing the dynasty's artistic and architectural excellence.

The Delhi Sultanate, which ruled northern India from 1206 to 1526, was a period of significant political and cultural transformation. The Sultanate was established by Qutb-ud-din Aibak, a former slave who became the founder of the Mamluk dynasty, the first of five successive Muslim dynasties that would rule Delhi: the Mamluks, Khiljis, Tughlaqs, Sayyids, and Lodis.

The Delhi Sultanate was marked by its attempts to consolidate and expand Muslim rule in India, often through military conquest and administrative reforms. The Khilji dynasty, under Alauddin Khilji (1296–1316), is noted for its aggressive expansionist policies, including successful campaigns in Gujarat, Rajasthan, and the Deccan. Alauddin Khilji also implemented significant economic and administrative reforms, such as price controls and market regulations, to stabilize the economy and strengthen central authority.

The Tughlaq dynasty, particularly under Muhammad bin Tughlaq (1325–51), is remembered for its ambitious and often controversial policies. Muhammad bin Tughlaq's decision to move the capital from Delhi to Daulatabad in the Deccan, and his subsequent reversal, caused significant upheaval. Despite these challenges, the Tughlaqs continued to expand their territory, although their reign was plagued by internal rebellions and external invasions.

The Delhi Sultanate also saw the rise of Indo-Islamic culture, characterized by a synthesis of Persian, Arabic, and Indian influences. This cultural amalgamation is evident in the architecture of the period, with iconic structures such as the Qutub Minar, Alai Darwaza, and the tomb of Ghiyasuddin Tughlaq showcasing a blend of Islamic and Indian architectural styles. The introduction of Persian art, literature, and administrative practices significantly influenced the cultural and intellectual landscape of northern India.

The Vijayanagara Empire, which flourished in southern India from 1336 to 1646, represents a period of immense wealth, military prowess, and cultural achievements. Founded by Harihara I and Bukka Raya I of the Sangama dynasty, the empire's capital at Vijayanagara (modern-day Hampi) became one of the most prosperous and impressive cities in the medieval world.

The Vijayanagara rulers, particularly under Krishnadevaraya (1509–29), oversaw a period of political stability, economic prosperity, and cultural renaissance. Krishnadevaraya's reign is often considered the golden age of the Vijayanagara Empire, marked by military victories, extensive building projects, and patronage of the arts and literature. The empire's military strength, including its formidable cavalry and use of war elephants, enabled it to defend its territory against various adversaries, including the Bahmani Sultanate and the Deccan Sultanates.

Architecturally, the Vijayanagara Empire is renowned for its distinctive style, characterized by massive temple complexes, intricate carvings, and impressive public works. The Virupaksha Temple, Vittala Temple, and Hazara Rama Temple in Hampi exemplify the empire's architectural grandeur. The stone chariot at the Vittala Temple complex, with its detailed carvings and unique design, is an iconic symbol of Vijayanagara architecture.

The empire also made significant contributions to literature and the arts. The court of Krishnadevaraya was a hub of literary activity, with the king himself being an accomplished poet. His reign saw the compilation of important works in Telugu, Kannada, Tamil, and Sanskrit, reflecting the empire's linguistic and cultural diversity. The patronage of various art forms, including music, dance, and sculpture, further enriched the cultural landscape of the Vijayanagara Empire.

The second millennium CE in India was thus a period of remarkable political, cultural, and architectural achievements. The Chola Empire, with its naval dominance, trade networks, and magnificent temples, left an enduring legacy in southern India and beyond. The Delhi Sultanate introduced significant administrative and cultural changes, shaping the course of Indian history through its synthesis of Indo-Islamic culture. The Vijayanagara Empire, with its wealth, military strength, and architectural marvels, represented a period of prosperity and cultural renaissance in southern India. Together, these dynasties and empires played a pivotal role in shaping the rich and diverse history of the Indian subcontinent.

SIXTEENTH CENTURY

The sixteenth century in Indian history is predominantly marked by the rise and consolidation of the Mughal Empire, which would become one of the most powerful and culturally rich empires in the Indian subcontinent. Established by Babur in 1526 after the pivotal Battle of Panipat, the Mughal Empire saw significant expansion and cultural flowering, especially under the reign of Akbar the Great. This period is notable for its military conquests, administrative reforms, architectural achievements, and a policy of religious tolerance that would leave a lasting impact on India's cultural and social fabric.

The Mughal Empire was founded by Zahir-ud-din Muhammad Babur, a descendant of Timur on his father's side and Genghis Khan on his mother's side. Babur's victory at the First Battle of Panipat in 1526 against the Sultan of Delhi, Ibrahim Lodi, marked the beginning of Mughal rule in India. Despite his relatively short reign (1526–30), Babur laid the foundation for the empire by consolidating power in northern India and introducing Persian culture and administrative practices, which would become hallmarks of Mughal rule.

Babur's son, Humayun, succeeded him but faced challenges in maintaining the newly established empire. Humayun's reign was marked by conflict and displacement, especially with the rise of Sher Shah Suri, who temporarily ousted the Mughals from power. However, Humayun managed to reclaim the throne in 1555, shortly before his death. His untimely demise led to the ascension of his son, Akbar, who would go on to become one of the most celebrated rulers in Indian history.

Akbar the Great (reigned 1556–1605) is often credited with transforming the Mughal Empire into a vast and stable realm. His reign is distinguished by extensive military conquests, administrative innovations, and efforts to foster religious harmony. Akbar's military campaigns expanded the empire to include much of the Indian subcontinent, from Afghanistan in the northwest to Bengal in the east and the Deccan Plateau in the south. Key victories included the annexation of Gujarat, Bengal, and Rajasthan, bringing diverse regions and cultures under Mughal control.

One of Akbar's most significant achievements was his policy of religious tolerance and his efforts to integrate the diverse religious communities of India into a cohesive empire. Akbar's policy, known as Sulh-e-Kul (peace for all), promoted a spirit of tolerance and understanding among different religious groups. He abolished the jizya (a tax on non-Muslims), married Hindu princesses, and appointed Hindus to high-ranking administrative positions. Akbar's court included scholars and representatives from various religious traditions, including Hindus, Muslims, Jains, Zoroastrians, and Christians, reflecting his commitment to inclusivity.

Akbar's interest in fostering a syncretic culture is exemplified by the creation of the Din-i-Ilahi, a syncretic religious doctrine that sought to blend elements of various faiths, including Islam, Hinduism, Zoroastrianism, and Christianity. Although the Din-i-Ilahi did not gain widespread acceptance, it underscored Akbar's innovative approach to governance and his vision of a unified and harmonious empire.

Administrative reforms under Akbar laid the groundwork for a highly efficient and centralized state. He implemented the Mansabdari system, a hierarchical structure for organizing the military and bureaucracy. Under this system, officials, known as mansabdars, were granted ranks and were responsible for maintaining a specified number of troops for the emperor. This system ensured loyalty to the emperor and efficient administration across the vast empire.

Akbar also undertook significant efforts to improve the economy and promote agricultural productivity. He standardized weights and measures, introduced a uniform tax system, and encouraged the cultivation of cash crops such as cotton and indigo. His policies fostered economic prosperity and helped in the establishment of vibrant urban centres and trade networks.

Culturally, Akbar's reign witnessed a flourishing of art, literature, and architecture, setting the stage for what is often referred to as the Mughal Renaissance. Akbar's court attracted poets, artists, musicians, and scholars from across the world, leading to a rich exchange of ideas and cultural practices. The Mughal court became a centre of Persianate culture, with Persian serving as the language of administration and high culture.

Architecturally, Akbar's legacy includes some of the most iconic structures in India. The city of Fatehpur Sikri, built by Akbar as his capital, is a UNESCO World Heritage Site and a masterpiece of Mughal architecture. The city features a blend of Persian, Indian, and Islamic architectural elements, with notable structures such as the Buland Darwaza, Jama Masjid, and Panch Mahal. Another significant architectural achievement from Akbar's reign is the Agra Fort, a massive red sandstone fortress that served as the main residence of the Mughal emperors.

The Mughal Empire under Akbar also saw advancements in literature and the arts. The emperor's patronage of the arts led to the development of the Mughal school of painting, characterized by its detailed and vivid miniature paintings that depicted court scenes, battles, and portraits. Literature flourished as well, with the translation of classical works from Sanskrit to Persian, and the creation of new literary compositions in Persian and Hindi.

In conclusion, the sixteenth century marked the establishment and consolidation of the Mughal Empire, a period that brought about significant military, administrative, and cultural advancements. Babur's initial conquests set the foundation, but it was under Akbar the Great that the empire truly flourished, expanding its territories, promoting religious tolerance, and fostering a golden age of cultural and intellectual achievements. Akbar's policies of inclusivity and his vision of a unified empire left a lasting legacy that shaped the course of Indian history for centuries to come.

SEVENTEENTH CENTURY

The seventeenth century in Indian history is marked by significant developments that would shape the subcontinent's future trajectory. This period witnessed the rise of the Maratha Empire under the leadership of Shivaji, which posed a formidable challenge to the dominant Mughal Empire. Additionally, the arrival and establishment of European trading companies, including the Portuguese, Dutch, French, and British, laid the groundwork for future colonial dominance. These developments not only altered the political landscape but also had profound economic, social, and cultural implications.

The rise of the Maratha Empire under Shivaji Maharaj is one of the most remarkable events of the seventeenth century. Shivaji, born in 1630, emerged as a formidable warrior and astute leader, establishing a robust Maratha state in western India. Shivaji's early life was marked by a strong influence from his mother, Jijabai, who instilled in him a sense of pride in Maratha heritage and a vision for a sovereign Maratha state.

Shivaji's military acumen was evident from his early campaigns. He utilized guerrilla warfare tactics, leveraging the rugged terrain of the Western Ghats to launch surprise attacks on his adversaries. His innovative strategies and superior knowledge of local geography enabled him to capture key forts, such as Torna, Raigad, and Pratapgad, establishing a strong territorial base. The capture of the strategic fort of Kondana, later renamed Sinhagad, further bolstered his position.

In 1674, Shivaji was formally crowned as Chhatrapati (king) at Raigad, marking the official establishment of the Maratha Empire. This coronation was a significant event, symbolizing the emergence of a new sovereign power in the region. Under Shivaji's leadership, the Maratha state was characterized by an efficient administration, a robust military, and a commitment to justice and welfare.

Shivaji's administrative reforms were groundbreaking. He established a council of ministers, known as the Ashta Pradhan, to assist in governance. This council included key positions such as the Peshwa (Prime Minister), Amatya (Finance Minister), and Senapati (Commander-in-Chief). Shivaji implemented a revenue system that was fair and efficient, ensuring that peasants were not unduly burdened. His emphasis on maritime strength led to the development of a strong navy, which protected the western coast from foreign invasions and facilitated trade.

Shivaji's legacy extended beyond his military and administrative achievements. He championed the cause of Hinduism, protecting temples and promoting religious tolerance. His policies were inclusive, ensuring that his administration reflected the diverse demographic composition of his empire. Shivaji's respect for women and his efforts to protect them from exploitation were also notable.

The seventeenth century also witnessed the increasing presence of European colonial powers in India. The Portuguese were among the first Europeans to establish a foothold in India, capturing Goa in 1510. By the seventeenth century, Goa had become a vibrant trading hub and the centre of Portuguese operations in India. The Portuguese influence extended to the west coast, where they controlled key ports and engaged in lucrative spice trade.

The Dutch East India Company (VOC) arrived in India in the early seventeenth century, establishing trading posts along the western and eastern coasts. The Dutch focused on the spice trade, particularly in the Malabar region, and competed fiercely with the Portuguese for control of the lucrative spice markets. The Dutch influence in India was primarily commercial, and they established key trading centres in Cochin, Pulicat, and Surat.

The French East India Company, founded in 1664, also sought to establish a presence in India. The French established trading posts in Pondicherry, Chandernagore, and Mahe. Pondicherry, in particular, became the focal point of French activities in India, and it developed into a significant centre of trade and culture. The French influence in India was characterized by a blend of commercial and military endeavours, with frequent conflicts with other European powers and Indian states.

The British East India Company, chartered in 1600, gradually emerged as the most dominant European power in India. The British initially focused on establishing trading posts along the eastern and western coasts, with significant centres in Surat, Madras (Chennai), Bombay (Mumbai), and Calcutta (Kolkata). The company's influence grew steadily, facilitated by its powerful navy and strategic alliances with local rulers.

The British East India Company adopted a policy of gradual territorial expansion, often through diplomacy and military force. The Battle of Plassey in 1757, which took place in the following century, marked a significant turning point, leading to British dominance in Bengal and laying the foundation for British colonial rule in India. However, the seeds of this dominance were sown in the seventeenth century, as the British expanded their commercial and political influence.

The increasing presence of European powers in India had profound economic and social implications. The Europeans introduced new goods, technologies, and agricultural practices, which influenced local economies and lifestyles. The demand for Indian textiles, spices, and other commodities fuelled economic growth, but also led to exploitation and economic disparities.

Culturally, the interaction between Europeans and Indians led to a rich exchange of ideas, art, and architecture. European influence is evident in the colonial architecture of cities like Goa, Pondicherry, and Kolkata. The fusion of European and Indian artistic styles resulted in unique cultural expressions, particularly in areas such as painting, music, and cuisine.

In conclusion, the seventeenth century was a dynamic period in Indian history, marked by the rise of the Maratha Empire under Shivaji and the increasing presence of European colonial powers. Shivaji's leadership and administrative reforms laid the foundation for a strong Maratha state, challenging Mughal dominance and shaping the political landscape of western India. The arrival of the Portuguese, Dutch, French, and British trading companies introduced new economic and cultural dynamics, setting the stage for future colonial rule. These developments had far-reaching impacts on India's history, culture, and society, influencing the subcontinent's trajectory for centuries to come.

EIGHTEENTH CENTURY

The eighteenth century in India was a period of significant transition marked by the decline of the Mughal Empire and the rise of the British East India Company as a dominant political and economic power. This era witnessed the gradual weakening of Mughal authority following the death of Aurangzeb, which led to regional fragmentation and the emergence of new power centres. Concurrently, the British East India Company expanded its influence through military conquests, strategic alliances, and treaties, culminating in the decisive Battle of Plassey in 1757. These developments set the stage for the eventual establishment of British colonial rule in India.

The decline of the Mughal Empire began in earnest after the death of Emperor Aurangzeb in 1707. Aurangzeb's extensive military campaigns had overstretched the empire's resources and weakened its administrative structure. His policies of religious intolerance and heavy taxation had also alienated various segments of the population, including the Rajputs, Marathas, and Sikhs. Following Aurangzeb's death, the Mughal Empire faced a series of succession crises and internal conflicts that further eroded its power.

Aurangzeb was succeeded by his son Bahadur Shah I, whose reign (1707–12) was marked by attempts to reconcile with the empire's various factions. However, Bahadur Shah's efforts were largely unsuccessful, and his death led to a period of instability and rapid succession of weak rulers. The Mughal Empire became increasingly fragmented as regional governors, or nawabs, asserted their independence and established quasi-autonomous states. Notable among these were the nawabs of Bengal, Hyderabad, and Awadh, who effectively ruled their territories with minimal interference from the central Mughal authority.

The Marathas, under the leadership of the Peshwas, emerged as a formidable power during this period. The Maratha Confederacy expanded its influence across much of India, challenging Mughal authority and establishing control over large territories. The Battle of Panipat in 1761, where the Marathas were defeated by the Afghan ruler Ahmad Shah Durrani, temporarily halted their expansion but did not significantly weaken their overall power. The Marathas continued to play a crucial role in the regional politics of India throughout the eighteenth century.

As the Mughal Empire weakened, European trading companies, particularly the British East India Company, took advantage of the political vacuum to expand their influence. The British East India Company had been granted a royal charter by Queen Elizabeth I in 1600, allowing it to trade with the East Indies. By the eighteenth century, the company's focus had shifted to India, where it sought to establish control over lucrative trade routes and resources.

The company's growing power was facilitated by its formidable private army, which it used to protect its interests and assert its dominance. The Battle of Plassey in 1757 was a turning point in the company's expansion. Led by Robert Clive, the British forces defeated the Nawab of Bengal, Siraj-ud-Daulah, with the help of local allies. This victory gave the British East India Company control over the wealthy province of Bengal, providing it with substantial revenue and a strategic base for further expansion.

The company's influence continued to grow through a combination of military conquests and strategic alliances. The Battle of Buxar in 1764 further consolidated British power in northern India, as the British defeated a coalition of Indian rulers, including the Nawab of Awadh and the Mughal Emperor

Shah Alam II. The Treaty of Allahabad, signed in 1765, granted the company the right to collect revenue (diwani) from Bengal, Bihar, and Orissa, effectively making it the de facto ruler of these regions.

The British East India Company's expansion was not limited to northern India. In the south, the company engaged in a series of wars with the Mysore kingdom under rulers Hyder Ali and his son Tipu Sultan. The four Anglo-Mysore Wars (1767–99) ultimately resulted in the defeat and annexation of Mysore by the British. Similarly, the company fought the Marathas in the three Anglo-Maratha Wars (1775–1818), gradually weakening the Maratha Confederacy and bringing large parts of western and central India under British control.

The company's expansion was facilitated by a combination of military strength, diplomatic manoeuvring, and economic exploitation. The British used a policy of 'divide and rule' to exploit the rivalries among Indian states and secure their dominance. The company's control over trade and resources allowed it to amass immense wealth, which it used to fund its military campaigns and administrative apparatus.

The British East India Company's growing power had profound economic, social, and cultural impacts on Indian society. The company's policies of land revenue collection, particularly the introduction of the Permanent Settlement in Bengal, led to widespread dispossession and impoverishment of Indian peasants. The focus on cash crops for export disrupted traditional agricultural practices and contributed to recurrent famines.

Culturally, the company's presence led to significant interactions between Indians and Europeans. British educational and missionary activities introduced Western education and ideas to Indian society, leading to the emergence of a new class of Western-educated Indians who would later play a crucial role in India's struggle for independence. The British also introduced new technologies, infrastructure, and administrative practices that had lasting effects on Indian society.

In conclusion, the eighteenth century was a period of profound transformation in Indian history. The decline of the Mughal Empire and the rise of regional powers such as the Marathas created a fragmented political landscape that the British East India Company exploited to establish its dominance. The Battle of Plassey and subsequent military victories allowed the company to expand its control over large parts of India, setting the stage for the eventual establishment of British colonial rule. These developments had far-reaching economic, social, and cultural implications, shaping the course of Indian history for centuries to come.

NINETEENTH CENTURY

The nineteenth century in India was a period of profound change marked by the expansion and consolidation of British colonial rule, significant economic exploitation, and the beginning of social and religious reforms that laid the groundwork for the Indian Renaissance. Key events such as the Indian Rebellion of 1857 and the establishment of the British Raj in 1858 were pivotal in shaping India's history during this period. Additionally, the century saw the emergence of influential reformers like Raja Ram Mohan Roy and Swami Vivekananda, whose efforts were instrumental in modernizing Indian society and culture.

The expansion of British control over India began in earnest in the late eighteenth century and continued throughout the nineteenth century. The British East India Company, which had already established a strong presence in Bengal, Bihar, and Orissa, extended its influence across the subcontinent through a combination of military conquests, diplomatic alliances, and economic manipulation. Key events such as the Anglo-Mysore Wars and the Anglo-Maratha Wars resulted in the annexation of significant territories and the weakening of regional powers.

The Indian Rebellion of 1857, also known as the Sepoy Mutiny or the First War of Indian Independence, was a major turning point. The rebellion was sparked by widespread discontent among Indian soldiers, or sepoys, in the British East India Company's army. Factors such as the introduction of new rifle cartridges rumoured to be greased with cow and pig fat, which offended both Hindu and Muslim religious sensibilities, along with broader grievances related to economic exploitation and social discrimination, fuelled the uprising.

The rebellion began in Meerut in May 1857 and quickly spread to other parts of northern and central India, including Delhi, Kanpur, Lucknow, and Jhansi. It was characterized by fierce battles and significant atrocities committed by both sides. Despite initial successes, the rebels lacked a unified command and adequate resources, and the British forces, reinforced by troops from Britain, eventually suppressed the uprising. The capture of Delhi in September 1857 and the fall of other key rebel strongholds marked the end of the rebellion by mid-1858.

The aftermath of the rebellion had far-reaching consequences. The British government took direct control of India from the East India Company, leading to the establishment of the British Raj in 1858. Queen Victoria was proclaimed Empress of India in 1876, symbolizing the formal integration of India into the British Empire. The British government implemented a series of administrative and military reforms to prevent future uprisings, including the reorganization of the Indian army to include more British soldiers and a policy of divide and rule to exploit religious and regional differences among Indians.

Under the British Raj, India underwent significant economic and social changes. The British focused on exploiting India's resources for their benefit, leading to the commercialization of agriculture and the development of infrastructure such as railways, telegraphs, and ports. While these developments facilitated the integration of India into the global economy, they also resulted in widespread economic exploitation and hardship for Indian peasants and artisans. The introduction of cash crops for export, such as cotton, indigo, and tea, disrupted traditional agricultural practices and contributed to recurrent famines.

Socially, British colonial rule brought about significant changes, both positive and negative. The introduction of Western education, legal systems, and administrative practices had a profound impact on Indian society. The establishment of institutions like the University of Calcutta (1857), the University of Bombay (1857), and the University of Madras (1857) provided opportunities for Indians to receive higher education and engage with modern scientific and intellectual ideas. This led to the emergence of a new class of Western-educated Indians who played a crucial role in the subsequent struggle for independence.

The nineteenth century also saw the rise of social and religious reform movements, collectively referred to as the Indian Renaissance. These movements aimed to address the social and cultural challenges posed by colonial rule and to reform Indian society from within. One of the most prominent reformers of this period was Raja Ram Mohan Roy (1772–1833), often called the 'Father of Modern India.' Roy founded the Brahmo Samaj in 1828, a socio-religious reform movement that sought to eliminate social evils such as sati (the practice of widow immolation), child marriage, and caste discrimination. He advocated for the spread of modern education, women's rights, and the abolition of oppressive customs.

Another key figure in the Indian Renaissance was Swami Vivekananda (1863–1902), a disciple of the mystic Ramakrishna Paramahamsa. Vivekananda played a pivotal role in revitalizing Hinduism and promoting a sense of national pride and unity among Indians. His speeches at the Parliament of the World's Religions in Chicago in 1893, where he spoke about the universal values of Hinduism and the need for interfaith harmony, brought him international acclaim. Vivekananda emphasized the importance of spiritual and moral development alongside material progress, and his teachings inspired many Indians to take pride in their cultural and spiritual heritage.

The Indian Renaissance was characterized by a diverse array of reform movements and intellectual currents. Reformers like Ishwar Chandra Vidyasagar, Jyotirao Phule, and Pandita Ramabai worked tirelessly to improve the status of women and marginalized communities. Vidyasagar championed women's education and the remarriage of widows, while Phule and his wife Savitribai Phule were pioneers in promoting education for lower-caste communities and women. Ramabai advocated for women's rights and founded institutions to support and educate destitute women and widows.

In addition to social and religious reforms, the nineteenth century witnessed the early stirrings of political consciousness and nationalism. The formation of the Indian National Congress (INC) in 1885 marked the beginning of organized political activity aimed at achieving greater self-governance and eventually independence from British rule. The Congress provided a platform for Indian leaders to articulate their demands for political and economic reforms, and it played a crucial role in mobilizing public opinion and fostering a sense of national unity.

In conclusion, the nineteenth century was a period of significant transformation in India, marked by the decline of Mughal power, the consolidation of British colonial rule, and the emergence of social and religious reform movements. The Indian Rebellion of 1857 and the establishment of the British Raj were pivotal events that reshaped India's political landscape. The Indian Renaissance, led by reformers like Raja Ram Mohan Roy and Swami Vivekananda, sought to modernize Indian society and culture while preserving its rich heritage. These developments laid the groundwork for the subsequent struggle for independence and the emergence of modern India.

TWENTIETH CENTURY

The twentieth century was a transformative period in Indian history, characterized by the Indian independence movement, the eventual partition and independence in 1947, and the establishment of the Republic of India in 1950. These events were marked by significant political, social, and economic changes that shaped modern India.

The Indian independence movement was a mass struggle against British colonial rule, led by the INC and key figures such as Mahatma Gandhi, Jawaharlal Nehru, and Subhas Chandra Bose. The movement drew from a variety of ideologies and tactics, from non-violent resistance to armed struggle.

Mahatma Gandhi emerged as the foremost leader of the independence movement. Born in 1869, Gandhi's philosophy of non-violent resistance (Satyagraha) became the cornerstone of the struggle for freedom. His early experiences in South Africa, where he fought against racial discrimination, shaped his approach to resistance and activism. Gandhi's return to India in 1915 marked the beginning of a new phase in the independence movement.

One of the first major campaigns led by Gandhi was the Non-Cooperation Movement (1920–22). This movement was a reaction to the Jallianwala Bagh massacre in 1919, where British troops killed hundreds of unarmed Indian civilians.

Gandhi called for the boycott of British goods, institutions, and services, urging Indians to withdraw their support from the colonial government. The movement saw widespread participation and significantly challenged British authority. However, it was called off by Gandhi in 1922 following the Chauri Chaura incident, where protesters killed 22 policemen.

In the 1930s, the Civil Disobedience Movement further intensified the struggle for independence. This movement was marked by the Salt March in 1930, where Gandhi led a 240-mile march to the Arabian Sea to produce salt in defiance of British laws. The act of making salt became a powerful symbol of resistance, and the movement saw mass participation across the country. The British responded with arrests and repression, but the movement significantly raised international awareness about the Indian independence cause.

Subhas Chandra Bose was another prominent leader who adopted a different approach to achieving independence. Bose advocated for more radical methods, including armed struggle, and believed that British rule could only be overthrown through force. He formed the Indian National Army (INA) with the support of Japan during World War II and sought to liberate India through military means. Despite initial successes, the INA was eventually defeated, but Bose's efforts inspired many and highlighted the diverse approaches within the independence movement.

The Quit India Movement of 1942 was another pivotal moment in the struggle for freedom. Initiated by Gandhi, the movement called for the immediate withdrawal of British rule from India. The slogan 'Do or Die' encapsulated the movement's urgency and determination. The British responded with mass arrests and violent repression, but the movement demonstrated the widespread desire for independence and the resilience of the Indian people.

The culmination of decades of struggle came in 1947 when India finally gained independence from British rule. However, independence came with the traumatic partition of India and Pakistan, a division based on religious lines that led to one of the largest mass migrations in history.

The partition caused immense suffering, with communal violence resulting in the deaths of hundreds of thousands and the displacement of millions. The creation of the two new states of India and Pakistan marked the end of British colonial rule but also left a legacy of conflict and division that persists to this day.

On 15 August 1947, India celebrated its independence, and Jawaharlal Nehru became the first Prime Minister of independent India. His speech, known as the 'Tryst with Destiny', reflected the aspirations and challenges of the new nation. The immediate task for the Indian leadership was to stabilize the country, address the needs of millions of refugees, and lay the foundation for a democratic and inclusive society.

The adoption of the Constitution of India on 26 January 1950 marked the formal establishment of the Republic of India. The Constitution, drafted by the Constituent Assembly under the chairmanship of Dr B.R. Ambedkar, laid down the framework for a sovereign, democratic, and secular state. It guaranteed fundamental rights to all citizens and established a parliamentary system of government. The adoption of the Constitution was a significant milestone in the consolidation of India as a modern nation-state.

Post-independence, India faced numerous challenges, including economic development, social integration, and political stability. Nehru's vision for India included the promotion of industrialization, scientific advancement, and social reform. His policies aimed at building a self-reliant economy and reducing poverty. Nehru's tenure also saw the establishment of key institutions, including the Indian Institutes of Technology (IITs) and the Planning Commission, which played crucial roles in India's development trajectory.

Socially, the abolition of untouchability and the promotion of women's rights were significant steps towards creating a more equitable society. The Constitution outlawed caste discrimination, and affirmative action policies were introduced to uplift marginalized communities. Women's participation in education and the workforce gradually increased, although significant challenges remained.

The twentieth century also witnessed significant cultural and intellectual developments in India. The Indian film industry, particularly Bollywood, emerged as a major cultural force, influencing millions across the country and the diaspora. Literature, art, and music flourished, reflecting the diverse and dynamic nature of Indian society.

In conclusion, the twentieth century was a period of profound change in Indian history. The struggle for independence, led by figures like Mahatma Gandhi, Jawaharlal Nehru, and Subhas Chandra Bose, culminated in the end of British colonial rule and the partition of India and Pakistan. The establishment of the Republic of India in 1950 marked the beginning of a new era of democratic governance and social reform. Despite numerous challenges, India embarked on a path of development, modernization, and cultural resurgence that continues to shape its identity and destiny in the twenty-first century.

TWENTY-FIRST CENTURY

The twenty-first century saw India continuing on the path of economic liberalization that began in the early 1990s. The reforms initiated under Prime Minister Narasimha Rao and Finance Minister Manmohan Singh dismantled the License Raj, which had stifled economic growth by imposing extensive bureaucratic controls on industry and trade. These reforms aimed to integrate India into the global economy, encourage foreign investment, privatize state-owned enterprises, and deregulate various sectors.

India's economy experienced robust growth throughout the 2000s and 2010s, establishing itself as one of the world's fastest-growing major economies. The GDP growth rate averaged around 6–8 per cent per annum, driven by strong domestic consumption, a burgeoning middle class, and rapid urbanization. Services, manufacturing, and agriculture sectors all contributed significantly to the economic expansion.

The IT and software services sector emerged as a cornerstone of India's economic growth. Cities like Bangalore, Hyderabad, Pune, and Chennai became global hubs for IT services, software development, and business process outsourcing (BPO). The outsourcing industry capitalized on India's large pool of English-speaking, skilled professionals and competitive cost advantages. This sector not only bolstered India's foreign exchange earnings but also created millions of jobs and propelled technological innovation.

Investments in infrastructure were prioritized to support economic growth and urbanization. Major projects included the construction of highways, airports, ports, and urban mass transit systems. Initiatives like the Golden Quadrilateral highway project and the Delhi Metro exemplified India's efforts to modernize its transportation infrastructure and enhance connectivity across the country.

Reforms in the financial sector aimed to strengthen India's banking system, improve access to credit, and enhance financial inclusion. The establishment of new private banks, expansion of rural banking networks, and introduction of financial services for underserved populations were key initiatives. The introduction of Aadhaar, a biometric-based unique identification system, facilitated direct benefit transfers and streamlined financial transactions.

The Indian Space Research Organisation (ISRO) achieved significant milestones in space exploration during the twenty-first century. Notable achievements include:

- Chandrayaan Missions: Chandrayaan-1 (launched in 2008) was India's first lunar probe, which discovered water molecules on the lunar surface. Chandrayaan-2 (launched in 2019) aimed to explore the south pole of the Moon and enhance understanding of lunar geology.
- Mars Orbiter Mission (Mangalyaan): Launched in 2013, Mangalyaan made India the first Asian country to reach Martian orbit and the fourth space agency globally to do so. The mission showcased India's technological prowess and cost-effectiveness in space exploration.

India's IT industry continued to evolve, encompassing software development, IT services, and digital transformation. The proliferation of mobile devices, expansion of internet connectivity, and adoption of digital payment systems revolutionized consumer behaviour, business operations, and governance. E-commerce platforms emerged as major drivers of economic activity, offering consumers access to a wide range of goods and services.

India made strides in biotechnology and pharmaceutical research, manufacturing, and exports. The country became a global hub for generic drugs and vaccines, supplying affordable healthcare solutions to domestic and international markets. Biotechnology research institutions and pharmaceutical companies collaborated on developing innovative therapies and addressing global health challenges.

India's demographic dividend, characterized by a large and youthful population, presented opportunities and challenges. Efforts were made to harness the demographic dividend through skill development programs, education reforms, and job creation initiatives. However, disparities in education, healthcare, and employment persisted, posing socio-economic challenges.

The political landscape in India witnessed significant shifts and electoral dynamics. The Bharatiya Janata Party (BJP), under leaders like Atal Bihari Vajpayee and Narendra Modi, emerged as a dominant force advocating for economic reforms, infrastructure development, and cultural nationalism. The Congress Party, historically influential, faced challenges from regional parties and new political formations.

India continued to grapple with issues of social justice, gender equality, and caste discrimination. Legal reforms and affirmative action policies aimed to empower marginalized communities and promote inclusive development. Initiatives focused on improving access to education, healthcare, and employment opportunities for women, Dalits, Adivasis, and other disadvantaged groups.

Concerns over environmental degradation, climate change, and natural resource management gained prominence. India committed to international climate agreements while implementing policies to promote renewable energy, sustainable agriculture practices, and conservation of biodiversity. Efforts were made to balance economic development with environmental stewardship, addressing challenges such as air and water pollution, deforestation, and urban sustainability.

India expanded its diplomatic engagements with major powers, neighbouring countries, and global institutions. Bilateral relationships with countries like the United States, Russia, Japan, and European Union nations deepened, focusing on strategic partnerships, trade agreements, defence cooperation, and cultural exchanges. India's active participation in multilateral forums such as BRICS, G20, and Shanghai Cooperation Organisation (SCO) underscored its role in shaping regional and global agendas.

India's relations with neighbouring countries, including Pakistan, China, Bangladesh, Nepal, and Sri Lanka, experienced varying dynamics influenced by historical, geopolitical, and economic factors. Efforts were made to strengthen regional cooperation, resolve border disputes, enhance connectivity through infrastructure projects, and promote economic integration through initiatives like the South Asian Association for Regional Cooperation (SAARC) and Bay of Bengal Initiative for Multi-Sectoral Technical and Economic Cooperation (BIMSTEC).

India's cultural heritage, soft power diplomacy, and contributions to global governance garnered international recognition. Cultural exchanges, yoga diplomacy, Bollywood films, and Indian cuisine promoted India's cultural diversity and heritage worldwide. The Indian diaspora played a significant role in fostering economic ties, promoting educational exchanges, and enhancing India's global influence.

Despite economic growth and development achievements, India faced persistent challenges related to poverty alleviation, income inequality, regional disparities, and access to basic services. Efforts to address these challenges included targeted social welfare programs, rural development initiatives, and reforms in healthcare and education.

Infrastructure gaps in transport, energy, water supply, and sanitation posed obstacles to sustained economic growth and urban development. Investments in infrastructure projects, public–private partnerships, and smart city initiatives aimed to improve connectivity, enhance quality of life, and promote sustainable urbanization.

The rapid pace of technological advancement presented opportunities for innovation and digital transformation, but also highlighted the digital divide between urban and rural areas, and among different socio-economic groups. Efforts were made to bridge the digital gap through initiatives promoting digital literacy, internet access, and affordable technology solutions.

Addressing environmental challenges, including air and water pollution, deforestation, and climate change, remained a priority. India committed to achieving sustainable development goals (SDGs), increasing renewable energy capacity, enhancing forest conservation efforts, and promoting eco-friendly practices in industry and agriculture.

Geopolitical shifts, regional conflicts, and global uncertainties posed strategic challenges for India's foreign policy and national security. Issues such as border disputes, terrorism, maritime security, and cybersecurity required proactive diplomatic engagement, defence preparedness, and international cooperation.

In conclusion, the twenty-first century has been a transformative era for India, marked by economic growth, technological advancements, and evolving social and political dynamics. As India continues to navigate global challenges and opportunities, its ability to leverage demographic dividends, promote inclusive development, foster technological innovation, and strengthen international partnerships will be crucial in shaping its future as a vibrant, resilient, and influential global player.

2 GEOGRAPHY

EVOLUTION OF THE EARTH

The evolution of the earth can be divided into three specific stages:

1. The period of acquisition of the present shape and size of the earth.
2. The period of formation of the earth's interior.
3. The period of formation of mountains, plateaus and plains.

The first oceans were formed from the primitive crevasses on the outer zone of the earth's surface. The water derived from condensation of water vapour filled up these crevasses forming the large lakes. These lakes filled up and joined with each other forming today's oceans. The deposition of weathered and eroded materials from the landmasses into the oceans made the continents more acidic because the basic ones were removed in solution. All these increased the weight of the oceans and made the continents lighter.

GEOLOGIC AGE OF THE EARTH

The table below shows the geologic age of the earth starting from the oldest to the present. The entire geological history is divided into eras. The eras are subdivided into epochs. These epochs are further subdivided into periods.

ERA	MAJOR INCIDENTS	PERIODS
Pre-Cambrian	No evidence of atmosphere. Granite and Gneiss were found. The Laurentian shield, Gondwana shield, Siberian shield, and Baltic shield were formed.	
Paleozoic	Beginning of early plant and animal life. Invertebrate animals were found. Other rocks like limestone and sandstone were formed.	Cambrian (basic light limestone and sandstone were formed) Ordovician (volcanic eruptions and submergence of large masses of land under water) Silurian (origin of fish and animals that could breathe; vegetation came into existence) Devonian (red sandstone were formed; folding and faulting for mountain building) Carboniferous or coal age (coal was formed; amphibians were formed) Permian (Earth's atmospheric temperature began to rise and evolution of the mountain building in North America, Central Europe)

ERA	MAJOR INCIDENTS	PERIODS
Mesozoic	Formation of reptiles.	Triassic (drifting of Gondwanaland towards the north) Jurassic (the growth of reptiles in large numbers dominating on land and water. Dense vegetation and flowering plants were evolved.) Cretaceous (deposition of chalk, formation of thick lava in south India; formation of deciduous trees; initiation of the formation of the Himalayas, Rockies, Alps)
Tertiary	Further evolution of plants and animals. Geosynclinal movements causing formation of mountains. Period when ape man formed and the major portions of the earth started getting covered with thick sheets of ice. Himalayas were formed and Africa started drifting away from Gondwanaland.	
Quaternary or Great Ice Age	Vast ice sheets covered most parts of the earth. Several animals and evolution of man happened. The alluvial deposits of the world were found. Gradually, the temperature stated rising and this age is continuing from then.	

The shape of the earth is **oblate spheroid**.

About 71.1 per cent of the earth's surface is covered with water while 28.9 per cent is covered with land masses.

Latitudes and longitudes:

Latitudes are horizontal imaginary lines separating the earth into unequal parts that run parallel to the most important one that is the equator 0° dividing the Earth into two equal hemispheres– the Northern and Southern hemispheres. The rest of the latitudes parallel to the equator are the angular distances north and south of the equator.

Longitudes are the imaginary vertical lines which converge at the poles 90°. They are the great circles dividing the earth into equal halves. The most important line of longitude is the prime meridian 0° which divides the Earth into the Eastern and Western hemispheres.

The intersection points of latitude and longitude known as the **coordinates** gives us the exact location of a place. For example, the coordinates or exact location of Delhi is 28.7041° N, 77.1025° E. Where 28.7041° N stands for latitude of Delhi in North and 77.1025° E stands for its longitude.

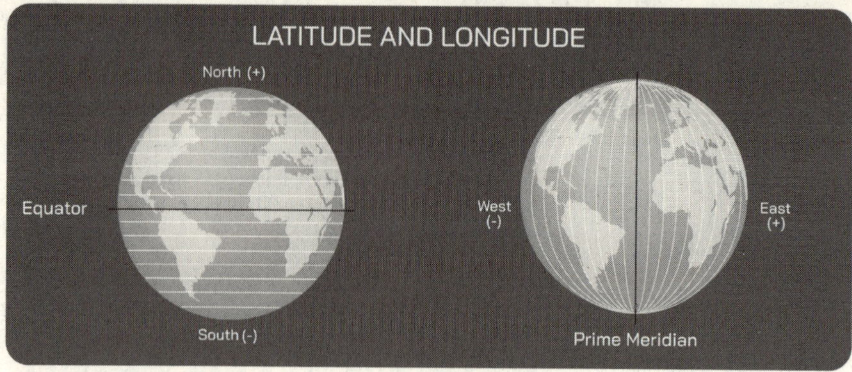

ROTATION AND REVOLUTION OF THE EARTH AND ITS CONSEQUENCE

The Earth rotates on its own inclined axis. At the same time, it also revolves around the sun. The time of rotation is 23 hours 59 minutes and 4 seconds while the time taken for revolution is 364.25 days. Since the orbit of the earth around the sun is elliptical in shape so the period when it is closest to the sun is called the **perihelion (3rd January)** and the time when it is farthest from the sun it is called the **aphelion (4th July)**.

Due to its revolution the seasons appear, and the length of the day and night varies.

21st March: the sun's rays fall vertical on equator so it is equal day and night called the **spring equinox**.

The apparent movement of the sun northwards till 21st June when the rays fall vertically on the Tropic of Cancer this is called the phenomena of **summer solstice**. This is the longest day and peak summer in the Northern hemisphere and just the reverse in the Southern hemisphere.

Then the sun's rays start moving southward again till it reaches the equator on 22nd September called **autumnal equinox**. This is again the period of equal day and equal night.

As the apparent movement of the sun starts its southward journey the sun reaches its southernmost limit that is the Tropic of Capricorn on 23rd December. This is called the **winter solstice**. It is the shortest day and longest night in the Northern hemisphere but peak summer in Southern hemisphere.

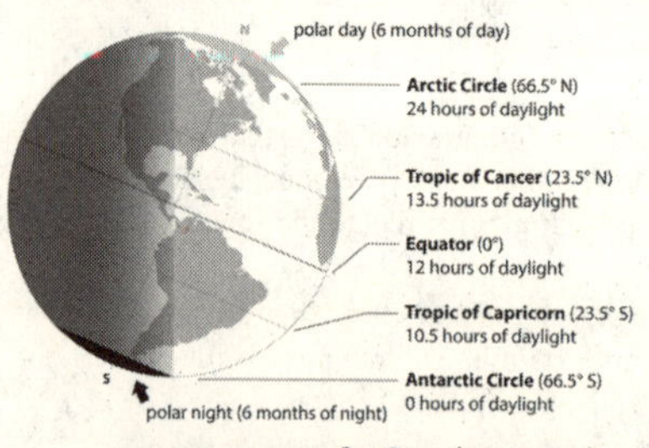

summer solstice (21 June)

N
polar night (6 months of night)
Arctic Circle (66.5° N)
24 hours of darkness
Tropic of Cancer (23.5° N)
13.5 hours of darkness
Equator (0°)
12 hours of darkness
Tropic of Capricorn (23.5° S)
10.5 hours of darkness
Antarctic Circle (66.5° S)
0 hours of darkness
S
polar day (6 months of day)

winter solstice (21 December)

So now you know why you feel cold in December in India while in Australia it is the reverse? (hint: check the location of the two countries in two different hemispheres)

INTERIOR OF THE EARTH

The earth's interior is divided into three concentric layers: the crust, mantle, and the core. The crust or the lithosphere is the outermost layer of the earth. The lighter part is the sial or the continental crust composed of silica and aluminium. The denser part is the sima or the oceanic part composed of silica and magnesium.
The layer below is the crust is the mantle. The boundary between the crust and mantle is called the **Mohorovicic discontinuity**. The mantle extends up to the depth of 2,900 km. Here the temperature and density increases with depth.

Asthenosphere is the zone of rocks at the upper part of the mantle. Here the materials are found in semi-molten state. The boundary between the mantle and the core is called the **Gutenberg discontinuity**. In core, the temperature and density are highest. The outer core is in liquid state. The inner core is in solid state due to extreme pressure. The core is composed of NIFE that is nickel and ferrous. It is also called the bar sphere.

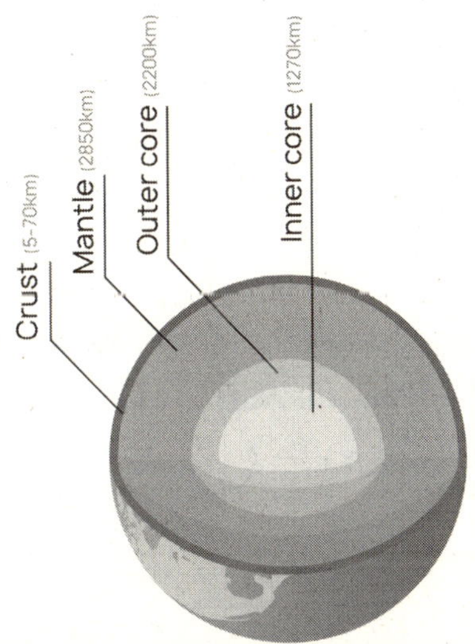

Structure of the earth

ROCKS OF THE EARTH AND THEIR CHARACTERISTICS

The materials on the crust are generally called rocks. Lithosphere means rocksphere as the word 'lithos' means rocks. The whole earth comprises of eight most abundant elements which are iron, oxygen, silicon, magnesium, nickel, sulphur, calcium, and ammonium. These constitute 99 per cent of the total mass of the earth whereas only four elements which are iron, oxygen, silicon, and magnesium account for 90 per cent of total mass of the earth. Whereas 99 per cent of the total mass of the crust are eight most abundant elements which are oxygen, silicon, aluminium, iron, magnesium, calcium, potassium, and sodium.

TYPES OF ROCKS

Igneous rocks: Formed due to solidification of lava/magma either on the earth's surface or below it. These are called primary rocks.

Sedimentary rocks: Formed due to lithification, compression, and cementation of sediments deposited mainly in aquatic areas.

Metamorphic rocks: Formed due to change in form, composition of either igneous or sedimentary rocks.

Igneous rocks do not have any layers and are quite hard and compact. They do not contain any fossils and are mostly found in volcanic areas. Igneous rocks are impermeable that is water cannot enter through these rocks unless basalt which become quite soft when they come in constant contact with water. These rocks are either fine grained or coarse grained depending on the rate and place of cooling.

Types of Igneous Rocks

On the basis of mode of occurrence, igneous rocks are classified into:

Intrusive igneous rocks: The cooling and solidification of the magma below the earth's surface causes these types of rocks. They are of further two sub-types. Plutonic intrusive igneous rocks – when they are formed very deep below the earth's surface (e.g., granite). Hypabyssal intrusive igneous rocks – the magma is cooled just below the surface (e.g., batholiths, laccoliths).

Extrusive igneous rocks: Rocks that are formed due to cooling and solidification of lava on the earth's surface (basalt, gabbro, and obsidian).

On the basis of chemical composition, igneous rocks are classified into the following:

- Acid igneous rocks have silica content between 65 and 85 per cent. They lack in iron and magnesium. Granite is an example. These rocks are erosion resistant.
- Basic igneous rocks contain silica between 45 and 60 per cent. They are easily eroded, heavy and darker in colour. Basalt is an example.
- Sedimentary rocks are formed of sediments derived from plant and animal remains so they may contain fossils. Sedimentary rocks are the most abundant rocks of the earth. They are called stratified rocks as they contain layers or strata. Most of these rocks are permeable and porous. They can be well consolidated or poorly consolidated depending upon the parent rock material.

Agents of Metamorphism

Heat: Sometimes the mineral composition is entirely altered due to intense heat. The source of this heat is the hot and molten magma when they come out through the cracks. These types of metamorphism are thermal metamorphism.

Pressure: The compressive forces during the process of mountain building release large amount of pressure which alters the original form of the rocks. This type of metamorphism is called dynamic or regional metamorphism.

Types of Metamorphism

As discussed earlier, metamorphism can be thermal or dynamic. It can also be hydro metamorphism, which happens when rocks come in constant contact of chemically active water.

Metamorphism of some common igneous and sedimentary rocks:

- Limestone (sedimentary rocks) → marble (metamorphic rocks)
- Granite (igneous rocks) → gneiss (metamorphic rocks)
- Sandstone (sedimentary rocks) → quartzite (metamorphic rocks)
- Shale (sedimentary rocks) → slate (metamorphic rocks) → schist (further metamorphism)

TYPES OF SEDIMENTARY ROCKS

	MECHANICALLY FORMED	CHEMICALLY FORMED	ORGANICALLY FORMED
1. On the basis of the nature of sediments	Sandstone Conglomerate Shale Loess	Gypsum Salt rock	Limestone Dolomite Coal Peat
2. On the basis of transporting agents	Argillaceous or Aqueous rocks	Aeolian	Glacial
	Marine Lacustrine Riverine	Loess	Till Moraines

Rock cycle

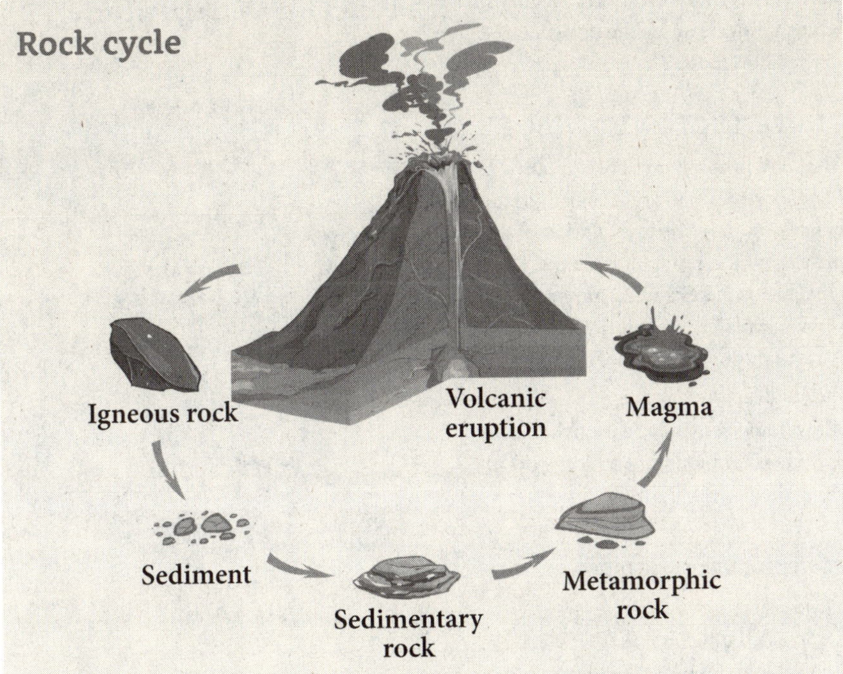

The concept of rock cycle was first propounded by an eighteenth-century scientist James Hutton. It is the continuous process of formation, alteration, and breaking down of the different types of rocks based on the application of heat, pressure, or both over time. We can safely say it is the process where rocks are constantly being recycled and reformed under given circumstances and location.

FORMATION OF THE CONTINENTS AND THE THEORY OF PLATE TECTONICS

The continents dominate over the Northern hemisphere and contrary to this, water bodies dominate over the Southern hemisphere. But there is a belief that these continents were never in the position that they are now. This drifting of the continents has been propounded by **Alfred Wegener**, a German meteorologist in his theory. He believed that there was a single landmass called the Pangea. The Tethys Sea separated the Pangea into two landmasses: the Gondwanaland to the south of Tethys Sea and Laurentia in north.

EVIDENCE IN SUPPORT OF THE CONTINENTAL DRIFT THEORY

See closely the continents of South America and Africa, and they seem to fit with each other as a jig-saw puzzle as if they were a single landmass.

Marked similarity between the fossils and vegetation remains on the eastern coast of South America and the western coast of Africa.

Carboniferous glaciations in Brazil, Falkland, South Africa, Australia, parts of India proved that there was a single unified landmass.

Palaeomagnetism: The study of old magnetic rocks called palaeomagnetism shows different directions of magnetism which points towards the presence of a unified landmass.

PLATE TECTONIC THEORY

The solid lithosphere slabs are called plates. Plate tectonics is the mechanism of the behaviour, movement, evolution of the plates, and the resultant reaction. There are 6 major plates and 20 minor plates. The six major plates are American, Eurasian, African, Indo Australian, Pacific, and Antarctic.

All tectonic activities be it earthquakes, volcanoes, or mountain building occur along the plate margins.

Constructive plate margins:

Two plates move away (diverge) from each other and there is constant upwelling of the lava on the surface. Volcanic and seismic activities are common along such edges.

Destructive plate margins:

Two plates move towards each other and there is a collision. There is lot of crumpling and folding. In case of oceanic crust, the lighter plate moves over the heavier one and trenches are formed at the zone of subduction. This is the zone of orogenesis or mountain building.

Conservative Plate Margins

Two plates move past each other without any interaction. So there is neither creation nor destruction.

PLATE BOUNDARIES

Divergent Plate Boundary

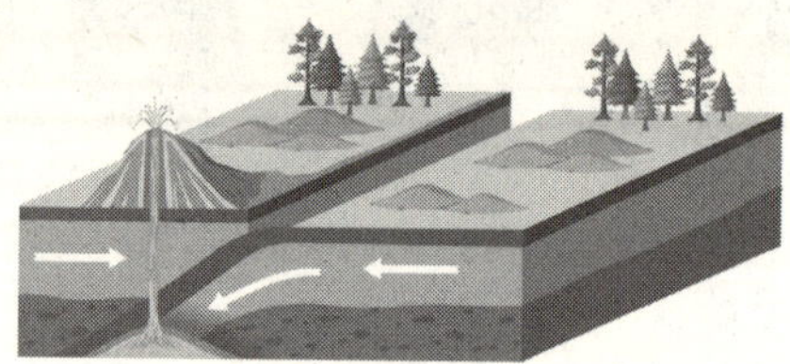

Convergent Plate Boundary

Transform Plate Boundary

WHY THE PLATE TECTONIC THEORY IS IMPORTANT?

On the basis of the knowledge of the crustal plate movements the future shape of the continents can be guessed or earthquakes and other seismic activities can be predicted.

MOVEMENTS OF THE EARTH

Earth's movements are divided into two forces:

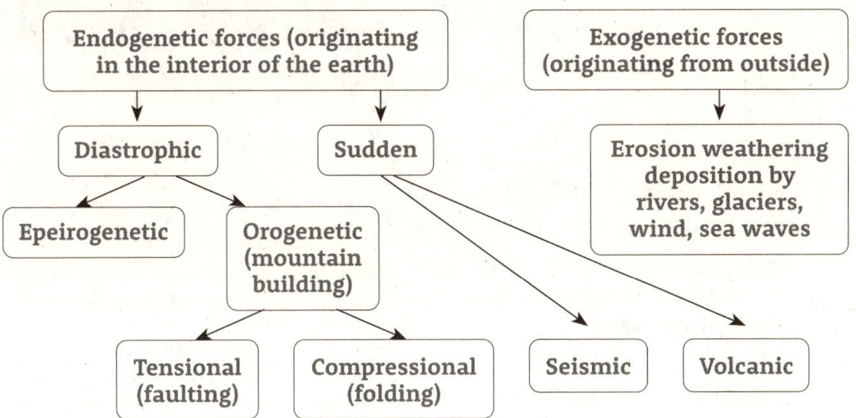

FACT FILE

The Indian plate is moving north eastwards towards the Eurasian plate at the speed of 5 cm per year. This is pushing the Himalayas higher and causing further subduction of the Indian plate under the Eurasian plate.

So we can encounter more earthquakes in this zone in the coming years!

FACT FILE

Sea Floor Spreading:

The continuous process of magma oozing out of the sea bed and getting solidified along the Mid-Atlantic Ridge. It is leading to the spreading of the Atlantic Ocean and diversion of continental block.

MAJOR LANDFORMS OF THE EARTH

- *Mountains:* A high landform that rises significantly than its surrounding area. A mountain can be either coastal (Appalachians, Rockies, Alpine), Inland (Himalayas, Urals, Kunlun, Tienshan), or oceanic (Mauna kea of Hawaii).

  On the basis of mode of origin, mountains are classified as the following:

  - *Fold mountains:* Formed due to folding of sedimentary rocks by the compressional forces coming from inside the earth. These are the most extensive and highest mountain ranges of the world. They are of two types: young fold and old fold mountains. Young fold mountains are characterized by steep slopes and pointed peaks. They are higher in height (e.g., Himalayas, Alps, Rockies). Old fold mountains have gentle slopes and round peaks. They are mostly affected by weathering and denudation (e.g., Aravallis, Vindhyas).
  - *Block mountains:* Also known as the fault block mountains, are formed due to tensional forces operated by endogenetic forces from deep within the earth's crust. They are formed when the two-side blocks on the either side of the two faults move downward while the middle block

remains in its position. Or they can form when the middle block moves down forming rift valley while the either side blocks remain intact forming horst (e.g., Vosges and Black forest mountains bordering the Rhine Rift Valley, Sierra Nevada mountain of California.

- *Volcanic mountains:* Formed due to accumulation of volcanic materials.
- *Dome mountains:* Up warping of the surface due to emergence and cooling of magma.
- *Relict mountains:* Formed due to denudation and erosion of higher mountains. Constant weathering of the mountains has lowered these mountains (e.g., Aravallis, Satpuras).

TYPES OF MOUNTAINS

Folded mountains

Upwarped mountains

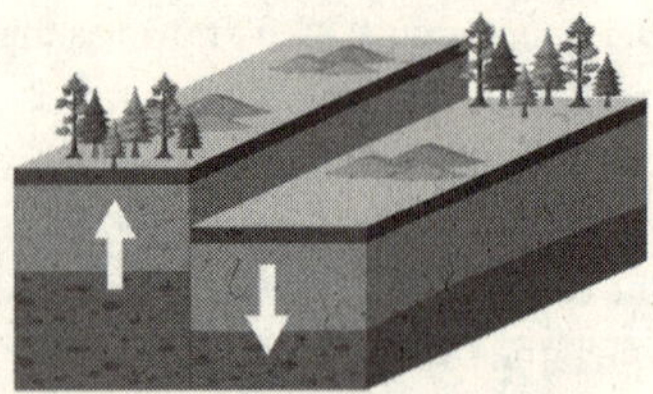

Fault-block mountains

Volcanic mountains

Plateaus: A table land feature with steep slopes higher than the surrounding areas with the upper part almost flat. On the basis of its location, plateaus can be:

- *Intermontane plateaus:* That are surrounded by mountains on all sides (e.g., Tibetan plateau).
- *Piedmont plateaus:* That are located at the foot of mountains (e.g., the Patagonian plateau).
- *Continental plateaus:* Away from mountains and are mostly surrounded by coastal plains (e.g., Arabian plateau, Australian plateau).
- *Volcanic plateaus:* Formed due to accumulation of thick basaltic lava (e.g., Columbian plateau [USA]).

Other types of plateaus: (according to mode of origin)

Glacial plateaus

Fluvial plateaus

Aeolian plateaus

The Deccan plateau, one of the oldest plateaus of the world, is highly dissected and is bordered by Western Ghats in the west and Eastern Ghats in the east.

- *Plains:* Flat areas with low undulating surface and very gentle slopes. They can be either higher or lower than the sea level. On the basis of mode of origin plains can be:

- *Diastrophic plains:* Formed due to upliftment or subsidence of land due to diastrophic movements (e.g., the Great Plains of the USA).
- *Erosional plains:* Lateral erosion by the rivers causes the formation of these plains.
- *Depositional plains:* Gradual deposition of sediments by rivers, wind, and glaciers causes such extensive plains.

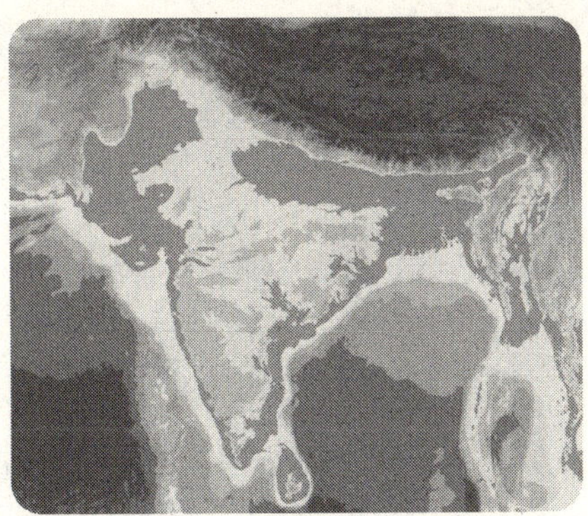

Other types of plains:

Delta plains
Lava plains
Lacustrine plains
Glacial plains

The Great Plains of India are formed due to the deposition of sediments brought down by the rivers flowing in that region.

The Great Ganga Brahmaputra plains are either Bhangar or Khadar type. Khadar plains are more fertile, get renewed every year with fresh alluvium. Bhangar plains are older alluvium and are filled with lime nodules and kankars.

WEATHERING AND EROSION

TYPES OF WEATHERING	SUB-TYPES	CHARACTERISTICS
Physical or mechanical weathering	Block disintegration Granular disintegration Frost action Exfoliation	Common in areas of high diurnal temperature changes like in hot deserts. Frost action occurs due to alternate freezing and thawing of water during night and day respectively in cold regions.
Chemical weathering	Solution Carbonation Hydration	Common in rocks which contain soluble minerals. The main agents are water vapour and water which mix with the minerals in the rocks causing chemical decomposition or disintegration. This type is most prevalent in areas of heavy rainfall like equatorial regions.
Biological weathering	Agents Plants Animals Man	Gradual breaking down of buildings, monuments and structure by plants, burrowing animals and even man due to development activities.

LANDFORMS CAUSED BY RIVERS, WIND, AND GLACIERS

FLUVIAL/RIVERINE LANDFORMS

The work of the river is divided into three stages: The youthful stage, maturity, and old age.

Youthful stage: Starting from the source of the river, the velocity of the running water is maximum. Steep gradient and downcutting is most active. Landforms formed are V-shaped valleys, waterfalls, and rapids. Erosion is the most dominant activity.

Matured stage: Transportation of load is most active, the gradient starts becoming gentler causing lateral cutting. The volume of water increases. Landforms formed are meanders and ox bow lakes.

Old stage: Deposition of sediments starts, the gradient is most gentle as the river approaches its mouth.

The river is unable to carry load any longer so there is a sluggish flow of the river. Landforms formed are deltas, braided stream, and vast alluvial plains.

MEANDERING STREAM

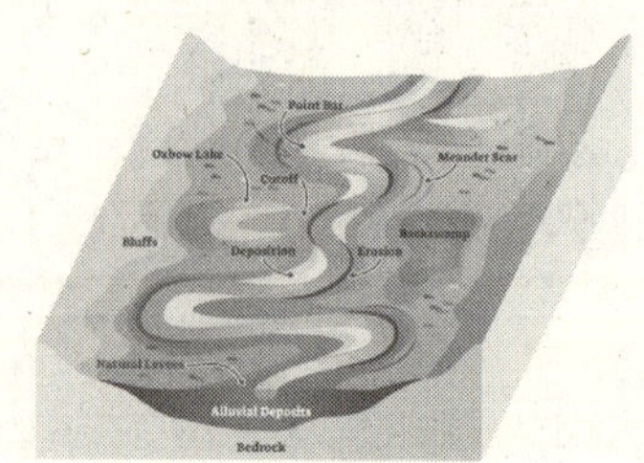

Important terms:

- *Source of the river:* Point of origin of a river which can be a mountain glacier or a lake.
- *Mouth:* When the river meets the sea or ends its journey typically when it is unable to carry its load.
- *Ox bow lake:* Extreme curvature creates close loop meander enclosing the land so only the neck of the land is left behind.
- *Delta:* A triangular relief feature with the apex pointing upstream.
- *Confluence:* When the river meets its tributary.
- *Tributary:* A river is divided into several small streams in its journey towards the sea.
- *Distributary:* Several smaller streams come out of the main river.
- *Estuary:* Sometimes river may not form delta, but it takes the shape of gradually widening mouth cutting inland.

AEOLIAN LANDFORMS

These are most active in arid and semi-arid regions. Velocity of the wind is more as there is no obstruction in the form of trees or vegetation. Some common landforms are:

Sand dunes: Depositional features made by wind.

Barkhan: Moon-shaped or crescent-shaped dunes having a sloping tail and a concave slope with two horns protruding outward.

Seif dunes: Long narrow sand ridges that lie parallel to the direction of the prevailing wind.

Deflation hollows: Depression formed due to loose sand particles blown away by wind.

In India, most of the sand dunes and seif dunes are common in the western part of the Thar Desert adjoining Pakistan.

The Qattara Depression of Egypt is a deflation hollow.

Loess are large extensive sand plains and are common in China.

GLACIAL LANDFORMS

EROSIONAL WORK OF GLACIERS	TRANSPORTATIONAL WORK OF GLACIERS	DEPOSITIONAL WORK OF GLACIERS
Cirque: Bowl-shaped feature resembling almost an arm chair where the snow collects. *U-shaped valley:* The moving glacier broadens the sides of the valley. Such valley has flat floor and almost vertical sides resembling a U. *Arêtes:* A saw tooth dividing two cirque basins resembling a comb. *Col:* Saddle-like narrow depression. *Bergschrund:* Mostly found in summer when there is no snow cover when a crevasse opens up along the headwall of a glacier. *Fjord:* A glacial trough found along a sea coast. *Horns:* A sharp pointed peak which forms when several cirques gorge a mountain peak from all sides.	Glaciers or moving ice carry with themselves large boulders of rock fragments along its journey.	When a glacier starts melting or retreats the load it was carrying starts getting deposited. These are called moraines. *Terminal moraines:* Here the debris gets deposited at the end of the glacier in the form of a ridge. *Lateral moraines:* Deposition of moraines on either side of a glacier. *Medial moraines:* Formed at the confluence of two glaciers. *Ground moraine:* Deposits left behind after the glaciers melt in an area.

MORAINE

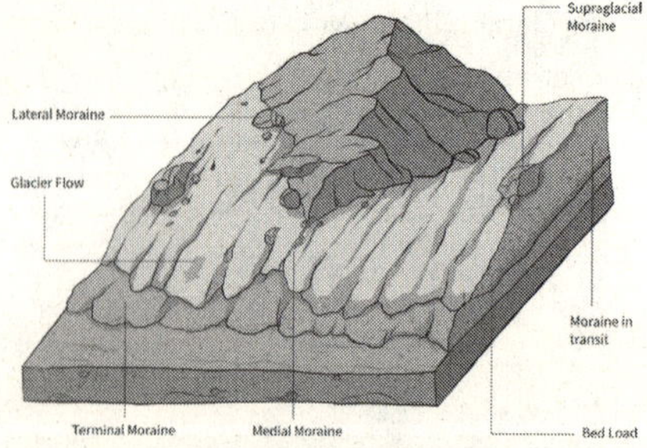

What is a hanging valley?

Sometimes the tributary glaciers also join a main glacier like that of a river and thus the tributary glacial valley joins the main glacial valleys of greater depth known as hanging valleys. This difference in over deepening between the main and the tributary glacier causes the tributary glacier to hang over the main valley. This happens as the main glacier is much broader and wider so it erodes its valley more extensively; hence, the valley of the main glacier becomes more deeper than the tributary valley.

What are drumlins?

Rounded hummocks from deposition of glacial till. They look like a spoon.

- Did you know what **glacial tills** are?

They are a mixture of soil that are unsorted and unstratified, made up of coarse materials.

Landforms made by sea waves:

Sand bars: They form barrier between the sea and the shore. They are caused by the deposits of gravel, rocks, and sand brought by waves and currents.

Spit: When an end of the sand bar extends to the sea and the other end is attached to the coast.

Lagoon: A saline shallow water lake separated from the sea or a larger water body by a sand bar or coral reef.

Beach: A flat or undulating platform plain formed of gravels and sand picked up and deposited by the sea causing the coastal area to rise than the adjoining sea that becomes shallow.

FACT FILE

The Marina Beach of Chennai is the longest beach of India.
Chilka Lake and Pulicat Lake are examples of a lagoon.

EARTHQUAKES AND SEISMIC WAVES

Sudden vibrations felt on the surface of the earth ranging from a mild tremor to a destructive motion. Earthquakes are caused due to transmission of waves of energy through the surface layer of the earth.

IMPORTANT TERMS TO REMEMBER

- *Focus:* The place of origin of an earthquake.
- *Epicentre:* The place on the ground that is perpendicular to the focus.
- *Seismic waves:* The waves generated during an earthquake.
- *Seismology:* The science dealing with the study of seismic waves.
- *Seismograph:* An instrument to measure the seismic waves.

Richter scale is used to measure the intensity of an earthquake. The scale ranges between 0 and 9.

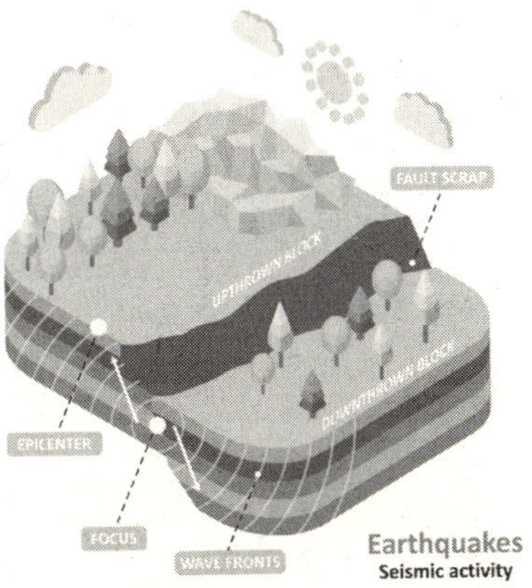

Earthquakes
Seismic activity

CAUSES OF AN EARTHQUAKE

Earthquakes are mainly caused due to two reasons: tectonic activities (like folding or faulting) and volcanic activity.

But the most possible answer to the cause of an earthquake is related to the plate tectonic theory. We know that the earth's crust is made up of several lithosphere slabs which are floating over the asthenosphere. These plates are either oceanic or continental. They are constantly moving either towards or away from each other. All tectonic activities take place along the plate margins.

- High magnitude earthquakes are formed along the margins of destructive plate boundaries. When two plates move towards each other and collide the heavier plate is subducted below the lighter plate. This zone of subduction becomes the focal point of tectonic activities.
- Moderate earthquakes are found along the constructive plate boundaries as the movement of the plates away from each other allows the rate of rupture to be low.

Earthquakes are all about release of energy waves. Let us know about the type of **seismic waves** generated at the time of an earthquake:

TYPES OF SEISMIC WAVES

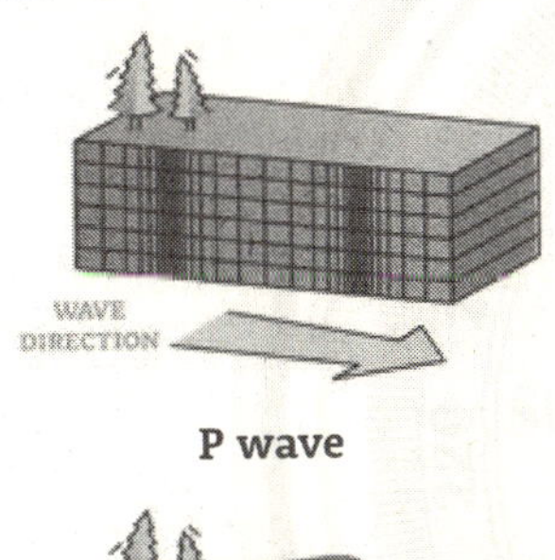

P wave

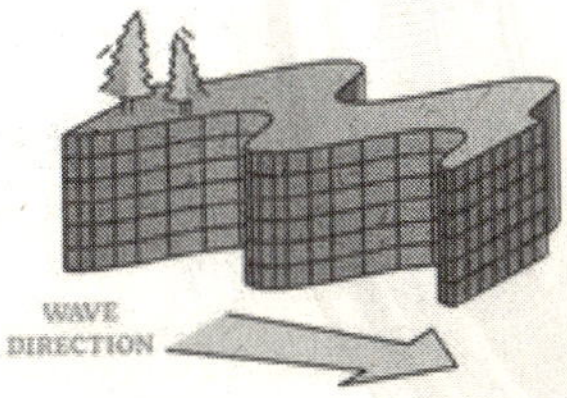

S wave

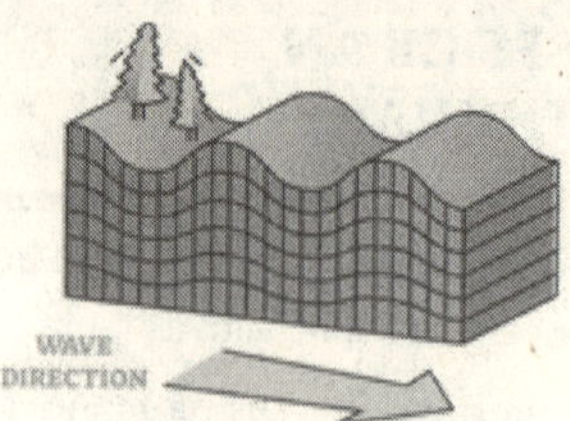

Rayleigh wave

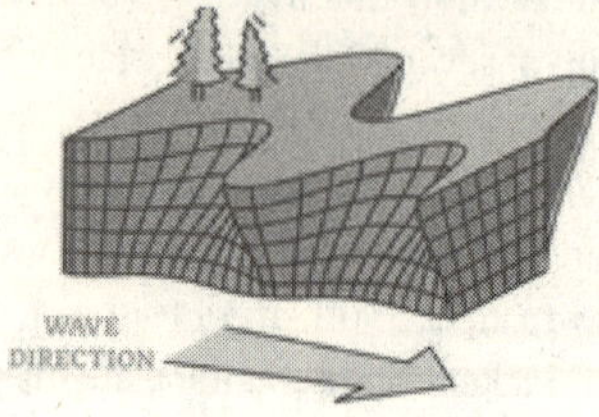

Love wave

P waves: These are longitudinal waves. They can travel through both solid and liquid medium.

S waves: These are transverse waves. They can travel through solids but not through liquid medium.

Surface waves: Long waves, these are mainly found on the surface of the earth. These are the most violent and destructive waves as they travel the longest distance. However, their speed is lesser than P and S waves.

CLASSIFICATION OF EARTHQUAKES

ON THE BASIS OF	TYPES	CHARACTERISTICS
Causes	• Natural earthquakes	Formed due to endogenetic forces
	➢ Volcanic earthquakes	Due to volcanic eruptions. The intensity of such earthquakes depend on the intensity of the volcanic eruption
	➢ Tectonic earthquakes	Due to movement of tectonic plates or faulting activity
	➢ Isostatic earthquakes	Sudden disturbance in the isostatic balance triggering an earthquake
	➢ Plutonic earthquakes	Deep focus earthquakes at the depth of 240–660 km
	• Artificial earthquakes	Due to human activities such as underground drilling of oil, mining, blasting of rocks for constructional purposes, etc.
Focus (according to Guttenberg)	➢ Moderate earthquakes	Foci at the depth between 0 and 50 km
	➢ Intermediate earthquakes	Foci at the depth between 50 and 250 km
	➢ Deep focus earthquakes	Foci at the depth between 250 and 700 km
Human casualties	➢ Moderately hazardous earthquakes	Human casualty is less than 50,000
	➢ Highly hazardous earthquakes	Human casualty is between 50,000 and 1,00,000
	➢ Most hazardous earthquakes	Human casualty is above 1,00,000

WORLD DISTRIBUTION OF EARTHQUAKES

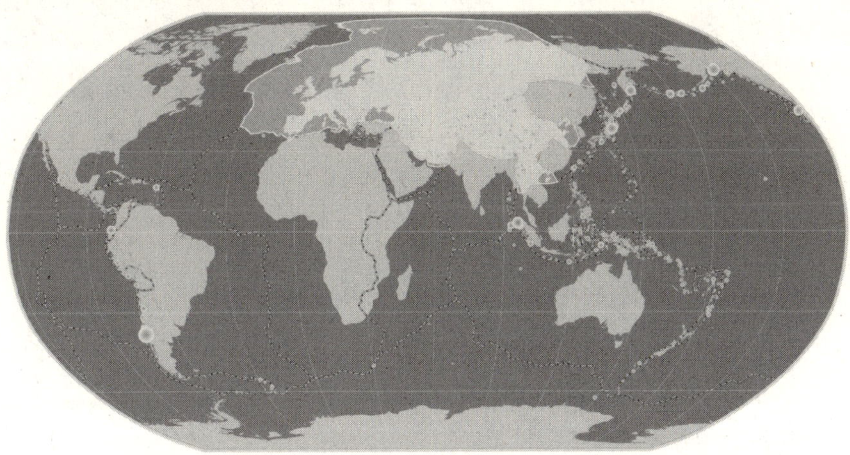

1. *The Circum-Pacific belt:* Includes the coastal margins of North and South America and Eastern Asia. More than 65 per cent of the earthquakes occur here. It is the zone of high tectonic movements, active volcanoes as well as the subduction zones of destructive plate boundaries. This zone is famously called the Pacific Ring of Fire.
2. *Mid Continental belt:* Or the Alpine Himalayan belt. This is the zone of subduction of continental plates.

The earthquakes occurring in the Indian Himalayas are due to the northward movement of the Indian plate so it is getting subducted below the Asiatic plate. The Indian Himalayan belt is an extensive area of some complex faults along the zone of collision.

INDIA IS DIVIDED INTO FIVE DAMAGE RISK ZONES OF EARTHQUAKE

ZONE I OF LEAST DAMAGE	ZONE II OF LOW DAMAGE	ZONE III OF MODERATE DAMAGE	ZONE IV OF HIGH DAMAGE	ZONE V OF VERY HIGH DAMAGE
Parts of Bihar, Punjab, Haryana, Uttar Pradesh, some portions of plains of West Bengal, delta areas of Godavari	Southern Punjab, Haryana, Uttar Pradesh, coastal districts of Tamil Nadu, Odisha	Most of Madhya Pradesh, Karnataka, Maharashtra	Jammu and Kashmir, Himachal Pradesh, hilly areas of Sikkim, Bihar, and Uttarakhand	Entire north eastern part, Kutch region of Gujarat, western north Bihar, parts of Jammu and Kashmir

Did you know?

Although the plains of West Bengal fall under least damage zone but a devastating earthquake struck the then Kolkata on 11 October 1737, killing almost 3,00,000 people!

As we know the Richter scale measures the intensity or magnitude of an earthquake the diagram above illustrates what each unit means.

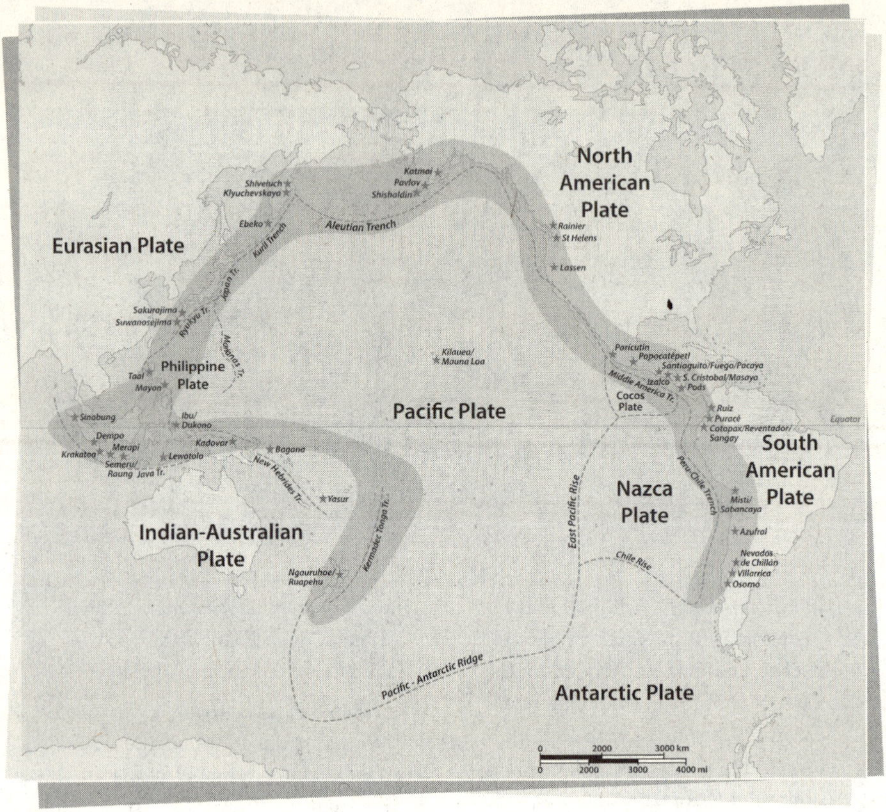

North American Plate
Eurasian Plate
Philippine Plate
Pacific Plate
Cocos Plate
South American Plate
Nazca Plate
Indian-Australian Plate
Antarctic Plate
Aleutian Trench
Kuril Trench
Japan Tr.
Ryukyu Tr.
Mariana Tr.
Java Tr.
New Hebrides Tr.
Kermadec Tonga Tr.
Middle America Tr.
Peru-Chile Trench
East Pacific Rise
Chile Rise
Pacific - Antarctic Ridge
Equator
Shiveluch
Klyuchevskaya
Katmai
Pavlov
Shishaldin
Ebeko
Rainier
St Helens
Lassen
Sakurajima
Suwanosejima
Taal
Mayon
Kilauea/
Mauna Loa
Paricutin
Popocatépetl
Santiaguito/Fuego/Pacaya
Izalco
S. Cristobal/Masaya
Poás
Ruiz
Puracé
Cotopax/Reventador/
Sangay
Sinabung
Ibu/
Dukono
Dempo
Merapi
Krakatoa
Semeru/
Raung
Lewotolo
Kadovar
Bagana
Yasur
Ngauruhoe/
Ruapehu
Misti/
Sabancaya
Azufral
Nevados
de Chillán
Villarrica
Osorno
0 2000 3000 km
0 2000 3000 4000 mi

EARTHQUAKE MAGNITUDE SCALE

Micro
Minor
Light
Moderate
Strong
Major
Great
1.0
2.0
3.0
4.0
5.0
6.0
7.0
8.0
9.0
10

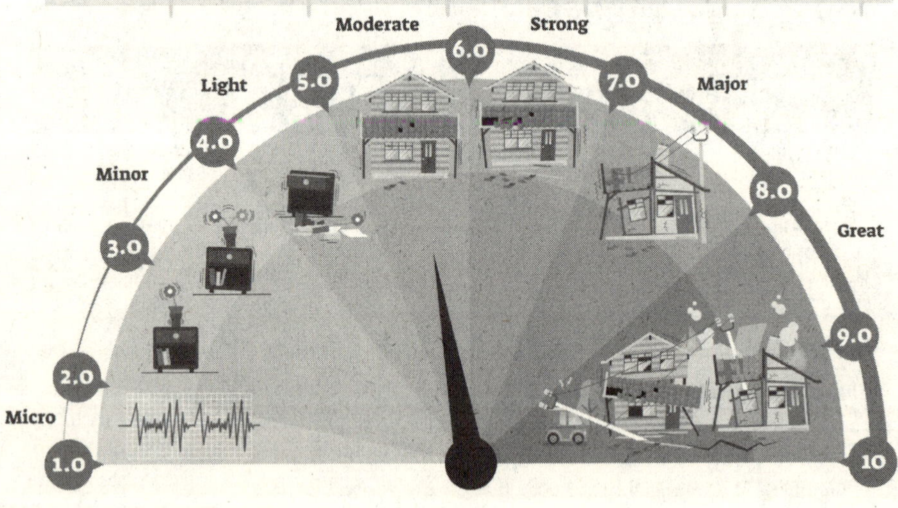

DESTRUCTIVE EFFECTS OF EARTHQUAKES

- Damage to human structures.
- Loss of life and property.
- Landslides and debris falls.
- Deformation of ground surface.
- Flash floods.
- Fire break out.

What are tsunamis?

Series of ocean waves that are triggered by an earthquake on the sea floor which causes upwelling of sea waves as high as 100 ft onto land. These waves cause massive destruction when they crash ashore. Since the Pacific Ocean is notoriously known for its Ring of Fire, tsunamis are most common here. When tsunamis appear in mid ocean they are only a foot high but as they approach the shore they slow down by entering the shallow water and start collecting energy and pace. The top of the waves moves faster than the bottom.

The retreating of sea waves is often seen as a warning sign of a tsunami because the trough of the tsunami often reaches the shore first. It creates a vacuum that sucks the coastal water seaward and exposes the sea floor.

A tsunami usually comprises of series of waves called wave trains so its destructive force increases with each successive wave.

VOLCANOES

Volcanoes are a vent or an opening from which heated materials, gases, smoke, liquid lava, and fragments of rocks come out of the interior of the earth to the surface. Hot molten materials called magma are thrown out to the surface with great force from the magma chamber below. These materials when they reach the surface, they are known as lava.

COMPONENTS OF A VOLCANO

An important component of a volcano is the presence of a volcanic cone. The volcanic materials are accumulated in the form of a cone or volcanic mountain. There is a vent or an opening which is either circular or nearly circular almost in the centre of the cone. This is called volcanic vent. It is connecting the interior of the earth with the vent by a narrow pipe called the volcanic pipe. All the hot molten materials are ejected through this pipe and the vent situated at the top of the pipe. When repeated explosions and weathering causes the vent to enlarge then it is called the volcanic crater or caldera.

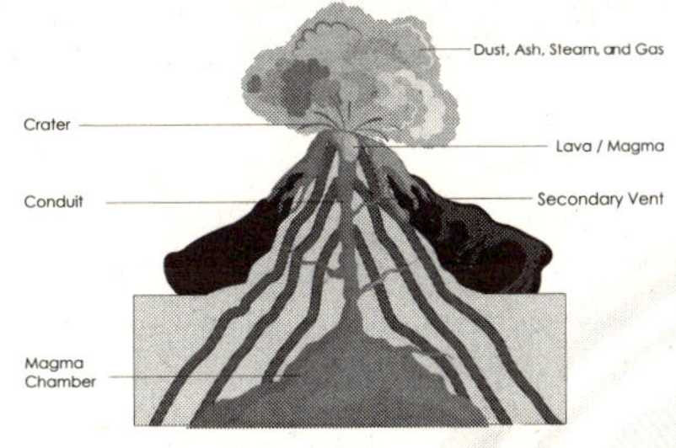

CLASSIFICATION OF VOLCANOES

On the basis of periodicity of eruptions volcanoes can be:

Active volcanoes are those which are constantly erupting and ejecting volcanic lava, gases, smoke, ashes, and fragmented materials. Etna and Stromboli volcanoes of the Mediterranean Sea are the classic examples. Stromboli volcano is known as the light house of the Mediterranean as it is constantly ejecting luminous and burning gases.

Dormant volcanoes are those which have not erupted in the recent past but can erupt at any time in future. These volcanoes are most dangerous as they can erupt suddenly and violently causing huge damage to life and property. Mt. Vesuvius is one such example which had erupted in 79 AD and then kept dormant for long before erupting once again in 1631 AD.

Extinct volcanoes are those which have not erupted in the recent geologic past. The crater of such volcanoes are filled with rain-water forming lakes. These are dead volcanoes.

On the basis of the mode of eruption:

1. *Central eruption type:* These are the explosive type of volcanoes where the materials come out through the central pipe and small opening. The crustal surface is broken because of the violent and explosive gases which tries to come out through the opening due to the accumulated pressure deep inside the earth. These volcanoes are most destructive and very violent. The eruption becomes so rapid and violent that large quantities of fragmented rock particles, lava, dust, and ashes are thrown up to several thousand metres in the sky.

The sub-types of these volcanoes are:

Hawaiian type: These volcanoes are most common in the Hawaiian Islands. These are generally silent type where less viscous lava and gases come out quietly. The red molten lava comes out and looks like long threads of hair as it waves by strong glides of wind in the air. Hawaiian people names this lava as Pele (goddess of fire in Hawaii).

Strombolian type: These volcanoes erupt with moderate intensity. These eruptions are mostly continuous ones. They eject lava, fragmented materials thousands of metres into the sky and when they come down they get accumulated in and around the volcanic craters.

Vulcanian type: These volcanoes erupt with great force and intensity. The lava here is so viscous that it immediately solidifies and hardens between two eruptions and plugs the volcanic vents. As a result, it creates an obstacle in the next eruption. Consequently, the accumulated pressure causes the materials to erupt violently, shattering the lava crusts into angular fragments and to appear as ash-laden clouds of dark colour in the sky, taking a convoluted or cauliflower shape.

Pelean type: Most violent and explosive type. These make roaring noise as the materials come out with explosion and great intensity. This type of volcano is often associated with avalanches on hill slopes.

Vesuvius type: They are almost similar to the strombolian or the vulcanian type. The only difference is that there is enormous volume of gases which erupt with massive expulsion of magma.

2. *Fissure type:* Slow expulsion of magma occurs along the fissures faults and cracks. The magma spreads over the ground as lava and forms extrusive landform features. The speed of the lava depends on the nature, volume of the magma, gradient of the slope, and the temperature conditions.

VOLCANIC MATERIALS

- Vapour and gases ➔
  Volcanic gases include carbon dioxide, nitrogen dioxide, hydrogen, carbon monoxides, etc.
- Magma and lava ➔
  On the basis of silica percentage magma and lava can be acidic or basic. Acidic magma and lava have greater percentage of silica.

- Magma and lava can also be classified on the basis of their colour into felsic and mafic lava. Mafic lava has maximum fluidity and is also the hottest lava.
- Fragmented materials ➔
  Volcanic dust (very fine particles), ash (2 mm in size), lapilli (peas size), and volcanic bombs (6 cm in size).

FACT FILE

In Hawaiian language, ʻAʻā lava is more viscous while Pahoehoe lava has more fluidity. It spreads like thin sheets on the surface thus also called ropy lava.

CAUSES OF VOLCANIC ERUPTION

Volcanic Eruption

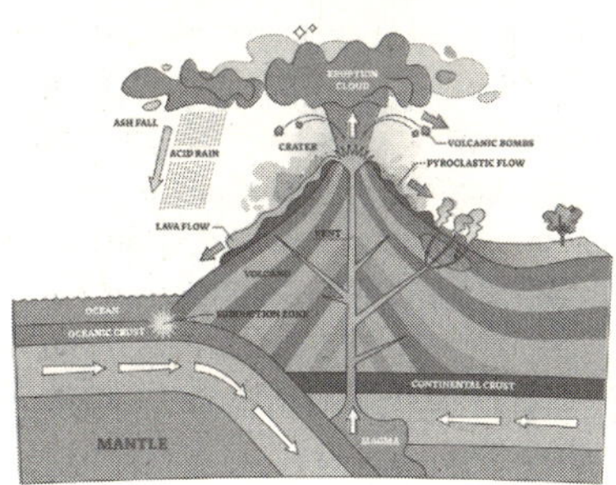

Just like earthquakes volcanoes are also associated with lines of weaknesses. These lines of weaknesses are found along the destructive plate margins.

- Destructive plate boundaries are associated with most violent form of volcanoes. When two plates collide against each other the heavier plate gets subducted below the lighter plate. This subducted plate melts and forms magma when it reaches up to a certain depth inside the earth. This magma is forced to expel out because of the tremendous pressure beneath along with explosive gases. This type of volcanic eruption is most prevalent in the Pacific Ring of Fire. The volcanoes of the islands of Pacific are mainly due to the collision and subsequent subduction of the Pacific plate below the lighter Asian plate.
- Constructive plate boundaries are associated with quiet fissure type eruption. This is because here the pressure release of magma is slow and gradual.

FACT FILE

The mid oceanic ridges are always known for their supply of basaltic lava. Hence most active volcanoes are found near these ridges. As the distance from the ridges increases, the volcanoes become more inactive and extinct.

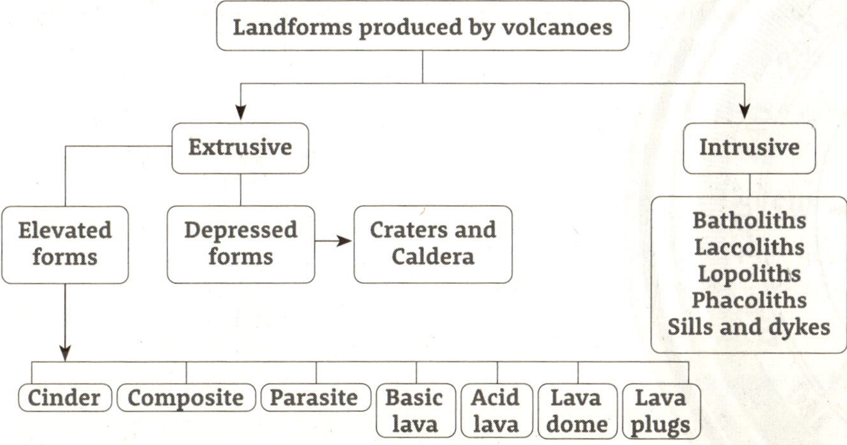

TERMS TO REMEMBER

Extrusive Landforms

- *Cinder cones:* Accumulation of finer particles around the volcanic vent. Cinder cones are of low height and are made up of volcanic dust, ash, and pyroclastic matter.
- *Composite cones:* Highest of all cones. They are composed of alternate layers of lava and pyroclastic materials where lava acts as the cementing factor for the compaction of fragmental materials.
- *Parasite cones:* Many branches of pipes come out from the main central pipe. The lava comes out through these small pipes and these materials are found around newly formed vents located on the outer surface of the main cone.
- *Basic lava cone:* Lighter magma consisting of less silica. It cools and solidifies after spreading on larger area.
- *Acid lava cone:* Lava is highly viscous and rich in silica. They get immediately cooled and solidified as they have less mobility.
- *Lava dome:* Are formed due to accumulation of solid lava around the volcanic vents.
- *Lava plugs:* Formed due to plugging of volcanic pipes and vents when they become extinct.
- *Volcanic neck:* The lava filled volcanic pipe.
- *Craters and caldera:* Craters are depressions found at the top of the volcanic vent. These are usually funnel shaped. Enlarged form of craters are called caldera.

Sometimes the crater of a volcano becomes so large that there are few eruptions of small intensity. After long time several smaller cones are found within the larger ones. So these formations of several small-sized craters found within one crater are called crater within crater or **nested craters**.

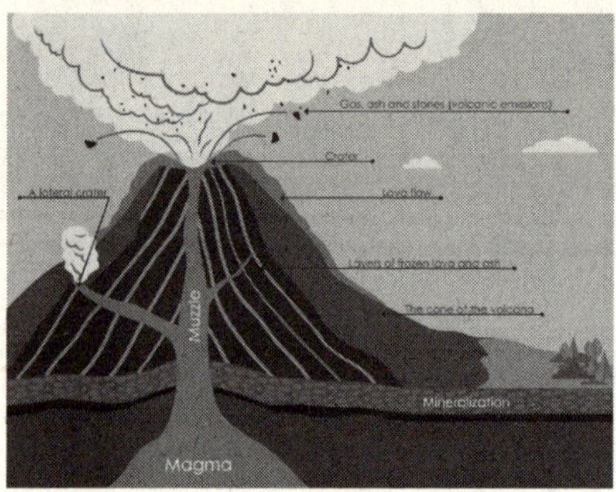

Intrusive Landforms

- *Batholiths:* Dome-shaped forms of solidified magma. The side walls are very steep and almost vertical. Sometimes the upper part of the batholiths can be seen protruding in the surface due to continuous denudation. However, their bases can never be seen as they are buried deep inside the earth. These batholithic domes are common in Ranchi plateau.
- *Laccoliths:* They are found along the bedding planes of horizontally bedded sedimentary rocks. The word 'laccos' means rock. These are mostly mushroom shaped.
- *Phacoliths:* Found due to magma intrusions along the anticlines and synclines of fold mountains.
- *Lopoliths:* Magma gets solidified in a shallow basin where the central part is bent downward. These are mostly coarse-grained magma because of the slow rate of cooling.

- *Sills and dykes:* Sills are found parallel to the beds of sedimentary rocks. Thin beds of magma are called sheets.

  Dykes are perpendicular to the beds of sedimentary rocks.

Plutonic Bodies

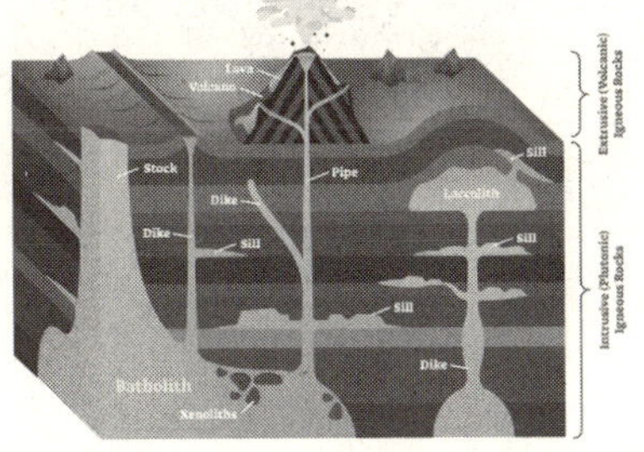

Destructive Effects of Volcanoes

- May bury human structures, killing people and animals.
- Destroys crops, vegetation, and forests due to emulsion of huge quantities of molten lava, pyroclastic materials that spreads on the surface.
- They may trigger landslides and acid rain.
- Volcanic eruptions may generate huge seismic waves on the sea floor leading to tsunamis.
- Radiation balance of the earth and atmosphere may change. Greater concentration of smoke and harmful gases in the atmosphere will affect the incoming solar radiation and the outgoing terrestrial radiation leading to climate change. The temperature will rise, leading to global warming.

World Distribution of Volcanoes

Volcanoes are associated with earthquakes as both are found along the lines of weaknesses like the fault zones or the meeting of continent and ocean plate boundaries.

The three major zones are:

Circum-Pacific belt: It is called the Pacific Ring of Fire. Most of the volcanoes here are found in chains. Cotopaxi is the highest volcanic mountain in the world located in this belt. This zone includes the mountain belt of both the eastern and western coastal areas of the Pacific Ocean, the western coastal margins of Asia, the islands on the east coast of Asia.

Volcanic eruptions and the consequent solidification and cooling of lava on the surface give birth to black lava soil which is good for cotton and sugarcane cultivation.

Good effects of volcanoes!

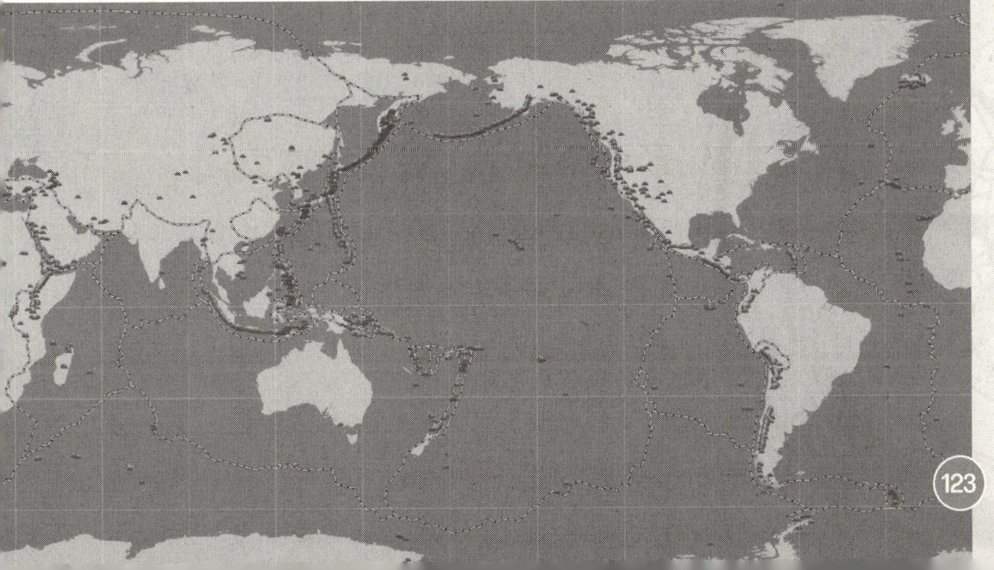

Mid Continental belt: This belt includes the Alpine mountain chain and the Mediterranean Sea. Here the volcanic eruptions occur due to the convergence of the Asiatic and Indian and African plates. The famous volcanoes of Stromboli, Etna, Vesuvius fall under this belt.

Mid Atlantic belt: Mainly fissure eruption type volcanoes along the divergent plate boundaries.

> ***What are geysers and hot springs?***
>
> Geysers and hot springs are features which constantly spouts hot water and vapour. These features are mainly found in regions which are typically associated with vulcanicity. The hot water and steam are rich in sulphur and are good for patients with arthritis.

DRAINAGE SYSTEM AND PATTERNS

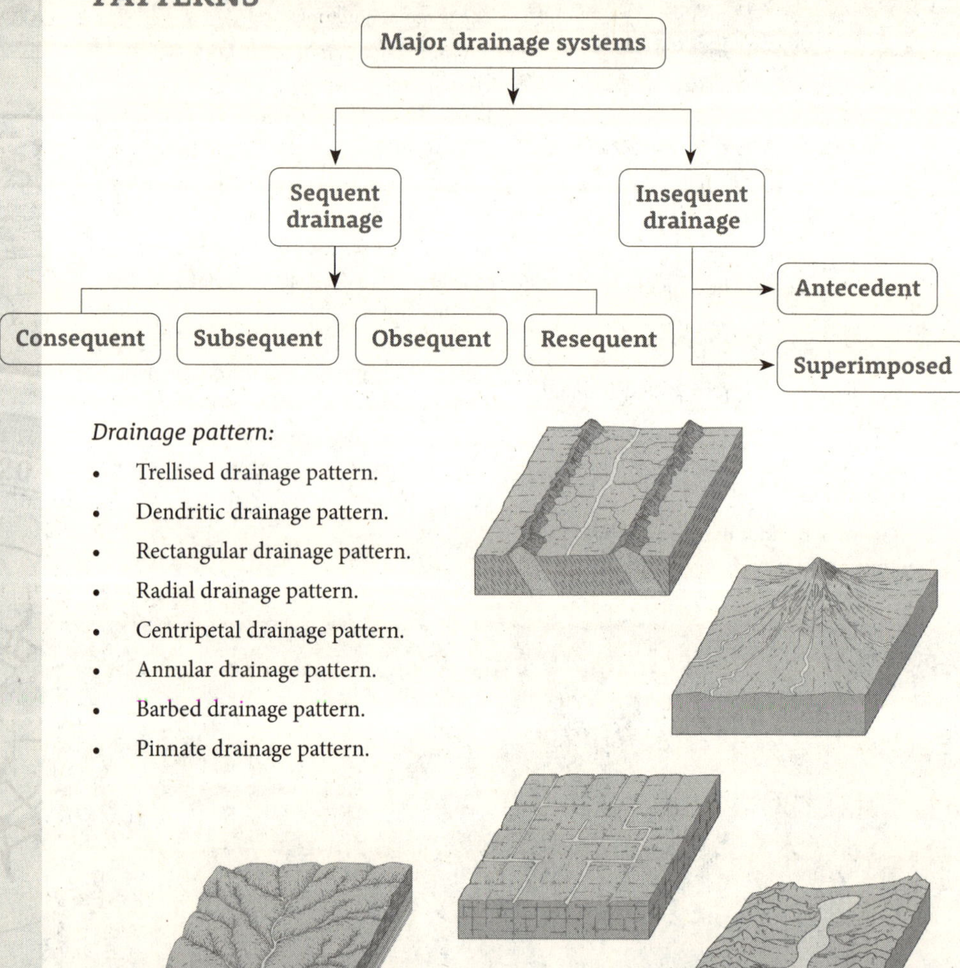

Drainage pattern:

- Trellised drainage pattern.
- Dendritic drainage pattern.
- Rectangular drainage pattern.
- Radial drainage pattern.
- Centripetal drainage pattern.
- Annular drainage pattern.
- Barbed drainage pattern.
- Pinnate drainage pattern.

Few important geographic terms:

- *Anticline:* The upper part or up fold rock strata of the fold mountains are anticlines.
- *Synclines:* The down folded rock strata.
- *Anticlinorium:* The folded structures where there are series of minor anticlines and synclines within one anticline. These are formed due to difference in the intensity and duration of compressive forces.
- *Synclinorium:* The folded structures where there are series of minor anticlines and synclines within one syncline.
- *Fault plane:* The plane along which the rocks are displaced by compression and tension acting horizontally and vertically.
- *Fault dip:* Angle between fault plane and horizontal plane.
- *Fault scarp:* Steep wall like slope formed by faulting of crustal rocks. Sometimes they are so steep they look like cliffs.
- *Geosynclines:* Long shallow and narrow depressions of water. These have subsided due to accumulation of sediments in water. They are believed to be the origin of the young fold mountains of the world.

ATMOSPHERE

Atmosphere is the mixture of gases that envelopes the earth from the surface to at least 1,000 km. More than 99 per cent of the atmospheric mass is found within 32 km due to the gravitational pull of the earth.

Composition of the atmosphere

MAIN GASES	AMOUNT IN %	SECONDARY GASES	AMOUNT IN %
Nitrogen	78.1	Argon	0.9
		Carbon dioxide	0.03
		Hydrogen	0.01
Oxygen	20.9	Neon	0.0018
		Helium	0.0005
		Ozone	0.00006

Water vapour: It is the source of all clouds and precipitation. It regulates the hydrological cycle. However, the composition of atmosphere varies from one place to another, for example, in desert areas where the composition of water vapour is less.

Dust particles: These contribute to the vibrant colours of the sky at dawn and dusk. Dust particles act as the condensation nuclei. These particles absorb the terrestrial radiation.

Layers of the Atmosphere

Troposphere:

- The lowest layer of the atmosphere and its average height is 16 km over the equator and 6 km over the poles.
- All the weather phenomena occur in this layer.
- Temperature decreases with an increase in height at the rate of about 6.5°C per 1,000 m known as normal lapse rate.

Stratosphere:

- The layer just above the troposphere. This layer is particularly devoid of any weather phenomena.
- It is suitable for flying aircrafts.
- The lower portion of the stratosphere has maximum concentration of ozone and is called the ozonosphere.
- The ozone is found within the limits of 15 – 35 km from sea level.
- The temperature rises with increasing height in the stratosphere which stops again at the stratopause.

Mesosphere:

- The coldest layer of the atmosphere.
- In the uppermost layer of the mesosphere the temperature goes down to –80°C.

Ionosphere:

- Extends from 80 to 640 km.
- This layer reflects the radio waves back to the earth.
- In this layer the temperature increases with increase in height and reaches up to 1,700°C.

Exosphere:

- Uppermost layer of the atmosphere.
- The density is very low and the air is almost rarefied.

What is ozone?

Ozone consisting of three oxygen atoms is a blue irritating gas with a pungent odour. It absorbs most of the harmful UV rays of the sun. The ozone molecules are unstable as they are constantly formed and destroyed in the stratosphere.

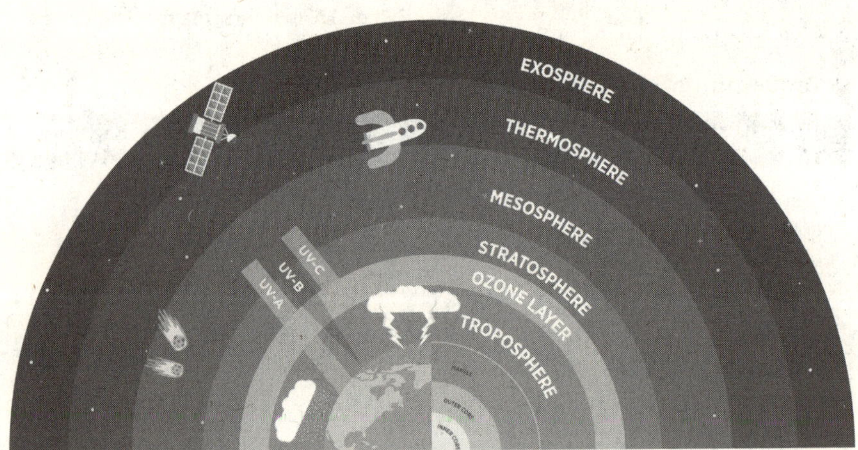

INSOLATION AND HEAT BUDGET

Factors affecting the distribution of insolation:

Insolation (also known as the incoming solar radiation) received at the earth surface decreases from equator towards the poles due to various factors:

- *Angle of the rays of sun:* The angle of the sun's rays decrease from equator towards the poles. The sun's rays are more or less vertical at the equator but they become more slanting at the poles. This causes the amount of insolation received at the equator to be more than the poles. Simple reason being the vertical rays concentrate on a smaller area where the intensity of heat is more while in poles the oblique rays spread over a large area so the intensity of the heat is less.

- *Length of day:* The amount of insolation will be more when the length of the day is more and vice versa. The length of the day and night is almost the same at the equator throughout the year while it increases as one marches towards the North Pole due to the northward apparent movement of the sun at the time of summer solstice. In winter solstice it is just the reverse when the length of the night is maximum at the North Pole.
- *Distance between earth and sun:* Since the orbit of the earth around the sun is elliptical in shape so the period when it is closest to the sun is called the perihelion (3rd January) and the time when it is farthest from the sun it is called the aphelion (4th July). When it is supposed to be receiving maximum insolation in the month of January (as we are closest to the sun) we don't feel the heat as there is winter season at that time in the Northern hemisphere due to the inclination of the earth's axis.

FACT FILE

Even if the length of the day is more at the poles, the amount of insolation will be less at the poles due to two reasons:

1. The ice cover reflects back most of the rays.
2. The sun's rays have to travel a long distance so remain parallel to the ground surface.

- *Effects of the atmosphere:* All of the sun's rays are not absorbed by the atmosphere they are partly absorbed, partly reflected, and partly scattered by the atmosphere.
    - *Absorption:* If we take the total units of incoming solar radiation to be 100 units then out of this about 14 per cent is absorbed by the earth's atmospheric gases and water vapour (mostly ozone).
    - *Scattering:* Some portions of insolation around 23 per cent is scattered by dust particles and haze. Six per cent of it is sent back to space while 17 per cent reaches the earth's surface. Scattering is possible when the diameter of the suspended dust particles and molecules of the gases present are shorter than wavelength of the solar radiation.
    - *Reflection:* When the diameter of the dust particles are longer than the wave length of the incoming solar radiation some portions are sent back to space while some remain back in the lower layers of the atmosphere. This is called diffuse reflection.

What is an albedo?

The portion of energy that is reflected back is known as albedo. The **albedo** of ice covered areas are always more than that of forest areas.

Why does the sky look blue?

Blue light of the incoming short wave length is more scattered than red light. The brilliant and vibrant hues of sunrise and sunset is due to the scattering of all colours except red and orange.

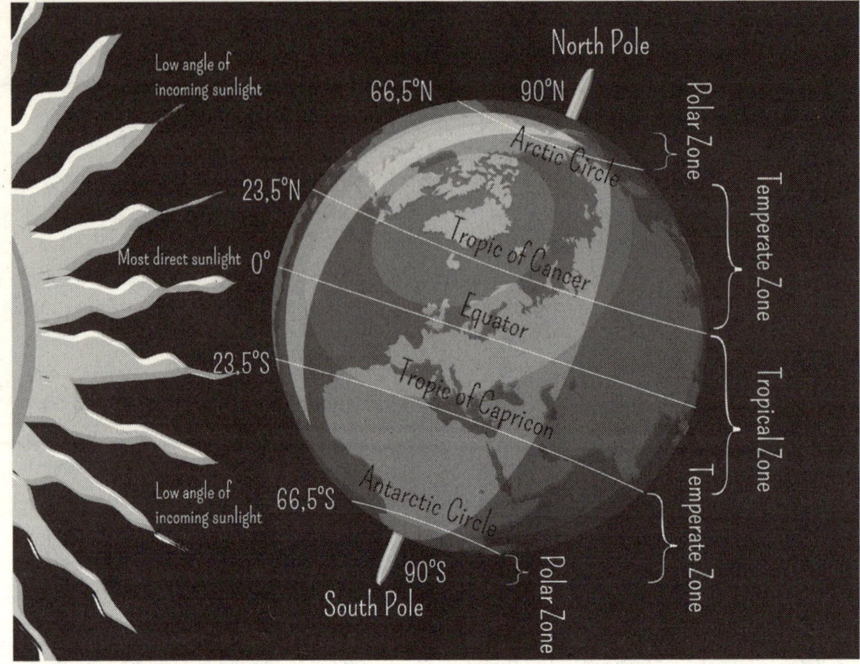

Heat Zones of the Earth

- *Torrid zone/tropical zone:* Extends between the Tropic of Cancer (23.5° N) and Tropic of Capricorn (23.5° S). Here the sun's rays are almost vertical throughout the year. Equator is the zone of no seasons. The temperature remains hot and humid throughout the year in equator.
- *Temperate zone:* Extends between 23.5° and 66.5° N and S in both the hemispheres. There are marked seasonal contrasts with the northward and southward apparent movement of the sun during the solstices. The range of temperature is high between summer and winter.
- *Frigid zone:* Extending between 66.5° latitudes and the poles in both the hemispheres. The sun's rays are slanting throughout the year. Days and nights are of 6 months, duration at the poles. The ground remains almost covered with snow at the poles throughout the year.

What is thermal anomaly?

It is the difference between the mean temperature of a latitude and the actual temperature of a place located at that latitude.

For example, if the mean temperature of latitude 30° N is 20°C and the actual temperature of place A located at that latitude is 30° C then the thermal anomaly is 10°C.

The imaginary lines joining places having the same thermal anomaly are called **isonomals**.

Heat budget of the earth:

Heat budget of the earth is the balance between the incoming solar radiation absorbed by the earth and outgoing terrestrial radiation. If this balance is not achieved, then the earth would become too hot or too cold to survive.

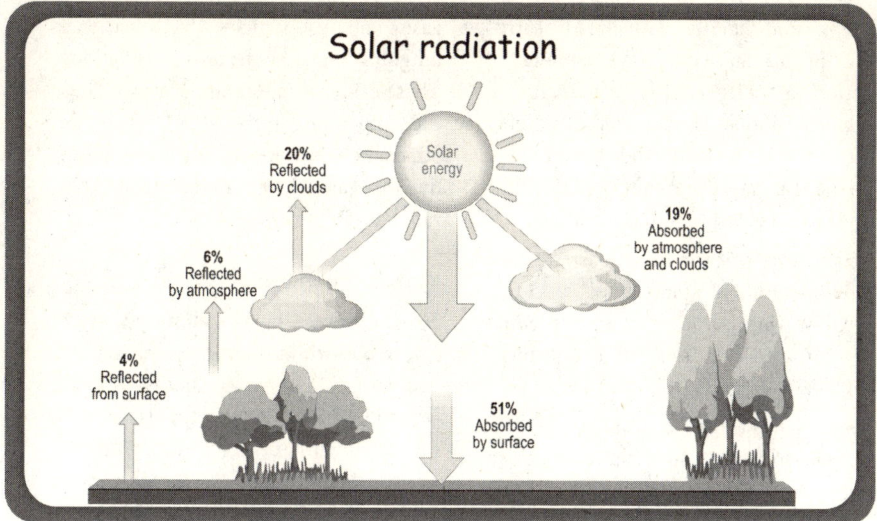

How Is the Balance Achieved?

It is important to remember that although the earth maintains its balance between the incoming solar radiation and outgoing terrestrial radiation but the amount of insolation always depends on the latitudes. In tropics the amount of insolation is higher than the outgoing radiation. So it is the region of heat surplus while poles are the regions of heat deficit.

Horizontal Distribution of Temperature

Latitude: The angle of incidence decreases from the equator to the poles. Higher the angle of incidence greater is the temperature. So as the latitudes increase the temperature starts falling.

Land and sea differences: Land gets heated and cools down more rapidly than water bodies. So the land temperature is always higher than water during day and water temperature is higher at night. Similarly, there is seasonal contrast between land and water temperature. During summer the land is heated more than the oceans. This contrast between the land and sea temperature causes differences in the rate of heating.

INCOMING SOLAR RADIATION	UNITS IN %
Let us take the total heat received	100
Reflected back to space	**35**
Back to space from top of the atmosphere	6
Reflected by clouds	27
Reflected by snow and ice cover	2
Reaches the earth's surface	**51**
Absorption by gases, water vapour, and dust particles	**14**
Outgoing terrestrial radiation	**100**
Terrestrial radiation	51
Absorption by the atmosphere	34
Directly goes to space	17
The atmosphere radiates back to space	48
Solar unit reflected back to space by atmosphere	17 + 48 = 65

Relief and altitude: We have already learnt about normal lapse rate in the previous portion. So we feel cold as we go up in higher elevations. The presence of a higher relief prevents the cold winds to enter like the Himalayas prevent the cold chilly winds to enter India from Central Asia.

Ocean currents: Warm ocean currents raise the temperature of a place along which they flow while cold ocean currents reduce the temperature of the coasts along which they flow.

Winds: Winds transport heat from one place to another so also affects the temperature of a place.

Vegetation cover: Soils devoid of any vegetation cover receives heat more rapidly and supports radiation from the earth. While a dense vegetation cover prevents heat to escape.

Gradient of slope: Steep slope will cause more angle of incidence of sun's rays than gentler slopes.

Distance from the sea: Places located near the coast will have maritime climate because there is more mixing of air masses between the sea and the coastal land. As the distance from the sea increases the range of temperature becomes more.

Vertical Distribution of Temperature

Temperature decreases with increase in height in the troposphere but the rate at which it decreases depends on the seasons, duration of day and location. As the distance from the earth's surface increases the temperature of air goes down. This is a proof of the fact that air is heated from the surface of the earth as there is a transfer of heat from surface to the air above through the processes of conduction, convection, and radiation.

The air in the lower layers of the atmosphere contains more water vapour, gases, and dust particles which absorb the outgoing long-wave terrestrial radiation. These decrease rapidly as we go up. Thus, the temperature of the lower layers of the atmosphere is more than the upper layers due to greater absorption of terrestrial radiation in the lower layers.

Inversion of temperature:

We know that the temperature decreases with increasing height but sometimes it is opposite to the normal trend that is the temperature is more in the upper layers. This occurs due to certain factors: long winter nights, clear skies, dry air, and absence of winds. This leads to quick radiation of the heat from the surface, so the air becomes cooler and denser at the surface while warm light air floats above. This phenomenon is of shorter duration because during day time again the earth's surface will get heated and will warm up the cold air near the surface. Inversion of temperature is common in valley bottoms. The valley floor remains colder than the top because of the descent of cold dense air at the bottom and due to lack of heat loss through terrestrial radiation. Inversion of temperature causes frost which is not economically viable for fruit orchards in valleys.

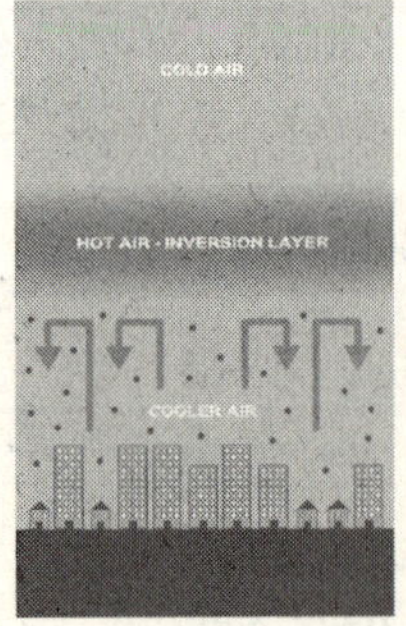

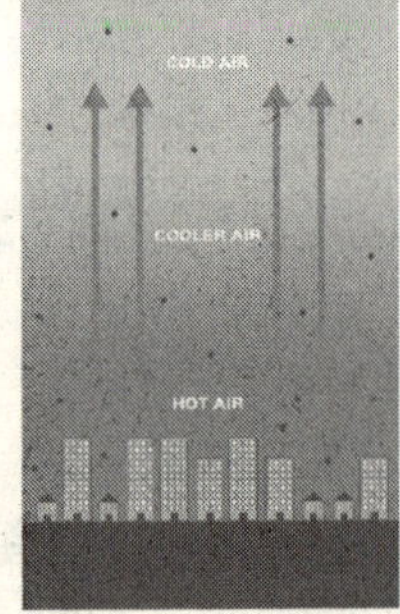

ATMOSPHERIC PRESSURE AND WINDS

The weight of a column of air at a given place and time is called atmospheric pressure. It is measured by an instrument called barometer. Atmospheric pressure is measured as force per unit area. The unit used for measuring pressure is millibar.

Factors Responsible for Variation in Air Pressure

- *Air temperature:* There is an inverse relationship between pressure and temperature. At higher temperature the air becomes warm and lighter. Lighter air expands in volume, rises up creating a vacuum. Hence equatorial regions have low pressure and polar regions have high pressure.
- *Earth's rotation:* Earth's rotation creates a centrifugal force. This creates deflection of air from its original place causing pressure to decrease. Earth's rotation causes convergence and divergence of moving air. Areas of convergence creates low pressure and vice versa.
- *Pressure of water vapour:* Air with more amount of water vapour has lower pressure and that of lower quantity has higher pressure. In winter the continents are much colder and tend to develop high pressure areas. In summer oceans are cooler than the continents so high pressure is developed over oceans.

Pressure Belts of the World

- *Equatorial low pressure belt:* This belt is known as doldrums or zone of calm as there is absence of moving surface wind here. The sun shines almost vertically throughout the year on equator. So the air remains warm near the surface, gets heated up, expands, and rises producing low pressure. This belt extends from 0° to 10° N and S latitudes. This zone is also known as the Inter Tropical Convergence Zone as the winds from sub-tropical high pressure belts converge here.
- *The sub-tropical high pressure belt:* This belt extends from the tropics to 35° latitudes in both the hemispheres. The warm air rising from the equator condenses, cools down, and settles down to the sub-tropical belt due to deflection of winds by earth's rotation. This creates a zone of high pressure. This belt is also known as the Horse Latitudes.
- *The sub-polar low pressure belt:* This belt extends between 45° N and the Arctic circle and 45° S and the Antarctic circle in the Northern and Southern hemispheres, respectively. This belt is produced due to the deflection of winds from sub-tropical high pressure belt. This belt is more developed in the Southern hemisphere because of the dominance of water bodies. There are small centres of low pressure over the oceans in the Northern hemisphere.

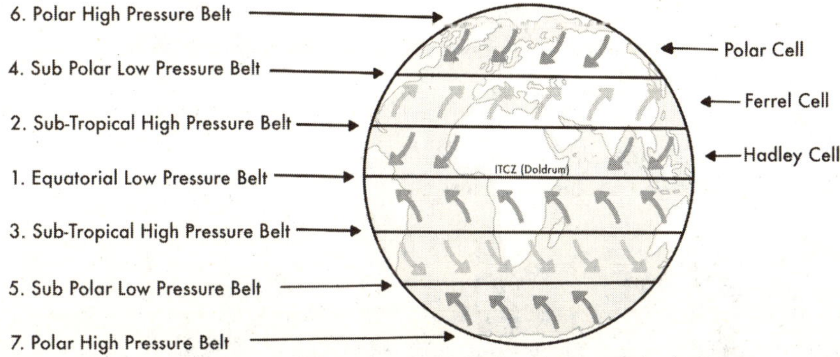

Imaginary lines joining places having same temperature on the earth are called **isotherms**.
Imaginary lines joining places having same atmospheric pressure are called **isobars**.

As this is the zone of the poles so, needless to say, the temperature remains low and the pressure is high.

- *Polar high pressure belt:* Very low temperature makes the air at the surface cold. Thus, cold air being heavier compresses and stays closer to the ground. Denser cold air creates high pressure in the poles.

Shifting of Pressure Belts

The northward and southward migration of the overhead sun causes the shifting of pressure belts at about 5°. All pressure belts move northward during the summer solstice due to northward migration of the overhead sun except polar high pressure belt. Similarly, during the time of winter solstice, all pressure belts except the polar high shift southward. At the time of vernal and autumnal equinoxes, the pressure belts remain almost in the same position.

The reason why Mediterranean region receives rainfall in winter is the shifting of pressure belt southward so they come under the influence of westerlies that brings moist rain-bearing wind.

Pressure gradient: Pressure gradient means the difference of pressure between two places. Steep pressure gradient is represented by closely spaced isobars while low pressure gradient is represented by widely spaced isobars. The direction of pressure movement is always perpendicular to isobars.

Wind always has the tendency to blow from regions of high pressure to regions of low pressure.

What is geostrophic wind?

Wind that blows parallel to the isobars at the height of 600 m.

Wind always get deflected due to rotation of the earth along its axis as well as due to the pressure gradient. The force which deflects wind is called Coriolis force. Due to this force, wind is deflected to the right in the Northern hemisphere and to the left in the Southern hemisphere.

The direction of the pressure gradient is also from high pressure to low pressure.

The slope of the land facing wind is called **windward** slope and the slope on the other side is called **leeward** slope.

Fact: We know that the speed of rotation of the earth is maximum at the equator and decrease at the poles. When the wind reaches the equator it does not reach its destination because before that only the destination place changes and moves ahead as the speed of rotation at the equator is more and the wind lags behind whereas in the poles the wind moves ahead because of the decreasing speed of rotation at the poles. This law was propounded by **Ferrel** in his statement where he said **'if one stands with one's back towards the direction from where winds are coming they (winds) are deflected to the right in the northern hemisphere and to the left in the southern hemisphere.'**

Classification of winds

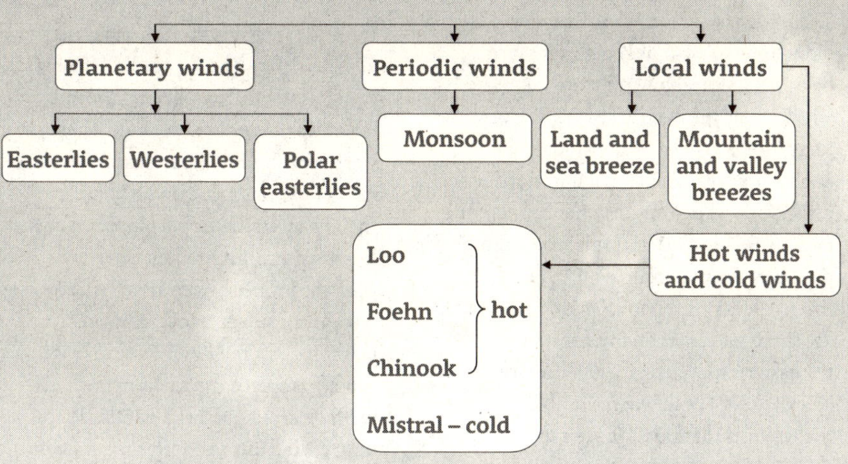

BEAUFORT WIND SCALE

Beaufort Number	Description	Wind speed	Wave height	Sea conditions	Land conditions
0	Calm	< 1 knot < 1 mph < 2 km/h	0 ft 0 m	Sea like a mirror	Smoke rises vertically
1	Light air	1–3 knots 1–3 mph 2–5 km/h	0–1 ft 0–0.3 m	Ripples	Direction shown by smoke drift
2	Light breeze	4–6 knots 4–7 mph 6–11 km/h	1–2 ft 0.3–0.6 m	Small wavelets	Wind felt on face
3	Gentle breeze	7–10 knots 8–12 mph 12–19 km/h	2–4 ft 0.6–1.2 m	Large wavelets	Leaves and small twigs in constant motion
4	Moderate breeze	11–16 knots 13–18 mph 20–28 km/h	3.5–6 ft 1–2 m	Small waves	Raises dust and loose paper
5	Fresh breeze	17–21 knots 19–24 mph 29–38 km/h	6–10 ft 2–3 m	Moderate waves	Small trees and leafs begin to sway
6	Strong breeze	22–27 knots 25–31 mph 39–49 km/h	9–13 ft 3–4 m	Large waves	Large branches in motion
7	High wind, moderate gale, near gale	28–33 knots 32–38 mph 50–61 km/h	13–19 ft 4–5.5 m	Sea heaps up	Whole trees in motion
8	Gale, fresh gale	34–40 knots 39–46 mph 62–74 km/h	18–25 ft 5.5–7.5 m	Moderately high waves	Twigs break off trees
9	Strong/severe gale	41–47 knots 47–54 mph 75–88 km/h	23–32 ft 7–10 m	High waves	Slight structural damage
10	Storm, whole gale	48–55 knots 55–63 mph 89–102 km/h	29–41 ft 9–12.5 m	Very high waves	Trees uprooted, considerable structural damage
11	Violent storm	56–63 knots 64–72 mph 103–117 km/h	37–52 ft 11.5–16 m	Exceptionally high waves	Widespread damage
12	Hurricane force	≥ 64 knots ≥ 73 mph ≥ 118 km/h	≥ 46 ft ≥ 14 m	Exceptionally high waves, sea is completely white	Devastation

The Beaufort wind scale table.

Planetary Winds

The trade winds/easterlies: These winds blow from sub-tropical high pressure belt to equatorial low pressure belt. The word 'trade' means track. Due to Coriolis force, the northern trade winds move away from sub-tropical high in north east direction and in Southern hemisphere the trade winds move from sub-tropical high pressure to equatorial low pressure from the south east direction. Trade winds are on-shore winds when they blow along the eastern margins so they bring rainfall. They are off-shore when they blow along the western margins. Hence most of the deserts of the world are found along the western margins of the continents.

The westerlies: These winds blow poleward from sub-tropical high pressure in the Northern hemisphere and are deflected to the right and blows from south west. In the Southern hemisphere these winds are deflected to the left and blow from north-west. Westerlies are more complicated in the Northern hemisphere due to dominance of land. They are less effective in summer and more active in winter. The westerlies bring rainfall to the Mediterranean lands in winter. In the Southern hemisphere, the westerlies become strong and vigorous due to dominance of water bodies. They bring gale and high velocity winds known by different names in different latitudes.

Roaring Forties between 40° and 50° S

Furious Fifties between 50° and 60° S

Shrieking Sixties at 60° S

The polar easterlies: These winds blow from polar high to sub-polar low pressure belt. These winds blow north easterly on the Northern hemisphere and south easterly in the Southern hemisphere. Polar winds are more common in the summer season while they disappear in the winter season.

What is Hadley cell?

It is a thermally induced cell named after its discoverer, G. Hadley. The equatorial winds get heated up and becomes lighter and rises up. These warm and moist wind releases latent heat after condensation so they rise further up in the troposphere. Over the equator they diverge northward and poleward. The surface winds meanwhile blow from sub-tropical high-pressure belt to equatorial low-pressure belt in order to replace the vacuum created by the warm equatorial winds. These upper wind after getting cooled down again descends down to the equatorial belt and consequently again gets heated up and ascends. So an entire cycle of air circulation is formed.

Periodic Winds

Monsoon winds: The word 'monsoon' is derived from the Arabic word 'mausim' meaning seasons. These winds change their direction with the change of seasons.

Origin of Indian Monsoon

- The role of Himalayas and the Tibetan plateau as physical barrier.
- Differential heating and cooling of large land masses and water bodies.
- Upper air jet stream in the troposphere.

Summer monsoons: When sun shines vertically over the Tropic of Cancer intense low pressure is developed over the Indian subcontinent. This is due to intense heating of the land during April-May. The surrounding seas are comparatively cooler and develops a high pressure over them. Winds have the tendency to blow from high- to low-pressure areas. So moisture-laden winds start blowing from sea towards the land during May-June. These winds are south east-trade winds while they cross the equator; they become south westerly due to

Coriolis force and rush towards India. The winds get divided into two branches: the Bay of Bengal branch and the Arabian Sea branch due to the tapering nature of the Indian peninsula.

The Arabian Sea branches rise abruptly after getting hit by the windward side of the Western Ghats and yield heavy rainfall there while the eastern side of the Western Ghats receive lesser amount of rainfall as the winds descend down along the eastern slopes and are warmed due to which the relative humidity increases. This leeward side of the relief is also known as the rain shadow area.

- Now we know why Pune on the leeward side of Western Ghats get lesser rainfall than Mumbai on the windward side!
- Why is Thar a desert?

The south-west monsoon winds of Arabian Sea branch move parallel to the Aravallis so it cannot shed its moisture on the Thar Desert that lies on the leeward side of the Aravallis. Hence, Thar is a desert area.

The Bay of Bengal branch of the south-west monsoon winds runs along the coast of Bangladesh and Myanmar. It strikes against the Arakan Yoma and is diverted towards the Indian subcontinent. As a result monsoon strikes India from south and south-east. Due to the presence of the Himalayas, the Bay of Bengal branch gets diverted into two sub branches. One moves westward along the Gangetic plains and the other moves towards the north-east up to the Brahmaputra valley. The winds strike against the Garo Khasi and Jaintia hills of Meghalaya making Mawsynram the wettest place on the earth.

The monsoon branches of the Arabian Sea and the Bay of Bengal meet each other over the northern part of the Gangetic plains bringing showers to Delhi, NCR region, and rest of North India.

Winter monsoon: The situation is reverse in winter. The seas are comparatively warmer than the landmass. So a high pressure is created over the land mass while the sea develops low pressure. Wind now starts blowing from land towards the sea. Since these winds are off-shore winds they do not shed much moisture, these winds blow in north east direction so are also known as NE monsoon winds. They pick up moisture while blowing over Bay of Bengal and sheds rainfall over the Coromandel coast during October-November.

MUSON RÜZGÂRLARI - YAZ DURUMU, KIŞ DURUMU
MONSOON WINDS - SUMMER CONDITION, WINTER CONDITION

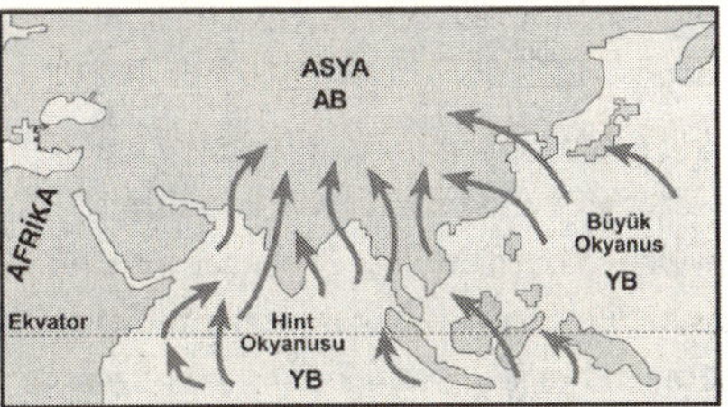

Muson Rüzgârları - Yaz Durumu
Monsoon Winds - The State of Summer

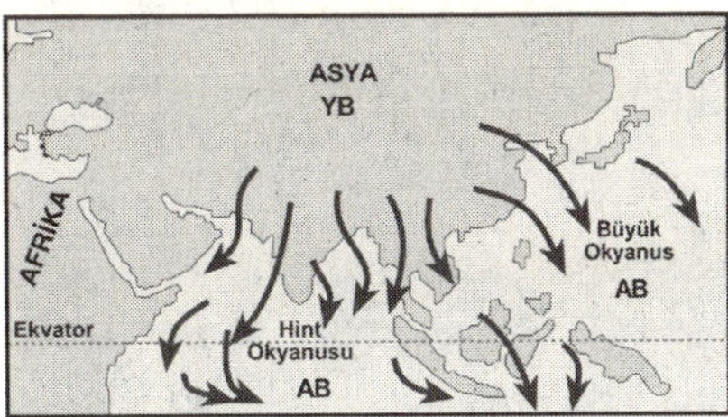

Muson Rüzgârları - Kış Durumu
Monsoon Winds - winter situation

Apart from the Coromandel (Tamil Nadu) coast, Punjab, Haryana, and western UP also receive mild to heavy rainfall in winter and snow fall in Jammu and Kashmir.

The reason is **western disturbances**. These are temperate cyclones which originate in the Mediterranean Sea and bring rainfall to India and Pakistan. These winter showers are extremely beneficial for rabi cultivation in North India.

Land and sea breezes: This is a daily cycle produced due to differential heating of land and sea causing high and low pressure.

Sea breeze: During day time, land gets heated up quicker than the adjacent sea. Warm air over the land expands and rises up so a low pressure is developed. While high pressure is developed over the sea. This difference in pressure system causes wind to blow from sea to land. This phenomenon continues till sunset when the sea becomes comparatively warmer than the land. Sea breezes are on-shore winds and they are most active in summer season.

Land breeze: During night time the sea breezes are weakened as low pressure is developed over the sea. The adjacent land has high pressure. So wind starts blowing from land to sea. These winds are off-shore and dry winds.

Land vs Sea Breeze

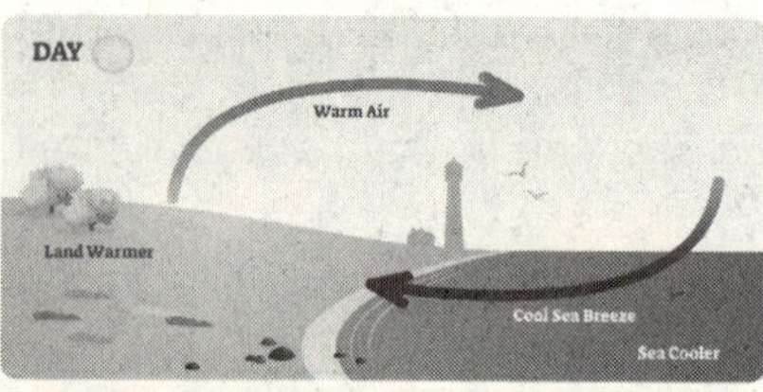

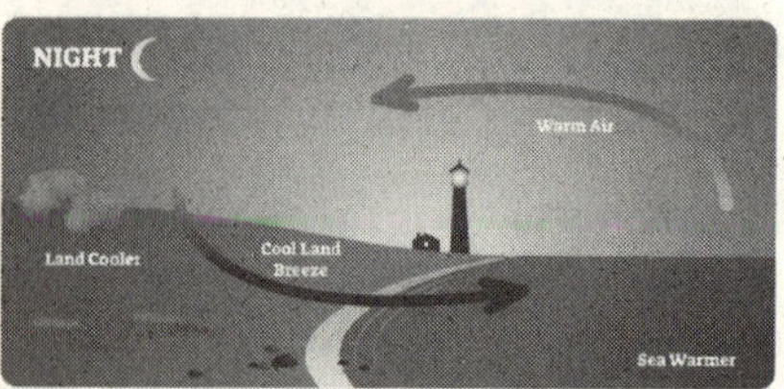

Mountain and valley breezes: The valley floors and the slopes are more heated during the day time due to insolation. As a result the warm wind of the valley bottoms rises up and expands. This upslope breeze during day time is called valley breeze. Valley breezes once they reach up cools down and condenses. They bring rainfall in the mountain peaks. When the valley breezes condenses and cools down due to loss of heat through outgoing radiation such winds are called mountain breeze. Valley and mountain breezes cause inversion of temperature.

Hot Winds

Loo: Hot, dry, local winds which blow over the northern and north-western plains of India in the months of May and June in afternoons.

Foehn: Strong, dry, dusty local winds which develop on the leeward side of the Alps mountains. Foehn winds help in early ripening of grapes as they descend down they melt the snow thus making pasture land ready for cattle grazing.

Chinook: Hot, dry local winds which blow down the eastern slopes of Rockies of United States and Canada. They are also known as snow eater since they keep the grassland snow free.

Cold Winds

Mistral: Very cold dry high velocity local winds originating on Alps and blowing towards the Mediterranean Sea through the Rhone valley. They bring down the temperature below the freezing point in areas under their realm.

Other notable hot winds:	Other notable cold winds:
Harmattan	Blizzard
Sirocco	Bora

Jet steam: These are fast moving circumpolar westerly wind circulation blowing in the upper layers of the troposphere. This circulation is observed between poles and 20° latitudes in both the hemispheres. They are circum-polar since they blow around the poles in both the hemispheres. There is change in the wind velocity of jet streams. They become strong in winter season and wind velocity becomes twice the velocity during summer season.

Easterly jet stream plays an important role in Indian summer monsoon. They are formed due to intense heating of the Tibetan plateau during summer that triggers the summer monsoon.

Westerly jet stream brings winter rainfall to north-western and northern India in the form of western disturbances.

What Is an El Nino?

Warm ocean winds develop on the surface waters of the tropical east Pacific Ocean, causing global changes in the world distribution of rainfall and temperature. Low air pressure is formed in the south-east Pacific mainly off the coast of Peru and Ecuador (South America). Upwelling of cold seawater is stopped, warm air rises up and becomes unstable bringing rainfall after condensation.

What Is La Nina?

The cold phase of El Nino is La Nina when sea surface temperature in south-east Pacific goes down and air pressure is high.

Both El Nino and La Nina trigger heavy floods on the west coast of South America or droughts in Australia and can also lead to weaker monsoons over the Indian subcontinent.

HUMIDITY AND RAINFALL

Humidity is the amount of water vapour present in the air. Water vapour is found only 2 per cent of the total composition of the atmosphere but this composition varies both spatially as well as locally. About 50 per cent of the water vapour is concentrated in the lower layers of the atmosphere up to the height of 2,000 m. Water vapour plays a vital role in the regulation of temperature, hydrological cycle, amount of precipitation, amount of loss of heat through radiation, etc. The water vapour present in the atmosphere has its source from rivers, lakes, streams, seas, and oceans through evaporation.

- *Evaporation:* This is the process of transformation of liquid water to its gaseous state. The rate of evaporation varies from place to place and depends upon several factors such as aridity, wind velocity, temperature. Higher the aridity, wind velocity more will be the rate of evaporation because dry air with high temperature has more capacity to hold water vapour than already humid air.
- *Condensation:* This is the process of transformation from gaseous state to liquid state or solid state.
- *Latent heat:* This is the hidden amount of heat in water vapour. The amount of heat which is needed for the process of evaporation is never lost rather it is always associated with water vapour. For example, when we sit under the fan after coming back home on a sultry summer afternoon we feel instant cool because our sweat gets evaporated. Latent heat of condensation is the heat energy released after condensation.
- *Absolute humidity:* The total amount of water vapour present in a column of air at a given temperature. Absolute humidity decreases from the equator towards the poles and from oceans to the continents.
- *Relative humidity:* Ratio of the amount of water vapour actually present in the air to the maximum amount of water vapour that the air can hold. Relative humidity is expressed in percentage. When relative humidity is 100 per cent the air is said to be **saturated**.
    - Relative humidity is inversely proportional to air temperature. It decreases with increasing temperature and increases with decreasing temperature.

- Relative humidity = absolute humidity/humidity capacity × 100
- Relative humidity is measured by an instrument known as hygrometer or wet and dry bulb thermometer.

- Relative humidity helps in predicting the climate of a place. For example, high relative humidity can predict wet conditions. Evaporation decreases with high relative humidity. It also controls human comfort and health. When it is too humid and the relative humidity is very high we feel uncomfortable and sweaty.

Condensation

Condensation depends on two factors:

1. The percentage of relative humidity in the air.
2. The degree of cooling of the air.

The temperature at which air gets saturated is called **dew point**.

What is adiabatic change of temperature?

When there is a change of temperature of the air due to contraction or expansion of air it is known as adiabatic change of temperature. This happens when air condenses and cools down it becomes heavier. The heaviness is due to the contraction of air but its temperature increases as it comes near the surface. This change of temperature is due to the descent and not due to any addition or subtraction of heat from it.

Stable and unstable air: Stable air is the one without vertical movement while unstable air is the one with any vertical movement. An air mass when becomes lighter it ascends and becomes unstable while an air mass when it descends it becomes stable.

The stability and instability of an air mass depends on the relationship between normal lapse rate and adiabatic temperature changes. The adiabatic temperature remains constant while the normal lapse rate might change.

Forms of Condensation

Fog: Thin clouds consisting of very small water droplets which remain suspended in the air near the ground surface and reduces horizontal visibility.

Lighter fog is called mist.

On the basis of visibility fog is classified into:

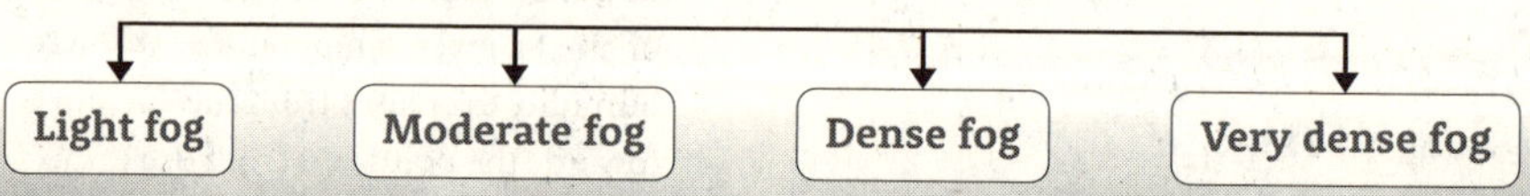

On the basis of processes of formation fog is classified into:

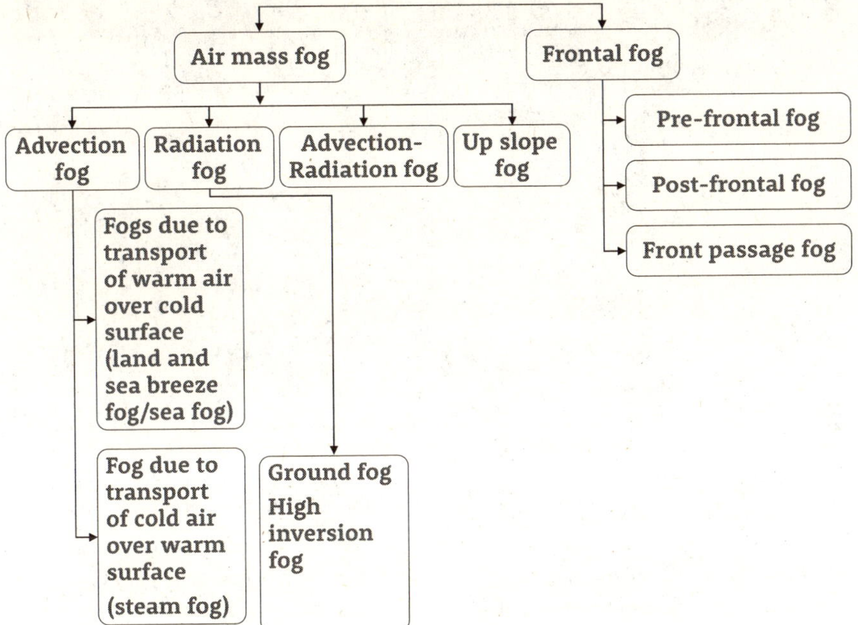

Effects of Fog

- Fog hinders navigation and transport.
- Dense fog and smoke create smog which creates health hazards.
- Fog also affects flight takeoffs and landing, causing delays in air traffic.
- Dense fog causes road accidents due to low visibility.

Clouds: Clouds are formed due to condensation of water vapour around hygroscopic nuclei caused by cooling of air due to ascent. All forms of precipitation originate from clouds. Clouds are microscopically minute droplets of water, ice particles or both that remain suspended in air above the ground. Clouds absorb and diffuse part of incoming solar radiation and also absorbs some amount of long-wave terrestrial radiation.

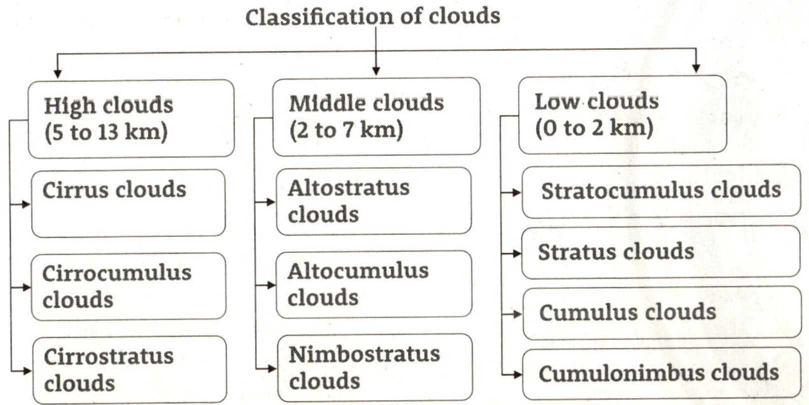

Forms of Precipitation

Rainfall: Rain is the most common form of precipitation. These are droplets of water formed due to condensation of water vapour. The process of condensation begins when the air is fully saturated. The clouds aggregate together to form large clouds. These large cloud droplets remain suspended in the air as they are microscopic in size. The clouds often collide with each other and form larger droplets. In this process, several cloud droplets coalesced that they are unable to hold them and they fall down as rainfall. Often the sky is over cast with thick clouds but there is no rainfall. This happens when the cloud droplets get evaporated before they reach the ground surface.

- Rainfall consisting of very small droplets of water are called drizzle.
- Heavy showers are very large raindrops or incessant rainfall.
- When condensation occurs below the freezing point the resultant precipitation is snowfall.

Types of Rainfall

- *Convectional rainfall:* This type of rainfall is most common in equatorial regions.

- The ground surface is intensely heated due to vertical rays of the sun.
- The air above the surface also gets heated. It becomes lighter as it expands and rises up.
- This ascending warm air after reaching a height starts cooling down when its relativity humidity increases. The air becomes saturated as it further rises up and when it reaches beyond the saturation point it condenses and precipitates in the form of rainfall.
- When the air further ascends it reaches a height where its temperature matches the temperature of the surrounding air. Here, the process of condensation is doubled and thick cumulonimbus clouds are formed.
- Convectional rainfall occurs almost every afternoon in equatorial regions where they are known as 4 o'clock showers.
- This type of rainfall is accompanied with thunder and lightning.
- They are associated with dark, thick cumulonimbus clouds and bring heavy showers of short duration.

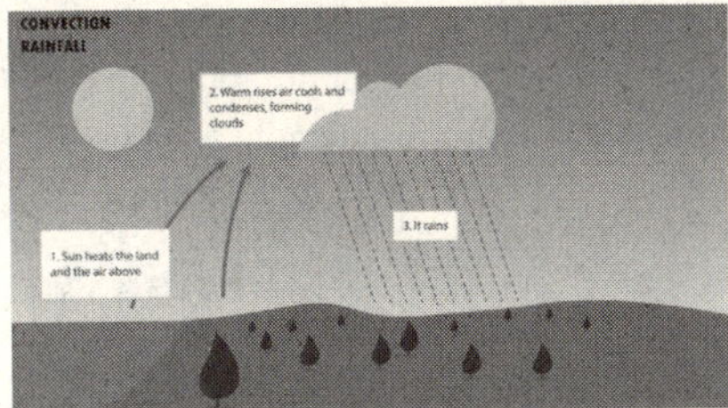

- *Orographic rainfall:* This type of rainfall is triggered by the presence of high relief in the path of moisture-laden winds.
  - When moisture-laden winds strike against a mountain barrier it is forced to rise up.
  - The ascent of the air cools the air and rises its relative humidity. The air becomes further saturated after reaching a certain height and condensation begins around hygroscopic nuclei.
  - The addition of latent heat of condensation causes the air to ascend further. This ascending air yields precipitation. The presence of the mountain barrier and its height trigger the moist warm air to ascend.
  - The windward side of the mountain receives heavier rainfall than the leeward side. When the moisture winds reach the leeward side they start descending down, consequently the relative humidity falls so most of the moisture is lost.
  - The amount of orographic rainfall is maximum near the mountain slopes and the amount starts decreasing away from the foothills.
  - Monsoons in India are orographic in nature mostly.

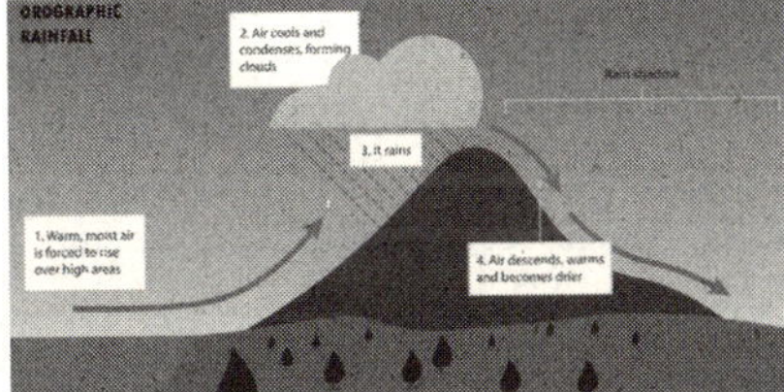

- *Cyclonic or frontal rainfall:*
  - This type of rainfall occurs due to the convergence of two air masses of distinct characteristics. When warm and cold air masses converge along a line a front is formed.
  - The warm wind ascends along the front while the colder denser wind settles down. This type of rainfall is temperate cyclonic in nature where cold polar winds and warm westerlies converge.
  - The warm air lying over the cold air is cooled and gets condensed around hygroscopic nuclei.
  - This process of condensation is slow and gradual so this type of rainfall is of long duration and weak spells. Sometimes the precipitation occurs in the form of snowfall and hail.
  - Precipitation associated with warm front brings drizzle of long duration while precipitation associated with cold front brings thunderstorms of short duration. This is because cold air mass pushes with great force the warm air mass to ascend.

Other Forms of Precipitation

Snowfall: When the saturation of air occurs at temperature below the freezing point the type of precipitation that occur is called snowfall. These are small opaque grains of ice that falls and settles down on the ground. Snowfall is common in high altitude regions.

Sleet: Mixture of snow and rain is called sleet.

Hail: Precipitation of small balls of ice having a diameter of 5–50 mm. Hail storms are bad for agricultural crops. These fall as alternate layers of transparent and translucent ice.

Drizzle: Numerous minute droplets of water having a diameter of less than 0.5 mm. They fall continuously from low altitude clouds.

Cyclones and Anti-cyclones

Cyclones: These are centres of low pressure surrounded by closely spaced isobars. The centre of the cyclone consists of low pressure and wind blows inward in anti-clockwise direction in Northern hemisphere and clockwise in Southern hemisphere. Cyclones are of two types: temperate cyclones and tropical cyclones.

Temperate Cyclones

These are atmospheric disturbances with low pressure in the centre and increasing pressure outward. These are formed due to convergence of warm and cold air masses along a front. They are found in mid latitudes as they move in east under the influence of westerly winds.

Temperate cyclones are of different shapes elliptical, oval, or v shaped. They have closely spaced isobars in which the wind blows inward. Since these cyclones are formed due to convergence of two contrasting air masses so the temperature recorded in each part of the cyclone is different. The southern part of the cyclone records higher temperature due to dominance of warmer air while the north, north-western parts of the cyclones records low temperature because of polar air masses. Notably the warm part of the front is associated with warm air and the cold part is associated with cold dense air. So there is a sudden change in the wind direction along the warm and cold fronts. This line along which the wind changes its direction is called **wind shift line**.

Temperate cyclones unlike tropical cyclones occur for longer duration and in weak spells. They are generally not always associated with thunder and lightning.

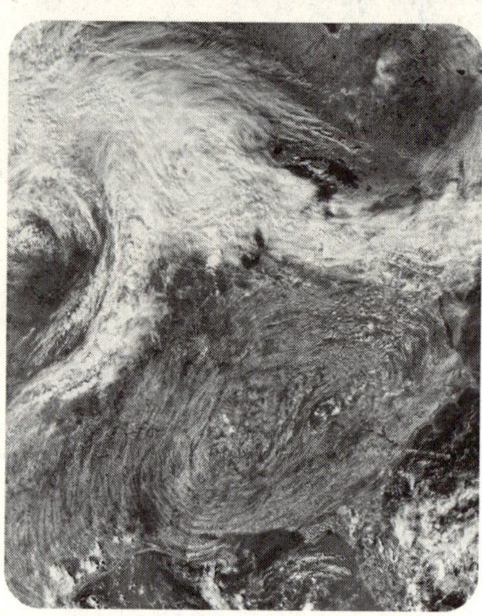

Tropical Cyclones

Cyclones lying between the Tropic of Cancer and Capricorn are called tropical cyclones. These cyclones are not regular and uniform. The centre of cyclone consists of low pressure surrounded by closely spaced isobar. The velocity of wind is very high as it moves inward. Tropical cyclones develop over seas, and gain intensity over seas, vigorously picking up moisture while moving towards land. Once they make landfall they become weak and feeble. They ultimately die out in the interior of the continent.

Tropical cyclones derive their energy from the latent heat of condensation. They are not stationary. The more they stay over the seas, the more they gain moisture and cause larger destruction to life and property.

Tropical cyclones are associated with incessant rainfall of shorter duration from dark, thick cumulonimbus clouds with thunder and lightning. The average wind velocity ranges from 35 km/h to more than 150 km/h.

The eye of the cyclone is characterized by calm conditions, high air temperature, low wind velocity, fine and calm weather. This situation changes very soon with building up of cirrus and later thicker clouds – the wind velocity becomes very high and there is heavy downpour.

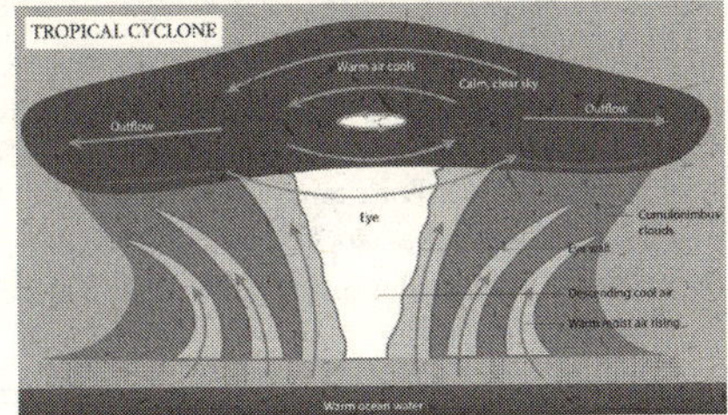

Tropical cyclones are known by different names in different parts of the world. They are called hurricanes and tornadoes in the United States, typhoons in Japan, Willy Willies in Australia, and tropical storms or cyclones in the Indian subcontinent.

TYPE	WIND SPEED IN KM/H	WIND SPEED IN KNOT (MPS)
Low pressure area (L)	Less than 31	Less than 17 (09)
Depression (D)	31–49	17–27 (9–14)
Deep depression (DD)	50–61	28–33 (15–17)
Cyclonic storm (CS)	62–88	34–47 (18–24)
Severe cyclonic storm (SCS)	89–118	48–63 (25–32)
Very severe cyclonic storm (VSCS)	119–221	64–119 (33–61)
Super cyclonic storm (Sup. CS)	222 or more	120 (62) or more

Table: The scale of tropical cyclones in Indian ocean.

Thunderstorms

Local storms characterized by heavy rainfall with thunder and lightning. In thunderstorms the wind instead of blowing inward rises upward as convectional currents. The showers are heavy like that of cloud burst but of short duration. As the name suggests such storms produce thundering sounds due to sudden and rapid expansions of air columns caused due to rapid heating of lightning.

Anti-cyclones

Anti-cyclones are those atmospheric phenomena which are characterized by high pressure in the centre and low pressure in the periphery. The wind blows outward in clock-wise direction in the Northern hemisphere and anti-clockwise in the Southern hemisphere. Anti-cyclones are most common in sub-tropical high-pressure belts and are literally not found in equatorial low-pressure area.

Anti-cyclones are calm and undisturbing weather phenomena. They have a sluggish movement and they are much larger in area and size. Their average velocity is 30–50 km/h. Sometimes they may remain stationary at a particular region for several days. They bring dry spells in weather, light breeze, and clear skies. Sometimes they create a halo around the sun.

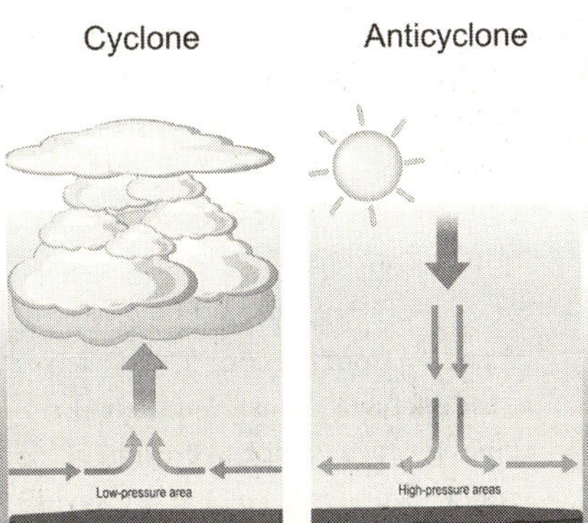

FACT FILE

Difference between **weather** and **climate**:
Weather is the short-term characteristic of a particular region with respect to its temperature, rainfall, humidity, moisture, cloudiness, etc. The weather of a particular place may vary at any time. For example, the weather of Delhi today is hot and dry.
Climate is the aggregate weather conditions for a long period of time of a region. For example, India has a tropical monsoon type of climate. So here we are identifying the climate of India in a broader perspective.

OCEANOGRAPHY

OCEANIC RELIEF AND FEATURES

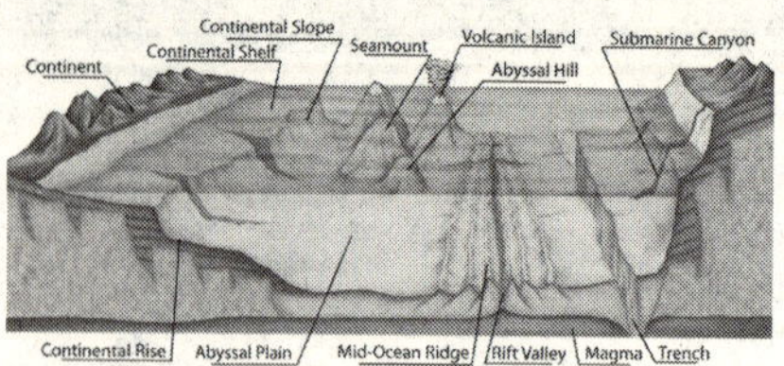

Oceanic relief

- *Continental shelf*: The shallow submerged extension of continents is called continental shelves. The continental shelf slopes gently sea wards with an angle of less than a degree. The shallow seawater over the continental shelf has a depth between 120 and 350 m. Continental shelves are sources of petroleum and natural gas. They are the sources of major fishing grounds of the world.

  Continental shelves are marked by the presence of submarine canyons. These canyons are steep sloped valleys in the sea floor. These canyons are formed due to earthquakes or landslides under water. The force of the moving sediments causes the valley to erode forming canyons.
- *Continental slope:* Steep slopes extending from the continental shelves to the deep sea plains. Continental slopes are formed due to erosion of sediments under sea by the sea waves.
- *Abyssal plains:* These are undulating deep sea plains found at a depth between 3,400 and 5,000 m. Abyssal plains are formed of sediments. Sometimes these plains are marked by the presence of fossils of marine life forming sediments which are called oozes.
- *Submarine ridges:* The presence of high relief under the sea are called submarine ridges. These are oceanic mountains which are intersected by faults and are interconnected between oceans to oceans. The ridges are those mountain chains beneath the oceans that are frequently affected by earthquakes and volcanism.

  The **Mid-Atlantic Ridge** is the largest submarine ridge that runs from north of Atlantic Ocean to its south.
- *Seamounts and guyots:* Submerged volcanoes with sharp pointed peaks are called seamounts. Sometimes they are visible to us as isolated islands.

  Guyots are the submerged volcanoes whose tops have been eroded and get covered by water.

Ocean deeps: The deepest parts of the ocean (also called oceanic trenches) are long, narrow, steep-sided depressions on the sea floor. Ocean deeps are not necessarily located in the middle of the ocean; they can be located parallel to the continental margins. They are the zone of tectonic activities. Pacific has the largest number of trenches.

The Challenger Deep in **Mariana Trench** of the western part of the Pacific Ocean is the deepest point of the earth.

TEMPERATURE OF OCEANS

IMPORTANCE OF TEMPERATURE OF THE OCEANS

- The temperature of the oceans is essential for the survival of marine plants and animals.
- It also affects the temperature of the coastal lands.

LAYERS OF OCEANIC TEMPERATURE

- *First layer:* The top layer of the warm oceanic water where the temperature varies between 20° and 25° C. This layer is mainly prevalent in tropical waters.
- *Second layer: Thermocline* layer characterized by rapid decrease of temperature with increasing depth.
- *Third layer:* This is a very cold layer where no sunlight can penetrate. This layer extends up to the ocean floor.

FACTORS AFFECTING THE TEMPERATURE OF OCEAN WATER

- *Latitudes:* We know that the amount of insolation decreases from the equator to the poles. This is due to the rays of the sun becoming more slanting at the poles. Similarly, the temperature of the surface water of the oceans decreases from the equator to the poles.
- *Prevailing wind:* Winds whether they are blowing from land to sea or from sea to land also affects the temperature of ocean water. Off-shore winds which blow from land to sea push away the warm surface water from the coast while the denser cold water from the bottom rises up. On-shore wind causes warm water to pile up near the coast and thus raises the temperature. The trade winds when blowing along the eastern coastal areas are on shore so they raise the temperature on the eastern coastal areas. Whereas trade winds which are off shore along the western margins of the continents and eastern margins of the seas lowers the temperature of the western coastal areas and eastern margins of the seas.
- *Distribution of land and water:* The temperature of oceanic water will always differ between the Northern and the Southern hemispheres. This is due to the dominance of sea over the Southern hemisphere. Due to dominance of land in the Northern hemisphere the oceans there receive more insolation. They are in contact with larger land masses than their counter parts in the Southern hemisphere. This is also a reason why enclosed seas in low latitudes have higher surface temperature than open seas as the former is connected with land mass than the latter.
- *Ocean currents:* Warm ocean currents such as Gulf Stream raise the surface temperature of the oceans while cold ocean currents such as Labrador Current lower the temperature of the oceans.
- *Other factors:* Other factors such as incidences of storms, cloudiness, rainfall, shape of land also influences temperature of oceans.

DISTRIBUTION OF TEMPERATURE

As it is a known fact that the temperature of the surface of the oceans will always be more than the bottom. This is due to the maximum amount of solar insolation received at the surface. Sun's rays can penetrate up to 20 m depth and beyond that there is a rapid fall in the temperature with increasing depth. However, the temperature falls with increasing depth very rapidly up to a depth of 200 m and beyond that the rate of decrease slows down.

Oceans are divided into two zones based on the solar penetration:

Photic zone: From the surface up to the depth of 200 m. This zone receives solar rays.

Aphotic zone: From 200 m till the ocean floor. This zone does not receive solar rays and is completely dark.

FACT FILE

There are some seas where the temperature of the sea floor also records high temperature. These seas are enclosed seas of low latitudes. For example, Mediterranean Sea, Sargasso Sea, Red Sea.

The enclosed seas of high latitudes remain frozen on the surface while their bottom records higher temperature!

Point to remember:

The rate of decrease of temperature is not uniform from the equator to the poles. The surface temperature of seas near equator is more than in poles but the temperature of the sea floor is almost uniform from the equator to poles. That means there is a rapid fall of temperature with increasing depth near the equator than at the poles.

SALINITY OF OCEANS

Not only sodium chloride as we believe the oceans consist of variety of other salts as well. The dominant salts found in oceans are sodium chloride (77.7 per cent) and magnesium chloride (10.9 per cent). Other notable salts are magnesium sulphate (4.7 per cent) and calcium sulphate (3.6 per cent). The proportion of sea salts remains more or less the same due to the free movement of oceanic water but the concentration of salts varies from one sea to another.

Salinity is defined as the following: 'the total amount of solid material in grams contained in 1 kg of seawater and is expressed as part per thousand (%0).' For example, 40 %0 means 40 gm of salt in 1,000 gm of seawater.

IMPORTANCE OF SALINITY OF THE OCEANS

- Salinity of seas and oceans affects the marine plants and animals.
- It also influences the physical properties of water such as temperature, density, waves, and currents.
- Ocean currents are affected by salinity.
- The more saline seawater freezes slowly as compared to freshwater.

FROM WHERE DO THESE OCEANIC SALTS COME?

The source of oceanic salts is land in solution form. When the rivers join the seas and oceans they bring with them salts. Where rivers contain lesser amount of salts (about 2 per cent) oceans contain almost 77 per cent of sodium chloride. Winds also blow away salts towards oceans. The rocks on the sea coasts get eroded and dissolved in seawater which is carried away by waves and ocean currents. Marine organisms may also release salts and calcium into the ocean floor.

An imaginary line joining places on map having equal oceanic salinity is called **isohaline**.

People seldom get drowned in very saline seawater, for example, Dead Sea, as the density of such seas are always more!

FACTORS INFLUENCING OCEANIC SALINITY

- *Evaporation:* There is a direct relationship between the rate of evaporation and the amount of salinity. Greater the evaporation, more is the salinity. So salinity of oceans is always higher in seas experiencing higher rate of evaporation. Salinity is higher in tropics than in equator due to dry conditions over the tropics although the rate of evaporation is high in both the areas. Salinity can go down in situations of cloudiness with high humidity.
- *Precipitation:* Abundant rainfall decreases salinity. So equatorial regions receiving heavy rainfall throughout the year record lower oceanic salinity than regions of low rainfall. The influx of freshwater from melting of glaciers or rainwater reduces oceanic salinity.
- *River water:* The influx of freshwater from the rivers reduce salinity. That is why the mouth of the rivers record low salinity due to the mixing of more river water. Some seas have more salinity when the rate of evaporation is more than the influx of fresh rainwater.
- *Wind direction:* Winds drive away more saline water into less saline areas, resulting in decrease in salinity in the former. Trade winds blow away high saline water from the western margins of the continents (eastern seas) and pile them up in the western seas. This results in more salinity in the eastern seas.
- *Atmospheric disturbances:* Incidences of cyclones can churn the salinity of seawater while anti cyclonic conditions that are characterized by no weather and calm conditions may increase the salinity of surface of the seas.

The variation in sea salinity depends on three factors:

- How much river water (freshwater) is mixing with the sea?
- The rate of evaporation.
- Mixing of the ocean water through currents.

Distribution of Salinity

Latitudinal distribution of salinity:

REGIONS OF LOW SALINITY	REGIONS OF MAXIMUM SALINITY	REGIONS OF LOW SALINITY	REGIONS OF MINIMUM SALINITY
Equatorial regions (heavy rainfall)	Tropical region (high evaporation and low rainfall)	Temperate region (less evaporation)	Polar and sub-polar regions (influx of melted fresh ice caps and glaciers)

SEAS HAVING ABOVE NORMAL SALINITY	SEAS HAVING NORMAL SALINITY	SEAS HAVING BELOW NORMAL SALINITY
Red Sea, Dead Sea, Mediterranean Sea, Persian Gulf	Caribbean Sea, Gulf of Mexico, Gulf of California	Arctic Ocean, Bering Sea, Japan Sea, Andaman Sea, China Sea, Baltic Sea, English Channel

Vertical Distribution of Oceanic Salinity

- Salinity increases with increasing depth at higher latitudes.
- Heavy rainfall reduces the salinity of the surface oceanic water in equatorial regions but high salinity can be recorded below.

OCEAN DEPOSITS

The sources of oceanic deposits are classified into three categories:

- *Terrigenous materials:* These are the rock fragments, gravels which are weathered and disintegrated forming fine sediments. These sediments are continental in origin as they are brought down by the rivers to the seas. These include:

  Gravels contain boulders, pebbles, stones, etc.

  Sands which may range from very fine sands to large coarse sands.

  Silt, clay, and mud.
- *Volcanic materials:* The source can either be volcanic eruptions occurring under the seas when the sediments are directly deposited or it can be volcanic eruptions near the coast. These volcanic materials are brought down by the winds to the oceans.
- *Organic materials:* Includes remains of marine plants and animals. These are of two sub-types:
  1. Pelagic deposits: which include remains of different types of algae.
  2. Neritic deposits: which include remains of dead marine plants and animals.

Pelagic deposits are called oozes. These are of two types:

Calcareous ooze: Consist of calcium deposits of marine skeletons. They get dissolved very fast so are seldom found at greater depths. These are generally white, grey in colour.

Siliceous ooze: These are mostly made up of silica. These are not soluble as calcium because of less calcium dominance. These oozes are found on both warm and cold waters at great depth.

- *Inorganic materials:* The source of these materials is rainfall or surface run-off. Often the rivers carry these sediments and deposit them into the seas. This include iron, manganese oxide, dolomite, phosphate, etc. The organic and inorganic materials are so mixed together that cannot be isolated. These include red clay. It covers the largest area of deep sea deposits. Red clay mostly consists of silicates of alumina and iron oxides.

Distribution of Ocean Deposits

Terrigenous deposits: Include gravels, sands which are derived through disintegration and weathering of rocks by various denudation processes. These are widely distributed from the shore to the sea as gravels, sand, silt, clay, and mud. These are subdivided into:

- *Littoral deposits:* These are basically mud, stones, gravels, silt, and clay. They are found on the continental shelves.
- *Shallow water deposits:* These are found between the depth of 100 fathoms and low tide water. These also consist of sand, gravels, silt, and clay.
- *Deep water deposits:* These are found below the depth of 100 fathoms. They include blue mud, green mud, red mud, coral mud, and volcanic mud.

Pelagic deposits: Consists of remains of dead marine plants and animals. The most dominant one is the red ooze followed by globigerina oozes and radiolarian oozes.

Classification of oceanic deposits.

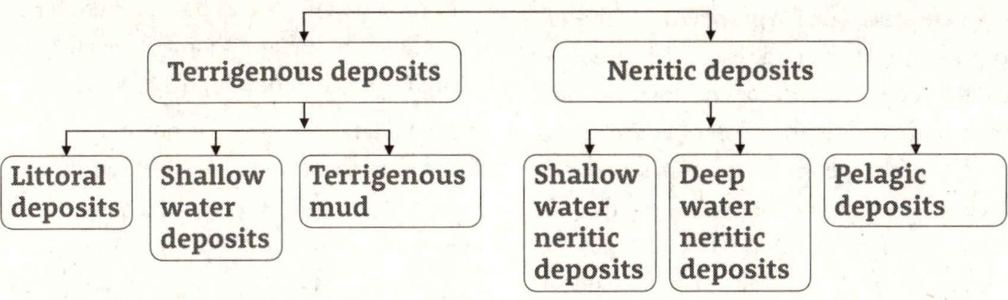

Classification on the basis of origin of deposits:

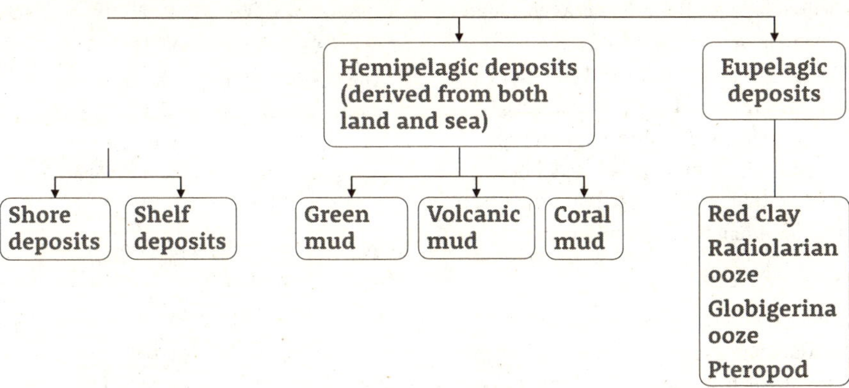

OCEAN TIDES AND CURRENTS

Waves: Waves are caused due to winds blowing on the surface of the seawater. As the water comes in contact with the wind it rises up and down in the form of crest and trough. The raised part of the wave is called a crest and the low area between two crests is called trough. The vertical distance between the crest and **trough** is called wave height. The horizontal distance between two crests or two troughs is called **wave length**. **Wave period** is the time taken for two crests to pass through a given point. When waves are fast moving the wave period is shorter.

Factors determining the force of sea waves:

- The wind velocity.
- The time taken by the wind to blow.
- Distance wind travelled across the open sea **(fetch)**.

When the sea waves dash up the shore after breaking down, it makes a great noise. It is called swash. When the sea waves retreat backwards or seawards it is called back swash. All waves are controlled by the velocity of the sea winds. Large-sized waves are called **stern waves**.

Tides: The periodic rise and fall of sea level is called tides. Such variation in sea level occurs daily and from hour to hour. At the time of rise in sea level the tidal water comes towards the shore as a flood tide. At the time of falling sea level the tidal water withdraws and is called tidal ebb. The flood tide is called high tide and low tide is called tidal ebb. Tides occur twice a day at regular intervals. It is important to note that twice a month the high tides are higher than the average and the ebb tides are lower than the average.

Causes of Tides

Tides are caused due to gravitational force of the moon and sun on the earth. The moon and the sun exerts gravitational force on the earth. Since the moon is closer to the earth so the gravitational pull of the moon is greater than sun. The part of the earth facing the moon experience high tide. The opposite side also has high tide at the same time due to centrifugal force. A low tide is seen on the upper and lower parts of the earth.

Theoretically the duration between a high tide and a low tide is 12 hours. Each day the high tide arrives about 51 minutes later than the previous day. It is because each day the rising and setting of moon lags behind by 51 minutes. It takes 24 hours and 50 minutes for the earth to bring the same meridian below the moon every day.

Types of Tides

There is a difference in the intensity and duration of tides due to the varying distance between earth and sun and moon. The types of tides based on these factors are:

- *Spring tide:* These are very high tides caused when the earth, sun, and moon are in the same line. This position when the sun, moon, and earth are in the same line it is called syzygy. When the sun and moon are in one side of the earth, the position is called conjunction. Conjunction occurs during new moon or Amavasya. When the earth is between the sun and moon, it is called opposition. Opposition occurs at the time of full moon or Purnima. The height of spring tides is always 20 per cent more than normal high tides.
- *Neap tides:* The sun, moon, and earth are in the position of a right angle or quadrature, low tide is caused. The height of neap tide is 20 per cent lower than normal low tides. The gravitational force of the sun and moon works in opposite directions thus the low tide is formed.
- *High tides:* When there is normal rise of the seawater due to the gravitational force of the sun and moon, it is called high tide. High tide occurs twice daily.
- *Low tides:* When there is normal fall of the seawater due to the gravitational force of the sun and moon, it is called low tide. Low tide occurs twice daily.
- *Apogean and perigean tides:* The position when the moon is closest to the earth is called perigee. At this time abnormally high tides occur due to increased gravitational pull.

  The position of the earth when the moon is at its farthest is called apogee. Exceptionally low tides are formed at this time due to decreased gravitational pull.

  When spring tides and perigean tides occur at the same time, the resultant tide is abnormally high.
- *Daily tides:* The tides arriving daily at the interval of 24 hours 52 minutes are called daily tides.

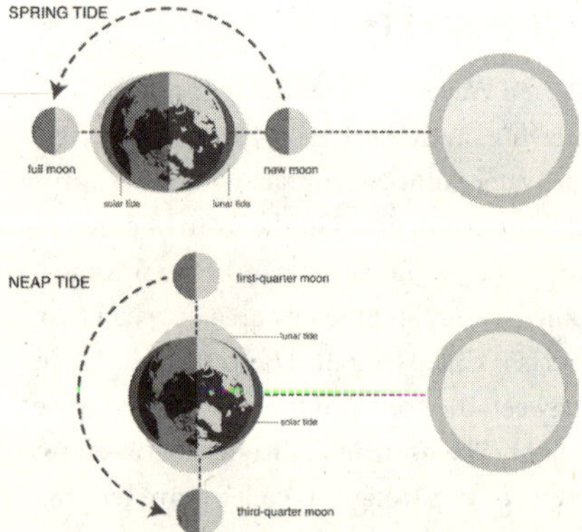

Factors affecting the variation in tides:

- The position of the sun and moon in relation to the earth.
- The distance between the earth and moon and sun which is not constant.
- The shape of the coastline.
- The dominance of sea and oceans.

Important Facts

Water has the tendency to flow from tidal crest to the tidal trough. If the wavelength of the wave is too long it takes greater time to travel from the crest to the trough. At this time the journey is affected by the Coriolis force. At the Northern hemisphere the tidal waves are defected to the right and in the Southern hemisphere it is defected to the left. When the tidal waves are defected to the right, the crest swirls anti-clockwise around a point. At this point, the water remains stagnant throughout the tidal cycle. This point is called **amphidromic** point.

Thus the tidal range is zero at the amphidromic point and it increases away from the point.

The earth rotates from west to east. The speed of rotation is also not the same at every latitude. The velocity of rotation decreases with increasing latitude so the tidal bulge is displaced farthest to the east while it is least affected at the poles.

The equilibrium theory of Newton:

Newton believed that every heavenly body has its own gravitational force. Both sun and moon exerts gravitational force on the earth. Although the gravitational force of the sun will be more than the moon but the effect will be greater of the moon on earth since it is closer to the earth and sun. The water of the surface facing the moon is attracted and high tide is caused. The opposite side of the earth is also pulled due to centrifugal force. The sea level is lowered on the other sides of the poles due to the balancing of the gravitational and centrifugal forces along a line joining the two poles. It is apparent that each place experiences two high tides every day.

Ocean currents: The movement of huge masses of oceanic water in a definite direction is called ocean currents.

On the basis of its temperature, ocean currents are of two types: warm and cold ocean currents.

On the basis of its velocity, ocean currents are of three types: currents, drifts, and streams.

- *Warm ocean currents:* When the large masses of oceanic water move from warm areas to cold areas they are warm ocean currents.
- *Cold ocean currents:* The movement of ocean water from cold areas to warm areas is called cold ocean currents.
- *Drift:* The movement of surface water of the oceans under the influence of the prevailing winds are called drift.
- *Current:* The movement of large volumes of oceanic water with great speed in a particular direction.
- *Streams:* These are same as drifts and currents but with greater velocity.

Factors Affecting Movement of Ocean Currents

- *Factors related to rotation of the earth:* The rotation of the earth from west to east creates Coriolis force which deflects any moving object winds and ocean currents. Ocean currents flowing from the equator to the North Pole are deflected to the right. The rotation of the earth causes movement of oceanic water near the equator in opposite direction from east to west direction and thus equatorial currents are formed.
- *Temperature differences between oceans:* Since the amount of insolation received at the equator is greater than the poles so the equator waters always have higher temperature. The higher temperature of the equatorial waters makes the water less denser because of

the expansion of the water molecules. The waters at the poles are heavier due to contraction. As a result, water with more expansion moves towards water which is more denser, that is from equatorial regions to polar regions. There is also movement of sub-surface water currents from polar areas to equatorial areas to balance the loss of water in the equatorial areas.

- *Salinity differences between oceans:* Saline water is more denser than less saline water. So even if the temperature between two oceanic bodies remains, the same but the salinity is different, water with greater salinity will be denser than the water with less salinity. The denser water sinks in and moves as sub-surface current towards areas of low density while the lesser denser water moves as surface current towards more saline water.
- *Density differences due to influx of freshwater:* Apart from salinity and temperature differences, density of oceans also vary due to the influx of freshwater into the seas and oceans from melting of ice caps or due to joining of rivers and streams. The density of water decreases due to influx of freshwater from melting of polar ice caps and glaciers into the oceans. But polar areas will also have highly dense water due to low insolation and low temperature of the polar seas. The water which is lesser denser moves towards the more denser water as surface current while the more denser water moves towards the lesser denser water as sub-surface current.
- *Amount of rainfall:* Heavy rainfall with low evaporation increases the sea level whereas if the rate of evaporation is high and rainfall is less the salinity of the seas will increase. This will cause the movement of surface currents from low density areas to high density areas. Ocean currents move from equatorial regions towards the higher latitudes due to the fact that in equatorial regions the sea level is always high due to heavy rainfall and low evaporation throughout the year. Polar ocean currents move towards the low latitudes because they have more water level due to low rate of evaporation and more influx of freshwater from melting of glaciers.
- *Other factors:* Shape of the coastline affects the movement of ocean currents. The Brazilian coast bifurcates the equatorial current into two branches. The northern branch flows as the Gulf Stream along the east coast of the United States and the southern branch moves parallel to the Brazilian coast.

  Seasons: In India the ocean currents follow the season of rains. In summer monsoon the direction of the monsoon drift is north east. And in time of north east winter monsoons they follow the direction of east to west.

MAJOR OCEANIC CURRENTS OF THE WORLD

Currents of the Pacific Ocean

Warm ocean currents: The *North Equatorial Current* originates from the western coast of Mexico and flows in westerly direction and reaches the Philippines coast.

FACT FILE

The transfer of water is evident between open seas and closed seas. For example, the Mediterranean Sea is more saline than Atlantic Ocean so it is much denser than Atlantic Ocean. The denser saline water sinks in and flows as under current into the Atlantic Ocean, and in order to compensate the loss, the less saline water of the Atlantic Ocean flows in to the Mediterranean Sea as surface current.

The *South Equatorial Current:* This current happens due to the influence of south-eastern trade winds and flows from east to west. This current is stronger than the North Equatorial Current. The volume of the water increases in the west as numerous minor currents join from the left.

Kuroshio Current: North-flowing current on the west side of the North Pacific Ocean basin.

North Pacific drift: Kuroshio Current extended eastward, reaching the western coast of North America.

Cold ocean currents: Oyashio Current, also known as Kurile Current, flows through the Bering Strait in southerly direction. It transports cold water of Arctic Ocean into Pacific Ocean.

Peru Current: A cold current flowing along the western coast of South America from south to north.

Californian Current: This is the eastward extension of north Pacific drift. This current is formed due to the movement of oceanic water from north to south along the Californian coast.

CURRENTS OF THE INDIAN OCEAN

Warm Ocean Currents

North east monsoon currents: Blow from land to sea in the Northern hemisphere during winter season formed between Andaman and Somali.

South-west monsoon currents: In summer season the general direction of monsoon winds is from south west to north east.

Cold ocean current: West wind drift: these are formed due to westerlies called Roaring Forties at 40° latitude.

CURRENTS OF THE ATLANTIC OCEAN

Warm Ocean Currents

North Atlantic drift: It originates from the eastern part of North America and moves in north-eastern direction towards the western coast of Europe.

Gulf stream: Originates near the Gulf of Mexico and moves towards the western Europe after flowing along the Grand banks region of North America.

Cold Ocean Currents

Labrador Current: Flows between western Greenland and Baffin Bay. It meets the warm gulf stream off the coast of New Foundland making that area one of the richest fishing grounds of the world.

Canaries Current: Extension of North Atlantic drift.

Falkland Current: Flows from Antarctic region up to Argentina. It makes the east coast of the South America cold.

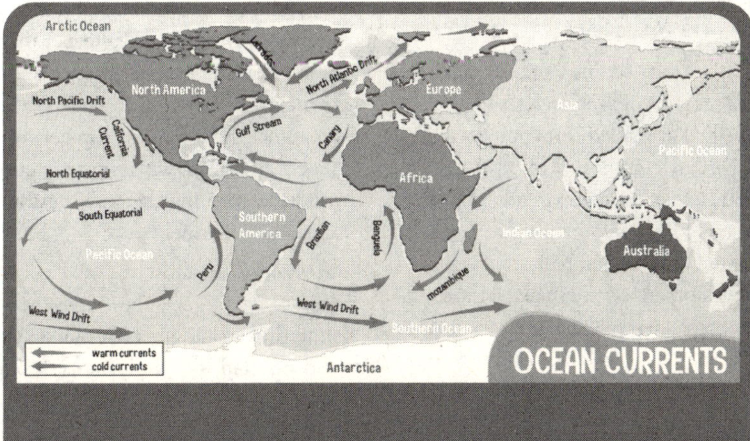

Effects of Ocean Currents

- *Modifies climate:* The warm ocean currents when they reach cold areas keeps the colder areas relatively warmer in winter months. Cold ocean currents lower the temperature of the affected areas and cause snowfall. Labrador Current keeps the ports frozen and causes snowfall in affected areas during winters. When warm wind blows over warm ocean current, it picks up moisture and brings rainfall in the coastal areas. For example, warm Kuroshio Current helps in causing rainfall along the east coast of Japan.

  Cold ocean currents cause aridity, for example, the Kalahari Desert is formed due to the Benguela Current and the Atacama Desert due to the cold Peru Current.
- *Fishing and supply of planktons:* The meeting of warm and cold ocean currents make the best fishing grounds of the world. For example, the meeting of warm Kuroshio Current and cold Oyashio Current makes Japan one of the richest fishing grounds of the world. Ocean currents help in transporting planktons from one part of the ocean to another.
- *Effects on navigation:* Dense fogs are formed at the meeting of warm and cold ocean currents. These affects navigation.

CORAL REEFS AND MARINE RESOURCES

Coral reefs are formed due to accumulation of skeletal remains of lime secreting organisms that are called coral polyps. Coral polyps are common in tropical waters. Numerous coral polyps are grouped together as colonies and form calcareous shells around them. Coral reefs are formed due to development of one shell over the other at suitable depth. Coral reefs cannot survive on the surface so they are always found at depths below the sea surface.

Favourable conditions helping the growth of corals:

1. Corals are found mainly in the tropical seas and oceans as they require about 20°–21°C for their survival.
2. Corals flourish in sediment free water. Muddy water hinder the growth of corals. Corals cannot flourish in freshwater also. So they are found far from the coastal lands and not near the mouth of rivers.
3. Corals do not live in deeper waters. They avoid greater depths due to lack of penetration of sunlight and oxygen.
4. Corals cannot survive in extremely saline water because saline water is poor in calcium carbonate specially lime.
5. Ocean currents and waves bring sufficient food for the coral polyps. So corals cannot survive in enclosed seas because of the lack of supply of food.
6. Submarine platforms favour the growth of coral polyps. The corals can grow when there is a strong base of rocks and grow upward till they reach the sea level.
7. Human activities such as deforestation, pollution of oceanic water, over fishing, urban wastes cause death of coral polyps.

Types of Coral Reefs

- *Fringing reef:* Coral reefs that are found along the continental margins or along the islands are called fringing reefs. Here the seaward slope is steeper than the landward slope. Fringing reefs are mainly attached to the coast but sometimes there can be a gap between the reef and the coast. This gap is filled with water forming lagoons. These are called **boat channel**.
- *Barrier reef:* The most extensive coral reefs are found here. These are generally found broken and not continuous. They are connected with the lagoons through

a tidal inlet. Sometimes the tidal inlet becomes so broad that ships can enter through these.

- *Atoll:* Atolls are formed around an island or on a submarine platform. These are rings of narrow growing corals. There is a lagoon in the middle of the ring.

  Atolls are of three types: Island atoll (having an island in the centre of the lagoon enclosed by reef).

  Coral island: Island is formed due to deposition by oceanic waves.

  True atoll: Circular reef enclosing a shallow lagoon but no island.

The Great Barrier Reef of Australia is the largest in the world.

Terms to remember:

Coral pinnacles: small ridges within the lagoons.

Coral banks: isolated shapeless reefs.

Faros: chains of small atolls having several small lagoons.

THE ORIGIN OF CORALS

Subsidence Theory by Darwin

According to Charles Darwin coral polyps can only grow in shallow seawaters. As contrary to this coral reefs are also found at great depths. He believed that fringing reefs, atolls are found in the land which are never stationary. In fact, these lands are always subsiding.

The stages of the formation of coral reefs and atolls are:

First stage: Formation of coral polyps on a suitable submarine platform and grows upward and reaches the sea level. So a fringing reef is formed.

Second stage: The land is subjected to gradual subsidence and coral reefs grow at greater depths.

Third stage: A lagoon is formed between the coast and the fringing reef. A barrier reef is formed.

Fourth stage: More subsidence of the land causes further submergence of the island and a ring of coral reef as atoll is formed.

Coral bleaching: Loss of algae from the corals lead to whitening of the corals which indicates the death of corals. A global

Classification of marine resources:

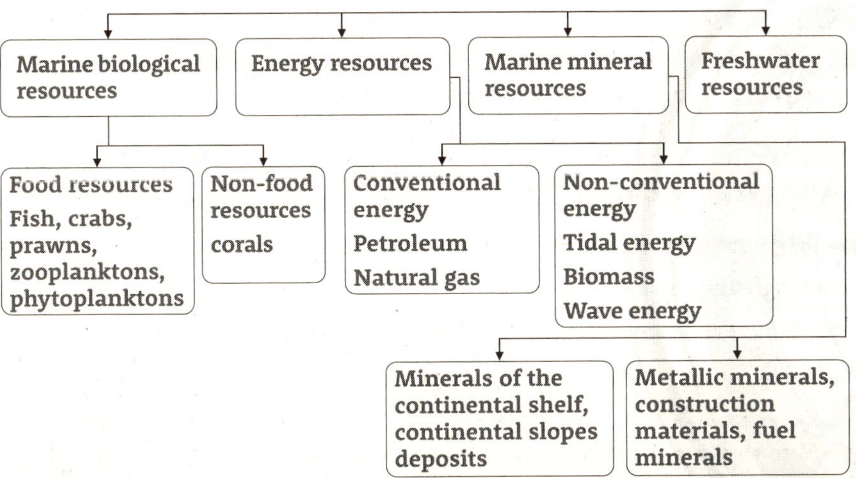

concern, coral bleaching is the direct consequence of global warming and other human malpractices. El Nino, outbreak of coral diseases, too much of human interferences like oil spills, over fishing, etc. cause coral bleaching.

Marine organisms are divided into three categories on the basis of their habitats:

1. *Planktons:* These are floating micro organisms of photic zone. These are the food of marine organisms.

   These are divided into phytoplanktons and zooplanktons.
2. *Nektons:* Include algae as well as fishes.
3. *Benthos community:* Includes all those marine organisms that live on the bottoms of the sea floor. Majority of the benthos include scavengers like sharks, sword fish, octopus, etc.

Corals are considered to be the most important marine organism. These are generally called rainforests of the ocean. The richness of the marine life depends on the variety of corals in the oceans. As we know the coral polyps grow in colonies, these conies form the habitat for several other marine organisms. Most of the sea fishes lay eggs on the coral colonies.

POPULATION GEOGRAPHY

Population geography is the geography that deals with earth's population. Here population include the geographical distribution, composition, migration, and various social and demographic attributes of a region.

IMPORTANT TERMS RELATED TO POPULATION

- *Census:* A source of data for population studies.
- *Crude birth rate:* Number of births per 1,000 total population.
- *Crude death rate:* Number of deaths per 1,000 total population.
- *Natural increase:* Difference between crude birth rate and crude death rate expressed in per cent in a year.
- *Reproduction rate:* Average number of girls born per woman.
- *Fertility rate:* Birth rate per 1,000 women from 15 to 49 years old.
- *Fertility:* Actual number of live birth produced by a woman in a population.
- *Fecundity:* Actual number of healthy baby born to a woman in a population.
- *Infant mortality rate:* The number of infant deaths in a year per 1,000 live births during a year.
- *Maternal mortality rate:* Annual number of maternal deaths per 1,00,000 live births.
- *Life expectancy:* Number of years a person is expected to live based on statistical average.
- *Population density:* Number of persons per unit area.
- *Age dependency ratio:* The ratio of the persons who are dependent (0–15 and 64 and above) to the persons who are economically independent (15–64) years in a population.
- *Population pyramid/age sex pyramid:* A bar chart arranged vertically that shows the distribution of population by age and sex. In the pyramid the males are shown to the left and females are shown to the right. The younger age groups are shown at the bottom.
- *Neonatal mortality rate:* The number of deaths of infants under 28 days at age per 1,000 live births in a year.

Marine pastures are areas of dense cover of algae and diatoms.

- *Perinatal mortality rate:* Number of foetal deaths after 28 weeks of pregnancy plus the number of deaths of infants under 7 days of age per 1,000 live births.
- *Post neonatal mortality rate:* The annual number of deaths of infants from 28 days to one year per 1,000 live births in year.
- *Sex ratio:* Number of females per 1,000 males in a population.

POPULATION COMPOSITION

RURAL-URBAN COMPOSITION

The composition shows the proportion of rural people and urban people to the total population. The rural population is the number of persons living in small-sized settlements in the countryside. Urban population is the number of persons living in cities and towns.

An important indicator of social and economic development is the number of persons living in rural or urban area. In India, since independence there has been a steady increase in population in urban areas than in rural areas. Level of urbanization increased from 31.16 per cent in 2011 census to 35.39 per cent in 2021. The proportion of rural population decreased from 68.84 per cent in 2011 census to 64.61 per cent in 2021.

RELIGIOUS COMPOSITION

The cultural and political life of a nation is always influenced by its religious composition of the population. The following table shows the religious composition of India, a Hindu-dominant nation.

RELIGION	COMPOSITION (IN %)
1. Hindus	79.8
2. Muslims	14.2
3. Christians	2.3
4. Sikhism	1.7
5. Buddhism	0.7
6. Jainism	0.4

The lowest sex ratio is in Haryana (879) and highest sex ratio is in Kerala (1,084).

The most educated and wealthy community of Jains registered the slowest growth rate of population in 2000–11. There has been a sharp fall in the fertility rate of Muslims; however, India still remains the country with highest proportion of Muslim population in the world as a non-Muslim nation. Populations of Sikhs, Jains, and Buddhists are expected to remain stable for the next decade.

Sex composition: The sex composition of a population is the indicative of the balance between males and females in a country. There has been a notable improvement in the sex ratio of India as 1,020 females per 1,000 males in India according to National Family Health Survey 2020–21. This has been a remarkable improvement since 1881. The low sex ratio till all these years has been due to (a) lack of fair treatment given to women; (b) superstitions attached to female child birth as male child had been considered as an asset and female child had been treated as a liability; (c) poor medical facilities; (d) sex determination before birth leading to termination of pregnancy.

Age sex pyramid: An age sex pyramid is the graphical representation of population composition of a region in terms of age and sex. The males are shown in the left of the pyramid and the females are shown to the right. The age is shown on the y axis and population is shown on the x axis. This graphical representation takes the shape of a pyramid because it represents the growth of the population.

Types of population pyramid: Population pyramid are of three types: expansive, constrictive, and stationary.

Expansive population pyramid: This pyramid represents growing population. In these countries the fertility rates are higher but life expectancy is low. Typically found in developing countries these pyramids have a broader base that tapers narrowly to the top. The proportion of population belonging to younger and reproductive age group is maximum. India almost has an expansive population pyramid.

Constrictive population pyramid: This pyramid represents declining population. Here the fertility rates and mortality rates are lower, life expectancy is higher. The pyramid is broader in the middle and has a narrow base. These are typically found in developed nations like Japan. The proportion of population belonging to elderly group and post reproductive stage is more.

Stationary population pyramid: This pyramid represents stationary population. Here the population is neither growing nor declining. The fertility rates and mortality rates are more or less the same. It is in the shape of a bell. Typically found in developed nations such as United States, the pyramid has more population in its working age group.

Significance of the population pyramid:

- Population pyramid tells us about the number of dependant and working population in a region.

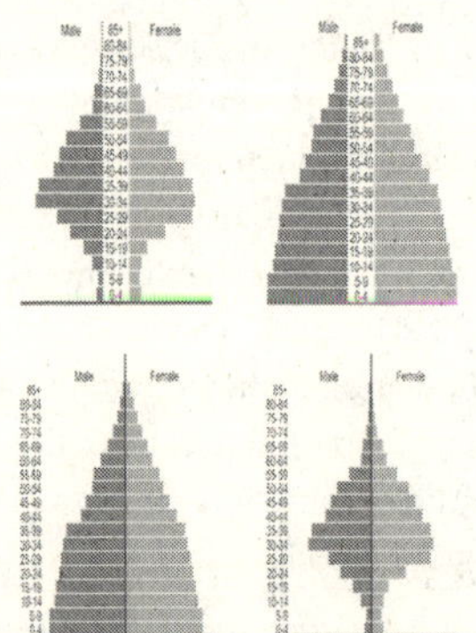

- It gives information about whether there is a balance in sex composition of a nation.
- It tells us about the birth rates and death rates.
- It helps in predicting about the future growth in population and population policies.

Child sex ratio: It is defined as number of females per 1,000 males in the age group of 0–6 years. There was a fall in child sex ratio in India when it dropped to 918 in 2011 from 927 in 2001.

The reasons for low child sex ratio has already been discussed in the segment of reasons for low sex ratio.

Consequences of low child sex ratio: The lack of balance between males and females in population can lead to greater violence against women. Women's lessened participation in political matters can lead to fall in democracy and country's economy.

FACT FILE

Arunachal Pradesh has the highest child sex ratio (972) while Haryana has the lowest child sex ratio (834) females per 1,000 males.

Literacy Composition

According to the Census of India, 'person aged seven and above who can both read and write with understanding in any language is considered a literate'. It should be kept in mind that the person need not receive any formal education to be considered a literate.

Crude literacy rate: number of literate persons/total population × 100

The literacy rate of India is 74.04 per cent in 2011 census.

FACT FILE

- Kerala record the highest literacy rate (93.91 per cent) while Bihar has the lowest (63.82 per cent).
- The gap between male and female literacy is lowest in Meghalaya and highest in Rajasthan.

POPULATION DENSITY

Asia remains the continent with highest population density of 145 persons per square kilometre. Europe with 116 persons per square kilometre comes second. Among the countries higher densities are found in relatively smaller nations such as Hong Kong and Singapore where the population densities are about 6,000 persons per square kilometre. Among the larger countries, population densities are higher in Bangladesh (1,237), South Korea (533), the Netherlands (532), India (382), Japan (348).

Even within a country there is spatial variation in distribution of population.

The world can be divided into two population zones:

Areas of high population density: In this regions the population density is about more than 300 persons per square kilometre. The areas which are mostly dense are the South-east Asian, South-Asian countries, and the European cluster.

- *South-east Asia:* About 25 per cent of the world's population are concentrated in this region. This region includes the countries of China, Korea, Vietnam, Japan, and Indonesia. Majority of the people here are engaged in agriculture and other allied activities. The fertile river soil, suitable climate, irrigational facilities, and well-developed transport system have contributed to the population growth in these countries.
- *South Asia:* Nearly one-fourth of the world population are found in this cluster where India is the most populous one. However, Bangladesh has higher population density than India owing to its smaller size. This zone comprises India, Pakistan, Bangladesh, Myanmar, and Sri Lanka. Agriculture is the most important occupation here due to the availability of fertile alluvial soil, fresh river water, suitable tropical climate to grow variety of fruits and vegetables, port facilities, transport network, readily available market.
- *European clusters:* High population density is found in the European cluster from the British Isles to European Russia. The development of industries, availability of oil, mineral resources has supported large population in this cluster. Agriculture is also developed in this region but the food production capacity is not much in this zone specially in few countries owing to climatic restrictions.

Areas of moderate population density: The population density is between 100 and 300 persons per square kilometre. Although this region has medium population density but the density in these areas are comparatively larger. Owing to its relatively small size and area as compared to the major clusters they are falling under the category of medium population density. This region has witnessed a rapid population growth mainly after the industrial revolution.

- *North-east United States and south-east Canada:* Large concentrations of minerals and agricultural resources have contributed to the population in this region. The region also supports industries and dense transport network provides support to urbanization.
- *South-east Australia:* The region is rich in industries, mineral resources, and suitable climate and soil for agriculture.
- *Nile valley region:* Fertile deltaic soil, irrigation, and strong agricultural base have contributed to the growth of population in this region.

Point to note:

Since ancient times the largest concentration of population has been concentrated in the cradles of ancient human civilization mainly India and China.

More than 75 per cent of the world's population are found in the tropical belt.

Areas of low population density: The very hot or very cold areas, infertile lands, rugged terrain have very low density of population. The large deserts of Sahara, Atacama, Kalahari are sparsely populated. Similarly, the cold arid regions of Siberia and northern parts of Canada, tundra regions are also least populated. The rugged mountainous regions of Rockies, Himalayas, Alps are uninhabited. The dense forested regions of Amazon rainforests are also least populated.

FACTORS AFFECTING POPULATION GROWTH

Physical Factors

- *Terrain:* Plain areas will always support higher population as compared to plateaus and mountainous regions. Plain lands are suitable for growing crops, for construction of roads, bridges, and buildings. They can also support the growth of industries which can generate employment opportunities.
- *Suitable climate:* Moderate climate neither too hot nor too cold will always attract more population. Desert regions and mountainous terrain which pose difficulties in cultivation and transport and communication do not attract large population. Similarly, regions receiving extremely heavy rainfall like the areas of dense rain forests are also sparsely populated. They produce very humid and oppressive conditions of survival.
- *Availability of fertile soil:* Agriculture has always been the most important economic activity since time immemorial. Agriculture needs fertile soil throughout the year. From ancient times the cradles of human civilization have been laid along the river banks due to the availability of fertile rich soil.
- *Supply of freshwater:* River valleys have always attracted population growth. In fact, in deserts population grows around any water body like an oasis. Water is essential both for domestic and non-domestic uses.
- *Mineral resources:* Availability of mineral resources is needed for the development of industries. Sometimes in mountainous regions high population densities are seen due to mining of precious minerals. In India the Chota Nagpur plateau is highly industrialized owing to the availability of minerals that has led to the growth of several towns and cities in this region.

Economic Factors

- *Government policies:* Favourable government policies, peaceful, and conducive socio-economic environment will help in supporting population growth.
- *Employment opportunities:* The growth of industries in a particular region will attract people towards it as it will help in generating employment opportunities. So the population growth is always higher in cities and towns.

POPULATION DISTRIBUTION IN INDIA

Areas of extremely low population density: These regions have a population density of less than 100 persons per square kilometre. These include:

- The desert areas of Thar, Kutch.

- States of Sikkim and Arunachal Pradesh due to their rugged mountainous terrain.
- The islands of Andaman and Nicobar due to their location far from the mainland.

Areas of low population density: These regions have a population density ranging between 100 and 250 persons per square kilometre.

- The forested and rugged regions of NE states of Meghalaya, Nagaland, Mizoram, and Manipur
- The cold and arid areas of Jammu and Kashmir
- The dry areas of interior of Chhattisgarh and Madhya Pradesh
- The north-western side of Rajasthan and Gujarat
- The mountainous terrain of Himachal Pradesh and Uttaranchal

Areas of medium population density: These regions have a population density ranging between 250 and 500 persons per square kilometre.

- The north-eastern states of Assam and Tripura
- Industrial and developed states of Telangana and Andhra Pradesh
- Odisha and Jharkhand

Areas of high population density: These regions have a population density ranging between 500 and 1,000 persons per square kilometre.

- The agricultural rich states of Punjab and Haryana
- The industrialized states of Gujarat, Tamil Nadu, and Karnataka
- The fertile plains of Uttar Pradesh and Kerala

Areas of very high population density: These regions have a population density above 1,000 persons per square kilometre.

- The industrial states of Maharashtra and West Bengal
- The state of Bihar
- The national capital region of Delhi

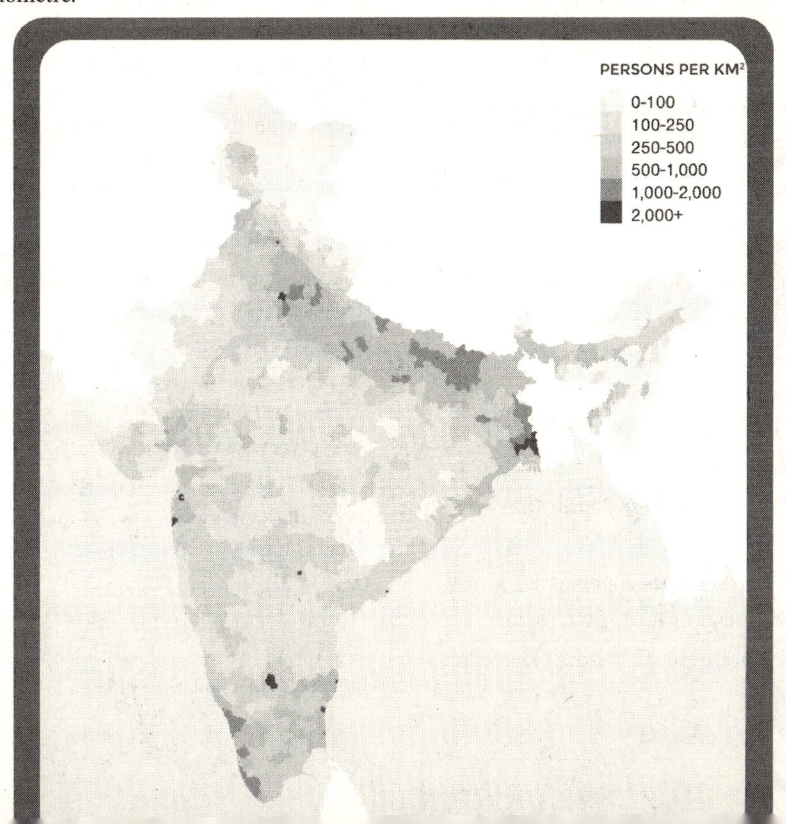

THE POPULATION GROWTH IN INDIA IN STAGES

The population history of India can be divided into four distinct phases:

The Period of Stagnant Population (1901–21)

- There was a stagnant and sporadic growth of population in India during, most of the nineteenth century.
- This period of population was considered to be stagnant as compared to the latter years which witnessed rapid population growth.
- Both the birth rates and death rates were high. The death rates were high due to poor medical facilities, lack of hygiene, and shortage of food supply. Drought, Famine and spread of endemic diseases like cholera, jaundice, influenza, small pox plagued the nation during this period.
- The year 1921 witnessed a negative population growth for the first time in demographic history in India so this period was also termed as demographic divide.

The Period of Steady Population (1921–51)

- There was a steady decline in mortality due to improvements in medical and sanitation facilities.
- The growth rate of population jumped by about 47.3 per cent.
- The fertility rates remained high so the population continued to grow.
- Population growth at this stage was mortality-induced growth.

The Period of Rapid Population (1951–81)

- There was a massive population growth at this stage owing to high fertility.
- There were growth of urban towns and cities, industries were developing all of which were conducive for population explosion.
- The standard of living was improved.
- Population growth at this stage was fertility-induced growth.

The Period of High But Steady Population (1981–2011)

- This was the phase when population continued to rise but after the arrival of twenty-first century the growth rate was not so rapid.
- The population control policies, high cost of living and family planning measure were effective.
- However, India's population continues to rise, surpassing China and becoming the most populated country of the world.

THE THEORY OF DEMOGRAPHIC TRANSITION

This theory of demographic transition deals with transformation of a society characterized by high fertility and mortality rates (agrarian economy) to a more developed and urbanized society. The theory was propounded by Thompson and Notestein. It shows the sequence of events of population growth. The stages of demographic transition are:

Agrarian Stage

- The first stage of demographic transition, the economy is agrarian or pre-industrial.
- At this stage, both the birth rates and death rates are high so the growth rate of population is low or fluctuating. Life expectancy is low.
- Agriculture is the most important economic activity, there is abundance of labour due to high population.
- Agriculture is mainly intensive in nature – mostly labour intensive and traditional ways of farming are practised on small plots of land.

- The per hectare productivity is low, farmers mainly grow crops for their own consumption.
- There is high incidence of illiteracy.
- Famines, droughts, and regular crop failures are common. Poor nutrition, medical and hygienic facilities lead to high infant mortality.

Industrial Stage

- This is the early industrial stage when the birth rates show a decline and there is a sharp fall in death rates. Life expectancy also goes up.
- This is the stage of population explosion since the decline in mortality is much more than that of fertility rates so the gap between the two increases leading to rapid population growth.
- The fall in death rates is due to the improvement in medical, health, and sanitation facilities.
- Growth of industries started which made way for better living standards.
- Better division of labour, use of technology in the fields of agriculture led to better productivity.
- Spread of education led to higher literacy.

Urban Stage

- This is the late industrial stage or urban stage when there is a slow growth rate of population.
- The mortality rates continue to fall while the fertility rates also show a sharp decline due to which there is a low and stable growth rate.
- High life expectancy is seen; remarkable improvements are made in the medical fields.
- Use of technology in the fields of agriculture and industries. Generation of employment opportunities from setting up of new industries.
- Development of towns and cities, better educational facilities lead to higher literacy and also cost of living.
- Higher cost of living leads to growing preferences for smaller families.

MIGRATION

Migration refers to the movement of people from one region to another that can be within or across nations.

Types: Migration can be of the following types:

- *Internal migration:* Movement of people within a country due to work, health, education, or any social purpose. Internal migration can be inter regional or intra regional in which the former means the movement of people happens between two regions within a country and the latter means the movement of people within a specific region of a country.
- *International migration:* Movement of an individual across nations.
- *Immigration:* When a person settles down in a new country and leaves his country of origin.
- *Forced migration:* Sometimes a person has to leave his place of origin forcefully and settle down somewhere else. They are also termed as refugees.
- *Migration can also be:*
  - Rural to rural migration
  - Rural to urban migration
  - Urban to urban migration
  - Urban to rural migration

CAUSES OF MIGRATION

The causes of migration can be classified as push factors and pull factors.

Push factors are those negative factors which forces a person to leave his place of origin.

Pull factors are those positive factors which attract a person to settle down there.

Push Factors

- Lack of proper medical facilities.
- High cost of living and lack of employment opportunities.
- Political instability, war, famine, crop failure, and faulty government policies.
- Inhospitable climate, poor soils, and lack of freshwater supply.
- Lack of proper educational facilities.
- Prone to natural disasters such as earthquakes, floods, cyclones, etc.

Pull Factors

- Proper medical facilities in the form of doctors, medical practitioners, hospitals, clinics.
- Generation of employment opportunities.
- Habitable climate, fertile soils, freshwater.
- Developed transport and communication facilities.
- Educational facilities and friendly government policies.
- Encouraging loans and incentives for research and career growth.

CONSEQUENCES OF MIGRATION

People always have the tendency to migrate from less advanced or less developed regions to more developed or advanced regions. The sole purpose of most of the migrations are the desire to lead a better life.

- *Economic consequences:* Remittances sent by the migrants to their home country adds to the national income of the country. This money helps in raising the standard of living. However, it may also lead to overcrowding and growth of slums and squatter settlements in the destination country. Overcrowding causes poor health and sanitation and lack of proper housing. Often people working in a new place displaces the people who originally belong there from their workplace leading to unemployment.
- *Demographic consequences:* Unbalanced sex ratio is seen in the home country as men leave their homes to work in a different city. This also causes lack of proper development in home country.
- *Social consequences:* When migrants come back to their place of origin they bring with them lots of ideas, innovation, life skills, etc. which can be applied in different fields. At the same time, their social outlook is broadened because of inter mixing of different cultures and races. But at the same it also creates missing out of family life, loneliness, fierce competitions, and depression that affect the mental health of an individual.
- *Environmental consequences:* Over use and exploitation of natural resources due to migration in destination countries often lead to pollution and causes environmental degradation.

SOME MAJOR MIGRATIONS OF THE WORLD

- In the post-Second World War period a large number of Jews migrated to Israel between 1948 and 1951. Most of the Jewish migrants were from Russia and the other European countries.
- Forced migrants were sent to America from African nations.
- In the mid-1970s large number of European settlers of the Portuguese African colonies migrated back to Europe and others went back to South Africa. This migration was caused due to civil war in Angola followed by its independence.
- The partition of India in 1947 caused the biggest migration in Indian history where lakhs of people were displaced from their lands overnight and were migrated forcefully to newly formed India, Bangladesh (East Pakistan), and west Pakistan.

BRAIN DRAIN

When talented and skilled individuals leave their country of origin and settle down in foreign country for better exposure, pay and working conditions, it is termed as brain drain.

Brain drain is caused mainly due to lack of facilities, lack of proper career growth, political instability in the home country. All these acts as the push factors while better facilities, money and exposure in the developed countries act as the pull factors.

Advantages and Disadvantages of Brain Drain

Advantages: Brain drain causes the migrants to send remittances to their families in the home country which adds up to the national income of the country. When the professionals return back to their own country they bring with them lots of expertise and skills which can be used here. Brain drain is advantageous for the countries experiencing the gain due to the influx of skilled workers. Emigration will also increase the wages of the workers remaining back in the place of origin.

Disadvantages: Brain drain causes loss of talented professionals from the country. It signals lack of economic development and also failure in government policies over time. There is an economic loss in the human capital. Critical fields such as medicine and health suffers a setback due to lack of skilled professionals which will hamper the country's growth.

How to Avoid Brain Drain?

- Changing the pattern of education system in the country that will be more vocational will teach life skills and student friendly.
- Research infrastructures should be invested upon,
- Better educational facilities, schools, and colleges offering more professional courses.
- Proper pay check and work culture.

POPULATION PROBLEMS AND POLICIES OF DEVELOPING NATION (INDIA)

POPULATION PROBLEM

- *Overcrowding:* When the carrying capacity of a region is less than its population the area suffers from overcrowding. This leads to exploitation of resources as there is increased pressure of population on resources.
- *Growth of slums and squatter settlements:* Developing nations mainly face rural to urban migration. Shortage of proper housing, health, and sanitation facilities in the cities lead to the growth of slums and squatter settlements. These are temporary settlements made up of tin, or cloth shades without any proper sanitation, drinking water, or electricity. They continue to grow along the railway tracks, roads, under bridges in the cities and its surroundings. These people neither have any permanent settlements nor do they have any legal ownership over the land where they build their settlements.
- *Lack of employment opportunities:* High population in developing nations leads to lack of job opportunities as the work place is already overburdened with too many people. All this leads to people getting involved in criminal and illegal activities such as theft or dacoity to escape poverty and hunger.
- *Low standard of living:* Poverty and unemployment increases the cost of living in cities. This leads to improper and uncompleted education to get early

jobs, lack of proper health care, and use of medical facilities.

- *Pollution:* One of the biggest problems faced by Indian cities and towns is the alarming rate of pollution be in air, water, or soil. Overexploitation of resources, huge vehicular traffic, unplanned setting up of factories within residential areas, cutting of trees to make way for more development, release of untreated wastes into water bodies lead to pollution of air, water, or soil.

Population control policy of India: At this time between 1961 and 2000 the prime focus was given to the following areas:

- Social acceptability for smaller families.
- Implementation of family planning measure by promoting the uses of contraceptives and birth control measures.
- Increased awareness in rural families about family planning.
- Improvement in maternity and child health care services.

In 1976, the National Population Policy was announced. Its salient features were:

- To raise the age of marriage for boys to 21 years and for girls to 18 years.
- Encouraging female education in all states.
- Additional incentives to couples undergoing sterilization.

NATIONAL POPULATION POLICY 2000

Salient Features

- Reproductive health services should be taken advantages of, promoting educated, decision making and public acceptance.
- Free and mandatory education for all children till 14 years, lowering the rates of failures and drop outs among both males and females.
- Lowering the infant mortality rate to under 30 per 1,000 live births.
- Lowering the maternal mortality rate to less than 100 per 10,000 live births.
- Widespread immunization to all infants.
- 100 per cent recording of births, deaths, marriages, and pregnancies.
- Encouraging females to postpone marriage preferably above 20 years.
- Preventing communicable diseases.
- Preference for smaller families.
- Implementation of AYUSH in Indian medicine system in reproductive and infant health care.
- Grow awareness on AIDS, other reproductive tract infections.
- Contraception awareness among individuals by providing incentives for sterilization.

FACT FILE

India has the largest diaspora in the world. That means Indians are the largest community to live abroad for work.

SETTLEMENT: RURAL AND URBAN; THEIR MORPHOLOGY

The growth of human settlements started with domestication of animals, agriculture and permanency in living in a particular region. Previously humans were mostly nomads, they practised hunting and grazing of animals so they moved from one place to another in search of greener pastures. Human settlements refer to a permanent collection of houses, huts, or buildings.

The growth of settlement is controlled by few factors such as availability of plain lands or suitable terrain, favourable climate, availability of fresh clean drinking water, mineral resources, or forest resources.

Human settlements can be either temporary or permanent. As the name suggests temporary settlements are those in which the people move or wander from one place to another in search of food or water, these are basically nomadic hunters or pasturers.

Permanent settlements are all those houses or buildings specially in cities or towns in which the inhabitants live permanently or for a long period of time.

Settlements can either be rural or urban also. Rural settlements are the ones found in villages in which agriculture, fishing, forestry is the main occupation. Most of the rural settlements are permanent in nature.

Urban settlements are the ones seen in cities and towns in which people living are mainly engaged in secondary and tertiary sectors such as banking, education, medical, law, industries, etc. The density of population in such settlements is always very high.

DIFFERENT TYPES OF SETTLEMENTS

Nucleated settlements: These are clustered settlements that comprises of many houses in compact form surrounding temples or important religious centres or a water body or farmlands. Nucleated settlements are common in Indo-Gangetic plains, Nile valley, etc. These settlements generally grow along river valleys and in flat terrain.

Dispersed settlements: Inhospitable areas such as forests, rugged terrain, arid areas are marked by these type of settlements. The houses are located far from each other. Mostly found in the remote villages where the farmers have to walk long distances to reach their fields. This may be due to absence of proper roads, dense forests, or hilly terrain.

PATTERN OF RURAL SETTLEMENTS

- *Rectangular pattern:* The roads are almost straight meeting each at right angles. These settlement patterns are mostly seen in fertile alluvial plains or valleys.
- *Linear pattern:* Houses are arranged along a major road, stream, railway line, and canal.
- *Star-like pattern:* These develop when metalled or unmetalled roads converge at a point and houses spread out along the sides of roads in all directions.
- *Triangular pattern:* At the confluence of rivers settlements take a triangular shape following the course of the rivers.
- *Nebular pattern:* Takes the shape of a nebula where houses are built around a nucleus. This nucleus can be a temple or a water body. The roads are arranged almost in a circular way which ends at the nucleus.
- *Semi-circular pattern:* These settlements are occupation specific. Often the people engaged in fishing build their houses on the sea coasts far from the village. This often takes the shape of a semi-circle.

GENERAL TRENDS IN URBANIZATION

The trend in urbanization varies between eastern and western countries. The industrial revolution caused massive upheaval in urbanization in Europe. Urbanization was associated with production of surplus food by the farmers. This allowed the farmers to make profits and use machineries in their agricultural fields. The towns became the focus of production and selling of goods there was diversification of work as more and more people got involved with other economic activities such as pottery, artisans, etc.

URBANIZATION IN INDIA

- Delhi and Chandigarh are the most urbanized.
- Maharashtra comes second as 45.23 per cent
- Gujarat 42.58 per cent
- Tamil Nadu 34.95 per cent
- Karnataka 31.5 per cent
- Punjab 37.49 per cent
- Kerala 47.72 per cent

IMPORTANT TERMS RELATED TO URBANIZATION

- *Metropolis:* Urban areas having a population of more than 1 million.
- *Megalopolis:* urban areas having a population of more than 10 million.
- *Satellite city:* An urban area typically smaller in size that grows near a metropolis city. They are economically or socially independent completely or partially from the main city but are well connected with the main city. Satellite cities are mainly developed to reduce the stress of population from the main city.
- *Smart city:* City which uses advanced technologies in its social, economic, and physical infrastructure. Sustainable development, enhanced connectivity, online government services, cyber security are the basic components of a smart city.
- *Edge city:* Concentration of firms, factories, entertainment, shopping centres in a previously known rural or residential area is called an edge city. Edge city is an American term where the most common type of edge cities is called 'boomers'. A boomer is an edge city that develops gradually around a road or a shopping mall.
- *Rural urban fringe:* It is the boundary zone where urban and rural land use intermixes. It is the area where there is a transition from city to village. The rural agricultural fields slowly change into medium-sized houses and then eventually bigger buildings.
- *Suburb:* A suburb develops in the outskirts of the city and is a mixed use or a residential area existing as a part of the city. The population density in a suburb is generally lower than the main city. People living in suburbs mostly commute daily to the main city for work.
- *Ghetto:* An urban district in which the population mainly consists of a particular ethnic group.
- *Urban sprawl:* Rapid expansion of the geographical extent of cities or towns characterized by low priced land, low population density, social segregation, use of private automobile.

FUNCTIONAL CLASSIFICATION OF TOWNS

- *Administrative towns:* This includes the capital city/town, centre of a state, province, district, tehsil, etc. All the government bureaucrats, officers, public buildings are located in the administrative towns (e.g., New Delhi in India).
- *Defensive towns:* They are located far away from the main city to maintain security. They contain cantonments, military base camps, training areas, barracks for the armed forces (e.g., Vishakhapatnam).
- *Cultural centres:* Cultural centres can either be religious centres or educational towns. For example, Oxford (England) or Kota in Rajasthan are educational centres while Mathura and Haridwar are religious towns.

- *Production centres:* Urban areas in which production or manufacturing is the most important economic activity. For example, Jamshedpur in India is considered to be the steel city for its iron and steel industry.
- *Collection centres:* The mining towns, fishing towns, come under this category. For example, Raniganj in West Bengal.
- *Distribution centres:* The main function of this town is trade and commerce. Market towns, financial towns or port cities come under this category. They mainly include port cities. Some of the world's largest cities have developed on ports, for example, Mumbai, New York, and Tokyo. Some towns have developed as financial centres.
- *Resorts:* Towns which have developed for the recreation needs of the people are resorts. These places are known for their natural scenery, historical monuments, sports, cultural attractions, mountain climbing and trekking, health treatments, etc. (e.g., Darjeeling, Srinagar).
- *Residential towns:* Towns which are mainly used for inhabitation. The land use comprises of houses, schools, and hospitals. Residential towns are connected to the main city which enables the daily commuters to go to work daily.

FACT FILE

India's three mega cities where the population is more than 10 million are:
Greater Mumbai (urban agglomeration), Delhi, and Kolkata.

CHARACTERISTICS OF URBANIZATION

- The level of urbanization is an indicator of economic development of a nation because as the economy develops the purchasing power of an individual also develops. There is an increase in per capita income of an individual.
- Industrialization leads to urbanization. The land use mainly comprises of manufacturing units, factories, mills, and industrial setups.
- An urban settlement consists of high population density caused due to natural increase as well as migration of people from surrounding rural areas.
- The cost of living is high in urban areas that causes disintegration of joint families, impersonal relations.
- Problem of over-population causes growth of slums, lack of housing facilities, pollution, growth in crime rates.
- Urban centres have easy availability of inputs such as skilled labour, capital, repair services from which profits are earned.
- There are ample job opportunities in urban centres as workers can easily switch from one work to another as there are wider choices. So rural people often settle down near urban centres.

What is counter urbanization?

Movement of people from urban areas back to rural towns or villages to seek a better quality of life in the countryside (may be after retirement).

What is repatriation?

A government policy of returning immigrants back to their country of origin.

MORPHOLOGY OF TOWNS

Morphology means the physical shape of towns. The difference of population groups within the towns causes the morphology. People belonging to a particular ethnic group, caste or linguistic group tend to live together because of their common backgrounds.

The difference in income also causes segregation in the population. The suburbs consist of larger houses, big lawns that are inhabited by high income groups while the older houses near the centre of the towns are the homes of the middle income groups.

In the model of general growth and land use pattern the most distinctive feature is the presence of CBD (central business district). The CBD has land use of tall buildings, offices, headquarters, offices, stores, and major crowded streets. The fringe of the CBD consists of warehouses, transportation terminals, light factories, durable commodities stores, etc. beyond the CBD consists of the residential areas.

The following is the five concentric ring of a model town:

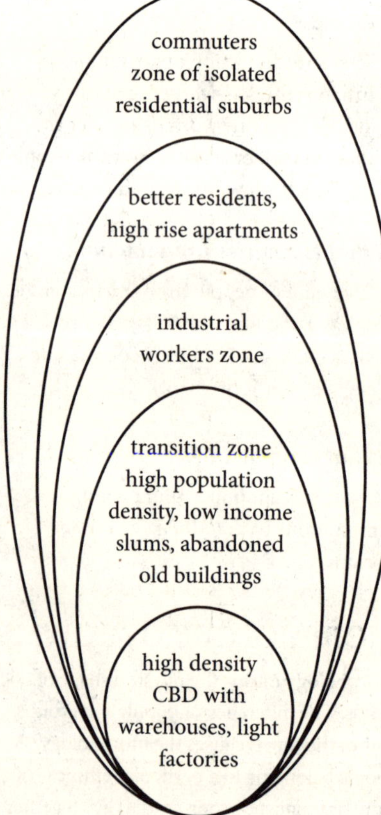

ECONOMIC GEOGRAPHY

SECTORS OF AN ECONOMY

- *Primary sector:* This involves primary activities such as hunting of animals, cattle grazing, fishing, harvesting of crops and trees, obtaining minerals from earth's crust, etc.; these activities are directly obtained from nature. The people engaged in this work are called red-collar workers.
- *Secondary sector:* This involves processing and shaping the commodities already obtained through primary activities. This includes production of steel goods, production of textiles by processing animal or plant fibres such as wool or cotton respectively. Workers in this group make use of machineries and capital and are termed as blue-collar workers.
- *Tertiary sector:* Include service sector such as barbers, secretaries, clerks, etc. These include range of business and personal services.
- *Quaternary sector:* Professional and administrative services includes teaching, legal services, doctors or health professionals, entertainment services, etc.; these workers are called white-collar workers.
- *Quinary sector:* They include chief executives and top professionals in government as well as private sectors. Researchers, financial planners, advisors, consultants come under this category. These people are called gold-collar workers.
- *Pink-collar sector:* Activities primarily involving women come under this category. This includes jobs in beauty, nursing, social work, teaching, child care industry.

AGRICULTURE AND OTHER ALLIED ACTIVITIES

It is the most basic of all primary activities. World agriculture is of the following types:

- *Nomadic herding:* The nomads move from one place to another in search of water or pastures. It is the simplest form of pastoralism.
- *Livestock ranching:* Animals are raised and taken for grazing on ranches. Ranches are more permanent than herding. The rearing of animals is done commercially using scientific techniques.
- *Shifting agriculture:* Also called slash and burn method, a small plot of forested land is cleared by fire and used for growing crops. When the land loses its fertility the farmers abandon the land and move to a fresh plot.
- *Intensive subsistence farming:* Here the farmers cultivate small plots of land using simple and primitive tools. They mainly produce crops for self-consumption. It is a labour-intensive method practised in high population density regions. The land holdings are small and uneconomical due to fragmented land holdings.
- *Commercial farming:* Capital intensive, use of modern machineries, irrigation methods, fertilizers, pesticides are used. Farming is mainly done on large plots of lands with the motive of earning profit.
- *Plantation farming:* A single crop is grown on large plots of land. Crops are mainly grown for profit and the methods of farming are mechanized. Large amount of capital, irrigation methods, fertilizers, high-quality seeds are used extensively.
- *Dairy farming:* Long-term production of milk for commercial sale of dairy products.
- *Commercial grain farming:* Farmers grow grains for selling in the market. It is done on large plots of lands using better machineries and huge capital investment.
- *Organic farming:* Agricultural method that uses organic fertilizers and methods for environmental friendly produce. It reduces human health hazards by using natural inputs. It also decreases cost of production and enhances soil fertility.
- *Market gardening:* Fruits, vegetables, and flowers are grown on smaller scale to sell to consumers directly. Often farmers practise market gardening to earn some additional income.

FISHING

Fishing is concentrated mainly in all those countries which lie close to sea or oceans or have good network of river system. Fishing can be either in-shore fishing or coastal fishing. The largest fishing industry are found in Japan, Russia, China, United States. The major fishing grounds of the world where fishing is done on a commercial scale are grand banks near New Foundland, the north of Japan and the sea around Iceland. Fishing grounds are mainly concentrated in the temperate latitudes mainly due to the following reasons: Cooler water contains more phytoplankton than warm water so more fishes are produced.

- The continental shelves are developed more in temperate latitudes.
- Fish storage is easier in cooler climate than in tropical climate as there is no storage problem.
- Coastal regions in higher latitudes do not grow much crops due to restrictions, so they consider fishing as an important occupation.

FACT FILE

Florida is the fishing capital of the world with its great resources, variety of fish, and use of modern techniques.

FORESTRY

Forestry not only involves cutting or lumbering of wood but also the industries related to forests such as harvesting of timber as well as forest management. Forestry includes paper and pulp industry, sports equipment industry, cosmetic industry in the form of essential oils, flavours, fragrances, camphor, gum, resins. Forestry has been a major environmental concern as a lot of trees are being cut down for lumbering. The ever increasing demand for wood and timber for the growing population is one of the reasons. The dense forests of the world are found in areas of heavy rainfall and long warm season. The luxuriant growth of vegetation is hindered by drought conditions or aridity.

Trees both hardwood and softwood are found in forests. Hardwood trees are mainly deciduous or tropical evergreen trees. They are found in both temperate as well as tropical latitudes. Temperate latitudes contain broad leaved and deciduous like oak, beech, elm. Tropical forests contain hard wood such as teak, ebony, rosewood, and mahogany. Soft wood trees are mainly conifers. These trees are needle shaped and are evergreen such as pine, deodar, fir, spruce, etc.

Forestry is a major economic activity in the Northern hemisphere. The entire belt of coniferous vegetation flourishes in the temperate latitudes from Alaska in North America to Labrador and New Foundland. This zone is known as the taiga and covers from Northern Europe through Scandinavia and Russia and across Asia through Siberia. Tropical hardwoods are found in areas of Africa, equatorial regions of South East Asia, South America such as Brazil.

Productive function of forests: Forest provides us with variety of products. The most important is timber followed by pulp for paper. Other than these many products are also extracted from trees which do not require felling. These are gums, resins rubber latex, turpentine, essential oils, fragrances, spices, etc. Many plants having medicinal properties are also obtained from forests such as cinchona, coca, and castor oil. Cinchona is used for treatment of malaria, for increasing appetite and treating bloating of stomach. A variety of fruits and nuts are also derived from forests. For example, the Brazilian nuts are hard nuts used for making buttons, studs.

Agro Forestry

It is the method in which crops are cultivated along with forest trees and animal rearing on a plot of land. The main aim of agro forestry is to earn additional income for the farmers and to ensure the most efficient land use in accordance with the socio-cultural practices of the local people. Agro forestry is practised to (a) reduce the pressure on forests; (b) to check soil erosion and deforestation; (c) to maintain ecological balance and to maintain the natural fertility of the soil; (d) Maximum utilization of the available land to obtain a variety of products such as wood, timber, fodder, livestock, etc.

Social Forestry

People oriented and joint management of forests with the major objective of satisfying the needs, desires, and aspirations of both the people and the government. It includes management of forests and afforestation on barren lands with the purpose of helping in the social, rural development.

Objectives are:

- Providing food, fodder, timber for rural people.
- Developing cottage industries.

- Generating employment opportunities to the rural people.
- Efficient conservation of land and water.
- Fulfilling the recreational needs of the people.
- Adding aesthetic value to the place.

MINERALS AND ENERGY RESOURCES

Minerals are considered to be a valuable natural resource. They are not distributed equally in all parts of the world. There is an inverse relationship between quality and quantity of minerals. The minerals of best quality are found in smaller quantities and vice versa. There are several factors such as climate, location, accessibility that determine how and whether the minerals can be exploited commercially or not.

MAJOR MINERALS OF THE WORLD

- *Iron ore:* When a particular mineral is derived from the mixture of different minerals it is known as ore of that mineral. Iron ore provides the base for the development of basic industries such as iron and steel industries. Australia is the largest producer of iron ore in the world. In India, iron ore is mainly concentrated in Odisha belt. The types of iron ore are haematite, magnetite, limonite, and siderite. Haematite is the black ore – the most superior variety consisting of more than 70 per cent of iron content.
- *Manganese:* Manganese is used as a raw material in iron and steel industry to make steel stronger. It is also used in dry cell batteries, bleaching powder, paints and emulsifiers, railway tracks, and ship building. South Africa is the largest producer in the world and Odisha in India.
- *Copper:* The first metal known to man, it is a good conductor of electricity so it is mainly used for electrical equipment, construction building purposes and industrial machines. It is both ductile and malleable.
  Chile is the largest producer in the world while in India copper reserves are found in Madhya Pradesh followed by Rajasthan and Jharkhand.
- *Aluminium:* It is mainly used for making alloys as it is strong, light, and ductile. It is used in aircraft industry, jewellery, everyday items, foil, etc. It is also free from corrosion so it is used for making high rise buildings and bridges. The main producers are China, Russia, and India. Bauxite is used in making aluminium metal. It is used for making chemicals, steel, cement, and as building material.
- *Zinc:* Paints, rubber, pharmaceuticals, cosmetics, soaps, batteries, garments are manufactured by using zinc oxides. China is the largest producer in the world while in India Rajasthan is the largest.
- *Diamonds:* The most precious of all minerals, South Africa is the leading producer in the world. Diamond is famously used in jewellery industry, glass industry, cosmetics, etc. It is the hardest of all metals. Diamonds are mined in Madhya Pradesh in India.
- *Gold:* Another precious metal, the largest reserves of gold mines are found in Australia. Gold is durable and non-corrosive so it is used in jewellery, aerospace, automotive, dentistry, medical tools sector. In India gold mines are found in Karnataka and Andhra Pradesh.
- *Silver:* Silver is also a precious metal. It is found either in pure form or in combination with gold, copper, or lead.

Silver is a ductile, malleable, and soft metal. Since it is a good conductor of electricity, it is used for making batteries, ornaments, mirrors, dental alloys, etc. Mexico is the leading producer in the world while in India Rajasthan is leading.

CLASSIFICATION OF MINERALS

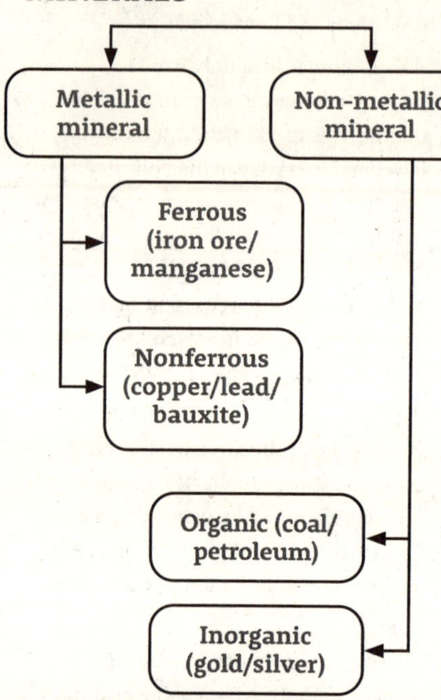

CONVENTIONAL AND NON-CONVENTIONAL SOURCES OF ENERGY

Conventional sources of energy: These are energy resources which are non-renewable in nature. These energy resources are being used by man since immemorial. The most important ones are:

Coal

One of the most important sources of energy coal is a sedimentary rock formed by the action of pressure and heat on the vegetative remains of dead plants and animals. Coal is also termed as a fossil fuel. The major types of coal are:

Anthracite coal: Best quality coal in which carbon content is about 92 per cent. It is black, lustrous, and shiny. It is smokeless, burns for a long time, has high calorific value and does not contain moisture. In India anthracite coal is found in small quantities specially in Jammu and Kashmir.

Bituminous coal: The carbon content is about 50–80 per cent. Its colour ranges between dark brown and black. It is the most abundantly used coal and is primarily used for domestic purposes or as a coking coal and for blasting furnaces. The type of coal used in India is mainly of bituminous type.

Lignite: The carbon content ranges between 25 and 35 per cent. It has a low calorific value due to its high moisture content. It is a poor grade coal. In India lignite is mined from Neyveli in Tamil Nadu.

Peat: This is the first stage of transformation from wood to coal. It is the most inferior variety of coal.

Uses of coal:

- Coal is used for power generation and electricity.
- Coal is used as a raw material in many basic and heavy industries such as iron and steel, ship building, railway tracks and parts, cement, chemical industries.
- It is used as a source of fuel for domestic purposes.
- Coking coal is used for smelting iron ore into iron and make steel.

Distribution of coal in India: Coal is found in two important reserves in India one as Gondwana coal reserves and the other as tertiary coal reserves.

Gondwana coal reserves: Ninety-eight per cent of the coal reserves in India are made up of Gondwana coal. These coal fields are about 400 million years old. This coal is free from moisture and has high calorific value. It contains sulphur and phosphorous. The entire Chota Nagpur plateau region consists of Gondwana coal fields.

Tertiary coal fields: These coal fields are comparatively new. They are about 55 million years old. These variety of coal have low calorific value as they contain moisture and less quantity of sulphur and phosphorus. The carbon content is also very low. These are found in small pockets in the north-eastern states.

Petroleum

The term 'petroleum' is derived from 'petra' and 'oleum' that means rock oil. Petroleum is a fossil fuel derived from below the earth's crust that is refined into fuel from crude form. It is formed due to decomposition of fossil fuel over millions of years. Petroleum forms the base of transport sector. Crude oil is refined in refineries to make petrol, diesel, kerosene, LPG, gasoline, lubricating oil, paraffin wax, etc.

Uses of petroleum:

- Petroleum is used as a source of fuel for vehicles as petrol and diesel.
- LPG or liquefied petroleum gas is used for cooking purposes.
- Petrol and diesel are used for dry cleaning and for running electric generators.
- Paraffin wax is used for making candles, ointments, crayons, and printing ink.

The oldest coal field in India is Raniganj coal field (West Bengal).

The largest coal field is Jharia in Jharkhand.

The oldest oil refinery in India is Digboi oil refinery in Assam. The largest oil refinery in India as well as in world is Reliance Industries oil refinery in Jamnagar (Gujarat).

What are petrochemicals?

These are derived from petroleum as well as its products which are used as major raw materials. Petrochemical products are lighter, durable and cost effective. Its raw materials are also easily available and are not dependent on agriculture as in the case of natural fibres such as jute. So they are now fast replacing the traditional products. Some of the common petrochemical products used in our daily life are synthetic rubber, synthetic fibres, plastic, detergents, resins. The petrochemical industries are located close to oil fields due to easy availability of raw materials and for reducing the cost of transportation.

Did you know?

Why can we detect cooking gas leakage at home?

Since LPG is highly inflammable but odourless it is added with **ethyl mercaptan** which gives the foul stingy smell so that we can easily detect that there is a leakage of gas!

Natural Gas

These are generally associated with oil fields or as an independent source. It mainly consists of methane. Natural gas is considered to be a safer option than coal because it is environmental friendly and does not leave ash behind. It is a mixture of hydrocarbon compounds formed under the earth's crust for millions of years due to the decay of plant and animal remains under extreme heat and pressure.

Uses:

- It is used as fuel in the form of CNG (compressed natural gas) in vehicles such as autorickshaws.
- Used in making chemicals and fertilizers.

- Used for generating electricity, cooking, and heating.
- Used in making paints, plastic, fabric, and steel.

Hydel Power

One of the cheapest sources of energy, hydel power is renewable. Hydro electricity is produced when water is made to fall from a certain point with great force that flows through a turbine that turns it activating the generator generating electricity. Hydel power is environmental friendly and does not emit any greenhouse gases.

The major hydro electric projects of India that are also multi-purpose river valley projects are: Bhakra Nangal dam project built on river Satluj benefitting Punjab, Haryana, and Rajasthan, Hirakud dam project built on river Mahanadi in Odisha, Damodar Valley Corporation on river Damodar benefitting West Bengal and Jharkhand.

Uses of multi-purpose river valley projects:

- To prevent soil erosion and promote afforestation.
- To control floods.
- To promote pisciculture.
- Generation of hydro electricity.
- To provide irrigational facilities.
- To provide for the recreational needs of the locals.

ADVANTAGES AND DISADVANTAGES OF CONVENTIONAL SOURCES OF ENERGY

ADVANTAGES OF COAL

- It is the most traditional source of fossil fuel.
- It is used in rural household for cooking purposes.
- It provides raw materials to several industries such as iron and steel, automobile, chemical, cement industries.
- Several byproducts such as phenol, benzene, tar are obtained from coal.

DISADVANTAGES OF COAL

- Indian coal is mostly of bituminous coal that too concentrated in specific regions and are not widely distributed all over the country.
- Coal is an exhaustible natural resource so there is always a risk of it getting depleted fast.
- Burning of coal releases harmful gases that cause greenhouse effect.
- The transportation cost is quite high and there are lots of corruption in the form of coal smuggling.

ADVANTAGES OF PETROLEUM

- Petroleum is used for power generation.
- Petrol, diesel, kerosene, gasoline, LPG are used as fuel for transport sector.
- It is easy and convenient to transport petroleum over long distances through pipelines or vehicles.
- Petrochemicals that are derived from petroleum has wide range of uses as they are cheaper and durable.

DISADVANTAGES OF PETROLEUM

- Petroleum is an expensive fuel and cannot be extracted from anywhere.
- It is an exhaustible resource and takes millions of years to form.
- It is highly inflammable.
- It causes harmful gases while burning which can cause greenhouse effect and pollution.
- It can damage the marine life through oil spills in oceans.

ADVANTAGES OF NATURAL GAS

- It is cheaper and a cleaner fuel.
- There is no storage problem and it can also be transported safely through gas lines.
- It is of abundant supply and is colourless, odourless, and lighter.
- CNG (compressed natural gas) is used as an alternative to fuel which is eco-friendly.
- It is a reliable source of energy used for running electrical appliances.

DISADVANTAGES OF NATURAL GAS

- Natural gas leakage cannot be detected as it is odourless so inhalation of natural gas is harmful for human body as methane is more dangerous than carbon dioxide.
- It is a non-renewable source of energy.
- The mileage given by CNG run vehicles is lesser than petrol, diesel.
- It is a highly volatile gas.
- Natural gas is mainly found near petroleum reserves so their distribution is not widely spread.

ADVANTAGES OF HYDEL POWER

- Cleanest and cheapest source of energy as it does not emit any harmful gases.
- It is a renewable and sustainable source of energy.
- Apart from generating electricity, hydel power has multiple uses.
- The maintenance cost is lesser.

DISADVANTAGES OF HYDEL POWER

- The cost of installation of hydel power projects are quite high.
- These projects often lead to displacement of people from their land for construction of dams, reservoirs, barrages, etc.
- They may also cause deforestation as huge plots of land is required for their installation.
- Serious geological damage can lead to earthquakes such as for bursting of dams due to human negligence.

NON-CONVENTIONAL SOURCES OF ENERGY

These are energy resources which are renewable, eco-friendly, and inexhaustible in nature. These are expensive at the time of installation but are cheaper in the long run. These include solar energy, wind energy, tidal energy, nuclear energy, biogas, and geothermal energy.

Solar Energy

Sun is the prime source of energy. In a tropical country like India that receives long duration of sunshine almost throughout the year solar energy can be generated and put to great use. Solar energy is used for cooking, heating water, for generating electricity. Solar energy is derived from solar voltaic cells. These cells make up the solar panels. Each solar cell converts the light energy into electrical energy by trapping the sun's rays. Solar cells are used in running calculators, street lights, traffic lights, watches, etc.

Advantages of solar energy:

- It is the most renewable, cleanest, and safest source of energy.
- It has a wide variety of uses as it can be used for cooking, heating, running electrical appliances, water pumps, street lights, etc.
- Its maintenance and repair cost is low as there is no wear and tear.

- It saves electricity bills and can be installed easily in houses especially in rural areas.

Wind Energy

It is a clean, environmental friendly form of energy. Wind energy can be harnessed in coastal areas or grassland where there is an uninterrupted flow of wind. Electricity is generated from wind mills. The wind turns the blades of the mills which in turn rotates the turbines that runs the generator. The installation cost of wind farms are quite high. The largest wind farm in India is found from Nagarcoil to Madurai in Tamil Nadu. Wind mills that are off shore are stronger and generate greater electricity than their counterpart.

Advantages of wind energy:

- It is a clean form of energy as it does not emit any harmful gases.
- The farmers often lend a part of their land for installing wind mills which help them in earning some extra income.
- The electricity bills are also cut down.
- Wind energy is renewable and does not require water.

Tidal Energy

High tides generate electricity in the form of tidal energy. There are tidal stream generators that turns the turbines by using the kinetic energy of the tidal water. The turbines run the generator like that of wind energy but the intensity is more in tidal energy due to greater density of water. The difference in height between the high tides and low tides generates the potential energy used in the tidal barrages. Tidal barrages are the most traditional method of harnessing tidal energy.

Advantages of tidal energy:

- Tidal energy does not release any harmful gases so it is clean and eco-friendly.
- It is a renewable source of energy.
- The maintenance cost is also low.
- Tides are easy to predict and thus reliable. Even if the tidal waters are low there is no difference in generation of power.

Nuclear Energy

Nuclear energy is generated by nuclear fission. The spitting of uranium atoms produces heat that forms steam. This steam turns the turbines that generates electricity.

Advantages of nuclear energy:

- It produces zero carbon emissions and so is pollution free.
- It is safe and reliable and is not dependent on weather.
- Used in wide range of industries from medicine and scientific research to consumer products.
- It is cheaper and convenient to use.

Geothermal Energy

The term 'geothermal' is derived from the combination of two terms: 'geo' meaning earth and 'thermos' meaning heat. So geothermal energy is the energy derived from within the earth's crust. Geothermal energies are often associated with volcanic areas. Hot magma along with steam comes out of the surface in the form of lava through fissures and cracks. This heated lava contains very high temperature as well as energy. This energy is tapped using geothermal power plants. Generally found in areas of hot lava, pipes are fitted that goes down and pulls up the required lava along with steam. The steam that comes out from below is used to turn the turbines that runs the generator.

Advantages of geothermal energy:

- Environmental friendly and does not have carbon emissions.
- Easy to maintain and reliable.

- Renewable source of energy.
- Cheaper in the long run and produces less electricity bills.

Biogas

A reliable source of energy used in rural households, biogas is derived from decomposition of organic matter, animal wastes, manure, vegetative matter without the presence of oxygen thus producing combustible gas. Biogas plants use cow dung in rural areas so are called gobar gas plants.

Advantages of biogas:

- It is a clean, convenient, cheaper source of energy.
- There is no storage problem as there is direct supply of gas to the plant.
- It is a renewable source of energy and is eco-friendly.
- The sludge left behind is used as an organic fertilizer for crops in rural areas.
- Organic manure is also produced.

INDUSTRIES

Industries form the basis of economic development of a nation. Industries are made to cater to human needs as they convert raw materials to more usable commodities. An industry can be a small cottage unit to a huge multinational unit with many factories.

FACTORS SUPPORTING THE GROWTH OF INDUSTRIES

- *Climate:* Needless to say, harsh climatic conditions can never support any industrial growth. For example, cotton textile mills have flourished in the Mumbai–Ahmedabad belt due to its humid climate. Humid keeps the thread strong. Extreme conditions can lead to decrease in human labour efficiency and will also discourage capital investment.
- *Availability of raw materials:* Nearness to the source of raw materials cut down the transportation cost. Industries can develop around a region where there is an easy availability of raw materials. For example, iron and steel industries flourish in regions which are rich in minerals such as coal, limestone, manganese, iron ore, bauxite, etc.
- *Power:* Location of industries depends on uninterrupted supply of power. For example, the location of iron and steel industry depends on regular and uninterrupted supply of coal. Similarly, many industries such as electrical industry, aluminium industry, ores industry, textile mills use hydel power as source of power.
- *Labour:* Both skilled and unskilled labour is required for the location of industries. Labour based industries are benefitted if there is abundant supply of cheap labour. Most of the iron and steel plants in India are concentrated in the Chota Nagpur plateau region that gets abundant supply of cheap labour from the neighbouring densely populated states of Bihar, Jharkhand, West Bengal, and Odisha.
- *Water:* Most of the industries develop in regions that are close to freshwater which can be a major river, canal, or lake. Industries such as textiles, iron and steel, chemical, paper and pulp require large quantities of water at its processing stage.
- *Transportation:* A well-developed transport system is required both for the supply of raw materials as well as for the distribution of finished goods to the market. A huge hinterland of Kolkata and Mumbai has been conducive for the growth of industries in this region. Port facilities also work as an added advantage as ports are needed both for import of raw materials, machineries and for export of finished goods.

- *Market:* Nearness to market is needed for the sale of finished goods. It is of no use if the markets are located far from the production site. It unnecessarily rises the cost of the commodity to the final customer. Heavy and perishable goods such as food items or dairy products must be sold at nearby market.
- *Capital:* Major industries always require huge investments. That is the reason why most of the industries of the world have developed in the major cities where there is regular flow of funds and capital.
- *Banking and loan facilities:* Often industries require huge investment. Banking, loan, and insurance facilities help any new startup. This provide a protective umbrella to the manufacturers, labourers, and investors from any kind of unavoidable losses.
- *Government policies:* The policies set up by the government for industrial growth in the five-year plans provides the base for the economy of the nation. It should aim at removing regional imbalances in industrial growth, generating employment opportunities, elimination of air, land, noise, and water pollution, looking for more sustainable use of resources.

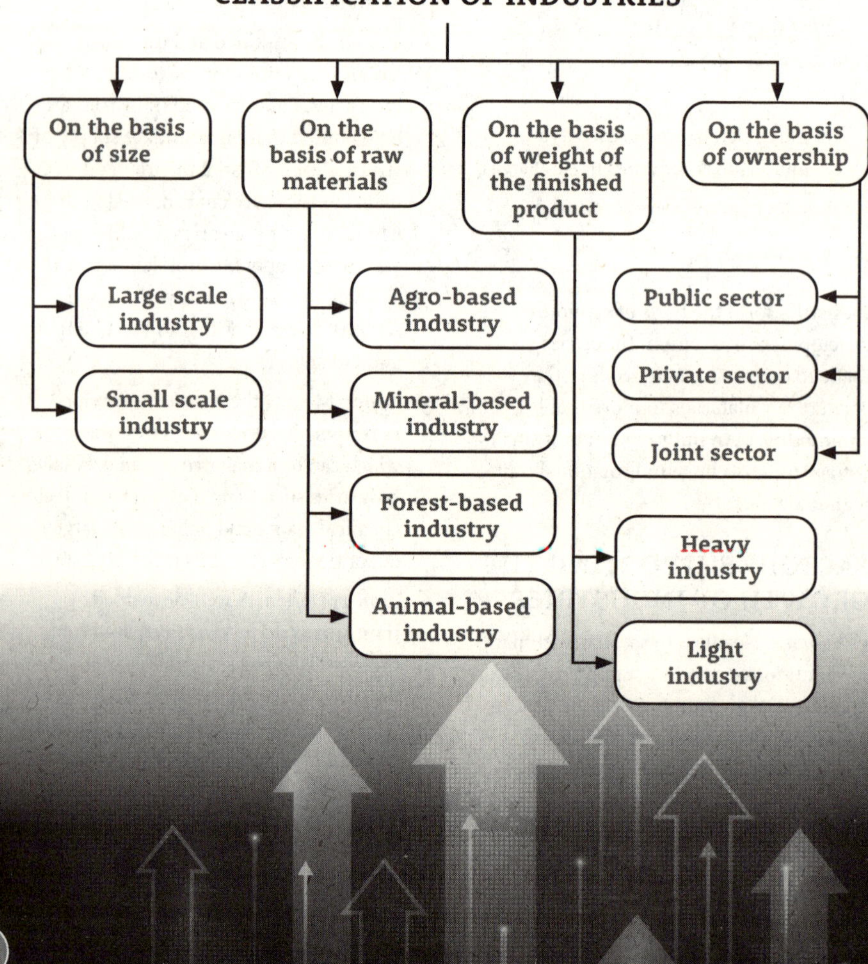

MAJOR INDUSTRIES

Iron and Steel Industry

The overall industrial development depends to a large extent on the growth of iron and steel industries of a country. This is chiefly because iron and steel provides the raw materials for numerous other industries. The location of iron and steel industry is governed by several factors such as availability of raw materials, power, water, cheap labour, nearness to port, market, capital. The iron and steel industries have flourished mostly in China, South Korea, Brazil, and India. The growth of iron and steel industry in china has been phenomenal. Today china produces 17 per cent of crude steel and 24 per cent of pig iron. Japan is the second leading producer of crude steel and pig iron. Although there is a dearth of raw materials in Japan the country mostly uses its port facilities to import raw materials. The finished products are sold in readily available markets.

India: India has a long history of iron and steel plants. The major plants are:

- The first steel plant (**Tata Iron and Steel Company ltd TISCO**) was set up by Jamshedji Tata in 1911 in the town of Sakchi (now Jamshedpur) in then Bihar.

The locational advantages of TISCO helped it to flourish as there were readily available raw materials from the Chota Nagpur plateau region, water from Subarnarekha River and Kharkhai dam, power from Jharia coal field, readily available market from nearby Kolkata, port facilities, cheap labour from the surrounding densely populated states of West Bengal, Bihar, Jharkhand, and Odisha. Jamshedpur was also well connected by dense network of roadways and railways.

- *IISCO:* Located at Burnpur, the Indian iron and steel company is formed due to the joint collaboration of three units at Kulti, Burnpur, and Hirapur. It gets its raw materials like iron ore, coal, limestone, manganese, bauxite from the plateau region, uninterrupted supply of thermal power from DVC, road and rail links as Kolkata is just 200 km away.
- *Bhilai steel plant:* Set up in Durg district of Chhattisgarh, this steel plant was set up in collaboration with the erstwhile Soviet Union. The setting up of the steel plant in otherwise backward district of Durg helped this region as well as its surrounding districts economically. Apart from its raw materials, thermal power is obtained from Korba thermal power station, coal from Jharia and Raniganj coal fields. It is located on the Kolkata Nagpur main railway line.
- *Rourkela steel plant:* Situated in Sundergarh district of Odisha, the Rourkela steel plant was made in collaboration with a German company Krupps and Demag. This plant uses hydel power from Hirakud dam, basic raw materials from Sundergarh, Keonjhar, Jharia fields. Kolkata provides the port facilities and its hinterland serve as the market.
- *The Viswesvaraya Iron and Steel Ltd:* Previously known as Mysore iron and steel company, this steel plant is located on the banks of Bhadravati River in Shimoga district of Karnataka. Previously it used charcoal as source of fuel from the nearby forested regions but now hydel power is used from Sharavati power project.
- The other notable steel plants are:
  - Durgapur steel plant.
  - Salem steel plant.
  - Bokaro steel plant.
  - Vishakhapatnam steel plant (the first shore-based steel plant of India).

Mini Steel Plants

These are decentralized secondary units that uses cheaply available raw materials such as scrap iron and electric arc furnaces for processing. Mini steels help in eradicating regional imbalances in industrial growth. They generate employment opportunities, reduces the pressure of production from the large integrated steel plants. They are easy to construct and do not require much capital investment as their gestation period is shorter. They mainly produce alloy steel and stainless steel.

Textile Industry

Cotton textile industry is the most important among all the textile industries. The locational factors of climate, supply of raw materials, power, water, cheap labour contribute to the growth of this industry. The major cotton textile industry countries are India, China, Pakistan, Japan, and Egypt. The early cotton textile mills flourished in New England region of the United States. The early development of the industry in New England, presence of hydel power and marine climate made this industry flourish there.

China is probably in the second spot. Like in India china cotton textile industry is both hand spun as well as machine spun. The most important centre was Shanghai. It enjoys the facilities of cheap power supply, labour force, large cotton growing areas and output and a vast market. Pakistan is the fourth largest producer of cotton textiles but it faced the wrath of partition when majority of the cotton textile mills remained with India while long staple cotton growing areas went to Pakistan.

India: India's largest organized modern industry is cotton textile industry. Along with China India is the world's leading producer of cotton textiles. Although it faced severe shortage of long staple cotton after partition of the country but it bounced back and today about 15 million people are employed in this sector. Eighty per cent of the cotton textile mills are concentrated in the cotton growing areas. The humid climate, cultivation of raw cotton on black soil, readily available market, labour forces all favour the growth of textile mills in Maharashtra–Gujarat region. Apart from this, cotton textile mills have also developed in Madhya Pradesh, Tamil Nadu, Uttar Pradesh, West Bengal, and Punjab.

FACT FILE

Mumbai is called the Cottonopolis of India and has the largest number of cotton textile mills.

Gujarat is the world's second largest producer of cotton with Ahmedabad as the second largest city in cotton textile production. Ahmedabad is called the Manchester of India.

Challenges faced by Indian cotton textile mills:

- Unavailability of best quality long staple raw cotton.
- Use of old and obsolete technologies.
- Management problems, labour strikes, low pay, and frequent shut downs of mills.
- Erratic and insufficient power supplies.
- Stiff competition from synthetic fibres which are cheaper, power loom, and handloom industries.

Silk Industry

India is the second largest producer of silk after China. Mainly four types of silk are produced in our country – mulberry, tussar, muga, and eri. Raw silk is a very light material so it can be transported easily. China is the leading supplier of silk to the international market. Uzbekistan,

Brazil, Iran, and Thailand are the leaders of silk Industry in the world.

India: The process of growing silk worms and processing silk worms is called **sericulture**. Majority of the silk in India is produced from the silk worms grown on mulberry leaves known as *Bombyx mori*. This industry employs about 55 million people. South India is country's leading silk producer in which Karnataka ranks the list. Tamil Nadu is the leading producer of white silk in the world while Assam leads in muga silk. Several byproducts are also obtained from sericulture apart from silk: mulberry fruits are high on vitamins and minerals, the roots, barks, and leaves are used for making herbal medicines, they are used as a fodder for animals, mulberry branches are used for burning as fuel.

FACT FILE

Bhagalpur in Bihar known for its Bhagalpuri silk is known as the silk city of India. Kanchipuram in Tamil Nadu is called the silk capital.

Challenges faced by Indian silk textile mills:

- Stiff competition from artificial silk and low cost Chinese silk.
- Demand for silk goods has been fluctuating in western market.
- Mulberry silk cultivation has been depleting fast due to lack of government initiatives, less interest among farmers and lack of expertise.

Sugar Industry

Sugar industry is India's second largest organized industry. India is also the leading producer of sugar in the world now followed by Brazil. An important cash crop, sugar industry produces sugar, gur, and khandsari by crushing sugarcane. The other byproducts are molasses, bagasse, and press mud. The major sugar-consuming countries are brazil, India, China, United States, Indonesia, Russia, EU 27.

The world demand for sugar depends on the availability and price of artificial sweeteners, the per capita income, population composition, and concerns for health.

In India, Uttar Pradesh was leading in sugar production but then it lost its position to Maharashtra. The use of old and obsolete technology, unavailability of raw materials, and shorter crushing periods were the reasons. The sugar industry has migrated to south due to the long crushing period, use of modern technologies, system of cooperatives in sugar industry, high sucrose content of the sugarcane.

Challenges faced by sugar industry:

- The prices of sugarcane are fixed by the government so the farmer cannot ear much profit.
- Labour unrest and management problems.
- Seasonal nature of production leads to labour inefficiency.
- The canes of India are not of superior quality as compared to the international standard.
- The demand for gur and khandsari is more in rural areas.
- Transport delay in reaching the sugarcanes to the mills since sugarcane is a weight losing crop so the cane needs to be crushed within 24 hours.

FACT FILE

Uses of the byproducts:

- **Molasses** are used for distillation of rum and ethyl alcohol, as cattle feed, fertilizers.
- **Bagasse** used as fodder or as source of fuel for sugar mills. Bagasse is used as a substitution of wood so used for making printing paper, white writing paper, newsprint, tissue paper, bags and cardboard, biogas or sludge.
- **Pressmud** used for making animal feed, fertilizers, tooth powder, board chalk.

Problems faced by handloom and khadi industry:

- Lack of availability of raw materials.
- Most of the workers are very poor and unskilled.
- Stiff competition from modern fashion and designs in international market.
- Lack of capital investments.

Handloom and Khadi Industry

Khadi means when a clot is woven using hand spun yarn and handloom means when a cloth is woven using machine spun yarn the handloom industry is one of the largest unorganized industries of India the handloom industry is one of the oldest and traditional industries of our country which is upholding the rich cultural heritage of our country through its usage of vibrant colours, patterns that are unique to India. It provides employment to millions of rural households. It also helps the country to earn foreign exchange. The government is promoting this industry globally through organizing fairs and exhibitions across the world platform.

Jute Industry

India is the leading producer of jute in the world market followed by Bangladesh and China. This **golden fibre** helps India to earn foreign revenue and provides employment to more than 40 lacs farmers. Jute industry in India has mainly flourished in the eastern side (West Bengal, Assam, Bihar) due to several factors such as: hot and humid climate which helps in producing high-quality jute, abundant supply of labour, water from Ganga and its tributaries, big market in and around Kolkata, power from nearby coal fields of Raniganj and Jharia.

Why is jute called the Golden Fibre?

Because of its shining lustrous texture, it is 100 per cent biodegradable and helps in earning foreign revenue.

Challenges faced by jute industry

After the partition of India more than 80 per cent of the mills stayed back in India while the jute producing areas went with erstwhile east Pakistan. Due to political dispute, the supply of raw materials was halted.

Two main problems now are high production cost and lack of capital investment.

Labour unrest, fluctuating demand, irregular supply of raw jute due to erratic nature of Indian monsoon.

Aluminium Industry

The second largest industry after iron and steel is aluminium. Aluminium is a good conductor of electricity so it is primarily used in making electrical equipment, aeroplanes, defence, rail coaches, household utensils, etc. The chief factors influencing the location of such industries are the availability of cheap labour, power, and supply of bauxite ores for obtaining alumina. Odisha is the leading bauxite-mining site in India, accounting for more than half of the total production. After Odisha, bauxite is found in the reserves of Ranchi, Palamu districts of Jharkhand.

The major aluminium companies of India are:

HINDALCO (Hindustan Aluminium Company) headquartered in Mumbai, it produces aluminium foil, wires, rolled products, and wheels.

Vedanta Aluminium Ltd, headquartered in Jharsuguda Odisha, this company operates in both Odisha and Jharkhand.

Electronics and Information Technology

The newest Entrant to the list, electronics and IT spreading very fast in India. Bengaluru is known as the IT hub of India. Apart from this the silicon triangle of Bengaluru, Hyderabad, and Pune form the apex of IT growth. Now IT is used in various fields such as medical diagnosis, space exploration, defence equipment, communication, etc.

The period between 1980 and 1990 witnessed the golden period of electronic growth in India. India has a big market for electronic items, price regulations as well as skilled and semi-skilled labour.

India has made tremendous progress in space research and technology. The space research station at ISRO Bengaluru, satellite launching station at Sriharikota and the National Remote Sensing Agency at Hyderabad provides major impetus to space research in the country. Both software as well as BPO (business process outsourcing) industry is booming in the Indian market.

Challenges faced by aluminium industry:

- Use of old and obsolete technology.
- Lack of uninterrupted and easy supply of power.
- Unavailability of bauxite ores.
- Strikes and labour unrest.
- International competition: Indian production lags behind Australia, France, Canada.
- Government sets and controls the price of bauxite that becomes unprofitable for the companies.

TERTIARY ACTIVITIES: TRADE, TRANSPORT AND COMMUNICATION

Trade: Trade involves exchange of goods, services, ideas, and innovations. It involves both import and export that is movement of goods and services from countries having surplus to countries having deficit.

REASONS TO TRADE

- Trade happens when there is difference in the production of manufactured goods: needless to say, natural resources are not evenly distributed all over the world. There are many places which are not well equipped with some basic necessities required for survival. So all these regions have to buy those items from other countries.
- Differences in climate and other natural factors: due to differences in climatic factors such as temperature, rainfall, humidity, agro-based as well as forest-based products differ between countries. Like the agro-based products of tropical countries like India will always differ from those of temperate nations like Canada. So both these countries have to involve in trade to buy each other's items.

- Differences in taste and preferences of the consumers: the taste and preference of the consumers also differ from one country to another that induces trade.
- Differences in the stages of industrial development: all countries are not equally industrially developed. The first-world countries such as the United States and Japan are highly industrialized and some countries such as India are developing and African nations are mostly underdeveloped. These differences cause trade. Goods from modern countries are bought by the less developed or developing countries in exchange for raw materials, agro-based items.
- Differences in transportation and labour skills: trade is always controlled by transportation. Transportation means have also evolved through civilizations so the need for trade has also evolved. Every country cannot possess same set of skilled or semi-skilled labour force. Every country is known for its own inherent skills of people as well as products that represents the culture and heritage of that nation. In the same way, the level of technological development is also not the same in every country. Trade arises when there are differences in this culture, skill, expertise of people.

Types of Trade

Trade can be either internal: when trade happens within a country. International trade: when trade happens across nations.

Common items involved in international trade

CATEGORY	ITEMS OF TRADE
Food items	Grains, pulses, spices, beverages, fruits.
Raw materials	Scrap iron, minerals, cotton, jute, tea, coffee, rubber, timber.
Fuel	Coal, petroleum, natural gas.
Consumer goods	Textiles, medicines, chemicals

WORLD'S MAJOR TRADING ZONES

Europe: Most industrialized and densely populated countries of Europe are found in its western part. International commercial centres at London, Paris, and Rotterdam are considered to be the hub of international trade.

North America: A large volume of trade takes place between the United States and Canada. Developed economy, varieties of consumer durables produced, and richness of natural resources provide impetus for exports between these nations.

World Trade Organization

The major objectives of WTO are:

- To dissolve trade disputes.
- To keep transparency in international trade agreements.
- To enforce rules for international trade.
- To provide the platform for international negotiations.
- To cooperate and coordinate with the other organs of world trade.

Other International Trade Organizations

- Asia Pacific Economic Organization (APEC)
- Association of South East Asian Nations (ASEAN)
- Asia Pacific Economic Cooperation (APEC)
- Organization of Petroleum Exporting Countries (OPEC)

TRANSPORT AND COMMUNICATION

Transport: The movement of goods and people from one place to another takes place through transportation. Transport network of a nation works as the arteries of heart. Just like the arteries pump blood for the body similarly transport plays a vital role in production and consumption.

- Producers produce goods by transporting the raw materials to their production units. These raw materials are processed and made into usable consumer goods. These goods are then transported to the market centres where they are bought by the final consumers.
- The social, cultural, political, and economic development of a nation depends largely on the availability of quick and smooth transport.
- Transport has also helped in decreasing fluctuations in prices.
- The success of industrial revolution in Europe paved the way for revolutionizing transport.
  Roads were developed followed by railways. The primitive method of boats carrying people and goods was also modernized by introducing steam ships, cruise liners, etc. Then came air transport that further shortened the distance between countries.

Modes of transport: There are three principal modes of transport:

Land transport: Both roadways and railways come under this category. A vast network of major roads such as highways and expressways has been constructed throughout the world.

Roadways are more comfortable than railways for shorter distances. Roadways provide feeder to railways as people have to get down at railway stations and use road transport to reach their destination. Roads provide door-to-door services and are good for transporting perishable goods.

When mass movements of people and bulky commodities need to be transported then railways are the most convenient. They are the main movers of goods and freight. Rail transport is comfortable for old people and children.

Air transport, though it is the most expensive and is also weather dependant, crosses every barrier be it mountains, vast seas, or oceans with ease. It helps in reaching far-flung countries at the shortest time possible.

Inflammable objects such as oil, petroleum, or natural gas can be transported through pipelines across nations.

Water transport is of two types: inland waterways (rivers, canals, lakes) and oceanic waterways (seas and oceans).

Water transport is one of the oldest and cheapest means of transport. It is suitable for carrying not only bulky commodities but also a huge number of people. However, there can be several limitations in the form of bad weather conditions, river siltation, unnavigable rivers, etc.

COMMUNICATION

Communication means exchange of ideas, information, thoughts, opinions experiences either verbally or non-verbally between two persons.

Verbal communication means when we are using words to communicate with each other face to face or by email or over telephone.

Non-verbal communication means when we are using sign language or gestures to communicate.

Radio, telephone, fax, email are the different modes of communication used in our daily life.

Important terms to remember:

- Basic industry: that depends on other industries for manufacturing process.
- Consumer industries: that manufacture commodities which are directly sold to the consumers.
- Tertiary industries: which provide public utility based services.
- Ancillary industry: production of spare parts which are used for manufacturing in large heavy industries, e.g., spare parts used in automobile.
- Consumer durables: commodities that are sold to the consumers and do not have to be purchased frequently and can be used for a long period of time. For example, washing machine, television set.
- Enterprise: an organization meant to earn profit that employs people.
- Joint sector enterprise: the ownership, management of such units are jointly done by the government as well as private entrepreneur, e.g., Ipitata Sponge Iron Ltd with TELCO
- Public sector enterprise: the ownership, management of such units is exclusively done by the central/state government, e.g., Steel Authority of India ltd (SAIL).
- Private sector enterprise: the ownership, management of such units is done by individual or group of individuals, e.g., Reliance industries.

Resources and Its Types

Resource refers to any natural substance which is used for human benefit and prosperity. Resources can be land, water, forest, soil, minerals, fish, agriculture, etc. Resources are classified into the following:

- *Renewable resources* are those which can be renewed regularly. For example, water, forest, and land are renewable. There are some renewable resources which are inexhaustible as they have unlimited supply, for example, solar energy, wind energy. Some renewable resources can become inexhaustible if they are not taken care of, for example, fish, forests, freshwater, etc.
- Non-renewable resources are those which are not easy to form and takes many years for their formation. Minerals such as coal and petroleum are all non-renewable resources.
- *Abiotic resources:* Resources which are non-living in nature, for example, land, soil, water, sunshine, minerals, etc.
- *Biotic resources:* Resources which are obtained from the biosphere. For example, plants, animals, human beings, micro organisms, fish from water bodies, birds.
- *Energy resources:* Every human activity as well as work by nature depends on constant flow of energy. Energy can be classified into: conventional (coal, petroleum) and non-conventional sources of energy (solar energy, wind energy).
- *Raw material resources:* These include raw materials needed for manufacturing goods. For example, iron ore, manganese, limestone are used as raw materials in iron and steel industry.
- *Actual resource:* Resources which are known to us and are being used by us at present, for example, coal.
- *Potential resources:* Are those which are known to us but are not being used to the fullest potential at present due to its limited availability (e.g., uranium).

- *Ubiquitous resources:* That is available all over the world and is widely distributed (e.g., water).
- *Localized resource:* That are only concentrated in a particular area like minerals in Ruhr region of Germany, Chota Nagpur plateau region. Several natural factors govern the availability of such resources.
- *Human resources:* Refers to the quality, skills and number of people who have the ability to transform goods, situations and services into anything which has more utility. Human resources are considered to be assets for a country's economy. Man with the help of his expertise, skills, efficiency, labour, judgment, and intellect has the power to transform the society conducive for human prosperity.
- *Economic resources:* Resources that are used for production of goods and services. These include land, labour, capital, and entrepreneurship. Both natural and man-made resources are needed for the growth of an economy.
- *Capital resources:* These include human capital, natural capital, and physical capital. Human capital includes skills, intelligence, expertise of man. Natural capital includes land, water, soil, forests, minerals, etc. Physical capital includes machines, tools, equipment needed for manufacturing.
- Resources that are assisted by technology:
  - *GIS:* (geographic information system) is used to create maps. It is used to collect, store, manipulate, interpret, and analyse geographical date.
  - *GPS:* (global positioning system) is a satellite-based system used for navigation, find locations, track movements on the earth's surface.
  - *Remote sensing:* Used to collect data on the earth's surface. It is used to study land use pattern, create maps and images, study environmental issues.

Conservation of Resources

Safeguarding of our precious resources should be a top priority for us. All natural resources such as land, soil, water, air, minerals, wildlife, forests should be conserved so that the needs of the future generation are not jeopardized. This is called **sustainable development**.

Conservation of resources happen in two ways: ex situ and in situ conservation.

In situ conservation is the one in which the resources are taken care of and conserved in their place of origin. For example, conservation of species, habitat, and ecology.

Ex situ conservation is the one out of their natural habitats.

Conservation of resources in which there should be judicious use of the resources to avoid any form of wastage can be done in the following ways:

- Preservation and maintenance of biological hotspots.
- Maintain and create buffer zones between man-made and natural land use.
- Conservation and protection of threatened species of plant and animal life.
- The three R's: Reduce, Reuse, and Recycle.

- *Reducing*: Here reducing means reducing the amount of wastage or judicious use of resources. For example, we should only buy things that is enough for us to live. Reducing our needs would also mean reducing the amount of garbage so reducing wastage. Reduce our uses of polythene, plastics, disposables, etc. which are harmful to the environment.
- *Reusing:* When we are reusing something for its original purpose or for some other purposes without dismantling its originality. For example, when we are reading our daily newspaper and after reading instead of disposing it off we are using that paper to wrap small furniture, crockery items, or any household items. Similarly, donating our old books and clothes to underprivileged children is also an example of re-use.
- *Recycling*: When we are changing the form of an already used commodity to make something new that might enhance its utility, it is called recycle. For example, we are recycling our plastic bottles, soda cans, making paper bags out of newspapers, making gardening pots from old containers, etc.

BIO GEOGRAPHY

The study of biosphere is called bio geography. Margaret Anderson has rightly remarked that biogeography is **'the essence of biological relations between man (considered as animal) and the whole of his animate and inanimate environment'.**

BIOSPHERE

This is that part of the earth that supports and contains living organisms. The biosphere consists of both living and non-living organisms and there is a constant interaction and flow of energy between the living beings and the physical environment and also within the living organisms themselves. The upper limit of the biosphere is determined by the availability of oxygen, suitable temperature, pressure conditions, and moisture. The lower limit of the biosphere is determined by the availability of water and light that is needed to sustain life. The deepest roots of the trees that can sustain life and micro organisms, the depth of the oceans and the deepest of the oceanic trenches that can sustain marine life are the lowermost extent of the biosphere.

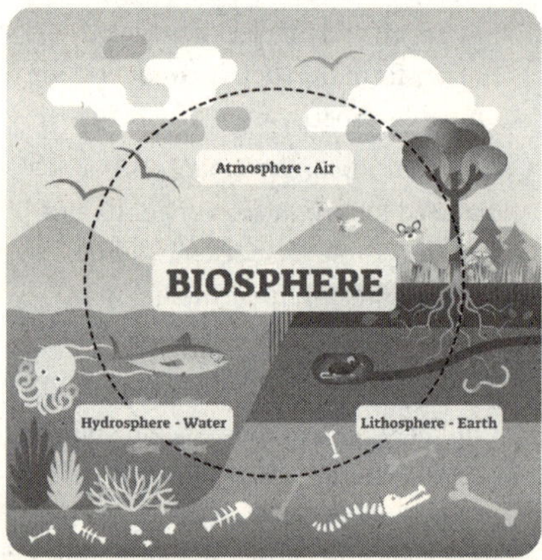

The biosphere is always affected and modified by the constant flow of energy. These factors are called modifiers. These are of three types: physical modifiers, chemical modifiers, and biological modifiers. The physical modifiers affect the physical properties of the atmosphere in the form of climate change, temperature, humidity changes, etc. When chemical elements of soil, water, or climate are modified they are called chemical modifiers. Biological factors affect the population, land use, distribution of animals.

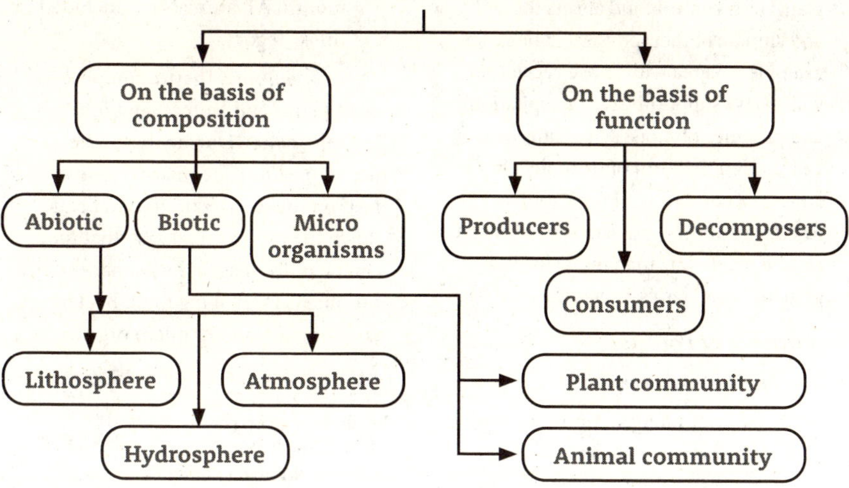

Abiotic Components

- *Lithosphere:* Consists of land, rocks, soil, minerals, erosional, transportational, and depositional features produced by exogenetic forces, mountains, plateaus, plains formed by endogenetic forces on and below the earth's crust. The earth's surface is a storehouse of minerals. Different land form features on and below the earth's crust adds to the dynamicity of the planet. The forces on and below the crust are constantly acting upon each other leading to the creation, transformation, destruction and recreation of features. Soil is an important component of the lithosphere. Soil made up of breaking down or disintegration of rocks and its particles form the base on which plants grow. Soil acts as the reservoir of nutrients for living organisms.
- *Atmosphere:* All the essential gases needed for the survival of the biosphere is provided by the atmosphere. The atmosphere filters the incoming solar radiation to the earth by preventing the harmful UV rays of the sun from reaching the earth. The atmosphere gives us all the weather phenomena be it temperature, rainfall, humidity, air pressure, winds, cyclones, anti-cyclones air currents, etc.
- *Hydrosphere:* Water is an essential component for all forms of life. Water is needed for the circulation of nutrients among the different components of ecosystem. Water is available as surface water or groundwater. Surface water is the one found in seas, oceans, lakes, rivers, streams, ponds, tanks, and reservoirs. Ground water is found in the underground reserves known as aquifers the hydrosphere also include the deep sea features such as continental shelf, continental slope, abyssal plains, oceanic trenches, coral reefs, atolls, etc.

Biotic Components

- *Plant community:* The social groupings of plant species are plant community. Plants are the primary producers since they produce their own food through the process of photosynthesis. Plant community includes plants of different species or a single species. There is a constant interaction between plants and their physical environment and also within themselves. Plants develop their own habitat depending on several factors of the environment. While soil and climate are the most significant ones, plants also controls and affects the soil and climate of their physical habitat. For example, an area with dense vegetation will always support heavy precipitation and presence of moist soil. Plants can be found in the form of naturally grown large area covered with vegetation as forests, meadows, grasslands or they can also be planted by man in the form of gardens, sanctuaries, nurseries.

Importance of Forests

- Forests increase precipitation.
- It helps in controlling soil erosion, erosion by wind, surface run off, and floods. The dense root system of trees helps in binding the soil particles together.
- Forests help in recharging underground water reserves.
- Forests are the natural habitats of rich wildlife.
- Forests act as the natural sink of carbon dioxide. They help in absorbing the greenhouse gases and helps in moderating temperature. It purifies the air. It is the source of food and shelter for both humans and wildlife.
- It helps in controlling air, water, and land pollution.
- *Animal community:* The animal community consist of autotrophs or plants and heterotrophs that depend on autotrophs for their food. The heterotrophic animals are also called primary consumers. These animals are further classified into:
  - *Saprophytes* are those animals that feed on the decayed remains of dead plants and animals. Example: plant fungus.
  - *Parasites* are those that depend on other plants and animals for their survival. Example: protozoa.
  - *Holozoic* animals are those which consume their food through their mouth. All animals are included in this category.
  - *Micro organisms:* They decompose dead plants and animals and other organic matter. During this process of decomposition, the micro organisms feed on the decayed parts and break down the organic matter so that they can be utilized again by primary producers for making food. Bacteria and fungi fall under micro organisms.

FACT FILE

Producers: green plants which manufacture their own food through photosynthesis and nutrients from the soil through their roots.

Consumers: includes man and other animals. They can be either herbivores (primary consumer that feed on plants only), carnivores (secondary consumer that feeds on primary consumer), and omnivores (that feed on both).

A deer is an herbivore, a lion is a carnivore, man is omnivore!

Decomposers: which decompose and feed on dead plants and animals.

ECOLOGY

DEFINITION

Haeckel has rightly defined ecology as 'the **study of the reciprocal relationship between living organisms and their environments**'. The word 'ecology' is derived from the combination of two Greek words: 'oikos' meaning home and 'logos' meaning study.

THE DIFFERENT FIELDS OF ECOLOGY

The concept of ecology can be applied in various fields whether it is in population, human behaviour, climate, human genetics, meteorology, etc. Ecology is divided into two broad categories: autecology and synecology.

Autecology: Auto means self so this ecology studies a particular species.

Synecology: 'Syn' means together, so this ecology studies a group of organisms. Basically autecology studies a particular species and its relation to the physical environment, the habitat in which it grows. Synecology is concerned with the study of the composition, characteristics, structure, and distribution of a group of organisms.

The Fields of Ecology

- *Paleoecology:* Studies the origin of plants and animals, past geological periods, and the different eras of evolution of flora and fauna.
- *Population ecology:* Studies the number of species in the ecosystem, their inter relationships, the factors influencing their distribution and growth.
- *Habitat ecology:* The study of habit that includes forests, grasslands, oceans, rivers, deserts, etc.
- *Cytoecology:* Studies the cytological details that is the microscopic cell structure of the organisms of the population species in relation to their physical environment.
- *Ecosystem ecology:* Studies the structure and function of an ecosystem, how they are inter related with each other, their functions, and inter relationship between the biotic and abiotic components.
- *Conservation ecology:* Studies the protection and management of natural resources so that the needs of the future generation are not jeopardized.
- *Production ecology:* Deals with the production of energy, conversion of energy, and the flow of energy through organisms which is essential for the survival and growth of organisms.
- *Radiation ecology:* Study of radioactive substances and the positive and negative impact of radiation for human welfare.
- *Gene ecology:* Studies the genetics of the population, the origin and evolution of species.

The Principles of Ecology

- Man being the most important member of an ecosystem has the power to change, modify the natural environment by using the resources efficiently or inefficiently. He can either introduce new farming techniques, cause deforestation, construct buildings, cultivate and introduce new breed of vegetation, or change habitats.
- Ecological study depends on the study of the ecosystem which is the most vital unit.
- Living organisms are always interacting with each other and influence each other. Similarly, they also interact with their physical environments.
- Sun is the prime source of energy for all organisms. Solar energy is needed for the process of photosynthesis. The flow of energy from the sun is non-cyclic and unidirectional. This flow also helps in the circulation of nutrients within the different trophic levels.
- There is a constant loss of energy as one moves up the trophic level.
- Productivity of an ecosystem refers to the rate of growth of organisms per unit per time by green plants through photosynthesis with the help of solar energy. It depends on how much solar energy is used or available and the efficiency of the plants to convert the solar energy into chemical energy.
- The ecosystem productivity decreases from the equator towards the poles due to lesser amount of solar rays received at the poles.

What is climax vegetation?

The vegetation community that has developed at the end of succession. This happens when the vegetation passes through several phases and ultimately reaches an equilibrium. Now this vegetation community will remain unaltered unless disturbed.

ECOSYSTEM

DEFINITION

Ecosystem has been recently defined by E. P. Odum (1971) as **'living organisms and their non-living (abiotic)environment are inseparably interrelated and interact upon each other. Any unit that includes all of the organisms (i.e., the community) in a given area interacting with the physical environment so that a flow of energy leads to clearly defined trophic structure, biotic diversity and material cycle (i.e., exchange of materials between living and non-living parts) within the system in an ecological system or ecosystem'.** So in simpler words, we can say that ecosystem is the process of interaction between organisms and their environment.

Types of ecosystem

NATURAL ECOSYSTEM	ARTIFICIAL ECOSYSTEM
Operate all by themselves without any human interferences. They can be terrestrial ecosystems such as forests, grasslands, deserts, or marine ecosystem such as oceans, rivers, etc.	These are maintained by man and his activities such as agriculture – cultivation of crops which modifies both the physical and social environment.

CHARACTERISTICS OF ECOSYSTEM

- Ecosystem is the sum of all living organisms and their physical environment in a given area.
- It is composed of abiotic, biotic components.
- It occupies a well-defined area.
- There is always an interaction between the organisms and among the organisms.
- These are natural resource systems.
- There is a continuous input and output of energy and matter.
- Sun is the prime source of energy.
- Ecosystem has a dimension or a particular unit area. It can be a small space such a little pond or as big as a desert.
- It is well organized and structured.

STRUCTURE OF AN ECOSYSTEM

The structure of an ecosystem is related to diversity of species. Greater the species diversity more is the complexity of the ecosystem. The structure of an ecosystem includes the species, their composition, numbers, their history, space, distribution as well as the distribution, quantity, nature of the non-living things.

FUNCTIONS OF AN ECOSYSTEM

The functioning of an ecosystem depends on the energy flow. The flow of energy is unidirectional while matter flows in

a cyclic path. Sun is the primary source of energy. The green plants or primary producers absorb the solar energy to produce food through the process of photosynthesis that converts the solar energy into chemical energy. This chemical energy helps in the production of food by the autotrophs. This is called **trophic level 1.** Some amount of energy is lost through respiration by the plants. This energy of the autotrophs is consumed by the animals of the first order or herbivores or primary consumers. Herbivores use this energy for building their own tissues. This is called **trophic level 2**. These are again transferred to the carnivores (secondary consumers). This is called **trophic level 3.**

- It is important to note that not all energy is transferred from plants to herbivores or from herbivores to carnivores. Some amount of chemical energy is lost through respiration.
- More the level of the animals more complex will be the transfer of energy, as animals of higher order will need more energy to perform their activities than the animals of the lower order.

Some portion of the energy is then transferred from trophic level 3 to **trophic level 4** that is the omnivores. Man is an important example of omnivores. They are also known as tertiary consumers.

Man takes energy from trophic level 1 as well as 2 also.

Some portion of energy is lost through respiration by omnivores. The stored chemical energy of the remains of dead plants and animals is transferred to the decomposers. These decomposers absorb the energy released by both plants and animals. The decomposers then release a substantial amount of energy to the atmosphere.

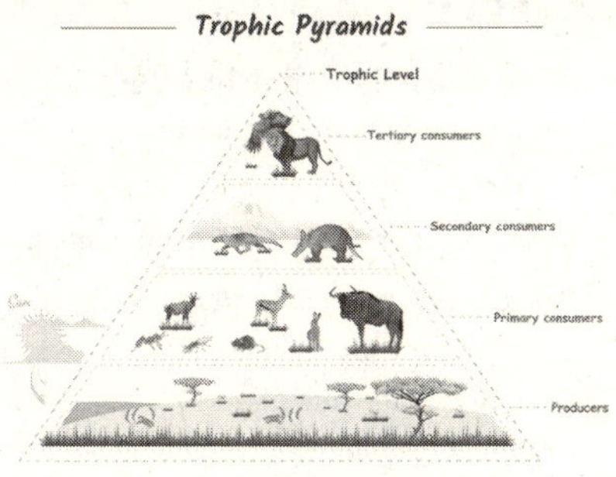

Matters or nutrients flow in a cyclic manner. Both organic and inorganic substances move in the biosphere, hydrosphere, lithosphere, and atmosphere through systems of cycle in such a way that the total mass of all the substances remains the same. The inorganic elements comprise waste materials as well as the dead remains of plants and animals. Plants derive energy from the sun as well as from the roots and soil through root osmosis. This is used to produce food and for development of tissues. The nutrients, derived through the roots of the plants, are then transferred to the various components of the biosphere through biogeochemical cycle.

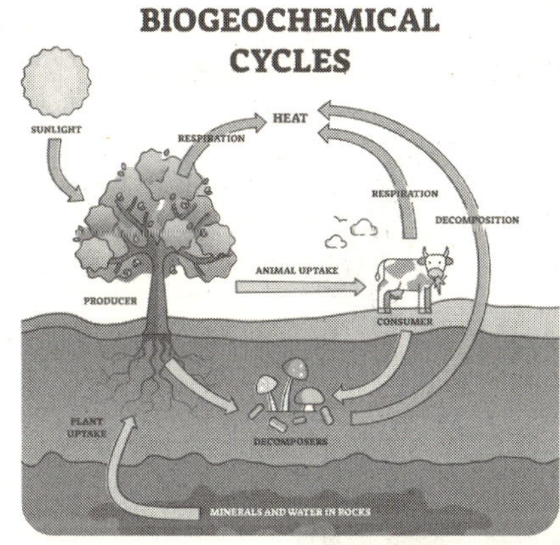

THE PRODUCTIVITY OF AN ECOSYSTEM DEPENDS ON FEW FACTORS

- Availability of the amount of solar radiation to the green plants.
- The efficiency of the plants to convert the solar energy into chemical energy.
- The climate governing the nutrient supply in the area, interactions between the organisms, role of various levels of organism hierarchy.

There are three levels of primary productivity in the world:

1. Regions of high primary productivity: these include tropical rainforests, shallow water bodies, alluvial plains, intensive cultivated areas.
2. Regions of low primary productivity: permafrost areas.
3. Regions of intermediate productivity: grasslands, lakes, extensive farming areas.

BASIC CONCEPTS OF FOOD CHAIN, FOOD WEB, TROPHIC LEVELS

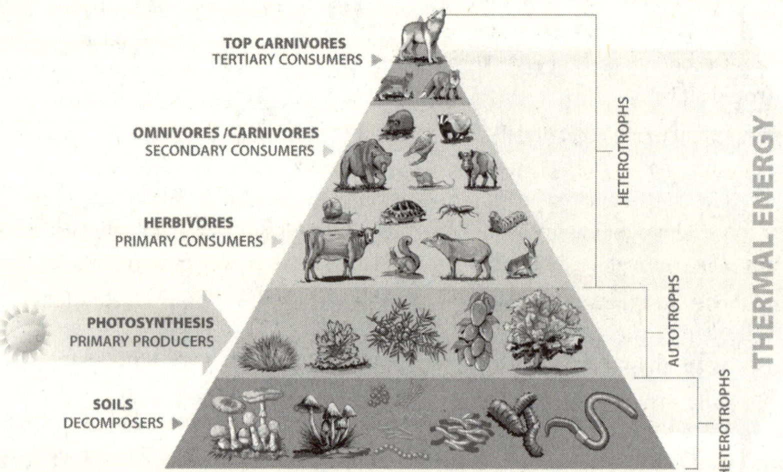

TROPHIC LEVEL

The chain of transfer of food energy from one group of organisms to the other is known as the trophic level.

What is a food chain?

The chain of transfer of energy from one group of organisms to the other in an ecosystem.

- *Trophic level 1:* This is the base of the food chain. It is composed of the green autotrophic plants. Green plants use the chlorophyll in them to absorb solar energy, water, carbon dioxide, and nutrients to produce food through the process of photosynthesis. They use the energy to build plant tissues. The green plants are the source of food for all organisms of the upper trophic levels.

- *Trophic level 2:* This includes organisms which cannot produce their own food but depend on green plants for their survival. They are herbivorous or primary consumers. This includes cattle, goats, sheep, grasshoppers, deer.
- *Trophic level 3:* These are the carnivores or secondary consumers. They feed on the primary consumers. They can be either land animals such as lion, tiger, eagles, or animals living in soils such as bacteria, fungi which feed on the decomposed and decayed remains of dead animals and marine animals such as sperm whales, sea otters.
- *Trophic level 4:* These animals are called omnivores. They take food from all the other levels as tertiary consumers. Man is the perfect example of an omnivore since man derives energy from either plants or by feeding on animals on second and third trophic levels.

What is a food web?

The process of transfer of food energy from one level to another is not a simple one and is complex process. There are several interconnected overlapping food chains. Such a food chain is called food web. For example, grass is eaten by grasshoppers. Grasshoppers also feed on grains. Rats feed on both. Owls feed on both grasshoppers and rats. Similarly, rabbits can feed on both grass and grains.

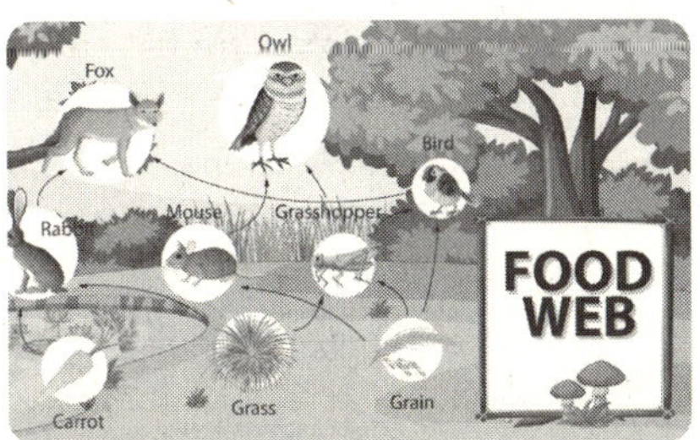

Food web maintains the stability of the ecosystem. More complex the food web, more will be the interdependence between the organisms and more will be the stability of the ecosystem.

The complexity of the food web depends on certain factors:

Length of the food chain: The food chain becomes longer if there is more diversity in the organisms. When a particular level acts as an alternative to animals belonging to multiple trophic levels, this will make the food web more complex.

Ecological Pyramids

As already mentioned before, at each step in the food chain, the organisms never consume the total amount of energy from its previous level. Some amount of energy is lost through respiration. So every organism passes on lesser amount of energy to the next level. Higher the trophic levels, lesser will be the energy available for the final members. This decrease in the amount of energy at the higher levels creates a tapering form in the shape of a pyramid. This is called an ecological pyramid. The base of the pyramid is broad because it contains many organisms while as one goes to the top the number of organisms decreases.

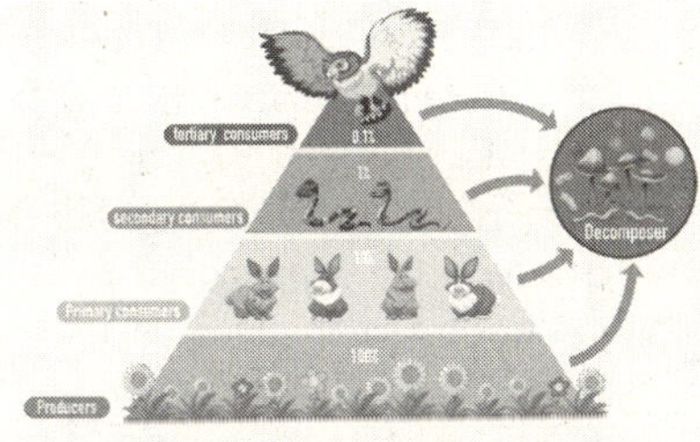

SIMPLIFIED ECOLOGICAL PYRAMID

TYPES OF ECOLOGICAL PYRAMIDS

- *Pyramid of numbers:* When only the number of species are included it is called pyramid of numbers. The base of the pyramid consists of autotrophs which are larger in number. On its top lies the primary consumers at trophic level 2 which are larger in size and comparatively lesser in number. (For example, at trophic level 1 lies grass. Grasses are found in thousands of blades which are fed by a single cow at trophic level 2.) Similarly at level 3 lies the secondary consumers which are lesser in numbers than trophic level 2 but the size gets bigger. Thus in this kind of pyramid, the size of animals gets bigger as one goes up and the numbers also deteriorate towards the top.

- *Exception to the law:* This happens in the forest ecosystem. Forest consists of many large trees. A single tree can be fed on by large number of herbivores at trophic level 2. So the base of the pyramid is tapered and broader at trophic level 2 due to many herbivores. A single tree can be consumed by many birds, hyperparasites, and parasites as primary and secondary consumers.
- *Pyramid of biomass:* When the weight of the organisms is taken into consideration it is called biomass pyramid. The shape of the pyramid implies the decrease in the biomass at each trophic level from the base to the apex. The total biomass of the producers is more than the primary consumers and the biomass of the primary consumers is more than the secondary ones. Since some amount of energy is always lost at each trophic level, the amount of biomass difference depends on the rate at which the energy is stored below.
- *Pyramid of energy:* When the total amount of energy used at each trophic level is taken into account it is called pyramid of energy. At trophic level 1 the amount of energy will be more than at trophic level 2. The primary producers may have smaller biomass but the amount of energy conserved and transferred may be greater than the organisms of trophic level 2 which may have a bigger biomass. The loss of energy through respiration is also maximum at the base and decreases towards the top.

ENERGY PYRAMID

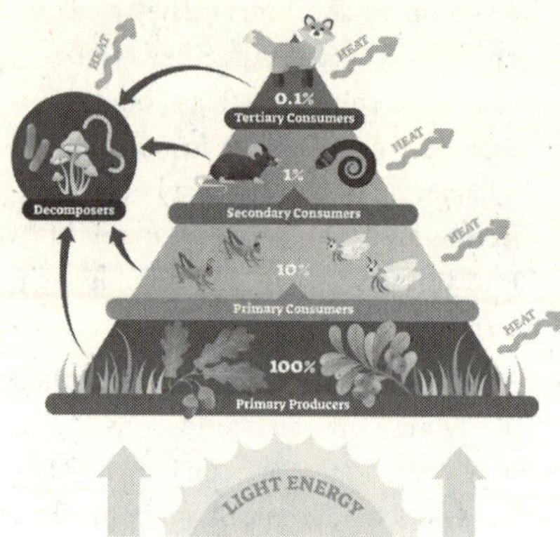

CIRCULATION OF MATTER

HYDROLOGICAL CYCLE/ WATER CYCLE

The hydrological cycle involves the following steps:

- Evaporation of the water from oceans, seas, lakes through insolation.
- The conversion of the water into water vapour through the process of condensation.
- The movement of the atmospheric moisture over seas and continents by air circulation.

- The release of the water back to earth through precipitation either in the form of snowfall or rainfall.
- The eventual returning back to the water to the seas and oceans.

When there is precipitation, the water that is directly falling on the oceans and seas are called **direct fall.** Some amount of rain also falls on vegetation and reaches the ground. The amount falling on the ground gets lost through surface runoff or can get percolated through the pores and crevasses into the underground.

FACT FILE

The hydrological cycle involves the movement of water across oceans, continents, and atmosphere but around 95 per cent of the total moisture of the biosphere is never available to the cycle. Only 5 per cent is available. Out of this 5 per cent, 97 per cent is stored in oceans, 2.15 per cent stored in the form of polar ice caps, 0.62 per cent in the form of groundwater, and 0.03 per cent in the form of freshwater lakes, rivers, and ponds.

Carbon Cycle

There are three phases of the transfer of carbon in the biosphere.

1. Gaseous phase: carbon in the form of carbon dioxide in the atmosphere.
2. Liquid phase: dissolved carbon dioxide in water.
3. Solid phase: carbon stored in fossil fuels, organic matter.

There are two ways in which the movement of carbon takes place. Either it takes place as gaseous phase in which the carbon dioxide moves as gas in the atmosphere and in dissolved form in water or as non-gaseous phase in which the carbon is stored in fossil fuels or in rocks.

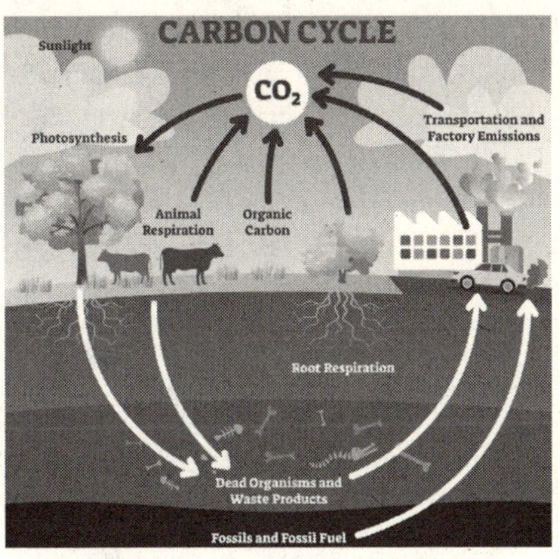

- The carbon dioxide enters the biosphere from the atmosphere through the process of photosynthesis with the help of sunlight by the green plants. The component which provides energy is called donor component and the one receiving the energy is called recipient component. The transfer of carbon from the donor to the recipient components is a two-way process. The the amount of carbon dioxide absorbed by the plants depends on the density of vegetation, activities, other natural factors, and concentration of CO_2 in the atmosphere.
- The carbon dioxide absorbed by the plants are stored in the tissues and barks of the tree as organic reservoir. This carbon is released due to breakdown of carbohydrates during respiration from living organisms. The respiration converts the carbohydrates to gaseous carbon dioxide that returns back to the atmosphere.
- Some amount of carbon dioxide is released back when there is a breakdown of the carbohydrates by the animals of trophic level 2, 3, and 4.
- Even decomposers break down the carbon to carbon dioxide.
- The sedimentary reserves store carbon in the form of fossil fuels, organic

matter for a long geological period of time. When these rocks are weathered or eroded and fossil fuels are burnt, the carbon dioxide is released back to the atmosphere.

FACT FILE

It is important to note that in carbon cycle the amount of carbon that is released back to the atmosphere is more than the amount removed. This is due to human interferences where deforestation and burning of fossil fuels increase carbon dioxide concentration, leading to global warming.

Oxygen Cycle

Oxygen is a vital element for living organisms as it supports life. Oxygen is a chemically active element because it easily combines with majority of elements in the biosphere. There are different forms of oxygen from the atmosphere to the biosphere: molecular oxygen, water, carbon dioxide, inorganic compounds such as oxides (ferrous oxides, calcium carbonates).

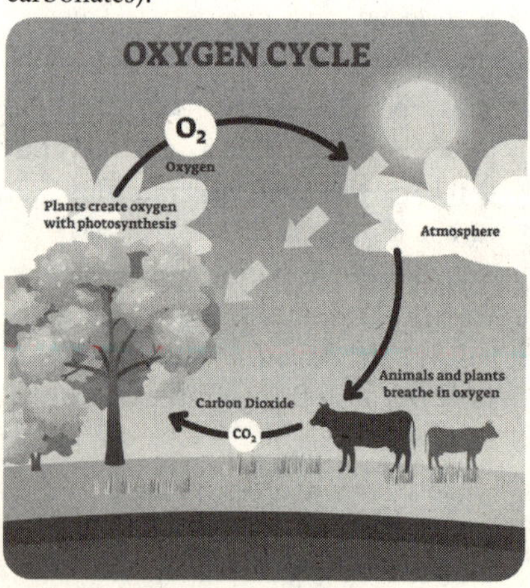

- Green plants release oxygen into the atmosphere at the time of photosynthesis.
- Some amount of oxygen is released into the atmosphere through volcanic eruptions.
- This oxygen is then utilized by the animals of terrestrial and marine ecosystem for respiration.
- Some amount is consumed during burning of fossil fuels.
- Some amount enters the sedimentary rock reservoirs through oxides.

THE MAJOR NATURAL REGIONS OF THE WORLD

What is a biome?

A large natural ecosystem consisting of an assemblage of plant and animal community is a biome.

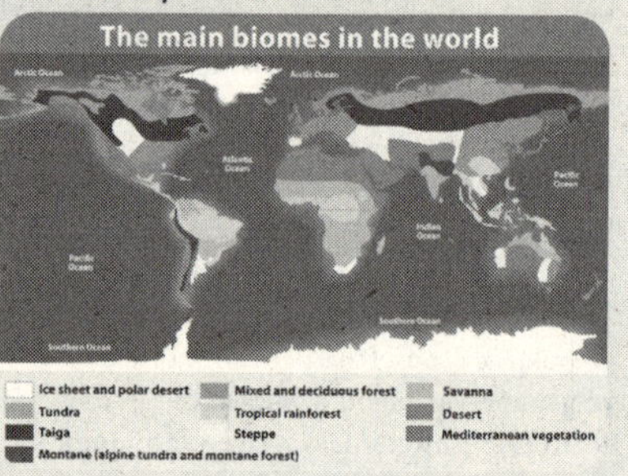

TROPICAL EVERGREEN RAIN FOREST BIOME

- *Location and extent:* This biome extends between 10° N and 10° S latitudes. This biome is the richest one in terms of its luxuriant plant growth and diversity in animal life since it remains hot and humid throughout the year. The equatorial regions of Congo basin, Amazon basin, the forests of the SE Asian countries come under this biome.
- *Climate:* The mean annual temperature remains about 20°C throughout the year. The average annual rainfall is about 200 cm. There are no seasons and the diurnal range of temperature is low. The length of days and nights is almost equal. Rainfall is of convectional type. It rains almost every day late afternoon which is known as 4 o'clock showers.

- *Plant life:* Numerous species of plants are found in this biome. Mostly evergreen, hard wood, and broad-leaved trees are found here. The rainforest is covered with big trees, creepers, climbers, and epiphytes. Each vertical layer of the forest presents a new and a different strata of plants from the soil surface to the upper most forest canopy. The typical trees found here are mahogany, ebony, rosewood, rubber, and cinchona.

  The first layer or the topmost strata: It is the uppermost canopy of the tallest trees of the forests. The canopy looks like an umbrella. This layer receives the maximum amount of rainfall and sunshine. The height of the tallest trees can be high as 60 m. This is the emergent layer.

  The second layer or the canopy layer: It is found below the first layer and has a height of about 20–35 m.

  Third layer: Here the height of the trees is about 15–20 m. Here the leaves are broad in surface area to trap as much sunlight possible. The amount of sunshine and rainfall decreases at this layer due to the thick and dense growth of the trees above. This is the under storey.

  Lowest layer or the forest floor: The absence of sunlight makes the ground layer very dark and moist. It consists of only few shrubs, grasses, and creepers that grow on taller trees.

RAINFOREST LAYERS

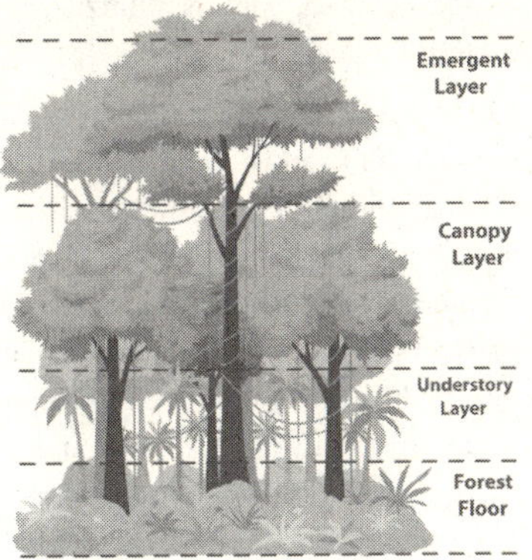

Animal life: This biome is full of different varieties of animals. The animals in this biome have some typical characteristics: since there is an abundant supply of food throughout the year, the animals found here are least mobile. They are larger and bulkier in size and are found to occupy the various strata of the forest. The floor of the forests are filled with large ground animals like deer, elephants, bisons, gorillas, wild pigs, leopards, tigers, etc. Most of the animals are arboreal such as monkeys, squirrels, etc. There are varieties of birds too like parakeets, toucans, barbets.

MONSOON DECIDUOUS FOREST BIOME

- *Location and extent:* This biome is associated with the monsoon biome and is found in the belts of south and South-east Asia except the equatorial zone, Northern Australia, and Eastern Africa.

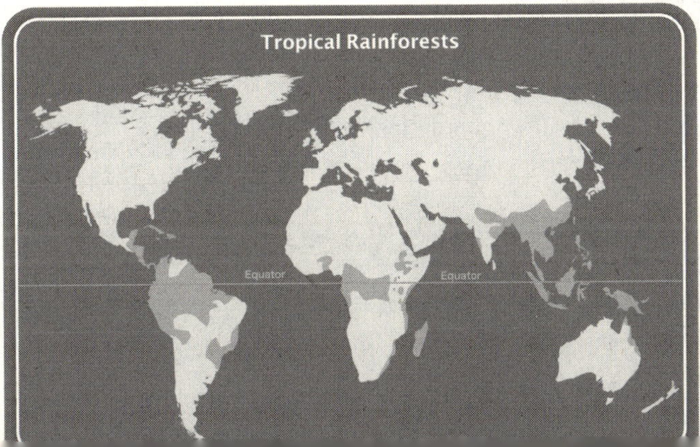

In addition, localized pockets are found in South Africa, Southern Brazil, South-eastern United States.

- *Climate:* The temperature ranges between 38°C and 45°C which is the maximum during summers. The average annual temperature during summers that are hot and humid stays between 20°C and 30°C. Rainfall mainly occurs during the southwest monsoon period from July to September and there is spatial variation in the amount of rainfall received. The mean annual rainfall is around 150 cm. The winters are cool and dry. Only few regions receive rainfall during winters from the retreating monsoon winds.
- *Plant life:* Most of the trees found here are deciduous in nature. The height of the trees ranges between 12 and 30 m. Trees are found in pure stands and are broad leaved; that is, the leaves are broad enough to absorb maximum water during the rainy season. The trees shed their leaves during the dry season to conserve moisture. The barks of the trees are thick, hard, and rough. There are also climbers in the form of epiphytes. The typical trees found here are sal, teak, rosewood, mango, neem, shisham.
- *Animal life:* The variety of animal species in the tropical deciduous forests are lesser than the equatorial rainforest. The animals range from small sizes like squirrels, rats to large and bulky ones like bisons, elephants, tigers, wild pigs, wild buffaloes, and different species of birds too. This region also sees a lot of migratory birds from the Arctic during its cool short winters.

TEMPERATE GRASSLAND BIOME

- *Location and extent:* The temperate grasslands are mainly found in the interior of the continents where the off-shore westerlies keep the climate hot and dry. The grasslands are treeless. In the Northern hemisphere, the grasslands are hot and dry while in the Southern hemisphere they have a comparatively better climate due to the maritime influences of the surrounding seas.

The Different Names of the World Temperate Grasslands

- Prairies – North America.
- Pampas – South America.
- Veldts – Africa.
- Downs – Australia.
- Canterbury – New Zealand.
- Steppes – Europe.
- *Climate:* In the Northern hemisphere the temperate grasslands have extreme climate because of its interior location and scanty rainfall while in the Southern hemisphere the climate is maritime. Summers are warm and temperature ranges between 20°C and 30°C. Winters are very cold and severe in the Northern hemisphere. The temperature in January is from −18°C to 10°C; the average annual rainfall ranges between 25 and 75 cm throughout the year in different locations of the temperate grasslands. Winter sees snowfall in the land-locked areas in the extreme north.
- *Plant life:* Grasses dominate the grasslands. The lack of rainfall makes the grasslands almost treeless. Different species of grasses are found in the temperate grasslands depending on the rainfall, location, temperature, and soil. The Australian Downs comprise a mixture of grasses and eucalyptus trees. The winter season is warmer here than their counterpart in the Northern hemisphere.

The North American Prairie are found between the foothills of Rockies to the temperate deciduous forest in the east. The tall grass prairie having a height of 1.5–2.5 m (bluestem), mixed prairie having grasses of height 0.6–1.2 m (needle grass/little blue stem), and short grasses of about 60 cm.

- *Animal life:* Herbivores mainly dominate the grasslands. Large mammals such as buffaloes, deer, antelopes and gazelles, kangaroos, emu (downs) are found in the grasses. The mammals are large and bulky in order to protect themselves from predators like wolves, leopards. Burrowing animals such as rats, moles, mongoose are found. They dig holes in the soft soils to store food and protect themselves from the extreme winter. There has been modification in the animal life of the grasslands. Large-scale hunting and deforestation to make way for agriculture has led to the disappearance of animals from this region.

SAVANNA

- *Location and extent:* Found between 10° and 20° latitudes in both hemispheres. It includes the Llanos of Venezuela and Columbia, Brazil, Paraguay of South America, Sudan, and other parts of Central and East Africa.
- *Climate:* The temperature remains high throughout the year with abundant sunshine. The cold dry season is characterized by day temperature of about 26°–32°C and night to be around 20°C. The warm dry season is marked by 32°–38°C. The amount of rainfall depends on the distance from the equator. The savanna grasslands close to equator, for example, the savanna grasslands of Brazil gets an annual rainfall of about 70–200 cm.
- *Plant life:* The savannas are dominated by tall grasses and herbaceous plants. The grasses are hard, rough, dominate the ground layer and generally attain a height of about 80 cm and sometimes up to 500 cm like the African elephant grass. Few trees of savanna have distinct characteristics which help them to reduce water loss through evapotranspiration so they remain green even during dry periods. The roots are long in order to penetrate deep into the ground to take underground water. Baobab tree is a significant tree found in the savannas.

- *Animal life:* The African savanna has the most variety of animals. Large herbivorous mammals such as zebra, giraffe, buffaloes, elephants, antelopes are found here. The Australian savanna is dominated by marsupials such as kangaroos, wallaby. Toucans, parakeets, kingfishers, woodpeckers, doves are common in South American savannas. There are also large variety of invertebrates found in the savannas like insects (locusts, grasshoppers, crickets) and arthropods (scorpions, spiders).

TROPICAL DESERT

- *Location and extent:* The tropical deserts are found on the western margins of the continents between 15° and 30° latitudes north and south of the equator. The flow of off-shore trade winds in the western margins of the continents makes the regions dry and hot. The regions include Sahara Desert (Africa), Namib and Kalahari (southern part of Africa), the deserts of Thar, Iran, Arabia (Asia), Peruvian (South America), Californian, Sonoran, Mexican deserts (from Mexico USA in North America), the Great Australian Desert in Australia.
- *Climate:* Extremes of temperature are found in deserts. The summers are hot and winters are cold. In summer the temperature ranges between 30°C and 45°C while in winter the temperature sometimes goes down to less than 15°C. The diurnal range of temperature is also very high. Frost is common in winter. In some areas the summer temperature shoots up to 58°C. The reason for high temperature at day is the absence of vegetation cover and the land absorbs heat very fast. While at night the long cloudless skies promote high terrestrial radiation causing the drop of temperature. Rainfall is scanty receiving less than 25 cm of annual rainfall. The off, shore trade winds and cold ocean currents make the climate dry. Local winds like sirocco, mistral, bora may bring pleasant weather conditions and can cause short wet spells in the coastal parts.
- *Plant life:* Because of the scanty rainfall and dry conditions, the kind of natural vegetation found in deserts are of **xerophytes** type. These are adapted to the natural arid conditions as they have long roots, thick barks, waxy leaves. They are mostly stunted trees that are leafless and have a strong odour to protect themselves from the grazing animals. The typical plants are cacti, date palms, prickly pear, acacia, grasses, and shrubs.

- *Animal life:* Burrowing animals are found in large numbers such as rats, snakes, squirrels. These animals protect themselves from the heat by staying indoors. Apart from these, camels, jackals, hyenas, antelopes are common.

MEDITERRANEAN BIOME

- *Location and extent:* This biome extends between 30° and 45° N and S latitudes in the western parts of the continents. The regions are lands around the Mediterranean Sea, central Chile of South America, central and Southern California of USA, the coastal lands of Africa and Asia bordering the Mediterranean Sea, some coastal parts of western and southern Australia.
- *Climate:* Summers are hot and dry while winters are cool and wet. Summers are sunny and the temperature during summer ranges between 20°C and 27°C. The temperature at winter ranges between 5°C and 10°C. Rainfall is received at winter due to the shifting of pressure belts ranges between 30 and 60 cm.
- *Plant life:* The vegetation of this biome has naturally adapted to survive the hot, dry summers. The trees have long roots, thick stems, waxy, smaller leaves to prevent the loss of water through evapotranspiration. The common trees found here are Karri, Jarrah varieties of eucalyptus, oak, chaparral shrubs, and several varieties of garden flower plants. With the advent of modernization, today the Mediterranean lands are known for the widespread cultivation of citrus fruits such as grapes, olives, oranges.
- *Animal life:* The animals found here are mainly mule deer, wood rats, squirrels, coyote, lizards, snakes, fox, rabbits. Most of the native mammals have now disappeared due to clearing of forests for farming. The Australian region can see kangaroos, wallaby, and mice. The typical birds are whistlers, honeyeaters, robins, etc.

TAIGA REGION

- *Location and extent:* It lies between 55° and 60° N in the Northern hemisphere. It merges with the tundra in the north around the Arctic circle. The region experiences continental climate so only conifers are found on the uplands of Europe, Russia, and North America. The regions include Northern Siberia, Southern Canada, Southern Alaska (North America), Sweden, Norway, Finland.

- *Climate:* The winters are very long and severe and the summers are shorter and warmer. Summers last for only 3–4 months, rainfall ranges between 25 and 100 cm. It mainly occurs as snowfall in winter since the temperature remains below the freezing point. Frost occurs in august. Rainfall is evenly distributed throughout the year. Cold anti-cyclones in the form of blizzards or snow storms blow all during winter.
- *Plant life:* The most dominant trees are evergreen conifers. These are naturally adapted to survive in the long chilly winters. They are found in continuous belt from North America to Asia. These trees are soft wooded, have needle shaped leaves and downward drooping limbs which help in snow shedding. Some broad leaved trees such as birch, willows are also found. The dominant trees are pines, spruce, cedar, oak, elms, and maple. The southern part of the taiga sees a smooth transition from conifers to temperate mixed vegetation due to slight rise in temperature.
- *Animal life:* The extreme winter makes wildlife difficult in the taiga. Only few species are found in the boreal/taiga forests such as Siberian fox, salamander, Canadian toad, wood frog, etc. They mostly hibernate in winter. Large number of herbivores mammals are found in taiga such as caribou, reindeer, wild boar, snow sheep. Small mammals such as beaver, squirrel, chipmunk, predatory mammals that travel to long distances to catch prey are also found such as European lynx, Siberian weasel, wolf, red fox, arctic fox, polar bear, black bear, Siberian tiger, etc. Many migratory birds from taiga region migrate to the warmer south to escape the harsh winters.

TUNDRA REGION

- *Location and extent:* The word 'tundra' means barren land. It includes the parts of Alaska, northern parts of Canada, Northern Siberia, the coastal strips of Greenland. The severity of climate causes change in the vegetation rapidly below the tree line. The tundra is found between the southern limit of the permanent ice caps in the north to the northern limit of taiga in the south.
- *Climate:* The climate is characterized by severe winters, very low temperature throughout the year, little insolation. The tundra remains a barren land due to severity of climate. The below freezing point temperature leads to permafrost. Precipitation occurs as snowfall below 40 cm. Winters are very long and severe and summers are cool. The region experiences 6 months of day light and 6 months of night due to its location at the poles.
- *Plant life:* During summers when the temperature rises a little, mosses and lichens grow on the soil. The vegetation found in tundra are **cryophytes** – the ones that are naturally adapted to survive in the harsh cold weather. Most of these are stunted plants with a height of about 5–8 cm. These plants do not grow tall and remain sticky to the surface to protect themselves from the blizzards.

- *Animal life:* Both resident as well as migratory animals are found in this biome. The resident animals have thick furry coat around their bodies that protect them from the severe winter. The thick coat acts as an insulator which is impervious to cold. For example, the American musk ox. The musk ox shed their heavy coat at summer to adjust with the warm summer. The arctic fox has much thicker fur coats to withstand the winter. Arctic fox can survive and remain active even during long winters. The resident birds have feathers that work as insulators.

  The migratory birds leave the tundra in autumn and are the first ones to come back in early spring. These include geese, ducks, swan. These birds do not have special features to protect themselves from the severe winter. The Arctic tern is the longest flying migratory bird. It flies from the Arctic tundra all the way to the Antarctica in the Southern hemisphere. The migratory animals include reindeer and caribou. These animals come down to the taiga biome to spend the winters.

MAJOR ENVIRONMENTAL ISSUES OF THE WORLD

- *Global warming:* The gradual rise in the temperature of the earth is called global warming. Global warming is related to the **greenhouse effect**. A greenhouse is a special glass house used in temperate regions where plants are kept. The house is made up of glass that traps the incoming solar rays and do not allow the rays to radiate back. This keeps the room warm and suitable for plant growth. Similarly, the increased concentration of several gases such as carbon dioxide, methane, carbon monoxide, chlorofluorocarbons, water vapour, nitrous oxide allows the solar rays to penetrate but does not allow outgoing terrestrial radiation. This results in the rise in the global temperature. The rise of greenhouse gases is due to burning of fossil fuels, deforestation, mining, burning of biomass, etc. It is estimated that if the greenhouse gases continue to rise in this way then the global temperature will rise by about 1.5°–4.5°C in the next 50 years and it will pose a serious threat to life.

Major greenhouse gases and their sources

GREENHOUSE GASES	SOURCES OF THE GASES
Carbon dioxide	Fossil fuel burning, deforestation, land use changes, release by plants and animals during respiration.
Methane	Garbage dumps, freshwater swamps, biomass burning, flooded paddy fields, enteric fermentation in cattle.
Chlorofluorocarbons	Non-toxic stable compounds used in making refrigerators, aerosol propellants in spray cans, insulators, fire extinguishers, air conditioners, production of plastic foams
Nitrous oxides	Biomass burning, agriculture (use of nitrous fertilizers), nylon production, livestock waste, contaminated ground water.

CONSEQUENCES OF GLOBAL WARMING

- *Rise in sea level:* Global warming causes rise in sea level due to melting of polar ice caps and glaciers. Melting of ice caps lead to global changes in water circulation. This is because the melted ice causes freshwater influx in seas and oceans. The freshwater which is less saline and less dense forms a layer at the surface thus preventing the pattern of deep ocean currents from rising to surface.

- *Rise is surface temperature of the oceans:* It causes coral bleaching and changes the pattern of rainfall distribution.
- *Change in weather patterns:* Global warming causes extremities in climate either desertification or severe floods. Stronger and frequent storms, warmer weather leading to higher rate of evaporation of water leading to cloudbursts or severe rainfall. There will be areas experiencing incidences of droughts due to rainfall failure.
- *Effects on animals and humans:* Warmer winters leads to death among animals who are adaptable to cold weather. The human health complications cannot be avoided. Agriculture will be affected as with rise in temperature, many places that were previously used for growing a particular type of crop will experience crop failure.
- *Ozone (O_3) depletion:* Ozone is an inorganic compound consisting of three atoms of oxygen instead of two. The stratospheric ozone is useful for us as it prevents the harmful ultra violet rays of the sun to reach us. However, the excessive use of CFCs and HFC (hydrochlorofluorocarbons) causes depletion of ozone layer. They release chlorine and bromine into the atmosphere that remove an oxygen atom from the ozone molecule with the help of sunlight. The 03 depletion leads to exposure to UV rays, skin cancer, eye cataracts, crop failure, spread of tropical diseases.
- *Urban heat island:* A metropolitan area that is comparatively warmer than its surrounding rural areas due to human activities. This difference in temperature is felt more at night than at day and when the wind is weak. Urban areas are considered to be concrete jungles. They promote surface run off, cutting down of trees for construction of bridges, buildings generating heat. Furthermore, increased concentration of pollutants in the lower layers of the atmosphere causes lesser outgoing terrestrial radiation.

CONSEQUENCES OF URBAN HEAT ISLAND

- The air quality deteriorates by increasing the concentration of pollutants such as carbon monoxide and ozone.
- Length of growing seasons is increased, incidences of cloud bursts or severe storms can occur.
- Excessive humidity in air leading to human discomfort, extended summers.
- *Pollution:* Certain substances when added to air, water, soil which are responsible for causing harmful or undesirable effects are called pollutants. These pollutants tend to cause damage to human or animal life and can pose serious threat to comfortable enjoyment of life, health, and society. Pollutants can either be from natural or manmade sources. Let's know about the sources and level of **air pollution.**

SOURCES OF AIR POLLUTANTS	EXAMPLES
Natural	Volcanic eruptions, natural forest fires, dust storms.
Man made	Factory smoke, burning of fossil fuels, combustion, transport.
Point sources	Volcanic eruptions, forest fires, Industrial activity, power plants chemical units, oil refineries, incineration plants, etc.
Non point sources	Hospitals, residential areas, disposal of wastes, agricultural operations, transport sector, emission of smoke.

LOCAL LEVEL	REGIONAL LEVEL	NATIONAL LEVEL	GLOBAL LEVEL
Waste disposal, sewage, burning of wood, coal.	Large-scale industries. Transport, emission of smoke.	Acid rain	Global warming, ozone depletion, radioactive pollution.

Sources of water pollution

SOURCES OF WATER POLLUTANTS	EXAMPLES
Natural	Runoff, volcanic activities, earthquakes, landslides, mudslides.
Man made	Domestic, medical sewage, industrial effluents, municipal waste, radioactive, mining wastes.

GEOGRAPHY OF INDIA

THE ORIGIN OF INDIA

The peninsular plateau of India was a part of the Gondwanaland which covered Australia, India, South America, and South Africa. The breaking of Gondwanaland millions of years ago led to the northward shifting of the Indo-Australian plate. The Indian plate collided with the Eurasian plate. This caused the formation of the fold mountains: the Himalayas.

Location and extent of India: The mainland of India extends between 8°4′ and 37°6′ N latitude and 68°7′ and 97°25′ E longitude. The **Tropic of Cancer** (23°30′ N) divides India in almost two halves. The total length of the Indian coastline is 7,517 km. The tapering shape of the Indian peninsula divides the Indian Ocean into two water bodies: the Bay of Bengal to the east and the Arabian Sea to the west.

The relief of India: There are six major physiographic divisions of India:

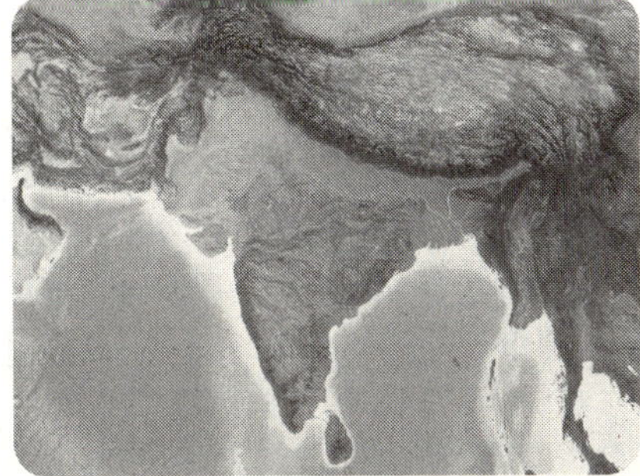

1. *The Himalayan mountain system:* The northern mountain wall stretches for about 2,500 km from Kashmir in the north to Arunachal Pradesh in the north east and extends as Arakan Yoma in Myanmar. The Himalayas act as a climate divide. It prevents the cold chilly winds of the north to enter India and also prevents the south-west monsoon winds to escape from India. The Himalayan mountain system can be divided into the following sections:
   - ➢ The Greater Himalayas or the Himadri with average peaks rising up to 6,000 m. Here lie the lofty Mount Everest and Kanchenjunga.
   - ➢ The Lesser Himalayas or the Himachal with average peaks as high as 4,000 m. Here lie the famous hill stations like Mussoorie, Shimla, and Nainital.
   - ➢ The outer Himalayas or the Shiwaliks. Here lie the duns: Dehradun and Patlidun.
   - ➢ Purvanchal covering the parts of north Bengal and north-east states.
2. *The northern plains:* The northern plains are formed by the deposition of alluvium brought down by the major river systems of India. The rivers – the Ganga, Indus, and Brahmaputra along with their tributaries – have their origin from the melting of glaciers in the Himalayas. The northern plains are subdivided into:
   - *The Punjab plains:* Formed by the deposition of alluvium by river Indus and its tributaries, the major part of it lies in Pakistan.
   - *The Ganga plains:* Spreads across the states of Haryana, Uttar Pradesh, Bihar, Jharkhand, Delhi, and West Bengal.
   - *The Brahmaputra plains:* Covers major parts of Assam and north-east states.
3. *Peninsular plateau:* The oldest landmass of India the plateau was formed due to the northward shifting of the Gondwanaland. The plateau is subdivided into:
   - *Central highlands:* North of Narmada river lies this highland and covers a large part of the Malwa plateau.
   - *Deccan plateau:* Lies to the south of Narmada river. It has a triangular feature taking the shape of the Indian peninsula bordered by the Western Ghats and Eastern Ghats in the west and east, respectively. The slope of the land is from west to east. The highest altitude at the Western Ghats is 1,600 m, while at the east it is around 600 m. The northern part is bordered by the Satpuras.
4. *The Great Indian desert:* The Thar Desert is the driest part of the country. The state of Rajasthan and parts of Gujarat are occupied by the Thar Desert. The desert is undulating sand plains with rolling sand dunes.
5. *Coastal plains:* The outer edges of the Western Ghats and the Eastern Ghats comprise of the western coastal plains and the eastern coastal plains. The western coastal plains is much narrower and it lies between the Arabian Sea to its west and the Western Ghats to its east. It is subdivided into:

- The Konkan plain covering states of coastal Maharashtra and Goa.
  - ➢ The Kannada plain covering the coastal part of Karnataka.
  - ➢ The Malabar Coast covering Kerala.
  - ➢ The eastern coastal plain is much broader it lies between the Bay of Bengal to its east and the Eastern Ghats to its west. It is further subdivided into:
    - *The Northern Circars:* Covering the districts of coastal Odisha.
    - *Coromandel coast* Covering the coastal strip of Tamil Nadu.

6. *Island group:* This include the two group of islands namely the Andaman and Nicobar Islands on the Bay of Bengal and Lakshadweep Islands on the Arabian Sea. The Lakshadweep islands are group of coral islands. The Andaman and Nicobar islands are larger in size and are an archipelago (chain of islands). They have rich biodiversity and are volcanic in origin.

FACT FILE

The northernmost limit of India is the Indira Col (Jammu and Kashmir) and the southernmost limit of India is Indira Point (Andaman and Nicobar).

The southernmost tip of the Indian peninsula is the Cape Camorin.

The westernmost point is Sir Creek in Kutch of Gujarat.

The easternmost point is south-east of Dong (Kibithu) in Arunachal Pradesh.

The Drainage System of India

The Indian drainage system comprises of some major rivers that either flow in the northern part of the country or flow in the peninsular part of the country. Interesting to note that majority of the rivers flow into the Bay of Bengal. This shows the general slope of the land is towards the east. Seventy-seven per cent of the drainage area consists of the rivers Ganga, Brahmaputra, the Mahanadi, Krishna, Kaveri, and Godavari that drains into the Bay of Bengal. Rest 23 per cent comprises of the Indus, Narmada, Tapi, Mahi, Periyar that drain into the Arabian Sea.

THE HIMALAYAN DRAINAGE SYSTEM

- *The Indus river system (1,114 km in India):* A Himalayan river, the Indus, has its origin in the glacier of Tibet in the Kailash mountain range. The lower part of the Indus has five tributaries: the Beas, Satluj, Chenab, Jhelum, and Ravi. The Indus discharges into Arabian Sea at Karachi. The largest tributary is Chenab. Jhelum is an important tributary that flows through Srinagar and Wular Lake into Pakistan. Although the majority of the tributaries of Indus flows through Pakistan the Satluj feeds the canal system of the Bhakra Nangal project helping Punjab, Haryana, and Rajasthan.
- *The Ganga (2,525 km):* The Ganga originates from the Gangotri glacier at Gomukh in Uttarakhand. At Devprayag the Bhagirathi joins the Alaknanda and forms the Ganges. The Ganga is one of the largest river systems of the world. It benefits the states of Uttar Pradesh, Uttarakhand, Bihar, and West Bengal. The longest tributary of Ganga is the Yamuna which has its own set of tributaries: Chambal and Betwa. The major left bank tributaries are Gomati, Gandak, Ghaghara, Ramganga, and Kosi. Son is the major right-bank tributary.

The Chambal is infamous for its badland topography called the **Chambal ravines**.

- *The Brahmaputra (916 km in India):* Originates from Chemayungdung Glacier near the Manasarovar lake. In Tibet, the Brahmaputra is called the Tsang Po. The Brahmaputra enters India through the Sadiya district.

  The Brahmaputra has its mouth in Bangladesh where it merges with the Padma river and forms the Ganga Brahmaputra delta, the largest in the world. The major right-bank tributaries of the Brahmaputra are Subansiri, Manas, Sankosh. The left-bank tributaries are Lohit, Dibang, Dihing, and Dhansiri. In Bangladesh, the Brahmaputra is called the Jamuna where it joins the Tista.

THE PENINSULA RIVER SYSTEM

- This system is older than the Himalayan river system. The Godavari (1,465 km) or the Dakshin Ganga is the largest peninsular river.
- The Godavari originates from the Trimbakeshwar near Nasik and falls into the Bay of Bengal. The Godavari covers the states of Maharashtra, Madhya Pradesh, Chhattisgarh, Odisha, and Andhra Pradesh.
- The second largest east-flowing river of Peninsular India is the Krishna. It originates from Mahabaleshwar in Western Ghats. The Krishna drains the states of Karnataka, Andhra Pradesh, and Maharashtra.
- The Kaveri originates from the Brahmagiri hills and mainly drains Tamil Nadu, Karnataka, and Kerala.
- The Mahanadi (851 km) an important river of Madhya Pradesh, Chhattisgarh, and Odisha falls into the Bay of Bengal.
- The Narmada (1,312 km) is a major west flowing river of the Peninsular India that has its origin in the Amarkantak plateau. The Narmada flows in a rift valley between the Satpuras and Vindhyas. It drains into the Arabian Sea near Gujarat.
- Tapi originates from Betul district of Madhya Pradesh and falls into the Arabian Sea.

FACT FILE

Luni is the longest river system in Rajasthan. The Luni originates near Pushkar in Aravallis as two branches: Sabarmati and Saraswati. The Luni falls into the Arabian Sea near Rann of Kutch.

CLIMATE OF INDIA

The climate of India is tropical monsoon type.

Factors Influencing the Climate of India

- *Latitude:* The Tropic of Cancer divides India into two halves. The northern part experiences temperate cool climate while the southern part experiences tropical part.
- *Role of the Himalayas:* The Himalayas acts as a climate divide. It prevents the cold chilly winds of the north to enter India and also prevents the south-west monsoon winds to escape from India.
- *Distance from the sea:* The sea exerts maritime climate on the coastal areas. The regions that are far away from the sea experience continental climate.
- *Altitude:* The regions that lie on higher altitude will always have a cooler climate than plain lands. This is due to normal lapse rate. Both Siliguri and Darjeeling lie in the same state of West Bengal and are three hours apart but Darjeeling experience cold climate throughout the year due to its high altitude.
- *Distribution of land and water:* Land heats up and cools down easily than water. India is a peninsula surrounded by water bodies on its three sides. The difference in the rate of heating and cooling of land and water causes different air pressure zones in the subcontinent. This difference triggers the monsoon mechanism.
- *Relief:* Relief affects the temperature, distribution of rainfall, wind movement, and air pressure. The presence of Western Ghats causes the windward side receiving heavier rainfall than the Deccan plateau. The Deccan plateau acts as the rain shadow region as it lies between the Western and Eastern Ghats.

Similarly, the south-west monsoon winds of Bay of Bengal branch blows parallel to the Eastern Ghats so the Tamil Nadu coast remains practically dry during the summer monsoon.

Seasons of India

- The cold weather season (winter season)
- The south-west monsoon season (rainy season)
- The retreating monsoon season
- The hot weather season

➢ *Winter season:* During winter, a high-pressure zone develops over the Indian land mass. This high pressure creates a flow of air towards the Indian subcontinent. These are westerly jet stream blows across the Asian landmass parallel to the Tibetan plateau. The jet stream gets divided into two branches due to Tibetan plateau. One branch moves north of the Tibetan plateau and the other to the south of the Himalayas. The temperate cyclones originating over the Mediterranean Sea brings rainfall to western and north-western India.

➢ *Hot weather summer season:* At this time an inter tropical convergence zone (ITCZ) moves northward parallel to the Himalayas. The ITCZ is the zone of low pressure. The apparent migration of sun at the Tropic of Cancer leads to the gradual rise in temperature. April, May, and June are the summer months. Hot, dry, dusty winds called loo blow over the northern plains. At this time, Kalbaisakhis or Norwesters brings showers in the months of April and May that brings temporary relief from the summer heat. These are called Bardoli Cheerha in Assam, mango showers in Kerala. These seasonal storms are good for early ripening of mangoes, for the cultivation of jute.

➢ *The south-west monsoon season:* The easterly jet steam is most active at this stage. It triggers the formation of tropical depressions. The south-east trade winds get deflected after crossing the equator and enter the Indian peninsula as two branches: the Bay of Bengal branch and the Arabian Sea branch. The windward side of the Western Ghats receives more rainfall.

➢ *The north east monsoon season:* The monsoon winds now retreat back move from land to sea due to differences in pressure conditions. The Coromandel Coast gets rainfall in winter as the winds passes over Bay of Bengal picks up moisture and shed rain over there.

FACT FILE

- *Burst of monsoon:* The sudden onset of monsoon associated with heavy rainfall, thunder and lightning.
- *Break of monsoon:* The dry spell when there is no rainfall for several days or weeks.
- The amount of rainfall decreases from east to west and from coast to the interiors. This is due to the increasing distance from the source of moisture-laden winds.

The Significance of Jet Streams

- The westerly jet streams bring rainfall in winter to the western and north-western parts of India. This rain is beneficial for the cultivation of wheat crop.
- The subtropical easterly jet stream blows at summer bringing some rain at this time.
- The subtropical jet stream blocks the monsoon cell situated between the South Asia and Indian Ocean. In summer, the jet stream deflects northwards and crosses Himalayas. This triggers the formation of monsoon cells over the Indian Ocean. The cell is filled with moisture by a low-level tropical jet stream.

Water resources of India: The Indian peninsula is known for its rich water resources. Apart from the three vast water bodies on its three sides, the country is endowed with several freshwater lakes, lagoons, backwaters, gulfs, and strait.

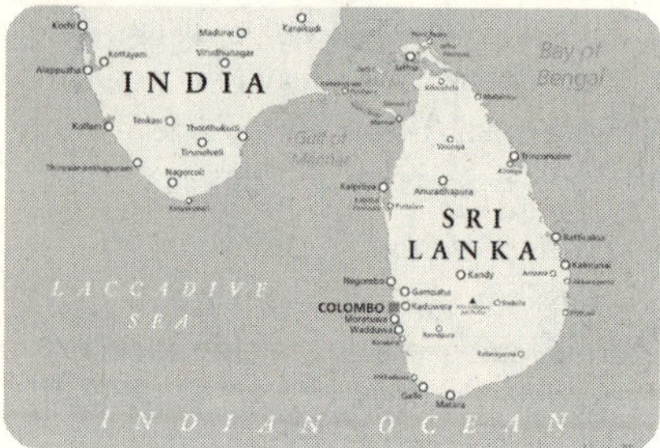

- *Gulfs:* Gulf of Kutch, Gulf of Khambhat, Gulf of Mannar.
- *Straits:* Palk Strait separating India and Sri Lanka, 10 Degree Channel separating the Andaman and Nicobar Islands.
- Smaller seas are the Andaman Sea and the Laccadive Sea.
- The largest salt water lake of India: Lake Sāmbhar in Rajasthan.
- *Other lakes:* Vembanad Lake in Kerala, Loktak Lake in Manipur, Dal Lake in Kashmir, Chilika Lake (lagoon) in Odisha.

Other Valuable Resources of India

Mangrove forests: Seven per cent of the world's mangrove cover is found in India. Mangroves are special variety of trees that have breathing roots or pneumatophores. The roots grow upward to protect themselves from sinking under water at high tides. In India, mangroves are found in Sunderban delta, Andaman and Nicobar Islands, Gulf of Kutch, deltas of Godavari, Krishna and Mahanadi rivers. The Sunderban is the world's largest mangrove forest encompassing the Ganga Brahmaputra delta. The majority of it lies in Bangladesh, this forest type has been recognized as the UNESCO World Heritage Site. The Sunderban is known for its rich flora, fauna the most famous being the Royal Bengal Tiger. The forest is named after sundari tree – a special variety of tree that produces durable hard wood used for making boats, houses, furniture, and firewood.

The north-western Gujarat is known for the **Rann of Kutch**. It is a salt marsh known all over the world for its white sand look. The Rann hosts international kite festival every year at Makar Sankranti that attracts tourists all over the world.

SOILS OF INDIA

Indian Soils Are of the Following Types

- *Alluvial soil:* It covers the largest area of India. These soils are formed due to the deposition of silt brought down by the rivers in the northern plains of India from Punjab to Assam valley. These soils are thus called riverine soils. They are generally fertile but lack nitrogen and are renewed every year by fresh alluvium. Alluvial soil is used for the cultivation of rice, jute, maize, sugarcane, pulses, and wheat.
- *Red soil:* It is the second largest soil group of India. It develops on crystalline metamorphic rocks; red soils are found in areas of low rainfall. The red colour is due to the presence of iron oxides. Wheat, cotton, tobacco, oilseeds grow on this soil. This is found in Tamil Nadu, Odisha, and Chhattisgarh.
- *Black soil:* Formed due to the weathering of volcanic lava rocks the black regur soil is found extensively over the Deccan plateau covering the states of Maharashtra, Karnataka, Andhra Pradesh, and some parts of Gujarat. Black soil has high water retention capacity and also develops cracks in summer. These cracks help in air circulation. Black soil has self-ploughing abilities. It is rich in iron, lime, calcium, and potassium but poor in nitrogen. The soil is good for the cultivation of cotton, pulses, and sugarcane.
- *Laterite soil:* Formed in areas of alternating periods of heavy rainfall. Laterite soil is formed due to intense leaching. Heavy rainfall leaches way the major nutrients making the soil unproductive. The humus content is low and organic matter is removed by bacteria at high temperature. The soil is mainly used for making bricks, for construction purposes, the crops grown on this soil are rice, ragi, cashew nuts, and tea. The laterite soil is found in some parts of Odisha's Eastern Ghats, some parts of north-eastern states, Western Ghats.
- *Desert soil:* Found in arid and semi-arid areas, contains a lot of salt. The soil is deficit in humus and moisture. Desert soil is found in Rajasthan, some patches of Gujarat.

DISTRIBUTION OF LIFE ON LAND

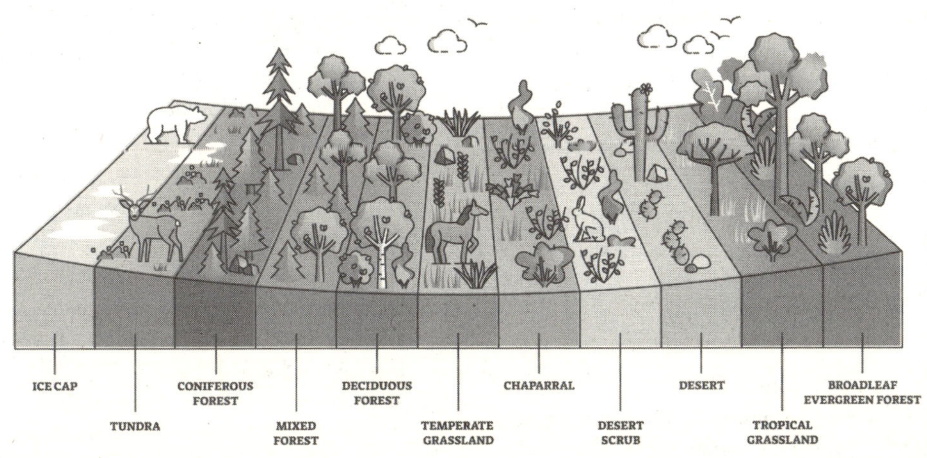

Natural vegetation of India

NATURAL VEGETATION OF INDIA	CHARACTERISTICS	LOCATION
1. Tropical evergreen rainforest	Trees are evergreen. Difficult to exploit, bear hard, durable, and fine-grained timber. Example: rosewood, mahogany, ebony, chaplas, gurjan.	Western slopes of Western Ghats, hills of NE states, island groups of Andaman and Lakshadweep.
2. Tropical deciduous forest	Most commercially exploited forest as they provide valuable timber. Example: teak, Sal, arjun, mahua, palash, neem, mulberry. Dry deciduous forest include rosewood, Sal, thorny bushes, bel, khair.	Foothills of Himalayas, Jharkhand, West Bengal (moist deciduous). Scattered along the foothills of Himalayas and Tamil Nadu (dry deciduous).
3. Tropical desert forest	Xerophytic vegetation, stunted growth of trees, coarse grains. Example: ber, khair, babool, date palm, neem. The trees are economically useful for making pickles, cosmetics, health products, etc.	Chhattisgarh, Gujarat, some parts of Rajasthan, Haryana, South west Punjab, rain shadow areas of Maharashtra, Karnataka, Andhra Pradesh.
4. Mangrove forest	These trees bear hard wood that are strong and durable. Examples: sundari, gorjan, hintal, Amur, rhizophora.	Sunderban delta, Andaman and Nicobar islands, Gulf of Kutch, deltas of Godavari, Krishna, and Mahanadi.
5. Mountain forest	Both evergreen and deciduous trees provide timber for construction. There are also mosses lichens, ferns at the higher altitude. Examples: cinchona, birch, chestnut, pine, oak, etc.	Mountain ranges of Kashmir, Himachal Pradesh, Darjeeling, Sikkim, Nilgiris.

FEATURES OF POPULATION OF INDIA

- *High population density:* India is known for its high population density. The density of population is about 460 persons per square kilometre. High density of population causes severe environmental degradation on land, water as well as other natural resources of the country.
- *Large size:* India is the most populous country of the world surpassing China. India entered the second phase of demographic transition after 1921. It was a stage of population explosion characterized by high birth rate and declining death rate.
- *Age of population:* The age sex pyramid shows the bottom heavy structure of the population. High birth rate of population has led to higher number of dependant population in the country.
- *Rural population:* The higher ratio of rural population in the country shows the dominance of agriculture and slow growth of urbanization in our country. Sixty-five per cent of India's population still lives in rural areas per the economic survey 2022–23.
- *Disparity in sex ratio within the states:* While there are states like Kerala, Union Territory of Puducherry have higher sex ratio, there are also states like Haryana, Bihar, Union Territory of Daman and Diu have unfavourable sex ratio due to low preferences given to female child.

- *Low literacy level:* The literacy level is not the same all over the country. In general, Indian literacy level is low. Poverty, unemployment, lack of proper educational facilities in rural areas, and the preference to work than education are the reasons why Indian literacy is low. Furthermore, the female literacy is lower than male literacy due to obvious reasons.
- *Life expectancy:* Indian life expectancy is lower than many developed countries such as Japan and United States. This is due to disparity in the development of medical facilities, awareness in public health, sanitation within the country.
- *Occupation:* More than 60 per cent of India's population is engaged in agriculture and other allied activities. This shows the dominance of rural population in the country.
- *Migration:* Although India has the highest diaspora in the world but a lot of migrants from Nepal, Bangladesh, and Bhutan migrate to India for work.

AGRICULTURE OF INDIA

The Features of Indian Agriculture

- *Domination of food crops:* Indian agriculture is dominated by food grains, manly rice and wheat. This is due to the demand for food grains by the growing population of the country.
- *Monsoon dependant:* Agriculture is primarily rain fed. Most of the farmers so not have adequate irrigational facilities so they are highly dependent on irrigational facilities. This often leads to crop failure or affects productivity at times of late arrival or early departure of monsoons.
- *Subsistence farming:* Farming is done on small plots of land that gives low productivity. Most of the output is used by the farmers for his own consumption; surplus is less that is sold to the market.
- *Use of old and primitive methods of farming:* Farming is still done in a traditional way except in few states. Farmers are poor and cannot afford to use high quality seeds, fertilizers, pesticides which affect the overall productivity. For example, animals are still used for ploughing, threshing, winnowing instead of machines.
- *Variety of crops:* India is a country with varied climate, relief, and soil. Each part of the country is known for its diversity. So a variety of crops are cultivated in different parts of the country. While the northern part of the country is dominated by wheat, jowar, bajra, ragi (in dry states), the eastern part is dominated by rice and jute. The southern states are known more for the cultivation of cash crops.
- *Role of agriculture in the country's economy:* About 70 per cent of the rural households are dependent on agriculture for their livelihood. It provides food to millions of people. Agriculture provides raw materials to several agro-based industries such as cotton, jute, tea, sugar, and also food processing industries. Agriculture is an essential sector to contribute to country's GDP.

Green Revolution

A period of 1960s when India was transformed from subsistence farming system to modern agricultural system by using technology in the form of introduction to HYV seeds, chemical fertilizers, insecticides, pesticides, modern irrigational methods, mechanized farm tools, and credit facilities.

Green revolution led to an increase in food production but the benefit was reaped by mainly wheat crop. The states of Punjab,

Haryana, and Uttar Pradesh were initially benefitted from the early phase. The agricultural productivity increased due to maximum utilization of agricultural inputs.

However green revolution led to environmental degradation in the form of soil toxicity, infertility, soil pollution due to overuse of chemical fertilizers, pesticides. It also led to disparities among farmers. Since the cost of HYV seeds, fertilizers, pesticides are quite high they can be afforded by rich farmers only. So the poor remained poor and the rich became richer. Furthermore, the northern states reaped the benefits of green revolution while the other states could not. Even in case of crops, commercial crops or even food crop like rice could not enjoy much from the revolution.

However, green revolution made the country self-sufficient in agricultural production. It generated employment opportunities, caused rural electrification, improved rural infrastructure, marketing of agricultural products to great extent.

White Revolution (Operation Flood)

In 1970, Operation Flood was launched under the able guidance of Mr. Verghese Kurien. It transformed India from a milk deficient nation to the world's largest milk producers. The main objective of white revolution was to give emphasis to animal husbandry, increase in milk production, and providing milk at fair prices to customers and generating rural employment. Mr. Kurien developed the National Dairy Development board (NDDB). He made cooperative society in rural areas to help the farmers in boosting milk production, providing modern inputs and to eradicate the concept of middle men. This led to the formation of AMUL (Anand Milk Union Limited) in Gujarat, the country's leading milk cooperative system that served as the engine for operation flood.

The Different Other Revolutions of India

- *Golden Fibre Revolution:* It revolves on jute production since jute is called the golden fibre. It has a high monetary value and helps the country in earning foreign exchange.
- *Golden Revolution:* The period of 1991–2003 witnessed the increased production of fruits, honey, and other horticulture products.
- *Blue Revolution:* Saw the increased production of fisheries and other marine organisms. The government had launched the *nil kranti* programme to boost the initiative for development of fisheries and to promote this sector in the economy.
- *Black Revolution:* In order to boost the production of petroleum and to reduce our dependence on imports. The main objective of this revolution is to increase the production of biodiesel by mixing ethanol with petrol. Ethanol is a renewable byproduct derived from molasses of sugarcane.
- *Pink Revolution:* Meant to boost poultry and meat processing. Durgesh Patel is known as the father of Pink Revolution. This revolution centres around the use of modernization and technology in the fields of meat processing, poultry, livestock production. It was also meant for boosting the production of onions, pharmaceuticals, and prawns.

Reforms in Indian agriculture

- *Consolidation of land holdings:* Small and fragmented land holdings resulted in low and inefficient agricultural productivity. So measures have been taken to provide consolidated land holdings to farmers so that they can use modern techniques on the farm lands to increase production. The areas are fixed by the state to a minimum unit according to the land reforms act.

- *Abolition of intermediaries or zamindari system:* The zamindars from time immemorial have been torturing and exploiting the farmers. The farmers were charged high rate of interest for the loans they would take from the zamindars. In case they failed to repay they would be subjected to torture and slavery. Abolition of this system was a necessity to provide better security to the farmers. Banks and credit institutions were formed to help the farmers in getting loans, incentives for buying agricultural inputs.
- *Security of tenure:* Most states have passed the legislation to protect the tenancy rights. The sub-tenants and tenants at will should not survive at the mercy of the landlords. Laws have been made to ensure that the land owned by the owner should be used for personal cultivation and the tenant must be assured of a prescribed minimum area if there is resumption as well as their ownership rights.

Cash Crops

These crops are grown mainly for commercial purposes that are for sale. They are also used as raw materials for agro-based industries.

Major cropping seasons of India

KHARIF SEASON	RABI SEASON	ZAID SEASON
Sowing season: July	Sowing season: October-December	Sowing season: March-April
Harvesting season: September-October	Harvesting season: April-June	Harvesting season: May-June
Crops: rice, cotton, maize, groundnut	Crops: wheat, barley, peas, mustard	Crops: vegetables, summer fruits

Major Crops of India

Food crops

NAME OF THE CROP	CLIMATIC CONDITIONS	SOIL	DISTRIBUTION
Rice	Temperature: 20°–35°C Rainfall: 150–300 cm	Fertile, clayey, loamy soil, mainly alluvial soil	West Bengal, Uttar Pradesh, Bihar, Odisha, Tamil Nadu, Haryana, Assam
Wheat	Temperature: 10°–15°C Rainfall: 80 cm of winter rainfall	Well drained loamy soil	Punjab, Haryana, Uttar Pradesh, Rajasthan
Jowar	Temperature: 27°–32°C Grows in arid and semi-arid regions receiving less than 50 cm of rainfall	Red sandy loamy soils	Rajasthan, Gujarat, Tamil Nadu, Andhra Pradesh, Maharashtra
Bajra	Temperature: 27°–32°C Grows in arid and semi-arid regions receiving less than 50 cm of rainfall	Red sandy loamy soils or black soils	Rajasthan, Gujarat, Punjab, Haryana
Ragi	Temperature: 27°–32°C Rainfall: 50–100 cm	Red sandy loamy soils or well drained alluvial soils	Karnataka, Tamil Nadu, Maharashtra, Andhra Pradesh
Pulses	Temperature: 20°–25°C Rainfall: 50–75 cm	Dry soil	Madhya Pradesh, Maharashtra, Uttar Pradesh, Rajasthan, West Bengal, Andhra Pradesh

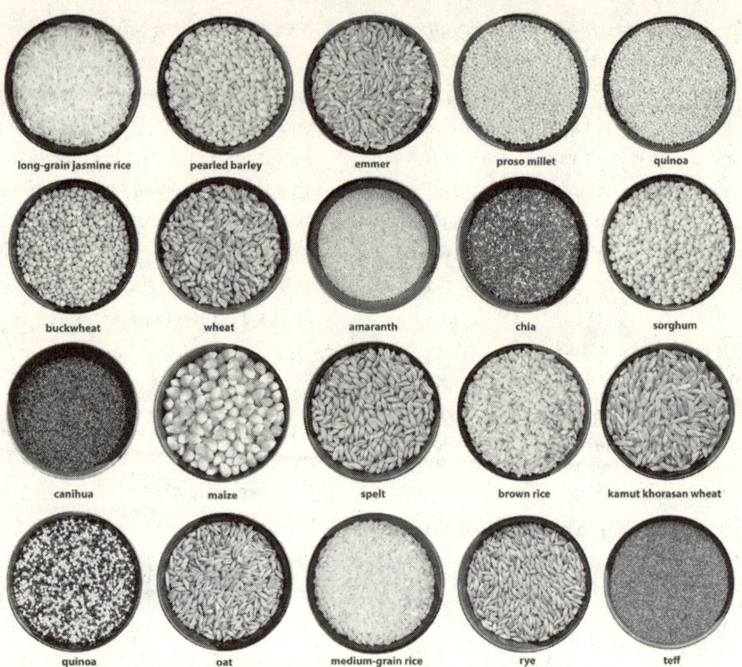

NAME OF THE CROP	CLIMATIC CONDITIONS	SOIL	DISTRIBUTION
Sugarcane	Temperature: 20°–24°C, frost-free days Rainfall: 100–150 cm	Loamy black soil or rich alluvial soil. Sugarcane is a soil exhausting crop and thus added fertilizers are needed	Maharashtra, Tamil Nadu, Uttar Pradesh
Cotton	Temperature: 21°–30°C Rainfall: 60–120 cm and at least 200 frost-free days. In Punjab and Haryana to escape the winter frost cotton balls are harvested before winter	Well-drained alluvia soil, black soil	Gujarat, Maharashtra, Andhra Pradesh, Telangana, Punjab
Groundnut	Temperature: 20°–25°C Rainfall: 50–100 cm. Frost is dangerous for the crop	Black soil, sandy loamy soil	Gujarat, Maharashtra, Karnataka, Andhra Pradesh, Tamil Nadu, Rajasthan, Punjab
Mustard	Temperature: 10°–20°C Rainfall: 25–40 cm	Deep, loamy alluvial soil	Punjab, Haryana, Uttar Pradesh, Rajasthan, West Bengal, Assam, Bihar
Soya bean	Temperature: 13°–25°C Rainfall: 40–60 cm	Alluvia soil can also grow on sandy soil	Madhya Pradesh, Maharashtra, Rajasthan
Jute	Temperature: 25°–35°C Rainfall: 150–200 cm High humidity is needed	Alluvial soil	West Bengal, Assam, Bihar, Odisha

NAME OF THE CROP	CLIMATIC CONDITIONS	SOIL	DISTRIBUTION
Tea	Temperature: 24°–30°C Rainfall: 150–500 cm (high humidity, fog, and morning dew are good for the growth of new leaves) tea cannot withstand standing water and direct long sunlight so gently slopes with shade trees are necessary	Well-drained deep friable loamy soil	Assam, West Bengal, Tamil Nadu, Kerala, Tripura, Arunachal Pradesh
Coffee	Temperature: 15°–28°C Rainfall: 150–200 cm Coffee cannot grow on longer days of sunshine, heavy rainfall, frost, or snow	Well-drained rich friable loamy soil	Karnataka, Kerala, Tamil Nadu, Andhra Pradesh

Fruits and Spices

High altitude areas of Himalayan valleys and duns, foothills of Nilgiris and cardamom hills in Tamil Nadu are considered as fruit and spices region.

Availability of food:

Refers to the supply of food. It covers production, distribution of food depending on soil, crop management, harvesting methods, use of better technology.

Access:

Refers to access of food to poor people depending on their purchasing power, whether the food is affordable to them, the repercussions on individual household in case of inflation.

Utility of the food:

The food that is made available to the people needs to be safe, hygienic to consume. It must be nutritious and meet the socio-cultural preferences of the households.

Stability:

The food must be available to the households throughout irrespective of the conditions. There should not be food insecurity in which food is not available either for a short span, e.g., during war, disasters or it can be chronic, i.e., for a long period of time.

THE FOUR PARAMETERS OF FOOD SECURITY

Food security: Refers to the condition where food is made available to the population.

INDUSTRIES OF INDIA

Major Industrial Regions of India

Mumbai-Pune industrial region:

- *Advantages:* Black lava soil and humid climate of the region.
- Developed infrastructural facilities.
- Readily available market.
- Huge hinterland and port facilities.
- Cheap labour force and use of hydel power.
- *Major industries:* Cotton textile, chemical, engineering goods, oil refineries, engineering goods, leather, chemicals, drugs, fertilizers, software, ship building, transport, food industries, entertainment industry.

The Hugli Industrial Region

- *Advantages:* Located in a narrow belt along the Hugli river it is well connected by the Ganga and its tributaries.
- Developed infrastructure and rich hinterland.
- The availability of coal and iron ore in Chota Nagpur plateau.
- Cheap labour from surrounding states.
- Port facilities and Kolkata being the capital of British India attracted large investments from the Europeans.
- *Major industries:* Jute, paper, chemicals, iron and steel, locomotives, cotton textiles.

Bangalore-Chennai Industrial Region

- *Advantages:* Large cotton growing areas.
- Availability of hydro electricity.
- Developed infrastructure.
- *Major industries:* Bharat Electronics, textiles, rubber goods, engineering goods, medicines, locomotives, glass, sugar, paper, petroleum refinery, etc.

The Gujarat Industrial Region

- *Advantages:* This industrial region centres around the cities of Ahmedabad and Vadodara, it has developed as a major cotton textile unit.
- Proximity to market.
- Port facilities – Kandla port.
- Discovery of oil fields and consequent development of petrochemical industry.
- *Major industries:* Cotton textiles, petrochemicals, pharmaceuticals, sugar, dairy products, food processing, diesel engines, etc.

Chota Nagpur Industrial Region

- *Advantages:* Extends over western West Bengal, Jharkhand, and northern Odisha, this region is known for its availability of minerals and abundance of coal.
- Cheap labour from the densely populated surrounding states.
- Large hinterland and nearness to Kolkata port.
- Readily available market.
- *Major industries:* Iron and steel industries, locomotives, fertilizers, cement, paper, machine tools.

Vishakhapatnam Guntur Region

- *Advantages:* Developed port facilities.
- Availability of mineral resources.
- *Major industries:* Ship building, petroleum refinery, cement, sugar, textiles, chemicals, light engineering, etc.

The other industrial regions are Gurgaon Delhi Meerut Industrial region that centres on light goods mainly woollen textiles, garments, hosiery bicycles, tractors, agricultural tools, glass, leather goods.

Kollam Thiruvananthapuram industrial region that centres on coconut products, cotton garments, match box, paper, aluminium, rubber, glass, fisheries.

Other Industries

Since the major industries have already been discussed in the previous part under Economic Geography let us have a quick glance on the other vital industrial units of India.

- *Ship building industries:* This industry thrives on the availability of bulky raw materials, skilled workers, level land, and nearness to port. The major units are: Hindustan Shipyard Limited, Mazagaon dock limited, Cochin shipyard, Garden reach workshop. These units specialize in the production of cargo ships, passenger vessels, fishing trawlers, navy ships, cruise liners, etc.
- *Railway locomotives:* Railways are one of the lifelines of the country's development. The major units are: Chittaranjan Locomotive Work, the Diesel Locomotive Work, the Integral Coach Factory. These unit make passenger coaches, meter gauge, broad gauge diesel engines, etc.
- *Air craft industry:* Hindustan Aeronautics Limited manufactures, designs, repairs various types of aircrafts, helicopters, aero engines, accessories.
- *Electronics:* The Indian telephone industry works for post and telegraph, defence, railways.
  The Electronic Corporation of India at Hyderabad
  The Bharat Electronics Limited works for defence, All India Radio, Meteorological Department of India.
- *Automobile industry:* India is the sixth largest manufacturer of consumer vehicles in the world. Maruti, Tata Motors, Mahindra are leading in the Indian and world market today.
- *Petrochemical plants:* Haldia petrochemicals, GAIL (Gas Authority of India Limited), Reliance Petrochemicals work for manufacturing of synthetic fibres, synthetic rubber, plastics, naptha, chemicals, etc.

TRANSPORT OF INDIA

Road Transport

The first major road was constructed by Sher Shah known as the Grand Trunk Road or **Sher Shah Suri Marg** connecting Kolkata to Peshawar. India has one of the largest road networks in the world. It carries about 85 per cent of passengers and 70 per cent of freight every year. The main advantages of roads are that they are suitable for short distance travel and provide door-to-door service.

National highways of India: These roads are constructed, maintained by the central government. These highways connect the state capitals, major cities, major ports, railway junctions. Meant for interstate travel the two main projects under this are:

FACT FILE

The National Highway Authority of India (NHAI) is an autonomous body under the central government that works for the maintenance, repair, construction, and development of the national highways of India.

- *The Golden Quadrilateral:* Connects India's four main metros: Delhi, Mumbai, Chennai, and Kolkata. The main purpose of this highway was to ease the movement of goods and better connectivity between the major cities of India.
- *The North-South and East-West corridors:* North-South corridor

connects Srinagar in Jammu and Kashmir to Kanyakumari in Tamil Nadu and the East-West corridor connects Silchar in Assam with Porbandar in Gujarat. The network facilitates the major cities and port towns that falls along the route.

State highways: Joins the national highways with the state capitals, important towns, and district headquarters. These roads are constructed, maintained by the state government.

District roads: Connects the district headquarters with the important towns, market centres.

Rural roads: Connects the main villages with the market centres.

Border roads: Roads that are constructed on the north-eastern hilly states. The Border Road Organization is responsible for the construction and maintenance of such roads. The preparedness during natural disasters, clearance of snow from high altitude roads, rescue operations at times of crisis are the area of work under BRO. the best example of BRO is the construction of high altitude road on the mountainous terrain of Leh to Manali and Chandigarh.

The **Northern Plains of India** is known for its high quality and dense road network because of its flat level land, high population density, industrial growth, and demand for road transport.

Railway Transport

The largest rail network in Asia, Indian railways are the most reliable passenger and freight transport in the country. It connects the major cities with almost every nook and corner of the country. The economic and industrial development of the country is accelerated by the development of Indian railways. The first railway track was laid between Bombay and Thane in 1853. Today there are more 12,000 trains running daily.

Indian railways are divided into 19 zones (including the Kolkata metro). The newest railway zone is the south coast railway zone headquartered at Vishakhapatnam. The biggest railway zone is the northern railway zone covering the states of Punjab, Haryana, Uttarakhand, Himachal Pradesh, Uttar Pradesh, and the union territories of Delhi, Chandigarh, and Jammu and Kashmir.

The most interesting rail routes of India:

- *The Himalayan Queen Railways:* Connecting Shimla to Kalka. This toy train passes through scenic beauty of the Himalayas crossing 102 tunnels and 82 bridges. This route has been recognized as the UNESCO World Heritage Site from 2008.
- *The Konkan Railway:* Made with the joint collaboration of Maharashtra, Goa, Karnataka, Kerala, this route is about 760 km long connecting Roha in Maharashtra to Mangalore in Karnataka.
- *The Darjeeling Himalaya:* Covers from Jalpaiguri to Darjeeling this train route passes through the rolling tea gardens, forests and towering conifers. It runs on meter gauge and an UNESCO world Heritage Site.
- *The Pamban Rameshwaram Railway line:* The most dangerous rail route in India, this route is dangerous as it runs

on the Indian Ocean connecting the Indian mainland to the Rameshwaram Island.

- *The Indian Maharaja Deccan odyssey:* One of India's few luxury trains, it offers the passengers with a wide variety of facilities starting from library, gymnasium, beauty parlour, on board health spa services, steam bath, luxury suits, conference rooms, etc.
- *Mumbai to Goa:* A stunning train ride covering the Arabian Sea to its one side and the Western Ghats on the other side it passes through 92 tunnels and 2,000 bridges this train ride gives a picturesque view of the western coastal plains.

Indian Rail Gauges: Indian Railways Run on Three Gauges

- *Broad gauge:* Distance between rails is 1.676 m.
- *Meter gauge:* Distance between rails is 1 m.
- *Narrow gauge:* Distance between rails is 0.762 or 0.610 m. This type of railway tracks is found on hilly areas.

Metro rail was first introduced in Kolkata as an underground metro rail similar to London tube services. Today almost the major cities of the country have metro operations. India's first underwater metro service – the **East West metro Corridor Project** connecting Salt Lake to Howrah via Kolkata will have a long stretch under the Hooghly River is expected to run soon for the passengers.

The Delhi metro rail is the largest and busiest metro of the country. All the cities under the NCR that is Noida, Gurugram, Ghaziabad, Ballabgarh, Bahadurgarh are connected through the Delhi metro.

Water Transport

India has a long coastline of about 7,517 km that boosts about 90 per cent of international trade. There are about 14 major and 190 minor ports in the coasts of the country. There are also natural ports on the western coast of the country. The natural presence of creeks and bays protect the ports from the strong waves of the sea. The difference between **a port and harbour** is that harbours are meant for safe anchorage to the ships and are generally natural while ports are meant for loading and unloading of cargo and are manmade mostly.

The Inland Waterways Authority of India takes care of the development, maintenance, repair of the national waterways in the country. The most important National waterways are:

National Waterways 1: Covers River Ganga from Allahabad (Uttar Pradesh) to Haldia (West Bengal) at a stretch of about 1,620 km. It covers Allahabad to Patna (through mechanized boats), from Patna to Farakka and finally from Farakka to Haldia. Up to Haridwar normal boats are used.

National Waterways 2: Covers river Brahmaputra from Dhubri to Sadiya covering about 891 km. It is navigable by steamers up to Dibrugarh district.

National Waterways 3: Kottapuram to Kollam stretch covering about 205 km.

Major Ports of India

Kandla Port: The tidal port of India located in the Gulf of Kutch in Gujarat. Items such as salt, mineral oil, chemicals, cement, sugar, cotton are traded here.

Mumbai Port: India's largest and second oldest port. Jawaharlal Nehru Port has been constructed later on to reduce the pressure from Mumbai port.

Kolkata Port: India's oldest and only riverine port, this port lies on river Hugli. Haldia Port has been constructed on the Haldi River to reduce the pressure from Kolkata Port where large ships can have access to. Mineral oil, industrial goods are traded through this port.

Chennai Port: An old and commercially important port located on the eastern coast of Chennai in Tamil Nadu. This port trades mineral, mineral oil, industrial goods, and agricultural goods.

Vishakhapatnam Port: A good natural harbour, this port handles about 16 per cent of India's trade. This port is used for ship building, for navy, repair and maintenance of commercial and naval ships.

Air Transport

India is a country with vast latitudinal and longitudinal extent with diversity in its physical features. There are numerous rivers, plans, plateaus, hills that need to be surpassed to reach the corners of the country. For this purpose, airways are the most convenient mode of transport. Air ways have been developed due to globalization to communicate with the different countries of the world.

Indian Airlines is the body for the transportation of goods, services, and postal services. Helicopter services are provided by Pawan Hans. India has many private organizations that run airline services all over the country such as IndiGo, SpiceJet, Vistara, and Akasa Air.

Top five airlines of India:

1. IndiGo airlines
2. Air India
3. Vistara
4. SpiceJet
5. Go First

Pipelines of India: Pipelines are used for the transportation of petroleum products, natural gas and other products. Pipelines are safer to transport inflammable commodities as there are fewer leakages and accidents. Pipelines are cost effective and can transport in bulk and large quantities. The maintenance is also low as pumps are used to transport liquids and gases over long distances.

The major pipelines of India are:

- *Naharkatia-Nunmati Barauni pipeline:* First pipeline constructed to bring crude oil from Naharkatia oil field to Nunmati. This pipeline also provides services up to Haldia petrochemicals in West Bengal.
- *Mumbai High-Mumbai-Ankleshwar-Koyali pipeline:* It connects the oil fields of Mumbai High and Gujarat with oil refinery at Koyali. Crude oil and natural gas is transported through this pipeline.
- *Salaya-Koyali-Mathura pipeline:* This pipeline supplies crude oil to refineries at Koyali and Mathura. From Mathura it extends to an oil refinery at Panipat in Haryana and further to Jalandhar in Punjab. It has an off-shore terminal for imported crude oil.

- Hajira-Bijapur-Jagdishpur gas pipeline-India's longest gas pipeline constructed by Gas Authority of India (GAIL). This pipeline provides gas and fertilizers across multiple states.
- *Jamnagar-Loni LPG pipeline:* This is the longest LPG pipeline in the world. It passes through the states of Gujarat, Rajasthan, Haryana, and Uttar Pradesh. It connects Jamnagar in Gujarat with Loni in Uttar Pradesh. This pipeline meets the LPG demands across multiple states.

Disadvantages of Pipeline Transport

- The old pipelines get corroded so there are frequent incidences of leakages. Poor maintenance and use of low cost pipes are responsible for corrosion.
- The corrosion of pipes causes cracks and holes through which valuable commodities like oil, gas leak out. Sometimes these old pipes also burst or rupture due to frequent corrosion and damage thus leading to major accidents and oil spills causing environmental pollution.
- Pipelines are often subjected to pilferages and tapping by criminals who extract oil illegally from the pipelines.
- There are often delays in completion of the pipeline projects. These delays are mainly due to held up capital investments, delays in getting necessary permissions, cost of labour, infrastructure, land acquisition problem, etc.
- There are technical problems on laying pipelines in hilly and forested areas of the north east so these regions of the country are always the worst sufferers in spite of being so rich in natural resources.

GLOBALIZATION ON INDIAN ECONOMY

A global village is what a government always desires for. A village which will be selling products to consumers all over the world at a price which is fixed by the people and not by the government. Globalization in India got its wings from the rise in foreign investments in retail and corporate sectors.

What do you mean by globalization?

Free movement of people, goods, and services across nations. The main purpose of globalization in simple language is to bring the local markets to the global world. The World Trade Organization (WTO) sets rules and regulations that benefits overseas trade conditions across countries. It was in 1990s under the financial leadership of Dr. Manmohan Singh globalization was fully implemented in India.

Benefits of Globalization in India

- *Generation of employment opportunities:* The special economic zones (SEZ) have been set up after which there were availability of new jobs. The presence of cheap labour in India has also motivated foreign companies to tie up with the country thus outsourcing work to companies present here. Export processing zones have been set up that generates employment.
- *Better purchasing power:* There has been an improvement in the standard of living of the people in the country especially those working under the foreign organizations. There has been generation of wealth which further improves the purchasing power. The Indian companies too in order to keep up their demands have hiked their salary structure to attract more employees.
- *Compensation benefits:* The level of knowledge, skills, and expertise brought from foreign companies are adding

values to the production process thus benefitting compensation among the employees.

Disadvantages of Globalization

- Globalization did not benefit the informal labourers much. The poor remained poor and the rich became richer.
- There were regional disparities in industrial growth. While states like Maharashtra, Gujarat, Punjab, Karnataka, Tamil Nadu were benefitted the most the other states like Bihar, Jharkhand, Uttarakhand lagged behind.
- Globalization did not address the common labour problems such as long working hours, child labour, bondage, poor health, working conditions, etc.

NATURAL DISASTERS IN INDIA

The diverse climate of India also makes it vulnerable to different natural disasters. Floods, cyclones, cloud bursts, earthquakes, landslides are some common disasters often striking India. These natural disasters pose serious threat to the people and the environment alike. Other than these, there are also localized dangers that cause frequent financial losses.

Frequent summer dust storms in northern and north western India increases the risk of desertification. They deposit large amount of dust from arid regions causing crop damage. Hail is also common in north India that causes severe damage to the standing crops such as paddy.

Some common natural disasters in India are:

- *Landslides:* These are common in the lower Himalayas. Incessant rainfall of shorter duration but higher intensity makes the soil on the lower Himalayas loose. These are further aggravated by deforestation, development activities such as construction of hotels, resorts on the hill slopes. As a result, there is a violent and rapid gush of soil along with rainwater falling down the slopes in high speed due to the absence of tree cover. Landslides are common in Sikkim, Darjeeling, Himalayas, Western Ghats, Himachal Pradesh, etc.

- *Floods:* Floods are an annual feature in several states of India such as Assam, and Bihar. The heavy rainfall during the south-west monsoon season causes the rivers to overflow their banks thus leading to flooding. Excess, erratic monsoons cause huge destruction to agricultural fields, washing away homes, crops, and farms. Several parts of the country are extremely flood prone. Apart from this, flash floods are also common in central India as well as in the hilly states. A rise in temperature with heavy and torrential rains has become a common feature in otherwise drought affected central India. Due to this there are more incidences of incessant rain of shorter duration but more intensity causing more damage.

- *Cyclones:* The entire eastern coast of India is affected by cyclones. Cyclones bring heavy rainfall, strong winds, high waves that cut the affected areas often from immediate relief and rescue operations. Tropical cyclones are common in Bay of Bengal more than Arabian Sea. The Bay of Bengal is subjected to intense heating, giving rise to hot, humid, and unstable air mass that causes cyclones. In terms of damage, cyclones have caused huge destruction to life and property in Odisha, coastal districts of West Bengal, Andhra Pradesh, and Tamil Nadu.

Some recent tropical cyclones that struck the Bay of Bengal coast:

- Cyclone Amphan in 2020
- Cyclone Yaas in 2021
- Cyclone Gulaab in 2021
- Cyclone Asani in2022
- Cyclone Sitrang in 2022
- Cyclone Biparjoy in 2023

Did you know?

The term 'cyclone' is derived from a Greek word 'cyclos' meaning coils of snake!

GEOGRAPHICAL TECHNIQUES AND METHODS OF MAPPING

Some important terms to remember:

- *Contours:* Imaginary lines joining places having equal elevation above sea level.
- *Isogones:* Imaginary lines joining places having equal compass declination.
- *Isoseismal:* Imaginary lines joining places having equal seismic strength.
- *Isochrones:* Imaginary lines joining places having equal time.
- *Isobaths:* Imaginary lines joining places having equal depth at sea bed.
- *Isohels:* Imaginary lines joining places having equal duration of sun light.
- *Isonephs:* Imaginary lines joining places having equal cloudiness.
- *Isopleths:* All those imaginary lines of equal value of any particular phenomena.

Map is the most important tool of a geographer. The person who makes maps is called a cartographer and the art of map making is called cartography.

The modern world has replaced the application of traditional map making with the use of digital images, remote sensing and Global Positioning System (GPS). In spite of that we must have an idea of what traditional maps are since they are the stepping stones of learning for every geographer. Maps are the two dimensional models of the earth. Not only about locations, maps give us a vivid idea about natural, man-made, socio-cultural features of a place.

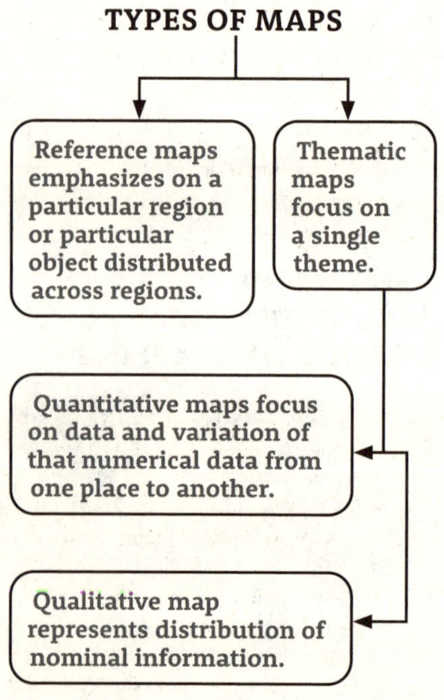

TECHNIQUES AND METHODS OF MAP MAKING

- *Isopleth maps:* As we know isopleth lines show equal value of any particular phenomena so isopleths maps show clear cut regions on the basis of any particular phenomena or objects.
- *Choropleth maps:* Here distribution is shown using various colours or shades of the same colour. The density of the shading varies with the density of the distribution, this technique is called choropleth method. It is different from isopleth maps as here the area is given importance and not the distribution.
- *Dot maps:* Absolute numbers on a map are shown by dot maps. The total population of a region can be shown by dot map where the value of each dot will represent a particular number of persons on the basis of a given scale (e.g., one dot represents 1,000 persons). The scale is to be decided keeping in mind the smallest and highest figures in the data and the size of the map. The size of the dot would also depend on the size of the map and number of dots to be placed in a particular space.
- *Isarithmic maps:* These are used to depict three dimensional values such as elevation on topographical maps. These maps use contour lines to depict continuous values such as rainfall, snowfall, etc.
- *Chorochromatic maps:* Qualitative area map, used to display nominal data with various colours or patterns. Colours are mapped according to the data for example soil maps, biome maps.
- *Dasymetric maps:* These are refined version of choropleth maps where the administrative areas are divided into smaller spatial units in which demographic data (e.g., population density) is shown by averaging the population to calculate a rate.
- *Flow maps:* Used to depict the flow or movement of any phenomena or objects such as migration of people, trading of products, etc. The direction of flow is depicted by using arrows from the point of origin to the point of destination. The flow can be unidirectional or multidirectional.

WHAT IS REMOTE SENSING AND WHAT ARE ITS APPLICATIONS?

Without any physical contact with an object or phenomena when we are collecting information that is called remote sensing. Remote sensing observations are made using satellites or aircrafts. Aerial photography is the most common form of remote sensing. They are used for topographical studies, engineering, and environmental studies.

Applications

- *Soils:* To map soils, classify soils, their distribution, to study soil conservation and soil moisture.
- *Geology:* Mapping of rock structure, rock types, igneous intrusions and bed rock, mapping of recent volcanic deposits.
- *Water resources:* Measurement of water depth, distribution of watershed, mapping of floods and flood plains, river bank, and coastal erosion.
- *Agriculture and natural vegetation:* Study and monitor the extent, distribution of different vegetation types, the cropping patterns, assessing forest fire damages, droughts, and other hazards.

DIGITAL IMAGING: USE OF GPS

Global Positioning System is a satellite based navigation system which provides detailed information in all weather conditions across the world in 3D format. GPS consists of satellites that are powered by solar cells, ground control stations and receivers that transmit and receive radio signals.

Applications

GPS are used for defence, navigation, astronomy, disaster relief, weather forecasting, etc.

3 Science

Chemistry

MATTER AND ITS STATES

Imagine a bustling universe made of an invisible dance of particles, each playing its part in the grand performance of existence. This dance is the essence of matter, the fundamental substance that makes up everything around us.

Matter is defined as any substance or material that **has mass**, **occupies space**, and is composed of **very tiny particles** such as molecules and atoms. These atoms, in turn, are built from even smaller particles: **protons**, **neutrons**, and **electrons**.

A state of matter is defined as one of the ways in which matter can interact with itself to form a homogeneous phase. It exists in three states – **solids**, **liquids**, and **gases**.

Matter changes its state from solid to liquid to gas when heated and from gas to liquid to solid when it is cooled.

For example, if you heat ice, it will absorb the heat and turn to water. Now when you heat water, it absorbs the heat and turns into gas. This is an **endothermic reaction**, as energy in the form of heat is absorbed from the surroundings.

When gas is cooled, it loses heat and turns to liquid. When a liquid is cooled, it loses heat and turns to solid. This is an **exothermic reaction**, as energy in the form of heat is released into the surroundings.

While solids, liquids, and gases are the most common states, the universe of matter has more to offer. **Plasma** is a state where the particles are so energized that they become charged, creating a soup of ions and electrons. It is the state of matter in stars and lightning.

Then there is the **Bose–Einstein Condensate (BEC),** a state achieved at temperatures close to absolute zero. Here, particles clump together and behave as a single quantum entity, showcasing the fascinating quirks of quantum mechanics.

> ***Did you know?***
>
> Gases can also change their state and turn into a plasma and BEC:
>
> When gases are heated to extreme temperatures, it causes a disruption in the normal balance of atoms. There are lots of free ions and electrons, turning them into plasma, which creates a light.
>
> If a gas of low density is cooled to ultra-low temperatures, you get a BEC super-atom wave. Warm it up, and the wave will return to a gas.

ATOMIC STRUCTURE

All matter consists of tiny particles called atoms which are made up of three main parts – neutrons, electrons, and protons – which are composed of even smaller particles, such as quarks. An atom is the smallest unit into which matter can be divided and that will have the characteristic properties of the element.

In a solid, these particles or atoms are closely packed together which is why a solid object can hold its shape. In a liquid, this arrangement is a bit disorganized, and there is some space between the atoms, giving

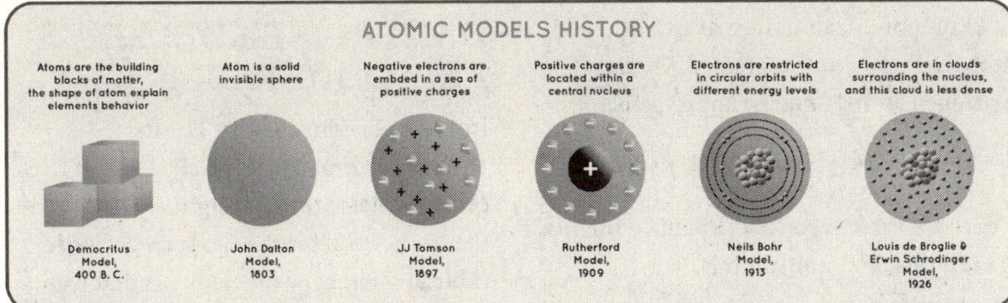

them the ability to move around and slide past each other. In gases, the arrangement of particles or atoms is extremely random, and there are large gaps between them.

An atom consists of a positively charged nucleus (protons and neutrons) around which negatively charged electrons orbit. The radius of an atom is about 0.1 nm or (1×10^{-10} m).

In 1897, **J. J. Thomson** discovered the existence of the electrons based on his experiments carried out in a discharge tube. In the 1920s, **Erwin Schrödinger** proposed the quantum mechanical model of the atom which describes the electron as a three-dimensional (3D) wave in the electronic field of the positively charged nucleus.

In 1917, **Ernest Rutherford** discovered protons when he detected the presence of hydrogen nuclei after firing alpha particles in the air. He then proceeded to fire alpha particle beams into pure nitrogen gas and found that a greater amount of hydrogen nuclei was created.

The presence of neutrons was discovered by **James Chadwick** in 1932, when he fired alpha radiation at a beryllium sheet from a polonium source. This led to the production of an uncharged, penetrating radiation, which he found had approximately the same mass as a proton.

Atomic mass is associated with the number of neutrons and protons that are present in the nucleus of an element. It is represented by A.

Atomic number of an element is the number of protons in an element's nucleus. It is represented by Z.

NAME	ATOMIC NUMBER (Z)	PROTONS	NEUTRONS	ELECTRONS
Hydrogen (H)	1	1	0	1
Helium (He)	2	2	2	2
Lithium (Li)	3	3	4	3
Beryllium (Be)	4	4	5	4
Boron (B)	5	5	6	5
Carbon (C)	6	6	6	6

ELEMENTS AND COMPOUNDS

An **element** is defined as a substance that is made up of **one kind of atom** and **cannot be broken down** into a simpler type of matter. Each element is distinguished by a **unique atomic number**.

A **compound** consists of **atoms of two or more different elements** bound together.

They are distinguished by a unique atomic number. The elements are organized by their atomic number in the periodic table, which highlights elements with similar properties. Water is an example of a compound, a mixture of two or more elements, and is created when two hydrogen atoms bond to an oxygen atom.

TYPES OF ELEMENTS

There are three types of elements – **metals, metalloids,** and **non-metals.**

Metals: Any substance that is characterized by high electrical and thermal conductivity, malleability, ductility, and high reflectivity of light.

Metals are electropositive elements that can donate electrons.

Metals include alkaline metals, transition metals, alkaline earth metals, etc., and are positioned on the left side of the periodic table.

Non-metals: Non-metals, including noble gases and halogens, are situated on the right side of the periodic table.

Non-metals are electronegative elements that can either accept or share electrons.

Metalloids or semi-metals: These are those elements whose properties lie between non-metals and metals. On the periodic table, they are usually represented in yellow.

DMITRI MENDELEEV'S PERIODIC TABLE

In 1869, Russian chemist **Dmitri Mendeleev** organized the elements in the order of their **atomic weights**. He created the framework for the **modern periodic table** and left gaps for elements that were yet to be discovered.

It was later observed that, for some elements, the position predicted by their atomic weight did not always match the position predicted by their chemical properties. In this case, the elements were positioned in the periodic table based on their chemical properties.

> ***Did you know***
>
> The year of the periodic table was observed, in 2019, by UNESCO to mark 150 years of Mendeleev's contribution to the periodic table.

In 1913, English physicist **Henry Moseley** used X-rays to measure the wavelengths of elements and correlated these measurements to their atomic numbers (number of protons). He then rearranged the elements in the order of their atomic numbers, which explained the disparities

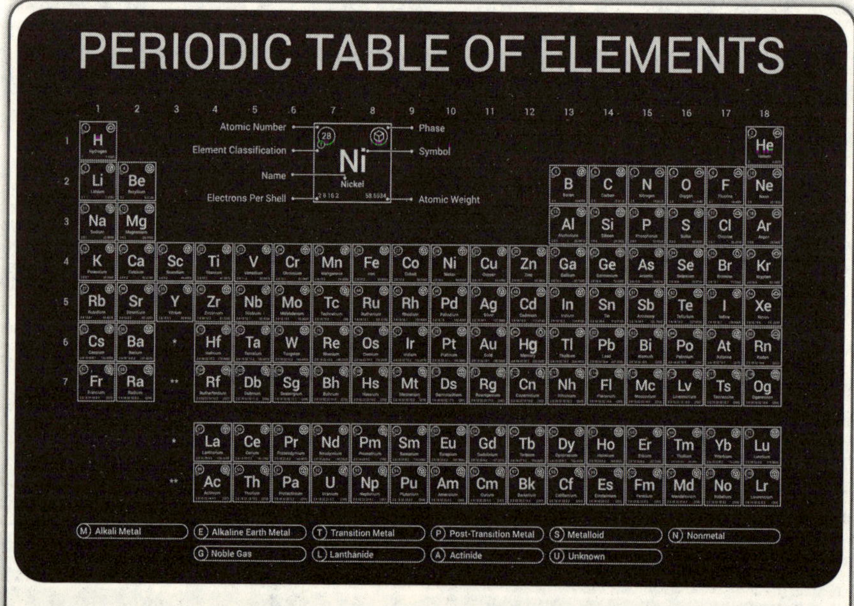

in earlier tables that had used atomic weights.

The elements on the periodic table are placed in seven periods (rows) and eighteen groups (columns). Two rows (periods 6 and 7) have been placed at the bottom of the periodic table. The **top row** is named **lanthanides** (elements 57 through 71) and the **bottom row** (elements 89 through 103) is named **actinides**.

The periodic table is used to predict the properties of elements, even those that have not yet been discovered. It also allows scientists to detect trends in element properties, including electronegativity, ionization energy, and atomic radius. Today, with **118 known elements**, the periodic table is widely regarded as one of the most significant achievements in science.

ACID, BASES, AND SALTS

A substance that **turns blue litmus red** and neutralizes bases is known as an acid. Acids are sour in taste.

There are two types of acid: **organic** and **inorganic.**

Organic acids are acids derived from plants and animals. Some examples are acetic acid, citric acid, and formic acid.

Inorganic acids, also referred to as **mineral acids**, are acids derived from minerals present in the earth's crust. Some examples are sulphuric acid (H_2SO_4), phosphoric acid (H_3PO_4), hydrochloric acid (HCl), and nitric acid (HNO_3).

A substance that **turns red litmus to blue** and neutralizes acids is known as a base. Bases are bitter in taste.

The reaction between an acid and a base to give a salt and water is known as a **neutralization reaction**. This can be written as

Base + Acid → Salt + Water

pH Scale

In chemistry, pH (potential of hydrogen) is a scale used to specify the acidity or basicity of an aqueous solution. The scale ranges from 0 to 14.

Solutions with a value of **pH ranging from 0 to 7 are termed as acidic** and the value of **pH ranging from 7 to 14 are known as basic solutions.** Solutions with a value of **pH equal to 7** are known as **neutral solutions.**

Some Important Reactions

When an acid reacts with a metal, hydrogen gas is released, and a corresponding salt is formed.

Metal + Acid → Salt + Hydrogen

When a base reacts with a metal, along with the evolution of hydrogen gas, a salt carrying a negative ion composed of the metal and oxygen is formed.

Metal + Base → Salt + Hydrogen gas

When an acid reacts with a metal carbonate or metal hydrogen carbonate, it gives the corresponding salt, carbon dioxide gas, and water.

Metal carbonate/metal hydrogen carbonate + Acid → Salt + Carbon dioxide + Water

Oxidation and Reduction

Oxidation takes place when a **reactant loses electrons** during the reaction.

$Ca \rightarrow Ca^{2+} + 2e^-$

Reduction takes place when a **reactant gains electrons** during the reaction.

$Zn^{2+} + 2e^- \rightarrow Zn$

Redox Reactions

A redox reaction (or oxidation–reduction) involves the **transfer of electrons** between the atoms, ions, or molecules involved in the reaction.

Example 1: Combustion of methane

$CH^4 (g) + 2O_2 (g) \rightarrow CO_2 (g) + 2H_2O (g)$

Example 2: Oxidation of copper

$$2Cu(s) + O_2(g) \rightarrow 2CuO(s)$$

ELECTROCHEMISTRY

Electrochemistry is a branch of chemistry concerned with the production of electricity from energy released during spontaneous chemical reactions and the use of electrical energy to bring about non-spontaneous chemical transformations.

There are two types of electrochemical cells: **galvanic (voltaic)** and **electrolytic**.

Galvanic cells or voltaic cells convert the chemical energy of spontaneous redox (oxidation–reduction) reactions into electrical energy.

Electrolytic cells involve non-spontaneous reactions and thus require an external source like a direct current (DC) or an alternating current (AC) power source. Electrolytic cells can be used for the electrolysis of certain compounds such as water which forms gaseous oxygen and gaseous hydrogen.

GALVANIC CELL OR VOLTAIC CELL	ELECTROLYTIC CELL
Converts chemical energy into electrical energy	Converts electrical energy into chemical energy
Contains negatively charged anode and positively charged cathode	Contains positively charged anode and negatively charged cathode
Features spontaneous cell reactions	Features non-spontaneous cell reactions

BATTERY

A battery is a device where the chemical energy of a redox reaction is converted into electrical energy. A battery can be made up of one or several electrochemical cells which consists of two electrodes separated by an electrolyte.

The chemical reactions that take place in a battery require the flow of electrons from anode (negative electrode) to another electrode called the cathode (positive electrode). This flow of electrons provides an electric current that can be used to do work.

To balance the flow of electrons, charged ions also flow through an electrolyte solution that is in contact with both electrodes.

Different electrodes and electrolytes produce different chemical reactions that affect how the battery works, how much energy it can store and its voltage.

There are two types of cells: **primary** and **secondary.**

In a **primary battery**, the reaction occurs only once, and after some time, the **battery becomes dead and cannot be reused**. For example, **the dry cell** (known as **Leclanché cell**) which is used in **transistors and clocks**.

A **secondary battery** can be recharged by passing current through it in the opposite direction (**negative terminal to the positive terminal**), **and it can be reused**. For example, the **lead storage** battery which is used in **automobiles and inverters**.

CARBON AND ITS COMPOUNDS

Carbon compounds are everywhere around us, weaving through our daily lives in fascinating ways. From the meals we enjoy to the clothes we wear, carbon is a fundamental building block. It even adds sparkle to diamond jewellery! You can find carbon in its free forms, such as coal and graphite, or in combined forms, such as the carbon dioxide we exhale.

Did you know?

Almost 20 per cent of the human body (by weight) is made of carbon. In fact, carbon atoms make up the backbone of major molecules in your body, including DNA, RNA, proteins, fats, and sugars.

Ionic and Covalent Bonds

Ionic (or electrovalent) bonds are formed between two atoms by the **complete transfer of one or more electrons** to attain their **nearest noble gas configuration (two or eight electrons in their valence shell)**.

Take, for example, NaCl.

Na has 11 protons and 11 electrons.

Its electronic configuration is $1s^2\ 2s^2\ 2p^6\ 3s^1$, which means it has a single valence electron in its 3s subshell.

Cl has 17 protons and 17 electrons.

Its electronic configuration is $1s^2\ 2s^2\ 2p^6\ 3s^2\ 3p^5$, which means it has seven valence electrons in its third shell.

To form an ionic bond, the sodium atom loses its valence electron to chlorine.

$$Na\cdot + :\ddot{\underset{\cdot\cdot}{Cl}}\cdot \longrightarrow Na^+ + :\ddot{\underset{\cdot\cdot}{Cl}}:$$

Covalent bonds are formed between two atoms by **sharing of an electron pair** to attain their nearest noble gas configuration.

There are three types of covalent bonds: **single, double**, and **triple.**

1. When **one pair of electrons** is shared between the atoms, it is known as a single covalent bond. These bonds have a smaller density and are weaker than double and triple bonds, but they are the most stable.

   Take, for example, NH_3.

   N has seven protons and seven electrons.

   Its electronic configuration is $1s^2\ 2s^2\ 2p^3$, which means it has five valence electrons in its second shell.

   H has one proton and one electron.

   Its electronic configuration is $1s^1$, which means it has one valence electron in its first shell.

   To form a covalent bond, the nitrogen and hydrogen atoms share one electron to complete their octet.

$$3\dot{H} + \cdot\dot{\underset{\cdot\cdot}{N}}\cdot \longrightarrow H\cdot\ \cdot\overset{\overset{\textstyle H}{\cdot}}{\underset{\cdot\cdot}{N}}\cdot\ \cdot H \longrightarrow H-\overset{\overset{\textstyle H}{|}}{\underset{\cdot\cdot}{N}}-H$$

2. When **two pairs of electrons** are shared between the atoms, it is known as a double covalent bond. They are stronger than single covalent bonds but are less stable. These are represented by double lines.

   Take, for example, CO_2.

   C has six protons and six electrons.

   Its electronic configuration is $1s^2\ 2s^2\ 2p^2$, which means it has two valence electrons.

   O has eight protons and eight electrons.

   Its electronic configuration is $1s^2\ 2s^2\ 2p^4$, which means it has six valence electrons in its second shell.

   To form a covalent bond, the carbon and oxygen atoms share two electrons.

$$\ddot{\underset{\cdot\cdot}{O}} = C = \ddot{\underset{\cdot\cdot}{O}}$$

3. When **three pairs of electrons** are shared between the atoms, it is known as a triple covalent bond. They are the least stable types of covalent bonds and are represented by three lines.

   Take, for example, N_2.

   N has seven protons and seven electrons.

   Its electronic configuration is $1s^2\ 2s^2\ 2p^3$, which means it has five valence electrons in its second shell.

   To form a covalent bond, the nitrogen atoms share three electrons.

$$:\dot{\underset{\cdot}{N}}\cdot + \cdot\dot{\underset{\cdot}{N}}: \longrightarrow :N\ :::\ N:$$
$$(:N \equiv N:)$$

Bonding Properties of Carbon

Carbon has six protons and six electrons, with configuration $1s^2\ 2s^2\ 2p^2$, which means it has four electrons in its valence shell. To become stable, carbon must gain four more electrons to complete the octet. Take, for example, methane (CH_4), where carbon forms covalent bonds with four hydrogen atoms to complete its outer shell.

Carbon also forms bonds with other atoms of carbon, giving rise to large molecules. This property is called **catenation.**

HYDROCARBONS

As the name suggests, hydrocarbons are organic compounds that are made up of only carbon and hydrogen atoms.

Take, for example, methane, which consists of a central carbon atom bonded to four hydrogen atoms. Because carbon atoms adopt positions that will maximize their distance from each other, CH_4 is tetrahedral in shape.

Types of Hydrocarbons

Saturated compounds are organic compounds that contain only carbon–carbon single bonds. These are also known as alkanes and comprise a homologous series having a general formula C_nH_{2n+2}.

ALKANE	MOLECULAR FORMULA	STRUCTURE
Methane	CH_4	CH_4
Ethane	C_2H_6	CH_3CH_3
Propane	C_3H_8	$CH_3CH_2CH_3$
Butane	C_4H_{10}	$CH_3(CH_2)_2CH_3$
Pentane	C_5H_{12}	$CH_3(CH_2)_3CH_3$
Hexane	C_6H_{14}	$CH_3(CH_2)_4CH_3$
Heptane	C_7H_{16}	$CH_3(CH_2)_5CH_3$
Octane	C8H18	$CH_3(CH_2)_6CH_3$

Unsaturated compounds are organic compounds that contain at least one double bond (alkenes) or triple bond (alkynes) between carbon atoms. The general formula for alkenes is C_nH_{2n} and for alkynes, the general formula is C_nH_{2n-2}.

ALKENE	MOLECULAR FORMULA	STRUCTURE
Ethene	C_2H_4	$CH_2{=}CH_2$
Propene	C_3H_6	$CH_2{=}CHCH_3$
1-Butene	C_4H_8	$CH_2{=}CHCH_2CH_3$
1-Pentene	C_5H_{10}	$CH_2{=}CH(CH_2)_2CH_3$
1-Hexene	C_6H_{12}	$CH_2{=}CH(CH_2)_3CH_3$

ALKYNE	MOLECULAR FORMULA
Ethyne	C_2H_2
Propyne	C_3H_4
1-Butyne	C_4H_6
1-Pentyne	C_5H_8
1-Hexyne	C_6H_{10}

Aromatic hydrocarbons, also called **arenes**, are compounds, which consist of carbon and hydrogen atoms in ring structures. **Aromatic compounds that contain a benzene ring** are known as **benzenoids**, and **aromatic compounds without a benzene ring** are known as **non-benzenoids.**

Cycloalkanes are the class of hydrocarbons that possess one or multiple carbon rings. The hydrogen atom is attached to the carbon ring.

Aliphatic hydrocarbons are organic compounds composed of carbon and hydrogen atoms, arranged in straight chains, branched structures or non-aromatic ring structures.

ENVIRONMENTAL CHEMISTRY

Environmental chemistry is the branch of science that involves the study of the effect of chemicals on air, water, and soil. and how it impacts the environment and human health.

Atmospheric pollution is mostly studied as **tropospheric** (lowest region of the atmosphere up to 10 km) and **stratospheric pollution** (extends above troposphere up to 50 km above sea level).

Global warming is the long-term warming of the planet's overall temperature. In the last hundred years, the pace has significantly increased due to the burning of fossil fuels.

Climate change refers to changes in weather patterns and growing seasons around the world.

Greenhouse Effect

The greenhouse effect occurs when certain gases – known as **greenhouse gases** – get trapped in the earth's atmosphere. Some of the greenhouse gases are carbon dioxide, nitrogen oxide, water vapour, methane, and chlorofluorocarbons.This excess heat in the atmosphere has led to an increase in the average global temperature and may eventually result in melting of glaciers and rising ocean levels.

Tropospheric pollution occurs due to the presence of undesirable (and harmful) solid or gaseous particles in the air. There are two types of tropospheric pollution:

1. **Gaseous air pollutants** are emitted from natural sources, such as volcanoes and forest fires. These include oxides of sulphur, nitrogen, carbon, hydrogen sulphide, hydrocarbons, ozone, and other oxidants.

Oxides of Sulphur

One of the most harmful gaseous air pollutants, SO_2 is a colourless but pungent gas. It is produced when fossil fuel – coal, oil, and diesel – or any substance that contains sulphur is burnt.

The presence of particulate matter in polluted air catalyses the oxidation of sulphur dioxide to sulphur trioxide.

$2SO_2\,(g) + O_2\,(g) \rightarrow 2SO_3\,(g)$

The reaction can also be promoted by ozone and hydrogen peroxide.

$SO_2\,(g) + O_3\,(g) \rightarrow SO_3\,(g) + O_2\,(g)$

$SO_2\,(g) + H_2O_2\,(l) \rightarrow H_2SO_4\,(aq)$

Oxides of Nitrogen

Dinitrogen and dioxygen are unreactive at a normal temperature. However, at a higher temperature (1,483 K), both these gases combine to produce significant quantities of nitric oxide and nitrogen dioxide.

$N_2\,(g) + O_2\,(g) \rightarrow 2NO\,(g)$

Nitric oxide that is produced reacts with oxygen and ozone in the stratosphere to produce nitrogen dioxide.

$2NO\,(g) + O_2\,(g) \rightarrow 2NO_2\,(g)$

$NO\,(g) + O_3\,(g) \rightarrow NO_2\,(g) + O_2\,(g)$

Oxides of Carbon

Hydrocarbons are produced by incomplete combustion of fuel used in automobiles. The most common cause of hydrocarbon pollution is the spillage of crude oil or other industrial commodities. Hydrocarbons are **carcinogenic** in nature which means they cause cancer. They are also harmful to plants, as they cause ageing, breakdown of tissues and shedding of leaves, flowers, and twigs.

2. **Particulate pollutants** consist of harmful solid and liquid particles suspended in the atmosphere such as dust, soot, metal particles, smog, and smoke. These particles originate from different sources and are present in many sizes and compositions. They are also formed by gaseous pollutants reacting with elements and becoming particulate matter.

IMPORTANT CHEMICAL TESTS (ORGANIC)

1. **Carbylamine reaction test**, also called Hofmann's isocyanide test, is used to detect primary amines.

   The analyte (a substance or solution whose chemical constituents are being identified and measured) is heated with alcoholic KOH and $CHCl_3$. If a primary amine is present, isocyanide (carbylamine) is produced, as indicated by a foul odour. The carbylamine test does not give a positive reaction with secondary and tertiary amines.

2. **Schiff's test** is a chemical test used to detect the presence of aldehydes.

   The presence of aldehydes is confirmed by the appearance of a purple or magenta colour when a few drops of Schiff's reagent (reaction product of a dye formulation such as fuchsin and sodium bisulphite) are added to the analyte.

3. **Bromine test** is a qualitative test to detect the presence of unsaturated carbon-to-carbon double or triple bond, phenols, and anilines.

   Add bromine water to the analyte drop by drop with constant shaking. If the orange red colour of bromine disappears, then the given organic compound is unsaturated.

4. **Lucas' test** is used to differentiate and categorize primary, secondary, and tertiary alcohols.

   Lucas reagent, a solution of anhydrous zinc chloride in concentrated hydrochloric acid, is added to the analyte.

   Primary alcohol: No visible reaction is observed, and the solution remains colourless.

   Secondary alcohol: Solution turns turbid or cloudy in 5–10 minutes.

   Tertiary alcohol: Solution turns turbid rapidly with the formation of two separate layers.

IMPORTANT CHEMICAL TESTS (INORGANIC)

1. **Molisch's test**, named after Czech-Austrian botanist Hans Molisch, is used to check for the presence of carbohydrates in a solution.

   A solution of α-naphthol in ethanol is added to the analyte. Then slowly add a few drops of concentrated H_2SO_4 to the mixture. If a purple ring appears, it is a positive indicator for the presence of carbohydrates in the solution.

2. **Brown ring test**, also known as the nitrate test, is used to detect the presence of nitrate ions in a solution.

   Add iron (II) sulphate to the analyte, then slowly add concentrated H_2SO_4 such that its forms a layer below the aqueous solution. The formation of a brown ring confirms the presence of nitrate ions in the analyte.

3. **Nessler's reagent** is used to test for the presence of ammonia.

   An alkaline solution of K_2HgI_4, called Nessler's reagent, becomes deeper yellow in the presence of ammonia. At higher concentrations, a brown precipitate may form when ammonia gas is passed through it.

CHEMICAL NAME OF SOME COMMON COMPOUNDS

COMMON NAME OF THE CHEMICAL	MOLECULAR FORMULA	CHEMICAL NAME
Baking powder	$NaHCO_3$	Sodium bicarbonate
Soap	$C_{17}H_{35}COONa$	Esters
Milk of magnesia	$Mg(OH)_2$	Magnesium hydroxide
Salt	$NaCl$	Sodium chloride
Chloroform	$CHCl_3$	Trichloromethane
Rochelle salt	$KNaC_4H_4O_6{\cdot}4H_2O$	Sodium potassium tartrate tetrahydrate
Marsh gas	CH_4	Methane
Alcohol	C_2H_6O	Ethanol
Bleaching powder	$CaOCl_2$	Calcium hypochlorite
Sugar	$C_{12}H_{22}O_{11}$	Sucrose
Aspirin	$C_9H_8O_4$	Acetyl salicylic acid
Mouthwash	H_2O_2	Hydrogen peroxide
Caustic soda	$NaOH$	Sodium hydroxide
Moth balls	$C_6H_4Cl_2$	1,4-dichlorobenzene
Limestone	$CaCO_3$	Calcium carbonate
Toilet cleaner	HCl	Hydrochloric acid
Antiperspirant & deodorants	Al_2ClH7O_6	Aluminum chlorohydrate
Borax	$Na_2B_4O_7{\cdot}10H_2O$	Sodium tetraborate decahydrate
Epsom salt	$MgSO_4$	Magnesium sulphate
MSG	$C_5H_8NO_4Na$	Monosodium glutamate
Marble	$CaCO_3$	Calcium carbonate
Sand	SiO_2	Silicon dioxide
Glycerine	$C_3H_8O_3$	Trihydroxy propanol
Heavy water	D_2O	Deuterium oxide
TNT	$C_6H_2(NO_2)_3CH_3$	Trinitrotoluene

FLUORESCENCE AND PHOSPHORESCENCE

Ever wondered why those plastic stars on your ceiling glow after lights out, or why fireflies and jellyfish light up? How about how forensic scientists use ultraviolet (UV) light to detect blood or urine at crime scenes?

These amazing phenomena stem from the ability of substances to absorb and emit light. In fluorescence, the glow stops immediately once the light source is off, while in phosphorescence, the glow can linger from a fraction of a second to several hours.

DIY

What would happen if you took a ripe banana with spots and shone a black light on it. Or if you took a US$20 bill and saw it under a black light?

In the former, you would observe that the area around the spots will glow, whereas in the latter, the security strip near the edge will glow bright green.

RADIOACTIVITY

The phenomenon of radioactivity was accidently discovered by **Henri Becquerel** in 1896. Following the discovery of X-rays in 1895 by **Wilhelm Conrad Roentgen**, Becquerel decided to further examine the correlation between X-rays and naturally occurring phosphorescence.

He illuminated uranium–potassium sulphate with visible light and wrapped it in black paper. Then he separated the package from a photographic plate by a piece of silver, and after several hours of exposure, the photographic plate was developed. The plate showed some penetrating radiation emitted by the compound that was able to pierce both the black paper and the silver.

Experiments performed subsequently showed that radioactivity was a nuclear phenomenon in which an unstable nucleus undergoes a decay. This is referred to as radioactive decay.

Did you know?

Even though Henri Becquerel is credited with the discovery of radioactivity, the term 'radioactivity' was coined by physicist and chemist Marie Curie.

There are three types of radioactive decay that occur in nature:

1. *α-Decay:* Helium nucleus ${}_2He^4$ is emitted.
2. *β-Decay:* Electrons or positrons (particles with the same mass as electrons, but with a charge exactly opposite to that of electron) are emitted.
3. *γ-Decay:* High-energy (hundreds of keV or more) photons are emitted.

IMPORTANT DISCOVERIES IN CHEMISTRY

Here is a summary of some key discoveries in chemistry by century, illustrating the progression of the field:

Thirteenth Century

Discovery of arsenic: Albertus Magnus (Albert the Great) is credited with discovering arsenic around 1250. He also described silver nitrate and sulphuric acid.

Development of fractional distillation: Taddeo Alderotti described methods for concentrating ethanol through repeated fractional distillation, achieving high purities of alcohol.

Seventeenth Century

Boyle's law: In 1662, Robert Boyle formulated Boyle's law, describing the relationship between the pressure and volume of a gas.

The Sceptical Chymist: Published by Robert Boyle in 1661, this work is considered a cornerstone in distinguishing chemistry from alchemy, introducing modern concepts of atoms and chemical reactions.

Eighteenth Century

Discovery of oxygen: Joseph Priestley and Carl Wilhelm Scheele independently discovered oxygen in the 1770s, which was crucial for the development of modern chemistry.

Law of conservation of mass: Antoine Lavoisier established this fundamental principle in the late eighteenth century, demonstrating that mass is conserved in chemical reactions.

Nineteenth Century

Atomic theory: John Dalton proposed his atomic theory in the early 1800s, stating that all matter is composed of atoms, which are indivisible and indestructible particles.

Periodic table: Dmitri Mendeleev created the first periodic table in 1869, arranging elements by atomic weight and predicting the existence of undiscovered elements.

Electromagnetic theory: James Clerk Maxwell formulated the theory of electromagnetism, which had significant implications for the understanding of chemical bonding and reactions.

Twentieth Century

Quantum mechanics: The development of quantum mechanics by scientists such as Max Planck, Niels Bohr, and Erwin Schrödinger revolutionized the understanding of atomic and molecular structures.

Discovery of DNA structure: In 1953, James Watson and Francis Crick discovered the double helix structure of DNA, which is crucial for genetics and biochemistry.

Development of penicillin: Alexander Fleming's discovery of penicillin in 1928 led to the development of antibiotics, transforming medicine and the treatment of bacterial infections.

Radioactivity: The work of Marie and Pierre Curie on radioactivity in the early twentieth century, following Henri Becquerel's discovery, advanced the understanding of atomic structure and nuclear chemistry.

Twenty-first Century

CRISPR-Cas9: The development of CRISPR-Cas9 gene-editing technology has revolutionized molecular biology and genetic engineering, with wide-ranging applications in medicine and agriculture.

Graphene: The isolation of graphene, a single layer of carbon atoms, in 2004 by Andre Geim and Konstantin Novoselov, opened up new possibilities in materials science and electronics.

NOBEL LAUREATES IN CHEMISTRY

As of 2024, the Nobel Prize in Chemistry has been awarded 114 times to 194 laureates between 1901 and 2023. The 2024 awards are to be declared yet. **Frederick Sanger** is the only laureate who has been awarded the Nobel Prize in Chemistry twice, in 1958 and 1980.

2023

Moungi G. Bawendi, **Louis E. Brus**, and **Alexei I. Ekimov**: discovery and development of quantum dots

2022

Carolyn R. Bertozzi, **Morten Meldal**, and **K. Barry Sharpless**: pioneering work on click chemistry and bioorthogonal chemistry

2021

Benjamin List and **David MacMillan**: development of asymmetric organo-catalysis

2020

Emmanuelle Charpentier and **Jennifer A. Doudna**: development of a method for genome editing

2019

John B. Goodenough, **M. Stanley Whittingham**, and **Akira Yoshino**: development of lithium-ion batteries

2018

Frances H. Arnold: the directed evolution of enzymes and **George P. Smith** and **Sir Gregory P. Winter**: phage display of peptides and antibodies

2017

Jacques Dubochet, **Joachim Frank**, and **Richard Henderson**: developing cryo-electron microscopy for the high-resolution structure determination of biomolecules in solution

2016

Jean-Pierre Sauvage, **Sir J. Fraser Stoddart**, and **Bernard L. Feringa**: design and synthesis of molecular machines

2015

Tomas Lindahl, **Paul Modrich**, and **Aziz Sancar**: mechanistic studies of DNA repair

2014

Eric Betzig, **Stefan W. Hell**, and **William E. Moerner**: development of super-resolved fluorescence microscopy

2013

Martin Karplus, **Michael Levitt**, and **Arieh Warshel**: development of multiscale models for complex chemical systems

2012

Robert J. Lefkowitz and **Brian K. Kobilka**: studying G-protein-coupled receptors

2011

Dan Shechtman: discovery of quasicrystals

2010

Richard F. Heck, **Ei-ichiNegishi**, and **Akira Suzuki**: palladium-catalysed cross couplings in organic synthesis

2009

Venkatraman Ramakrishnan, **Thomas Steitz**, and **Ada Yonath**: studying the structure and function of the ribosome

2008

Osamu Shimomura, **Martin Chalfie,** and **Roger Tsien**: discovery and development of the green fluorescent protein

2007

Gerhard Ertl: studying chemical processes on solid surfaces

2006

Roger D. Kornberg: studying the molecular basis of eukaryotic transcription

2005

Yves Chauvin, **Richard R. Schrock**, and **Robert H. Grubbs**: development of the metathesis method in organic synthesis

2004

Aaron Ciechanover, **Avram Hershko**, and **Irwin Rose**: discovery of ubiquitin-mediated protein degradation

2003

Peter Agre: discovery of water channels and **Roderick MacKinnon**: structural and mechanistic studies of ion channels

2002

John B. Fenn and **Koichi Tanaka**: development of soft desorption ionization methods for mass spectrometric analyses of biological macromolecules

Kurt Wüthrich: development of nuclear magnetic resonance (NMR) spectroscopy for determining the 3D structure of biological macromolecules in solution

2001

William S. Knowles and **Ryoji Noyori**: chirally catalysed hydrogenation reactions and **K. Barry Sharpless**: chirally catalysed oxidation reactions

2000

Alan J. Heeger, **Alan G. MacDiarmid**, and **Hideki Shirakawa**: discovery and development of conductive polymers

1999

Ahmed H. Zewail: studying the transition states of chemical reactions using femtosecond spectroscopy

1998

Walter Kohn: for his development of the density-functional theory and **John A. Pople**: for his development of computational methods in quantum chemistry

1997

Paul D. Boyer and **John E. Walker**: elucidation of the enzymatic mechanism underlying the synthesis of adenosine triphosphate (ATP) and **Jens C. Skou**: first discovery of an ion-transporting enzyme, Na^+, K^+ - ATPase

1996

Robert F. Curl Jr., **Sir Harold W. Kroto**, and **Richard E. Smalley**: discovery of fullerenes

1995

Paul J. Crutzen, **Mario J. Molina**, and **F. Sherwood Rowland**: work in atmospheric chemistry, particularly concerning the formation and decomposition of ozone

1994

George A. Olah: contribution to carbocation chemistry

1993

Kary B. Mullis: invention of the polymerase chain reaction (PCR) method and **Michael Smith**: fundamental contributions to the establishment of oligonucleotide-based, site-directed mutagenesis and its development for protein studies

1992

Rudolph A. Marcus: contribution to the theory of electron transfer reactions in chemical systems

1991

Richard R. Ernst: for his contributions to the development of the methodology of high-resolution NMR spectroscopy

1990

Elias James Corey: developing the theory and methodology of organic synthesis

1989

Sidney Altman and **Thomas R. Cech**: discovery of catalytic properties of RNA

1988

Johann Deisenhofer, **Robert Huber**, and **Hartmut Michel**: determination of the 3D structure of a photosynthetic reaction centre

1987

Donald J. Cram, **Jean-Marie Lehn**, and **Charles J. Pedersen**: development and use of molecules with structure-specific interactions of high selectivity

1986

Dudley R. Herschbach, **Yuan T. Lee**, and **John C. Polanyi**: contributions concerning the dynamics of chemical elementary processes

1985

Herbert A. Hauptman and **Jerome Karle**: outstanding achievements in the development of direct methods for the determination of crystal structures

1984

Robert Bruce Merrifield: development of methodology for chemical synthesis on a solid matrix

1983

Henry Taube: mechanisms of electron transfer reactions, especially in metal complexes

1982

Aaron Klug: development of crystallographic electron microscopy and structural elucidation of biologically important nucleic acid-protein complexes

1981

Kenichi Fukui and **Roald Hoffmann**: theories, developed independently, concerning the course of chemical reactions

1980

Paul Berg: fundamental studies of the biochemistry of nucleic acids, with recombinant deoxyribonucleic acid (DNA) and **Walter Gilbert** and **Frederick Sanger**: contributions concerning the determination of base sequences in nucleic acids

1979

Herbert C. Brown and **Georg Wittig**: development of the use of boron- and phosphorus-containing compounds into important reagents in organic synthesis

1978

Peter D. Mitchell: contribution to the understanding of biological energy transfer through the formulation of the chemiosmotic theory

1977

Ilya Prigogine: contribution to non-equilibrium thermodynamics, particularly the theory of dissipative structures

1976

William N. Lipscomb: studying the structure of boranes illuminating problems of chemical bonding

1975

John Warcup Cornforth: work on the stereochemistry of enzyme-catalysed reactions and **Vladimir Prelog**: research into the stereochemistry of organic molecules and reactions

1974

Paul J. Flory: theoretical and experimental achievements in the physical chemistry of the macromolecules

1973

Ernst Otto Fischer and **Geoffrey Wilkinson**: pioneering work, performed independently, on the chemistry of the organometallic, so-called sandwich compounds

1972

Christian B. Anfinsen: work on ribonuclease, especially concerning the connection between the amino acid sequence and the biologically active conformation and **Stanford Moore** and **William H. Stein**: contribution to the understanding of the connection between chemical structure and catalytic activity of the active centre of the ribonuclease molecule

1971

Gerhard Herzberg: contributions to the knowledge of electronic structure and geometry of molecules, particularly free radicals

1970

Luis F. Leloir: discovery of sugar nucleotides and their role in the biosynthesis of carbohydrates

1969

Derek Barton and **Odd Hassel**: contributionto the development of the concept of conformation and its application in chemistry

1968

Lars Onsager: discovery of the reciprocal relations bearing his name, which are fundamental for the thermodynamics of irreversible processes

1967

Manfred Eigen, **Ronald George Wreyford Norrish**, and **George Porter**: studying extremely fast chemical reactions, effected by disturbing the equilibrium by means of very short pulses of energy

1966

Robert S. Mulliken: fundamental work concerning chemical bonds and the electronic structure of molecules by the molecular orbital method

1965

Robert Burns Woodward: outstanding achievements in the art of organic synthesis

1964

Dorothy Crowfoot Hodgkin: determinations by X-ray techniques of the structures of important biochemical substances

1963

Karl Ziegler and **Giulio Natta**: discovery in the field of the chemistry and technology of high polymers

1962

Max Ferdinand Perutz and **John Cowdery Kendrew**: studying of the structures of globular proteins

1961

Melvin Calvin: research on the carbon dioxide assimilation in plants

1960

Willard Frank Libby: method to use carbon-14 for age determination in archaeology, geology, geophysics, and other branches of science

1959

Jaroslav Heyrovsky: discovery and development of the polarographic methods of analysis

1958

Frederick Sanger: work on the structure of proteins, especially that of insulin

1957

Lord Todd: work on nucleotides and nucleotide co-enzymes

1956

Sir Cyril Norman Hinshelwood and **Nikolay Nikolaevich Semenov**: research into the mechanism of chemical reactions

1955

Vincent du Vigneaud: work on biochemically important sulphur compounds, especially for the first synthesis of a polypeptide hormone

1954

Linus Carl Pauling: research into the nature of the chemical bond and its application to the elucidation of the structure of complex substances

1953

Hermann Staudinger: discovery in the field of macromolecular chemistry

1952

Archer John Porter Martin and **Richard Laurence Millington Synge**: invention of partition chromatography

1951

Edwin Mattison McMillan and **Glenn Theodore Seaborg**: discoveries in the chemistry of the trans-uranium elements

1950

Otto Paul Hermann Diels and **Kurt Alder**: for their discovery and development of the diene synthesis

1949

William Francis Giauque: contribution to the field of chemical thermodynamics, particularly the behaviour of substances at extremely low temperatures

1948

Arne Wilhelm Kaurin Tiselius: research on electrophoresis and adsorption analysis, especially for his discoveries concerning the complex nature of the serum proteins

1947

Sir Robert Robinson: investigations on plant products of biological importance, especially the alkaloids

1946

James Batcheller Sumner: discovery that enzymes can be crystallized and **John Howard Northrop** and **Wendell Meredith Stanley**: preparation of enzymes and virus proteins in a pure form

1945

Artturi Ilmari Virtanen: research and inventions in agricultural and nutrition chemistry, including fodder preservation method

1944

Otto Hahn: discovery of the fission of heavy nuclei

1943

George de Hevesy: work on the use of isotopes as tracers in the study of chemical processes

1939

Adolf Friedrich Johann Butenandt: work on sex hormones and **Leopold Ruzicka**: work on polymethylene and higher terpenes

1938

Richard Kuhn: work on carotenoids and vitamins

1937

Walter Norman Haworth: investigations on carbohydrates and vitamin C and **Paul Karrer**: investigations on carotenoids, flavins and vitamins A and B2

1936

Petrus Josephus Wilhelmus Debye: contributions to molecular structure through investigations on dipole moments and on the diffraction of X-rays and electrons in gases

1935

Frédéric Joliot and **Irène Joliot-Curie**: synthesis of new radioactive elements

1934

Harold Clayton Urey: discovery of heavy hydrogen or deuterium

1932

Irving Langmuir: discoveries and investigations in surface chemistry

1931

Carl Bosch and **Friedrich Bergius**: contributions to the invention and development of chemical high-pressure methods

1930

Hans Fischer: research into the constitution of haemin and chlorophyll and especially the synthesis of haemin

1929

Arthur Harden and **Hans Karl August Simon von Euler-Chelpin**: investigations on the fermentation of sugar and fermentative enzymes

1928

Adolf Otto Reinhold Windaus: research into the constitution of the sterols and their connection with the vitamins

1927

Heinrich Otto Wieland: investigations of the constitution of the bile acids and related substances

1926

Theodor Svedberg: work on disperse systems

1925

Richard Adolf Zsigmondy: demonstration of the heterogeneous nature of colloid solutions and for the methods he used, which have since become fundamental in modern colloid chemistry

1923

Fritz Pregl: invention of the method of micro-analysis of organic substances

1922

Francis William Aston: discovery, by means of his mass spectrograph, of isotopes, non-radioactive elements, and for enunciation of the whole-number rule

1921

Frederick Soddy: radioactive substances, and investigations into the origin and nature of isotopes

1920

Walther Hermann Nernst: work in thermochemistry

1918

Fritz Haber: synthesis of ammonia from its elements

1915

Richard Martin Willstätter: research on plant pigments, especially chlorophyll

1914

Theodore William Richards: accurate determinations of the atomic weight of chemical elements

1913

Alfred Werner: work on the linkage of atoms in molecules by which he has thrown new light on earlier investigations and opened up new fields of research especially in inorganic chemistry

1912

Victor Grignard: discovery of Grignard reagent and **Paul Sabatier**: method of hydrogenating organic compounds in the presence of finely disintegrated metals whereby the progress of organic chemistry has been greatly advanced in recent years

1911

Marie Curie, née Sklodowska: discovery of the elements – radium and polonium – by the isolation of radium and the study of the nature and compounds of this remarkable element

1910

Otto Wallach: work in organic chemistry and the chemical industry by his pioneer work in the field of alicyclic compounds

1909

Wilhelm Ostwald: work on catalysis and for his investigations into the fundamental principles governing chemical equilibria and rates of reaction

1908

Ernest Rutherford: investigations into the disintegration of the elements, and the chemistry of radioactive substances

1907

Eduard Buchner: biochemical research and his discovery of cell-free fermentation

1906

Henri Moissan: investigation and isolation of the element fluorine, and for the adoption in the service of science of the electric furnace named after him

1905

Johann Friedrich Wilhelm Adolf von Baeyer: advancement of organic chemistry and the chemical industry, through his work on organic dyes and hydroaromatic compounds

1904

Sir William Ramsay: discovery of the inert gaseous elements in air, and his determination of their place in the periodic system

1903

Svante August Arrhenius: electrolytic theory of dissociation

1902

Hermann Emil Fischer: work on sugar and purine syntheses

1901

Jacobus Henricus van't Hoff: discovery of the laws of chemical dynamics and osmotic pressure in solutions

WHAT IS MATTER?

Matter, the fundamental substance that fills space and possesses mass, forms the backbone of all physical structures.

Dive deeper, and you will discover that this matter is composed of **atoms** and **molecules**. Zoom in even further, atoms reveal themselves to be intricate systems of protons, neutrons, and electrons, the essential building blocks of everything around us.

GENERAL PROPERTIES OF MATTER

Matter can neither be created nor destroyed; it can only be changed from one form to another. Matter has chemical and physical properties.

Physical properties are qualities of matter that can be measured without changing the chemical composition, such as **volume**, **density**, **mass**, **colour**, **melting**, and **boiling points**.

Chemical properties define the characteristic ability of a substance to react to form new substances, such as **flammability**, **toxicity**, **acidity**, and **susceptibility to corrosion**.

Phases of Matter

Matter exists in several phases, such as **solid**, **liquid**, and **gas**. Most substances change between these phases based on the amount of heat the material absorbs or loses or based on the pressure applied.

Apart from the three basic states of matter, there is a **fourth state of matter – plasma**. This is not a common state of matter on earth, but the stars and the sun exist in this state.

There are additional states or phases of matter: **BECs**, **fermionic condensates**, and **quark-gluon plasma**.

MASS AND WEIGHT

Mass is defined as the **measure of inertia possessed by a substance or object**, or by **quantity of matter in a body**. The SI unit of mass is kilogram which is denoted by kg.

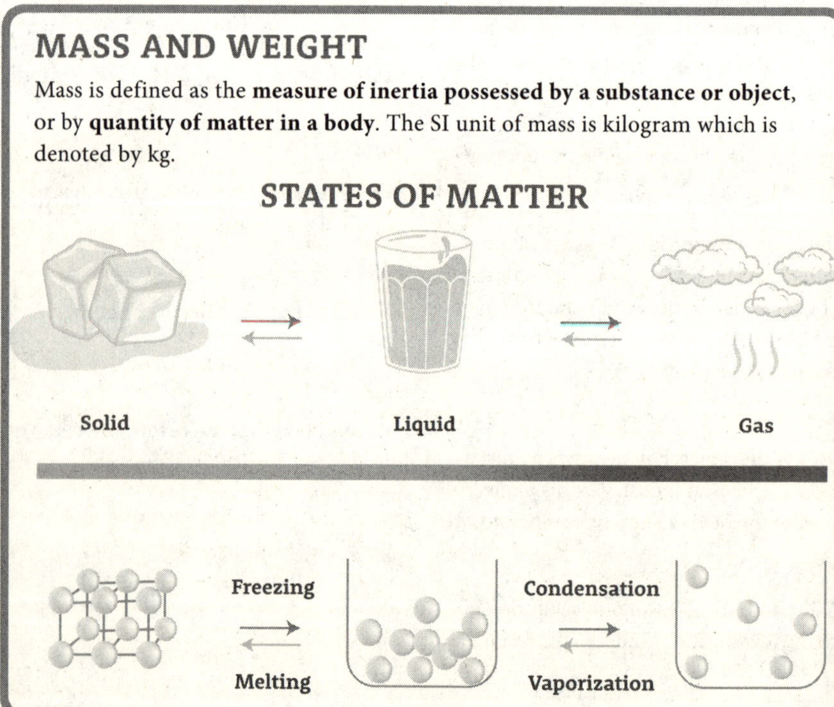

Weight is defined as the **product of mass of the body and the acceleration due to gravity**. This means that the weight of an object is due to the weight exerted by it towards the ground or the surface of the earth. The SI unit of mass is Newton, which is denoted by N.

DENSITY AND RELATIVE DENSITY

Density is the ratio between the mass and the volume of a body.

It can be expressed as

Density (ρ) = mass/volume or D = m/v

The unit of measurement of density is kg/m^3 (SI unit).

Relative density is the ratio between the density of an object and the density of another reference object (mostly water) at a given temperature.

Relative density is a dimensionless quantity. Water has a density of 1 gm/cm^3, which means that it has 13.6 times as much mass as possessed by equal volume of water.

It can be expressed as

$RD = \rho_{sample}/\rho_{reference}$

where ρ_{sample} is the density of sample object and $\rho_{reference}$ is the density of the reference object.

If relative density of material is less than 1, then the sample object is less dense than the reference object, and if more than 1, then the sample object is denser than the reference object. If it is equal to 1, the densities of both the measured and reference substances are the same.

FORCE

Force is defined as the external influence (push or pull) capable of changing the state of rest or motion of a body. It is a vector quantity.

It can also be written as

force = mass × acceleration

or

F = ma

Centrifugal and Centripetal Force

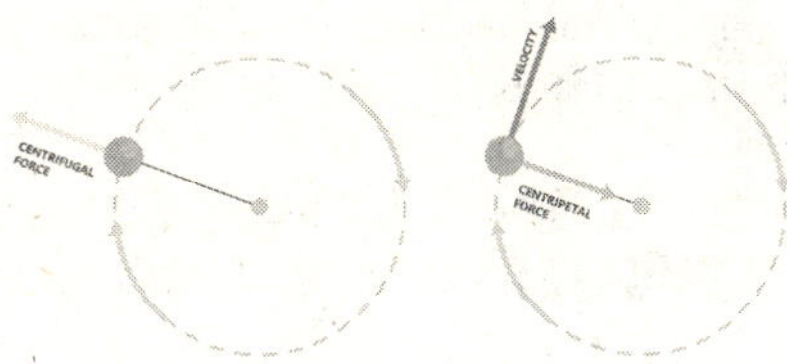

Centrifugal Force **Centripetal Force**

To explain centrifugal and centripetal forces, let us take the example of an object tied with a string. When you swing the piece of string in a circular motion, you have to pull the string inwards. This force which causes you to pull the stone is called **centripetal force**, whereas the equal and opposite force exerted by the stone is called **centrifugal force**.

Take another example of a merry-go-round at an amusement park. When the ride starts, you will feel an outward pull away from the centre of the ride. This force is centrifugal, whereas the force acting towards the centre is centripetal.

The main difference between centripetal and centrifugal forces is that centripetal force is the force acting towards the centre of the circular path keeping the object in motion, while the centrifugal force is the sensation an object feels during the circular motion, acting away from the centre.

Friction

The force that resists the motion of one object or body against another is known as friction.

It is because of friction that vehicles come to a halt when you apply the brakes or a rolling ball will stop after a few seconds. Without friction, a body in motion would continue to remain in motion.

Friction is caused due to the irregularities on the two surfaces in contact. Even surfaces that appear to be smooth have minute irregularities on them, causing friction.

Viscosity

Similar to friction, viscosity is defined as the **fluid's internal resistance** to flow.

NEWTON'S LAWS OF MOTION

Newton's laws of motion describe the motion of massive bodies and how they interact. For example, kicking a stationary object like a wall or a football. The wall will remain in place, but your foot will feel a force in the opposite direction and the football will move. Both of these can be explained with the laws of motion.

In 1686, Isaac Newton presented his three laws of motion in the *Philosophiæ Naturalis Principia Mathematica*, also referred to as Newton's *Principia*.

Newton's First Law of Motion

A body at rest will remain at rest, and a body in motion will remain in motion unless it is acted upon by an external force.

This means that an object or body cannot start, stop or change direction without an unbalanced, external force acting upon it. This property of bodies to resist changes in their state of motion is known as **inertia**. So, a stationary ball will not start rolling unless someone kicks it. Or a car in motion will not stop unless someone applies the brakes. Or a kite will not change direction unless the wind changes.

Newton's Second Law of Motion

The force acting on an object is equal to the mass of that object times its acceleration.

This means that larger the mass of the object, greater the force needed for it to accelerate.

So, moving a heavier object would require more force than a lighter one. The law also explains slowing down moving objects. For example, walking downhill is easier because gravity acting on it is in the same direction (positive acceleration), whereas walking uphill is harder because gravity acting on it is in the opposite direction (negative acceleration).

Newton's Third Law of Motion

For every action, there is an equal and opposite reaction.

This means that forces always occur in pairs. When one body pushes against another, the other body pushes back just as hard. For example, when you push a box, the box pushes back against you. Or when you are standing, you are exerting force on earth and at the same time, earth is pushing back against you with the same amount of force.

WORK

In everyday life, 'work', 'power', and 'energy' are interchangeable.

In the field of physics, work is defined as a force that causes movement – or displacement – of an object. There are many examples of work that we come across our day-to-day life: pushing a grocery cart; lifting a package; and throwing a ball.

Work is a scalar product (since work does not have a direction) of the force acting on an object and the displacement caused by that force. This means that pushing against a wall does not count as work since no movement has taken place. But a glass of water falling off the table would count as work because a force acts on the glass causing a downward displacement.

It can also be written as

$W = \text{force} \times \text{distance}$

or

$W = F \times d$

The SI unit of work is joule and is denoted by J. We can say that joule is defined as the work done by a force of 1 N causing a displacement of 1 m.

Numerical

A person throws a ball with a force of 5 N. The ball travels 10 m. What is the total work done?

$W = F \times d$

$W = 5\ N \times 10\ m$

$W = 50\ J$

ENERGY AND POWER

Energy is defined as the ability to do work, which is the ability to exert a force causing displacement of an object. Energy can neither be created nor destroyed; it can only be transformed from one form to another. Like work, energy is also a scalar quantity since it does not have any direction. The SI unit of energy is joule and is denoted by J.

There are typically two forms of energy:

Kinetic energy is defined as the energy possessed by a moving body by virtue of its motion. Work must be done on the object to change its kinetic energy.

It is expressed in the form of an equation as

$KE = \frac{1}{2} \times m \times v^2$

where m denotes the mass of the object and v denotes the velocity of the object.

Numerical

A ball of mass 3 kg is travelling at a velocity of 10 m/s. Calculate its kinetic energy.

$KE = \frac{1}{2} \times m \times v^2$

$KE = \frac{1}{2} \times 3 \times 10^2$

$KE = 150\ J$

Potential energy is defined as the energy stored by an object by virtue of its position.

It is expressed as

$PE = m \times g \times h$

where m denotes the mass of the object, g denotes the acceleration due to gravity, and h denotes the height in metres.

For example, you are holding an object in the air and because of its position, it has the potential to drop. If you let the object drop, potential energy is converted into kinetic energy.

Numerical

A container of mass 30 kg is kept at a height of 10 m. Calculate the potential energy of the tank. Consider the value of acceleration due to gravity (g) = 9.8 m/s^2.

$PE = m \times g \times h$

$PE = 30 \times 9.8 \times 10$

$PE = 2,940\ J$

Other Types of Energy

Mechanical energy is defined as the energy possessed by an object due to its motion or due to its position.

Chemical energy is defined as the energy released from chemical reactions, mostly in the form of heat.

Thermal energy is defined as the energy possessed by an object or system due to the movement of particles within the object or the system.

Light energy is defined as the electromagnetic radiation including wavelengths that the human eye can detect.

Electrical energy is defined as the energy stored in an electric field or transported by an electric current.

Nuclear energy is defined as the energy released from the nucleus or core of an atom.

TEMPERATURE AND HEAT

Temperature is defined as the degree of hotness or coldness of an object or environment. Temperature describes the

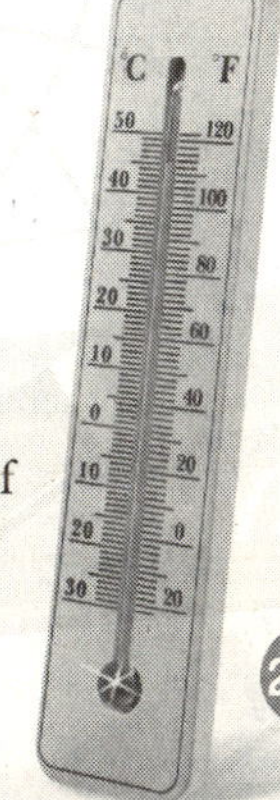

average kinetic energy of molecules within a material or system. The three most common temperature scales are Celsius (°C), Fahrenheit (°F), or Kelvin (K).

CONVERSION	EQUATION
Celsius to Fahrenheit	$T_{°F} = \frac{9}{5}T_{°C} + 32$
Fahrenheit to Celsius	$T_{°C} = \frac{5}{9}T_{°F} - 32$
Celsius to Kelvin	$T_K = T_{°C} + 273.15$
Kelvin to Celsius	$T_{°C} = T_K - 273.15$
Fahrenheit to Kelvin	$T_K = \frac{5}{9}(T(°F) - 32) + 273.15$
Kelvin to Fahrenheit	$T_{°F} = \frac{9}{5}(T(K) - 273.15) + 32$

Numerical

If the room temperature is 30°C, what is the room temperature in °F and in K?

Temperature in °F = 1.8 × 30 + 32 = 86°F

Temperature in K = 30 + 273.15 = 303.15K

On the other hand, **heat** is defined as the **thermal energy transferred** from a **hotter system to a cooler system** that are in contact. The SI unit of heat is **joule**.

Heat transfer takes place in three ways:

1. **Conduction** is when heat transfer takes place between substances in direct contact with each other.
2. **Convection** is when heat transfer takes place in liquids or gases.
3. **Radiation** is when transfer of heat energy takes place through electromagnetic waves.

Zeroth law of thermodynamics states that two separate bodies are in equilibrium with a separate third body, then the first two bodies are also in thermal equilibrium with each other.

First law of thermodynamics states that energy can neither be created nor destroyed; it can be converted from one form to another. It is also known as the law of conversion of energy.

Second law of thermodynamics states that the entropy in an isolated system always increases. This means that heat will not spontaneously flow from a cold object to a hot object, rather it will gradually flow from a cold to a hot object.

Third law of thermodynamics states that entropy of a system approaches a constant value as the temperature approaches absolute zero.

GRAVITATION

In 1687, while lounging beneath the shade of an apple tree, Isaac Newton witnessed a seemingly ordinary event that would change the course of science forever. An apple fell, not sideways or upwards, but straight down to the ground. This simple observation sparked a revelation in Newton's mind: an unseen force was at work, guiding the apple's descent. Thus, the concept of gravity was born, a force that governs the motion of the cosmos.

In scientific terms, **gravity** is defined as the force by which any planet or any other physical body attracts another body towards its centre. It is because of gravity that we are able to walk without flying off the surface of the earth or an object thrown in the air will fall to the ground.

Gravity in Universe

The gravitational force holds the planets in orbit around the sun and the moon in orbit around the planets. It also keeps the atmosphere in place, keeping us at a safe distance from the sun.

Newton's Law of Universal Gravitation

Every particle of matter attracts any other particle with a force that is directly proportional to the product of the masses of the particles and inversely proportional to the square of the distance between them.

It can be expressed as

$F = Gm_1m_2/r^2$

where F is the force, m_1 and m_2 are the masses of the objects interacting, r is the distance between the centre of the masses, and G is the gravitational constant.

This means that objects with more mass will have more gravity. The smaller the distance between the two objects, the heavier the gravitational pull. We can say that gravity gets weaker with distance.

UNITS

A physical quantity is any physical property of a material or system that can be measured. It can be expressed as a value – the algebraic multiplication of a numerical value and a unit. For example, mass which can be measured in grams or kilograms, and depending on the situation, it is important to identify which was used for the measurement.

There are various systems of measurement that are used around the world: **CGS** (centimetre, gram, second), **FPS** (foot, pound, second), and **MKS** (metre, kilogram, second).

The mathematical quantities used to describe the motion of objects can be divided into two categories:

Scalars are quantities that are described by a magnitude (or numerical value).

Vectors are quantities that are described by both a magnitude and direction.

SI Units

With the advances in science and technology, it was essential for scientists to develop a standardized unit of measurement. The units used all over the world have been standardized in the Système Internationale d'Unités which is known as SI units. There are seven fundamental units of measurement:

QUANTITY	SI UNIT	SYMBOL
Length (l)	Meter	m
Mass (M)	Kilogram	kg
Time (T)	Second	s
Electric current (I)	Ampere	A
Thermodynamic temperature (Θ)	Kelvin	K
Amount of substance (N)	Mole	mol
Luminous intensity (J)	Candela	cd

Derived Units

A derived unit is a unit of measurement derived from one or more of the seven base units and are either dimensionless or else are the product of base units. Some examples are watt, ohm, and hertz.

Some of the common derived units are:

QUANTITY	SI UNIT	SYMBOL
Area	Square meter	m^2
Volume	Cubic meter	m^3
Density	Kilogram per cubic meter	kg/m^3
Speed	Distance per unit time (second)	m/s
Acceleration	Speed changed per unit time	m/s^2
Force	Mass times acceleration of object	m/s^2
Pressure	Force per unit area	kg/ms^2
Energy	Force times distance travelled	kgm^2/s^2

SATELLITE

A satellite is defined as an object that orbits or circles around a bigger object.

There are two types of satellites:

A **natural satellite** is defined as a celestial body in space that orbits around a larger body like the moon that orbits the earth.

This means that the moon is a natural satellite of the earth.

A **man-made satellite** is defined as an object that man has built and launched into orbit using rockets.

There are hundreds of man-made satellites in operation, which are used for diverse purposes such as **weather forecasting, broadcasting signals,** and **Global Positioning System (GPS)**. The satellites also serve a range of other purposes such as **space data collection and research, earth surveillance**, and **internet communications.**

Types of man-made satellites

Navigation satellite – used to determine the exact location of a GPS receiver on earth

Communication satellite – used for television, phone, or internet transmissions

Weather satellite – used to capture image clouds and measure temperature and rainfall

Astronomical satellite–used to monitor and image space

Earth observation satellite – used to photograph and capture images of earth

WAVE MOTION

Wave motion is defined as the transfer of energy and momentum from one point of the medium to another point of the medium without actual transport of matter between two points. Take, for example, throwing a pebble in water or plucking a guitar string.

Wave motion can be classified into three ways:

1. Medium of propagation – **mechanical wave** and **non-mechanical wave**
2. Dimensions in which a wave propagates energy – **one-dimensional wave, two-dimensional wave, and 3D wave**
3. Transfer of energy – **standing wave** and **progressive wave**

Transverse Wave

In a transverse wave, the particles of the medium vibrate **perpendicular to the direction of propagation** of the wave. The **region of maximum upward displacement** is called crest and the **region of maximum downward displacement** is called trough. For example, a wave formed on a string.

Longitudinal Wave

In a longitudinal wave, the particles of the medium vibrate in the **same direction as the direction of the displacement** of the wave. For example, sound waves or ultrasonic waves.

Wave Interference

Wave interference is when two waves meet while travelling along the same medium, which leads to the medium taking on a shape as a result of the net effect of the two individual waves upon the particles of the medium.

There are two types of interference:

1. Constructive interference is when the two interfering waves are in phase and have a displacement in the same direction.
2. Destructive interference is when the two interfering waves have a displacement in the opposite direction and cancel each other.

SOUND WAVE

In the field of physics, sound is any vibration that is transmitted as an audible wave of pressure, through a medium – solid, liquid, or gas. The SI unit of measurement for sound is **hertz** which is denoted by Hz.

It can be said that a sound wave is the pattern of disturbance produced by the energy travelling from the source of the sound. Because sound waves are longitudinal, the propagation of vibration of particles is parallel to the energy wave propagation direction. Sound waves can be characterized by its frequency, wavelength, and amplitude.

1. The number of waves produced in one second is known as the **frequency** of a sound wave.

   It can be expressed as

   Frequency (f) = 1/Time period or 1/T

2. The distance between the adjacent identical parts of a wave is known as the **wavelength** of a sound wave.

   It can be expressed as

   $\lambda = v/f$

   where v is the velocity of the sound wave and f is the frequency of the sound wave.

3. The **amplitude** of sound is the magnitude of the maximum displacement of the particles in a sound wave.

Ultrasonic and Infrasonic Sounds

Sound waves with frequency higher than 20,000 Hz are known as ultrasonic, and these are inaudible.

Sound waves with frequency lower than 16 Hz are known as infrasonic, and these are inaudible.

HEAT

Heat is the form of energy transferred between **two materials of different temperature** (higher temperature to lower temperature).

The movement of energy from one material or place to another as a result of a difference in temperature is known as heat transfer. This transfer of energy occurs due to the differences in the average translational kinetic energy per molecule in the two materials. Heat flow takes place from the material or place with higher temperature to the material or place with lower temperature until thermal equilibrium is reached.

The SI unit of heat is **joule**, where 1 joule = 1 N × m.

LIGHT

In daily life, light allows us to see around us. It is simple, really. When light falls on an object, it is reflected by the object and is then received by our eyes, allowing us to see.

Light is a **transverse, electromagnetic wave** that can be seen by the typical eye.

Speed of Light

The speed of light, an astonishing 29,97,92,458 m/s, is one of the universe's fundamental constants. This incredible velocity means that light can travel around the Earth more than seven times in just one second. It is the ultimate speed limit in the cosmos, dictating how quickly information and energy can traverse the vast expanses of space. Whether illuminating our world or revealing the mysteries of distant galaxies, the speed of light is a cornerstone of our understanding of the universe.

There are several common phenomena associated with light such as image formation by mirrors, the twinkling of stars, the formation of rainbows, bending of light by a medium, and so on.

Reflection

Reflection is the change in the direction of propagation of a wave that strikes the boundary between two different media, which is known as the normal.

The incoming light ray makes an angle θ_i with the normal of a plane tangent to the boundary. The reflected ray makes an angle θ_r with this normal and lies in the same plane as the incident ray and the normal.

According to the **law of reflection**: $\boldsymbol{\theta_i = \theta_r}$.

Refraction

Refraction is the change in direction of propagation of a wave when the wave passes from one medium into another and changes its speed. For example, waves passing from air into water. The speed of light in water is less than the speed of light in air, so the ray of light bends towards the normal.

This means that if light enters a substance with a **lower refractive index** (such as from water into air), **light speeds up** and it **bends away from the normal line.**

According to Snell's law, or the law of refraction.

$n_1 \sin\theta_1 = n_2 \sin\theta_2$

where n_1 is the incident index, n_2 is the refracted index, θ_1 is the incident angle, and θ_2 is the refracted angle.

Total Internal Reflection

When a beam of light strikes the surface of water, a **part of the light is reflected** and **some part of the light is refracted**. This phenomenon is known as total internal reflection.

Dispersion

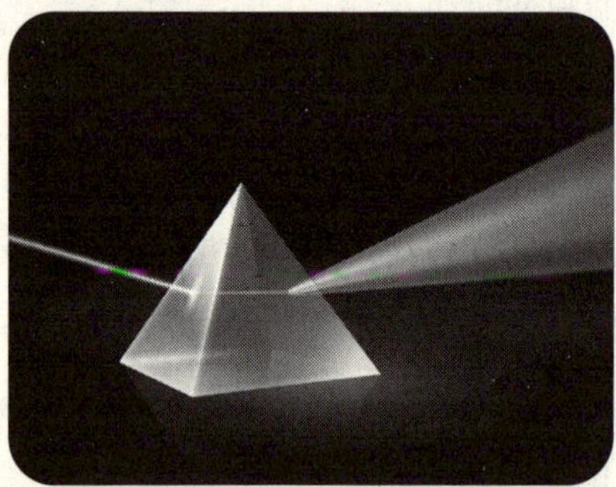

The splitting of white light into component colours is known as dispersion. The most common example of this phenomenon is the **formation of a rainbow**.

If you want to observe dispersion, it can be done by passing a narrow beam of light through a glass prism. Broadly, the different component colours that appear in sequence are **violet**, **indigo**, **blue**, **green**, **yellow**, **orange**, and **red** (VIBGYOR), where red light bends the least and violet light bends the most. This pattern of colour components of light is called spectrum of light.

Diffraction

It is the spreading out of waves of light when they pass through a narrow aperture or around an obstacle.

Wavefront

A wavefront is defined as an imaginary surface that represents corresponding points of a wave surface over which the phase of the wave is constant. This could be where all the crests or all the troughs lie, or any phase in between.

Depending on the source of light, wavefronts can be classified into the following:

When the light source is a point, it sends out waves in three dimensions. The resultant wavefronts are spheres centred on the source called a **spherical wavefront**. For example, ripples formed when a pebble is dropped in water.

When the source of light is linear, all the points equidistant from the linear source lie on the surface of a cylinder which is called a **cylindrical wavefront**. For example, a tube light.

When a fraction of a spherical or cylindrical wavefront originates from a distant source, it produces a **plane wavefront**. For example, the rays that reach us from the sun.

OPTICS

Optics is the branch of science that deals with the behaviour and properties of light and its interaction with matter. Visible light, infrared light, gamma rays, X-rays, and UV are all types of light. Some of the most common examples would be a digital camera, spectacles, or a rear-view mirror. All of these are applications of optics.

In ray optics, a light wave can be considered to travel from one point to another, along a straight line joining them, with an arrow representing the direction of propagation. The path of light is known as ray of light and a bundle of rays is known as beam of light.

Wavelengths of visible light range from about 400 nm (violet) to 700 nm (red).

A spherical mirror is defined as a mirror, which has the shape of a piece cut out of a spherical surface. There are two types of spherical mirrors – concave and convex. If the inside surface of the mirror, is reflective, the mirror is concave; if the outside is reflective, the mirror is convex.

Mirror Equation

Mirror equation or mirror formula is the equation that expresses the **relationship between object distance**, **image distance**, and **focal length**.

It can be expressed as

$1/u + 1/v = 1/f$

where u is the object distance, v is the image distance, and f is the focal length.

Focal length is related to its radius of curvature by the relation R/2.

So, we can say that $1/u + 1/v = 1/f = 2/R$

The **mirror equation** for **concave and convex mirrors** is the **same** and **remains unaffected whether the image formed is real or virtual**.

ELECTRICITY

In physics, electricity is defined as the flow of electric charge or electrons in a conductor. Thus, the several manifestations of electricity are due to the result of the accumulation or motion of a numbers of electrons. **Electric charge can be positive or negative.**

The continuous and closed path through which electric current flows is known as an electric circuit. The SI unit of electric charge is **coulomb** which is denoted by C.

Imagine a small area held normal to the direction of flow of charges, where both positive and negative charges flow across the area.

In a given time interval t, let q_+ be the net amount of positive charge that flows in the forward direction across the area. Similarly, let q_- be the net amount of negative charge flowing across the area in the forward direction.

The net amount of charge flowing across the area in the forward direction in the time interval is denoted by $q = q_+ - q_-$

If a charge q flows through the cross-section of a conductor in time t, the current will be denoted by $I = q/t$.

The SI unit of current is **ampere** which is denoted by A.

Ohm's Law

Imagine a conductor through which a current I is flowing and let V be the potential difference between the ends of the conductor. Then Ohm's law states that

$V \propto I$

or

$V = RI$

where the constant of proportionality R is known as the **resistance** of the conductor. The SI unit of resistance is **ohm** which is denoted by Ω.

Effects of Electric Current

When current flows through a conductor, there are a number of effects that take place.

- *Heating effect of electric current:* When an electric current flows through a conductor, heat is generated in the conductor. This heating effect can be represented with the equation

  $H = I^2RT$

  where I is the current, R is the resistance, and T is the time.

  This means that the longer the current flows in a conductor, more heat is produced; higher the resistance, more heat is produced; and larger the amount of current, more heat is produced.
- *Magnetic effect of electric current:* Another prominent effect of flow of electric current through the conductor is the build-up of the magnetic field. This can be observed when we place a compass close to a wire carrying DC, in which case, the compass needle will deflect.
- *Chemical effect of electric current:* When an electric current passes through a solution, the solution ionizes and breaks down into ions. This is because a chemical reaction takes place when an electric current passes through the solution.

  Depending on the nature of the solution and the electrodes used, the following effects can be observed in the solution – change in the colour of the solution, metallic deposits on the electrodes and release of gas or production of bubbles in the solution. An application of this effect would be in **electroplating** and **electrolysis**.

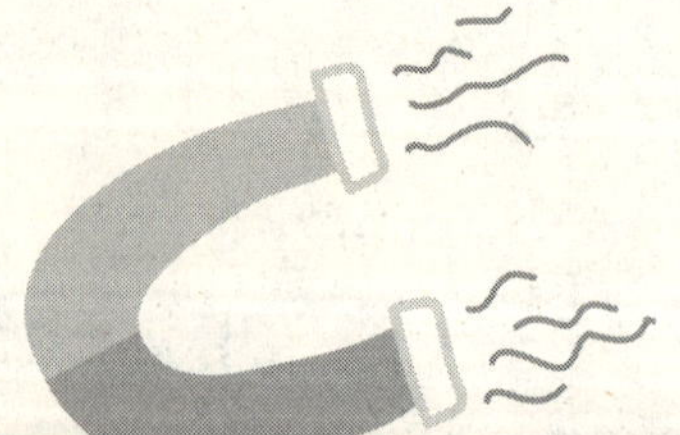

TYPES OF ELECTRICITY

Static Electricity

When charged particles are transferred between two objects, it creates static electricity. For example, when you rub a balloon against your head, it generates static electricity.

What happens in this case is that when these two objects are rubbed together, one object (hair) gives up electrons and becomes more positively while the other object (balloon) collects electrons and becomes more negatively charged.

Current Electricity

Current electricity is defined as the flow of negatively charged electrons across an electric field, through a conductor. It can be classified into:

DC is when electric charge flows in one direction.

AC is when electric charges flow in both directions periodically.

ATOMIC AND NUCLEAR PHYSICS

Atomic physics is the field of physics related to the study of atoms as an isolated system of electrons and an atomic nucleus.

Nuclear physics is the field of physics related to the study of protons and neutrons and interactions of atomic nuclei.

RADIOACTIVITY

Radioactivity is the phenomenon of the spontaneous disintegration of unstable atomic nuclei to atomic nuclei to form more energetically stable atomic nuclei. It was discovered – by accident – in 1896 by A. H. Becquerel while he was studying the fluorescence and phosphorescence of compounds irradiated with visible light. He observed that the photographic plates in which uranium–potassium sulphate was placed had turned black.

In nature, there are three types of radioactive decays that take place.

1. *α-Decay* – a helium nucleus $_2He^4$ is emitted
2. *β-Decay* – electrons or positrons (positively charged electrons) are emitted
3. *γ-Decay* – high-energy (hundreds of keV or more) photons are emitted

Law of Radioactive Decay

The number of nuclei undergoing decay (α, β, or γ-decay) per unit time is proportional to the number of unchanged nuclei present at that instant of time.

$\Delta N/\Delta t \propto N$

or $\Delta N/\Delta t = \lambda N$

where λ is the **radioactive decay constant** or **disintegration constant**.

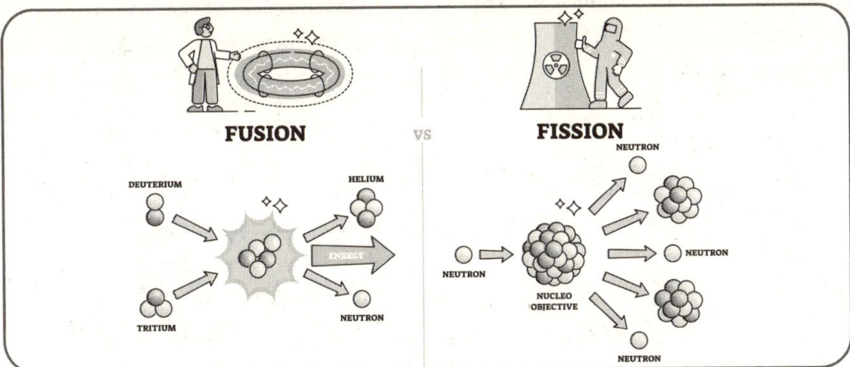

Nuclear Fission

Nuclear fission is defined as the process of splitting a heavy nucleus into two nuclei of comparable size. This process results in the release of large amounts energy.

An example of nuclear fission is the splitting of U^{235} and U^{233}.

$$^{235}_{92}U + ^{1}_{0}n \rightarrow ^{144}_{56}Ba + ^{89}_{36}Kr + 3^{1}_{0}n + 210MeV$$

$$^{233}_{92}U + ^{1}_{0}n \rightarrow ^{137}_{54}Xe + ^{94}_{38}Sr + 3^{1}_{0}n$$

Nuclear Fusion

Nuclear fusion is defined as the process in which two or more lighter nuclei combine to form a heavy nucleus. The sun and the stars are both examples of nuclear fusion reactions.

Fusion reactions are of two types:

1. Those that preserve the number of protons and neutrons

   An example of this is the D-T fusion reaction which produces helium and a neutron and is written

   $D + T \rightarrow He + n$

2. Those that involve a conversion between protons and neutrons

   An example of this is the reaction that takes place in stars which involves the fusion of two hydrogen nuclei to form deuterium (the H-H fusion reaction):

   $H + H \rightarrow D + \beta^+ + \nu$

   where β^+ represents a positron and ν is a neutrino.

NANOTECHNOLOGY

Nano means billionth, so a nanometre is one billionth of a metre.

Nanotechnology is the branch of **science and engineering**, which includes **designing**, **producing** and **using structures**, **devices**, and **systems by manipulating atoms and molecules** at a **nanoscale** (100 nanometres or less) level. This branch of physics can be used across all other science fields.

IMPORTANT DISCOVERIES IN PHYSICS

Pre-Scientific Era

- **384–322 BCE – Aristotle:** Laid the foundation for natural philosophy.
- **250 BCE – Archimedes:** Archimedes' principle, a key discovery in fluid mechanics.
- **500 CE – John Philoponus:** Theory of impetus, an early concept of motion.

Sixteenth Century

- **1514 – Nicolaus Copernicus:** Heliocentrism
- **1589 – Galileo Galilei:** Demonstrated the uniform acceleration of objects due to gravity.

Seventeenth Century

- **1609, 1619 – Johannes Kepler:** Kepler's laws of planetary motion described the orbits of planets.
- **1613 – Galileo Galilei:** Principle of inertia established the concept of uniform motion.
- **1621 – Willebrord Snellius:** Snell's law formulated the law of refraction.
- **1632 – Galileo Galilei:** Galilean principle asserted that the laws of motion are the same in all inertial frames.
- **1660 – Blaise Pascal:** Pascal's law introduced the concept of fluid pressure.
- **1660 – Robert Hooke:** Hooke's law defined the linear relationship between force and displacement in springs.
- **1662 – Robert Boyle:** Boyle's law described the inverse relationship between pressure and volume of gases.
- **1676 – Ole Rømer:** Determined the speed of light by observing the moons of Jupiter.
- **1678 – Christiaan Huygens:** Wave theory of light proposed light as a wave phenomenon.
- **1687 – Isaac Newton:** Formulated the laws of motion and universal gravitation, unifying celestial, and terrestrial mechanics.

Eighteenth Century

- **1782 – Antoine Lavoisier:** Conservation of mass laid the groundwork for modern chemistry.
- **1785 – Charles-Augustin de Coulomb:** Coulomb's law described the electrostatic force between electric charges.

Nineteenth Century

- **1801 – Thomas Young:** Demonstrated the wave nature of light through interference experiments.
- **1803 – John Dalton:** Proposed the atomic theory, describing matter as composed of atoms.
- **1806 – Thomas Young:** Kinetic energy concept formalized.
- **1814 – Augustin-Jean Fresnel:** Developed the wave theory of light, explaining optical interference.
- **1820 – André-Marie Ampère, Jean-Baptiste Biot,** and **Félix Savart:** Established the laws of electromagnetic interaction (Biot–Savart law).
- **1824 – Nicolas Léonard Sadi Carnot:** Analysed the ideal gas cycle (Carnot cycle), foundational for thermodynamics.
- **1826 – André-Marie Ampère:** Ampère's circuital law related magnetic fields and electric currents.
- **1827 – Georg Ohm:** Ohm's law described the relationship between voltage, current, and resistance.
- **1831 – Michael Faraday:** Faraday's law of induction explained electromagnetic induction.
- **1838 – Wilhelm Eduard Weber** and **Carl Friedrich Gauss:** Mapped the Earth's magnetic field.

- **1842 – Christian Doppler:** Doppler effect described the change in frequency of waves relative to an observer.
- **1845 – Michael Faraday:** Faraday rotation demonstrated the interaction of light and magnetic fields.
- **1850–51 – William Thomson (Lord Kelvin)** and **Rudolf Clausius:** Second law of thermodynamics.
- **1861–62 – James Clerk Maxwell:** Maxwell's equations unified electricity and magnetism.
- **1863 – Rudolf Clausius:** Entropy, a measure of disorder in a system.
- **1864 – James Clerk Maxwell:** Electromagnetic field theory.
- **1887 – Michelson–Morley experiment:** Disproved the existence of the ether, a medium once thought necessary for light propagation.
- **1887 – Heinrich Rudolf Hertz:** Demonstrated the existence of electromagnetic waves.
- **1895 – Wilhelm Röntgen:** Discovered X-rays, a form of high-energy electromagnetic radiation.
- **1896 – Henri Becquerel:** Discovered radioactivity.
- **1897 – J. J. Thomson:** Discovered the electron, a fundamental subatomic particle.

Twentieth Century

- **1900 – Max Planck:** Quantum theory introduced the concept of energy quanta.
- **1905 – Albert Einstein:** Special relativity revolutionized the concepts of space and time, introduced mass–energy equivalence ($E = mc^2$).
- **1911 – Ernest Rutherford:** Discovered the atomic nucleus.
- **1915 – Albert Einstein:** General relativity described gravity as the curvature of spacetime.
- **1924 – Louis de Broglie:** Proposed the wave nature of particles.
- **1925 – Werner Heisenberg:** Developed matrix mechanics, a formulation of quantum mechanics.
- **1926 – Erwin Schrödinger:** Schrödinger equation described the behaviour of quantum systems.
- **1927 – Werner Heisenberg:** Uncertainty principle stated the fundamental limits of measurement in quantum mechanics.
- **1932 – James Chadwick:** Discovered the neutron.
- **1938 – Otto Hahn, Lise Meitner,** and **Fritz Strassmann:** Discovered nuclear fission.
- **1947 – Pion discovered:** Key particle in nuclear physics.
- **1956 – Electron neutrino discovered:** Confirmed the existence of neutrinos.
- **1967 – Electroweak theory:** Unified the weak nuclear force and electromagnetism.
- **1970–73 – Standard Model:** Formulated the theory of elementary particles.
- **1981 – Fractional quantum Hall effect discovered:** Revealed new quantum states of matter.
- **1998 – Accelerating expansion of the universe:** Supernova observations revealed the universe's accelerating expansion, implying dark energy.

Twenty-first Century

- **2004 – Graphene isolated:** A two-dimensional form of carbon with remarkable properties.
- **2012 – Higgs boson discovered:** Confirmed the mechanism that gives particles mass.
- **2015 – Gravitational waves observed:** Confirmed a key prediction of general relativity.

- **2019 – First image of a black hole:** Captured by the Event Horizon Telescope.
- **2020 – Room-temperature superconductor identified:** A breakthrough in materials science.
- **2021 – Muon's anomalous magnetic moment confirmed:** Suggested new physics beyond the Standard Model.

NOBEL LAUREATES IN PHYSICS

YEAR	LAUREATE	RATIONALE
1901	Wilhelm Röntgen	The discovery of the remarkable rays subsequently named after him
1902	Hendrik Lorentz Pieter Zeeman	Research into the influence of magnetism upon radiation phenomena
1903	Antoine Henri Becquerel	Discovery of spontaneous radioactivity
	Pierre Curie Marie Skłodowska-Curie	Joint research on the radiation phenomena discovered by Professor Henri Becquerel
1904	Lord Rayleigh	Investigations of the densities of the most important gases and for the discovery of argon in connection with these studies
1905	Philipp Eduard Lenard	Work on cathode rays
1906	Joseph John Thomson	Theoretical and experimental investigations on the conduction of electricity by gases
1907	Albert Abraham Michelson	Optical precision instruments and the spectroscopic and metrological investigations carried out with their aid
1908	Gabriel Lippmann	Method of reproducing colours photographically based on the phenomenon of interference
1909	Guglielmo Marconi Karl Ferdinand Braun	Contribution to the development of wireless telegraphy
1910	Johannes Diderik van der Waals	Work on the equation of state for gases and liquids
1911	Wilhelm Wien	Discoveries regarding the laws governing the radiation of heat
1912	Nils Gustaf Dalén	Invention of automatic valves designed to be used in combination with gas accumulators in lighthouses and buoys
1913	Heike Kamerlingh-Onnes	Investigations on the properties of matter at low temperatures which led, inter alia, to the production of liquid helium
1914	Max von Laue	Discovery of the diffraction of X-rays by crystals, an important step in the development of X-ray spectroscopy
1915	William Henry Bragg William Lawrence Bragg	Analysis of crystal structure by means of X-rays; an important step in the development of X-ray crystallography

SCIENCE

YEAR	LAUREATE	RATIONALE
1917	Charles Glover Barkla	Discovery of the characteristic Röntgen radiation of the elements; another important step in the development of X-ray spectroscopy
1918	Max Planck	For the services rendered to the advancement of physics with the discovery of energy quanta
1919	Johannes Stark	Doppler effect in canal rays and the splitting of spectral lines in electric fields
1920	Charles Édouard Guillaume	Precision measurements in physics with the discovery of anomalies in nickel-steel alloys
1921	Albert Einstein	Service to theoretical physics, and for the discovery of the law of the photoelectric effect
1922	Niels Bohr	Service in the investigation of the structure of atoms and of the radiation emanating from them
1923	Robert Andrews Millikan	Elementary charge of electricity and on the photoelectric effect
1924	Manne Siegbahn	Discoveries and research in the field of X-ray spectroscopy
1925	James Franck	Discovery of the laws governing the impact of an electron upon an atom
	Gustav Hertz	
1926	Jean Baptiste Perrin	Discontinuous structure of matter, and especially for his discovery of sedimentation equilibrium
1927	Arthur Holly Compton	Discovery of the effect named after him
	Charles Thomson Rees Wilson	Method of making the paths of electrically charged particles visible by condensation of vapour
1928	Owen Willans Richardson	Work on the thermionic phenomenon and especially for the discovery of the law named after him
1929	Louis Victor Pierre Raymond, 7th Duc de Broglie	Discovery of the wave nature of electrons
1930	Chandrasekhara Venkata Raman	Work on the scattering of light and for the discovery of the effect named after him
1932	Werner Heisenberg	Creation of quantum mechanics, the application of which has led to the discovery of the allotropic forms of hydrogen
1933	Erwin Schrödinger	Discovery of new productive forms of atomic theory
	Paul Dirac	
1935	James Chadwick	Discovery of the neutron
1936	Victor Francis Hess	Discovery of cosmic radiation
	Carl David Anderson	Discovery of the positron
1937	Clinton Joseph Davisson	Experimental discovery of the diffraction of electrons by crystals
	George Paget Thomson	
1938	Enrico Fermi	Demonstration of the existence of new radioactive elements produced by neutron irradiation, and for the related discovery of nuclear reactions brought about by slow neutrons

YEAR	LAUREATE	RATIONALE
1939	Ernest Lawrence	Invention and development of the cyclotron and for results obtained with it, especially with regard to artificial radioactive elements
1943	Otto Stern	Contribution to the development of the molecular ray method and the discovery of the magnetic moment of the proton
1944	Isidor Isaac Rabi	Resonance method for recording the magnetic properties of atomic nuclei
1945	Wolfgang Pauli	Discovery of the Exclusion Principle, also called the Pauli principle
1946	Percy Williams Bridgman	Invention of an apparatus to produce extremely high pressures, and for the discoveries made within the field of high-pressure physics
1947	Edward Victor Appleton	Investigations of the physics of the upper atmosphere especially for the discovery of the Appleton layer
1948	Patrick Maynard Stuart Blackett	Development of the Wilson cloud chamber method, and discoveries in the fields of nuclear physics and cosmic radiation
1949	Hideki Yukawa	Prediction of the existence of mesons on the basis of theoretical work on nuclear forces
1950	Cecil Frank Powell	Development of the photographic method of studying nuclear processes and discoveries regarding mesons made with this method
1951	John Douglas Cockcroft	Pioneer work on the transmutation of atomic nuclei by artificially accelerated atomic particles
	Ernest Thomas Sinton Walton	
1952	Felix Bloch	Development of new methods for nuclear magnetic precision measurements and discoveries in connection therewith
	Edward Mills Purcell	
1953	Frits Zernike	Demonstration of the phase contrast method and invention of the phase contrast microscope
1954	Max Born	Fundamental research in quantum mechanics and statistical interpretation of the wave function
	Walther Bothe	Coincidence method
1955	Willis Eugene Lamb	Discoveries concerning the fine structure of the hydrogen spectrum
	Polykarp Kusch	Precision determination of the magnetic moment of the electron
1956	John Bardeen	Research on semiconductors and their discovery of the transistor effect
	Walter Houser Brattain	
	William Bradford Shockley	
1957	Tsung-Dao Lee	Penetrating investigation of parity laws which led to important discoveries regarding the elementary particles
	Chen-Ning Yang	

SCIENCE

YEAR	LAUREATE	RATIONALE
1958	Pavel Alekseyevich Cherenkov	Discovery and the interpretation of the Cherenkov effect
	Ilya Frank	
	Igor Yevgenyevich Tamm	
1959	Emilio Gino Segrè	Discovery of the antiproton
	Owen Chamberlain	
1960	Donald Arthur Glaser	Invention of the bubble chamber
1961	Robert Hofstadter	Pioneering studies of electron scattering in atomic nuclei and for discoveries concerning the structure of the nucleons
	Rudolf Ludwig Mössbauer	Research concerning the resonance absorption of gamma radiation and discovery in this connection of the effect which bears his name
1962	Lev Davidovich Landau	Pioneering theories for condensed matter, especially liquid helium
1963	Eugene Paul Wigner	Contributions to the theory of the atomic nucleus and the elementary particles, particularly through the discovery and application of fundamental symmetry principles
	Maria Goeppert-Mayer	Discoveries concerning nuclear shell structure
	J. Hans D. Jensen	
1964	Nicolay Gennadiyevich Basov	Work in the field of quantum electronics, which led to the construction of oscillators and amplifiers based on the maser–laser principle
	Alexander Prokhorov	
	Charles Hard Townes	
1965	Richard Phillips Feynman	Fundamental work in quantum electrodynamics, with deep-ploughing consequences for the physics of elementary particles
	Julian Schwinger	
	Shin'ichirō Tomonaga	
1966	Alfred Kastler	Discovery and development of optical methods for studying Hertzian resonances in atoms
1967	Hans Albrecht Bethe	Contributions to the theory of nuclear reactions and discoveries concerning the energy production in stars
1968	Luis Walter Alvarez	Contributions to elementary particle physics and the discovery of a large number of resonance states, made possible through the development of the technique of using hydrogen bubble chamber and data analysis
1969	Murray Gell-Mann	Contributions and discoveries concerning the classification of elementary particles and their interactions
1970	Hannes Olof Gösta Alfvén	Fundamental work and discoveries in magneto-hydrodynamics with fruitful applications in different parts of plasma physics
	Louis Néel	Fundamental work and discoveries concerning ferromagnetism and anti-ferromagnetism which have led to important applications in solid state physics

YEAR	LAUREATE	RATIONALE
1971	Dennis Gabor	Invention and development of the holographic method
1972	John Bardeen	Theory of superconductivity, usually called the BCS theory
	Leon Neil Cooper	
	John Robert Schrieffer	
1973	Leo Esaki	Experimental discoveries regarding tunnelling phenomena in semiconductors and superconductors, respectively
	Ivar Giaever	
	Brian David Josephson	Theoretical predictions of the properties of a supercurrent through a tunnel barrier, in particular those phenomena which are generally known as the Josephson effect
1974	Martin Ryle	Pioneering research in radio astrophysics: Ryle for his observations and inventions, in particular of the aperture synthesis technique, and Hewish for his decisive role in the discovery of pulsars
	Antony Hewish	
1975	Aage Bohr	Discovery of the connection between collective and particle motion in atomic nuclei and the development of the theory of the structure of the atomic nucleus based on this connection
	Ben Roy Mottelson	
	Leo James Rainwater	
1976	Samuel Chao Chung Ting	Pioneering work in the discovery of a heavy elementary particle of a new kind
	Burton Richter	
1977	Philip Warren Anderson	Fundamental theoretical investigations of the electronic structure of magnetic and disordered systems
	Nevill Francis Mott	
	John Hasbrouck Van Vleck	
1978	Pyotr Leonidovich Kapitsa	Inventions and discoveries in the area of low-temperature physics
	Arno Allan Penzias	Discovery of cosmic microwave background radiation
	Robert Woodrow Wilson	
1979	Sheldon Glashow	Contributions to the theory of the unified weak and electromagnetic interaction between elementary particles, including the prediction of the weak neutral current
	Abdus Salam	
	Steven Weinberg	
1980	James Watson Cronin	Discovery of violations of fundamental symmetry principles in the decay of neutral K-mesons
	Val Logsdon Fitch	
1981	Nicolaas Bloembergen	Contribution to the development of laser spectroscopy
	Arthur Leonard Schawlow	
	Kai Manne Börje Siegbahn	Contribution to the development of high-resolution electron spectroscopy
1982	Kenneth G. Wilson	Theory for critical phenomena in connection with phase transitions

SCIENCE

YEAR	LAUREATE	RATIONALE
1983	Subrahmanyan Chandrasekhar	Theoretical studies of the physical processes of importance to the structure and evolution of the stars
	William Alfred Fowler	Theoretical and experimental studies of the nuclear reactions of importance in the formation of the chemical elements in the universe
1984	Carlo Rubbia	Decisive contributions to the large project, which led to the discovery of the field particles W and Z, communicators of weak interaction
	Simon van der Meer	
1985	Klaus von Klitzing	Discovery of the quantized Hall effect
1986	Ernst Ruska	Work in electron optics, and for designing the first electron microscope
	Gerd Binnig	Design of the scanning tunnelling microscope
	Heinrich Rohrer	
1987	Johannes Georg Bednorz	Important break-through in the discovery of superconductivity in ceramic materials
	Karl Alexander Müller	
1988	Leon Max Lederman	Neutrino beam method and the demonstration of the doublet structure of the leptons through the discovery of the muon neutrino
	Melvin Schwartz	
	Jack Steinberger	
1989	Norman Foster Ramsey	Invention of separated oscillatory fields method and its use in the hydrogen maser and other atomic clocks
	Hans Georg Dehmelt	Development of the ion trap technique
	Wolfgang Paul	
1990	Jerome I. Friedman	Pioneering investigations concerning deep inelastic scattering of electrons on protons and bound neutrons, which have been of essential importance for the development of the quark model in particle physics
	Henry Way Kendall	
	Richard E. Taylor	
1991	Pierre-Gilles de Gennes	Discovering that methods developed for studying order phenomena in simple systems can be generalized to more complex forms of matter, in particular to liquid crystals and polymers
1992	Georges Charpak	Invention and development of particle detectors, in particular the multiwire proportional chamber
1993	Russell Alan Hulse	Discovery of a new type of pulsar
	Joseph Hooton Taylor Jr	
1994	Bertram Brockhouse	Development of neutron spectroscopy and for pioneering contributions to the development of neutron scattering techniques for studies of condensed matter
	Clifford Glenwood Shull	Development of the neutron diffraction technique and for pioneering contributions to the development of neutron scattering techniques for studies of condensed matter

YEAR	LAUREATE	RATIONALE
1995	Martin Lewis Perl	Discovery of the tau lepton and for pioneering experimental contributions to lepton physics
	Frederick Reines	Detection of the neutrino and for pioneering experimental contributions to lepton physics
1996	David Morris Lee	Discovery of superfluidity in helium-3
	Douglas D. Osheroff	
	Robert Coleman Richardson	
1997	Steven Chu	Development of methods to cool and trap atoms with laser light
	Claude Cohen-Tannoudji	
	William Daniel Phillips	
1998	Robert B. Laughlin	Discovery of a new form of quantum fluid with fractionally charged excitations
	Horst Ludwig Störmer	
	Daniel Chee Tsui	
1999	Gerard 't Hooft	Elucidating the quantum structure of electroweak interactions in physics
	Martinus J. G. Veltman	
2000	Zhores Ivanovich Alferov	Developing semiconductor heterostructures used in high-speed- and opto-electronics
	Herbert Kroemer	
	Jack St. Clair Kilby	Invention of the integrated circuit
2001	Eric Allin Cornell	Achievement of Bose–Einstein condensation in dilute gases of alkali atoms and for early fundamental studies of the properties of the condensates
	Carl Edwin Wieman	
	Wolfgang Ketterle	
2002	Raymond Davis Jr	Pioneering contributions to astrophysics, in particular for the detection of cosmic neutrinos
	Masatoshi Koshiba	
	Riccardo Giacconi	Pioneering contributions to astrophysics, which have led to the discovery of cosmic X-ray sources
2003	Alexei Alexeyevich Abrikosov	Pioneering contributions to the theory of superconductors and superfluids
	Vitaly Lazarevich Ginzburg	
	Anthony James Leggett	
2004	David J. Gross	Discovery of asymptotic freedom in the theory of the strong interaction
	Hugh David Politzer	
	Frank Wilczek	
2005	Roy J. Glauber	Contribution to the quantum theory of optical coherence
	John L. Hall	Contributions to the development of laser-based precision spectroscopy, including the optical frequency comb technique
	Theodor W. Hänsch	
2006	John C. Mather	Discovery of the blackbody form and anisotropy of the cosmic microwave background radiation
	George F. Smoot	

SCIENCE

YEAR	LAUREATE	RATIONALE
2007	Albert Fert	Discovery of giant magneto-resistance
	Peter Grünberg	
2008	Makoto Kobayashi	Discovery of the origin of the broken symmetry, which predicts the existence of at least three families of quarks in nature
	Toshihide Maskawa	
	Yoichiro Nambu	Discovery of the mechanism of spontaneous broken symmetry in subatomic physics
2009	Charles K. Kao	Groundbreaking achievements concerning the transmission of light in fibres for optical communication
	Willard S. Boyle	Invention of an imaging semiconductor circuit – the CCD sensor
	George E. Smith	
2010	Andre Geim	Groundbreaking experiments regarding the two-dimensional material graphene
	Konstantin Novoselov	
2011	Saul Perlmutter	Discovery of the accelerating expansion of the universe through observations of distant supernovae
	Brian P. Schmidt	
	Adam G. Riess	
2012	Serge Haroche	Experimental methods that enable measuring and manipulation of individual quantum systems
	David J. Wineland	
2013	François Englert	Theoretical discovery of a mechanism that contributes to the understanding of the origin of mass of subatomic particles; confirmed through the discovery of the predicted fundamental particle at CERN's Large Hadron Collider
	Peter Higgs	
2014	Isamu Akasaki	Invention of efficient blue light-emitting diodes, enabling bright and energy-saving white light sources
	Hiroshi Amano	
	Shuji Nakamura	
2015	Takaaki Kajita	Discovery of neutrino oscillations, showing that neutrinos have mass
	Arthur B. McDonald	
2016	David J. Thouless	Theoretical discoveries of topological phase transitions and topological phases of matter
	F. Duncan M. Haldane	
	John M. Kosterlitz	
2017	Rainer Weiss	Decisive contributions to the LIGO detector and the observation of gravitational waves
	Kip Thorne	
	Barry Barish	
2018	Arthur Ashkin	Inventions in the field of laser physics, in particular for the optical tweezers and their application to biological systems
	Gérard Mourou	Inventions in the field of laser physics, in particular for their method of generating high-intensity, ultra-short optical pulses
	Donna Strickland	

YEAR	LAUREATE	RATIONALE
2019	James Peebles	Theoretical discoveries in physical cosmology
	Michel Mayor	Discovery of an exoplanet orbiting a solar-type star
	Didier Queloz	
2020	Roger Penrose	Discovery that black hole formation is a robust prediction of the general theory of relativity
	Reinhard Genzel	Discovery of a supermassive compact object at the centre of our galaxy
	Andrea Ghez	
2021	Syukuro Manabe	Physical modelling of Earth's climate, quantifying variability and reliably predicting global warming
	Klaus Hasselmann	
	Giorgio Parisi	Discovery of the interplay of disorder and fluctuations in physical systems from atomic to planetary scales
2022	Alain Aspect, John F. Clauser, and Anton Zeilinger	Pioneering experiments with entangled photons, establishing the violation of Bell inequalities and pioneering quantum information science
2023	Pierre Agostini, Ferenc Krausz, and Anne L'Huillier	Experimental methods that generate attosecond pulses of light for the study of electron dynamics in matter

Biology

Biology, a term rooted in Greek with 'bios' meaning life and 'logos' meaning study, unfolds as the fascinating science of life and living organisms. Imagine biology as a grand narrative that chronicles the myriad forms of life, from the simplest single-celled bacteria to the complex multicellular giants such as elephants, towering trees, and intricate fungi networks.

At the heart of this science lies the concept of the organism. This term encompasses the entire spectrum of life forms, celebrating the diversity of existence. Whether it is the invisible, yet immensely important, bacteria thriving in various environments or the majestic, sprawling trees that anchor ecosystems, organisms come in an incredible variety of shapes, sizes, and complexities.

Biology invites us to explore these living entities, diving into their structures, functions, and interactions. It is like being handed the keys to a hidden world teeming with unseen wonders and intricate balances. As we delve deeper, we uncover the secrets of how life thrives, adapts, and evolves on this ever-changing planet, making biology not just a study, but an adventure into the essence of life itself.

Besides **Botany** (study of plant life) and **zoology** (study of animal life), biology embraces many diverse fields, such as human physiology, medicine, ecology, genetics, and others.

- *Morphology* is the branch of biology that deals with the study of the form and structure of organisms and their specific structural features.
- *Physiology*, on the other hand, is the branch of biology that deals with the study of the functions and mechanisms occurring within a living organism.

Together, morphology and physiology provide a comprehensive understanding of the biology of organisms.

SEVEN CHARACTERISTICS OF ALL LIVING ORGANISMS

1. *Nutrition:* Living organisms take in materials (food) that they use for growth or for energy, from their surroundings. This process is nutrition and the food is processed inside them to obtain energy and as raw materials for proteins, carbohydrates, and fats.
2. *Respiration:* Breathing in and out is respiration, and it releases energy from food that is taken in by all living cells. Living things break down food within their cells to release energy for functioning through respiration.
3. *Movement:* All living things move. Even plants move – swaying in the wind, for instance. Animal movement is easy to see.
4. *Excretion:* All living things excrete. Many chemical reactions are constantly taking place within them (in their cells), and these produce waste matter. Such wastes are naturally flushed out of their systems as excreta, including toxic substances.
5. *Growth:* Growth is seen in all living things. It involves using food to produce new cells. The permanent increase in cell number and size is called growth.
6. *Reproduction:* All living organisms have the ability to produce offspring.
7. *Sensitivity:* All living organisms are able to sense and respond to stimuli around them such as light, temperature, water, gravity, and chemicals.

Only living organisms exhibit all of these characteristics.

CLASSIFYING LIVING ORGANISMS

It is obvious that there is a difference between plants and animals – that they belong to two different groups of living things. It is also obvious that many living organisms share some common features. This has led to a system of classification, as under:

Kingdoms

Largest group; there are five kingdoms: Monera, Protista, Fungi, Plantae, and Animalia

Man is a member of Animalia

▼

Phylum

There are 10 types of phylum. Important ones are Protozoa (single-celled creatures) and Anthropoda (insects, fly, bugs)

Man: Chordata – *animals with a backbone (vertebrae)*

▼

Order

Man: Primate – *mammal with hands and feet*

▼

Family

Man: Hominidae *(includes Apes such as gorillas and chimpanzees)*

▼

Genus

All mankind: *Homo*

▼

Species

Modern man: *sapiens*

Ancient man: Neanderthals, etc.

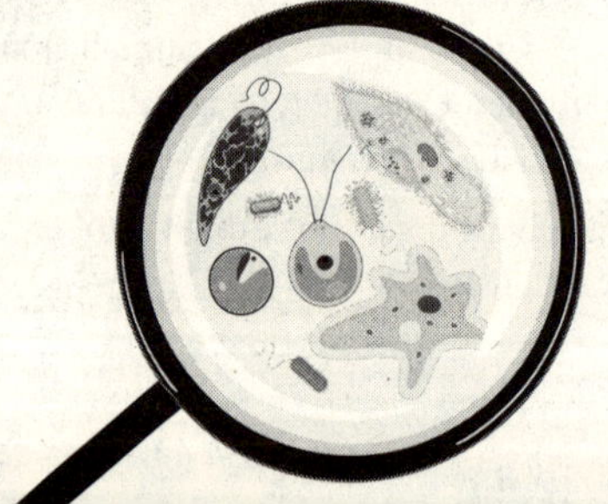

Mammal: A warm-blooded vertebrate animal of a class that is distinguished by the possession of hair or fur, a specialized region of the brain called the neocortex, three middle ear bones, females that secrete milk for the nourishment of the young, and (typically) the birth of live young.

THE CELL

Cells are the building blocks that make up all living organisms. A cell is the smallest and the most basic structural and functional unit of life.

- **1665:** English scientist **Robert Hook** sees many similar tiny pieces in cork, while examining it under his self-made microscope. He calls these cells.
- **1824: R. J. H. Dutrochet** concludes that plants and animals are made up of cells.
- **1835:** Czech physiologist **J. E. Purkinje** coins the term **protoplasm**, with reference to the embryonic material found in eggs.
- **1846:** German botanist **Hugo von Mohl** extends protoplasm to mean the material of cells.

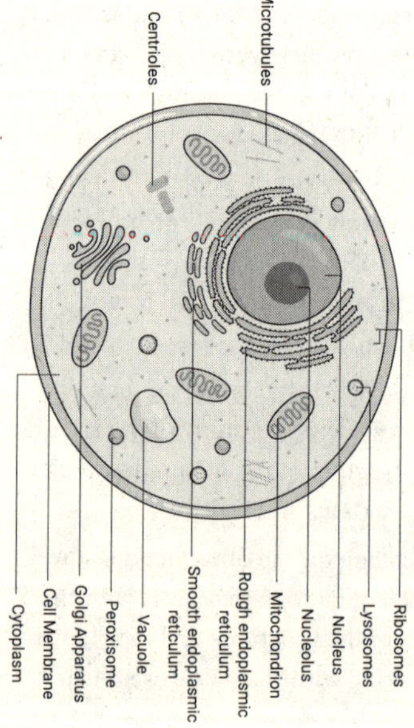

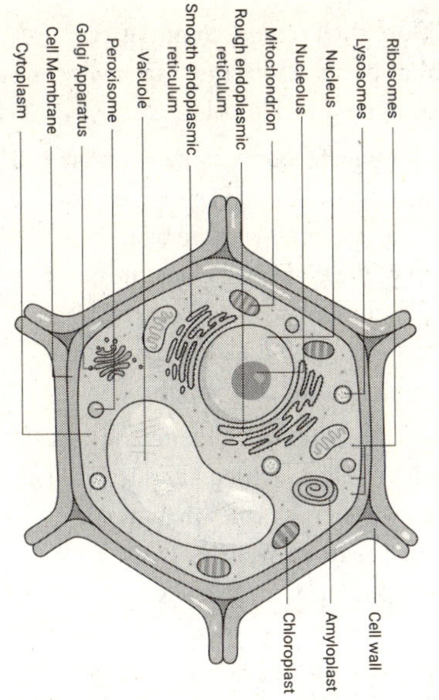

Bacteria and protozoa are single cell organisms. In more complex plants and animals, groups of specialized cells make up tissues and organs. A membrane marks the boundary of a cell. These are permeable and exchange of materials takes place between the cell and its surroundings. In plant cells, this membrane is inside a rigid cell wall. Two structurally distinct types of cells are:

- *Prokaryotic cells*
    - Simpler than those of eukaryotes
    - Lack a nucleus
    - Lack internal cellular bodies (organelles)
    - Examples: **bacteria** and **archaea**
- *Eukaryotic cells*
    - More complex than those of prokaryotes
    - Possess a nucleus
    - Contain internal cellular bodies (organelles)
    - Examples: **protists**, **fungi**, **plants**, and **animals** (all except prokaryotes)
- However, the cells of all prokaryotes and eukaryotes possess two basic features: a **plasma membrane** (or **cell membrane**) and **cytoplasm** (the gelatinous liquid that fills the inside of a cell).
- Though the structures of prokaryotic and eukaryotic cells differ, their molecular compositions and activities are very similar.

PLASMA MEMBRANE

The plasma membrane is the outermost cell surface, which separates the cell from the external environment. The plasma membrane is composed primarily of proteins, lipids, and phospholipids. The lipids occur in two layers *(bilayer)*. Proteins embedded in the bilayer appear to float within the lipid, so the membrane is constantly in flux and so, referred to as a *fluid mosaic structure*. These proteins carry out most of the membrane's functions.

CYTOPLASM AND ORGANELLES

A gel-like substance called **cytoplasm** (or **cytosol**) fills up the insides of a cell. Within the ***cytoplasm of eukaryote cells*** are a number of membrane-bound bodies called **organelles** ('little organs') that have special functions.

- One such organelle is the **endoplasmic reticulum (ER).** The ER is a series of membranes extending throughout the cytoplasm of eukaryotic cells.
    - In some places, the ER is studded with submicroscopic bodies called **ribosomes**. This type of ER is called **rough ER**. In other places, there are no ribosomes. This type of ER is called **smooth ER**.
    - The rough ER is the site of protein synthesis in a cell because it contains ribosomes.

- The smooth ER lacks ribosomes and is responsible for producing lipids.
- Within the ribosomes, amino acids are actually bound together to form proteins. **Cisternae** are spaces within the folds of the ER membranes.

- Another organelle is the **Golgi apparatus** (also called **Golgi body**).
  - The Golgi apparatus is a series of flattened sacs, usually curled at the edges. In the Golgi body, the cell's proteins and lipids are processed and packaged before being sent to their final destination.
  - To do so the outermost sac of the Golgi body often bulges and breaks away to form drop-like vesicles known as *secretory vesicles.*
- Another organelle is the **lysosome** connected to the Golgi body. It is a sac of **enzymes** in the cytoplasm. These enzymes are used for digestion within the cell. They break down particles of food taken into the cell and make the products available for use; they also help break down old cell organelles for disposal. Enzymes are also found in **peroxisome**, a cytoplasmic organelle.
- The organelle that releases energy to form **ATP** is the **mitochondrion** (plural: **mitochondria**). Because mitochondria are involved in energy release and storage, ATP is commonly referred to as the 'energy currency' of the cell.
- Green plant cells contain organelles known as **chloroplasts**, which are responsible for photosynthesis. Chloroplasts contain the pigment chlorophyll, which captures the energy from sunlight, converts it, and stores it in the ATP, while freeing oxygen from water in the cells. The ATP in turn release energy when required. Chlorophyll is most common in chloroplasts, and is the reason why most plants are green in colour.
- An organelle found in mature plant cells is a large, fluid-filled central **vacuole**, which may occupy more than 75 per cent of the plant cell. Here, the plant stores nutrients, as well as toxic wastes. Pressure within the growing vacuole may cause the cell to swell.
- The **cytoskeleton** is an interconnected system of fibres, threads, and interwoven molecules that give structure to the cell. The main components of the cytoskeleton are microtubules, microfilaments, and intermediate filaments assembled from subunits of protein.
- The **centriole** organelle is a cylinder shaped structure that occurs in pairs. Centrioles function in cell division.

Cilia and Flagella

Both are found outside the cell. Responsible of cell movement, but how are they different?

Cilia

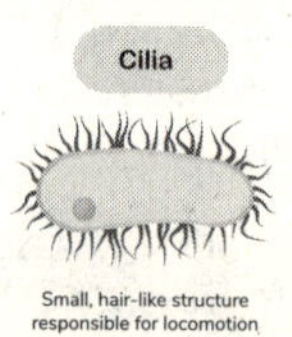

Small, hair-like structure responsible for locomotion

Flagella

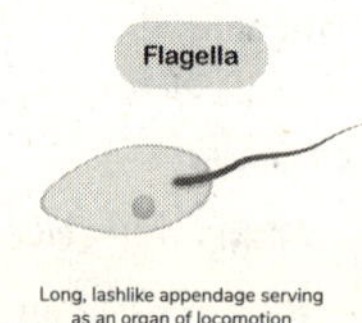

Long, lashlike appendage serving as an organ of locomotion

- *Flagella* are long, hair-like organelles that extend from the cell, permitting it to move. In prokaryotic cells, such as bacteria, the flagella rotate like the propeller of a motorboat. In eukaryotic cells, such as protozoa and sperm cells, the flagella whip about and propel the cell.
- *Cilia* are shorter and more numerous than flagella. In moving cells, the cilia wave in unison and move the cell forward. Cilia are also found on the surface of cells that line the human respiratory tract.

NUCLEUS

The nucleus is the control centre of the cell. It is surrounded by a nuclear membrane that allows molecules to enter and leave the nucleus similar to the plasma membrane.

Prokaryotic cells do not have a nucleus, while eukaryotic cells do.

- The nucleus of eukaryotic cells is composed primarily of protein and DNA, which is tightly wound around special proteins called **histones**.
- The mix of DNA and histone proteins is called **chromatin**.
- The chromatin is folded into distinct threads called **chromosomes.** Humans have 46 chromosomes in every cell, while roundworms have two. Although prokaryotic cells, have no nucleus, they do have DNA, which exists freely in the cytoplasm as a closed loop.
- Functional segments of the chromosomes are referred to as **genes**. About 21,000 genes are located in the nucleus of all human cells.

Inside the nucleus are dense organelles known as **nucleoli** (the singular form is *nucleolus*). In nucleoli, submicroscopic particles known as *ribosomes* are assembled before their passage out of the nucleus into the cytoplasm.

Cell Wall

Many kinds of prokaryotes and eukaryotes contain a structure outside the cell membrane called the **cell wall**. Almost all prokaryotes have thick, rigid cell walls that give them their shape. Among the eukaryotes, some protists, and all fungi and plants, have cell walls. Cell walls of fungi consist of a polysaccharide called **chitin**. Cell walls of plant cells consist of the polysaccharide **cellulose**.

CELL DIVISION

Cell division is the process by which new cells are formed for growth, repair, and replacement in the body. This process includes division of the nuclear material and division of the cytoplasm.

Types of Cell Division

- *Mitosis:* Through this process, cells make exact replicas of themselves. All cells in the body (somatic cells), except those that give rise to the eggs and sperm (gametes), reproduce (multiply) by mitosis.
- *Meiosis:* In this type of cell division, sperm or egg cells are produced instead of identical daughter cells as in mitosis. It leads to creating four daughter cells out of a single cell. Each daughter though has a set of chromosomes that is only half that of its parent.
- *Binary fission:* Single-celled organisms such as bacteria replicate themselves for reproduction.

DNA AND RNA

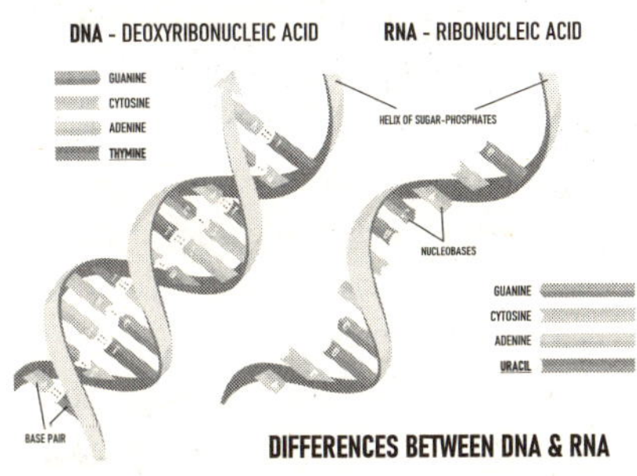

DNA and RNA are nucleic acids that carry genetic information. DNA is the master blueprint for life containing genetic material in all living organisms and most viruses. RNA acts as messenger between DNA and ribosomes to make protein.

	DNA	RNA
Name	Deoxyribonucleic acid	Ribonucleic acid
Function	Long-term storage of genetic information; transmission of genetic information to make other cells and new organisms.	Used to transfer the genetic code from the nucleus to the ribosomes to make proteins. RNA is used to transmit genetic information in some organisms and may have been the molecule used to store genetic blueprints in primitive organisms.
Structural Features	B-form double helix – a double-stranded molecule with a long chain of nucleotides.	A-form helix. RNA usually is a single-strand helix consisting of shorter chains of nucleotides.
Composition of Bases and Sugars	Deoxyribose sugar phosphate backbone adenine, guanine, cytosine, thymine bases	Ribose sugar phosphate backbone adenine, guanine, cytosine, uracil bases
Propagation	DNA is self-replicating.	RNA is synthesized from DNA on an as-needed basis.

- Actually, DNA was first identified in the late 1860s by Swiss chemist **Friedrich Miescher**. American biologist **James Watson** and English physicist **Francis Crick** (in 1953) determined that it was responsible for genetic inheritance and proposed the **double helix model** of the DNA.

VIRUS

A virus is a tiny particle made up of a DNA or RNA genome inside a protein shell called a **capsid**. Some viruses have an external membrane **envelope**.

- Viruses are very diverse. They come in different shapes and structures, and have many different kinds of genomes, and infect different hosts.
- Viruses reproduce by **infecting** their host cells and reprogramming them to become virus-making factories.

  But the common features that viruses share are:

  - A protective protein shell or **capsid**.
  - A nucleic acid genome made of DNA or RNA, tucked inside of the capsid.
  - A layer of membrane called the **envelope** (many, but not all viruses).

Because they cannot reproduce by themselves (without a host), viruses are not considered as being alive (living). Nor do viruses have cells: they are smaller than even the cells of living things, and are basically just packages of nucleic acid and protein.

VIRAL INFECTION

At the microscopic scale, a viral infection occurs when a load of virus invade a host (which could be bacterial, plant, or animal – including ourselves). These then manipulate the cells of their host to make more copies of themselves. The viral **lifecycle** is given below:

- *Attachment:* The virus recognizes and binds to a host cell via a receptor molecule on the cell surface.
- *Entry:* The virus or its genetic material enters the cell.
- *Genome replication and gene expression:* The viral genome is copied, and its genes are expressed to make viral proteins.
- *Assembly:* New viral particles are assembled from the genome copies and viral proteins.
- *Release:* Completed viral particles exit the cell and can infect other cells.

VIRAL DISEASE

Humankind knew nothing about viruses when vaccination began in **1796** once English doctor **Edward Jenner** noticed that milkmaids who had been infected by cowpox were immune from smallpox.

Discovery of Virus

- **1892: Dmitri Ivanovsky** experiments on the sap of diseased tobacco plants by passing them through very fine filters.
- The filters have pores small enough to retain bacteria.
- He still finds that sap from a diseased plant will infect healthy tobacco plants. This tells him that the infectious agent is smaller than bacteria. It is the **tobacco mosaic virus**.
- **Martinus Beijerinck** gives it the name – 'virus'. So begins the subject of Virology.
- Many **bacteriophages** (viruses that destroy bacteria) are quickly found.
- **1926: Thomas M. Rivers** defines viruses as obligate parasites. It is known by now that viruses are particles, rather than fluids.
- **1931:** Invention of the electron microscope allows seeing their structures.

DEADLY VIRUSES

Smallpox: Wiped out whole societies in the course of history, such as almost 90 per cent of the Inca population when the Spaniards invaded the South American continent. Europeans did have a level of immunity, but it would cause severe illness, disfigurement, and even death to many. It has been near-eradicated by successful vaccination programmes.

Rabies: Has been around from the time mankind began domesticating animals. It is invariably fatal once symptoms appear and its gestation period can vary from a week to more than a year. Those bitten or licked by a suspected rabid animal must immediately take a course of injections.

Influenza: It has likely been around for centuries in different forms and been responsible for epidemics – but virology was yet to develop.

- In **1918–19**, an influenza pandemic runs through the world. It will kill nearly 50 million people.
- **1931:** American pathologist Ernest W. Goodpasture grows influenza in fertilized chickens' eggs. It is only now that study of the virus begins.
- For the first time, enzymic activity is associated with the virus particle. In the 1950s, it is found that the virus recombines at high frequencies, and that it has a segmented genome. It has similarities with its cousin – the SARS COVID-19.
- The virus mutates quickly and vaccines lose effectiveness. But the disease no longer seems to be quite as deadly.

Poliomyelitis: The twentieth century witnesses a striking growth in number of severe polio cases.

- Even President F. D. Roosevelt of the United States was crippled because of it.
- In 1949, the polio virus is cultured for the first time in human embryo cells.
- It is then learnt that many have been asymptomatic carriers of the disease.
- The 1949 technique allows Jonas Salk to create an effective polio vaccine.

Epstein–Barr virus: Irishman Denis Burkitt is the first to describe a cancer now called Burkitt's lymphoma. Endemic in equatorial Africa among children, Burkitt sends tumour cells to British virologist Anthony Epstein.

- Working with Yvonne Barr, Epstein finally finds a virus similar to the herpes virus in the sample cells. This virus is later identified as yet another herpes virus.
- The Epstein–Barr virus is then found to be a very common but relatively mild to Europeans. But it can be a devastating illness in Africans.
- The Epstein–Barr virus is important because it is the first virus shown to cause cancer in humans.

Human immunodeficiency virus infection and acquired immunodeficiency syndrome (HIV/AIDS): Caused by the HIV retrovirus, the syndrome AIDS can manifest in a number of ways.

- After infection, individuals may or may not notice any symptoms. This is followed by a prolonged incubation period with no symptoms.
- Meanwhile the virus goes about destroying the immune system. This can manifest in a number of ways – ranging from tuberculosis to opportunistic tumours (such as Kaposi's sarcoma) and infections. Full blown AIDS is often also associated with drastic weight loss, unintended weight loss.

- HIV spreads through contaminated blood and body fluids, including mother to child during pregnancy, delivery, or breastfeeding. Saliva, sweat, and tears do not transmit the virus.
- There is no cure or vaccine, but antiretroviral treatment can slow the course of the disease and lead to an improved life expectancy. Without treatment, the average survival time after infection is 11 years.
- In 2021, about 38 million people worldwide were living with HIV and 650,000 deaths occurred that year. Between 1981, when it was first identified, and 2021, AIDS has led to an estimated 40 million deaths. As of the latest data, around 39 million people globally were living with HIV at the end of 2022. In that same year, approximately 630,000 people died from HIV-related causes. The cumulative impact of HIV/AIDS since its identification in 1981 has resulted in about 40.4 million deaths, according to the World Health Organization (WHO).
- HIV made the jump from other primates to humans in West-Central Africa in around mid-twentieth century.

As of 2024, significant developments have occurred regarding COVID-19, SARS-CoV-2 variants, and vaccination:

SARS-CoV-2 Variants

Omicron dominance: The Omicron variant remains the predominant strain globally. Within this category, subvariants such as JN.1 and its descendant KP.2 have become prevalent (WHO, CDC, IDSA Home).

JN.1 and KP.2 variant characteristics: Despite their increased ability to spread, these variants do not necessarily cause more severe disease than earlier strains (IDSA Home).

COVID-19 Severity and Immune Response

Reduced disease severity: Due to widespread immunity from vaccinations and past infections, the severity of COVID-19 has generally decreased. However, protection against infection wanes over time, underscoring the importance of booster vaccinations (CDC, IDSA Home).

Hyper-inflammatory response: Severe cases of COVID-19 are often linked to an acute hyper-inflammatory response, known as a cytokine storm, which can lead to complications such as acute respiratory distress, blood clotting, strokes, and heart attacks.

Vaccination Efforts

Vaccine efficacy: Numerous vaccines are available, including updated versions targeting the latest variants. These vaccines continue to be effective in reducing the severity of the disease but are less effective at preventing infection entirely (IDSA Home).

Impact on public health: Vaccination efforts have significantly mitigated the impact of the pandemic. A study reported that vaccines prevented nearly 20 million deaths between December 2020 and December 2021 (CDC).

Public Health Measures

Ongoing surveillance: Continuous monitoring and genomic sequencing are crucial for detecting new variants and understanding their impact. (WHO, CDC).

Preventive actions: Public health recommendations include getting vaccinated, improving indoor air quality, testing for COVID-19 when symptomatic, and adhering to other preventive measures such as wearing masks and maintaining good hand hygiene (CDC).

BACTERIA

Bacteria are one of the first forms of life to originate on earth and the earliest estimated to be about three billion years old. They are one of the most successful life forms on earth, as they have colonized almost the entire planet.

Bacteria are ***microscopic, prokaryotic type, single-celled*** organisms classified as belonging to Kingdom Monera. Their (usually circular) DNA can be found throughout the cytoplasm and not within a membrane-bound nucleus (they do not have a nucleus). They reproduce by binary fission.

In one form or another, they are capable of living in almost every environment that our world has to offer, from soil to seawater; boiling springs to radioactive waste; deep in the Earth's crust, to the stratosphere, and even in the bodies of other organisms.

Using primitive microscopes, Antony van Leeuwenhoek was the first to discover bacteria in 1676.

Classification of bacteria: There are many ways of classifying bacteria.

- One way is ***shape***:
  - ➢ Spherical **(cocci)**
  - ➢ Rod-like **(bacilli)**
  - ➢ Spiral **(spirochetes** and **spirilla)**
  - ➢ Comma-shaped **(vibrios)**
- Another way is whether or not they are **gram positive** or **gram negative**. Gram-positive ones are stained by dyes and appear coloured under a microscope.
  - ➢ Gram-negative bacteria are generally more resistant to antibiotics.
- Still other ways are whether they are aerobic or anaerobic (whether they need oxygen, can tolerate oxygen, or get poisoned by it); the temperature range they can tolerate, among others.

Essentialness of Bacteria

Though we tend to associate bacteria with diseases, most are crucial to the well-being of other living things.

- ➢ *Commensal* bacteria help us digest food that keeps us going.
- ➢ *Microbiome* in our gut also provides defence against other pathogenic bacteria. Such gut bacteria are called probiotics. Probiotics are the food on which the microbiome of our gut survives.

- *Nitrogen-fixing bacteria* help fix atmospheric nitrogen in soil and thus makes it fertile for plants to grow.
- *Food technology* – making **yogurt** and **cheese** from milk; **chocolate making**; **vinegar**; and bread
- *Industry and research:* Bacteria work like cheap molecular machines and are extremely cost-effective. They are used to manufacture: **alcohol, insulin, antibiotics, organic compounds** such as butyric acid, acetone, iso-propanol.
- *PCR* (thanks to COVID-19, you are probably familiar with the RT-PCR test), and **papermaking**.
- The largest single bacterial cell is the Thiomargarita namibiensis (Gram-negative coccoid Proteobacterium), which can grow up to 0.75 mm (750 μm) in diameter.

How Are Viruses Different from Bacteria?

At the biological level, bacteria and viruses are very different. Bacteria are small and single-celled, but they are living organisms that do not depend on a host cell to reproduce. Viruses, on the other hand, are even tinier and must have a host to survive and replicate.

Typical viruses are between about 20 and 300 nanometres in size, whereas the typical *E. coli* bacterium is about 1,000 nanometres (10^{-9} m) in size.

Because of these differences, bacterial and viral infections are treated very differently. Antibiotics are only helpful against bacteria, not viruses.

PLANTAE

Imagine Earth 450 million years ago, a time when the first brave pioneers of plant life began their slow but steady conquest of land. Before these green pioneers, the world was ruled by algal scum, which had been flourishing in the oceans for a staggering 1,200 million years. But the land was barren, a blank canvas waiting to be painted with life.

Recent studies of carbon isotope ratios in ancient Precambrian rocks have unveiled an astonishing revelation: photosynthetic plants had already developed a billion years ago, quietly laying the groundwork for a greener future.

Fast forward to the end of the Devonian Period, and the botanical landscape had transformed dramatically. Plants had evolved essential features we recognize today – roots delving into the earth, leaves capturing sunlight, secondary wood providing strength, and seeds ensuring the next generation. This period saw the rise of the first true forests, with towering trees casting shadows and creating habitats for a host of new life forms.

However, the botanical story did not end there. The last major group of plants to grace our planet were the grasses, which appeared relatively recently in the grand timeline of life, about 40 million years ago. These humble plants would go on to dominate vast landscapes and become the foundation of numerous ecosystems.

From the first algal whispers to the mighty forests and expansive grasslands, the story of plant evolution is a testament to the relentless march of life, adapting and flourishing in ever-changing environments.

The Plant Kingdom may be classified as shown:

PLANTAE		
VASCULAR		NON-VASCULAR
FERNS	SEED-BEARING	BRYOPHYTES
GYMNOSPERMS (Conifers) ANGIOSPERMS (Flower bearing)		Mosses Liverworts Hornworts

They are also known as Marchantiophyta (liverworts), Anthocerotophyta (hornworts), Bryophyta (mosses), Filicophyta (ferns), Cycadophyta (cycads), Ginkgophyta (ginkgos), Pinophyta (conifers), Pteridophytes (also ferns), Gnetophyta (gnetophytes), and Magnoliophyta (Angiosperms, flowering plants).

- Flowering plants now dominate terrestrial ecosystems, comprising 80 per cent of vascular plant species.

Vascular plants differ from non-vascular ones in two ways:

1. They have **xylem** and **phloem vessels** that allow glucose (produced during photosynthesis), gases, water, minerals, and nutrients to be circulated throughout the plant.
2. They are all seed-bearing.

Cotyledon: The first leaf or one of the first pair of leaves developed by the embryo of a seed plant. Just as leaves of plants provide food for the entire plants, so does the cotyledon for germinating seed.

Understanding such differences helps in better nurturing them. For example, spraying herbicide meant for a monocot weed on a dicot, will not kill it.

Monocot or dicot: Monocotyledons (monocot in short) have only one cotyledon, while dicots or dicotyledons have two cotyledons. Leaves of dicots have veins that are branched. Sometimes the veins branch out on either side of the leaf from a middle vein, in an arrangement resembling a feather. Other dicots have veins that branch out from a single vein, like fingers on a hand. Monocots have veins that are parallel to one another.

One can also tell if it is a monocot or dicot by the number of petals and other flower parts. Monocots have flower parts in threes or multiples of three, while dicots have flower parts in multiples of four or five.

Examples of monocots are rice, corn, banana, sugarcane, and wheat.

Examples of dicots are tomato, pea, lettuce, onion, and garlic.

PLANT PARTS

The principal parts of a plant are as follows:

Roots

- The radical or primary root anchors the plant to soil. These are usually the tap-root (a straight tapering root growing vertically downwards and forming the centre from which subsidiary rootlets emerge).
- Feeder roots draw nutrients from soil.
- Storage roots store nutrients – examples are tubers such as potato and radish.

Stem

Stems hold up the plant and provide support for leaves, fruits, and flowers. They may have connections such as:

- *Rhizomes* – that store nutrients
- *Tubers* – also store nutrients; they are larger than rhizomes
- *Corm* – underground leaves
- *Bulbs* – that store food and can grow into plants
- *Cladophyll* – spiny leaves such as in cactus that also act as stems
- *Tendrils* – thin stems such as in creepers such as cucumber

Leaves

Generally green in colour because they contain chlorophyll, food is photo-synthesized in them.

Flowers

Consisting of stamen, pistils, sepals, and petals, flowers are the reproductive organs of a plant. They are bright in colour to attract pollinators, like insects. After being fertilized, their ovaries develop into fruits and their ovules into seeds.

Angiosperms can be herbs or shrubs and trees. They can also be:

Perennials that bloom many times over the years.

Annuals that bloom just once – completing their life-cycle in one year.

Biennials grow leaves, stems, and roots the first year; then go dormant, before flowering and producing seeds the next year before dying.

ANIMALIA

METAZOA

Animals with bodies that are composed of many differentiated cells arranged into definite organs and that have a digestive system are known as Metazoa. These include chordates – homo sapiens, dogs, horses, and such; spiralia – worms and molluscs; and arthropods.

INVERTEBRATES

Invertebrates are animals that lack a backbone and include arthropods and molluscs. They make up 95 per cent of animal species over 30 different phyla.

- **Arthropoda**

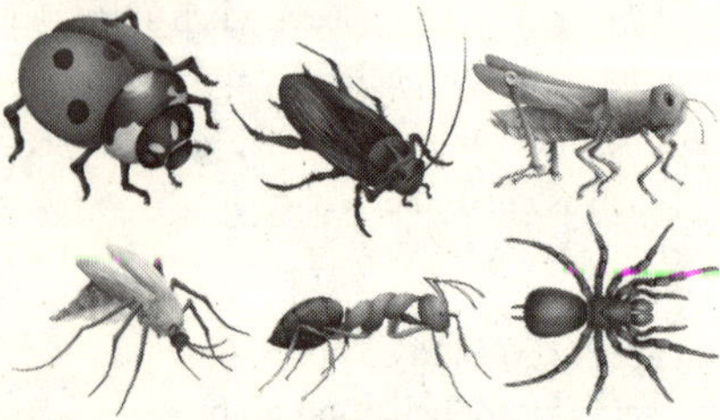

Constitute the largest phylum in the animal kingdom, and include invertebrates such as lobsters, crabs, spiders, mites, insects, centipedes, and millipedes. Many have exoskeletons (external skeletal support – not internal skeletons like the chordates). About 84 per cent of all known species of animals are arthropods.

VERTEBRATES

All animals that have a backbone or spinal column can be called vertebrates. They include mammals, birds, reptiles, amphibians, and fishes.

- **Pisces (fish)**

Pisces are a class of vertebrates comprising the true fishes. These have jaws supported by a skeleton and two sets of paired fins, pectoral and pelvic, as well as dorsal, caudal, and anal fins in the midline.

- **Whales** and **dolphins** are not fish at all. They are vertebrate warm-blooded aquatic mammals that bear babies (not hatched from eggs).
- **Sharks** are a special fish whose bones are made of cartilage, not bone. Sharks existed even 400 million years ago.
- **Amphibia**

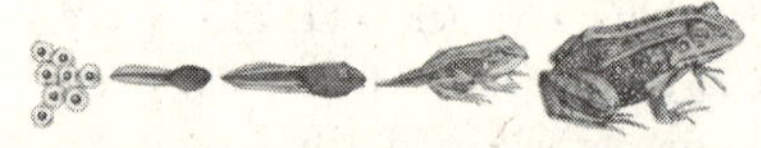

Amphibians are ectothermic (cold-blooded), tetrapod (four limbs) vertebrates. Characteristics are:

- External egg fertilization. Do not require mating for reproduction. They release clear eggs with a jelly-like texture into water.
- Adults have four legs.
- Ectothermic (cold-blooded). Their blood takes on the temperature of their surroundings.
- Carnivorous.
- Primitive lungs.
- Adults are capable of living in both water and land.

Frogs, toads, and newts are examples.

- **Reptiles**

  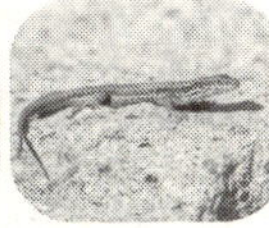

These are air-breathing, ectothermic vertebrates that have scaly bodies rather than hair or feathers. Examples include snakes, lizards, and crocodiles.

- Reptiles do not maintain a constant internal body temperature. Without fur or feathers for insulation, they cannot stay warm on a cold day, and without sweat glands or the ability to pant, they cannot cool off on a hot one. So, they move into the sun or into the shade as needed.
- Because of their slow metabolism and heat-seeking behaviour, during cooler parts of the year, they become inactive.
- Boas, pythons, most vipers, and some sea snakes give birth to live young.
- Other reptiles lay eggs in a nest, and leave while the young may hatch days or months later. Soil temperature is critical during this time and affects the gender of the hatchlings – whether they will be male or female.
- Reptiles first appeared about 315 million years ago and were the dominant animals during the Mesozoic era of dinosaurs. Dinosaurs were reptiles.

- **Aves (birds)**

There are more than 10,400 living species of birds. The major feature that sets them apart from all other animals is that ***all have feathers***.

- Birds are **endothermic** (warm-blooded) animals that maintain constant body temperature independent of the environment.
- Their forelimbs are modified into wings.
- They have well-developed flight muscles that help during the flight.
- Their hind limbs are adapted for walking, hopping, perching, grasping, wading, and swimming.
- There are epidermal scales on their legs.
- They reproduce by laying eggs.

An interesting trivia! Birds are actually theropod dinosaurs, though highly modified.

Bats also have similar characteristics but are classified as mammals because they give birth to live young and produce milk to feed their babies.

MAMMALS

These are vertebrate animals in which the young are nourished with milk from special mammary glands of the mother, for example, humans, cats, dogs, horses, apes, etc. There are three types of mammals:

- **Monotremes**

These (such as the platypus) lay eggs which hatch giving birth to offspring. Because such babies feed on their mother's milk, they are classified as mammals.

- **Marsupials**

- Such as kangaroos, give live birth with very short gestation durations. After birth, the essentially helpless embryo, climbs from the birth canal to a pouch on the mother's body until it has grown sufficiently.
- **Placentals**

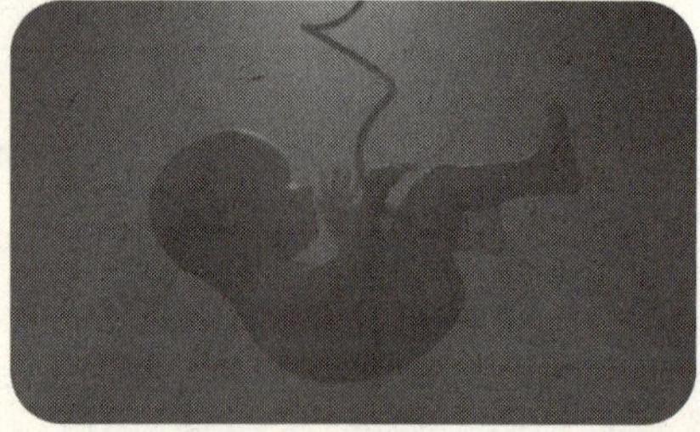

- The embryo grows into a well-formed structure over a gestation period of several months inside the mother's body, before the mother gives birth when the baby is ready. The baby in the womb gets nourishment from the mother's diet via the umbilical cord (attached to the mother) inside the placenta (the organ where the baby grows).

All mammals:

- Are warm-blooded (endothermic)
- Have some form of hair or fur

EVOLUTION OF LIFE: THEORIES

Anaximander's Theory

In the bustling Greek city of Miletus around 500 BCE, the philosopher Anaximander made an astute observation: human babies are born helpless. From this, he surmised that humans must have descended from some other creature whose young could survive independently. He proposed that our ancestors were fish, as freshly hatched fish begin living without any parental help. Remarkably, modern science supports this ancient idea, revealing that humans indeed trace their ancestry back to aquatic origins.

Historical Perspectives

Throughout history, religious beliefs and dogma have often shaped theories about the origin of life. For example, many Christians believe in the biblical creation story, where God creates the Earth in a day and Eve from Adam's rib. Hindus might attribute creation to Vishnu. These stories provided meaning and explanation long before scientific theories emerged.

Lamarck's Theory

In 1809, French naturalist Jean Baptiste Lamarck boldly challenged the prevailing notion that species were immutable. Based on fossil records, he argued that traits could be acquired during an organism's lifetime and then passed on to the next generation. Despite facing ostracism for suggesting that natural processes, rather than divine design, drove the evolution of life, Lamarck's ideas laid crucial groundwork for future evolutionary theories.

Darwin's Theory

Known today as the 'father of evolution', Charles Darwin revolutionized our understanding of life with his theory of natural selection.

- In 1831, Darwin embarked on a five-year scientific expedition aboard the HMS Beagle.
- His observations during this journey, meticulously recorded and analysed, led him to uncover compelling evidence of a process he called natural selection.
- Simultaneously, Alfred Russel Wallace arrived at similar conclusions, which further validated Darwin's ideas.

In 1859, Darwin published 'On the Origin of Species', where he articulated his groundbreaking theory:

- Evolution is a process of 'descent with modification'.
- Within a species, some organisms possess trait variants that enhance their survival.
- Over time, these advantageous traits become dominant, leading to the emergence of new species.
- Darwin proposed that all life evolved from a common ancestor millions of years ago.

This theory also explains extinction. For instance, in a heavily grazed area, plants without thorns might be consumed before they can reproduce. Thus, only those with crucial survival traits like thorns can thrive and pass on their genes.

Natural Selection

Darwin's theory of natural selection posits that organisms produce more offspring than can survive in their environment. The 'fittest' organisms – those best adapted to their surroundings – survive, mature, and reproduce. This 'survival of the fittest' concept explains how beneficial traits become more common over generations, driving the evolution of species.

Primordial Earth

Scientific consensus now holds that our universe is nearly 14 billion years old. Around 4.6 billion years ago, our sun formed from a vast cosmic cloud. Shortly after, the solar system, including Earth, took shape. Initially, Earth was a hot, molten mass without an atmosphere. Over hundreds of millions of years, the planet cooled, forming a crust with continuous volcanic activity.

Primordial earth refers to this early stage:

- The initial atmosphere was primarily hydrogen and helium.
- Volcanic eruptions released methane, water vapor, ammonia, and carbon dioxide, altering the atmospheric composition.
- By about 3.5 billion years ago, Earth's atmosphere was a mix of hydrogen sulphide, methane, water vapour, and massive amounts of carbon dioxide.

The 1952 Miller-Urey experiment demonstrated that amino acids, the building blocks of proteins, could form from inorganic compounds under conditions similar to early Earth. Life on Earth, largely based on organic chemistry and water, involves four key families of chemicals:

1. Lipids for cell membranes
2. Carbohydrates and sugars
3. Amino acids for protein metabolism
4. Nucleic acids (DNA and RNA) for heredity

Energy sources such as solar radiation, volcanic activity, underwater thermal vents, and lightning likely drove the synthesis of these compounds. Around 3.5 billion years ago, primitive life emerged. Between 2.2 and 2.7 billion years ago, photosynthesizing bacteria evolved, releasing oxygen and dramatically changing the Earth's atmosphere to its current composition of 78 per cent nitrogen, 21 per cent oxygen, and traces of other gases.

Soviet biochemist Alexander Ivanovich Oparin's 1924 book '*The Origin of Life*' synthesized ideas from Wallace, Darwin, and others, presenting a modern theory of life's origins. Oparin's work marked a significant advancement in our understanding of how life began on Earth, bridging the gap between ancient philosophical musings and contemporary scientific inquiry.

THE HUMAN BODY

As one of the most complex organisms on this planet, the human body is a single structure made out of myriad microscopic individual parts that work together in organized manner for the existence of the whole being – starting from cells, to tissues, to organs and then to systems.

Did you know that the versatile genius Leonardo da Vinci was also trained in anatomy and drew many sketches of skeletal structures, muscles, and organs of humans after he dissected them?

Cells are the basic unit of living matter that can reproduce itself. The human body (that will eventually consist of between 30 and 40 trillion cells) begins life as a single, newly fertilized cell.

Tissues are collections of billions of cells that come together as building matter for organs.

Organs are collections of different kinds of tissues in a manner that together they perform special functions. The stomach, for example, is made up of muscle and connective tissue that form its wall, while epithelial and connective tissues make up its lining; all of which have nervous tissue.

Systems are collections of organs that together carry out the most complex functions of the body. Ten major systems compose the human body.

THE SKELETAL SYSTEM

The human skeletal system consists of **bones, cartilage, ligaments,** and **tendons** and accounts for about 20 per cent of the body weight.

Humans are vertebrates and have a vertebral column or backbone, centred on a prominent spine. Bones make up the skeleton and serve as:

- Providing a ***rigid frame for supporting the human body*** against the pull of gravity
- *Protecting its soft organs:* The fused bones of the cranium contain and protect the brain; vertebrae do so for the spinal chord; the rib cage protects the heart and lungs in the thorax.
- Together with muscles, ***as mechanical levers*** for movement and working.
- The red marrow in bones is factories for **hematopoiesis** (formation of blood cells), manufacturing red blood cells, white blood cells, and blood platelets.
- *Regulating calcium in the body:* More than 50 per cent of human bone consists of calcium phosphate and 33 per cent is organic matter. When blood calcium levels fall below normal, bones release calcium to ensure adequate supply for metabolic needs. When blood calcium levels are excessive, calcium is stored in the bone matrix.

Babies are born with 300 bones, but as they grow some fuse. Adult humans have 206 bones.

- Bones are living things in our bodies. Requiring blood supply for oxygen and nutrients, they produce metabolic waste.
- Largest bone in humans: thigh bone or femur (average length 50 cm).
- Smallest bone in humans: stirrup bone in middle ear.

THE MUSCULAR SYSTEM

Composed of muscle fibres, muscles are attached to bones, internal organs and blood vessels, and responsible for movement – walking, running, eye and facial expressions, and respiration.

Other functions of muscle and tendons:

- Posture and stability.
- Muscles ***maintain body temperature*** through metabolism. Nearly 85 per cent of body heat is through muscle contraction.

THE CARDIO-VASCULAR SYSTEM

Also known as the circulatory system, it consists of

- The heart – pumping blood throughout the body to reach every cell.
- A closed system of vessels called arteries, veins, and capillaries.
- Components that regulate supply of blood to specific body areas according to need.

Circulation of blood maintains **homeostasis** and favourable cellular conditions. As such, the vascular system develops very early (by fourth week) in embryos. Besides supplying oxygen and nutrients, blood also carries away wastes to organs meant for its disposal.

Homeostasis: Self-regulating process by organisms to achieve conditions best for its survival. If homeostasis is successful, life continues.

HEART

The heart is a fist-sized organ that pumps blood throughout the body. It is the primary organ of the circulatory system. Controlled by the brain and the nervous system, it consists of four main sections (chambers) made of muscle and powered by electrical impulses.

- The heart is divided into four chambers.
  - *Right atrium or auricle:* Two large veins deliver oxygen-poor blood to the right atrium on the upper side. The superior vena cava carries blood from the upper body while the inferior vena cava brings blood from the lower body. The right atrium pumps the blood to your right ventricle.
  - *Right ventricle:* This is the lower right chamber and it pumps the oxygen-poor blood to the lungs through the **pulmonary artery**. The lungs reload blood with oxygen.
  - *Left atrium:* After the lungs have filled blood with oxygen, pulmonary veins carry the blood to the left atrium. This upper chamber pumps the blood to your left ventricle.
  - *Left ventricle:* The left ventricle is slightly larger than the right. It pumps oxygen-rich blood to the rest of your body.
- Heart valves open and close between the chambers to minimize backflow.
- The heart pumps blood through:
  - *Arteries* carrying oxygen-rich blood from the heart. The exception is the pulmonary arteries going to the lungs.

- *Veins* carrying oxygen-depleted, carbon dioxide-rich blood back to heart.
- *Capillaries* that are small blood vessels where oxygen is exchanged.

- *Systolic blood pressure* is when the heart contracts (pumping out blood). Diastolic blood pressure is when it relaxes. Optimum is around 120/80 mm Hg (this can vary from person to person and with age).
- To control the rhythm and pace of heartbeat, the heart has an electrical conduction system consisting of:
  - *Sinoatrial (SA) node:* Sends the signals that make the heart beat.
  - *Atrioventricular (AV) node:* Carries electrical signals from your heart's upper chambers to its lower ones.
  - And, a network of electrical bundles and fibres.
  - *Purkinje fibres:* These react to signals and pump out blood.
  - Normal rate of heart beat is about 70 beats per minute. It is likely to be less in athletes and young adults.

BLOOD

Blood makes up about 7 per cent of the human body weight.

- It has:
  - an average density around 1,060 kg/m^3, which is very close to the density of pure water of 1,000 kg/m^3.
  - Adults have a blood volume of between 5 and 6 litres.
- It is composed of:
  - **Plasma** (54 per cent of its volume). This is yellowish in colour.
  - **Red blood** cells or ***corpuscles*** also called **erythrocytes** (about 45 per cent of whole blood). The red colour of blood is due to **haemoglobin**.
  - *White blood cells* (about 0.7 per cent of its volume) are called **leukocytes**
  - And, cell fragments called **platelets** that help with clotting. This is vital in the case of injury to prevent bleeding to death.

Haemoglobin: It is an enzyme (being an iron-containing protein). It transports oxygen to cells of the body by reversibly binding. In contrast, carbon dioxide is mostly transported as bicarbonate ions in plasma. Vertebrate blood is bright red when its haemoglobin is oxygenated and dark red when it is deoxygenated.

Normal haemoglobin content in male adults is around 15 per cent; in female adults around 14 per cent. People living at higher altitudes have higher percentages.

Leukocytes: Humans have an adaptive immune system, based largely on white blood cells. These help to resist infections and parasites. They range between 4,000 and 11,000 per microlitre of blood. Leukemia is cancer of white blood cells.

Blood pH is regulated through homeostasis to stay within a narrow range (7.35–7.45). A pH below 6.9 or above 7.8 is usually lethal.

THE RESPIRATORY SYSTEM

Respiratory and circulatory systems work together to:

- Provide a continuous supply of oxygen to body cells.
- Remove waste products of metabolism.
- Regulate blood pH.

LUNGS

Respiration takes place in the lungs. It is the sequence of events that occur in the exchange of oxygen and carbon dioxide between the atmosphere and the body cells.

- Every 3–5 seconds, nerve impulses stimulate breathing (ventilation).

- Then there is an exchange of oxygen from air between the lungs and the blood (external respiration).
- Blood transports this oxygen to all the tissue cells in the body where it is used for metabolic purposes.
- In doing so, the oxygen is converted to carbon dioxide.
- Exchange of gases between tissue cells and blood is internal respiration.
- Bloodstream then carries this waste carbon dioxide back to the lungs, which remove it from the bloodstream and then exhale it along with left over nitrogen from the air.
- The whole vital process is called **gas exchange**.

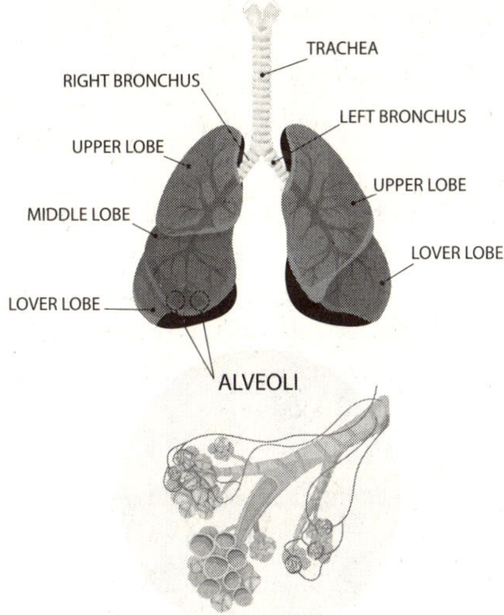

- At the end the bronchioles lie **alveoli**, very small air sacs where exchange of oxygen and carbon dioxide takes place.
- **Capillaries** are blood vessels in the walls of the alveoli.
- Deoxygenated blood enters the lungs via the right ventricle through pulmonary artery and oxygenated blood is then returned to the left atrium.

THE INTEGUMENTARY SYSTEM: SKIN

The integumentary system consists of hair, nails, oil glands, sweat glands, and the skin. The skin is the body's largest organ. It is made of water, protein, fats, and minerals. Three layers of tissue make up the skin:

- *Epidermis:* It is the top layer the skin that can be seen and touched. Mostly consisting of keratin, the epidermis.
  - *Dermis:* making up 90 per cent of skin's thickness
  - *Hypodermis:* at the bottom is the fatty layer

Skin Disorders

- Allergies and rashes
- Bug bites
- Cancer, such as melanoma
- Skin infections such as cellulitis
- Skin disorders such as acne, eczema, psoriasis and vitiligo
- Wounds, burns and blisters

THE ENDOCRINE SYSTEM

Working together with the nervous system, the endocrine system acts through ***chemical messengers called hormones*** released from glands. These influence growth, development, and metabolic activities and their effect may take weeks to show.

- Hormones consist of
  - **Peptides**; insulin being an important one
  - **Steroids**; cortisone being well-known
  - **Amino acid derivatives**; adrenaline is one

Exocrine glands have ducts that carry their secretions to a surface. These include sweat, sebaceous, digestive, and mammary glands.

Endocrine glands are ductless glands that secrete hormones directly into blood which then carry them throughout the body where they influence only those cells that have receptor sites for that particular hormone. These are:

- *Hypothalamus:* Part of the forebrain – regulates the pituitary and balances body temperature.
- *Pituitary (hypophysis):* The master gland regulating other glands such as the gonads, thyroid and adrenal, it is a pea-sized organ in the brain.
- *Thyroid:* The largest endocrine gland, it is located in the neck and regulates metabolism.
- *Pancreas:* Located in the abdomen just below the liver, it regulates blood sugar. Its beta-cells secrete insulin bringing glucose levels down, while its alpha cells secrete glucagon that raises glucose levels. The pancreas is both exo- and endocrine.
- *Adrenal glands:* Small, triangular glands located on top of both kidneys, they produce hormones that help regulate metabolism, immune system, blood pressure, and importantly ***response to stress.***
- *Pineal:* Located in the brain this affects the body's circadian rhythm (when to sleep and rest).

THE NERVOUS SYSTEM

It is the controlling, regulating, and communicating system in the body and the centre of all mental activities, including thought, learning, and memory. It is the sensing agency that supplies internal information to the endocrine system in order to maintain **homeostasis**. It also senses external conditions to keep the individual safe. Its principal organs are:

- The brain
- Spinal cord
- Nerves
- Ganglia

Its overlapping functions are:

- *Sensory:* Millions of sensory receptors detect changes, inside and outside the body, monitoring temperature, light, sound, etc., from the external environment. Inside the body, receptors detect variations in pressure, pH, gas concentration, etc.
- *Integrative:* These data are converted into electrical signals (nerve impulses) and are transmitted to the brain, where they create sensations, produce thoughts, or add to memory. This leads to decisions.
- *Motor:* The nervous system now generates signals to send to **effectors** (muscles/glands), for action.

BRAIN

Located inside the top of the skull, the human brain consists of:

Forebrain

- *Cerebrum:* Largest part of brain; has two hemispheres, left and right – separated by the **corpus callosum** (median furrow). It is the centre for intelligence, thinking, memory, imagination, and controls all voluntary (willed) action.
- *Thalamus:* Regulates the *circadian rhythm* (sleeping and waking).
- *Hypothalamus:* Regulates water balance, sleep, stress and emotions, release of hormones, and body temperature.

Midbrain

- Containing optic lobes, tectum, and cerebral peduncle

Hindbrain

- *Cerebellum:* A furrowed mass attached to the cerebrum, it is located towards the rear of the head. It controls the muscles, body movement, and balance.

- *Medulla oblongata:* Lowest part of brain; connected to the spinal cord, it controls involuntary and reflex functions of the body, such as breathing and heart rate and salivary secretion.

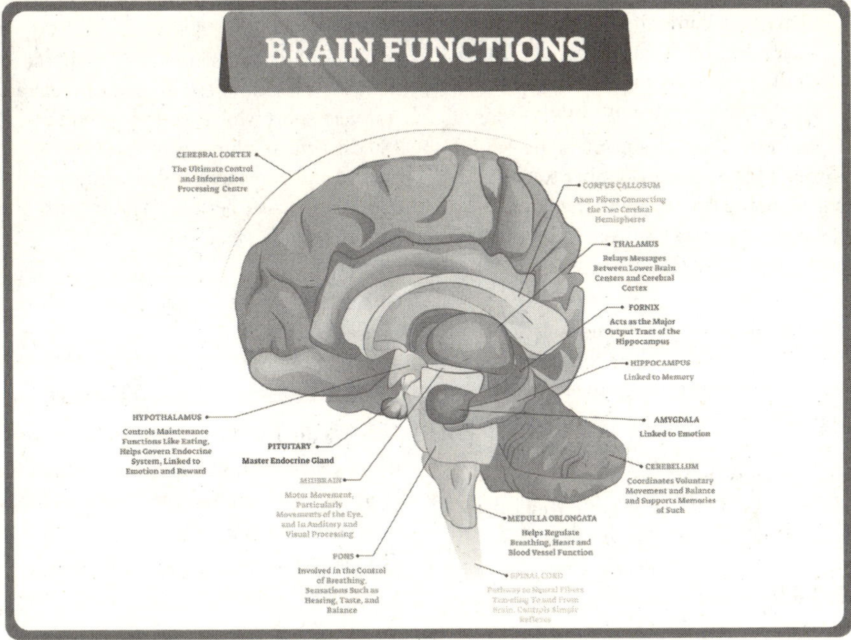

Spinal Cord

It is the bundle of nerves that runs from the brain down to the end of the trunk. It is enclosed (and so protected from injury) in the vertebra.

Sensory Organs

These consist of the tongue *(see digestive system)*, nose *(respiratory system)*, skin *(see integumentary system)*, eyes, and ears.

EYES

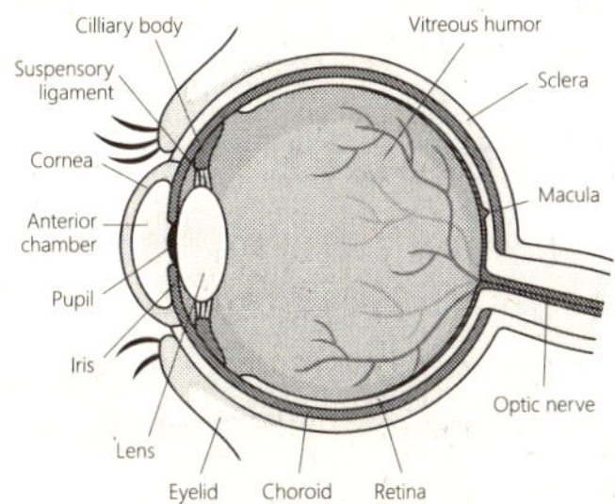

The Human Eye

The human eye (often called the **eyeball**) is a spherical organ about an inch in diameter and consists of three layers:

1. *Sclerotic* (outermost)
2. *Choroid* (middle)
3. *Retina* (innermost)

All the above have a gap in which sit the:

- *Cornea:* This is covered by a membrane called the **conjunctiva**. This membrane is sometimes infected by virus leading to the condition known as conjunctivitis; when the eye becomes inflamed and appears red in colour. Between the conjunctiva and the cornea is the **aqueous chamber** containing fluid known as **aqueous humour**.
- *Pupil*: Adjusted by the iris so that just the correct amount of light goes through. They dilate (grow bigger) in darkness and contract in harsh light.

- *Iris:* It is the coloured part of the eye (commonly – black, brown, and blue) and adjusts the size of the pupil.
- *Lens:* This is a transparent flexible piece convex in shape. By flexing, it changes in convexity to focus on objects depending on far away they are. The rest of the eyeball behind it is filled with a fluid called the **vitreous humour**.

Light from objects seen, enters the eye through the aqueous chamber to the cornea and passes through the pupil to the lens. The image is inverted by the lens at this point and this passes through the vitreous humour to the **retina**.

The retina contains millions of photoreceptors known as cones and rods, which convert this image to electrical signals that pass through the **optic nerve** to the brain which corrects the inversion and presents the image humans see. **Cones** differentiate the colours seen. **Rods** allow sight even when light is dim.

EARS

Ears serve two purposes:

- *Hearing*: Sound is detected and sent to the brain for analysing.
- *Balance:* A set of three semi-circular canals, along with an utricle and a saccule, are filled with fluids. Movement causes displacement of these fluids and signals are sent to the brain. Having thus detected changes in the body orientation, the brain decides on corrective action.

Did you know that three of the smallest bones of the human body (stapes, incus, and malleus) are all located in the ear?

The ear has three regions – outer, middle, and inner ear. Sound waves collected by the **pinna** in the outer ear are passed in and vibrate the eardrum. These vibrations are in turn transmitted to the **cochlea** and the **basilar membrane** of consisting of about 10,000 different sensory units for different frequencies. These convert the vibration into electrical signals for the **auditory nerve** to send to the brain for processing.

The normal hearing range for humans is between 20 Hz and 20 kHz. *Hz stands for Hertz (1 cycle per second); so 20 kHz is 20,000 cycles per second.*

In terms of loudness, humans can detect faint sounds as low as 0 dB and can tolerate (for very short whiles) sound as loud as 180 dB. But, anything over 85 dB can be hurtful and damaging and anything over 120 dB can cause permanent damage to the ears. *dB stands for decibels.*

Hearing deteriorates with age, and it starts with the higher frequencies. This is known as **presbycusis**.

THE LYMPHATIC SYSTEM

This has three primary functions:

- As a drain for interstitial fluid (fluid that accumulates around capillaries and does not return via veins).
  - Build up of interstitial fluid reduces blood volume since this fluid comes from blood itself.
  - This gradually brings about a drop in blood pressure which may show up as oedema (swelling).
  - Lymph capillaries pick up the excess interstitial fluid and proteins and feed them back to venous blood.
- The second function of the lymphatic system is to absorb fats and vitamins from the digestive system through **lacteals**.
- The third function of the lymphatic system is to filter out invading micro-organisms and release lymphocytes that destroy such invaders.

THE DIGESTIVE SYSTEM

In the digestive tract (also called alimentary canal or gastrointestinal tract) food is broken down, bit by bit, until the molecules are small enough to be absorbed.

Food undergoes the following processes in the body:

- *Ingestion:* The act of eating. Larger food pieces have to be broken into mush for enzymes to be effective. This is done by teeth that bite, chew and grind.
  - The mixture with salivary enzymes (now called **bolus**) then moves to the pharynx, oesophagus, and finally, to the stomach. This is deglutition or swallowing.
  - Movements that push food particles through the digestive tract are called **peristalsis**.
  - *Tongue:* Food flavours are sensed through its taste buds – sweet at the tip, then salty and sour in the middle, and bitter at the end. The tongue also produces saliva, containing enzymes that act to begin breaking down complex food molecules.
  - *Teeth:* First appear as 'milk teeth' in babies between 6 and 8 months old. At about the age of 6 years, these begin to fall and permanent teeth emerge. Adults have 32 teeth (16 each in upper and lower jaws) consisting of:
    - Incisors (2), for biting and cutting
    - Canines (1), for tearing
    - Premolars (2), for chewing
    - Molars (3), for chewing and grinding; on each side of each jaw

Tooth enamel is the hardest substance in the body.

- *Process of digestion:* Churning and mixing continues in the stomach. Combinations of carbohydrates, proteins, and fats are broken down into smaller molecules that can be absorbed and utilized by the cells. This is chemical digestion and involves a process called **hydrolysis** using water and **digestive enzymes**.
- *Absorption:* Chemical digestion produces simple molecules that pass through cell membranes lining the small intestine into blood or lymph capillaries. This is how the body gets its nutrition.
- *Elimination:* The leftover waste after digestion is eliminated from the body, through the anus, in the form of faeces, by a process called **defaecation**.

LIVER

The liver is located in the upper right-hand portion of the abdominal cavity, beneath the diaphragm, but on top of the stomach. Shaped like a cone, it is a dark reddish-brown organ that weighs more than 1 kg, and is the metabolic centre of the body.

Functions of the liver:

- More than 500 vital functions have been identified with the liver.
- All blood leaving the stomach and intestines passes through the liver, which processes this blood to produce nutrients.
- It breaks down, balances, and neutralizes toxins, and metabolizes drugs into nontoxic and even useful forms for the body.
- The liver regulates most chemical levels in the blood and excretes a product called bile.
- Bile carries away waste products from the liver.

Further, the liver:

- Produces cholesterol and special proteins to carry fats through the body.
- Converts excess glucose into glycogen for energy storage (glycogen can later be converted back to glucose for energy).
- Regulates levels of amino acids (building blocks of proteins).
- Is a storehouse for iron (component of haemoglobin).
- Converts poisonous ammonia to urea for excretion in urine.
- Regulates blood clotting.
- Removes bilirubin from red blood cells.

Hepatitis: If there is over-accumulation of bilirubin, the skin and eyes turn yellow. Also known as jaundice, it can happen from various causes such as virus and cancer.

Consisting of two main lobes, the liver holds nearly 13 per cent of the body's blood supply at any given moment. These are made up of eight sections of 1,000 lobules which are connected to ducts that finally connect to the hepatic duct.

The bile duct transports bile made by liver cells to gallbladder and duodenum (the first part of the small intestine). Blood supply to the liver, includes:

- Oxygenated blood flowing in from the hepatic artery
- Nutrient-rich blood flowing in from the hepatic portal vein

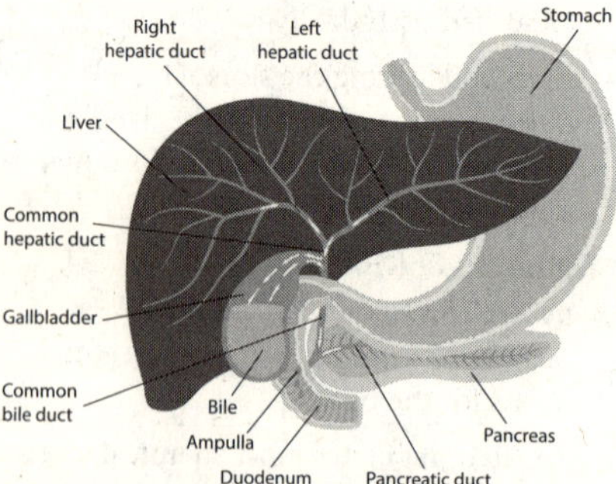

Once the liver has broken down harmful substances, the by-products are excreted into the bile or blood. Bile enters the intestine with the waste (by-products), and leaves the body as faeces. Blood by-products are filtered out by the kidneys, and leave the body in the form of urine.

SPLEEN

The spleen is an organ in the upper far left part of the abdomen, to the left of the stomach about 4 inches long protected by the rib cage.

- It acts as a filter for blood as part of the immune system.
- Old red blood cells are recycled in it.
- Platelets and white blood cells are stored there.
- Helps fight bacteria that cause pneumonia and meningitis.

THE URINARY SYSTEM

Its principal function is to maintain the volume and composition of body fluids within safe limits. A part of doing so is to rid the body of waste products and so it is an excretory system as well.

- The urinary system maintains an appropriate fluid volume by regulating the amount of water that is excreted in urine.
- It also regulates concentrations of various electrolytes in the body fluids and maintains blood pH within a safe range.
- It controls red blood corpuscle production by secreting the erythropoietin hormone.
- Maintains normal blood pressure by secreting the enzyme rennin.

KIDNEYS

These are chocolate brown bean-shaped organs just below the diaphragm on the right and left of the vertebra. The left kidney is a little higher than the right one. They consist of **nephrons** that filter the blood flowing through and pass on the waste to urine for disposal. A tube that carries urine is called **ureter**. Urine generated is stored in the **urinary bladder** (healthy ones can hold nearly a litre of it) until passed through the **urethra** while urinating. The structure of the urethra is different for the two genders – the male one is also a carrier of sperm.

- **Urine** should normally be light yellow in colour. Depending on the level of dehydration, it turns progressively darker. But continuous passage of very dark urine could be due to leakage of blood.
- Over 95 per cent of urine is water. It is acidic (pH ~ 6), denser than water because of substances such as **urea**, **creatinine**, and beta molecules in it. The urea gives off ammonia that has a pungent smell. Associated unpleasant smells can be due to bacteria in it that acts on the waste products.

Reproductive System

For the propagation of the species, humans have a reproductive system that is of the sexual type *(versus asexual types in some beings)*. Thus, the organs differ depending on gender.

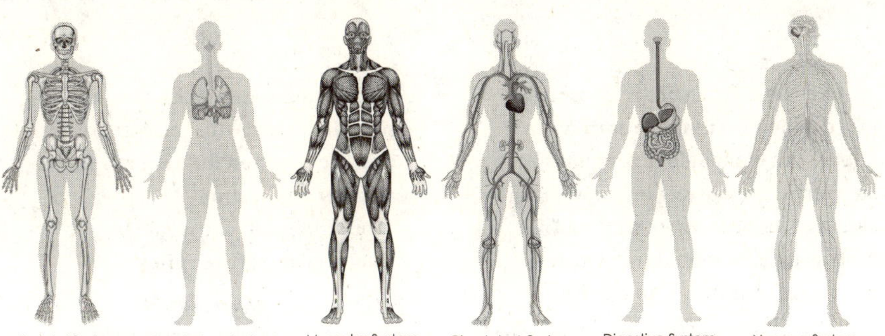

DISEASE

Broadly, three classes of disease afflict humankind:

- *Congenital disease:* Abnormalities present from birth. These could be due to:
  - Injury to the mother. There is greater prevalence of babies with heart defects among alcoholic mothers.
  - Gene mutation (sickle-cell anaemia, thalassaemia).
  - Chromosomal aberration (such as in Down's syndrome, formerly known as Mongolism).
  - Environmental factors. Exposure to hazardous waste carries more risk for abnormalities such as cleft-palate and harelips, and diseases such as leukaemia.
- *Communicable acquired disease:* These are contagious and infections spread from person to person. Causes:
  - Viruses. *Examples*: COVID-19, influenza, HIV-AIDS, polio, smallpox. *Prevention*: vaccines. *Treatment*: alleviation of symptoms.
  - Bacteria. *Examples*: typhoid, cholera. *Prevention*: hygiene, safe practices, sterilization. *Treatment*: antibiotics, antipyretics, and hydration.
  - Parasites. *Examples*: amoebic dysentery, malaria, filaria. *Prevention*: safe practices, sterilization. *Treatment*: antiparasitic drugs, hydration.
  - Fungus. *Examples*: candidiasis, ringworm, some forms of pneumonia, especially hospital acquired pneumonias. *Prevention*: screening and intensive sterilization. *Treatment*: antifungal creams, drugs, tablets, and injections depending on nature of case.
- *Non-communicable disease:* These are conditions that the human body picks up over a course of time and are usually age or lifestyle related. These include:
  - Arthritis – pain in the musculoskeletal system.
  - Cancer – uncontrolled growth of abnormal cells in the body.
  - Diabetes – inability of the body to produce insulin adequately to digest sugar. Over a period, this results in the failure of other organs as well.
  - Heart disease – general term for many conditions affecting the heart, such as mechanical (valve failure) or electrical (arrhythmia).

Lifestyle cases are preventable to an extent.

4 Information and Communication Technology (ICT)

An electronic device that can process **raw data** to give **usable information** is known as a computer. A computer has an internal memory, which stores data and instructions temporarily **waiting** processing. It also holds information before it is transmitted to the user.

All computers consist of three components – **hardware**, **software**, and **central processing unit** (CPU).

In simple terms, all the **physical components** of a computer system that contain a **circuit board**, **integrated circuits** (ICs), or other **electronic devices** are known as **hardware**.

It can be classified into two: **input devices** and **output devices**.

Input devices are used to send data to a computer system for processing. Some examples of input devices are **keyboard**, **mouse**, **scanner**, and **microphone**.

Output devices are used to display the information for the user to interpret. Some examples of output devices are **monitor**, **printer**, **speaker**, and **headphones**.

Software, on the other hand, is a **set of instructions**, **data**, or **programs** given to a computer to **execute specific tasks**.

There are two types of software: **application software** and **system software**.

System software is designed to **help the user and the hardware to function and interact** with each other in order to **perform tasks**. An example of system software would be **operating system (OS)**.

Application software is a computer software package that performs a **specific function for a user or for another application**. An example of application software would be **web browsers** and **office suites**.

Apart from these two, there are two other types of software: **driver software** and **programming software**.

Driver software, also known as **device drivers, controls the hardware devices and peripherals connected to a computer**, enabling them to perform specific tasks.

Programming software, also known as **software development tool, allows users and developers to write codes, test, and debug other software and application programs** to perform tasks.

CPU is referred to as the brain of the computer since it processes the instructions and commands given by the user.

History of CPU

The world's first commercially produced microprocessor – Intel 4004 – was released in 1971. It was a 4-bit general-purpose CPU on a single chip, and was made with cutting-edge silicon-gate technology.

There are two primary components: **arithmetic logic unit** (ALU) and **control unit** (CU).

ALU performs all the **mathematical**, **logic, and decision operations** that need to be carried out according to the instruction in a program.

CPU regulates the **operations of the computer** by generating the **appropriate timing and control signals**. It also **interprets instructions** and **guides data flow through** the **computer's memory**, **ALU**, and **input or output devices**.

COMPUTER MEMORY

Any device that can store information is called memory. There are three types of memory – **primary memory**, **secondary memory**, and **cache**.

1. Primary memory is the memory that the CPU will access first. This means that the program or data that needs to be accessed are loaded into the primary memory before processing. The CPU interacts directly with the primary memory to perform read or write operation. Primary memory is of two types: **temporary (random access memory** or **RAM)** and **permanent (read-only memory** or **ROM)**.
2. Since primary memory has limited storage, **secondary memory** is used to store data or instructions. It is **non-volatile and has larger storage capacity than primary memory**. Secondary memory cannot be accessed directly by the CPU which is why first it must be connected to the main memory. It is slower and cheaper than the main memory.
3. To enhance the performance of the CPU, a **high-speed memory** is placed between **the CPU** and **primary memory** which is known as the **cache**.

Memory can be volatile and non-volatile. **Volatile memory** loses its contents when the computer or hardware device loses power. An example would be RAM. **Non-volatile memory** keeps its contents even if the power is lost. An example would be **erasable programmable read-only memory (EPROM)**.

UNITS OF MEMORY

A **memory unit** is the amount of data that the memory can store. A computer system uses **binary numbers (0 and 1)**, called **bits**, to store and process data.

A **4-bit** combination is called a **nibble** and an 8-bit combination is called a **byte**. These units start from a bit, byte, and go up to the multiples of bytes, where the prefixes correspond to the international systems of units and can go up to cover all the finite numbers.

UNIT	DESCRIPTION
Kilobyte (KB)	1 KB = 1024 bytes
Megabyte (MB)	1 MB = 1024 KB
Gigabyte (GB)	1 GB = 1024 MB
Terabyte (TB)	1 TB = 1024 GB
Petabyte (PB)	1 PB = 1024 TB
Exabyte (EB)	1 EB = 1024 PB
Zettabyte (ZB)	1 ZB = 1024 EB
Yottabyte (YB)	1 YB = 1024 ZB

GENERATIONS OF COMPUTERS

The history of the computer goes back several decades and can easily be classified into five definable generations.

Each generation of computers went through an upgrade which was an improvement on the previous generation – leading to more compact, less expensive, but more powerful, efficient, and robust machines.

FIRST-GENERATION COMPUTERS – VACUUM TUBES (1940–56)

The earliest computers were developed using vacuum tubes and magnetic drums. These machines were enormous in size and would take up an entire room. In addition to using huge amounts of electricity, the first-generation computers generated lots of heat which would often lead to malfunctions.

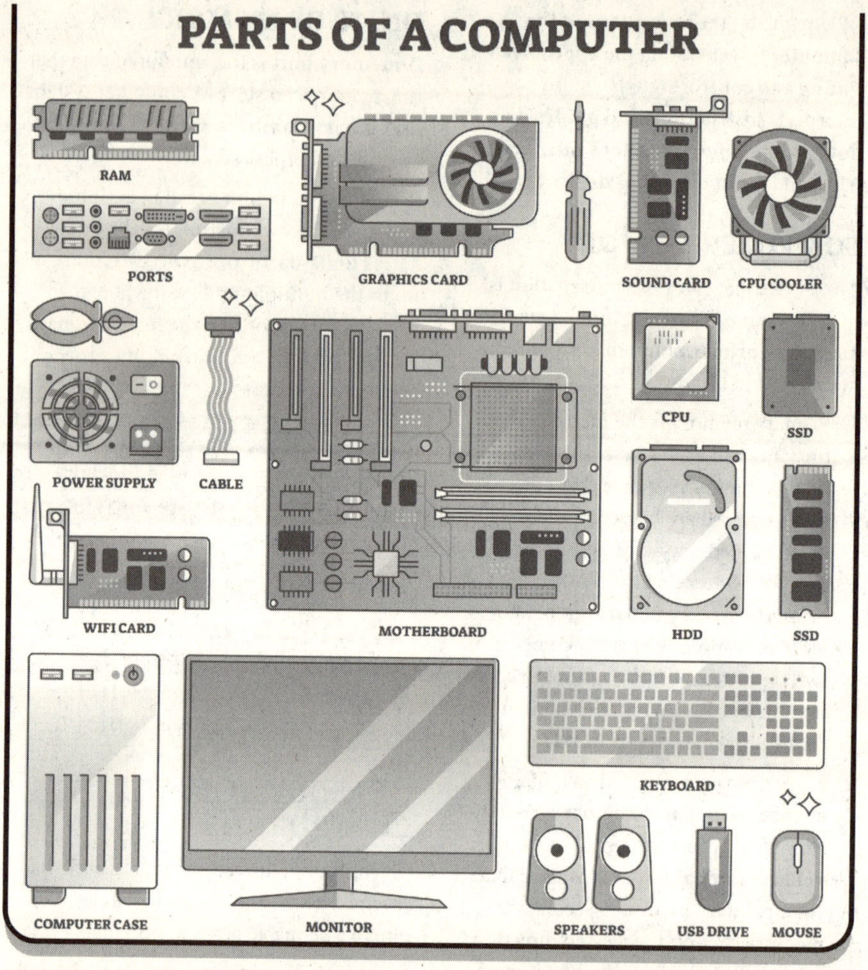

PARTS OF A COMPUTER

RAM
PORTS
GRAPHICS CARD
SOUND CARD
CPU COOLER
POWER SUPPLY
CABLE
CPU
SSD
WIFI CARD
MOTHERBOARD
HDD
SSD
KEYBOARD
COMPUTER CASE
MONITOR
SPEAKERS
USB DRIVE
MOUSE

The computers relied on machine language and could only solve one problem at a time.

The two notable machines were the UNIVAC, which was the first commercial computer and the ENIAC.

Main electronic component	Vacuum tube
Programming languages	Machine language
Main memory	Magnetic tapes and magnetic drums
Input	Paper tape and punched cards
Output	Printouts
Examples of first-generation computers	IBM 650, ENIAC, UNIVAC

SECOND-GENERATION COMPUTERS – TRANSISTORS (1956–63)

The computers developed during this period replaced the vacuum tubes with transistors, which is a semi-conductor device that regulates or controls current or voltage flow. Due to the use of transistors, these computers were smaller, cheaper to build, faster, more energy-efficient, and more reliable than their predecessors. These computers relied on assembly languages such as FORTRAN (1956), ALGOL (1958), and COBOL (1959), which made programming simpler for programmers.

Main electronic component	Transistor
Programming languages	Machine language and assembly language
Main memory	Magnetic core and magnetic tape/disk
Input	Magnetic tape and punched cards
Output	Printouts
Examples of the second generation	IBM 1620, IBM 7090, CDC 3600

THIRD-GENERATION COMPUTERS – INTEGRATED CIRCUITS (1964–71)

The third-generation computers were developed using IC technology, where a variety of transistors were placed on silicon chips or semiconductors. These devices were faster, cheaper, and more efficient than the second-generation devices. A user could interact with the computer using keyboards and monitors which interfaced with an operating system, which meant that it could run several applications at once.

Main electronic component	Integrated circuits
Programming languages	High-level language
Main memory	Large magnetic core, magnetic tape/disk
Input	Magnetic tape, keyboard
Output	Monitor, printer
Examples of the third generation	IBM 370, PDP-11, UNIVAC 1108

FOURTH-GENERATION COMPUTERS – MICROPROCESSORS (1971–PRESENT)

Fourth-generation computers were released in 1972 and were made using very large scale integrated (VLSI) circuits, earning them the name microprocessors. These computers were compact and portable, more adaptable, and had large storage capacity. They were also faster and more reliable than the third-generation devices.

Main electronic component	VLSI and microprocessor (thousands of transistors on a single microchip)
Programming languages	HLLs such as BASIC, PASCAL, COBOL, FORTRAN, and C
Memory	Semiconductor memory – RAM, ROM
Input/output devices	Mouse, optical scanning, keyboard, monitor, printer
Examples of fourth generation	IBM PC, APPLE II, Apple Macintosh

FIFTH-GENERATION COMPUTERS – ARTIFICIAL INTELLIGENCE (PRESENT AND BEYOND)

Fifth-generation computers are based on AI technology, which – although it has shown remarkable success in the fields of science, security, finance, travel, medicine, and gaming – is still in the development stage. Some applications of AI are widely being used today such as voice recognition and autonomous vehicles.

TIMELINE

Here's a chronological list of significant milestones in the history of computing, organized by year:

Early Developments

- **1837:** Charles Babbage designs the analytical engine, an early mechanical general-purpose computer concept.
- **1936:** Alan Turing introduces the concept of the Turing machine, laying the foundation for theoretical computer science.

1940s

- **1943:** The Colossus, the first programmable digital electronic computer, is developed by Tommy Flowers to break German codes during WWII.
- **1945:** ENIAC (Electronic Numerical Integrator and Computer) is completed, the first general-purpose electronic digital computer.
- **1947:** The transistor is invented by John Bardeen, Walter Brattain, and William Shockley, revolutionizing electronics and computing.

1950s

- **1951:** UNIVAC I (Universal Automatic Computer) is delivered, the first commercial computer produced in the United States.
- **1958:** Jack Kilby and Robert Noyce develop the integrated circuit, enabling the miniaturization of electronic circuits.

1960s

- **1964:** IBM introduces the System/360, a family of mainframe computers that standardizes computer architecture.
- **1969:** The ARPANET, the precursor to the modern internet, is established, connecting four university computers.

1970s

- **1971:** Intel releases the 4004 microprocessor, the first commercially available microprocessor.
- **1975:** The Altair 8800 is released, sparking the home computer revolution.
- **1976:** Steve Jobs and Steve Wozniak release the Apple I, a pre-assembled computer board.
- **1977:** The Apple II is introduced, becoming one of the first highly successful mass-produced microcomputers.

1980s

- **1981:** IBM releases the IBM PC, which becomes the standard for personal computers.
- **1984:** Apple launches the Macintosh, featuring a graphical user interface and a mouse.
- **1989:** Tim Berners-Lee proposes the World Wide Web, a system for interlinked hypertext documents accessed via the internet.

1990s

- **1990:** The World Wide Web is developed by Tim Berners-Lee at CERN.
- **1991:** Linus Torvalds releases the Linux kernel, leading to the development of the open-source Linux operating system.
- **1993:** The Mosaic web browser is released, popularizing the World Wide Web.
- **1995:** Microsoft releases Windows 95, featuring a user-friendly interface and built-in internet support.

2000s

- **2001:** Apple introduces the iPod, revolutionizing digital music consumption.
- **2004:** Facebook is launched, becoming a major social networking platform.
- **2007:** Apple releases the iPhone, revolutionizing mobile computing and communication.

2010s

- **2010:** Apple launches the iPad, popularizing tablet computing.
- **2011:** IBM's Watson wins 'Jeopardy!', showcasing advances in artificial intelligence.
- **2014:** Amazon introduces the Echo and its voice assistant, Alexa, bringing AI-driven voice control to the mainstream.
- **2015:** Google releases TensorFlow, an open-source machine learning framework.

2020s

- **2020:** Quantum computing milestones are achieved, with companies like Google and IBM making significant advancements.
- **2021:** The rise of AI-driven technologies continues, with significant developments in autonomous vehicles, natural language processing, and other fields.

COMMONLY USED TERMS

- **Applications** are complete, self-contained programs that perform specific tasks.
- A **bug** is part of a program that usually causes the computer to malfunction; often resolved in patches or updates to the program.
- **Booting** is the process of loading or initializing an OS on a computer; usually as soon as a computer is switched on.
- **Browser** is a program used to view World Wide Web pages, such as Google Chrome.
- **Crash** is when a computer malfunctions due to a software or hardware problem, causing information to be lost.
- **Database** is an organized set of structured data or information, typically stored electronically in a computer system.
- **Decryption** is the process of converting encrypted data into its original unencrypted form.
- A **domain name system (DNS)** is a hierarchical and decentralized naming system used to identify computers reachable through the internet or other networks.
- **Download** is when the user transfers data from another network to their computer.
- **Encryption** is the process of transmitting data by converting the original representation of the information (**plain text**) into an encrypted form (**cipher text**).
- A **file** is a resource or element of data storage which can be accessed and transferred as a single unit.
- A **firewall** is a network security device that monitors and restricts traffic to or from your network.
- A **folder** is the virtual location where files, applications, documents, and other sub-folders can be organized and stored.
- **Graphical user interface (GUI)** is a system of interactive visual components that allows the user to interact with a computer through the use of graphical symbols.
- **Hard disk drive (HDD)** is a non-volatile data storage device that reads and writes information, including the operating system, program files, and data files.
- **Hypertext markup language (HTML)** is a standard of text markup conventions for documents designed to be displayed in a web browser.
- An **icon** is a graphical symbol on the computer screen used to represent a file or program in a GUI interface.
- **Internet**, also referred to as a **network of networks,** is a worldwide system of computer networks encompassing the World Wide Web, telnet, File Transfer Protocol (FTP), Transmission Control Protocol/Internet Protocol (TCP/IP), and other protocols.
- An **IP address** is a unique string of numbers associated with a specific computer or computer network.
- **Modem** is an electronic device that converts digital signals to analog signals and vice versa.

- **Network interface card (NIC)** is a board inserted in a computer that provides a physical connection to a network.
- **Printer** is a peripheral device that converts output from a computer into a printed image.
- A **peripheral device** is an external or internal device connected computer to provide additional functionality.
- **Rebooting** is the process of restarting and reloading the OS; usually performed after a computer crashes.
- A **server** is a computer or system that provides access to resources, data, services, or programs to other computers, known as **clients**, over a network.
- **Spyware** is software that is installed on a computer and secretly monitors activity, attempting to gain private information without the user knowing.
- **Switches** are devices that are used to connect multiple devices, such as computers, wireless access points, and printers on the same network.
- A **Trojan**, also referred to as **Trojan Horse**, is a piece of software that gains access to a computer by disguising itself as a legitimate program or hiding within another application.
- **Upload** is when a user transfers data from a computer to a network.
- **Uniform resource locator (URL)**, or web address, is a unique identifier used to locate a resource on the internet. A simple web address has three main parts: **protocol**, **domain name**, and **path**.
- A **virus** is a type of malicious software, or malware, which attaches itself to other programs to survive and replicate, sometimes causing damage to data and software.
- **Virtual private network (VPN)** is a technology that uses real-time encryption on unsecured networks to protect your online identity, hide your IP address and shield your online data from third parties.
- A **worm** is similar to a virus, but it can exist independently which means it doesn't need to attach to a separate program. It is a type of malware whose primary function is to self-replicate and infect other computers while remaining active on infected systems.
- **Window** is a screen in a software program that permits the user to view several programs at one time.
- **Wireless fidelity or Wi-Fi** transmits data using radio waves that are sent from a wireless router to a nearby device and translates the signal into data you can use.

COMPUTER LANGUAGES

A computer does not understand the commands that a user inputs, so then the question is how the computer can process the commands that we give. It's simple. A computer has its own set of instructions or language for communication, which we call computer languages.

There are two types of computer languages: **low-level** and **high-level language**.

Low-level languages are **machine-oriented programs or instructions** that are used to **operate**, **sync**, **and manage the hardware and system components** of the computer. These languages carry out all the instructions which form the architecture of the hardware systems.

There are two types of low-level languages: **machine language** and **assembly language:**

1. Machine language is **written in binary code (0 or 1)** which was first used to interact with **first-generation computers**.
2. Assembly language is a **second-generation programming language** where, in addition to binary digits, **words**, **names**, and **symbols** are used.

3. **Assembly languages** are **converted into machine languages** with the help of an **assembler**.

High-level languages (HLLs) are **programmer-friendly languages** that are easier to manage and understand by the user as they allow the use of **symbolic operators to signify operations** and **symbolic names to represent data and data structures**. HLLs are **translated into machine code** with the help of a **compiler or interpreter**.

Some commonly used HLLs are Python, JavaScript, Java, C++, C, and so on.

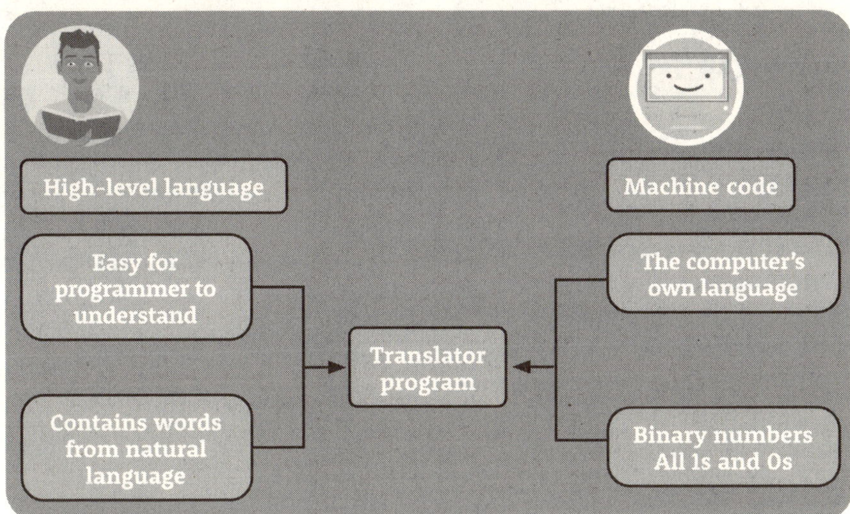

IMPORTANT TERMS TO REMEMBER

An **algorithm** is a finite set of instructions, typically used to solve a specific problem or to perform a computation by providing more information to a function.

Arrays are a collection of similar data items or elements stored at contiguous memory locations.

Arithmetic operators are mathematical functions that perform addition, subtraction, multiplication, division, exponentiation, and modulus operations.

Assignment operators are used to assign a value to an operator or a variable. Some examples are +=, −=, *=, /=.

Augmented reality (AR) is an interactive experience which allows the integration of digital information with the user's environment in real time. AR uses existing real-world environment and adds new information on top of it to create an enhanced perception of reality. An example of AR would be the IKEA mobile app and Nintendo's Pokémon Go app.

Coding is how a user creates instructions for computers to perform tasks and this is done through **coding languages**.

A **script** is a program or set (or sequence) of instructions interpreted or executed by the computer without being compiled.

Source code is a set of instructions that are written in human-readable programming language.

Statement is the way through which a user gives instruction to a computer to perform an action or to explain a desired action.

A **variable** is a value (single number, word, or any other information) that can change, depending on conditions or on information passed to the program. There are three parts of a variable: **type**, **name**, and **value**.

Once a variable is declared, the next step is to specify the **variable type**. Some basic variable types include **string (words** and **phrases)**, **char (character**; used for a **single letter** or **symbol)**, **int (integer**; used for **whole numbers)**, **double** or **float** (used for **decimal numbers)**, and **bool (boolean**; used for **true** or **false values)**.

NETWORK

A network is a system that connects numerous independent computers or other computer networks to share data, information, and resources.

There are three types of networks based on area covered: **local area network (LAN)**, **wide area network (WAN)**, and **metropolitan area network (MAN)**.

A **LAN** is a network that covers an area of up to 10 km. An example of this would be a college network or an office network.

A **MAN** is a network that covers an entire city. An example of this would be a cable television provider.

A **WAN** is a network that connects countries or continents. An example of this would be the internet. We see two distinct examples of WANs today: point-to-point WANs and switched WANs.

Point-to-point connects two connecting devices through transmission media.

Switched WAN is a network with more than two ends.

There are two types of networks based on the communication medium: **wired** and **wireless networks**.

1. A **wired network** uses wires to link devices to the internet or any another network, such as laptops or desktop PCs.
2. A **wireless network** links devices to the internet or any other network without any wires connected between them, such as TV remotes and mobile phones.

There are three types of networks based on the type of architecture: **peer-to-peer**, **client-server**, and **hybrid networks**.

1. **Peer-to-peer network** is when two or more PCs are connected and can share resources and access to devices without going through a separate server computer.
2. **Client-server network** is when multiple client programs share the services of a common server program.
3. **Hybrid network** is a combination of peer-to-peer and client-server networks.

CELLULAR NETWORKS: OVERVIEW

A cellular network functions similarly to a computer network or other wireless networks, primarily providing telecommunication services and internet access through mobile data. The evolution of these networks is categorized into generations, each offering improved speed and functionality.

TYPES OF CELLULAR NETWORKS

3G (Third Generation)

- *Introduction:* Introduced as CDMA2000 in the US and Universal Mobile Telecommunications Service (UMTS) in Europe.
- *Frequency bands:* Operated at the 1,900 MHz and 2,100 MHz bands.

- *Technology:* Utilized packet-based IP connectivity.
- *Speed:* Capable of up to 14 Mbps.
- *Features:* Enabled reliable transfer and download of music and video.

4G (Fourth Generation)

- *Introduction:* Released in the late 2000s.
- *Speed:* Almost 500 times faster than 3G, offering speeds up to 100 Mbps.
- *Technology:* Relies on IP-based communication systems for both voice and data.
- *Features:* Provides faster download and upload speeds, enabling high-definition video and audio streaming.

4G LTE (Long-Term Evolution)

- *Development:* Designed to facilitate the transition from 3G to 4G.
- *Speed range:* Covers speeds from 3G's average of 3 Mbps up to 4G's 100 Mbps.
- *Features:* Offers a vast range of potential speeds, bridging the gap between 3G and 4G capabilities.

5G (Fifth Generation)

- *Introduction:* The latest generation, currently being rolled out.
- *Speed:* Significantly faster than 4G, with speeds that can exceed 1 Gbps.
- *Technology:* Utilizes higher frequency bands (millimetre waves) and advanced technologies like massive MIMO (multiple input multiple output) and beamforming.
- *Features:* Supports ultra-reliable low-latency communication (URLLC), enhanced mobile broadband (eMBB), and massive machine-type communications (mMTC), enabling applications like autonomous driving, IoT, and smart cities.

Messaging Systems: SMS, MMS, and RMS

Messaging systems are vital for communication in our modern world, and they come in various forms such as SMS (short message service), MMS (multimedia messaging service), and RMS (rights management service). Each of these messaging systems serves different purposes and has unique features and advantages.

SMS (Short Message Service)

Overview:

- SMS is a text messaging service component of most telephone, internet, and mobile device systems.
- It uses standardized communication protocols to enable devices to exchange short text messages.

Key Features

- *Text-only messages:* Limited to 160 characters per message.
- *Wide compatibility:* Supported by virtually all mobile phones and networks globally.
- *Reliability:* Messages are delivered even in areas with low network coverage.
- *No internet required:* Operates over cellular networks, not requiring an internet connection.

MMS (Multimedia Messaging Service)

Overview:

- MMS is an extension of SMS that allows for the sending of multimedia content, such as images, audio, video, and text.

Key Features:

- *Multimedia content:* Supports various media types, enhancing the richness of communication.
- *Longer messages:* No strict character limit, allowing for more detailed messages.

- *Internet connectivity:* Requires mobile data or Wi-Fi for sending and receiving messages.

RMS (Rights Management Services)

Overview:

- RMS is a technology used to protect digital content and ensure that only authorized users can access it. In messaging systems, RMS helps to secure and manage the distribution of sensitive information.

Key Features:

- *Encryption:* Encrypts messages and attachments to protect them from unauthorized access.
- *Access control:* Sets permissions to control who can read, modify, forward, or print messages.
- *Usage restrictions:* Prevents copying, printing, or screenshotting of protected messages.
- *Audit trails:* Provides logs and reports on how data is accessed and used.

5 Space and Space Technology

- In August 1961, the government of India entrusted the responsibility of taking up research on space with the Department of Atomic Energy, headed by Dr. Homi Jehangir Bhabha.
- INCOSPAR (Indian National Committee for Space Research) was established in 1962 to start space research activities in India. Dr. Vikram Sarabhai was appointed as its first chairman.
- On 21 November 1963, a two-stage sounding rocket 'Nike Apache' was sent into space from the Thumba Equatorial Rocket Launching Station (TERLS), Kerala.
- On 15 August 1969, INCOSPAR was metamorphosed into the Indian Space Research Organisation (ISRO). Dr. Vikram Sarabhai was appointed its first chairman, and it started functioning under the Department of Atomic Energy.
- In June 1972, the Government of India established the Department of Space (DoS), and the Space Commission and ISRO were brought under DoS in September 1972.
- The Space Science and Technology Centre (SSTC) was established on 1 January 1965, at Veli Hills near Thiruvananthapuram, Kerala, to develop launch vehicles (commonly called rockets) for launching satellites. To recognize the contributions of Dr. Vikram Sarabhai to the Indian space sector, TERLS, SSTC, and other units were merged into a single entity named Vikram Sarabhai Space Centre (VSSC) in July 1972.

INDIAN SPACE RESEARCH ORGANISATION (ISRO)

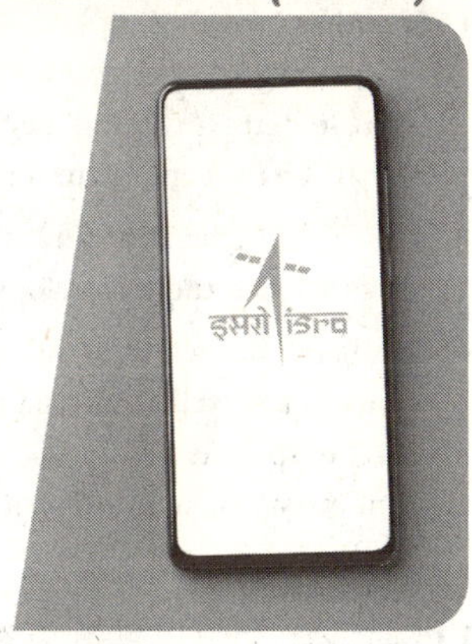

ISRO app

BRIEF INTRODUCTION

- ISRO is the national space agency of India and is the primary research and development division of the DoS, which directly reports to the Prime Minister of India.
- The chairman of ISRO is the chief executive of the DoS.
- The headquarters of ISRO are situated in Bengaluru, Karnataka.
- Dr. Vikram Sarabhai is the founding father of the Indian space programme.

OBJECTIVES OF ISRO

- It focusses on the design and development of various types of satellites and launch vehicles.
- It enhances communication infrastructure through the development

and deployment of communication satellites.

- It utilizes remote sensing satellites for natural resource management, agriculture, disaster management, and environmental monitoring.
- It conducts missions to explore the Moon, Mars, and other celestial bodies, to enhance scientific understanding of the solar system.
- It utilizes space technology for monitoring and protecting the environment, including the tracking of climate change and natural resources.
- It promotes education and training in space science and technology.
- It collaborates with the Indian industries as well as internationally, to develop space technologies, conduct joint missions, and foster innovation.

ORGANIZATIONAL STRUCTURE OF ISRO

- The chairman of ISRO is the secretary of the DoS and the chairman of the Space Commission. He/she is responsible for the overall direction and administration of ISRO. As of July 2024, the chairman of ISRO is Sreedhara Panicker Somanath.
- The Space Commission formulates the policies and supervises the implementation of the Indian space programme to promote the development and application of space science and technology for the socio-economic benefit of the country.
- The DoS is responsible for the implementation of these policies.
- The secretariat of DoS and the ISRO headquarters are located at Antariksh Bhavan in Bengaluru.

LAUNCH AND CONSTRUCTION			
NAME	**LOCATION**	**DIRECTOR**	**HIGHLIGHTS/FEATURES**
Satish Dhawan Space Centre (SDSC) or Sriharikota range	Sriharikota, Andhra Pradesh	Arumugam Rajarajan	• Named after Dr. Satish Dhawan, former ISRO chairman. • Primary spaceport of ISRO. • Two functioning launch pads used for launching sounding rockets, polar satellites, and geosynchronous satellites. • Launch pad for missions such as Chandrayaan-1, Chandrayaan-2, Chandrayaan-3, Mars Orbiter Mission, and Aditya L-1. • Created a world record with the launch of 104 satellites in one single mission in 2017.
U R Rao Satellite Centre (URSC)	Bengaluru, Karnataka	M. Sankaran	• Named after Dr. Udupi Ramachandra Rao, founding director of ISAC and former ISRO chairman. • Formerly known as ISRO Satellite Centre (ISAC). • Centre for the design, development, and construction of Indian satellites.

LAUNCH AND CONSTRUCTION			
NAME	**LOCATION**	**DIRECTOR**	**HIGHLIGHTS/FEATURES**
Laboratory for Electro-Optics Systems (LEOS)	Bengaluru, Karnataka	A. S. Laxmi Prasad	Design and development of optics and sensor modules that can be deployed either onboard a satellite or with the launch vehicle.
Thumba Equatorial Rocket Launching Station	Thumba, Thiruvananthapuram		Launch of sound rockets.

RESEARCH FACILITIES			
NAME	**LOCATION**	**DIRECTOR**	**HIGHLIGHTS/FEATURES**
Vikram Sarabhai Space Centre (VSSC)	Thiruvananthapuram, Kerala	S. Unnikrishnan Nair	• Formerly known as Thumba Equatorial Rocket Launching Station (TERLS). • Renamed in honour of Dr. Vikram Sarabhai. • Responsible for design, development, and testing of launch vehicles. • Plays a crucial role in ISRO's missions to place satellites into orbit.
National Atmospheric Research Laboratory (NARL)	Tirupati, Andhra Pradesh	A. K. Patra	• Research facility focussed on atmospheric sciences and related research. • Develops models to understand and predict atmospheric phenomena, contributing to improved weather forecasting and climate studies.
Liquid Propulsion Systems Centre (LPSC)	Headquarters: Thiruvananthapuram, Kerala; other units: • Bengaluru, Karnataka • Mahendragiri, Tamil Nadu	Dr. V. Narayanan	• Design and development of liquid propulsion systems for launch vehicles and spacecraft.
Physical Research Laboratory (PRL)	Ahmedabad, Gujarat	Dr. Anil Bhardwaj	• Conducts research on planetary exploration, studying the surfaces, atmospheres, and compositions of celestial bodies such as planets, moons, and asteroids. • Manages the Udaipur Solar Observatory and Mount Abu InfraRed Observatory.
North Eastern Space Applications Centre (NESAC)	Umiam, Meghalaya	Dr. S. P. Aggarwal	• Harnessing space technology for the development and welfare of the northeastern region of India. • Joint initiative of DoS and North Eastern Council (NEC).
Space Applications Centre	Ahmedabad, Gujarat	Nilesh M. Desai	Design, development, integration, and testing of payloads for various satellites, including communication, remote sensing, and meteorological satellites.

TEST FACILITY			
NAME	**LOCATION**	**DIRECTOR**	**HIGHLIGHTS/FEATURES**
ISRO Propulsion Complex	Mahendragiri, Tirunelveli, Tamil Nadu	J. Asir Packiaraj	• Formerly, it was known as Liquid Propulsion Systems Centre. • Development and testing of propulsion systems for launch vehicles and spacecraft.

TRACKING AND CONTROL FACILITIES		
NAME	**LOCATION**	**HIGHLIGHTS/FEATURES**
ISRO Telemetry, Tracking and Command Network (ISTRAC)	Bengaluru, Karnataka	• Responsible for tracking, telemetry, command, and control of satellites and spacecraft during all phases of their missions. • Provides critical support for ISRO's satellite and launch vehicle missions.
Indian Deep Space Network (IDSN)	Byalalu, Ramanagar district, Karnataka	• Dedicated to tracking and communicating with deep space missions. • Provided support for tracking ISRO's Mangalyaan, Chandrayaan-1, and Chandrayaan-2 missions.
National Remote Sensing Centre (NRSC)	Hyderabad, Telangana	Satellite data acquisition, processing, and dissemination for various applications, such as forestry, land-use planning, disaster management, urban development, agriculture, and more.
Master Control Facility (MCF)	Hasan, Karnataka and Bhopal, Madhya Pradesh	Responsible for the command, control, and monitoring of geostationary satellites in orbit.

COMMERCIAL WING OF ISRO			
NAME	**LOCATION**	**CHIEF MANAGING DIRECTOR (CMD)**	**HIGHLIGHTS/FEATURES**
Antrix Corporation	Bengaluru, Karnataka	Sanjay Kumar Agarwal	• Responsible for marketing and promoting space products, technical consultancy services, and satellite launches to both domestic and international customers. • It is a Public Sector Undertaking (PSU) and was awarded Miniratna Category-I status.
NewSpace India Limited	Bengaluru, Karnataka	Radhakrishnan Durairaj	• Promote the commercialization of space products, services, and technologies. • Scale up private sector participation in Indian space programmes.

LAUNCH VEHICLES OF ISRO

SATELLITE LAUNCH VEHICLE (SLV)

- It was India's first launch vehicle and was designed to carry small payloads into low Earth orbit.
- The first experimental flight of SLV was conducted on 10 August 1979, and it failed.
- ISRO was successful in its second attempt on 18 July 1980, when it placed the Rohini-1 satellite into orbit. With this, India became the sixth country to achieve this milestone.

AUGMENTED SATELLITE LAUNCH VEHICLE (ASLV)

- ASLV is also known as the Advanced Satellite Launch Vehicle.
- The ASLV was designed to enhance the payload capacity in comparison to the SLV. It aimed to place satellites into LEO.
- It featured a five-stage solid propulsion system, including two strap-on boosters, a core motor, and two upper stages.

POLAR SATELLITE LAUNCH VEHICLE (PSLV) (WORKHORSE OF ISRO)

- PSLV is India's third-generation launch vehicle and the first to be equipped with liquid stages.
- Since its successful launch in October 1994, PSLV has established itself as a dependable and versatile launch vehicle for both the Indian and international satellites.
- It is a four-stage vehicle that has a multiple satellite launch capability and multiple orbit capability. It can take up to 1,750 kg of payload to Sun-Synchronous Polar Orbits at 600 km altitude. It is designed to launch satellites into geosynchronous and geostationary orbits.
- Notably, PSLV launched the Chandrayaan-1 spacecraft to the Moon in 2008 and the Mars Orbiter Mission (MOM) to Mars in 2013, marking significant milestones in India's space exploration efforts.
- It earned its title 'the Workhorse of ISRO' by consistently launching various satellites to low Earth orbits.

GEOSYNCHRONOUS SATELLITE LAUNCH VEHICLE (GSLV)

- GSLV Mark II (GSLV Mk II) is a fourth-generation Indian launch vehicle designed to deploy communication satellites into Geosynchronous Transfer Orbit (GTO) using a cryogenic third stage.
- Initially, ISRO relied on Russian-supplied cryogenic stages, but starting with the GSLV-D5 mission in January 2014, ISRO began using an indigenously developed cryogenic stage.
- It features a three-stage design with four liquid strap-ons and has the capability of placing up to 6 tonnes in low Earth orbits broadening the scope of payloads from heavy satellites to multiple smaller satellites.
- While the primary objective of the GSLV series is to deploy communication satellites into GTO, it has also been used for launching weather, navigation, and experimental satellites.
- The series includes different versions, primarily the GSLV Mk I, GSLV Mk II, and the more advanced GSLV Mk III, each with progressively improved capabilities and performance.

LAUNCH VEHICLE MARK-3 (LVM-3)

- LVM-3 is also known as Geosynchronous Satellite Launch Vehicle Mark III. It is the most advanced and powerful launch vehicle developed by ISRO. It is designed to deploy heavier payloads into GTO and LEO.
- It is capable of placing the 4-tonne class satellites of the GSAT series into GTO. It can place 8,000 kg of payloads into LEO of 600 km altitude.
- The first successful test of LVM-3 was conducted on 5 June 2017, from the Satish Dhawan Space Centre.
- LVM-3 is designated as the launch vehicle for the Gaganyaan mission, India's first manned space mission.

SOUNDING ROCKETS

- Sounding rockets are one- or two-stage solid propellant rockets used for probing the upper atmospheric regions and conducting space research.
- They are cost-effective platforms to test and validate prototypes of new components or subsystems intended for launch vehicles and satellites.
- Initially, ISRO used two-stage model rockets that were imported from Russia (M-100) and France (Centaure).
- ISRO began launching indigenously made sounding rockets in 1965. RH-75 was the first Indian sounding rocket, with a diameter of 75 mm.
- The sounding rocket programme laid the foundation for ISRO's launch vehicle technology. It allows for coordinated campaigns by simultaneously launching rockets from different locations and enables multiple launches in a single day.
- Currently, ISRO offers three versions of operational sounding rockets, which cover a payload range of 8–100 kg and an apogee range of 80–475 km.

IMPORTANT MISSIONS

LUNAR EXPLORATION

Chandrayaan-1

- Chandrayaan-1 was India's first mission to the Moon. It was launched on 22 October 2008, from the Satish Dhawan Space Centre, Sriharikota, using the PSLV-C11 launch vehicle.
- It entered lunar orbit on 8 November 2008.
- The mission included an orbiter and an impactor, the Moon Impact Probe. On 14 November 2008, the impactor separated from the orbiter to hit the Shackleton Crater on the Moon. This point was named as Jawahar Point.
- The orbiter was orbiting around the Moon at a height of 100 km from the lunar surface for chemical, mineralogical, and photo-geologic mapping of the Moon.
- The mission was initially intended to last for 2 years, but it was concluded on 29 August 2009, due to a communication failure.
- One of the most significant discoveries was the detection of water molecules on the lunar surface, a finding that has profound implications for future lunar exploration and habitation.
- It provided high-resolution data that has been used for various scientific studies and lunar mapping.
- It carried instruments from other space agencies, including National Aeronautics and Space Administration (NASA) and European Space Agency (ESA), highlighting international cooperation in space exploration.

Chairman, ISRO: G. Madhavan Nair

Project director: Mylswamy Annadura (Moon Man of India)

Mission director: Srinivasa Hegde

Chandrayaan-2

- Chandrayaan-2 was India's second lunar exploration mission. It was launched on 22 July 2019, from the Satish Dhawan Space Centre, Sriharikota, using the GSLV Mk III-M1 launch vehicle. It successfully entered lunar orbit on 20 August 2019.
- The mission consisted of an orbiter, lander, and rover. The orbiter was designed to orbit the Moon and relay scientific data. It was equipped with eight scientific instruments to study the lunar surface and exosphere. The lander was named after Dr. Vikram Sarabhai, the founding father of the Indian space programme. It was expected to make a soft landing on the surface of the Moon. The rover was named as Pragyan rover. It was a six-wheeled robotic vehicle designed to explore the lunar surface. It was equipped with instruments to analyse the lunar soil and relay data to the lander, which then sent it to the orbiter.
- On 6 September 2019, the Vikram lander began its descent to the lunar surface, but the communication was lost when it was just 2.1 km above the surface. The point where the Vikram lander crashed was named the Tiranga Point.

Chairman, ISRO: K. Sivan

Project director: Muthayya Vanitha

Mission director: Ritu Karidhal

Chandrayaan-3

- Chandrayaan-3 was India's third mission to the Moon. It was launched on 14 July 2023, from the Satish Dhawan Space Centre, Sriharikota, using the LVM3 M4 launch vehicle. It successfully entered lunar orbit on 5 August 2023.
- The mission comprised three components: a propulsion module, a Vikram lander module, and a Pragyan rover.
- On 23 August 2023, India became the first country to successfully land a spacecraft on the south pole of the Moon. The point where Vikram lander landed was named 'Statio Shiv Shakti'. This day was honoured by recognizing it as the 'National Space Day' of India.
- The Pragyan rover and Vikram lander were to study the Moon's surface for a single lunar day, equivalent to approximately 14 Earth days.
- The mission confirmed the presence of sulphur on the lunar surface using the laser-induced breakdown spectroscopy instrument onboard. Other elements such as aluminium, calcium, iron, chromium, titanium, manganese, silicon, and oxygen had been detected.

Chairman, ISRO: S. Somnath

Project director: P. Veeramuthuvel

Mission director: S. Mohanakumar

Chandrayaan-3

MARS EXPLORATION

Mars Orbiter Mission (MOM) or Mangalyaan

- MOM is India's first interplanetary mission to Mars, also known as the Red Planet. It was launched on 5 November 2013, aboard a Polar

Satellite Launch Vehicle (PSLV-C25) from the Satish Dhawan Space Centre, Sriharikota.

- The mission comprised an orbiter that orbited Mars to study and examine the Martian surface features and landscapes.
- It travelled for about 300 days before entering Martian orbit on 24 September 2014, making India the first country to successfully reach Mars on its first attempt.
- Initially, the mission was planned for six months, it officially ended in 2022 when ISRO lost contact with the orbiter.
- MOM successfully captured images of Mars and its moons, Phobos and Deimos. It provided crucial information on the Martian atmosphere, including insights into methane levels and seasonal variations.
- The mission proved the feasibility of low-cost interplanetary missions, highlighting ISRO's technological prowess.

Chairman, ISRO: K. Radhakrishnan

Mission director: V. Kesava Raju

Project director: Subbiah Arunan

SOLAR PROBE

Aditya-L1

- Aditya-L1 is India's first space-based mission dedicated to studying the Sun. It is a coronagraphy spacecraft that carries seven payloads designed to observe the photosphere, chromosphere, and corona (outer layers of the sun). These payloads use electromagnetic, particle, and magnetic field detectors.
- It was launched on 2 September 2023, aboard the PSLV-XL C57 from Satish Dhawan Space Centre, Sriharikota.
- The spacecraft is positioned in a halo orbit around the Lagrange Point 1 (L1) of the Sun–Earth system. L1 is a location in space where the gravitational forces of two celestial bodies, such as the Sun and Earth, are in equilibrium. This allows an object placed there to remain relatively stable for both celestial bodies. This point is located about 1.5 million kilometres from Earth and its unique position allows the satellite to continuously observe the S without interruptions from eclipses or occultations, providing real-time data on solar activities and their impact on space weather.
- On 6 January 2024, Aaditya-L1 was inserted at the L1 point.
- Four payloads will directly observe the Sun, capturing data on solar activities. Three payloads will conduct in situ studies of particles and fields at L1, providing insights into the propagation of solar dynamics through the interplanetary medium.

Chairman, ISRO: S. Somnath

Project director: Nigar Shaji (Sunny Lady)

SPACE TELESCOPE

Astrosat-2

It is India's first dedicated multi-wavelength space observatory. It was launched on 2 September 2015, in the LEO at an altitude of approximately 650 km. It is designed to observe celestial sources in different wavelengths, enhancing our understanding of the universe.

SATELLITES OF ISRO

Communication Satellites

- These satellites support telecommunication, television broadcasting, satellite news gathering, societal applications, weather forecasting, disaster warning, and search and rescue operation services.

- The major communication satellite series are the INSAT Series and GSAT Series.
- INSAT stands for Indian National Satellite. It was established in 1983 with the commissioning of INSAT-1B. It has nine operational communication satellites placed in the geostationary orbit. These provide telecommunications, broadcasting, meteorology, and search and rescue operations.
- GSAT stands for geosynchronous satellite. These are indigenously developed communication satellites that enhance telecommunications, television broadcasting, and broadband services.

Earth Observation Satellite

- These satellites monitor and manage natural resources, aid disaster management, and contribute to environmental and weather studies.
- They provide critical data for various applications, including agriculture, forestry, water resources, urban planning, and climate monitoring.
- The major Earth Observation Satellite series are the IRS series, Resourcesat series, Cartosat series, RISAT series, Oceansat series, and INSAT and METSAT series.
- IRS satellite stands for Indian Remote Sensing Satellites. These provide high-resolution imagery for resource monitoring and management. IRS-1A was the first satellite in this series and was launched in 1988.
- Resourcesat satellites provide resource monitoring, agricultural applications, and disaster management. The first satellite in this series Resourcesat-1 (IRS-P6) was launched in 2003.
- Cartosat satellites provide high-resolution satellite imagery for urban planning, rural development, and infrastructure monitoring. The first satellite, Cartosat-1, was launched in 2005.
- RISAT stands for Radar Imaging Satellite. These satellites provide all-weather surveillance and reconnaissance using Synthetic Aperture Radar. These are the first all-weather Earth observation satellites from ISRO. The first RISAT satellite RISAT-2 was launched in 2009.
- Oceansat series are the satellites used for monitoring oceanographic parameters, including sea surface temperatures, phytoplankton blooms, and wind vectors. The first satellite in this series was OceanSat-1 and was launched in 1999.

Scientific Spacecraft

- These are designed to explore space and advance the understanding of the universe.
- These missions span various domains, including planetary exploration, space science, and astronomy, contributing significantly to global scientific knowledge.
- Some of them are MOM, Chandrayaan series, Aditya-L1.

Navigation Satellites

- These satellites are designed to provide navigation services to address the growing needs of civil aviation and fulfil user demands for precise positioning, navigation, and timing through an autonomous satellite navigation system.
- ISRO has developed **NavIC (Navigation with Indian Constellation)**, which was erstwhile known as the Indian Regional Navigation Satellite System. NavIC is

designed to provide accurate position information services to users in India and the surrounding region. It consists of seven satellites that are designed to provide continuous coverage over India and an area extending up to 1,500 km around it. It has a network of ground stations operating 24 × 7 to monitor these satellites.

- **GAGAN (GPS Aided GEO Augmented Navigation)** is a Satellite-Based Augmentation System (SBAS) being developed by ISRO in collaboration with the Airport Authority of India. It will provide precision and reliability essential for civil aviation leading to a much better Air Traffic Management in Indian airspace.

Experimental Satellites

- These are small satellites to test and demonstrate new technologies, conduct scientific experiments, and validate engineering concepts.
- These play a crucial role in advancing India's space capabilities and paving the way for future missions.
- Some of them are YOUTHSAT, APPLE, INS-1B, INS-1A, etc.

Small Satellites

- These satellites provide platforms for standalone payloads dedicated to Earth imaging and scientific missions with rapid turnaround time.
- Depending on the weight of the payload, two types of satellite buses have been designed and developed. These are IMS-1 and IMS-2.
- IMS-1 stands for Indian Mini Satellite-1. They are a versatile bus of 100 kg that can carry a payload capacity of approximately 30 kg. The first mission of the IMS-1 series was launched successfully on 28 April 2008, as a co-passenger along with Cartosat 2A.
- IMS-2 stands for Indian Mini Satellite-2. These are a standard bus of 400 kg that can carry a payload capability of around 200 kg. The first mission in this category was SARAL, a cooperative mission between ISRO and CNES (National Centre for Space Studies, France).

Student Satellites

- ISRO has actively engaged with educational institutions and students through its Student Satellite Programme, providing opportunities to design, develop, and launch small satellites.
- These initiatives foster hands-on learning in satellite technology, space science, and engineering.

QUICK FACTS

- Aryabhatta was India's first satellite launched by a Soviet Kosmos-3M rocket from Kapustin Yar on 19 April 1975. It was completely designed and fabricated in India. It was named after the famous Indian astronomer Aryabhata who invented zero and discovered the approximate value of pi.

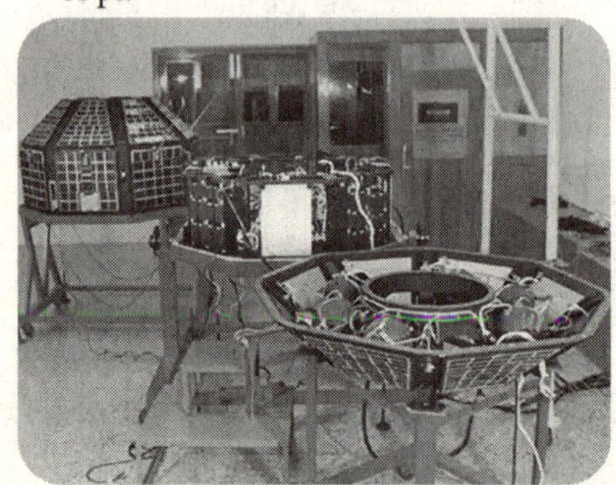

Aryabhatta – first satellite

- GSAT-11 is India's heaviest and most advanced high-throughput communication satellite with a weight of 5,854 kg. It was launched on 4 December 2018, from the Guiana Space Centre, French Guiana.

- ISRO launched 'Kalamsat', which is the world's smallest and lightest communication satellite. It weighed 1.26 kg and was made by Space Kidz India.
- BHUVAN is an Indian web-based geoportal, providing visualization services and earth observation data. It was launched in 2009 and developed by ISRO. It offers high-resolution satellite imagery of the Indian subcontinent. It allows users to view 3D models of terrain and buildings.

ISRO IN NEWS

- **Gaganyaan** is India's first human space flight programme. ISRO aims to send three astronauts to an orbit of 400 km and bring them back after 3 days. Before sending the humans, ISRO will send Vyommitra, the female humanoid to space. ISRO is working closely with the Defence Research and Development Organisation and Hindustan Aeronautics Limited to make this mission a success.
- Four air force officers – Group Captain Prashanth Balakrishnan Nair, Group Captain Ajit Krishnan, Group Captain Angad Pratap, and Wing Commander Shubhanshu Shukla – have been shortlisted for the Gaganyaan mission.
- **Bharatiya Antariksh Station (BAS)** will be India's first space station. ISRO is working to establish this station in a phased manner by 2035.
- ISRO successfully conducted the third and final landing experiment of the Reusable Launch Vehicle (RLV LEX-03) named **'Pushpak'**.
- ISRO will establish **India's second space station** at Kulasekarapattinam, Thoothukudi district, Tamil Nadu.
- ISRO carried mapping exercise with the NASA to successfully generate the most detailed map of **Adam's Bridge**, which is popularly known as **Ram Setu**. Adam's Bridge spans from Dhanushkodi, a southeastern point of Rameshwaram Island in India to the northwestern end of Talaimannar in Mannar Island of Sri Lanka.

INTERNATIONAL SPACE AGENCIES

NASA (NATIONAL AERONAUTICS AND SPACE ADMINISTRATION)

NASA is the national space agency of the United States responsible for space exploration, scientific discovery, and aeronautics research. It operates different research centres and facilities across the country to promote scientific research, exploration, and development.

It collaborates with international space agencies such as ESA, Roscosmos, JAXA, and ISRO, as well as private companies such as SpaceX and Boeing, to advance space exploration and technology.

Established: 29 July 1958

Headquarters: Washington DC, United States

Administrator: Bill Nelson

NASA building, Kennedy Space Centre, Cape Canaveral, Florida, United States

Some of its notable interplanetary exploration programmes and missions are as follows.

HUMAN SPACEFLIGHT

Project Apollo

- This project focussed on successfully landing humans on the Moon and returning them to Earth.
- It was run from 1961 to 1972. In all, there were a total of 14 missions in the Apollo programme. However, the first crewed flight took off in 1968.
- Apollo 11 mission was the first successful mission to land humans on the Moon. Neil Armstrong and Edwin Buzz Aldrin were the first two people to land on the Moon with Armstrong being the first person to land on the Moon. Apollo 11 was launched from Cape Kennedy on 16 July 1969.

Space Shuttle Programme (Space Transportation System)

NASA launched STS on 12 April 1981, to provide routine transportation for Earth-to-orbit crew and cargo. It enabled reusable space travel, deployed satellites, serviced the Hubble Space Telescope, and constructed the International Space Station (ISS). The space shuttle fleet had flown 135 missions till it made a final landing on 21 July 2011.

International Space Station (ISS)

ISS is a large spacecraft in low Earth orbit that serves as a habitable artificial satellite and research laboratory. It was built in two phases: Phase 1 (1995–98) and Phase 2 (starting from 1998). It works on a unique international collaboration involving multiple space agencies namely:

- NASA (National Aeronautics and Space Administration), United States
- Roscosmos (Russian Federal Space Agency), Russia
- ESA (European Space Agency), Europe
- JAXA (Japan Aerospace Exploration Agency), Japan
- CSA (Canadian Space Agency), Canada

The ISS orbits Earth at an average altitude of approximately 400 km (about 248 miles) and travels at a speed of about 28,000 km/h (17,500 miles/h). It has the following objectives:

- *Scientific research:* The ISS serves as a microgravity and space environment research laboratory where scientific research is conducted in astrobiology, astronomy, meteorology, physics, and other fields.
- *International cooperation:* It exemplifies international cooperation in space, bringing together countries to work on common goals and share resources.
- *Technological development*: The ISS helps develop technologies needed for long-duration human and robotic exploration into deep space, including missions to Mars.
- *Artemis programme:* Artemis is a Moon exploration programme that was formally established in 2017 via Space Policy Directive 1. The Artemis programme is intended to re-establish a human presence on the Moon and establish a permanent base on the Moon to facilitate human missions to Mars. With this mission, NASA will also land the first woman and first person of colour on the Moon.

ROBOTIC EXPLORATION

Mars Exploration

Over the years, NASA has sent five robotic vehicles, called rovers, to Mars. These are Sojourner, Spirit, Opportunity, Curiosity, and Perseverance.

SPACE EXPLORATION

Hubble Space Telescope

- It was developed by NASA in association with the ESA and is named after the American astronomer Edwin Hubble.
- It was launched on 24 April 1990, onboard Space Shuttle Discovery (STS-31) and placed in low Earth orbit.
- It has a 2.4-m primary mirror, which collects light from astronomical objects. It is equipped with Wide Field Camera 3 (WFC3), the Advanced Camera for Surveys (ACS), and the Cosmic Origins Spectrograph (COS) to study different astronomical objects.
- Its data has helped determine the age of the Universe to be approximately 13.8 billion years.
- It has provided critical evidence for the expansion of the Universe, supporting the Big Bang theory. It has been instrumental in studying the atmospheres of exoplanets and detecting signs of potential habitability.
- Its detailed images have revealed the processes of star formation, evolution, and the life cycle of stars.

James Webb Space Telescope (JWST)

- The JWST is an orbiting infrared observatory that complements and extends the discoveries of the Hubble Space Telescope. The telescope is named after James E. Webb, who was the administrator of NASA from 1961 to 1968.
- It is a collaboration between NASA, the European Space Agency (ESA), and the Canadian Space Agency (CSA).
- It is positioned at the second Lagrange Point (L2), approximately 1.5 million kilometres from Earth, providing a stable environment for observations.

PLANETARY EXPLORATION

Galileo Mission

It was the first mission to study Jupiter and its moons, as the asteroids Gaspra and Ida.

Cassini–Huygens Mission

It explored Saturn and its moons, especially Titan and Enceladus, revealing their potential for harbouring life.

JAXA (JAPAN AEROSPACE EXPLORATION AGENCY)

- JAXA is Japan's national aerospace agency, responsible for space and planetary research, satellite development, and the promotion of the aerospace industry.
- JAXA was formed due to the merger of three previously independent organizations: the National Space Development Agency of Japan (NASDA), the National Aerospace Laboratory of Japan (NAL), and the Institute of Space and Astronautical Science (ISAS).
- Mission and Goals: JAXA aims to contribute to society through space exploration and research, advancing scientific knowledge, and fostering innovation in aerospace technology.
- Some of its important programmes were/are:
  - *Hayabusa:* It was the first mission to return samples from an asteroid, Itokawa to Earth in 2010.
  - *Hayabusa2:* It successfully collected and returned samples from asteroid Ryugu to Earth in 2020.
  - *Akatsuki:* It is also known as the Venus Climate Orbiter (VCO) and was launched to study the atmosphere and climate of Venus in 2010.
  - *IKAROS (Interplanetary Kite-craft Accelerated by Radiation of the Sun):* It was launched in 2010 and was the

first spacecraft to demonstrate solar sail technology in interplanetary space.

- *Kibo Module, ISS:* It is the largest module on the International Space Station (ISS) and is used for scientific experiments in space.
- *SLIM (Smart Lander for Investigating Moon):* It is Japan's lunar mission and was launched on 6 September 2023. It successfully made a soft landing on the surface of the Moon on 19 January 2024.

Established: 1 October 2003

Headquarters: Tokyo, Japan

Administrator: Hiroshi Yamakawa

ROSCOSMOS

- Roscosmos is the governmental body responsible for the space science programme of the Russian Federation. It is a successor to the Soviet space programme.
- After the disintegration of the Soviet Union, it began as the Russian Space Agency to be eventually restructured into Roscosmos. Some of its notable programmes were/are:
  - *Sputnik 1:* This spacecraft was the world's first artificial satellite launched from Baikonur Cosmodrome at Tyuratam in Kazakhstan, then part of the former Soviet Union. It was successfully placed in an elliptical low Earth orbit around the Earth.
  - *Vostok programme:* Russian Soviet Cosmonaut Yuri Gagarin was the first human to fly in space on 12 April 1961. He was launched from what is now Kazakhstan in his Vostok 1 spacecraft.
  - *Soyuz 1:* It was the first crewed flight into space. It was launched on 23 April 1967, with cosmonaut Vladimir Komarov and ended with his death as the module faced some technical glitch.
  - *Luna programme:* Luna 2 was launched in 1959, and it was the first human-made object to reach the Moon. Luna 16 successfully returned lunar soil samples to Earth in 1970.
  - *Salyut programme:* It was the world's first space station and was launched in 1971.
  - *Mir space station:* It was launched in 1986 and served as a significant long-term research facility in orbit. It contributed to international space cooperation and scientific experiments.
  - *Zvezda Module, International Space Station (ISS):* It provides living quarters and life support for astronauts on the ISS.
  - *Fobos-Grunt or Phobos-Grunt:* It was launched to get soil samples from Mars' moon Phobos. However, it faced a launch failure.
  - In 2023, Russia launched Luna 25 to land on the south pole of the Moon. However, it failed as the lander crashed on the Moon's surface.

Established: 2 February 1992

Headquarters: Moscow, Russia

Administrator: Yury Borisov

EUROPEAN SPACE AGENCY (ESA)

- ESA is an intergovernmental organization with 22 countries dedicated to exploring space and advancing Europe's space capabilities.
- It receives funds from the contributions of its member states, along with revenue from European Union contributions and other sources.

- ESA collaborates with NASA, Roscosmos, JAXA, ISRO, and other space agencies on various missions and projects, promoting international cooperation in space exploration.
- Some of its space programmes are:
  - *Copernicus programme:* It provides accurate and timely environmental data and monitoring services. Sentinel satellites are a part of the Copernicus programme, and these monitor various environmental parameters.
  - *Herschel Space Observatory:* It was a space observatory that provided valuable data on the formation of stars and galaxies.
  - *Cosmic Vision (2015–25):* The programme is focussed on exploring the Universe and understanding its fundamental processes through innovative space missions and scientific research initiatives.
  - *ExoMars programme:* A joint mission with Roscosmos to search for signs of life on Mars.
  - *BepiColombo:* A joint mission with JAXA to explore Mercury.
  - *JUICE (Jupiter Icy Moons Explorer):* The mission is scheduled to explore Jupiter and its largest moons: Ganymede, Callisto, and Europa.

Established: 30 May 1975

Headquarters: Paris, France

Administrator: Josef Aschbacher

ESA sign outside an ESA factory building in Bremen, Germany

6 Transport

Transportation is vital for the country's economic, social, and cultural progress. Due to India's extensive size and varied geography, a well-functioning transportation network is crucial for linking different regions and enabling the movement of people, goods, and services. A good transportation infrastructure forms the backbone of trade and commerce that ultimately contributes to economic growth. It promotes connectivity among rural and urban India, thereby bridging the divide. It generates significant employment opportunities, from construction and maintenance to operation and management.

ROADWAYS

India has the second-largest road network in the world covering approximately 66.71 lakh km.

The Ministry of Road Transport and Highways is responsible for formulating broad policies relating to road transport regulation in the country. The different types of roads in India are as follows:

- *National highways:* These are wide four-to six-lane roads managed by the National Highways Authority of India (NHAI). These are generally meant for long travels and freight transport.
- *Golden quadrilateral:* It is a national highway connecting the four major cities of India: Delhi (north), Kolkata (east), Mumbai (west), and Chennai (south). Its approximate length is 5,846 km.
- *North-South and East-West Corridor (NSEW):* It is one of the largest ongoing highway development projects in India that aims to connect Srinagar in the north, Kanyakumari in the south, Porbandar in the west, and Silchar in the east – through a network of highways. The total length of this corridor is approximately 7,142 km. The project aims to improve connectivity and reduce travel time across the country.
- *Expressways:* These are high-speed corridors that connect the major economic hubs and cities. They have faster traffic flow and have higher safety standards.
- *State highways:* These connect major towns within a state and link them to the national highways. These are managed by respective state's Public Works Departments (PWDs).
- *District roads:* These connect district headquarters with other significant areas within the district and with the state highways. They provide connectivity within smaller towns and villages in the district. The district authorities or local government bodies manage these roads.
- *Village/rural roads:* These connect rural areas with nearby towns and villages and are generally maintained by the local panchayats.
- *Border roads:* These are near the international border of India and are important for India's defence and strategic purposes. These are managed by the Border Roads Organisation (BRO).

The length of roads under various categories is as follows:

- National highways: 1,46,145 km
- State highways: 1,79,535 km
- Other roads: 63,45,403 km

IMPORTANT IT INITIATIVES

NEXT-GEN MPARIVAHAN

It is a one-stop transport solution for citizens and provides instant access to information, services, and utilities related to the transportation sector. It provides all the information related to the vehicle registration number such as registration date, owner's name, vehicle age, vehicle class, insurance validity, fitness validity, etc.

FASTAG

It is a cashless electronic toll-collection system that uses Radio Frequency Identification (RFID) technology to make toll payments directly from the linked prepaid or savings account associated with the vehicle. FASTag (RFID Tag) is attached to the windscreen of the vehicle and enables the transfer of toll payments while it is in motion. This offers several benefits such as saving time and fuel. It also helps in doing away with long queues at the tolls as the customer does not have to stop at the toll plaza. This system is covered under the National Electronic Toll Collection (NETC) programme of the National Payments Corporation of India (NPCI).

RAJMARGYATRA

It is a one-stop repository of essential information for national highway users. The mobile application provides real-time weather conditions, timely broadcast notifications, and access to details about nearby toll plazas, petrol pumps, hospitals, hotels, and other essential services that ensure a seamless and safe journey on national highways. It also has an inbuilt complaint redressal and escalation mechanism.

BHARAT NEW CAR ASSESSMENT PROGRAMME (BNCAP)

It is a voluntary rating-based safety assessment programme for Indian cars. It will provide consumers with an indication of the level of protection offered to the customers by evaluating the vehicle in the following areas: Adult Occupant Protection (AOP), Child Occupant Protection (COP), and Safety Assist Technologies (SAT). The Central Institute of Road Transport (CIRT) is the designated agency of BNCAP.

BHARATMALA PARIYOJANA

It is a comprehensive and umbrella programme for the development of roads and highways in India. It is a successor to the erstwhile National Highways Development Project (NHDP). Under the Bharatmala Pariyojana, the government aims to develop economic corridors, border and international connectivity roads, greenfield expressways, brownfield expressways, widening of four-lane roads to six-lane roads, etc. The project aims to connect 550 districts in the country through national highways (NH) linkages. It also focuses on improving connectivity in the north-east. Through this programme, the government aims to bring 70–80 per cent of freight movement on the national highways.

NATIONAL HIGHWAYS AUTHORITY OF INDIA (NHAI)

NHAI is an autonomous organization responsible for the development, maintenance, and management of national highways in India. It is headquartered in Delhi and its current chairman is Santosh Kumar Yadav.

RAILWAYS

- Indian Railways is the largest railway network in Asia and the second largest globally. The first steam-operated railway was operated in 1837. The first passenger train was run from Howrah station to Hooghly on 15 August 1854. It covered a distance of 24 miles. There are 18 administrative zones in the Indian Railways.
- The headquarters of Indian Railways is the Rail Bhawan, New Delhi.

Types of Coaches

There are two types of coaches in Indian Railways:

1. *ICF (Integral Coach Factory):* It is a conventional coach of the Indian Railways. The designs of these coaches were developed by the Integral Coach Factory, Perambur, Chennai, India, in collaboration with the Swiss Car & Elevator Manufacturing Co, Schlieren, Switzerland. However, India is working towards phasing out these coaches by 2030.
2. *LHB (Linke-Hofmann-Busch):* It is a passenger coach developed by Linke-Hofmann-Busch, Germany, and will be subsequently replacing ICF. These are produced at Kapurthala, Chennai, and Raibareli.

Railway coach manufacturing units in India are as follows:

1. Integral Coach Factory (ICF), Chennai, Tamil Nadu
2. Rail Coach Factory (RCF), Kapurthala, Punjab
3. Banaras Locomotive Works (BLW), Varanasi, Uttar Pradesh
4. Modern Coach Factory (MCF), Rae Bareli, Uttar Pradesh

Types of Trains

1. *Vande Bharat (Train 18):* It is India's first inter-city semi-high-speed train whose maximum operational speed is 160 km/h. During the trials, the train

achieved the highest speed of 183 km/h. It has automatic doors, on-board Wi-Fi, a GPS-based passenger information system, and bio-vacuum toilets. The first Vande Bharat Express was run between New Delhi and Varanasi.

2. *Rajdhani Express:* It is a high-speed, long-distance train connecting the national capital, New Delhi, with the capitals of various states. The first train in this category was run on 1 March 1969. The Rajdhani Express is being upgraded to Tejas-Rajdhani Express. The new coaches are equipped with bio-toilets, CCTVs, reading lights, dedicated power sockets, etc.
3. *Shatabdi Express:* It is a high-speed, intercity train connecting major cities with shorter travel times. The trains run at a permissible speed of 110–150 km/h. The first train was introduced on 10 July 1988. It provides high-priority service with limited stops.
4. *Slow and fast passenger train:* These are passenger trains that connect small towns and cities to metropolitan cities in India. They halt at all or most of the stations on the railway routes.
5. *Amrit Bharat Express:* It is a super-fast express train which was introduced on 30 December 2023. These offer non-air-conditioned, sleeper, low-cost unreserved service. These connect the cities that are 800 km apart.
6. *Tejas Express:* These are semi-high-speed trains aimed at providing a premium travel experience. These are modern, fully air-conditioned coaches with premium seating.
7. *Freight trains/cargo trains:* These trains are used to carry cargo. These are suited to carrying bulk and heavy loads over longer distances.

Railway Gauge

It is the distance between two railway tracks, basically the inner side of the railway track. Globally, about 60 per cent of railways use a standard gauge of 1,435 mm. In India, there are four types of gauges:

1. *Broad gauge:* The distance between two tracks is 1,676 mm. It is the most widely used gauge in India. It provides higher stability and is suitable for high-speed trains and heavy freight. It is used for express and superfast trains like Rajdhani, Shatabdi, and freight corridors.

2. *Metre gauge:* The distance between two tracks is 1,000 mm. However, this is being phased out and converted to broad gauge under Project Unigauge. Metre gauge is used in regions with lower traffic volumes and in areas where narrow curves are required.
3. *Standard gauge:* The distance between two tracks is 1,435 mm. It is mostly used for urban rail transit systems such as metro, monorail, and tram. It is useful in cases when there is a requirement of frequent stops, high acceleration, and deceleration. It is mostly found in the Delhi metro, Namma metro, and Mumbai metro.
4. *Narrow gauge:* The distance between two tracks is 762 mm and 610 mm. It is suitable for sharp curves and steep gradients. It is commonly used to accommodate smaller, lighter trains in hilly regions and areas with difficult terrain.

URBAN TRANSIT IN INDIA

- The Ministry of Urban Development's Urban Transport wing is the nodal division for coordination, appraisal, and approval of urban transport matters including Metro Rail Projects at the central level.
- The Delhi–Meerut RRTS (RapidX) is the fastest urban transit system in India currently that can run at a speed of 160 km/h with an average operational speed of 100 km/h.
- The monorail runs on a narrow and single track. The Mumbai Monorail is the first and only operational monorail system used for urban transit in India.
- Rapid transit or mass rapid transit (MRT) are the metro trains which provide public transport. Some of them are the Delhi metro, Namma (Bengaluru) metro, Mumbai metro, etc. Kolkata metro was India's first underground rail system.
- Mumbai–Ahmedabad High-Speed Rail Corridor (MAHSR) or Mumbai–Ahmedabad HSR is India's first high-speed rail line. It will be a 508.18-km line and E5 Series Shinkansen train will run at a speed of 320 km/h. It is expected to be operational by 2026.

AIRWAYS

India has a well-developed network of international and domestic airports, connecting major cities and regions. For longer routes, people prefer to travel on domestic airlines to save time. Air travel also helps connect remote areas and enhance global business and tourism opportunities.

Types of Airlines in India

1. *Full-service carriers (FSC):* These airlines offer a wide range of services, including multiple classes of seating (economy, business, first class), in-flight meals, and additional amenities such as lounges and baggage allowances.
2. *Low-cost carriers (LCCs):* These airlines focus on providing affordable air travel by offering basic services with optional add-ons.
3. *Regional airlines:* These airlines operate short-haul flights, connecting smaller cities with regional hubs. They focus on regional connectivity, often serving tier-2 and tier-3 cities.
4. *Cargo airlines:* These specialize in transporting goods, mail, and cargo rather than passengers. They offer domestic and international cargo routes, including express delivery services.

NAME	HEADQUARTERS	IMPORTANT PEOPLE
Air India	Gurugram, Haryana	Founder: J. R. D. Tata Chairman: N. Chandrasekaran CEO & MD: Campbell Wilson
IndiGo	Gurugram, Haryana	Founders: Rahul Bhatia and Rakesh Gangwal Co-founder & MD: Rahul Bhatia CEO: Pieter Elbers
Vistara	Gurugram, Haryana	Chairman: Bhaskar Bhat CEO: Vinod Kannan
SpiceJet	Gurugram, Haryana	Chairman & MD: Ajay Singh CFO: Sanjeev Taneja
Go First	Mumbai, Maharashtra	Chairman: Bhisham Bharadwaj
Air Asia	Kuala Lumpur International Airport, Selangor, Malaysia	Executive Director & CEO: Tony Fernandes Executive Chairman: Kamarudin Meranun

IMPORTANT AIRPORTS IN INDIA

NAME	CITY
Kempegowda International Airport	Bengaluru, Karnataka
Chhatrapati Shivaji Maharaj International Airport	Mumbai, Maharashtra
Indira Gandhi International Airport	New Delhi
Rajiv Gandhi International Airport	Hyderabad, Telangana
Chennai International Airport	Chennai, Tamil Nadu
Netaji Subhash Chandra Bose International Airport	Kolkata, West Bengal

REGULATORY BODIES

International Civil Aviation Organization (ICAO)

The ICAO is a specialized agency of the United Nations that creates rules and regulations for safety, security, efficiency, and environmental protection in the aviation sector. ICAO is responsible for the establishment and maintenance of international Standards and Recommended Practices (SARPs), as well as Procedures for Air Navigation (PANS). The Chicago Convention of 1944 served as a starting point for the creation of the ICAO.

Ministry of Civil Aviation

The ministry is responsible for the formulation and administration of national policies, programmes, and legislations for the development and regulation of the civil aviation sector in the country.

Directorate General of Civil Aviation (DGCA)

DGCA is the statutory regulatory body that oversees civil aviation in the country. It is responsible for regulating air safety, issuing licenses, and ensuring compliance with aviation standards. It also co-ordinates all regulatory functions with the International Civil Aviation Organization (ICAO). It is headquartered in New Delhi and its current director-general is Vikram Dev Dutt.

Airports Authority of India (AAI)

AAI is a statutory body responsible for managing and operating airports across India. It also provides air navigation services. It is headquartered in New Delhi and its chairman is Sanjeev Kumar.

WATER TRANSPORT

India boasts an extensive network of rivers, canals, backwaters, and coastlines that serve as crucial trade routes, particularly in the north-eastern and eastern regions. Water transportation offers a more cost-effective alternative to road or rail, especially for transporting bulky and heavy goods, thereby lowering overall transportation expenses. Additionally, waterways have a smaller carbon footprint compared to road and rail, making them a more environmentally friendly option. Shifting bulk cargo to waterways alleviates congestion on roads and railways, reducing infrastructure strain and maintenance costs. Furthermore, waterways are essential for providing connectivity to areas with limited road and rail access, such as the north-eastern states and remote coastal regions.

TYPES OF WATER TRANSPORT IN INDIA

Inland Waterways

These refer to the natural waterways such as rivers and lakes, and artificial or man-made channels such as canals and backwaters. India has about 14,500 km of navigable waterways which comprise rivers, canals, backwaters, creeks, etc. According to the statistics, about 133.03 million metric tonnes (MMT) of cargo is being moved annually by Indian water transport (IWT). It is the most economical mode of transportation, especially for bulk cargo such as coal, iron ore, cement, food grains, and fertilizers. The Inland Waterways Authority of India (IWAI) is responsible for the development and maintenance of IWTs in India. IWAI works under the jurisdiction of the Ministry of Ports, Shipping and Waterways. Some of the important inland waterways are as follows.

NATIONAL WATERWAY NO.	LENGTH (KM)	LOCATION
NW-1: Ganga-Bhagirathi-Hooghly River System (Haldia–Allahabad)	1,620	Uttar Pradesh, Bihar, Jharkhand, West Bengal
NW-2: Brahmaputra River (Dhubri–Sadiya)	891	Assam
NW-3: West Coast Canal (Kottapuram–Kollam), Champakara and Udyogmandal canals	205	Kerala
NW-4: Phase-1 development on the stretch from Muktiyala to Vijyawada of River Krishna	82	Andhra Pradesh
NW-68: Mandovi–Usgaon Bridge to Arabian Sea	41	Goa
NW-111: Zuari–Sanvordem Bridge to Mormugao Port	50	Goa
NW-10 (Amba River)	45	Maharashtra
NW-83 (Rajpuri Creek)	31	Maharashtra
NW-85 (Revadanda Creek–Kundalika River System)	31	Maharashtra
NW-91 (Shastri River–Jaigad Creek System)	52	Maharashtra
NW-73 (Narmada River)	226	Gujarat and Maharashtra
NW-100 (Tapi River)	436	Gujarat and Maharashtra
Sunderbans Waterways (NW-97): Namkhana to AtharaBankiKhal in West Bengal	172	West Bengal (through Indo-Bangladesh Protocol Route)

Coastal Waterways

India has a long coastline of approximately 7,500 km which offers a wide potential for coastal shipping. It involves the movement of goods between different coastal regions or nearby international ports, helping to decongest road and rail networks. It is important to transport bulk goods, such as coal, iron ore, and fertilizers, between major ports.

NAME OF THE PORT	CITY
Chennai Port	Chennai, Tamil Nadu
Cochin Port	Kochi, Kerala
Deendayal Port (Kandla Port)	Kandla, Gujarat
Jawaharlal Nehru Port (Nhava Sheva Port)	Mumbai, Maharashtra
Kamarajar Port	Ennore, Chennai, Tamil Nadu
Mormugao Port	Mormugao, Goa
Mumbai Port	Mumbai, Maharashtra
New Mangalore Port	Mangalore, Karnataka
Pradip Port	Pradip, Odisha
Haldia Port	Haldia, West Bengal
Syama Prasad Mookerjee Port	Kolkata, West Bengal
Visakhapatnam Port	Visakhapatnam, Andhra Pradesh
V. O. Chidambaranar Port	Thoothukudi, Tamil Nadu

RORO (ROLL-ON/ROLL-OFF) FERRY SERVICE

The RORO ferry services are vessels made to carry wheeled cargo that are driven on and off the ferry on their wheels or using a platform vehicle. India's first RORO ferry service was launched between Ghogha in Bhavnagar district and Dahej in Bharuch district, Gujarat, in 2019. It reduced the distance between the two coastal towns from 310 km by road to 30 km, thus saving time and money.

SEAPLANE

A seaplane is a fixed-wing aeroplane designed for taking off and landing on water. Prime Minister Narendra Modi launched India's first seaplane service between the Sabarmati Riverfront in Ahmedabad and the Statue of Unity near Kevadia in Gujarat's Narmada district. The plane will be operated by SpiceJet.

PROJECT SAGARMALA

It was launched in 2015 by the Ministry of Ports, Shipping and Waterways to develop the 7,500-km-long coastline and 14,500-km-long potentially navigable waterways of India. The core vision of the Sagarmala programme was to reduce the logistics cost for export-import (EXIM) and domestic trade with minimal infrastructure investment.

INTERNATIONAL PROJECTS

TRANSCONTINENTAL RAILWAYS

These are the railroads that connect distant countries and regions spanning across continents. These help facilitate long-distance travel and trade, often traversing diverse terrains, climates, and time zones. These connect different cultures and regions and promote national unity and cultural exchange.

Postal stamp commemorating the completion of the first transcontinental railroad

NAME OF THE ROUTE	LENGTH	IMPORTANT FEATURES
Trans-Siberian Railway (Great Siberian Route)	9,289 km	• Longest railway line in the world and transcends from Moscow (West Russia) to Vladivostok (East Russia). • It takes eight days to complete the journey. • It serves as the economic artery of Russia and also forms a key route for freight and passengers traveling between Europe and Asia.
Canadian Pacific Railway	20,100 km	• Canada's first transcontinental railways was built between 1881 and 1886. • Runs between Vancouver (Western Canada), Montreal (Eastern Canada), and Edmonton (north). • During the construction, railway workers faced obstacles such as bears, forest fires, and impenetrable forest. • The construction of railway tracks led to the discovery of natural gas in Alberta.
First Transcontinental Railroad (Pacific Railroad/ Overland Route)	3,077 km	• The first railway to link the Eastern US rail network (at Omaha, Nebraska) with the Pacific coast (Sacramento, California). • It was built between 1863 and 1869. • Reduced travel time by approximately two weeks. It was a connecting link for travel, commerce, and trade.
Indian Pacific	4,352 km	• Weekly passenger train between Sydney (Pacific Ocean) and Perth (Indian Ocean). • It also crosses the world's longest straight stretch of 478-km railway track of the Trans-Australian Railway. • It offers experiential tourism and is named after the two oceans it encounters on its journey. • It takes almost 65 hours to complete the journey.

CHINA'S BELT AND ROAD INITIATIVE (BRI)/NEW SILK ROAD

- It was launched in 2013 by Chinese President Xi Jinping and was also known as the One Belt, One Road (OBOR) initiative. It is a global infrastructure development strategy of the Chinese government that includes developing land and sea-based trade routes. BRI aims to strengthen trade ties and economic cooperation through infrastructure development and enhanced connectivity among the participating countries.
- The New Silk Road is inspired by the ancient Silk Road that connected China to the Mediterranean during the Han dynasty (206 BCE–220 CE). The ancient Silk Road promoted and facilitated an exchange of goods, culture, spices, and other luxury items.

BRI has two basic components:

1. *Silk Road Economic Belt:* It is a land-based route to connect China and Europe through Central Asia while passing through countries such as Kazakhstan, Russia, and Poland. China intends to build rail routes to promote trade, energy cooperation, and

infrastructure among the Central Asian countries. India has strongly opposed China's OBOR on the pretext of the China-Pakistan Economic Corridor (CPEC) passing through the Pakistan-occupied Kashmir (PoK).

2. *Maritime Silk Road:* This is a sea route that will connect China, Southeast Asia, South Asia, Africa, and Europe through key maritime corridors, including the South China Sea, Indian Ocean, and the Mediterranean.

Some of the key projects that China has undertaken under OBOR are the China-Pakistan Economic Corridor (CPEC), Chongqing–Xinjiang–Europe railway (Yu–Xin–Ou railway), Kazakhstan's Khorgos Gateway, Kyaukpyu Port (Myanmar), etc.

INDIA-MIDDLE EAST-EUROPE CORRIDOR (IMEC)

- IMEC is an economic corridor that aims to enhance the connectivity between Asia, the Persian Gulf, and Europe. It is designed to strengthen economic, energy, and digital connectivity between India, the Middle East, and Europe.
- It will comprise two corridors: the east corridor connecting India to the Gulf and the northern corridor connecting the Gulf to Europe.
- This project was proposed and signed at the G20 Summit held in New Delhi in 2023. The project has currently been put on hold due to the ongoing Israel-Hamas war.

7 Indian Economy

The term *economics* originated from the Ancient Greek word *oikonomia*, which stood for the management of a family or a household.

- Greek philosophers such as **Aristotle** (384–322 BC) studied household management.
- This becomes 'study of wealth' between the sixteenth and eighteenth centuries by mercantilists in Europe. The great Scottish economist **Adam Smith** (1723–90) was one such mercantilist.
- He conducted deep studies about processes of production, consumption, and accumulation of wealth. He said that the wealth of a nation lies in the goods and services that command value in exchange, not mere accumulation of precious metals, such as gold and silver.
- English economist **Alfred Marshall** (1842–1924) said that wealth is not an end in itself as was perceived earlier; it is a means to an end (that of human welfare).

CURRENT DEFINITION OF ECONOMICS

Paul Samuelson ***(American Nobel Prize winner in Economics 1970)*** defined: 'Economics is the study of how men and society choose, with or without the use of money, to employ scarce productive resources which could have alternative uses, to produce various commodities over time, and distribute them for consumption, now and in the near future, among various people and groups in society'.

Economics is a social science.

What is an economy? It is the term for any and all activity between humankind and the resources that keep society going, whether at the level of an individual entity or to aggregations of humans such as regions, states, nations, and the world. Individuals, businesses, institutions, and the government are all parts of economies.

MICRO- AND MACRO-ECONOMICS

The studies of the Greek philosophers with their focus at household levels may be likened to 'micro-economics'; the mercantilists culminating with Smith, on the other hand, looked at issues at a national scale – introducing the concept of 'macro-economics'.

OPEN AND CLOSED ECONOMIES

- Open economies are those that freely trade with other economies. They are free from trade barriers, and imports and exports (international trade) make up a significant part of their GDP.
- At the other extreme are closed economies that do not trade at all with other nations.
- Most economies are somewhere in between, having a number of trade partners, but with some trade barriers/ restrictions in place. Balance of payment situations, susceptibility to international economic cycles, and country-to-country relations play their part in determining how open an economy is.

THE INDIAN ECONOMY

The Indian economy has three characteristics, which are as follows:

1. A **mixed economy** (term coined by John Maynard Keynes):
   - Consisting of a distinct private sector and a distinct public sector
   - Displaying a high degree of Government involvement
2. A **developing economy** (as reflected by):
   - Low per capita income
   - Continued dominance of agriculture despite small landholding as source of livelihood for a significant proportion of its populace
   - High (and rising levels of) population
   - Inadequate employment opportunities
   - Poor capital per person ratios
   - Inequitable distribution of wealth
   - Improving capital formation (this is a positive aspect)
3. An **agrarian economy:**

The Annual Report for 2020–21 presented by the Ministry of Agriculture, Government of India, states: 'Agriculture plays a vital role in India's economy. **Approximately 54.6 per cent of the total workforce is engaged in agricultural** and allied sector activities (**Census 2011**).

Sector-wise, the Indian economy may be viewed as follows:

- A **primary sector** that produces raw materials and includes activities such as mining, agriculture, and forestry
- A **secondary sector** that produces finished goods and includes manufacturing – from capital goods to consumer goods, building and construction, fuels (oil and gas) and energy (electricity), and pharmaceuticals
- A **tertiary sector** that provides services such as transport, communication, banking, and more

NATIONAL INCOME OF INDIA

A **three-member National Income Committee** was constituted **in 1949** with **Prof. P. C. Mahalanobis** as **Chairman** and **Prof. V. K. R. V. Rao** and **Prof. D. R. Gadgil** as members.

- Dr. Rao had previously worked in 1931 on scientifically estimating it by examining it in the form of sectors.

Pre-Independence Estimates of National Income (India)

ESTIMATED BY	YEAR OF ESTIMATE	NATIONAL INCOME (₹ CR.)	PER CAPITA INCOME (₹)
Dadabhai Naoroji	1868	340	20
Wadia and Joshi	1913–14	1,067	44
Shah and Khambata	1921–22	2,364	72
V. K. R. V. Rao	1931–32	1,689	64
MoC, Govt. of India	1945–46	6,234	198

Note

- Economics hugely depends on statistics. Collection, compilation, and collation of information were still to be properly developed at the time of the earlier estimates.
- All three attempts before Rao's were by people from the richer Bombay region and so were likely to be so biased.
- Rao, first divided the Indian economy into two parts – agriculture and industry, further subdividing these into activity sectors such as farming, fishing, forestry, construction, manufacturing, transport, and public services (13 in all). He used the **Production Method** for agricultural estimation and the **Income Method** for industrial estimation. Finally, he factored in the income from overseas trade.

National income is measure of the flow of goods and services in an economy.

In India, ***national income estimates are related to a financial (or fiscal) year that starts on 1 April to 31 March the next year***.

- **1951:** The National Income Committee submits its first report estimating the ***national income of India at ₹8,710 crores*** and the ***per capita income at ₹225 for 1948–49***.
- **1955:** The Central Statistical Organisation, or CSO, is given the task of estimating India's national income and related parameters.
- Data are generated by the National Sample Survey Organisation, or NSSO.
- **May 2019:** The CSO and the NSSO are merged into a single entity, the National Statistical Office, NSO.
- **2020:** Per the World Bank, the **GDP of India was US$2,623 billion**. On the basis of the population of India being 1.38 billion people, the **per capita GDP in India was US$1,901.** The per capita GDP of Bangladesh is slightly better at US$1,964.

METHODS OF MEASURING NATIONAL INCOME

Quite obviously, national income is the sum of the income from all three sectors of the economy – the primary sector (agriculture, forest, fisheries, mining, etc.), the secondary sector (industries, manufacturing, construction, etc.), and the tertiary sector (trade, transport, communications, banking, insurance, real estate, community, and personal services).

There are three ways that the income from these sectors and their sub-sectors may be measured. Developed by economist Simon Kuznets, they are as follows:

- *Production Method:* Here, the net value of final goods and services produced in a country during a year called the total final product is first derived. Then net income earned through foreign sources is added and depreciation is subtracted to arrive at the gross domestic product (GDP).
- *Income Method:* In this method, the total net incomes earned by people across sectors and commercial enterprises are collated. Incomes of both categories of people – paying taxes (quite accurate) and not paying taxes (less so in case of evasion) – are added to obtain national income. Here, **GDP = Wages + Rent + Interest + Profit.** To make this herculean task manageable, only sampling is conducted at a large number of locations all over India, and the data generated are extrapolated over the population.
- *Consumption Method:* Also called expenditure method, it is based on the premise that income is either spent on consumption or saved. Hence, national

income is sum of total consumption and total savings. But this needs authentic data from the majority of the populace. And so, it is not suitable for a populous country such as India.

In India, a combination of the Production Method (better suited to the primary sector) and the Income Method (better suited to the other sectors) is used.

GDP VERSUS GNP

Gross domestic product (GDP) is the total money value of all final goods and services produced within the geographical boundaries of the country during a given period of time.

Thus, **GDP = C + I + G + (X – M)**

where C = total expenditure on consumption; I = total expenditure on investment; G = total expenditure by government; and X and M are the values of exports and imports, respectively.

However, resources such as remittances from citizens living abroad are additional in an economy's kitty. To arrive at the **gross national product (GNP)**, the net balance between inward and outgoing remittances must be added to the GDP.

Thus, **GNP = GDP + (R – P)**

where R = incoming remittances and P = outgoing ones. R – P is called the **net factor income** from abroad.

Income generated and received by nationals of a country resident in a foreign nation should be added to the GDP of the country. Similarly, income received by foreign nationals within India should be excluded from India's GDP.

REAL GDP VERSUS NOMINAL GDP

- When GDP is computed at ruling market prices, the derived result is known as **nominal GDP**.
- In times of high inflation, this presents an exaggerated picture of growth. With double-digit inflation, while the economy may actually be shrinking, the NGDP will still indicate growth.
- *Real GDP* is measured on the basis of prices in a base year and so is a better (realistic) indicator of the health of any economy.

Happy Planet Index

Happy Planet Index (HPI) measures life satisfaction, feeling of happiness, and overall well-being of a person: physiological well-being, environment, community, and social support.

Gross National Happiness

The term 'Gross National Happiness' was coined by Bhutan's then King Jigme Singye Wangchuck in 1972. It was set as an indicator to measure quality of life, well-being, and overall progress.

INDIAN STRATEGIES OF STATE PLANNING

The struggle for independence was undertaken by the people of India because they had many aspirations. The **common aspiration for all was improvement in economic conditions for themselves** and their society.

For this to take place:

- goals had to be first set in a time frame
- ways forward had to be devised (the how, where, and when)
- resources were to be allocated and if scarce, these had to be generated
- and all this had to be done in harmony because India is a federal democratic nation and such processes call for consensus between the central and state governments and cohesion between agencies.

Realizing this, Indian leaders set about state planning as under:

- **March 1950: Planning Commission established** as a non-statutory, extra constitutional body.
- Prime Minister Jawaharlal Nehru became its first chairman.
- In addition to chairman and deputy chairman, the portfolio of Minister of State for Planning – who would be a member – was created.
- A National Development Council (1952), a National Planning Council (1965), and State Level Planning Commissions were established side by side. The NDC included the chief ministers of the states of India, while the NPC consisted of experts across every sector of the Indian economy.
- Their objectives were:
  - Preparing comprehensive plans
  - Economic growth
  - Self-reliance
  - Eradicating poverty and inequality
  - Building infrastructure

Five-Year Plans: From being a backward nation before the 1917 revolution, the Soviet Union had made tremendous progress by the 50s through the implementation of their five-year plans. This influenced Nehru, who chose to follow a similar path.

- Eleven such five-year plans were to be prepared in all until 2016.
- In the First Plan (1951–56), priority was given to agriculture. This led to a dramatic growth in irrigation and was effective in raising food production.
- The Second Plan (1956–61) focussed on establishing heavy industry. It had a growth target of 4.5 per cent (nearly achieved at 4.3 per cent). Our steel industry, oil refining, and many others are the result of this phase.
- Then came a series of plans aimed at the long-term growth of India and 'Gareebee Hatao'. By the Sixth Plan (1980–85), growth targets being set for India were 5 per cent or more. Importantly, these were being achieved.
- The Eighth Plan (1993–97) introduced a focus on exports, while the Ninth Plan introduced empowerment (of women and the disadvantaged). The Tenth Plan (2002–07) set a very high growth target of 8.1 per cent but failed to achieve it, although it did manage a respectable 5.4 per cent.
- It was during the Eleventh Plan (2007–12) that India achieved its best sustained growth of 8 per cent. Thereafter, the Twelfth Plan (2012–16) set a target of 8 per cent, but the Planning Commission itself was disbanded in 2014.

Niti Aayog

On 1 January 2015, the National Institution for Transforming India (NITI) Aayog came into being doing away with the Planning Commission that had served India so well by bringing. Its salient features are:

- The Prime Minister of India is its chairman and its governing council consists of chief ministers of states, and administrators of UTs. Its CEO is an IAS officer of secretary rank.
- Its vice president and experts (in domain knowledge) who operate as special invitees are all the nominees of the prime minister.
- It operates on the basis of a 15-Year Vision Document with effect from 2018. This document has a seven-year part (till 2024–25) with visionary strategy, schemes, and programmes.
- It is meant to act as a facilitator for development, with a holistic approach away from restrictions of government.

- Meant to focus on priority issues, it will function as a 'matchmaker' rather than as a doer.
- It has three arms: the **Research Wing** consisting of expert subject matter specialists; the **Consultancy Wing** for government at the centre and the states, as well as for the public and the private sectors in India and also internationally; and the **Team India Wing** as a permanent platform for national collaboration.

DEMOGRAPHY

Demography is the study of the characteristics of a population and the different groups within it. This is largely done through the statistics that are collected in a **census**. When sheer numbers make head counts difficult, 'representative' samples are taken and estimates that are quite accurate are obtained.

THE INDIAN CENSUS

- It is the basis estimating India's population and demographic changes that have taken place over the last decade. As such it is a measure of the progress of the nation and a way of assessing ongoing government schemes. It also provides indications for plans for the future.
- The census provides detailed and fairly accurate demographic data on:
  - Population numbers (district-wise, state-wise, and national) – overall and broken up age-wise; Scheduled Castes and Scheduled Tribes; language and religion
  - From these migration patterns can be understood
  - Economic activity
  - Literacy and education
  - Housing and household amenities
  - Urbanization
  - Fertility, mortality, disability, and other socio-cultural parameters
- The **first complete census of India was conducted in 1830 by Henry Walter** in Dhaka. This collected gender-wise, age-wise population numbers together with housing details. A second census followed in 1836–37.
- The first complete (house to house) census was conducted **by W. C. Plowden, Census Commissioner of India**. It began on **17 February 1881.**
- Since then censuses have been undertaken uninterruptedly once every 10 years until 2011.
- These indicated that there was ***no population growth*** in India between 1891 and 1921. Then the population began growing steadily until 1951. Since independence (1951 onwards), there was high population growth with a jump in the rate of growth. This rate has tapered off since, but we continue adding more than 1 per cent to our population every year.
- **The Census of 2011** was the 15th National Census of the country since 1872 and the seventh after Independence. It began on 9 February 2011, and took 19 days to finish.

SOME INTERESTING REVELATIONS OF THE 2011 CENSUS

- The total population of India stood at 1.21 billion people.
- Indian population was growing at the rate of 17.7 per cent per decade. At this rate, we should be a nation of 1.45 billion people now (2022).
- UP was the most populous state with nearly 200 million people (16.5 per cent of India's people); followed by Maharashtra with 112, Bihar with 104, and Bengal with 91 million, respectively.

- Kerala with its 33 million people had the highest literacy rate of 94 per cent. Literacy rate in Maharashtra was 83 per cent; in Bengal it was 76 per cent; in UP, it was 68 per cent (about the same as the figure for J&K); and in Bihar, it was only 62 per cent (the lowest in India).
- Women outnumbered men (1,000:943) almost everywhere except in Kerala and Puducherry; there is parity in Tamil Nadu.

AADHAAR CARD: UNIQUE IDENTIFICATION

An Aadhaar number is a 12-digit random number issued by the **UIDAI (Unique Identification Authority of India)** to residents of India, following a verification process for applicants.

- It is based on biometrics and the Aadhaar system is the largest and most sophisticated biometric ID system in the world.
- Entirely free of cost.
- **Only one Aadhaar number** is generated per person so it is **unique**.
- **Aadhaar Cards** are plastic ID cards with embedded memory carrying details such as residence. However, Aadhaar is considered to be proof of residence only but not of citizenship.

Targets

A National Population Policy was prepared in 2000 (NPP 2000).

- This set a target of 2.1 to be achieved in India by 2010 with regards to the **fertility rate** (that on average a woman will give birth to 2.1 babies in her lifetime). In 2020, this was 3.3 (data from NHFS and MI surveys). It was as high as 4.8 in UP and well above 4 in Bihar, MP, and Rajasthan.
- *Infant mortality rate:* A target was set for 28 deaths per thousand infants born. This figure remains at around 34.
- *Population stabilization:* Hopeful of achieving a drop in fertility rates, India had projected that its population would stabilize by 2045 (in the region of 1.5 billion). Now the projections are for this to happen in 2060 (at about 1.65 billion), ***provided*** there is an improvement in its fertility rate.

POVERTY

Poverty is that state of being poor, when people lack the means to satisfy basic needs necessary for survival. **The poverty line** is the estimated minimum income required to secure such necessities of life.

During heydays of the Mughal Empire, the Indian subcontinent was thought to be the richest region in the world. The basis for this affluence lay in:

- Its bountiful agricultural produce enabled by fertile river plains and climate suitable for (in many places) as many as three grain harvests a year.
- It had and continues to have a higher ratio of cultivable land to total territory as compared to any other sizable nation. Thus, most sections of its farmers were comfortable financially, while its rulers and traders were rich.
- By the beginning of the twentieth century, however, India was recognized as poor. Given the rapid increase in population (especially 1921 onwards – see *Demography*), by independence, large sections of people in both urban and rural India were living in grinding poverty amidst huge income disparities.

Causes of Poverty in India

Rise of poverty in India may be traced to rise in **rural poverty** to begin with.

Root Causes of Rural Poverty

- *Fragmentation of land:* Large landholdings yielding much surplus turn smaller and smaller with each generation (when there is more than one successor). Surplus keeps diminishing for the next owners. Eventually, there is no ***agricultural surplus***** – the landowner has become poor.

***Agricultural surplus:* When harvested yield is more than what is required for own subsistence, the balance is the surplus. This may be traded (sold or bartered) for other goods or services, and the accumulation of capital.

- *Growth in population:* The faster this happens, the greater the number of inheritors, leading to quicker fragmentation of land. Also population pressures had become evident even in arid areas that did not support farming.
- *Agrarian economy and its backwardness:* Agriculture was the force behind India's riches in medieval times and by independence 80 per cent of its people were dependent on it for livelihood and so adversely impacted by land fragmentation. Practices were traditional and technology advances unused. Irrigation was insufficient in arid zones. Yields were low per norms elsewhere.

OTHER RELATED CAUSES (RURAL)

- *Lack of alternate skills:* Most of those from farming backgrounds were unable to shift to more lucrative professions.
- *Lack of capital and evil of money lending:* Other than usurious moneylenders, there was little source of capital for the poor to set up alternate activity. Most were in any case borrowing at huge rates of interest for farm inputs (seeds and such).
- *Destructive social customs (such as Dowry)*: Rooted in tradition dowry prevailed, especially among the poor, who borrowed what they could from moneylenders. Such borrowing became debt-traps. **Illiteracy** and **superstition** also contributed.

RELATED CAUSES (URBAN)

- *Influx of rural migrants:* Rural folk, below and around the poverty line migrate to cities looking for sustenance – increasing population pressure.
- *Lack of training and its affordability:* Rural or urban, the poor have to mostly opt for menial employment.
- *Competition for even menial jobs:* Drives down wages further.
- *Availability and affordability of housing:* Forcing the poor to live in slums.

Pranab K. Sen, once chief statistician of India, chaired the Pranab Sen Committee which in 2010 defined a slum as 'a compact settlement of at least 20 households with a collection of poorly built tenements, mostly of temporary nature, crowded together usually with inadequate sanitary and drinking water facilities in unhygienic conditions'.

- *Lack of adequate social security umbrellas.*

STUDIES OF POVERTY IN INDIA

Rangarajan Report

- Released in 2014 under chairmanship of Dr. C. Rangarajan – still the most recent exhaustive study.
- Estimated that 363 million Indians (29.6 per cent) are poor. Rural poor at 31 per cent and urban poor at 26.4 per cent.
- Estimated poverty line for preceding period at ₹972 for rural and ₹1,407 for urban India.

Tendulkar Report

- Released in 2009 under chairmanship of Dr. Suresh D. Tendulkar.

- Previous methods of estimating the poverty line were based on calorie consumption. Tendulkar's formula included **spending on education, health, and clothing in addition to food**.
- This formula resulted in higher estimates for those below the poverty line than previous calorie consumption–based estimates.
- Tendulkar's method would be retained by Rangarajan for his own work.

Amartya Sen: Nobel Prize in Economics

Born on 3 November 1933, in Shantiniketan, West Bengal, Amartya Sen won the Nobel Prize in Economics in 1998 for **his contributions to welfare economics**. His works on poverty and its amelioration and on the causes and prevention of famines have been inspirational for economists (including Manmohan Singh) that followed.

In 1999, he was awarded the Bharat Ratna, the highest civilian award in India.

UNEMPLOYMENT

In economic terms, when a person is ready to work but does not get a job, he or she is said to be unemployed. **Unemployment rate** is the term for the percentage of the unemployed in the total workforce. Large unemployment rates indicate poor economic health in society. Since not all the unemployed register themselves with employment agencies, numbers are best assessed through sample surveys (provided they are well designed and representative).

Broadly, unemployment can be either:

Voluntary: When people choose not to work (in which case, they are not categorized as unemployed) or

Involuntary: When people on the search for jobs are unable to find any.

Involuntary unemployment can be further categorized as:

- *Cyclical:* Also known as Keynesian unemployment, this occurs during recession phases of an economy, when numbers of jobs available drops.
- *Frictional:* This occurs, for example, when people are between jobs, go on study leave without pay, and so on.
- *Seasonal:* This occurs in cases of seasonal activity such as for farm labour, which is in demand during planting or harvesting but laid off in between.
- *Disguised:* This occurs in cases of underemployment such as when graduates work as delivery boys because suitable employment is not available. It is also so for the qualified disabled and those with difficulties about migration.
- *Structural:* It is long-term unemployment when particular job skills are no longer required. An example is that of product assembly workers released from a clothing manufacturing unit because they have specialized production assembly equipement.
- *Technological:* By eliminating the need for human intervention, technology invariably takes away jobs. Examples are the use of robots in industry and machines in construction.

RURAL DEVELOPMENT PROGRAMMES

To address issues of poverty, unemployment, and under-development, the Government of India launched:

- Twelve anti-poverty and employment programmes between 1997 and 2015.
- Principal among them is MGNREGS (Mahatma Gandhi National Rural Employment Guarantee Scheme) in 2009.

- Another 12 programmes aimed at development (irrigation, housing, electricity, roads, communication, food security & the PDS, drinking water, sanitation, etc.).
- Another 11 programmes for empowering women, two for child welfare, eight for education, and five for healthcare. Along with miscellaneous others, the aggregate is more than 50.

MGNREGA

The National Rural Employment Guarantee Act 2005 (or, NREGA No. 42) is an Indian law enacted to guarantee the 'right to work'. On 2 October 2009, following some amendment, its nomenclature was changed to MGNREGA (MG stands for Mahatma Gandhi).

The guarantee given is to providing at least ***100 wage-days of employment per year to every adult (over 18 years old)*** who chooses to do unskilled manual work. Its salient points are as follows:

- The act was first proposed in 1991 by P. V. Narasimha Rao and finally accepted in parliament in 2006.
- It was run in pilot form for two years first.
- It was applied to all (the then) 625 districts of India w.e.f. 1 April 2008.
- Hailed by the government as 'the largest and most ambitious social security and public works programme in the world'. The World Bank called it a 'stellar example of rural development' in its Development Report 2014.
- Another objective of MGNREGA is to build infrastructure (such as roads, canals, ponds, and wells).
- The principles and agencies for execution, list of allowed works, financing pattern, monitoring, and evaluation, as well as detailed measures to ensure transparency and accountability are elaborately described in the act.

Operation

- MGNREGA is operated by Gram Panchayats (GPs).
- The involvement of contractors is banned.
- It conducts labour-intensive tasks such as water harvesting, drought relief, and flood control measures.
- Those interested in enrolling have to submit a written application in the respective panchayat office.
- Employment is to be provided within 5 km of an applicant's residence, and minimum wages are to be paid. If work is not provided within 15 days of applying, applicants are entitled to an unemployment allowance. Thus, employment under MGNREGA is a legal entitlement.

Benefits from MGNREGA

- Apart from providing economic security and creating rural assets, MGNREGA helps in protecting the environment, empowering rural women, reducing rural–urban migration, and fostering social equity.
- One-third of all employment in it is reserved for women.
- An equal wage is paid to all enrolled – men and women.
- Provides jobs to unemployed youth.

How MGNREGA Has Performed

Despite controversies, some of which involve delayed payment, MGNREGA has proven to be a good scheme for rural India. Thousands owe their daily survival to it while providing and contributing to many civic amenities.

It has been shown to arrest migration to cities from rural areas by providing a local employment alternative.

AGRICULTURE

ARABLE LAND IN INDIA

India has the second largest area of arable land in the world after the United States – an area of **159.7 million hectares.** Of this, **82.6 million hectares** is the gross irrigated crop area – the largest in the world. Whereas much of the world is limited to a single crop in a year, more than **56 million hectares** in India are ***multi-cropped***. For millennia, India has been an agricultural powerhouse.

AGRICULTURE & INDIAN ECONOMY

- While the **contribution of Agriculture to Indian GDP** has slipped to **16.3 per cent** in 2022, it still provides **employment to 43 per cent** of Indians.
- India's agricultural **exports were valued at $50.3 billion** during FY 2021–22. Agricultural **imports** (food oils, pulses, etc.) hit an all-time high of **$32.4 billion**. Imports of vegetable oils alone used up $19 billion. Still, agriculture contributed a net **foreign exchange** gain of **$18 billion**.
- The previous record for exports was $43.3 billion in 2013–14 against imports of only $15.5 billion, resulting in an agricultural trade surplus of $27.7 billion.
- Importantly, agriculture not only feeds the nation but also provides raw material for myriad industrial activity (e.g. pharmaceuticals). A shortage of agricultural commodities fuel inflation.

First Five-Year Plan

- Parts of India having faced serious famines in the recent past, the planners recognized the need for modern farming practices, and most importantly, **irrigation**.
- Accordingly, about 31 per cent of the expenditure under the plan was spent on agriculture, much of it to develop irrigation.
- Nearly half a million hectares of land was reclaimed and brought under farming, and irrigation systems were provided to a further 6 million hectares. New techniques such as the Japanese method of rice cultivation were introduced.
- Targets set for food grain and pulses were met. Overall growth rate was 2.7 per cent.
- The best growth rate of 4.6 per cent would be achieved in the Eighth Plan.

THE GREEN REVOLUTION

- Although India had made progress on the agricultural front, the decade from 1951 to 1961 saw a jump of 22 per cent in population.
- Indians were also consuming more food per person.
- Agriculture production was barely keeping pace and food prices were spiralling up.
    - To avoid shortage, wheat was being imported from the United States under their **Public Law 480.** This was mostly to be paid for, but the United States allowed some of the dues to be used as development funds in India.
    - The dilemma facing members of the **Planning Commission**, such as geneticist **Dr. M. S. Swaminathan**, was 'what if the US withdrew PL480?'
    - Since 1944, American **Norman Borlaug** had been working in Mexico to increase wheat yields. He had developed 'dwarf' wheat varieties that were yielding three times more than traditional ones.

- Swaminathan had studied the work of Dr. Borlaug, and in **1963**, he wrote a letter to the director of the **Indian Agricultural Research Institute (IARI)**, insisting that Borlaug be invited to India to address the problem of insufficient yields from conventional farming.
- Borlaug came immediately and was introduced to **Dr. M. S. Randhawa** who had established **PAU Ludhiana**. Randhawa ensured that facilities at PAU were put at Borlaug's disposal. Borlaug and Swaminathan visited hundreds of farmers and tried out the seeds that Borlaug supplied. Results were spectacular.
- This Indian initiative was sponsored by both **Ford and Rockefeller Foundations**, who also established **IRRI** in the **Philippines** to work on paddy along the lines of Borlaug's techniques.
- It was **Dr. William Gaud** of the USAID who coined the term '*Green Revolution*'.
- **Wheat yields** would go up from the **1.2 tonne** per hectare prevalent in India during 1960–61 to **5.1 tonnes per hectare in 2016–17**. For **paddy**, it went up from **1.1 tonne** per hectare to **4.1 tonnes per hectare**.
- The Green Revolution has given India **food security** for nearly six decades. Also, forests no longer have to be cut down to make way for more farming land. Regrettably, urban sprawls are now eating into prime agricultural land. Such sprawls also deplete water tables.
- Incidentally, the city of Chandigarh was Dr. Randhawa's brainchild.

Operation Flood – White Revolution

- The **National Dairy Development Board** (NDDB) is a statutory body set up by an act of the Parliament of India. Headquartered in Anand, Gujarat, it is owned by Ministry of Fisheries, Animal Husbandry and Dairying, Government of India.
- **1965:** NDDB is created to finance and support farmer cooperatives. Prime Minister Shastri appoints **Dr. Verghese Kurien** as its chairman. He successfully ran the Kaira Cooperative Milk Producers' Union (**Amul**), which has become a household brand by now.
- **1970:** NDDB launches Kurien's brainchild umbrella, **Operation Flood.** It is conducted in three phases:
  - **Phase I** (until **1980**); 18 milk sheds linked to four metropolitan cities – Delhi, Mumbai, Kolkata, and Chennai space under the **Mother Dairy** banner.
  - **Phase II** (**1981–85**); number of milk sheds increase from 18 to 136. It extends to more urban markets. By 1985 end, it had become a self-sustaining system of 43,000 village co-operatives with 42,50,000 milk producers.
  - **Phase III** (**1986–96**); number of milk sheds go up to 173; markets are now everywhere in India. Another 30,000 co-operatives are added. Emphasis has shifted to veterinary care and nutrition.
- Operation Flood transformed India from a milk-deficient nation into the world's largest milk producer, surpassing the United States of America in 1998. It produced 22 per cent of global milk output in 2018.
- Meenesh Shah was appointed the chairman of NDDB in 2021.

National Food Security Act 2013

- **1967:** India begins operating a Public Distribution System (**PDS**) through government regulated ration shops.

Meant primarily for weaker sections of society, it supplies essentials like foodgrains and kerosene at lower than market prices.

- **1997:** This is now modified and called the **T** (Targeted) **PDS**. People below poverty line (**BPL**) will now be issued these 'ration' cards.
- **2013:** Passage of the NFS Act which sets specific targets of covering 75 per cent of rural and 50 per cent of urban population. Eligible will be entitled to 5 kg of foodgrain per person per month at subsidized price of ₹3 for rice; ₹2 for wheat, and ₹1 for coarse grain. The poorest will receive 35 kg of grain per household free of charge.
- The Indian PDS is the largest in the world.

FISHERIES

India is the second largest producer of inland fish and the third largest overall producer of fish in the world.

THE INDIAN FINANCIAL SYSTEM

Its components are the currency, banking systems, financial and regulatory bodies, and the insurance sector.

Currency: The legal tender is the Indian rupee (INR) consisting of 100 paise. Coins and one-rupee notes are issued by the Government of India; banknotes higher in value are issued by **the Reserve Bank of India (RBI)**.

- All banknotes issued by RBI are backed by assets such as government securities, foreign currency assets, and gold, as defined in Section 33 of RBI Act, 1934.
- Trading in **crypto currency** (**virtual digital assets operating on a decentralized network without any governing authority**) is not prohibited in India, but not recognized as legal tender. Gains taxed at 30 per cent. VDAs remain grey area – unregulated at the moment.
- With the establishment of RBI, the rupee became independent currency in 1935, although linked to the pound sterling.
- India becomes **IMF (International Monetary Fund)** member in 1947; exchange rate henceforth set per IMF standards.
- Until 1956, post-Independence Indian rupee consisted of 16 annas of 12 paise each. **In 1957, rupee decimalized**, now consisting of 100 paise. Both systems run side-by-side until 1962.

Rupee devaluation: Pegged to the dollar, the value of the rupee is around 84 to the dollar, as of December 2024. This is due to **depreciation** owing to forces of a **floating exchange** rate system.

If the ***value of a currency is weakened through administrative action***, it is called **devaluation**. This has taken place four times in the past.

- June 1949: by 30.5 per cent
- June 1966: by 57 per cent
- July 1991: twice – by 9 per cent and 11 per cent, respectively

Rupee demonetization: When banknotes (or coins) are pulled out of circulation/ declared illegal through administrative action, it is called **demonatization.**

- January 1978: higher denomination banknotes (₹1,000; ₹5,000; ₹10,000) demonetized – declared no longer legal tender.
- November 2016: higher denomination banknotes (₹500; ₹1,000) demonetized – declared no longer legal tender. Later followed by fresh introduction of new-design ₹500 banknote. It was ostensibly meant to eradicate 'black money', eliminate terrorism.

BANKING SECTOR

Reserve Bank of India

- Constituted on 1 April 1934, the Reserve Bank for India was originally in Kolkata before shifting headquarters to Mumbai in 1937.
- Just 5 per cent was owned by the GoI, and its share capital of ₹5 crore, which was mostly held by private shareholders.

Its functions were to:

- Regulate the issue of banknotes.
- Maintain reserves so as to provide monetary stability to the currency and credit system of the country.
- Prepare modern monetary policy frameworks.
- Maintain price stability while keeping in mind the objective of growth (manage inflation without hurting growth).
- It was nationalized in February 1947, before independence. By the **Reserve Bank of India (Transfer to Public Ownership**) Act 1948, its entire share capital was transferred to the Government of India in 1948.
- This act empowered the central government to direct the RBI if in the public interest.
- C.D. Deshmukh was its governor from 1943 to 1949. Governors and deputy governors may hold office terms of five years.
- Sanjay Malhotra is the current RBI governor.

Current Functions of RBI

Primary:

- Central banker for state and central governments.
- Central banker or all commercial banks and co-operative banks.
- National Monetary Policy formulator and administrator.
- Determines the optimum strength of the INR and acting in accordance
- Represents India in the IMF.
- Nurturing the economic growth of the nation within the overall policy of the central government (managing inflation).

Secondary

- Monitoring the overall credit situation (both rural and banking) and correcting when/where required.
- Collating and providing monetary information.
- Supply of paper currency or denominations above ₹1.
- Stock market regulator – securities, derivatives, and market instruments.
- Last-resort lender for afflicted commercial banks.

RBI's Control Instruments

- *Bank rate (rediscount rate):* Rate at which RBI lends to commercial banks ***without asking for security***. It is always higher than the repo rate. As of November 2024, it is 6.75 per cent.
- *Repo rate:* Introduced in 1992, it is the rate at which RBI lends to commercial banks ***with security/collateral***. As of November 2024, it is 6.50 per cent. It is given for short-term loans.
- *Reverse-repo rate:* It is the rate at which banks can park any short-term surplus cash with RBI and earn on. As of November 2024, it is 3.35%. It is the inverse contract to the repo rate.

- *Cash reserve ratio (CRR):* Introduced in 1962, it is MANDATORY FOR BANKS to deposit a part of their total deposits with the RBI. This varies between 3 and 15 per cent.
- *Statutory liquidity reserve ratio (SLR):* It is the ratio of liquid assets (cash, gold, and government bonds) to the total credit that a bank is allowed to extend to borrowers.

To control inflation, the RBI may choose to enter into **open market operation** by selling government bonds to mop up excessive market liquidity.

Scheduled Banks of India

These are **banks listed under Schedule II of the Reserve Bank of India Act, 1934 (duly amended)**. The bank's paid-up capital and raised funds must be at least ₹5 lakh to qualify. These enjoy preferential rates of interest on loans from RBI. There are five such clusters regulated by RBI:

- *State Bank of India:* It came about in 1955, when the Imperial Bank of India was renamed. It is the largest employer in the banking sector in India (close to 2.5 lakh people) as well as the largest lender.
- **Nationalized banks:** such as Bank of Baroda (BOB), Punjab National Bank, (PNB), Canara Bank, etc.
  - 14 banks which held 85 per cent of national deposits were nationalized in 1969 (during Indira Gandhi's era).
  - Another six banks were nationalized in 1980.
  - After mergers and changes in name, there are 12 of these left now.
- **Private sector banks:** such as HDFC Bank, ICICI Bank, Axis Bank
- **Foreign banks:** such as Citi Bank, HSBC, Bank of America, etc.
- **Regional rural banks (RRBs):** Scheduled Commercial Banks (Govt.) that have been created primarily cater to the rural areas of India with basic banking and financial services. Such as Arunachal Pradesh Rural Bank under the sponsorship of SBI.

MUDRA Initiative

The Pradhan Mantri MUDRA Yojana (PMMY) is a scheme launched in April 2015 for providing loans up to 10 lakh to non-corporate, non-farm small/micro enterprises. Classified as MUDRA loans, they are given by Commercial Banks, RRBs, Small Finance Banks, MFIs, and NBFCs. Provisional disbursement or the year 2022–23 stood at ₹67,000 crore as of 1 July 2022.

Cooperative Banks

Cooperative banks play a significant role in credit delivery to rural populace.

- There are around 1,500 urban cooperative banks (UCBs) and 97,006 rural cooperative banks.
- The rural ones make up 65 per cent of the total asset size of all cooperatives.
- There have been issues of mismanagement with a few and a process of de-listing and listing is continuous.
- With increased urbanization and improving communication, the share of rural cooperative lending in total agricultural lending is on the decline (from as high as 64 per cent in 1992–93 to 11.3 per cent in 2019–20).

Small Finance Banks

- These were set up for specifically addressing the needs of underserved sections of small and micro-business units, and small and marginal farmers; sections of society struggling for funds that larger banks do not entertain.

Examples include AU Small Finance Bank Ltd., Equitas Small Finance Bank Ltd., Ujjivan Small Finance Bank Ltd., etc. There are 10 banks in this category and depending on compliance with rules and performance, these will be get the opportunity to become full-fledged banks.

Non-banking Financial Companies

These are mostly private sector firms that provide financial services such as:

- Loans for consumer goods
- Hire-purchase deals for capital goods
- Housing finance
- Vehicle finance
- Finance-related advisory services
- Loans against gold

Besides the many above, there are Residuary NBCs, Infrastructure Debt Fund-NBFCs, and NBFIs extending credit and include insurance firms, venture capitalists, currency exchanges, micro-loan organizations, and pawn shops.

Payment Banks

The RBI has allowed the establishment of E-portals to facilitate cashless transactions (payment for everyday purchases and such). These include agencies such as Paytm, Google Pay, and even the Department of Posts. Such entities:

- May accept deposits from individuals and firms. Such deposits should not exceed a total of ₹1 lakh.
- May issue instruments for transaction such as debit cards.
- Transact electronically for their clients on ECS, NEFT, and RTGS.
- Make payments to utilities on behalf of clients.
- Conduct mobile banking.

They are prohibited from:

- Offering clients any kind of time deposit.
- Lending activity.
- Accepting NRI deposits.
- Transacting cash more than ₹1 lakh.

FINANCIAL INSTITUTIONS

Many such have been instituted after independence. Some have become new entities, like the Industrial Credit and Investment Corporation of India (ICICI) became the ICICI Bank w.e.f. 2002, and the **IDBI** – now a subsidiary of LIC.

Noteworthy financial institutions include the following.

INDUSTRIAL FINANCIAL CORPORATION OF INDIA (IFCI)

- It is a public sector non-banking financial company listed on the NSE and BSE.
- A nodal agency that nurtures entrepreneurs in the SC/ST category IFCI provides guarantees to banks against loans offered.
- Its assistance is mostly for projects in the airport, road, power, telecom, real estate, and manufacturing sectors.
- This covers **Project Finance**, **Corporate Finance**, and **Syndication Advisory**.

UNIT TRUST OF INDIA (UTI)

- UTI was established in February 1964 under the Unit Trust of India Act, 1963 as statutory public sector investment institution.
- Objective: encouraging and mobilizing savings of citizens to put into productive corporate investment.

NATIONAL HOUSING BANK (NHB)

- After passage of the National Housing Bank Act 1987, the NHB was established in July 1988.
- It is the apex agency for all housing finance institutions at both regional and local levels, providing them with financial and related assistance.
- It was previously an integral part of the Reserve Bank of India until the Government of India purchased it in 2019 for ₹1,450 crore.
- NHB raises capital through borrowings, but most importantly through debentures, and bonds.
- These NHB bonds are accepted as security in commercial banks and can be used to meet statutory liquidity.
- These bonds also qualify for external assistance from international bodies such as USAID and OECF Japan.

EXIM BANK

- Following passage of the Export-Import Bank of India Act 1981, EXIM Bank was established by the Government of India, to extend export credit.
- It also facilitates import of technology and export product development, export production, export marketing, pre-shipment and post-shipment, and overseas investment.
- By extending lines of credit (LOCs) to financial institutions, banks, sovereign governments, and other entities overseas, the Exim Bank enables foreign buyers to import Indian goods.
- During FY 2021-22, EXIM Bank had sanctioned loans of ₹68,863 crore under various lending programmes.

TOURISM FINANCE CORPORATION OF INDIA (TFCI)

- Tourism Finance Corporation of India (TFCI) was established in 1989, to provide financial services to the tourism sector and promote tourism infrastructure throughout the country.
- It was a joint initiative of a group of government organizations like IFCI, LIC, OIC, SBI, BOI, Canara Bank, etc.
- It has facilitated millions of jobs being generated through funding to diverse segments such as heritage tourism, cruises, adventure, medical, wellness, sports, MICE, eco-tourism, film, and religious tourism.
- TFCI has been associated with creating many firsts in the tourism sector such as the Indian Railways' Palace on Wheels, Esselworld, spa resort Ananda in the Himalayas, and many more. And, it has assisted major domestic as well as international brands such as ITC, Leela, Taj, Lalit, Lemon Tree, Hyatt, Marriott, Hilton, Radisson, and Holiday Inn.
- It is an advisor to the central government, state governments, and their affiliated agencies in tourism matters.

INSURANCE

Modern insurance can be traced back to the **Great Fire of London** (1666) which destroyed over 30,000 homes. This led Nicholas Barbon to start an insurance business.

Broadly, the insurance businesses are of four categories:

1. Personal insurance, i.e. life and health
2. General insurance, e.g. motor vehicles, fire, theft, etc.
3. Credit insurance – ECGCI (Export Credit Guarantee Corporation of India)

4. Crop insurance – Agriculture Insurance Company Limited

- Life Insurance in India began in **1818**, when **Oriental Life Insurance Company** was started by Europeans in Calcutta.
- General insurance in India began in **1850** when **Triton Insurance Company** was established by the British in Calcutta.
- **1912: Life Insurance Companies Act** and **Provident Fund Act** are passed. The first makes it mandatory that premium rate tables and of company valuations must be certified by an actuary.
- All insurance premiums are based on **actuarial tables** nowadays. For personal insurance (life and health), these are ***demographic*** tables showing, for each age, the probability of death or disease.
- In the case of general insurance (e.g. motor vehicles), these tables are constructed from ***statistical*** records such as on accidents.
- The size of the insurance sector in India has now grown to 24 life insurance and 34 non-life insurance companies.
    - The market for fresh life insurers grew by **6.94 per cent** in **2021–22 to ₹2,27,188 crore (US$29.54 billion)**.
    - From July **2020 to 2021** non-life insurance premiums grew to **₹20,171 crore (US$2.71 billion), 19.5 per cent** up YoY – driven by strong performance of health and motor segments. Of this private sector companies made up a market share of 49.31 per cent in FY21.

LIC – LIFE INSURANCE CORPORATION OF INDIA

- In 1938, India had 176 insurance companies operating and failures were regularly taking place. By 1956, the number had swollen to 245.
- Life Insurance Corporation Act was passed in June 1956 to nationalize the sector, restoring order and introducing regulation.
- Thus, LIC was established in September 1956, headquartered in Mumbai. It absorbed most of these entities.
- LIC operates with 2,048 fully computerized branch offices, 113 divisional offices, 8 zonal offices, 1,381 satellite offices, and 9 offices abroad.
- In FY 2020–21, LIC's first-year premium income was ₹56,406 crore (US$7.75 billion) and growth 10.11 per cent.
- LIC maintains *settlement ratios* of more than 96 per cent by number of policies.

LIC IPO (largest IPO ever in India)

Following its policy of divestment of public assets, the Union Government had set itself the target of $29.6 billion for FY 2020–21. LIC has 'embedded value' of more than ₹5 trillion ($66.8 billion), so GoI feels partial divestment in LIC can raise $12 billion. GoI is the sole shareholder. Accordingly,

- *February 2020:* The Indian government announces plans to sell part of its stake in LIC through an IPO.
- *April 2020:* COVID-19 pandemic intervenes – delaying IPO.
- *February 2021:* The government states intention of selling 10 per cent of its share in LIC by March 2022.
- *February 2022:* LIC files its draft IPO papers and public awareness campaign follows. Meanwhile, Russia invades Ukraine battering stock markets world-wide. Union Cabinet approves (through amendment) selling 20 per cent of LIC stock to public. Bankers advise holding off because of situation.

- *April 2022:* Government decides to sell just 3.5 per cent of its shares.
- *May 2022:* Subscriptions open; issue is oversubscribed by three times. Issue price offered is ₹949 per share.
- It raised ₹20,500 crores ($2.7 billion) for GoI and is the largest IPO ever in the nation, but list price per share is ₹872 (a loss of 7.8 per cent for its buyers).

GIC RE – GENERAL INSURANCE CORPORATION OF INDIA

One hundred and seven companies were engaged in general insurance business in India when the General Insurance Business (Nationalization) Act, 1972 (GIBNA) was passed. This allowed the Union Government to take over their ownership by setting up the GIC. It began functioning on 1 January 1973. From inception, GIC was also the **Indian reinsurer** receiving obligatory cessions.

The companies absorbed were consolidated and restructured into four units as under:

- **New India Assurance Company Limited, Bombay**
- **United India Fire & General Insurance Company Limited, Madras**
- **Oriental Fire & General Insurance Company Limited, Bombay**
- **National Insurance Company Limited, Calcutta**

As holding company, GIC's role was to monitor and direct them. However,

- *March 2003:* The four subsidiaries were delinked from GIC and the Union Government became their owner.
- Functioning now as obligatory reinsurer, it has become **GIC Re**.
    - *Obligatory reinsurer:* Accepts all risks of other insurance companies, especially high-severity, low-frequency risks. Reinsurers participate in international insurance pools sharing risk.
    - GIC Re is manager for Indian Market Terrorism Risk Insurance Pool (IMTRIP), the FAIR Natural Catastrophe Reinsurance Pool (FNCRIP), and India Nuclear Insurance Pool (INIP).
    - *Obligatory cession:* Fee paid by others for such reinsurance. For every general insurance policy sold, 5 per cent of the premium is ceded to GIC Re, as the national reinsurer.

INSURANCE REGULATORY & DEVELOPMENT AUTHORITY OF INDIA (IRDAI)

In 1991 the Union Government opened the insurance sector to private sector companies and foreign promoters. With rising number of new entrants, it set up a Committee on Reforms in the Insurance Sector, headed by Mr. R. N. Malhotra, in 1993 to look into:

- Encouraging competition for more consumer choices and lower premiums.
- Safeguard and protect the interests of policy holders.
- Establishing an independent regulatory body answerable to Parliament.
- Promoting and ensuring orderly growth of the insurance industry.
- All insurance-related matters.

The IRDA was accordingly, set up in 2000, as an autonomous body under the IRDA Act 1999.

Trade (Credit) Insurance

In September 2021, the Union Cabinet approved an investment of ₹6,000 crore (US$804.71 million) into entities, offering export insurance cover to facilitate additional exports worth ₹5.6 lakh crore (US$75.11 billion) over the next five years.

CROP INSURANCE

- The first crop insurance programme was introduced in 1972–73 by the 'General Insurance' Department of LIC on H-4 cotton in Gujarat.
- There are two major types of crop insurance: **multiple peril crop insurance (MPCI)** and **crop-hail insurance**.
- A variety of schemes have since been introduced but most have petered out because there is always a season or two when it becomes completely unviable for the insurer, who then raises premiums making it unviable for the insured (farmer).
- The PCIS which ran from 1979 to 1984 charged premiums of 10 per cent.
- October 2020: Andhra Pradesh introduces free-of-cost crop insurance for state farmers.
- **Reliance General Insurance** and SatSure partner to launch satellite-based crop monitoring and predictive analytics support for better risk management.

Pradhan Mantri Fasal Bima Yajana (PMFBY) is supposed to:

- Protect farmers from production risk.
- Ensure their continuance in farming.
- Encourage farmers to adopt innovative and modern agricultural practices.

Crops covered and premiums charged (% age insured value):

- Kharif foodgrains, pulses, and oilseeds – 2 per cent
- Rabi foodgrains, pulses, and oilseeds – 1.5 per cent
- Commercial and horticultural – 5 per cent

It is applicable for farmers who are enrolled in the National Crop Insurance Portal (NCIP).

INSURANCE SECTOR OVERVIEW

Recognizing the potential of insurance sector in

- Employment creation
- Pension and social security

Accordingly, in 2021, the Union Government

- Announces it will infuse ₹3,000 crore (US$413 million) into state-owned general insurance companies.
- Increases FDI limit in insurance from 49 to 74 per cent (Union Budget 2021).

Insurance Sector as Employer

- Life insurance (registered) agents alone numbered 25 lakh in India in March 2021 – an increase of 8 per cent from 23 lakh in March 2020. Combined with general insurance agents, surveyors, and office personnel, the sector is estimated to employ 3.5 million.
- Indian start-ups also interested in the business of insurance reach. In November 2021, an online platform, vKover, announced plans to recruit 10,000 agents in the next two years, in Kerala. It looks to establish network of 100,000 digital agents in India, by 2026.

Pension and Social Security

Going forward, increasing life expectancy, favourable savings, and greater employment in the private sector is expected to fuel demand for pension plans.

Strong growth in the automotive industry over the next decade will be a key driver for the motor insurance market.

Bancassurance

Mutually beneficial arrangement between a bank and an insurance company, allowing the insurance company to sell its products to the bank's clients. For example, Bharti AXA Life Insurance partnership with

Fincare Small Finance Bank to offer life insurance products to 26.5 lakh customers.

STOCK EXCHANGES

Stock exchanges are places where shares of companies are traded, and the first such large-scale organized activity in India may be traced to Calcutta in 1836. It was however unregulated.

Besides trading and investment in equity, stock exchanges have moved on to dealing in indices, mutual funds, ETFs, IPOs, security lending and borrowing, equity derivatives, currency derivatives, commodity derivatives, interest rate futures, and corporate bonds.

Securities such as equity and bonds are part of national wealth.

In April 1992, the BSE (see below) suffered a '***market crash***' and 'the ***bubble*** burst' (collapse in the worth of most stocks) owing to unregulated speculation which occurred as a consequence of malpractices by primarily one individual.

SEBI

The Securities and Exchanges Board of India had been set up in April 1988 to regulate stock market activity in India, protect investors against fraudulence, and promote investor interests. The crash prompted an act of Parliament in 1992, giving SEBI statutory powers to fine violators of its guidelines. Powers were further granted in 2014, allowing for stringent investigation, audit of suspect records, and even imprisonment of identified violators.

At the moment, there are seven stock exchanges that are recognized by SEBI regulation, namely:

- *BSE (Bombay Stock Exchange):* Asia's first-ever stock exchange, it was established in the year 1875.
  - First stock exchange in the country to be granted permanent recognition under the Securities Contract Regulation Act, 1956 in 1957.
  - In February 2017, BSE became the first listed stock exchange of India.
  - By January 2022, BSE's market cap was ₹276.7 lakh crore. (US$3.7 trillion), with 5439 listed shares on it.
  - BSE is one of the fastest stock exchanges in the world with a transaction speed of 6 microseconds.
  - *SENSEX: Benchmark index of the BSE in India,* it comprised 30 of the largest and most actively traded stocks on the BSE (reflects to an extent the state of India's economy).
  - Currently, it is around 54,000 points (up from median levels of 17,000 in 2012).
- *NSE (National Stock Exchange):* Incorporated in 1992 and given SEBI recognition in April 1993, the NSE commenced operations in 1994.
  - It was the first dematerialized (***demat***) electronic exchange in the country providing a modern, fully automated screen-based electronic trading system anywhere in India.
  - *NIFTY: Benchmark index of the NSE in India,* it comprised 50 of the largest and most actively traded stocks on the NSE. It is used by investors the world over as a barometer of the Indian capital market.
  - By 2021, the NSE was the world's largest derivatives exchange in terms of the number of contracts traded (per statistics of FIA).
  - It stood fourth in the world in cash equities by the number of trades per statistics released by the World Federation of Exchanges (WFE) for 2021.

- NSE market cap was US$3.4 trillion (as of August 2021), with 2,002 listings on the exchange, as of October 2021.
- Currently, it is around 16,000 points (up from median levels of 5,300 in 2012).

- *CSE (Calcutta Stock Exchange):* Founded in December 1863 by 16 of Calcutta's leading stockbrokers.
  - 1997: Introduced completely computerized online trading reporting system called C-STAR n-Based Trading And Reporting).
  - 2013: Trading on CSE ceases following ₹120-crore scandal involving notorious stockbroker Ketan Parekh.
  - Currently being resurrected.
- *ICEX (Indian Commodity Exchange Limited)* is a SEBI regulated online commodity derivative exchange headquartered in Mumbai, basically dealing in hedging. It offers risk management for supply chain operators through commodities.
- *MSE (Metropolitan Stock Exchange of India Limited)* is recognized by SEBI and offers a transparent hi-tech electronic platform for trading in Capital Market, Futures & Options, Currency Derivatives, and Debt Market segments.
- *MCX (Multi Commodity Exchange of India Limited)* is a commodity derivatives platform for online trading of commodity derivatives contracts across varied segments including bullion, industrial metals, energy, and agricultural commodities. It is India's first exchange to offer commodity options contracts, bullion index futures, and base metals index futures.
- *NCDEX (National Commodity & Derivatives Exchange Limited)* is an exchange for that allows trading on 23 agricultural commodities including pulses, spices, and guar, which are not traded on any other global platform.

UNION BUDGET

The finance minister of India presents the Union Budget in Parliament every year, on the first working day of February. Before 2016, this used to be done on the last working day of February.

- It is a statement of accounts for all likely to be revenues collected and expenditures made by the Government of India during the **fiscal year** that is about to end.
- It is also an estimate of the government's intentions about generating revenue and spending/allocating this. It seeks permission from the Lok Sabha to pursue such intentions.

The **fiscal year** in India is the period **from 1 April of one year to 31 March of the next year**. It is often used interchangeably with financial year which is correct when the two periods are the same. Tax returns (individuals and organizations) generally conform to this.

- 'Budget' is a popular reference. It is actually called '**Annual Financial Statement under Article 112 of the Constitution of India**'.
- The budget division of the department of economic affairs (DEA) in the finance ministry is the nodal body responsible for producing this after consulting other ministries.

Union Budget 2022–23 presents:

- Statement I – CONSOLIDATED FUND OF INDIA – **REVENUE ACCOUNT** – RECEIPTS and DISBURSEMENTS.
  - Referred to as **Revenue Budget**, this shows amounts received or spent under each head in rupees crores.
  - **Heads** range from: ***Taxes***, ***General Services*** (e.g. police, jails, public services); ***Social Services*** (e.g.

housing, broadcasting); ***Economic Services*** (e.g. dairy development, warehousing, roads & bridges , civil aviation); and ***Grants-in-Aid & Contributions*** as **Receipts.**

- Many of these heads also show up in disbursement (indicating that government both earns and spends on such activity).
- Other disbursement heads include: ***Organs of State*** (a part of General Services, this is the 'spend' on salaries, support staff and offices, etc.), ***Tax Collection***, ***Interest*** (paid by the government on what it borrows), and ***Administrative Services.***

Note: Since the budget was presented to Lok Sabha on 1 February, it was (educated) guesswork how much the government would receive and spend in the next two months. As such the budget provides four sets of figures.

- **Actuals 2020–21** – catches up with the previous year's guessed estimate.
- **Budget Estimate 2021–22** – figures presented in the previous budget (which indicated intentions then; and ratified by Lok Sabha).
- **Revised Budget Estimate 2021–22** – corrected for some actual shift of intention.
- **Budget Estimate 2022–23** – what the government hopes to receive and wants to spend in terms of rupee-value, and seeks Lok Sabha approval, in order to proceed.
- Statement II – CONTINGENCY FUND OF INDIA – NET
- Statement III – PUBLIC ACCOUNT OF INDIA – RECEIPTS and DISBURSEMENTS
  - Often referred to as **Capital Budget** (format identical to Statement I).
  - Heads range from (On the both Receipts and Disbursements): ***NSS***, ***Reserves***, ***Provident Funds***, ***Deposits***, etc.

Budget 2020–23 (nutshell)

In Lakh Crores of Rupees	Revenue Receipts	Capital Receipts	**Total Receipts**	Revenue Disbursement	Capital Disbursement	**Total Disbursement**
Actuals 2020–21	108.95	28.49	**137.44**	100.92	28.45	**129.37**
	Indicating Fiscal Surplus – GOI spent less than revenue					
Budget Estimate 2021–22	107.33	23.86	**131.19**	108.90	23.30	**132.2**
	GOI Intention: small Fiscal Deficit					
Revised Budget Estimate 2021–22	102.36	24.59	**126.95**	103.47	25.51	**128.98**
	Ended up with Deficit only slightly higher than planned					
Budget Estimate 2022–23	113.16	26.24	**139.4**	113.65	25.75	**139.4**
	Informing Lok Sabha of GOI intention to sharply increase government spending but still '**balance**' the Budget – no Fiscal Deficit					

Budget-Related Issues of the Indian Fiscal System

- *Fiscal policy* is the set of strategic steps that government will take to manage earning – its policies regarding taxes, bondrates, etc., and also manage spending – its policies on whether to spend on healthcare or highways (for example) and if so, how much?
- *Plan expenditure* is what government spending for productive purposes, e.g. road building, infrastructural projects, etc.
- *Non-plan expenditure* is what the government spends on the so-called non-productive areas (mostly obligatory in nature) such as salaries, subsidies, repayment of loans, and interest are called non-plan expenditure.
- *Public debt* is when government borrows from the open market. This takes various forms.
  - *Government bonds* are issued by the Central and State Governments of India, to raise funds for infrastructure development. These are long term (five years or more) and at higher rates of interest.
  - *Treasury bills (T-bills)* are short-term borrowing, such as from RBI. Government of India issues four types of treasury bills, namely, 14-day, 91-day, 182-day, and 364-day. T-bills are available in multiples of ₹25,000. T-bills are issued at a discount and are redeemed at par.
  - *Schemes* such as the NSS and Post Office Savings.
- *External debt:* Such as loans taken from the World Bank, IMF, ADB, or on bilateral basis.
- *Fiscal (budget) deficit:* When government spending exceeds revenues the gap is known as the deficit.
  - This may be a part of policy or due to emergencies (war for instance).
  - But, high deficits are indicators of poor management.
  - They tend to accumulate raising the debt burden which in turn leads to increasing interest to be paid. Countries, then fall into a debt trap where there is very little useful expenditure (Sri Lanka for example).
  - Some deficit may not be 'bad' if incurred for development.
- *Revenue deficit:* Revenue deficit is the excess of estimated government expenditure over receipts in the revenue account. This happens when the actual revenue is less than the projected one and indicates how much extra the government needs to borrow to remain liquid.
- *Capital deficit:* It is the shortfall when there is a shortfall of foreign exchange.
- *Primary deficit:* Fiscal deficit – interest burden; indicates how much is available for plan expenditure (development work).
- *Eliminating/reducing deficits* can be done by
  - Cutting back on public expenditure.
  - Doing away with subsidies and welfare programmes.
  - Introducing fresh taxes and increasing rates of existing ones.
  - Selling public assets – lands, utilities and public sector units.

BUDGET ENACTMENT

- According to **Article 112 of the Indian Constitution, the president is responsible** for submitting the budget to the Lok Sabha.

- However, **Article 77 (3)** allows the president to delegate the responsibility to the union finance minister and steering it through parliament.
- At the same time as in the Lok Sabha, a copy of the budget is placed on the Rajya Sabha's table. All members of parliament are given printed copies.
- Once the budget has been presented, a ***proposed*** **Finance Bill** is also presented. This has details of proposed new taxes, changes to (or repeals of) current taxes. Then follows active debate by MPs on **revenue and expenditure** aspects along with Grant requests/Cut motions.
- The Parliament votes on grant/cut requests, after which the **Appropriation Bill** is introduced, debated, and passed by the Parliament's Appropriation Committee. This is the legal basis for the withdrawal of funds from the **Consolidated Fund of India**.
- Once the appropriation bill is passed, the proposed **Finance Bill** is debated. MPs can ask for adjustments at this point, which the finance minister may accept or reject.
- The **Appropriation Bill** is now sent to Rajya Sabha along with the **Finance Bill** and it is given 14 days time to return these bills to the Lok Sabha, with or without revisions. It is left to Lok Sabha to accept or reject these.
- The president now signs the Finance Bill for it to become a **statute**. The president lacks authority to veto the bill.

FINANCE COMMISSION

The Finance Commission is a body that has been constituted by the president under Article 280 of the Constitution, every five years. The First Finance Commission was constituted vide presidential order dated 22 November 1951 under the chairmanship of Shri K. C. Neogy in April 1952. We are into the Fifteenth Finance Commission in 2022 which has tenure till 2026.

FUNCTIONS OF THE FINANCE COMMISSION

- To act as an advisory body for the President of India in matters of:
  - *Distribution of collected taxes between the Union and the States.*
  - The ***principles*** behind grants-in-aid of given to the states out of the Consolidated Fund of India.
  - ***Develop measures*** to augment these State Funds to supplement the resources of panchayats and municipalities in the state (State Finance Commissions provide the basis).
  - Any other matter, referred to the commission by the president of India in the interests of sound finance.
  - Parliament empowers the commission to ***set necessary procedure***.
  - ***Parity of all public services*** across the states.

APPOINTMENT OF THE FINANCE COMMISSION

The Finance Commission is constituted as per the provisions of the **Finance Commission [Miscellaneous Provisions] Act, 1951**:

- The chairman of the commission is selected from among persons who have had experience in public affairs.
- Four other members are selected from among persons who are either qualified to be appointed as judges of a high court; or, are specialists in finance and accounts of government; or are recognized economists.

IMPLEMENTING THE FINANCE COMMISSION RECOMMENDATIONS

- **By presidential order:** Category includes distribution of union taxes and duties and grants-in-aid.
- **By executive orders:** Other matters depending on the terms set it.

PRESENT (16TH) FINANCE COMMISSION: WHO'S WHO

Chairman: Dr. Arvind Panagariya, former Vice-Chairman, NITI Aayog and Professor of Economics and the Jagdish Bhagwati Professor of Indian Political Economy at Columbia University

Member: Ajay Narayan Jha, former Finance Secretary and member of the Fifteenth Finance Commission of India

Member: Annie George Mathew, former Special Secretary-Department of Expenditure, Ministry of Finance

Member: Dr. Manoj Panda, former Director of the Institute of Economic Growth, Delhi and the Centre for Economic and Social Studies (CESS), Hyderabad

Part-time Member: Dr. Soumya Kanti Ghosh, Group Chief Economic Adviser of SBI

NPCI

Founded in December 2008, National Payments Corporation of India (NPCI) is a Section 8 company under the Indian Companies Act, 2013, and has been set up by the Reserve Bank of India and Indian Banks' Association. The Certificate of Commencement of Business was issued in April 2009. Its products and services include retail, retail payment services like unified payments interface (UPI), and cheque truncation (electronic image of the cheque is transmitted to the drawee bank by NPCI along with relevant other information). It also acts as the national automated clearing house.

As part of the financial inclusion drive, the entire UPI ecology was planned to take the banking system to the doorstep of the citizens of India even in the remotest part of the country. Owned and operated by the National Payments Corporation of India (NPCI) and introduced in 2016, it facilitates inter-bank transactions. A single app helps access multiple bank accounts of the owner. It supports both collect and pay requests. From 8 June 2022, the Reserve Bank of India allowed linking RuPay credit cards to UPI as well.

UPI is being actively marketed through a subsidiary of NPCI called NPCI International Payments Limited (NIPL) in other countries as well. And now it is accepted in the following seven countries:

1. Bhutan
2. France (e-commerce)
3. Mauritius
4. Nepal
5. Singapore
6. Sri Lanka
7. UAE

Per the global payments hub Paysecure, India's unified payments interface processed 3,729.1 transactions per second during the April–July 2024 period.

UPI processed nearly Rs 81 lakh crore transactions in the April–July 2024 period, thus leading all other global digital payment platforms. More than 40 per cent of all payments in India are done through UPI, per the Press Information Bureau, 30 October 2023.

STOCK EXCHANGE

A stock exchange is a marketplace where securities (tradable financial assets) such as stocks, bonds, and derivatives are bought and sold.

Stock Exchanges in India

Sr. No.	Name of the Recognized Stock Exchange	Address	Recognition Valid Upto	Segments Permitted
1	BSE Ltd.	P J Tower, Dalal Street, Mumbai 400001 Website: http://www.bseindia.com	Permanent	a. Equity b. Equity Derivatives c. Currency Derivatives (including Interest Rate Derivatives) d. Commodity Derivatives e. Debt f. Electronic Gold Receipt (EGR)
2	Calcutta Stock Exchange Ltd.	7, Lyons Range, Dalhousie, Kolkata-700001, West Bengal Website: http://www.cse-india.com/	Permanent	a. Equity b. Equity Derivatives c. Currency Derivatives (including Interest Rate Futures) d. Debt
3	Metropolitan Stock Exchange of India Ltd.	205A, 2nd Floor, Piramal Agastya Corporate Park, Sunder Bung Lane, Kamani Junction, LBS Road, Kurla (West), Mumbai 400070 Website: http://www.msei.in/index.aspx	15 September 2024	a. Commodity Derivatives
4	Multi Commodity Exchange of India Ltd.	Exchange Square, Suren Road, Chakala, Andheri (E), Mumbai 400093 Website: https://www.mcxindia.com/	Permanent	
5	National Commodity & Derivatives Exchange Ltd.	Akruti Corporate Park,1st Floor, Near G.E.Garden, L.B.S. Marg, Kanjurmarg (West), Mumbai 400078 Website: http://www.ncdex.com/	Permanent	a. Commodity Derivatives
6	Indian Commodity Exchange Limited	Reliable Tech Park, 403-A, B-wing, 4th Floor, Thane-Belapur Road, Airoli (E), Navi Mumbai 400708	Permanent	
7	National Stock Exchange of India Ltd.	Exchange Plaza, C-1, Block G, Bandra Kurla Complex, Bandra (East), Mumbai 400051 Website: https://www.nseindia.com	Permanent	a. Equity b. Equity Derivatives c. Currency Derivatives (including Interest Rate Derivatives) d. Commodity Derivatives e. Debt

BOMBAY STOCK EXCHANGE

The Bombay Stock Exchange (BSE) was born under the shade of a giant banyan tree way back on 9 July 1875 by Premchand Roychand, a cotton merchant. Educated in Elphinstone College, Bombay (now Mumbai), he was the first Indian broker able to write, read, and speak in English. Indian brokers doing business in stocks and shares decided to form an association in Bombay to protect the interests of Indian share brokers and stockbrokers. It was also Asia's first stock exchange and tenth oldest in the world.

NATIONAL STOCK EXCHANGE

The National Stock Exchange (NSE) is India's largest and fifth largest among world stock exchanges by market cap. It was established in 1992, and currently it comprises 50 of the largest Indian companies. The NSE was the first to adopt fully automated screen-based electronic trading, which replaced the traditional open outcry system.

Largest employers of India

The record for the largest employer in India belongs to the country's government-controlled sector – Indian Railways. On 1 July 2023 the number of gazetted and non-gazetted employees of the Indian Railways stood at 12,18,221.

In the private sector, Tata Consultancy Services continues to be the largest employer with 6,01,546 employees in March 2024 – a significant drop from 6,15,316 in June 2023.

8 Indian Polity

INTRODUCTION

India has come a long way from the Indus Valley Civilization, 3,300 years ago, to being the world's largest working democracy. Home to 1.2 billion people, India stands second in the list of most populous countries in the world after China. A country with 780 languages, 730 tribes, India's population represents a good mix of all four major racial groups, namely, Mongoloid, Negroid, Australoid, and Caucasian.

In order to understand the present-day socio-cultural, political, as well as economic make-up of the people of India, it is important to delve into the past of this enormous landmass geographically situated in the south of the Asian continent.

TIMELINE OF MOVEMENT OF RACES/TRIBES AND DYNASTIES THAT RULED INDIA

73000–55000 years ago: Modern humans arrived in Indian subcontinent.

45000 BCE: Settled life spread in South Asia.

7000–5500 BCE: Village life developed in Mehrgarh (present-day Balochistan, Pakistan) with focus on agriculture and domestication of animals.

3300–1300 BCE (Bronze Age): Evolution of Indus Valley Civilization (covering present-day northeast Afghanistan, Pakistan, and northwest India).

2600 BCE: Emergence of highly developed early cities of Harappa and Mohenjo-Daro (present-day Sindh and Pakistan).

1900 BCE–1500 BCE: Decline of Indus Valley Civilization.

1500–500 BCE: Indo-Aryan migration from Central Asia; emergence of Vedic period (Hindu texts – the Vedas in written form; Gandhara civilization in present-day northern Pakistan and Afghanistan).

1200–900 BCE: Kuru dynasty ruled in present-day Delhi, Haryana, and western Uttar Pradesh.

First recorded state-level society in the Indian subcontinent.

500 BCE (approximately): Sage Valmiki composes the epic, *Ramayana*.

530 BCE: Indus Valley conquered by Persia.

520 BCE–325 CE: Persian King Cyrus expands his Achaemenid Empire to Gandhara region.

327–326 BCE: Alexander the Great conquers Achaemenid Persian Empire and expands his Macedonian (Greek) Empire to Punjab and Sind in present-day Pakistan.

326 BCE: Alexander returns from the banks of Beas River in Punjab.

320–180 BCE: Mauryan rule in Gandhara region; Chandragupta Maurya first ruler.

320 BCE: Chandragupta Maurya expands empire to Magadha (present-day Bihar) and northern India.

268–232 BCE: Rule of Mauryan King Ashoka the Great.

200 BCE: Invasion of Greco-Bactrian King Demetrius via Khyber Pass (after decline of Mauryan Empire); established empire in southern Afghanistan and northwest India (Bactria was an Iranian civilization in Central Asia).

180–80 BCE: Indo-Greek rule in the region of Gandhara.

186 BCE: Demetrios begins Greek era in India (also referred to as Yavanarajya).

160–130 BCE: Menander, the Indo-Greek king, rules Punjab.

80 BCE–75 CE: Shaka Pahlava or Scytho-Parthians invade northwest India; Shakas were nomadic Iranian people; Parthians (called Pahlavas in India) were a major political power of Iran.

75–450 CE: Kushan rule in Gandhara, also called golden era of Gandhara. Kushans are believed to be nomadic pastoralists of western China who migrated to Bactria (Iran). Kanishka, the most prominent Kushan king, spread of Buddhism.

320 CE: Gupta Empire in North India (controlled the Kushans); white Huns caused huge damage to Gupta Empire.

450 CE: White Huns (Central Asian tribe) invade India across Hindu Kush mountains.

550 CE: End of Gupta rule.

554–606 CE: Rule of Maukhari dynasty, ruled the Ganga-Yamuna plains.

610–681 CE: Rule of Chalukyas.

712 CE: First Muslim invasion in India under Muhammad bin Qasim (Arab); conquered Sindh; Islam arrives in India.

848–1279 CE: Chola dynasty rule; controlled most of India; empire extended to Indonesia and Cambodia.

1000–1025 CE: Invasions of Mahmud of Ghazni.

1175 CE: Invasion of Muhammad Ghori (central Afghanistan).

1193 CE: Muslim General Muhammad Bin Bakhtiyar Khilji destroys Vikramshila University.

1206–1526 CE: Rule of Delhi Sultanate; established by Qutb ud-Din Aibak (slave/ Mamluk dynasty).

1221 CE: Genghis Khan (also known as Chinggis Khan) invades Punjab.

1229 CE: Ruler of Kamarupa (present-day Assam) defeated Muslim invasions to his territory.

1236 CE–1240 CE: Rule of Razia Sultan (first Muslim woman ruler).

1311 CE: Malik Kafur, most trusted general of Alauddin Khilji, attacked and looted Warangal, Halebidu, and Madurai.

1336 CE: Vijayanagara Empire, a Hindu empire established by brothers Harihara I and Bukka Raya I that ruled almost entire South India.

1398 CE: Turco-Mongol conqueror Timur looted and plundered Lahore.

1498 CE: Entry of the first European sailor Vasco da Gama (Portuguese explorer) to India.

1503 CE: Cochin becomes the first European (Portuguese) settlement in India.

1518 CE: Rana Sangha defeats Ibrahim Lodi and regains control of northeast Rajasthan.

1520 CE: Krishnadevaraya of Vijayanagara Empire defeats the Sultan of Bijapur; same year Rana Sangha leading the coalition of Rajput army invades Gujarat Sultanate.

1526–1757 CE: Mughal rule in India; started with Babur (Mughal ruler of Kabul) being called in by local nobles to defeat Ibrahim Lodi in the Battle of Panipat.

1556 CE: Mughal Ruler Humayun dies: succeeded by his son Akbar.

1556: Hindu King Hemu defeated Mughals in the Battle of Tughlaqabad and established Hindu Raj in North India, conferred the title of Vikramaditya; however, he was killed in the Second Battle of Panipat by Akbar.

1582 CE: Akbar's forces defeated by Maharana Pratap in Rajasthan.

1600 CE: East India Company formed in England and wins exclusive trading rights with India.

1606 CE: Mughal King Jahangir (son of Akbar) ordered torture and killing of Sikh Guru Arjan Singh as he refused to convert to Islam.

1616 CE: Mughal forces were defeated in a land and navy battle with Ahom King Susenghphaa in Assam.

1674 CE: Maratha Empire that began in 1674 (with coronation of Shivaji) reached its zenith in 1760 CE; starting with Maharashtra, the Marathas controlled almost half of Indian subcontinent.

1757–1947 CE: British era in India.

1818: Maratha ruler Bajirao II defeated in the third Anglo-Maratha War; collapse of Maratha Empire and establishment of East India Company control over almost whole of India.

1834: Sikh Empire won the Battle of Peshawar and included Peshawar as a part of the Sikh Empire.

1849: Sikh Empire defeated East India Company in the Battle of Chillianwala.

1857: Last Mughal emperor, Bahadur Shah Zafar deposed by East India Company after Sepoy Mutiny; India comes directly under British Crown.

1947: India won independence from British after a long struggle for freedom; India was divided on religious basis as India and Pakistan (Muslim-dominated East Bengal, present Bangladesh, included in Pakistan).

1947: 15th August, a democratic form of government established in India.

1950: Constitution of India (the world's longest written constitution) comes into force; India becomes a Republic.

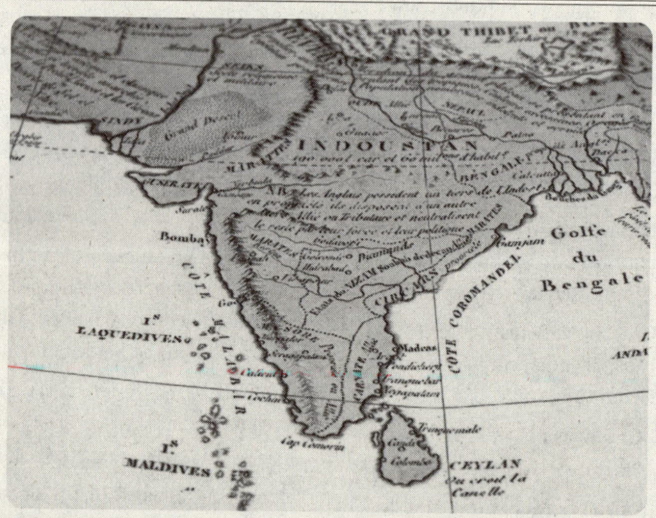

***Trivia:** The mastermind of the Kurukshetra war in the epic, Mahabharata, Shakuni, the maternal uncle of Crown Prince Duryodhana, was the King of Gandhara (present-day Northern Pakistan and Afghanistan).*

***Trivia:** Kuru dynasty finds its place in the Mahabharata that describes the battle between the Kurus (Kauravas) and the Pandavas. Kurukshetra, the battleground, still exists in the state of Haryana.*

The evolution of the political system that India has today is a process of culmination of various influences and processes that have been experienced and passed on from generations.

The flow of this evolution of systems of government that India witnessed over the centuries may be summarized through this flow chart:

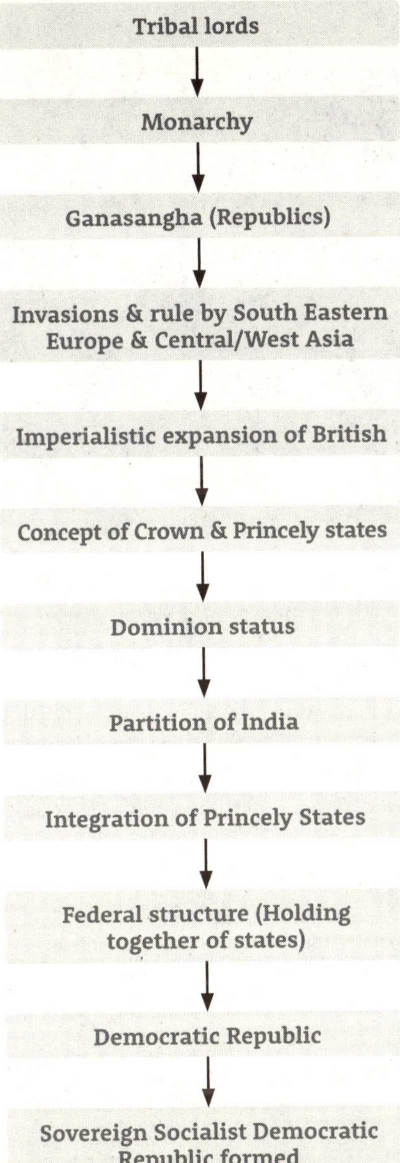

Where the term Bharat comes from

{Sanskrit Shloka from *Vishnu Puran* (fifth-century Hindu text)}

उत्तरं यत्समुद्रस्य हिमाद्रेश्चैव दक्षिणम् ।
वर्षं तद् भारतं नाम भारती यत्र संततिः ।।

Uttaraṃ yatsamudrasya himādreścaiva dakṣiṇam
varṣaṃ tadbhārataṃ nāma bhāratī yatra santatiḥ

Meaning: The country (Varsam) that lies north of the ocean and south of the snowy mountains is called Bharatam; there dwell the descendants of Bharata.

Bharatvarsha is believed to be identified as part of Jambudweepa, a larger geographical area. The text gives elaborate account of King Bharata who conquered and ruled the entire region. It was considered to be the reign of peace and development. King Bharata was the son of King Dushyanta and Queen Shakuntala. Kauravas and Pandavas are believed to be his descendants.

Depiction from Vishnu Puran:

Hindu religious text compiled around fifth century BCE

The above map is of ancient Indian subcontinent. This map shows all the kingdoms and regions mentioned in the epics *Mahabharata* and *Ramayana* written between 500 and 400BCE.

The timeline gives an account of the change of political power the country has gone through over the centuries. In trade, commerce, political might, scientific research, astronomy, astrology, medicine, higher education, philosophy, literature, and the like, India excelled during the period. Maritime trade through the Indian Ocean dominated the entire world. In fact, till the eighteenth century, India and China were among the richest countries of the world. However, China maintained isolation voluntarily in terms of overseas trade from the fifteenth century onwards.

As the British Crown took over the reign of power in India, the once rich economy was reduced to a colony of the foreign powers. And this gave the opportunity to the western world, namely, Europe and North America to emerge as trade giants. There was a shift of supremacy from Asia to the West. Europe established itself as the centre of world trade.

As mechanized industries developed in England, India's agriculture, natural forests, mineral resources were looted and plundered to provide raw materials to the factories in England. The country's natural vegetation was destroyed for growing commercial crops and plantations which the colonialists termed as 'Science Forestry'.

Interesting Fact:

German Botanist Dietrich Brandis gave the concept of 'Scientific Forestry' to India. Under this system natural forests were cleared and only a single variety of commercial tree such as sal was planted for timber. Basically, the colonialists wanted timber for expanding their railway network.

Note

Portuguese, Dutch, Danish, and French traders cannot be omitted from a discussion on India's past and the various influences the country had experienced.

It is to be noted that all these European powers entered India with the purpose of trade. So, it is seen that they settled in the port cities so that they could export items easily through ships. Most of them traded in spices, cotton, diamond, etc. They set up trading centres and factories in several places. Initially, British East India Company also came with the same purpose but with the turn of events starting from the Battle of Plassey in 1757, they controlled the entire country. Most of the other European traders left for markets in South-East Asia. Portuguese and Dutch were limited to small colonies in the coastal cities.

FACT FILE

- Masulipatnam is present-day Machilipatnam in Andhra Pradesh (Coromandel Coast).
- Tranquebar is present-day Tharangambadi in Tamil Nadu (Coromandel Coast)

German Botanist Dietrich Brandes (1824 – 1907). He founded the Imperial Forest School in 1906 in Dehradun (Uttarakhand), now known as the Forest Research Institute.

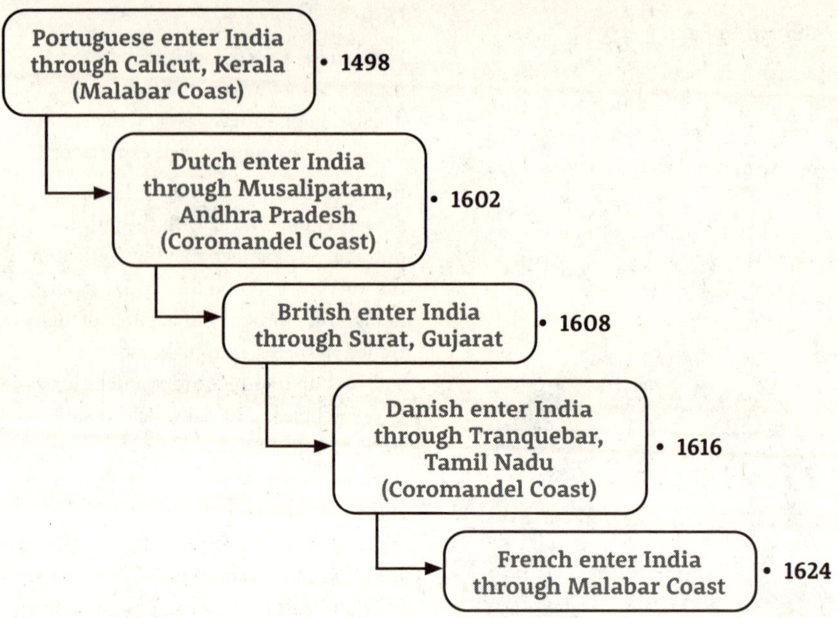

CONCEPT OF DEMOCRACY AND INTERNATIONAL INFLUENCES ON INDIAN CONSTITUTION

The Concept of Democracy

The term 'democracy' comes from the Greek terms 'demos' meaning 'people' and 'kratos' meaning 'rule'. Together it means, 'rule of people'. Democracy is a form of government that is ruled by the people. This system of government existed as early as the fifth century BCE in ancient city-state of Athens, Greece. Direct democracy was practised then. However, with the emergence of much bigger countries, direct democracy gave way to representative democracy by the eighteenth century.

Origin of Democracy as a Form of Government

The prehistoric society is not always backward contrary to certain beliefs. Even the indigenous communities have had a leader and protector. The concept of a written constitution emerged much later. However, there were customary rules in every society that the leader followed while administering justice. A tyrant may not be expected to follow such rules.

Let us understand the different types of government (rule) that prevailed in the most developed early civilizations of the world around fifth to tenth century BCE.

COUNTRY	GOVERNMENT
Egypt	Theocratic monarchy (the king was believed to have been chosen by God and he is supposed to protect and administer justice to people in accordance to Ma'at (God of Wisdom & Justice).
Greece	Direct democracy was practised in ancient Athens, Greece. A fixed number of citizens were chosen who actively participated in all activities of the state to serve the people. However, women, children, and slaves were not considered as citizens and so were not allowed to vote. Democracy was not permanent in Greece as it was taken over by oligarchy.
China	Dynastic rule dominated entire Chinese civilization. The Zhou dynasty was the longest ruling dynasty that ruled for 790 years. A very important Chinese political ideology was 'Mandate of Heaven'. It means that the emperor is given mandate by heaven to rule. So, the emperor was considered 'Son of Heaven'. If the emperor is overthrown or the country faces natural disasters such as floods, droughts, etc., it is believed that he is unworthy of the post and that heaven is no longer giving him mandate to rule. This doctrine kept the emperor under control and made him deliver his duties diligently. Mandate of Heaven allowed men of common origin to overthrow an unjust ruler.
India	India saw the rise of large Janapadas also referred to as ganapadas (aristocratic republics) during this period. This was a step forward from smaller Samrajyas (kingdoms) of the early Vedic period (late Bronze Age to early Iron Age). The Kuru kingdom was the first state-level political power. The kuru kings took advice of the royal priest in all matters of governance. Apart from this, the king had the village headman, chief of army, food distributor, and also spies and duta (ambassadors/ messengers) to maintain foreign relations. There were two types of assemblies in the Kuru empire: the Samiti and Sabha. Samiti was the legislative assembly of jana members. They had the power to dethrone or elect the king. The Sabha was an assembly of wise men who would advise the king in taking decisions. It was a smaller body than the Samiti. Gana and sangha are words used to denote 'republic'. The Licchavis are known for establishing Ganasangha. This system strongly believed in decentralization of power.

Note

- Women were not considered citizens in Athenian state. They were seen as 'second-rated' humans who were to obey the orders of husbands and fathers in the family. They had no role in public life.
- Janapada comes from the words 'Jana' meaning people and 'Pada' meaning foot. So, it literally means 'foothold of people' referring to a stable and settled human life.
- In the Licchavis Janasangha, women participated in social life but not in political assemblies.

Interesting Facts

- Women in ancient India were given the right to choose her husband. During the Swayamvar ceremony, the lady was free to choose her husband from among the invited guests. She put the garland around the man she liked.
- Vedic society also practised the concept of Niyog, in which a widow or a woman whose husband is not capable of producing a child, may enter into a physical relation with a person of her choice for procreation so that the family lineage continues. However, the child so born would be considered the legal child of the married couple and the biological father would have no claims over the child.

So, it is evident that though the concept of democracy originated in ancient Athens (Greece), equally advanced civilizations, such as Egypt, Indian subcontinent, and China, also had people-centric governments and not just hereditary or absolute monarchy. In fact, India initiated a republican form of government with very systematic and organized structure of administration.

As modern countries emerged, monarchy gradually declined and people demanded equal rights for all. The First and Second World Wars changed the world view on traditional systems of government like monarchy, oligarchy, and aristocracy. The world also realized the violent effects of dictatorship and Russian communism. Democracy was seen as the best alternative.

However, with increased territorial size of countries and large population, the Athenian concept of direct democracy was practically impossible. So, in the twentieth century, indirect or representative democracy became very popular.

To run these huge democracies, the modern world initiated several institutions and certain set of rules and procedures for directing and controlling these institutions. This rule book was the Constitution. All democratic nations adhere to their constitutional provisions, which may be written or unwritten.

Evolution of democracy all over the world also empowered the citizens of the countries to voice their opinion on the state and its concerns. During the initial days of democracy, a section of citizens or

Do you know?

Chanakya (also known as Vishnugupta or Kautilya) wrote *Arthashastra* between third and fourth century BCE. *Arthashastra* is a treatise on statecraft, economics, politics, and military strategies. Chanakya was a scholar of Taxila University and guide and mentor of Chandragupta Maurya. He helped Chandragupta establish the Mauryan Empire in Magadha, overthrowing the Nanda dynasty. The original book was rediscovered in 1905. It was written in Sanskrit and later translated to other languages.

a minority established power over majority. Political rights were given to a selected few. Non-propertied people and small-time wage earners who could not pay taxes were not allowed to vote. Women, even though educated, were not given the voting right till the 1920s in some of the most developed countries like the United States of America and the United Kingdom. It is an irony that the United Kingdom colonized half of the world in the name of the Queen. However, women in general were not even given the voting right!

Women in USA demanding Right to Vote

As feminist movements gained momentum, equal voting rights were given to women in the United States as well as in the United Kingdom. Women were given the voting right in the United States in 1920. Unitary parliamentary democracy in Great Britain gave voting rights to women in 1928.

However, the case of racial neglect and lack of opportunities for the African-origin people derogatorily referred to as 'Blacks' remained unresolved in Europe and the United States.

Civil Rights Movement in the United States of America (1954–1968) to fight against racial segregation of African people.

However, gradual developments of events in America and Europe offered political right of choosing the representatives to almost all citizens.

Note

Indian Constitution offered equal voting and citizenship rights to both men and women immediately after achieving independence from British colonial power in 1947.

Original copy of the Articles of Confederation came into force on 1st March, 1781 that served as the first constitution of the United States of America.

In 1789, the present-day constitution came into effect.

INDIA GAINS INDEPENDENCE FROM BRITISH COLONIALISTS

From around 1600–1947 British looted, plundered, and controlled the society, economy, and politics of India. The reigns of the country passed on from the British East India Company to the British Crown in 1857 after the Sepoy Mutiny that united several kingdoms and states of India.

Trivia

Sepoy Mutiny means mutiny or revolt of the 'sepoys' or soldiers. A soldier is called 'Sipahi' in Hindi. The British pronounced 'Sipahi' as 'Sepoy' and hence the name 'Sepoy Mutiny'.

INTERESTING FACTS

- Revolt of 1857 or sepoy mutiny.
- First major united rebellion in India against the East India Company.
- Immediate cause of the revolt was introduction of greased cartridges.
- The cartridges were believed to contain animal (pig and cow) fat which had to be removed with mouth before throwing. Both Hindu and Muslim soldiers found it against their religious beliefs.
- Rebellion started in Meerut (Uttar Pradesh) and spread all across the country with local leaders and royalty joining in big numbers.
- Rani Lakshmi Bai, Mangal Pandey, and Bahadur Shah Zafar were some of the prominent leaders of the revolt.
- British Crown took over the rule of India from the East India Company after the revolt.
- The Indian rebels were defeated by British in 1858.

Rani Lakshmi Bai, the Queen of Jhansi, who fought valiantly and sacrificed her life in the battlefield

After the revolt of 1857, sporadic revolts for independence continued in several parts of the country. This was also the period of social reformations brought in by educated Indian intellectuals. Great personalities like Swami Dayanand Saraswati, Raja Ram Mohan Roy, and Jyotiba Phule contributed immensely in abolishing social evils such as sati, child marriage, purdah system, caste system, and untouchability. They also motivated people for encouraging women's education and widow remarriage. Social reformations went parallel to political struggle.

PERSONALITY	FIELD OF WORK
Swami Dayananda Saraswati	Reformation in Hinduism; founded Arya Samaj
Jyotiba Phule	Abolition of untouchability and encouraged women's education; opened schools for women
Raja Ram Mohan Roy	Socio-religious reformation movement; founded the Brahmo Samaj; considered as 'Father of Indian Renaissance'
Ishwar Chandra Vidyasagar	Educator and social reformer worked for simplification of Bengali alphabets; worked tirelessly to legalize widow remarriage and was instrumental in passing the Age of Consent Act 1891 (minimum age for consummation of marriage was set at 12 years)
Anne Besant	British socialist who worked for Indian Nationalism; first women President of Indian National Congress

Struggle for Independence

As we move ahead with the timeline of events of this great country, it is imperative to mention the struggle for independence from British colonialists in the early twentieth century. Without getting into the details of the freedom struggle, this chapter tries to touch upon certain prominent events and personalities who played a significant role in gaining freedom from the shackles of British imperialists.

A picture diary of the major events would be able to provide information on what the country went through during the period (1900–47).

1915: Gandhi returns to India from South Africa and plunged into the struggle for freedom. He introduced the concept of Satyagraha and non-violence.

1905: Abanindranath Tagore draws the image of Bharat Mata personifying the feeling of nationalism.

Bankim Chandra Chattopadhyay gave the concept of Bharat Mata as a personification of Bharat/India the nation before the pictorial representation of the same by Abanindranath Tagore.

1917: Satyagraha in Champaran

Satyagraha refers to holding on to truth. Gandhi introduced the concept of Satyagraha and practised resistance through non-violence.

Similar Satyagrahas also took place in Ahmedabad Cotton Mills (1918) and Kheda, Gujarat (1917).

13 April 1919, General O Dwyer ordered the troops to fire on peaceful protestors in the Jallianwala Bagh (park), Amritsar, Punjab. The only exit from the park was closed. The Baisakhi mela was also going on and there was a crowd of men, women, and children. The troops fired continuously at everyone until they ran out of ammunition.

It was one of the most horrific incidents of India's freedom struggle. The bullet marks on the walls still remain.

Gandhi realized that the British was successful in dominating India with the help of Indians. So, if the Indians resorted to non-cooperation with the British, the colonialists would not be able to run the administration. So, he called upon the people of India to peacefully non-cooperate with the government.

On 1 August 1920, Mahatma Gandhi called for nation-wide Non-Cooperation Movement. People were asked to give up titles, jobs given by the government, not to attend courts, schools, and colleges run by the government, and discard foreign-made goods including clothes.

The movement was called off in 1922 after the Chauri Chaura incident when protestors turned violent and burnt a police station at Chauri Chaura wherein 22 policemen were burnt alive.

This movement became a mass movement.

The British believed and propagated the policy of 'divide and rule'. As India is a country of diversity in terms of religion, race, culture, language, etc., it was easy for British to spread the feeling of doubt, suspicion, and hatred among the different communities. Gandhi realized the significance of a united people in front of the common enemy. So, in order to foster a spirit of Hindu-Muslim unity, he convinced the Indian National Congress to join the Khilafat Movement.

The Khilafat Movement of 1920 was called by the Indian Muslims to support the cause of the Ottoman Empire in Turkey. The two brothers Mohd Ali and Shaukat Ali were the Khilafat leaders. The Indian National Congress under Gandhi's leadership supported the movement.

In **1927**, the British parliament sent a commission of seven members to India to review and recommend constitutional reforms. The commission was led by Sir John Simon.

The Simon Commission boycotted by Indian National Congress and Muslim League due to non-inclusion of any Indian member. There were large-scale protests, hartals all over the country.

The protestors moved with the slogan 'Go Back Simon'.

Trivia:

One of the members of Simon Commission was Clement Richard Attlee who later became the prime minister of Great Britain.

1929: In October, Lord Irwin announced a vague offer of dominion status for India. This led to Declaration of 'Purna Swaraj' or complete independence in the Lahore Session of Congress the same year. Under the leadership of Jawaharlal Nehru, the date 26 January 1930 was announced as the Independence Day of India.

1930s is the period of severe turmoil in various parts of India, spreading to the countryside as well. Dr. B.R. Ambedkar formed the **Depressed Classes Association** so that the Scheduled Classes get equal representation in the elections and they may take part in the decision making of the country.

Dr. Ambedkar later became the chairman of the Constituent Assembly that drafted the Constitution of India.

DISCUSSION

Mahatma Gandhi encouraged a peaceful mass movement. He very well realized that to defeat the economically strong British, only a handful of people resorting to violence would not serve the purpose. He wanted each and every family to come out on the streets to protest and create such disobedience that it becomes unmanageable for the British. In order to touch the heart of every Indian, he thought of one thing that all Indians rich and poor alike. So, he focussed on breaking salt law (salt is a product used by all). Any other issue would have been class specific, but salt was for all. Indians till then were using salt provided by the government.

Gandhi marching towards coastal village Dandi from Sabarmati Ashram (Gujarat) to make salt and break the Salt Law on 12 March 1930. This was the beginning of Civil Disobedience Movement that aimed at disobeying the government.

Women preparing salt at home.

Breaking the salt law and making salt indigenously was a historic move. All sections of society overwhelmingly supported Gandhi. Civil Disobedience Movement became a countrywide agitation.

On 5 March 1931, Gandhi-Irwin Pact was signed and Civil Disobedience Movement was called off. There was a large-scale resentment among the revolutionaries who were confident of earning freedom through this mass movement that touched every corner of the country. Gandhi was called for the Second Round Table Conference in London. However, the conference failed to achieve desired outcome; Gandhi returned to India and relaunched the Civil Disobedience Movement. But this time, Gandhi did not receive support from several sections of people. By 1934, the movement lost momentum.

The Government of India Act was passed in 1935. This act gave provincial autonomy aiming at establishing Federal Polity in India. Elections were held in 1937. Out of 11 princely states, Congress won in 8. So, every princely state had a prime minister who had to work under a British governor. The act provided separate electorate for Sikhs, Muslims, and others but not to depressed classes.

On **8 August 1942, Quit India Movement** was launched under the leadership of Gandhi demanding complete independence from British Crown. 'Quit India' was a demand by Indians to British to 'quit' or leave India forever.

The Quit India Movement or popularly called Bharat Chodo Aandolan ended in 1945. However, it opened doors for the eventual independence of India in 1947. The movement saw emergence of new leaders from Muslim League, Hindu Mahasabha, and Rashtriya Swayam Sevak Sangh as most of the leaders of Indian National Congress were arrested.

The British realized the difficulty of controlling India after this united mass movement. Moreover, United Kingdom's involvement in the Second World War impacted its treasury heavily. Maintaining India became an economic challenge for Britain. This led to the final step of declaration of independence of India on **15 August 1947**.

But, the colonialists created unrest at this juncture by dividing the country on communal lines. There were several unresolved issues related to borders between India and Pakistan. These issues still remain unresolved.

Partition of India had been one of the darkest chapters of British rule in the country. Communal violence reached such a level that trains full of dead bodies crossed the borders. Thousands of people were killed in riots on both sides. People were left homeless over-night.

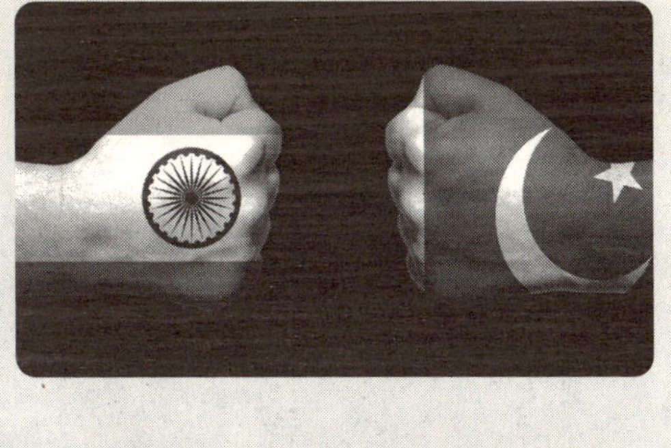

Though independence was a long cherished dream, yet the price paid was too heavy.

Note:

Communal feelings developed among the general masses due to a complex combination of factors including religious tensions fueled by political rhetoric and instances of communal violence. This feeling of fear and doubt of one community over the other reached its peak leading to division of the country on communal lines as India and Pakistan.

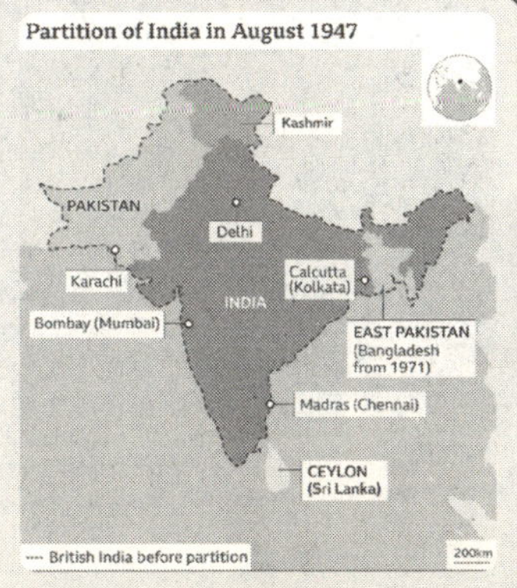

> ***Food for Thought***
>
> The Indian democracy that we see today is an outcome of all the past historical events and influences. It is pertinent to know the historic past in order to understand the democracy of present times.
>
> The Constitution of India is a document that encapsulates all the past experiences to give a society and polity that is based on equality, liberty, and justice to all so that peaceful co-existence is ensured.

INTEGRATION OF THE PRINCELY INDIAN STATES INTO THE INDIAN UNION POST-INDEPENDENCE

What Is a Princely State?

During the rule of the British Crown, some of the states or kingdoms of India were directly under the British government and the rest were run by their hereditary rulers under the guidance of the British Crown. These were the princely states. The British did not participate in the internal matters of the princely states. There were over 500 princely states in India prior to independence. These princely states had revenue-sharing agreement with the British Crown. There were also a few enclaves run by France and Portugal as their colonies.

The Indian Independence Act 1947 gave the option to the princely states to join either India or Pakistan or to remain as sovereign states.

The Constitution makers of India had foreseen the danger and impending instability that came with this option with princely states. They wanted to create a strong India leaving no scope for cessation or revolt or any foreign intervention.
The first home minister of India, Sardar Vallabhbhai Patel along with V. P. Menon, Secretary of State Department, set out to integrate all the princely states into the Indian Union. In January 1947, months before the declaration of independence, Jawaharlal Nehru refused to accept the 'Divine Right of Kings'. Over the next few years, Patel and Menon were successful in bringing most of these princely states under the Union of India, sometimes using coercion and sometimes diplomacy. These efforts by Patel earned him the title **Iron Man of India** who helped India to be one strong union of states.

However, Jammu and Kashmir and Manipur remained out of this arrangement due to insurgency and other factors.

Note:

Manipur became a union territory in 1956 and full-fledged state in 1971. Jammu and Kashmir is administered by Indian government as a union territory.

PRINCELY STATES THAT WERE NOT READY TO JOIN INDIAN UNION INITIALLY

Hyderabad	Wished to join Pakistan	Annexed by Indian Army
Travancore	Wished to stay independent	Convinced through talks
Jammu & Kashmir	Wished to stay independent	Series of discussion and dialogue for decision making
Junagadh	Wished to join Pakistan	Annexed by Indian Army
Bhopal	Wished to stay independent	Convinced through talks
Jodhpur	Wished to join Pakistan	Convinced through talks
Manipur	Faced threat from communists Party of Burma	Joined through talks

The Statue of Unity stands tall in Gujarat (India) today as a mark of respect for Sardar Vallabhbhai Patel (1875–1950).

CONSTITUTIONAL DESIGN (EVOLUTION OF INDIAN CONSTITUTION)

The Constitution of India is known as a 'living document' as it has been given the scope of innumerable amendments by the constitution makers so that it can serve the changing needs of time.

The journey of evolution of the Constitution of India embodies the values, ethos of the rich cultural past coupled with the various acts and policies of the East India Company and British administration that ruled India till 1947. It is because of this reason the historical past of this country has been discussed. This entire process of evolution can be divided into two phases: one from 1773 to 1858 and the second one from 1858 to 1947. The first phase can be referred to as Company rule and the second phase can be called British Crown rule.

Following is a timeline of all the policies and acts passed by the aforementioned to rule over Indian subjects.

Company Rule

1773: Regulating Act was passed by British parliament to regulate affairs of the East India Company.

1781: Amending Act passed to amend the faults of the Regulating Act.

1784: Pitts India Act introduced the system of decentralized administration.

1786: Act of 1786 brought in judicial reforms; codification of civil and criminal laws; appointment of collector and registrar courts.

1793: Charter Act extended the company's trade monopoly in India for 20 years.

1813: Charter Act ended company's trade monopoly in East. Tea trading was allowed.

1833: Charter Act drafted Indian Penal Code (IPC); Governor General of India appointed.

1853: Charter Act formed Indian (Central) Legislative Council; legislative and executive functions separated.

Crown Rule

1858: Government of India Act transferred power of governance to British Crown.

1861: Indian Council's Act included Indians in the law-making process; representative institutions came in.

1892: Indian Council's Act included more Indians in legislative councils.

1909: Indian Council's Act legalized 'Communalism'; also called Morley-Minto Reforms.

1919: Government of India Act is also called 'mini constitution'; formed the basis of Indian Constitution.

1935: Government of India Act established the Federal Court (leading to Supreme Court of India); Burma (Myanmar) was separated from India; steps taken towards establishment of 'Federation of India' (British India provinces and princely states).

1947: Government of India Act brought in the Mountbatten Plan of partition of India.

The process of drafting and adopting the Constitution after Independence and Partition of the country as India and Pakistan

1947 (29 August): Drafting Committee appointed Dr. B.R. Ambedkar as chairman.

1948 (16 July): Vice presidents of the Constituent Assembly appointed. They were H.C. Mookerjee and V.T. Krishnamachari.

1949 (26 November): Constitution of India passed and adopted by assembly.

1950 (24 January): Constitution of India signed and accepted.

1950 (26 January): Constitution of India came into force .

FIRST HAND-WRITTEN CONSTITUTION OF INDIA

FACT FILE

- The first demand for a Constituent Assembly for drafting of Indian Constitution was raised by the communist leader Mahendra Nath Roy in 1934.
- Prem Behari Narain Raizada was the calligrapher who wrote the Constitution of India in his beautiful flowing handwriting.
- It took 2 years 11 months 17 days were taken to complete the Constitution.
- The original text of the Constitution contained 395 articles in 22 parts and eight schedules. The number has increased since then because of amendments over the years.

Establishment of Democratic Form of Government in India

The Drafting Committee of the Constitution of India, realizing the diversity of Indian populace in all aspects of culture, tradition, community, religion, race, and language, adopted the parliamentary democratic form of government. It has a federal structure with unitary features.

India as a Quasi-Federation

India has a three-tier system of government. The central government, the state governments, and local/rural governments. For maintaining unity and upholding diversity of the states, the administration functions in accordance to the three lists mentioned in the Constitution of India. These are Union List, State List, and Concurrent List.

This was taken from the Government of India Act 1935.

Union List

Union/central government can make laws

- Defence, Foreign affairs, communications

State List

State governments can make laws

- Agriculture, police, public health, sanitation, etc.

Concurrent List

Both centre and state can make laws (in case of differences, union government's decision prevails)

- Marriage, adoption, forests, education, etc.

Residuary subjects: There are some subjects known as residuary, in which union government makes laws. Example: IT, software.

TIERS OF INDIAN GOVERNMENT

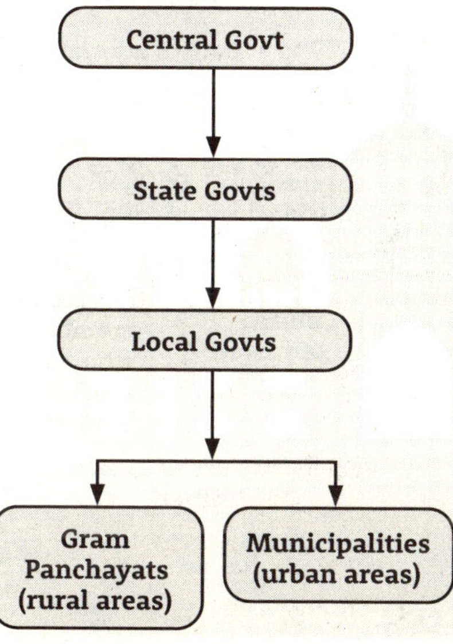

BRANCHES OF INDIAN GOVERNMENT

- **Executive**
  - President/ Vice President
  - Prime Minister
  - Council of Ministers
- **Legislature**
  - 2 Houses of Parliament
    - Lok Sabha (Lower House)
    - Rajya Sabha (Upper House)
- **Judiciary**
  - Supreme Court
  - State High Courts
  - District Courts/ Sessions Courts

FACT FILE

- Lok Sabha members are directly elected by the citizens of India.
- 238 members of Rajya Sabha are elected by the state legislative assemblies and union territories.
- 12 members are nominated to Rajya Sabha by the president for their contributions to the various fields of art, culture, sports, social work, etc.

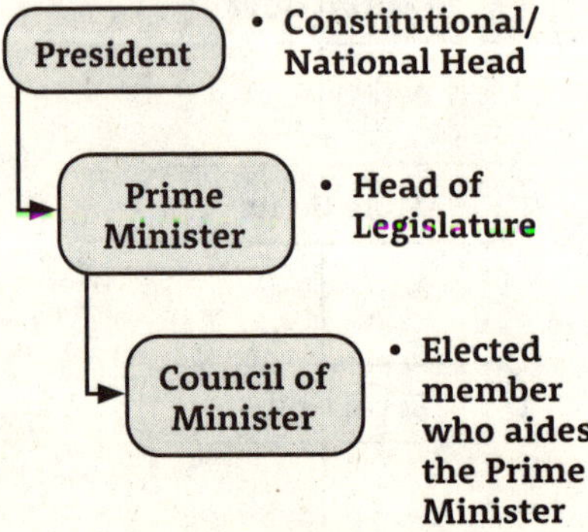

Basic Structure of Indian Government

FACT FILE

The Government of India is structured in the Westminster system, which is still followed in England; a parliamentary democracy with elected legislature, independent judiciary, and ceremonial head of the state, the Crown, though India has an elected nominal head of state as president.

PREAMBLE TO THE CONSTITUTION OF INDIA

The Constitution of India starts with the Preamble:

'WE, THE PEOPLE OF INDIA having solemnly resolved to constitute India into a SOVEREIGN SOCIALIST SECULAR DEMOCRATIC REPUBLIC and to secure to all its citizens:

JUSTICE, social, economic and political;

LIBERTY of thought, expression, belief, faith and worship;

EQUALITY of status and of opportunity; and to promote among them all

FRATERNITY assuring the dignity of the individual and the unity and integrity of the Nation;

IN OUR CONSTITUENT ASSEMBLY this twenty-sixth day of November, 1949, do HEREBY ADOPT, ENACT AND GIVE TO OURSELVES THIS CONSTITUTION'

The Preamble is an introduction or preface to the Constitution of India. It is the soul of the Constitution that carries the underlying values that the Constitution stands for. Though it is not enforceable in the court of law, yet it has been serving as a guiding force in interpreting the Constitution by the courts.

Brief Explanation of the Terms Mentioned in the Preamble

Sovereign: India is an independent country and is not subject to the control of any external power. This is taken from the Constitution of Ireland.

Socialist: India follows democratic socialism so that socialist goals are achieved through democratic means without any violence. This is added to the Preamble by the 42nd Amendment in 1976.

Secular: Refers to equality of all religions within the country. Every citizen is free to practise his/her own religion. So, there is no state religion in India. This was added to the Preamble by the 42nd Amendment in 1976.

Democratic: India is run by elected representatives chosen by the people of the country. Universal Adult Suffrage is practised in the country without any biases.

Republic: The head of the state in India is democratically elected for a fixed term. No hereditary or propriety right is practised in the country.

Justice: The Constitution of India ensures social, political, and economic justice to the people of India.

- Social Justice means no one can be discriminated on the basis of caste, creed, race, religion, gender, or place of birth. There is no concept of any privileged class in society.
- Political justice means all citizens have equal right to vote and participate in the electoral process.
- Economic justice means equal distribution of wealth and resources in the country. Equal opportunities are given to all citizens to earn their living.

Liberty: Refers to the freedom to do things that one wants within constitutional limits and without harming anybody.

Equality: Every citizen is equal in the eyes of law and everybody would be given equal opportunities.

Fraternity: Spread the feeling of brotherhood and oneness in the country.

FACT FILE

- 26th November is celebrated as 'Samvidhaan Day' or 'Constitution Day' in India.
- The original handwritten Preamble to the Constitution was designed by Artist Beohar Rammanohar Sinha and carries his signature as 'Ram' in the extreme left corner.

Fundamentals Rights and Duties

Fundamental Rights mean the basic rights that a person requires to live. Article 12–35 of the Constitution provides the Fundamental Rights for the citizens of India. Article 12 and 13 define state and laws.

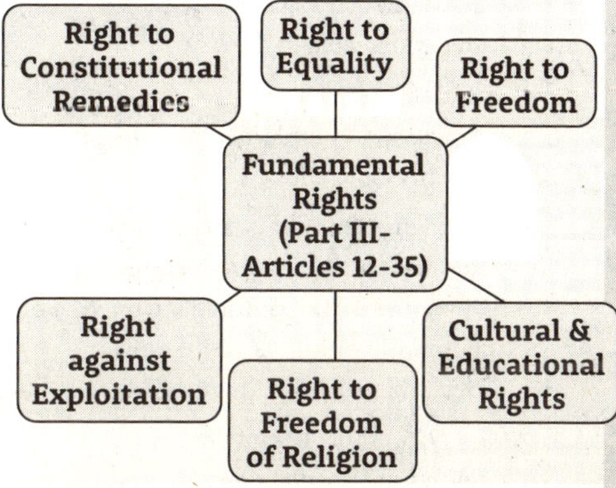

Right to equality (Articles 14–18): All citizens of India are equal. There cannot be any discrimination on the basis of caste, creed, gender, place of birth, religion, or language.

Right to freedom (Articles 19–22): Constitution guarantees all citizens of the country freedom of expression, speech, to assemble without arms, to practice any profession, and to reside in any part of the country. However, there are certain limitations on these as one's freedom cannot be harmful to others in society.

Right against exploitation (Articles 23–24): Exploitation in any form is strictly prohibited under the Constitution of India. Child labour, human trafficking, and any kind of forced labour are prohibited. Even forced service by government is not allowed by the Constitution.

Right to freedom of religion (Articles 25–28): Citizens are given the right to practice any religion of their choice.

Cultural and educational rights (Articles 29–30): Constitution gives equal rights to people including those belonging to minority groups to practise and protect their culture, traditions, and heritage.

Right to constitutional remedies (Articles 31–35): This right gives the citizens the right to approach the court if any of their fundamental rights are violated.

FACT FILE

- Fundamental Rights are enforceable in the court of law.
- Violation of Fundamental Rights is a punishable offence.
- Fundamental Rights mentioned in the Constitution are inspired by England's Bill of Rights, United States' Bill of Rights, and France's Declaration of the Rights of Man.
- In 1925, Annie Besant demanded seven fundamental rights in drafting the Commonwealth of India Bill.

Fundamental Duties

The constitution makers put forth certain moral obligations on the citizens of India. These are called Fundamental Duties, mentioned in Part IV (A) of the Constitution.

Citizens are advised and expected to carry on these duties so that the peaceful co-existence of all is made possible and the basic values of a democratic way of life are maintained. These duties are not enforceable in the court of law.

Fundamental Duties Mentioned in the Constitution

Article 51A says,

'It shall be the duty of every citizen of India—

(a) to abide by the Constitution and respect its ideals and institutions, the National Flag and the National Anthem;

(b) to cherish and follow the noble ideals which inspired our national struggle for freedom;

(c) to uphold and protect the sovereignty, unity and integrity of India;

(d) to defend the country and render national service when called upon to do so;

(e) to promote harmony and the spirit of common brotherhood amongst all the people of India transcending religious, linguistic and regional or sectional diversities; to renounce practices derogatory to the dignity of women;

(f) to value and preserve the rich heritage of our composite culture;

(g) to protect and improve the natural environment including forests, lakes, rivers and wild life, and to have compassion for living creatures;

(h) to develop the scientific temper, humanism and the spirit of inquiry and reform; (i) to safeguard public property and to abjure violence;

(j) to strive towards excellence in all spheres of individual and collective activity so that the nation constantly rises to higher levels of endeavour and achievement;

(k) who is a parent or guardian to provide opportunities for education to his child or, as the case may be, ward between the age of six and fourteen years.'

(Source: The Constitution of India)

FACT FILE

Fundamental Duties (FD)

- Added to the Constitution by the 42nd Amendment 1976 on the recommendation of Swaran Singh Committee
- The idea was taken from Russian and Japanese constitutions
- Not enforceable in court

Directive Principles of State Policy (DPSP): (Part IV, Articles 36–51)

The Constitution of India gives certain directions to the state/government to take into consideration these principles while formulating new laws. These Directive Principles were put forward so that social order is maintained and welfare of all citizens is ensured. It is the moral duty of the state to apply these principles in making laws. So, these are fundamental to good governance.

These principles aim at establishing a welfare state wherein socio-economic justice is ensured to all citizens.

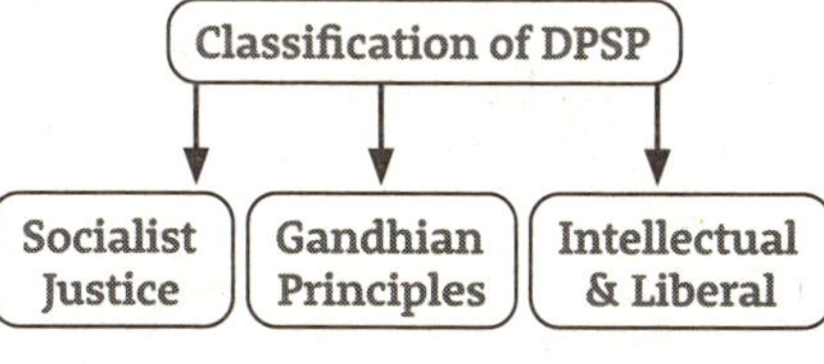

FACT FILE

- Directive Principles of State Policy are inspired by Constitution of Ireland & United Nations Universal Declaration of Human Rights.

States and Union Territories

India is the seventh largest country in the world with 28 states, 7 Union Territories (UT), and 640 districts, as per Census 2011. All the states as well as UTs have their state governments run by different political parties.

Interesting Facts

Largest state: Rajasthan (3,42,239 sq. km)

Smallest state: Goa (3,702 sq. km). Goa had been a Portuguese colony even after independence of India from British. In 1961, Indian Army attacked and ended Portuguese control over Goa. It was merged with India as a UTand declared a state in 1987.

Smallest UT: Lakshadweep (32 sq. km)

- Each of the eight northeastern states share international borders with one or more countries like China, Myanmar, Bhutan, Nepal, and Bangladesh.
- Eight UTs of India are Andaman and Nicobar Islands, Chandigarh, Dadra and Nagar Haveli and Daman and Diu (one UT), Delhi, Puducherry, Jammu and Kashmir, Ladakh, Lakshadweep.

Do you know?

Difference between state and union territory:

- State is a larger division within the country. It has its own elected state government. Union territory is smaller than a state and is directly run by the union government through a governor as the representative of the president.
- Delhi, Puducherry, Jammu and Kashmir are UTs that received partial statehood. So, they have their own elected legislative assembly and council of ministers with a chief minister.
- Jammu & Kashmir Reorganization Act, 2019, was passed to reconstitute J & K as two UTs, namely, Jammu & Kashmir and Ladakh.
- Delhi was redefined as National Capital Territory and larger areas like Ghaziabad, Noida (in UP) and Faridabad, Gurugram (in Haryana) were added as National Capital Region (NCR).

Important Institutions (Legislature, Executive, Judiciary)

Legislature: Parliament

Legislature: Parliament at Union Level

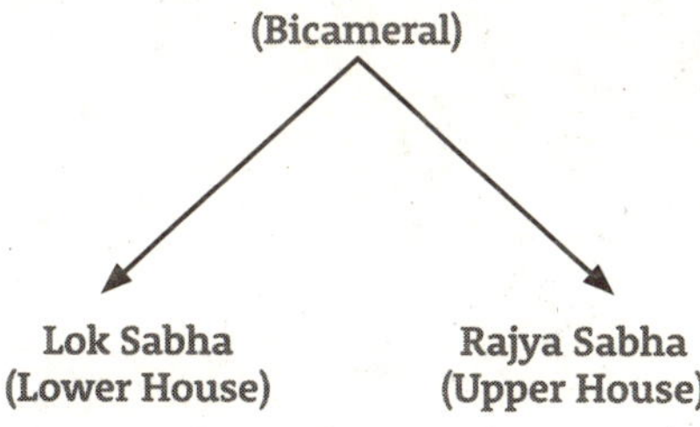

Assemblies: at State Level

Unicameral Legislative assembly/ Vidhan Sabha

Bicameral Legislative Council

(Note: 22 states and 3 UTs have Unicameral legislature; 6 states have bicameral legislatures; 5 UTs are directly run by union government.)

Legislature is called the Parliament in India. The country has a bicameral legislature, meaning, it has two houses, namely, Lok Sabha and Rajya Sabha.

Lok Sabha

- Also called Lower House of Parliament.
- All elected representatives from all over the country sit here together to take part in debate and discussions.
- Lok Sabha has 543 members.
- The political party (or combination of parties aligned together) with majority seats (members) form government.
- Leader of the majority party (chosen by the party/parties in case of alliance) becomes the prime minister and leads the Council of Ministers.
- A core group of members from the Council of Ministers forms the cabinet that aids and advises the prime minister.
- Rest of the parties sit as opposition members.
- Members are elected for five years (ministry might fall before five years for various reasons).

- All bills are discussed in the Lok Sabha.
- A bill becomes a law when passed by majority members in the Parliament and is signed by the president.

Rajya Sabha

- Also called the Upper House.
- It is composed of 245 members; 233 are elected by state and UT assemblies and 12 are nominated by the president.
- President nominates people who have contributed significantly in the fields of art, literature, sports, science, and social service.
- Members occupy office for a fixed term six years. One-third of elected members retire after every two years.
- Vice president of India presides over the sessions.
- All bills are discussed here, but no bill can be rejected; bills can be sent back to Lok Sabha for reconsideration.
- President can call for joint sessions of both houses.

Indian Parliament in Session

- The Parliament sessions are held normally three times a year – monsoon, winter, and budget sessions
- Budget session: January to April
- Monsoon session: July to August/September
- Winter session: November to December
- The president may call for emergency sessions during a national emergency

Executive

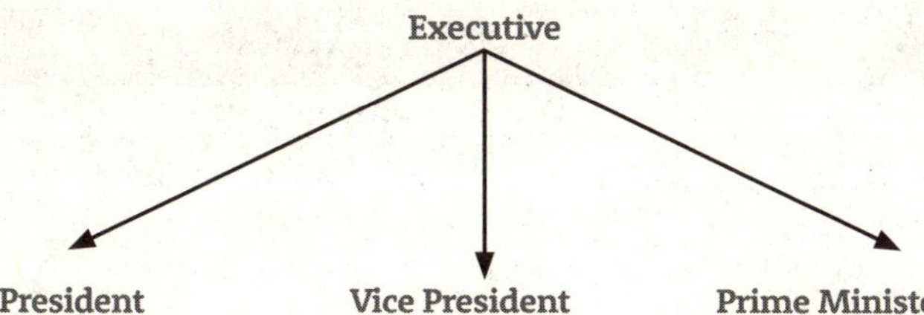

President

- Fixed tenure of five years
- Elected by Electoral College (elected members of Parliament + state assembly members)
- Ceremonial or nominal powers
- Works on advice of PM, except during emergency
- Is the supreme commander of defence forces
- Proclaim national emergency or impose president's rule, dissolve Lok Sabha
- Can grant mercy for capital punishment

Vice President

- Fixed tenure of five years
- Is the chairperson of Rajya Sabha
- Acts as president when there is sudden vacancy in the president's office
- May be removed from office by a resolution passed by both houses of the Parliament

Prime Minister with Council of Ministers

- Leader of majority party is appointed as prime minister by president
- Forms government with his Council of Ministers
- Cannot exceed five years tenure, may be removed anytime before that by own party members
- Rest of the ministers are appointed by president on the advice of PM
- A person may be appointed as minister if the PM wants even if he/she is not an elected member. Must be elected to either house within six months
- Most powerful post in India

President's House/Rashtrapati Bhavan

FACT FILE

- Presently, the official residence of the president of India, in New Delhi
- Architects were Sir Edwin Lutyen and Sir Herbert Baker (construction period 1913–30)
- Known as Viceroy's House during British rule

Presidents of India

NAME	TENURE
Dr Rajendra Prasad	26 January 1950–13 May 1962
Dr S. Radhakrishnan	13 May 1962–13 May 1967
Dr Zakir Hussain	13 May 1967–3 May 1969
Varahagiri Venkata Giri	3 May 1969–20 July 1969
Mohammad Hidayatullah	20 July 1969–24 August 1969
Varahagiri Venkata Giri	24 August 1969–24 August 1974
Fakhruddin Ali Ahmed	24 August 1974–11 February 1977
Basappa Danappa Jatti	11 February 1977–24 July 1977
Neelam Sanjiva Reddy	25 July 1977–25 July 1982
Giani Zail Singh	25 July 1982–25 July 1987
Ramaswamy Venkataraman	25 July 1987–25 July 1992
Shankar Dayal Sharma	25 July 1992–25 July 1997
Kocheril Raman Narayanan	25 July 1997–25 July 2002
Dr A. P. J. Abdul Kalam	25 July 2002–25 July 2007
Pratibha Patil	25 July 2007–25 July 2012
Pranab Mukherjee	25 July 2012–25 July 2017
Shri Ram Nath Kovind	25 July 2017–21 July 2022
Droupadi Murmu	21 July 2022–present

India's first president, Dr Rajendra Prasad, was the longest serving president. He served for two consecutive tenures of 12 years (1950–62).

Judiciary

The Supreme Court of India Dharma Chakra (Architect: Ganesh Bhikaji Deolalikar)

Emblem of Supreme Court–Ashoka Stambh with Dharma Chakra Inscription: 'Yatodharmastato jayah' (Truth Alone I Uphold)

- India has an independent judiciary system that interprets the Constitution in total neutrality. At the helm of judiciary is the Supreme Court of India headed by the Chief Justice of India. Every high court also has a chief justice.
- There are high courts in almost all states and UTs of India.
- Lower in the hierarchy stands the district courts and then revenue courts.

EVOLUTION OF THE JUDICIAL SYSTEM OF INDIA

Judicial System in Ancient India

- Vedas, shashtras, and smritis were consulted and interpreted before delivering justice.
- The ancient king was not above law but was subject to law.
- Manusmriti, a significant legal text of ancient India, clarifies that rule of law or 'dharma' is most superior. It is the ultimate power and even the king must obey.
- Kautilya in *Arthasashtra* (fourth to third century BCE) mentions that the welfare of the king depends on the welfare of his people.
- In the Mauryan Empire (322–298 BCE), administrative units were divided as
  - *Sthaniya* (centre of 800 villages) – modern districts
  - *Dronamukha* (centre of 400 villages) – tehsils
  - *Kharvatika* (centre of 200 villages) – Parganas
  - *Sangrahana* (centre of ten villages) – law courts were established here. Courts had three dharmastha (jurists) and three amatya (ministers).
- Some of the famous jurists of ancient India were Manu, Yajnavalkya, Katyayana, Brihaspati.
- The family court was the lowest court and highest was the king's court.
- *Pradvivaka*, the chief justice, other judges, ministers, and the Brahmanas (council members) guided the king in delivering justice.

Judicial System in Medieval India

- Medieval times are dominated by the court system of the Delhi Sultanate (1206–1526) and Mughal period's court administration (1526–1755).
- Sultan (king) as head of the state, was the sole authority to deliver justice in both the times of Delhi Sultanate as well as in the Mughal era.
- Religious convictions formed the basis of Islamic law.

Judicial System in Colonial Period

- The East India Company introduced 'common laws'.
- In 1726, the company established mayor's courts in Madras, Bombay, and Calcutta (modern day Chennai, Mumbai, and Kolkata).
- British gradually replaced Hindu laws (based on dharma) and Muslim laws with Western laws.
- The Regulatory Act of 1773 paved way to establish a Supreme Court in Calcutta.

(Note: Major Acts of British era are already mentioned above that were instrumental in the establishment of present judicial system of India.)

Electoral Politics

Elections form the most important phase of a democratic country. In India, Lok Sabha and Vidhan Sabha elections become a grand occasion with huge gatherings in election rallies to non-stop media coverage.

The constitutional democracy in India necessitates regular free and fair elections to choose members of the Parliament, assemblies of states and union territories, and the office of the president and vice president of India.

General elections in India for election of members of Lok Sabha leading to a new central government are one of the biggest events in the world as India is the second most populous country in the world. The Election Commission of India is responsible for conducting this huge event in the most efficient way.

Election Commission of India:

- Established in 1950, under Article 324 of the Constitution of India
- Headquartered in New Delhi
- Headed by the Chief Election Commissioner
- Assisted by chief electoral officers in states
- Candidates file their nominations with EC

Consider the following facts to understand the vastness of this event in India

- Population of India is estimated to be 1.4286 billion (2023).
- The size of the Indian electorate is as big as 36 democracies in the world combined.
- The voting age was reduced from 21 years to 18 years in 1989 by 61st Constitutional Amendment.
- The Election Commission (EC) announces the date of elections, starting and ending dates of election campaigns.
- There are 543 constituencies in India; one member from each is elected.

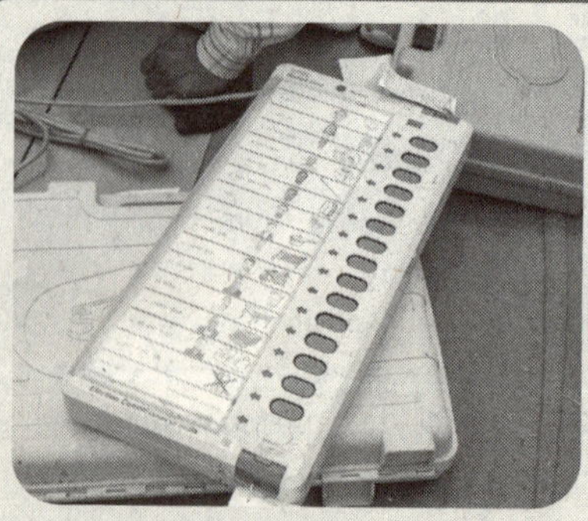

Electronic voting machine (EVM):

- First used in 1982, Kerala elections, now used all over India.
- 'None of the above' (NOTA) option in EVM was first used in 2014 elections.
- EVMs are not connected to any Wi-Fi or Bluetooth in India; these are stand-alone machines.
- Small printer (voter verified paper audit trail or VVPAT) is attached to EVMs, which gives a paper slip printout of the choice made by voter. Within 10 seconds this slip falls into the sealed box attached.

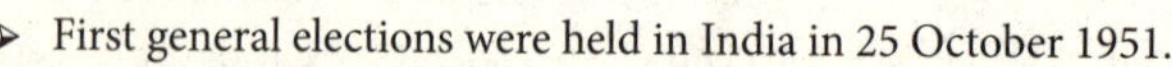

- First general elections were held in India in 25 October 1951.

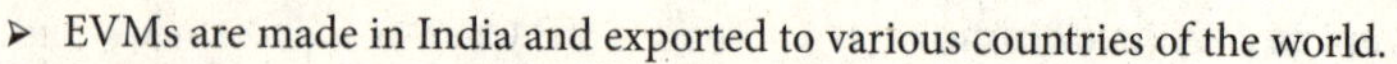

- EVMs are made in India and exported to various countries of the world.
- There were around 912 million eligible voters in India in 2019.

Political Parties in India

India follows a multi-party system. All parties must be registered with EC. A party is given the status of national party and state or regional party by the EC on the basis of certain criteria.

Current Statistics Published by EC

- There are six national parties in India.
- There are 58 state parties.
- All parties choose a symbol from the list of symbols given by EC.

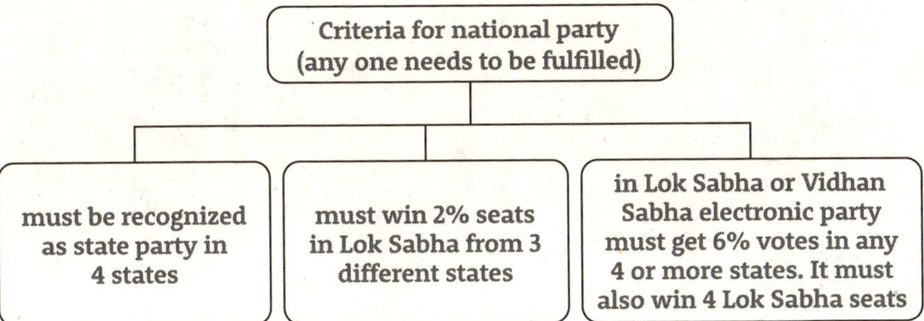

LIST OF POLITICAL PARTIES IN INDIA

National Parties

SYMBOL	NAME	ABBREVIATION	YEAR OF FOUNDATION
	Indian National Congress	INC	1885
	Communist Party of India–Marxist	CPI-M	1964
	Bhartiya Janta Party	BJP	1980
	Bahujan Samaj Party	BSP	1984
	National People's Party	NPP	2013
	Aam Admi Party	AAP	2012

Regional Parties

SYMBOL	NAME	ABBREVIATION	YEAR OF FOUNDATION
	Trinamool Congress	TMC	1998
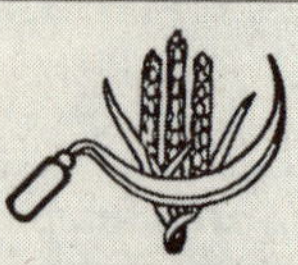	Communist Party of India	CPI	1925
	Janta Dal (Secular)	JD(S)	1999
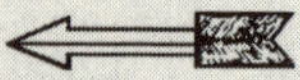	Janta Dal (United)	JD(U)	2003
	All India Anna Dravida Munnetra Kazhagam	AIADMK	1972
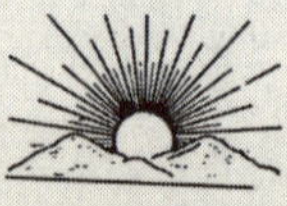	Dravida Munnetra Kazhagam	DMK	1949
	Lok Janshakti Party (Ram Vilas)	LJP	2000
	Naga People's Front		2002
	Nationalist Congress Party		1999

	Rashtriya Janata Dal	RJD	1997
	Telugu Desam Party	TDP	1982
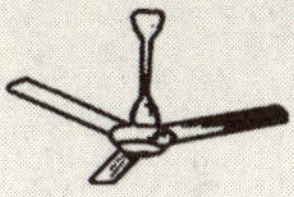	YSR Congress Party		2011
	All India Forward Bloc		1939
	All India Majlis-e-Ittehadul Muslimeen	AIMIM	1927
	All India N.R. Congress		2011
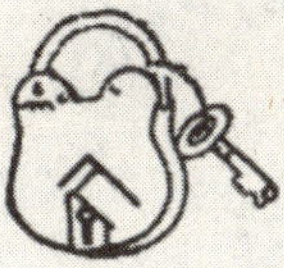	All India United Democratic Front		2005
	All Jharkhand Students Union		1986
	Apna Dal (Sonelal)		2016
	Asom Gana Parishad	AGP	1985

	Bharat Rashtra Samithi	BRS	2001
	Biju Janata Dal	BJD	1997
	Bodoland People's Front	BPF	2005
	Communist Party of India (Marxist–Leninist) Liberation		1974
	Desiya Murpokku Dravida Kazhagam		2005
	Goa Forward Party		2016
	Hill State People's Democratic Party		1968
	Samajwadi Party	SP	1992
	Shiromani Akali Dal	SAD	1920
	Shiv Sena		1966
	Shiv Sena (Uddhav Balasaheb Thackeray)		2022

(List is not exhaustive)

- As of March 2024, there are 2,764 registered unrecognized parties in India.

Fun Facts about Prime Ministers and Chief Ministers of India

Gulzari Lal Nanda has the record of being the prime minister of India for the shortest period of time. He served from 27 May 1964 to 9 June 1964 when Prime Minister Jawaharlal Nehru suddenly died during his tenure and again from 11 January 1966 to 24 January 1966 when Lal Bahadur Shastri died.

Choudhury Charan Singh was the fifth prime minister of India and the only prime minister who never faced the Parliament.

Arvind Kejriwal, chief minister of Delhi, is the first chief minister to run the government from jail. He had been put in jail on corruption charges.

Interestingly, the Constitution of India allows a person to run government from jail till the time he is proved guilty.

Pawan Kumar Chamling, former chief minister of Sikkim, has made a record of being the longest serving chief minister. He served for 24 years.

Naveen Patnaik, former chief minister of Odisha, is the longest serving chief minister of the state. He is a prolific writer as well.

Patnaik is the only chief minister of a state who does not speak the state language fluently. He reads out his Odia speeches written in Roman alphabets.

Lalu Prasad Yadav, a former chief minister of Bihar, is the first chief minister known to have held a court under a tree.

Lalu Prasad Yadav openly says that he does not know his actual date of birth and that he follows the date given in his academic documents, which is 11 June 1948.

He is known for his sense of humour. His wife's name is Rabri Devi (a former chief minister of Bihar).

The names of his sisters-in-law are Jalebi, Raasgulla, and Paan (all food items).

He named his daughter Misa (meaning Maintenance of Internal Security Act).

Indira Gandhi (daughter of Jawaharlal Nehru) was the first and only women prime minister of India from 1966 to 1977, then again from 1980 to 1984.

Indira Gandhi was instrumental in the formation of Bangladesh as an independent country from being a part of Pakistan.

Mrs. Gandhi was the first prime minister of India to impose National Emergency from 1975 to 1977.

Local Self-Government (Rural and Urban)

Local self-government refers to government or administration at the local or grassroots level. Local self-government truly realizes the essence of democracy as government 'of the people, by the people, and for the people'.

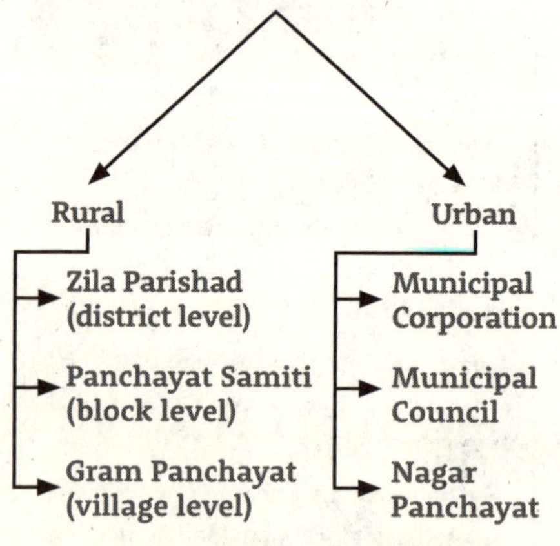

- Municipal corporation: where population is over 1 million (large areas are further divided into wards).
- Municipal council: where population is less than 1 million.
- Nagar (town) panchayat: areas in the middle of transition from rural to urban.

History of Local Self-Government in India

- Local self-government in villages have been practised in India since ancient times.
- 'Panch' means five or rule by an assembly of five village elderly.
- First elected local self-government was introduced by Lord Ripon in 1882 .
- Mahatma Gandhi supported and encouraged local self-government.
- The Constitution of India made it compulsory to hold elections in the local level after every 5 years.

- **There are 2,50,000 local self-government bodies in India.**
- **Over 3.1 million elected members.**
- **1.3 million members are women.**
- All India Institute of Local Self Government, established in 1926, guides the local bodies.
- Lord Ripon is known as 'Father of local self-government'.

Significant Government Departments/Organizations

There are 58 union ministries and 93 departments in the Indian government, headed by a union minister, minister of state bureaucrats, and other government employees. Following are some of the other significant government organizations in India:

NAME	ESTABLISHMENT DATE	FUNCTION
National Bank for Agriculture and Rural Development (NABARD)	1982	Promotion and development of agriculture, small-scale industries, etc.
Reserve Bank of India (RBI)	1935	Maintain currency and credit system of India
Securities & Exchange Board of India (SEBI)	1988	Promote and regulate investments, securities
Small Industries Development Bank of India (SIDBI)	1990	Promote and finance MSME (Micro, Small & Medium Enterprises)
Federation of Indian Chambers of Commerce and Industry (FICCI)	1927	Promote and support country's economic growth
National Association of Software and Service Companies (NASSCOM)	1988	Promote technology industry
Council of Scientific and Industrial Research (CSIR)	1942	Promote scientific research
Telecom Regulatory Authority of India (TRAI)	1997	Promote growth of telecommunication and broadcasting
Food Safety & Standards Authority of India (FSSAI)	2008	Maintain food standards and safety
Defence Research and Development Organization (DRDO)	1958	Development of defence technologies
Geological Survey of India	1851	Promote geographical surveys
Indian Council of Medical Research (ICMR)	1911	Promotion of biomedical research
Indian Council of Agricultural Research (ICAR)	1929	Promote research or agricultural development
Life Insurance Corporation of India (LIC)	1956	Promote life insurance of citizens
Central Bureau of Investigation (CBI)	1963	Investigate crimes
Directorate General of Civil Aviation (DGCA)	1946	Regulate air transport service
Union Public Service Commission (UPSC)	1926	Conduct exams for selection of administrative officers
National Human Rights Commission (NHRC)	1993	Safeguard human rights
National Green Tribunal (NGT)	2010	Conservation of environment
Sports Authority of India (SAI)	1984	Promote sportsmen through training and infrastructure
Press Council of India (PCI)	1966	Set standards for media
National Council of Educational Research and Training (NCERT)	1961	Promote quality education at school level

Interesting Facts

Ayush Ministry:

A: Ayurveda

Y: Yoga & naturopathy

U: Unani

S: Siddha

H: Homeopathy

This ministry was formed in 2014 to promote and revive ancient knowledge of medicine. Earlier it was the Department of Indian System of Medicine & Homeopathy.

First general elections of India were held between October 1951 and February 1952.

Congress under the leadership of Jawaharlal Nehru won 364 out of 489 seats.

Nehru became the first democratically elected prime minister of India.

There were 1,874 candidates and 53 parties.

27,527 polling booths were exclusively reserved for women.

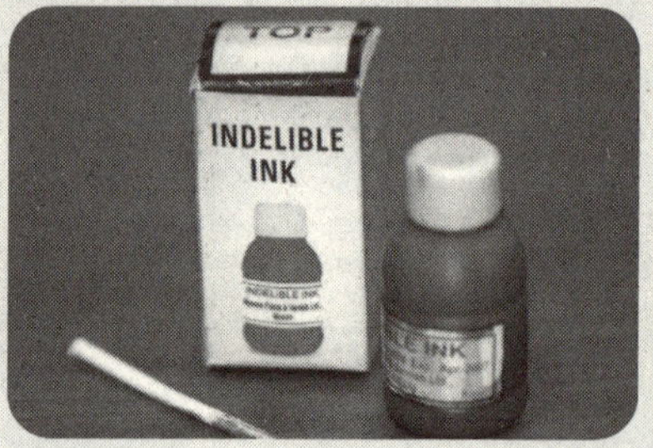

Indelible ink is applied on the left finger nail of each voter after casting vote so as to prevent duplication of vote.

It is generally believed that indelible ink was used for the first time in the third Lok Sabha elections in 1962. Mysore Paints and Varnish Ltd, based in Mysore (now Mysuru), Karnataka, was authorized to manufacture the ink. The company continues to supply this ink to this date. However, there are sources that date similar use of indelible ink back to the 1952 general election.

The Election Commission of India has set up polling booth in Banej village under Junagarh parliamentary constituency for a single voter. The voter is a priest in a temple inside Gir Forest, Gujarat.

Do you know?

The voting age in India during the first general elections in 1952 was 21 years. It was lowered to 18 years in 1988.

Here are a few more terms that will you to understand the election process in India better:

Notified Voters

Class of persons notified by the Election Commission, in consultation with the government, that they are eligible for postal ballot (they can be people from the electricity department, railways, Doordarshan, fire services, and so on).

Service Voters

Members of the armed forces, members of a force to which provisions of the Army Act, 1950, apply with or without modification, members of a state armed police force residing outside the state, or any government employee posted outside India.

Special Voters

President, vice president, governors of states, ministers of the Union or states – people holding offices to which subsection (4) of Section 20 of the Representation of the People Act, 1951, applies.

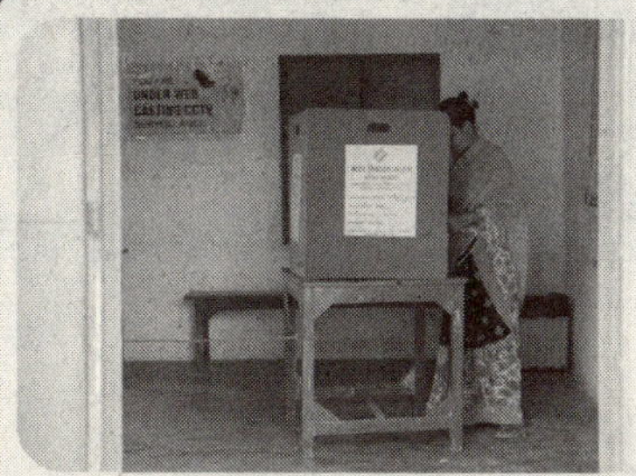

For the first time in 2014 general elections, transgenders were allowed to vote in India.

In 2019, general elections 38,325 voters registered as 'Others'.

Nirmala Sitharaman is the Union Minister for Finance & Corporate Affairs. She holds the title of giving the longest budget speech in 2020.

Her speech continued for 2 hour 42 minutes.

9 Defence and Security

DEFENCE AND SECURITY

India's defence and security system is a comprehensive and well-organized network dedicated to safeguarding national sovereignty, maintaining territorial integrity, and ensuring regional peace and stability. The Indian armed forces comprise three branches: the army, air force, and navy. The president of India serves as the supreme commander of the armed forces, while executive authority and responsibility for national security rest with the prime minister and the cabinet ministers. The Ministry of Defence specifically manages the operations of the Indian armed forces.

The armed forces are undergoing extensive modernization programmes to enhance technological capabilities and promote self-reliance. The initiatives such as 'Make in India' aim to boost domestic production of defence equipment and reduce dependency on imports. India's defence and security strategies are continually evolving to address emerging threats, reinforcing its role as a key player in both regional and global security dynamics.

EQUIVALENT RANKS OF THE INDIAN ARMED FORCES

Commissioned Ranks

INDIAN NAVY	INDIAN ARMY	INDIAN AIR FORCE
Admiral of the Fleet	Field Marshal	Marshal of the Indian Air Force
Admiral	General	Air Chief Marshal
Vice Admiral	Lieutenant General	Air Marshal
Rear Admiral	Major General	Air Vice Marshal
Commodore	Brigadier	Air Commodore
Captain	Colonel	Group Captain
Commander	Lieutenant Colonel	Wing Commander
Lieutenant Commander	Major	Squadron Leader
Lieutenant	Captain	Flight Lieutenant
Sub-Lieutenant	Lieutenant	Flying Officer

Junior Commissioned Ranks

Master Chief Petty Officer First Class	Subedar Major	Master Warrant Officer
Master Chief Petty Officer Second Class	Subedar	Warrant Officer
Chief Petty Officer	Naib Subedar	Junior Warrant Officer

Non-Commissioned Ranks

Petty Officer	Havildar/Daffadar	Sergeant
Leading Seaman	Naik/Lance-Daffadar	Corporal
Seaman 1	Lance Naik/Acting Lance-Daffadar	Leading Aircraftsman
Seaman 2	Sepoy/Sowar	Aircraftsman

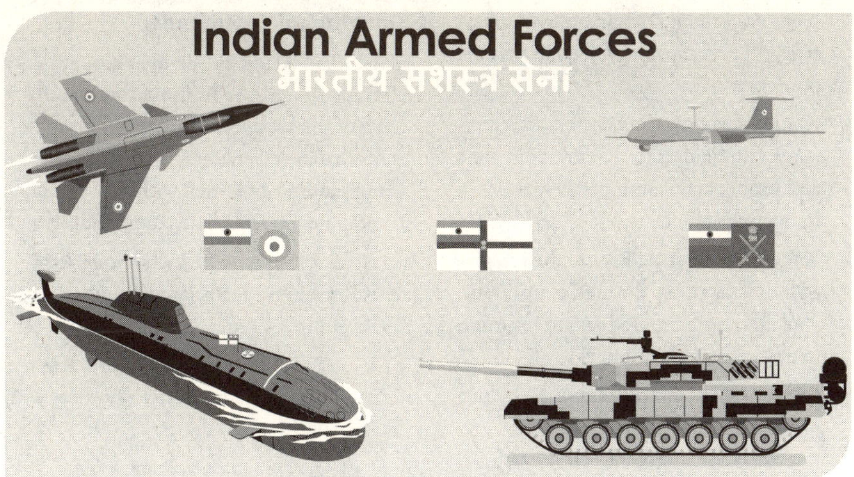

STRATEGIC DEFENCE STRUCTURE

INDIAN ARMY

The Indian Army is the largest component of India's Armed Forces and is primarily responsible for land-based military operations. It plays a crucial role in ensuring national security, maintaining peace, and defending the country against external aggression and internal threats on land.

Brief History

On 1 April 1895, the Indian Army was established under the East India Company as the British Indian Army. After the partition of India, when India became a republic on 26 January 1950, the army was established in its current format. Lieutenant General K. M. Cariappa was the first Indian Chief of the Army Staff and Commander-in-Chief of the Indian Army.

Quick Facts

Army Day: 15 January

Headquarters: New Delhi

The motto of the Indian Army: Sevā Paramo Dharmah (Service Before Self)

March of the Indian Army: Quick: Qadam Qadam Badhaye Ja (Keep stepping forward) and Slow: Samman Guard (The guard of honour)

Role of the Indian Army

The Indian Army aims to protect the nation's interests from external threats and ensure national security and integrity. Some of its primary tasks are:

- *War fighting*. Engage in combat to counter external aggression.
- *Border security*: Protect India's borders against external threats and aggression, particularly along the Line of Control (LoC) with Pakistan and the Line of Actual Control (LAC) with China.
- *Internal security management:* Address internal threats and maintain peace within the country.

- *Force projection*: Demonstrate military strength and capability beyond national borders.
- *Humanitarian assistance and disaster relief*: Offer aid during natural disasters and support civil authorities with humanitarian efforts.
- *Territorial integrity:* Ensure the integrity of India's territory through continuous vigilance and preparedness to respond to any incursions or attacks.
- *Counter-terrorism operations:* Conduct operations to neutralize terrorist threats, particularly in regions such as Jammu and Kashmir and the northeastern states.
- *Peacekeeping missions:* Contribute troops to the United Nations peacekeeping missions, helping maintain global peace and security.
- *Defence research:* Collaborate with research organizations to develop advanced military technology and strategies.
- *Construction projects:* Involved in building and maintaining critical infrastructure in remote and strategic areas, such as roads, bridges, and airstrips.
- *Educational and medical support:* Provide educational and medical services in remote and underserved regions as part of its nation-building efforts.

ORGANIZATION OF INDIAN ARMY

Chief of the Army Staff (CoAS)

The Chief of the Army Staff (CoAS) heads the Indian Army and the position is generally held by a four-star general officer. As of July 2024, the CoAS is General Upendra Dwivedi. The Vice Chief of the Army Staff (VCoAS) assists the CoAS and oversees day-to-day operations.

Operational Commands

The Indian Army has six operational commands and one training command. Each of the six operational commands is headed by a General Officer Commanding-in-Chief, with the rank of a Lieutenant General. The commands are:

- *Northern command:* Udhampur, J&K. It is responsible for Jammu and Kashmir.
- *Western command:* Chandigarh. It is responsible for the western borders with Pakistan.
- *Eastern command:* Kolkata, West Bengal. It is responsible for the eastern borders with China, Myanmar, and Bangladesh.
- *Southern command:* Pune, Maharashtra. It is responsible for the southern part of India.
- *Central command:* Lucknow, Uttar Pradesh. It is responsible for central India.
- *South western command:* Jaipur, Rajasthan. It is responsible for parts of Rajasthan and Gujarat.
- *Army training command (ARTRAC):* Shimla, Himachal Pradesh. It is responsible for training and doctrine development.

Corps

Below the operational commands, there are corps. A command generally consists of two or more corps. The corps comprises three to four divisions and is commanded by an officer of the rank of lieutenant general and comprises divisions, brigades, and battalions.

Divisions

Each corps consists of multiple divisions, each commanded by a major general. Divisions are further divided into brigades.

Brigades

A brigade is commanded by a brigadier and consists of several battalions. A division usually consists of three to four brigades.

Battalion and Regiments

Battalions and regiments are the basic fighting units within brigades. Infantry battalions are the basic fighting units. They typically consist of around 800–1,000 soldiers and are commanded by a lieutenant colonel. The armoured regiments comprise tank units and are also commanded by a lieutenant colonel. Artillery regiments provide fire support and are similarly structured.

Companies, Platoons, and Sections

Companies are the sub-units of a battalion. These are commanded by a major or captain. Platoons are the sub-units of a company. These are commanded by a lieutenant or junior commissioned officer. Sections are the smallest tactical units. These are commanded by a non-commissioned officer (NCO).

COMBAT EDGE OF THE INDIAN ARMY

Indian Army Armoured Corps

- The armoured corps is a premier combat arm of the Indian Army, specializing in armoured warfare and mechanized operations.
- It provides battlefield mobility, firepower, and protection using armoured fighting vehicles (AFVs), such as tanks and infantry fighting vehicles (IFVs). These units are utilized in offensive manoeuvres, defensive roles, and exploitation of breakthroughs in mechanized warfare scenarios.
- The armoured corps has 67 armoured regiments, including the prestigious president's bodyguard.
- An armoured corps regiment is led by an officer of colonel rank, who serves as the commandant of the unit. The regiment is structured into three sabre squadrons and a headquarter squadron. Each sabre squadron is commanded by an officer of major rank, designated as the squadron commander. An armoured regiment typically has 45–50 tanks. Each sabre squadron includes 14–15 tanks and one armoured recovery vehicle. The headquarters squadron, which includes the commandant's tank, has three tanks. Each squadron is further divided into four troops, with each troop consisting of three tanks.
- The training centre of Armoured Corps Centre & School (ACC&S) is in Ahmednagar, Maharashtra. Armour Day is celebrated on 1 May.

Infantry of the Indian Army

- It is the largest combat arm of the Indian Army. The infantry's primary role is to engage and defeat enemy ground forces in close combat. Infantry units operate on foot and are trained for combat operations.
- They are responsible for securing and holding territory, conducting offensive operations, defending positions, and performing surveillance and patrolling tasks.
- The Infantry School is the alma mater of infantry and is situated in Mhow, Madhya Pradesh.
- Infantry Day is celebrated on 27 October every year to commemorate the landing of infantry troops at Srinagar airport in 1947.

INFANTRY REGIMENTS OF THE INDIAN ARMY

NAME	YEAR OF ESTABLISHMENT	REGIMENTAL CENTRE	WAR CRY	MOTTO
Madras Regiment	1758	Wellington, Tamil Nadu	'Veera Madrassi, Adi Kollu, Adi Kollu' ('Brave Madrassi, Strike and Kill, Strike and Kill!')	'Swadharme nidhanam shreyaha' ('It is a glory to die doing one's duty')
Punjab Regiment	1761	Ramgarh Cantonment, Jharkhand	'Jo Bole So Nihal, Sat Sri Akal' ('Shout Aloud in Ecstasy, True is the Great Eternal God!'); 'Bol Jawala Ma ki jai' ('Say victory to Mother Jawala')	'Sthal wa jal' ('By land and sea')
Maratha Light Infantry	1768	Belgaum, Karnataka	'Bola Shri Chhatrapati Shivaji Maharaj ki jai, ('Say victory to Great King Shivaji,); 'Temlai Mata ki Jai' ('Victory to Mother Temlai'); 'Har Har Mahadev' ('O Lord Mahadev you are omnipresent')	'Duty, honour, courage'
Rajputana Rifles	1775	Delhi Cantonment	'Raja Ramachandra ki jai' ('Victory to King Ramachandra')	'Veer bhogya vasundhara' ('The brave shall inherit the earth')
The Grenadiers	1778	Jabalpur, Madhya Pradesh	'Sarvada shaktishali' ('Always strong')	'Naam, Namak, Nishan' ('Name, Salt, Mark')
Rajput Regiment	1778	Fatehgarh, Uttar Pradesh	'Bol Bajrang Bali Ki jai' ('Say victory to Hanuman')	'Sarvatra vijay' ('Victory everywhere')
Jat Regiment	1795	Bareilly, Uttar Pradesh	'Jat balwan, jai bhagwan' ('The Jat is strong, victory to the Fortunate God')	'Sangathan va veerta' ('Unity and valour')
Kumaon Regiment	1813	Ranikhet, Uttarakhand	'Kalika Mata ki jai' ('Victory to Mother Kali'); 'Bajrang Bali ki jai' ('victory to Lord Hanuman'); 'Dada Kishan ki jai' ('Victory to Dada Kishan')	'Parakramo vijayate' ('Valour triumphs')
1 Gorkha Rifles (The Malaun Regiment)	1815	Subathu, Himachal Pradesh	'Jai Ma Kali, ayo Gorkhali' ('Hail Mother Kali, here come the Gorkhas')	'Kayar hunu bhanda marnu ramro' ('Better to die than live like a coward')

NAME	YEAR OF ESTABLISHMENT	REGIMENTAL CENTRE	WAR CRY	MOTTO
3 Gorkha Rifles	1815	Varanasi, Uttar Pradesh	'Jai Ma Kali, ayo Gorkhali' ('Hail Mother Kali, here come the Gorkhas')	'Kayar hunu bhanda marnu ramro' ('Better to die than live like a coward')
Mahar Regiment	1815	Saugor, Madhya Pradesh	'Bolo Hindustan ki jai' ('Say victory to India')	'Yash sidhi' ('Success and attainment')
Jammu & Kashmir Rifles	1821	Jabalpur, Madhya Pradesh	'Durga Mata ki jai' ('Victory to Mother Durga')	'Prashata ranvirta' ('Valour in battle is praiseworthy')
8 Gorkha Rifles	1824	Shillong, Meghalaya	'Jai Ma Kali, ayo Gorkhali' ('Hail Mother Kali, here come the Gorkhas')	'Kayar hunu bhanda marnu ramro' ('Better to die than live like a coward')
Sikh Regiment	1846	Ramgarh Cantonment, Jharkhand	'Jo Bole So Nihal, Sat Sri Akaal' ('Whoever utters, shall be fulfilled, True is the Great Timeless One') 'Waheguru Ji Da Khalsa Waheguru Ji Di Fateh' ('The Khalsa belongs to the Wondrous Enlightener! Victory belongs to the Wondrous Enlightener')	'Nischay kar apni jeet karon' ('With determination, I will be triumphant')
4 Gorkha Rifles	1857	Sabathu, Himachal Pradesh	'Jai Ma Kali, ayo Gorkhali' ('Hail Mother Kali, here come the Gorkhas')	'Kayar hunu bhanda marnu ramro' ('Better to die than live like a coward')
5 Gorkha Rifles (Frontier Force)	1858	Shillong, Meghalaya	'Jai Ma Kali, ayo Gorkhali' ('hail Mother Kali, here come the Gorkhas')	'Shaurya evam nistha' ('Courage and determination')
Dogra Regiment	1877	Ayodhya, Uttar Pradesh	'Jawala Mata ki jai' ('Victory to Mother Jawala')	'Kartavyam anvatma' ('Duty before death')
The Garhwal Rifles	1887	Lansdowne, Uttarakhand	'Badri Vishal Lal ki jai' ('Victory to the Great Lord Badri Nath')	'Yudhaya krit nischya' ('Fight with determination')
Assam Regiment	1941	Shillong, Meghalaya	'Rhino charge'	'Assam vikram' ('Unique valour')

NAME	YEAR OF ESTABLISHMENT	REGIMENTAL CENTRE	WAR CRY	MOTTO
Bihar Regiment	1941	Danapur, Bihar	'Bajrang Bali Ki Jai' (Victory to Lord Hanuman) ; 'Har Har Mahadev' ('O Lord Mahadev, you are omnipresent')	'Veerta se yudh par' ('To war with valour')
Sikh Light Infantry	1944	Fatehgarh, Uttar Pradesh	'Jo Bole So Nihal Sat Sri Akal' ('Whoever utters, shall be fulfilled, True is the Great Timeless One!')	'Deg Tegh Fateh' ('Victory to charity and arms')
Parachute Regiment	1945	Bengaluru, Karnataka	'Balidan Param Dharma' ('Sacrifice, Supreme Duty')	'Shatrujeet' ('The conqueror')
Jammu and Kashmir Light Infantry	1947	Avantipur, Jammu and Kashmir	'Bharat Mata ki jai' ('Victory to Mother India')	'Balidanam vir lakshanam' ('Sacrifice is a characteristic of the brave')
11 Gorkha Rifles	1948	Lucknow, Uttar Pradesh	'Jai Ma Kali, Ayo Gorkhali ('Hail Mother Kali, here come the Gorkhas')	'Yatraham vijayastatra' ('Victory resides where I reside')
Ladakh Scouts	1963	Leh, Ladakh	'Ki ki so so Lhargyalo' ('Victory to God')	
Naga Regiment	1970	Ranikhet, Uttarakhand	'Jai Durga Naga' ('Victory to Durga Naga')	'Parakramo vijayate' ('Valour triumphs')
Arunachal Scouts	2010	Rayang, Pasighat, Arunachal Pradesh		
Sikkim Scouts	2013			

Regiment of Artillery

- The Regiment of Artillery is the second largest arm of the Indian Army. It provides immense firepower during all ground operations of the army.
- It wields a wide array of weapons, including guns, mortars, rocket launchers, unmanned aerial vehicles, surveillance systems, and missiles.
- The School of Artillery was established at Deolali in Nashik, Maharashtra.
- Its motto is 'Sarvatra Izzat-o-Iqbal' (Everywhere with Honour and Glory).
- Gunner's Day is observed on 28 September every year, as on this day, the 5 (Bombay) Mountain Battery, the first unit of the Indian Regiment of Artillery, was raised.

Army Aviation Corps (AAC)

- It is the youngest arm of the Indian Army and was established on 1 November 1986.
- It supports ground operations by providing reconnaissance, close air support, and troop transport capabilities.

- AAC helicopters are utilized for reconnaissance missions, casualty evacuation (CASEVAC), troop insertion and extraction, logistics support, and special operations.
- Their motto is 'Suveg Va Sudrid', which means 'Swift and Sure'.

Corps of Army Air Defence (AAD)

- AAD is a specialized branch of the Indian Army dedicated to safeguarding the ground forces from airborne assaults and enhancing aerial surveillance capabilities.
- It protects the Indian air space from enemy aircraft and missiles, especially the ones below 5,000 feet.
- Its primary mission is to protect friendly forces, vital infrastructure, and mobile units from aerial threats through offensive and defensive measures. These include countering enemy aircraft, missiles, and drones, as well as providing crucial early warning and surveillance functions.
- AAD was carved out as a separate arm from the Regiment of Artillery on 10 January 1994, to become a critical and technical advanced Combat Support Arm of the Indian Army.
- Its motto is 'Annihilate the Airborne Enemy' and the war cry is 'Akashe Shatrun Jahi', meaning 'Shoot the Enemy in the Air'.

Indian Army Corps of Engineers

- It is responsible for providing combat engineering support, infrastructure development, and construction tasks during both peace and war times.
- College of Military Engineering, Pune (CME) is the premier technical and tactical training institution of the Indian Army Corps of Engineers.
- Their motto is 'Sarvatra' ('Everywhere').

Indian Army Corps of Signals

- The Indian Army Corps of Signals manages military communications and information technology infrastructure.
- It is responsible for deploying and maintaining robust communication networks and ensuring cybersecurity capabilities, essential both during peace and war.
- Additionally, the corps facilitates connectivity for soldiers stationed in remote areas to stay connected with their families.
- They have developed the Samyukta Electronic Warfare System along with Bharat Electronics Limited. It is a mobile-integrated electronic warfare system.
- Their motto is 'Teevra Chaukas', which means 'Swift and Alert'.
- The Military College of Telecommunication Engineering (MCTE), Mhow in Madhya Pradesh, is a premier training institute of the Corps of Signals.

Mechanized Infantry

- The Mechanized Infantry Regiment is an infantry regiment of the Indian Army and is often referred to as 'tomorrow's arm in today's army'.
- It has two regiments: the Brigade of the Guards and the Mechanized Infantry Regiment. Overall, it has 48 infantry battalions. The Mechanized Infantry is the brainchild of General Krishnaswamy Sundarji, the former CoAS (1986–88).
- The Brigade of the Guards along with Armoured Cops form the Mechanized Forces.

NAME	YEAR OF ESTABLISHMENT	REGIMENTAL CENTRE	WAR CRY	MOTTO
Brigade of the Guards	1949	Kamptee, Maharashtra	'Garud ka hu bol pyare' ('I am the son of Garuda say O my friend')	'Pahla humesha Pahla ('First, always first')
Mechanized Infantry Regiment	1979	Ahmednagar, Maharashtra	'Bolo Bharat Mata ki jai' ('Say Victory to Mother India')	'Valour and faith'

Army Medical Corps (AMC)

- AMC is a specialized branch of the Indian Army tasked with delivering medical services to army personnel, their families, and, occasionally, civilians during humanitarian missions.
- Together with its counterparts in the Indian Navy and Indian Air Force, the AMC is an integral part of the Armed Forces Medical Services (AFMS).
- The motto of AMC is 'Sarve Santu Niramaya' which means 'Let all be free from disease and disability'.

Army Ordnance Corps (AOC)

- AOC provides logistical and supply chain support for ammunition, weapons, and equipment.
- It oversees the procurement, storage, and distribution of arms, ammunition, vehicles, clothing, and other equipment necessary for the Indian Army.
- The AOC manages the maintenance and repair of military equipment and vehicles, ensuring they remain operational and have a long service life.
- This encompasses items, from small arms to tanks and aircraft spare parts.
- Their motto is 'Shastra se Shakti' which means 'Strength through Arms'.
- The AOC centre in Secunderabad is the training academy of the corps.

Indian Army Corps of Electronics and Mechanical Engineers (EME)

- The corps of Electronics and Mechanical Engineers (EME) maintain and service all mechanical, electrical, and electronic equipment used by the Army.
- They ensure the operational fitness of a wide range of equipment. Additionally, it leads the management of technology transitions to support the force modernization programme.

Army Dental Corps (ADC)

- The Army Dental Corps (ADC) is a team of dedicated professionals committed to maintaining the dental health of armed forces officers, personnel, and their families.
- The primary mission of the ADC is to provide comprehensive dental care to army personnel, which includes preventive care (such as check-ups and cleanings), restorative treatments (such as fillings and crowns), and specialized dental procedures (such as root canals and oral surgery).

Rashtriya Rifles (RR)

- The Rashtriya Rifles is a specialized counter-insurgency force dedicated to combating terrorism and insurgency in Jammu and Kashmir.
- It comprises troops from various Indian Army regiments, and these soldiers undergo specialized training in counter-insurgency operations, jungle warfare, and handling asymmetric threats.

- Additionally, the Rashtriya Rifles maintain public order under the authority granted by the Armed Forces (Jammu and Kashmir) Special Powers Act, 1990 (AFSPA).
- The motto of RR is 'Dridhta aur Virta' (Courage and Valour) and the war cry is 'Bajrangbali ki Jai' (Glory to Lord Hanuman).

Indian Army Service Corps (IASC)

- The Army Service Corps (ASC) is a vital support branch of the Indian Army, tasked with logistics and supply chain management.
- Its primary role is to provide logistical support, which includes transporting troops, ammunition, fuel, and supplies to various units across diverse terrains and operational areas.
- They manage the entire supply chain for the army, ensuring that essential items such as food, clothing, medical supplies, and equipment are delivered promptly. This responsibility encompasses inventory management, procurement, and distribution logistics.
- The motto is 'Seva Asmākam Dharma', which means 'Service is our duty'.

Indian Army Pioneer Corps (IAPC)

- The Pioneer Corps is a specialized branch dedicated to maintain discipline, law enforcement, and security within the military.
- It supplies disciplined and well-trained personnel in situations where civilian labour is unavailable or unsuitable due to security concerns.
- These units primarily operate in forward and operational areas, and are often tasked with guarding headquarters, installations, ammunition trains, and convoys.
- They also provide escort services for military convoys, VIPs, and prisoners, ensuring their security and safety during transportation.
- The Pioneer Corps Training Center (PCTC) is currently located in Bengaluru, Karnataka. Their motto is 'Shram Sarva Vijayee', meaning 'With labour, everything can be won'.

Territorial Arms (TA)

- The Territorial Army (TA) in India is a part-time volunteer reserve force comprising civilians who undergo military training and can be mobilized during national emergencies or when regular army units need reinforcement.
- The concept of TA was introduced in 1897.
- It consists of two types of units: departmental units, which include employees of public sector undertakings (PSUs) and the Indian Railways, along with ex-servicemen and non-departmental units, composed of privately employed civilians.
- It is led by a Director General of the Territorial Army, typically a lieutenant general–ranking officer from the Indian Army, and operates under the Chief of Defence Staff within the Department of Military Affairs of the Ministry of Defence.
- The motto of TA is 'Savdhani va Shoorta' (Vigilance and valour).

DRDO (DEFENCE RESEARCH AND DEVELOPMENT ORGANISATION)

- DRDO is the premier military research and development organization of the Government of India. It functions under the Ministry of Defence.
- It was established by the amalgamation of the then already functioning

Technical Development Establishment (TDEs) of the Indian Army and the Directorate of Technical Development & Production (DTDP) with the Defence Science Organisation (DSO).

- It has a network of more than 40 laboratories throughout India that are extensively involved in developing new defence technologies for the Indian armed forces. It is working towards building state-of-the-art indigenous defence technologies and systems.
- It has been successful in the development of a range of missile systems such as the Agni series, Prithvi series, BrahMos, Akash, and Nag.
- It has successfully developed Tejas, the light combat aircraft, Rustom, the unmanned aerial vehicle (UAV), etc.
- As a part of 'Atma Nirbhar Bharat', it collaborates with various public sector undertakings and private industries to develop and produce defence equipment. It also engages in technology transfer and joint development projects with other countries.

Established: 1958

Motto: Strength's Origin Is in Science

Headquarters: New Delhi

Chairman: Sameer V. Kamat

DIRECTORATE OF MILITARY INTELLIGENCE (DMI), INDIA

DMI is a key branch of the Indian Army responsible for providing intelligence support to military operations and ensuring national security. It was established on 1 March 2002, and is headquartered in New Delhi. It is headed by the Director General of Military Intelligence (DGMI), a senior officer of the rank of lieutenant general. The first director general of the DMI was Lt. Gen. Kamal Davar. As of July 2024, the Director General of DMI is Lt. Gen. D. S. Rana. It performs the following functions:

- Collect and analyse information on enemy forces, capabilities, and intentions.
- Provide actionable intelligence to support tactical operations and strategic planning.
- Conduct operations to detect and neutralize espionage, sabotage, and other subversive activities against the Indian Army.
- Offers real-time intelligence support to ongoing military operations, ensuring commanders have the necessary information to make informed decisions.
- Provides training to military personnel in intelligence gathering, analysis, and counter-intelligence techniques.
- Utilizes various methods, including human intelligence (HUMINT), signals intelligence (SIGINT), and imagery intelligence (IMINT), to monitor and assess potential threats.
- Engages in electronic warfare and cyber intelligence operations to safeguard military communications and information systems.
- Provides mapping, terrain analysis, and geospatial information to support military operations and strategic planning.

ACTIVE INDIAN ARMY EQUIPMENT

INFANTRY WEAPON (ASSAULT RIFLES)

NAME	MANUFACTURER	ORIGIN	TYPE
AK-203	Kalashnikov Concern and Indo-Russia Rifles	Russia	Assault rifle
1B1 INSAS (Indian Small Arms System)	Armament Research and Development Establishment Ordnance Factories Board	India	Assault rifle Light machine gun
SIG 716i	SIG Sauer	United States	Assault rifle and battle rifle
IWI X95	Israel Weapon Industries (IWI)	Israel	Bullpup assault rifle Carbine
IMI Tavor TAR-21/ IWI Tavor	Israel Weapon Industries (IWI)	Israel	Bullpup assault rifle
T91 assault rifle	205th arsenal	Taiwan	Assault rifle
M4 carbine	Colt's Manufacturing Company, FN Herstal, Remington Arms	United States	Assault rifle Carbine
AR-M1	Arsenal AD	Bulgaria	Assault rifle
AKM	Mikhail Kalashnikov	Soviet Union	Assault rifle
AK-47 (Avtomat Kalashnikova)	Mikhail Kalashnikov	Soviet Union	Assault rifle
MPi-KMS-72	Mikhail Kalashnikov	Soviet Union	Assault rifle
Vz. 58	Czech armory	Czechoslovakia	Assault rifle

INFANTRY WEAPON (SNIPER RIFLES)

NAME	MANUFACTURER	ORIGIN	TYPE
Dragunov Sniper Rifle	Kalashnikov Concern Norinco	Soviet Union	Designated marksman rifle Sniper rifle
IMI Galil 7.62 Sniper	Israel Military Industries	Israel	Assault rifle Carbine Battle rifle
Heckler & Koch PSG1	Heckler & Koch	Germany	Sniper rifle
Mauser SP66	Mauser	Germany	Bolt-action sniper rifle
SIG Sauer SSG 3000	SIG Sauer	Germany	Sniper rifle
Sako TRG 42	Sako	Finland	Sniper rifle
Beretta Scorpio TGT	Beretta	Italy	Sniper rifle
SSS Defence 338 Saber	Stumpp Schuele & Somappa Defence	India	Sniper rifle

INFANTRY WEAPON (MACHINE GUNS)

NAME	MANUFACTURER	ORIGIN	TYPE
FN Minimi	FN Herstal	Belgium	Light machine gun Squad automatic weapon
INSAS LMG	Armament Research and Development Establishment Ordnance Factories Board	India	Assault rifle Light machine gun
IMI Negev NG5	Israel Weapon Industries	Israel	Light machine gun
IMI Negev NG7	Israel Weapon Industries	Israel	Light machine gun
MG 2A1	Fabrique Nationale (FN)	Belgium	General-purpose machine gun
MG 5A	Fabrique Nationale (FN)	Belgium	General-purpose machine gun
MG 6A	Fabrique Nationale (FN)	Belgium	General-purpose machine gun
Mk 48 machine gun	Fabrique Nationale Manufacturing	Belgium and United States	General-purpose machine gun
PK machine gun	Mikhail Kalashnikov	Soviet Union	General-purpose machine gun Squad automatic weapon Medium machine gun
NSV machine gun/ NSV Utyos	Metallist, Uralsk, Kazakh SSR	Soviet Union	Heavy machine gun
M2 Browning	General Dynamics, Ohio Ordnance Works, U.S. Ordnance, and FN Herstal	United States	Heavy machine gun

INFANTRY WEAPON (KNIVES AND BAYONETS)

NAME	ORIGIN	TYPE
Khukri	Gorkha kingdom	Bladed melee weapon, utility tool
Kirpan	Khalsa	Dagger
M9 Bayonet/M9 Phrobis III	United States	Bayonet
Glock Knife	Austria	Combat knife
Naga Dao	Northeast India	Sword

INFANTRY WEAPON – SMALL ARMS (HANDGUNS/ PISTOL)

NAME	ORIGIN	TYPE
Pistol Auto 9mm 1A	India	Semi-automatic pistol
Glock	Austria	Semi-automatic pistol
Beretta Px4 Storm	Italy	Semi-automatic pistol

INFANTRY WEAPON – NON-LINEAR LINE OF SIGHT WEAPONS

NAME	ORIGIN	TYPE
Shoot Edge	India	CornerShot
DRDO CSWS (CornerShot Weapon System)	India	CornerShot

INFANTRY WEAPON – SHOTGUNS

NAME	ORIGIN	TYPE
12 Bore PAG	India	Pump action shotgun

INFANTRY WEAPON (SUBMACHINE GUN)

NAME	ORIGIN	TYPE
Micro-Uzi	Israel	Submachine gun
Brügger & Thomet MP9	Switzerland	Submachine gun
Heckler & Koch MP5	Germany	Submachine gun
SAF Carbine 2A1	United Kingdom	Submachine gun
ASMI (Asmita)	India	Submachine gun and machine pistol
Taurus T9	Brazil	Submachine gun

ARTILLERY (ROCKET ARTILLERY)

NAME	ORIGIN	TYPE
Pinaka Multi-Barrel Rocket Launcher (MBRL)	India	Multiple launch rocket system
BM-21	Soviet Union	Multiple rocket launcher
Smerch 9K58 MBRL	Soviet Union	Multiple rocket launcher

ARTILLERY (SELF-PROPELLED ARTILLERY)

NAME	ORIGIN	TYPE
K9 Vajra-T	South Korea	Self-propelled howitzer

ARTILLERY (TOWED ARTILLERY)

NAME	ORIGIN	TYPE
BAE Systems M777	United Kingdom	Towed howitzer
OFB Dhanush	India	Howitzer
Haubits FH77 B02	Sweden	Howitzer
IOB Sharang	Soviet Union	Towed field gun
OFB Indian Field Gun Mk 1/2/3	India	Field gun

ARTILLERY (STATIC ARTILLERY)

NAME	ORIGIN	TYPE
Vijayanta	United Kingdom	Self-propelled howitzer
T-55 MBT	Soviet Union	Medium tank and main battle tank

BALLISTIC AND CRUISE MISSILES

NAME	MANUFACTURER	ORIGIN	TYPE
BrahMos	BrahMos Aerospace Ltd.	India and Russia	Supersonic cruise missile
Prahaar	Bharat Dynamics Limited	India	Tactical ballistic missile
Nirbhay	Bharat Dynamics Limited	India	Long-range all weather subsonic cruise missile
Pralay	Defence Research and Development Organisation (DRDO)	India	Tactical to short-range ballistic missile
Prithvi II	Bharat Dynamics Limited	India	Short-range ballistic missile
LORA (Long Range Artillery)	Israel Aerospace Industries	Israel	Theatre quasi-ballistic missile
Shaurya	Bharat Dynamics Limited	India	Surface-to-surface missile
Agni I	Bharat Dynamics Limited	India	Short range ballistic missile
Agni II	Bharat Dynamics Limited	India	Medium-range ballistic missile
Agni III	Bharat Dynamics Limited	India	Intermediate-range ballistic missile

AIR DEFENCE SYSTEM (ANTI-SATELLITE MISSILE SYSTEMS)

NAME	DESIGNER	TYPE
Prithvi Defence Vehicle Mark 2	Defence Research and Development Organisation	Exo-atmospheric anti-ballistic missile

AIR DEFENCE SYSTEM (ANTI-BALLISTIC MISSILE SYSTEMS)

NAME	DESIGNER	TYPE
Prithvi Defence Vehicle (PDV)	Defence Research and Development Organisation	Exo-atmospheric anti-ballistic missile
Advance Air Defence (AAD)	Defence Research and Development Organisation	Endo-atmospheric anti-ballistic missile

MAN-PORTABLE AIR DEFENCE SYSTEM

NAME	MANUFACTURER	TYPE
Akashteer	Bharat Electronics Limited	Automated air defence control and reporting system
S-400 Triumph	Fakel Machine-Building Design Bureau	Mobile long-range surface-to-air/anti-ballistic missile system
Barak-8 (MR-SAM)	Bharat Dynamics Limited, Bharat Electronics Limited, and Rafael Advanced Defence Systems	Medium to long-range surface-to-air missile
Akash	Bharat Dynamics Limited	Mobile surface-to-air missile system
Surface-to-Air Python and Derby (SPYDER)	Rafael Advanced Defence Systems	Short- and medium-range air defence system
Quick Reaction Surface-to-Air Missile (QRSAM)	Bharat Dynamics Limited	Surface-to-air missile
2K12 Kub	Ulyanovsk Mechanical Plant (SURNs) and ZiK (TELs)	Tracked medium-range surface-to-air missile system
S-125 Neva/Pechora	JSC Defence Systems	Short-range SAM system
9K33 Osa	Znamya Truda Plant	6×6 amphibious SAM system
9K35 Strela-10	Saratovskiy Zenit Machine Plant	Vehicle-mounted SAM system

MAN-PORTABLE AIR DEFENCE SYSTEM

NAME	MANUFACTURER	TYPE
FIM-92 Stinger	Raytheon Missiles & Defence	Man-portable surface-to-air missile
9K38 Igla	KB Mashinostroyeniya	Man-portable surface-to-air missile

AIR-DEFENCE ANTI-AIRCRAFT GUN SYSTEMS

NAME	MANUFACTURER	ORIGIN	TYPE
ZSU-23-4 'Shilka'	Ulyanovsk Mechanical Plant (UMZ), Mytishchi Machine-Building Plant (MMZ)	Soviet Union	Self-propelled anti-aircraft gun
2K22 Tunguska	Ulyanovsk Mechanical Factory	Soviet Union	Tracked self-propelled anti-aircraft gun
Bofors L70	BAE Systems AB	Sweden/ United Kingdom	Autocannon
Sudarshan CIWS	Larsen & Toubro (L&T)	India	Close-in weapon system

MISSILE SYSTEMS (ANTI-TANK GUIDED MISSILE)

NAME	MANUFACTURER	ORIGIN	TYPE
Man-Portable Anti-Tank Guided Missile (MPATGM)	Bharat Dynamics Ltd.	India	Anti-tank guided missile
MILAN 2T	MBDA	France and West Germany	Anti-tank guided missile
9M133 Kornet	Degtyarev plant	Russia	Anti-tank guided missile
Spike	Rafael Advanced Defence Systems	Israel	Anti-tank guided missile
9M113 Konkurs	Tula Machinery Design Bureau (Tula KBP) and Bharat Dynamics Ltd.	Soviet Union	Anti-tank guided missile
9K120 Svir, 9K119 Refleks or 9K119M Refleks-M	Degtyarev plant	Soviet Union	Anti-tank guided missile
9K114 SHTURM	Kolomna Machine Design Bureau	Soviet Union	Anti-tank guided missile vehicle

AIRCRAFT

HELICOPTERS

NAME	MANUFACTURER	ORIGIN	TYPE
Boeing AH-64 Apache	Boeing Defence, Space & Security	United States	Attack helicopter
HAL Prachand	Hindustan Aeronautics Limited	India	Attack helicopter
HAL Rudra	Hindustan Aeronautics Limited	India	Attack helicopter
HAL Dhruv	Hindustan Aeronautics Limited	India	Utility helicopter
HAL Light Utility Helicopter	Hindustan Aeronautics Limited	India	Utility helicopter
HAL Chetak	Hindustan Aeronautics Limited	France	Light utility helicopter
HAL Cheetah	Hindustan Aeronautics Limited	France	Utility helicopter

UNMANNED AERIAL VEHICLES (UAVs)

NAME	MANUFACTURER	ORIGIN	TYPE
IAI Heron TP	IAI	Israel	Unmanned surveillance and reconnaissance aerial vehicle and unmanned combat air vehicle (armed variant)
Elbit Systems Hermes 900 Kochav	Elbit Systems	Israel	Unmanned surveillance and reconnaissance aerial vehicle
IAI Searcher or Marsh Tern	IAI	Israel	Reconnaissance UAV
NIMBUS	Newspace Research and Technologies (NRT) Pvt Ltd.	India	Swarm drones
BELUGA	Newspace Research and Technologies (NRT) Pvt Ltd.	India	Swarm drones
mPhibr MR-20	Raphe mPhibr	India	Cargo

OPERATIONS OF THE INDIAN ARMY

NAME OF THE OPERATION	YEAR	IMPORTANT HIGHLIGHTS
Operation Polo	September 1948	• Incorporation of the princely state of Hyderabad into the Indian Union. • Ending the rule of Nizam of Hyderabad.
Operation Vijay	December 1961	• Liberation of Goa, Daman and Diu from the Portuguese rule. • First integrated tri-service operation of India.
Operation Blue Star	June 1984	• Conducted at the Golden Temple in Amritsar, Punjab to expel the hidden militants from the gurudwara. • These militants were led by Jarnail Singh Bhindranwale.
Operation Meghdoot	April 1984	• Gain the control of Siachen Glacier in Ladakh. • Joint operation of Indian Army and Air Force.
Operation Rajiv	June 1987	• Aimed to capture the highest point along the Actual Ground Position Line (AGPL) of the Siachen Glacier from Pakistan forces. • This point was renamed as Bana Top after Naib Subedar Bana Singh who led the operation.

NAME OF THE OPERATION	YEAR	IMPORTANT HIGHLIGHTS
Operation Cactus	November 1988	• India's successful tri-service military intervention in Maldives. • It aimed to prevent the military coup against the ruling Maldivian government headed by the then President Abdul Gayoom. • The coup was attempted by Abdul Luthufi, a Maldivian businessman, with the help of Sri Lankan separatist group People's Liberation Organisation of Tamil Eelam (PLOTE).
Operation Pawan	October 1987	• Operation by the Indian Peace Keeping Force (IPKF) in Sri Lanka. • Through the operation, IPKF wanted to take control of the Jaffna Peninsula from the Liberation Tigers of Tamil Eelam (LTTE) or Tamil Tigers. • However, operation ended in 1990 with the withdrawal of the IPKF following the assassination of Indian Prime Minister Rajiv Gandhi and a deteriorating security situation in Sri Lanka.
Operation Vijay	May–July 1999	• Operation by the Indian army to evict Pakistani forces from Kargil, Jammu and Kashmir. • 26 July is celebrated as Vijay Diwas as, on this day, Indian army announced the complete eviction of Pakistani forces from the Indian side of the Line of Control (LoC).
Operation Calm Down	September 2016	• Launched to calm down the situation in Jammu and Kashmir after the execution of Burhan Wani.
Operation Zafran	February 2019	• Launched in response to the Pulwama terror attack by the Pakistan-based terrorist organization Jaish-e-Mohammed, in which 40 CRPF personnel were martyred.

MILITARY EXERCISES

BILATERAL

NAME OF THE EXERCISE	COUNTRIES
Ajeya Warrior	India and United Kingdom
Al-Nagah	India and Oman
Bold Kurukshetra	India and Singapore
Ekuverin	India and Maldives
Dharma Guardian	India and Japan
Garuda Shakti	India and Indonesia
Hand In Hand	India and China
Kazind (Army and Air Force)	India and Kazakhstan
Khanjar	India and Kyrgyzstan
Lamitiye	India and Seychelles
Maitree Exercise	India and Thailand
Mitra Shakti	India and Sri Lanka
Nomadic Elephant	India and Mongolia
Sampriti	India and Bangladesh
Shakti	India and France
Vajra Prahar	India and USA
Vinbax	India and Veitnam
Yudh Abhyas	India and USA

WAR MEMORIALS

National War Memorial

- It is a war memorial dedicated to honour the soldiers of the Indian armed forces who have laid down their lives in the line of duty since India's independence in 1947.
- The memorial was inaugurated on 25 February 2019, by the then Prime Minister Narendra Modi.
- It was designed by Yogesh Chandrahasan and is located at India Gate, New Delhi.
- The memorial has a C-hexagon shape and spans over 40 acres. It is spread out in a radial pattern with four concentric circles, known as the 'Chakravyuh' model. The four circles are:
  - *Amar Chakra (Circle of Immortality):* It has an obelisk with an eternal flame, Amar Jawan Jyoti at its base. This symbolizes the immortality of the fallen soldiers.
  - *Veerta Chakra (Circle of Bravery):* It includes a gallery with bronze murals depicting the valiant deeds of the armed forces.
  - *Tyag Chakra (Circle of Sacrifice):* It consists of granite tablets inscribed with the names of martyrs from various operations such as the Indo-Pak Wars, the Sino-Indian War, the Kargil Conflict, and other military operations.

- IV. *Rakshak Chakra (Circle of Protection):* It consists of rows of trees, symbolizing the soldiers who protect the nation.

- The memorial has an area dedicated to the recipients of the Param Vir Chakra, India's highest military decoration for valour. It is known as Param Yodha Sthal.

Marwar Memorial

- The Marwar Memorial was erected to honour the soldiers who gave their lives on 18 December 1961, during 'Operation Vijay'. Their valour led to the liberation of Diu Island and forced the Portuguese governor General Manuel Antonio Vassalo e Silva, to surrender Diu to the Union of India.
- The island of Diu, located off the southern coast of Gujarat, was under Portuguese colonial rule for over 450 years.
- The memorial symbolizes national pride and the end of colonial rule in this region.

Victory War Memorial

- The Victory War Memorial is an obelisk-shaped memorial in Chennai, Tamil Nadu. It was formerly called the Cupid's bow.
- It was originally built to commemorate the victory of the Allied Armies in the First World War and later expanded to honour the sacrifices of soldiers in the Second World War, the 1948 Kashmir conflict, the 1962 war with China, and the Indo-Pakistan Wars of 1965 and 1971.

National War Memorial Southern Command

- The National War Memorial Southern Command is a war memorial in Morwada Junction, Pune, Maharashtra. It is the only war memorial in South Asia that has been erected by citizens' contributions.
- It was inaugurated on 15 August 1998, and serves as a significant landmark for commemorating the bravery and sacrifice of Indian soldiers.

Longewala Memorial

- The Longewala War Memorial is dedicated to the soldiers who fought in the Battle of Longewala during the Indo-Pakistani War of 1971. The memorial is in the Thar Desert, near Longewala, Jaisalmer district, Rajasthan, India.
- The memorial features plaques, statues, and displays that detail the events of the battle.
- It also includes a collection of military hardware such as tanks and artillery used during the conflict.

Darjeeling War Memorial

- The Darjeeling War Memorial is located in Batasia Loop, a scenic spot in Darjeeling, West Bengal. It honours the Gorkha soldiers who have fought in various conflicts, both before and after India's independence.
- It serves as an educational site for visitors, providing insights into the history and bravery of the Gorkha Regiment and its pivotal role in the Indian armed forces.

Walong War Memorial

- The Walong War Memorial is located in Walong, a small town in the Anjaw district of Arunachal Pradesh, India.
- It is a tribute to the bravery and sacrifice of Indian soldiers who fought in the Battle of Walong during the Sino-Indian War of 1962.
- The Walong War Memorial commemorates the courage and determination of the Indian soldiers who defended the region against overwhelming odds. Their resistance

is remembered as a symbol of national pride and military bravery.

Tawang War Memorial

- The Tawang War Memorial is a Buddhist shrine (stupa) dedicated to the memory of Indian soldiers who lost their lives during the Sino-Indian War of 1962.
- It is a 40-foot-high memorial locally referred to as the 'Namgyal Chortan'.
- It has the names of 2,420 dead soldiers etched in gold on 32 black granite plaques. It also includes a gallery that displays photographs, personal belongings, and other memorabilia of the soldiers who fought in the 1962 war.

Dograi War Memorial

- Dograi War Memorial is located at Khasa, Amritsar. It is dedicated to brave soldiers who laid their lives during the 1965 Indo-Pak War.

Operation Rakshak Memorial

- The Operation Rakshak Memorial was constructed in Badami Bagh Cantonment, Srinagar.
- It is dedicated to the Indian Army soldiers who sacrificed themselves during their valorous efforts to bring normalcy to the Kashmir Valley.

INDIAN AIR FORCE (IAF)

Brief Introduction

The Indian Air Force (IAF) is the air arm of the Indian armed forces and was established as an auxiliary force on 8 October 1932. It was renamed as the Indian Air Force on 26 January 1950. Air Marshal Subroto Mukherjee, one of the founding members of the Air Force, took over as the first Indian Chief of Air Staff (CAS) on 1 April 1954.

Role of IAF

- Secure Indian airspace and conduct aerial warfare during conflicts.
- Conduct strategic bombing missions to destroy enemy infrastructure, supply lines, and military installations during wars and conflicts.
- Operate a fleet of transport aircraft for moving troops, equipment, and supplies quickly across vast distances.
- Instrumental in disaster relief operations, conducting airlift missions to deliver aid and evacuate civilians during natural disasters such as earthquakes, floods, and cyclones.
- Conduct surveillance missions to gather intelligence on enemy movements and positions.
- Conduct and participate in joint military exercises with other nations' air forces to enhance interoperability and learn new tactics.
- Participate in the United Nations peacekeeping missions by providing air support and logistical assistance in conflict zones.
- Protect the Air Force's communication and control systems from cyber threats, ensuring secure and reliable operations.
- Upgrade its fleet and systems to incorporate the latest technologies and maintain operational superiority.

Quick Facts

Air Force Day: 8 October

The motto of the Indian Air Force: Nabhah Sparsam Diptam ('Touch the sky with Glory')

March: Quick – Dēśa Pukārē Jaba Saba Kō (When the nation calls) and Slow – Vāyu Sēnā Niśāna (The Air Force Emblem)

Headquarters of IAF: Vayu Bhawan, New Delhi

ORGANIZATION & STRUCTURE OF IAF

- The Chief of the Air Staff (CAS) heads the IAF. This position is held by the senior-most officer, who is generally a four-staff air chief marshal. As of July 2024, the position of CAS is held by Vivek Ram Chaudhari.
- The Vice Chief of the Air Staff (VCAS) assists the CAS and oversees various administrative functions.
- The Deputy Chiefs of the Air Staff (DCAS) manages operations, personnel, and maintenance.

Commands

- The Indian Air Force is divided into five operational and two functional commands. Each of the commands is headed by an Air Officer Commanding-in-Chief (AOC-in-C) of the rank of Air Marshal.
- The five operational commands are:
  I. Western Air Command (WAC), New Delhi
  II. Eastern Air Command (EAC), Shillong, Meghalaya
  III. Central Air Command (CAC), Prayagraj, Uttar Pradesh
  IV. Southern Air Command (SAC), Thiruvananthapuram, Kerala
  V. South Western Air Command (SWAC), Gandhinagar, Gujarat
- The two functional commands are:
  I. Training Command, Bengaluru, Karnataka
  II. Maintenance Command, Nagpur, Maharashtra

Wings

- A wing is a unit of a command and each command is divided into several wings. Wings are operational units comprising multiple squadrons and support units.
- Wings are typically located at airbases and headed by an Air Commodore or Group Captain.

Stations

- These provide logistical support and house various operational units. There may be 9 to 16 stations in each operational command.
- These are commanded by an Air Commodore or Group Captain.

Squadrons

- It is the basic flying unit within the wing and consists of a group of aircraft and their crews. Each squadron is headed by a commanding officer with the rank of wing commander.

Flights and Sections

- Flights are led by squadron leaders and are categorized under squadrons. Each flight is composed of two sections.
- Sections are the smallest unit and consist of three aircraft. It is commanded by a squadron leader.

Specialized Branches

- *Flying branch:* Includes all personnel directly involved in flying duties, such as pilots and navigators.
- *Technical branch:* Responsible for the maintenance and technical management of aircraft and other equipment.
- *Ground duty branch:* Includes various sub-branches such as Administration, Logistics, Meteorology, Accounts, Education, and Medical services.

Surya Kiran Aerobatic Team (SKAT)

- It is the aerobatic demonstration team of IAF and was formed in 1996. It is based out of Air Force Station Bidar in Karnataka.
- SKAT performs at various national and international air shows, military events,

and public celebrations, showcasing the prowess of the IAF.

- SKAT is supported by a dedicated ground crew responsible for maintenance, logistics, and coordination.

Sarang Helicopter Display Team

- It is the helicopter aerobatic team of IAF and was formed in 2003. It is based at Sulur Air Force Station in Tamil Nadu, India.
- The team flies Dhruv, an indigenously developed Advanced Light Helicopter (ALH) by the Hindustan Aeronautics Limited (HAL).

GARUD Commando Force

- It is the special force of IAF and was officially formed on 6 February 2004.
- They are trained to execute missions that enhance the operational capability of the IAF.
- It protects critical IAF installations, undertakes special reconnaissance missions, conducts direct action tasks, and engages in combat search and rescue operations.

Airmen

Airmen are personnel who carry out the essential tasks that ensure the operational readiness and efficiency of the IAF. They form the backbone of the service by providing crucial support in technical and non-technical roles. Some of their important functions are:

- Maintenance and repair of aircraft and their systems, including avionics, engines, and armaments.
- Manage and maintain radar, communication, and electronic warfare systems.
- Ensure the functionality of mechanical and electrical systems in various IAF installations and aircraft.
- Handle clerical and administrative tasks, including personnel management and record-keeping.
- Manage the supply chain, including procurement, storage, and distribution of equipment and materials.
- Provide security and law enforcement within IAF bases.
- Support medical operations and provide first aid and emergency care.

Airmen can be promoted through various ranks, starting from Aircraftman to Senior Non-Commissioned Officers (NCOs), such as Sergeant, Junior Warrant Officer (JWO), Warrant Officer (WO), and Master Warrant Officer (MWO). Exceptional airmen can be selected for commissioning

PATROL BOATS

NAME	ORIGIN	TYPE
Immediate Support Vessel	India	Patrol boats
Super Dvora class	Israel	Patrol boats
Solas Marine fast interceptor boat	Sri Lanka	Patrol boats

RESEARCH, SURVEY, & TRACKING VESSELS

SHIPS	PENNANT NUMBER	TYPE	ORIGIN
INS Anvesh	A41	Missile range instrumentation vessel/ floating test range	India
INS Dhruv	A40	Missile range instrumentation vessel	India

SHIPS	PENNANT NUMBER	TYPE	ORIGIN
INS Sagardhwani	A74	Research vessel	India
INS Sandhayak	J18	Survey vessel	India
INS Makar	J31	Survey vessel	India
INS Investigator	J15	Survey vessel	India
INS Jamuna	J16	Survey vessel	India
INS Sutlej	J17	Survey vessel	India
INS Darshak	J21	Survey vessel	India
INS Sarvekshak	J22	Survey vessel	India

TRAINING VESSELS

SHIPS	PENNANT NUMBER	CLASS	TYPE	ORIGIN
INS Tir	A86	Tir class	Training vessel	India
INS Tarangini	A75	Tarangini class	Training vessel (Sail)	India
INS Sudarshini	A77	Tarangini class	Training vessel (Sail)	India
INS Varuna		Varuna class	Training vessel (Sail)	India
INSV Mhadei	A76	Mhadei class	Training boat (Sail)	India
INSV Tarini		Mhadei class	Training boat (Sail)	India

as officers through schemes such as the Airmen Education and Cadre Commissioning Scheme (AECCS).

AIRCRAFT AND WEAPON SYSTEMS OF IAF

FIGHTER/COMBAT AIRCRAFT

NAME	COUNTRY OF ORIGIN	MANUFACTURER	ROLE
Mikoyan-Gurevich MiG-21 (Balalaika)	Soviet Union	Mikoyan	Fighter and interceptor aircraft
Mikoyan MiG-29 (Baaz)	Soviet Union	Mikoyan	Superiority fighter
Dassault Rafale	France	Dassault Aviation	Multirole fighter
HAL Tejas	India	Hindustan Aeronautics Limited	Multirole combat aircraft
SEPECAT Jaguar	France and United Kingdom	SEPECAT	Attack aircraft
Sukhoi Su-30MKI	India and Russia	Hindustan Aeronautics Limited	Multirole fighter

TRANSPORT AIRCRAFT

NAME	COUNTRY OF ORIGIN	MANUFACTURER	ROLE
C-17 Globemaster III	United States	McDonnell Douglas/ Boeing	Strategic and tactical airlifter

NAME	COUNTRY OF ORIGIN	MANUFACTURER	ROLE
C-130J Super Hercules	United States	Lockheed Martin	Military transport, aerial refuelling aircraft
Ilyushin Il-76	Soviet Union	Tashkent Aviation Production Association and Aviastar-SP	Strategic and tactical airlifter
Antonov An-32	Soviet Union/Ukraine	Aviant	Military transport aircraft

RECONNAISSANCE AND SURVEILLANCE AIRCRAFT

NAME	COUNTRY OF ORIGIN	MANUFACTURER	ROLE
Boeing 707	United States	Boeing Commercial Airplanes	Narrow-body airliner
Gulfstream G100	Israel	Gulfstream Aerospace	Business jet
Gulfstream III	Israel	Gulfstream Aerospace	Business jet
Global 5000	Canada	Bombardier Aviation	

AWACS (AIRBORNE EARLY WARNING & CONTROL)

NAME	COUNTRY OF ORIGIN	MANUFACTURER	ROLE
Beriev A-50	Soviet Union	Beriev	Airborne early warning and control
Embraer R-99	Brazil	Embraer	Airborne early warning and control, remote sensing, and maritime patrol

TANKER

NAME	COUNTRY OF ORIGIN	MANUFACTURER	ROLE
Ilyushin Il-78	Soviet Union	Ilyushin	Aerial refuelling tanker

TRAINER AIRCRAFT

NAME	COUNTRY OF ORIGIN	MANUFACTURER	ROLE
Pipistrel Virus	Slovenia	Pipistrel	Ultralight civil utility aircraft
HAL HJT-16 Kiran	India	Hindustan Aeronautics Limited	Intermediate jet trainer
Pilatus PC-7 Turbo Trainer	Switzerland	Pilatus Aircraft	Trainer aircraft
BAE Hawk	United Kingdom	Hindustan Aeronautics Limited (2008–present) and BAE Systems, UK	Advanced trainer aircraft
HAL HTT-40	India	Hindustan Aeronautics Limited	Basic training aircraft

HELICOPTERS

NAME	COUNTRY OF ORIGIN	MANUFACTURER	ROLE
Aérospatiale SA 315B Lama	France	Aérospatiale	Utility helicopter
Mil Mi-24	Soviet Union/Russia	Mil Moscow Helicopter Plant	Attack helicopter with transport capabilities, helicopter gunship
Boeing AH-64 Apache	United States	Boeing Defence, Space & Security (1997–present)	Attack helicopter
Mil Mi-17	Soviet Union/Russia	Mil Moscow Helicopter Plant	Utility, transport, armed capable helicopter
Boeing CH-47 Chinook	United States	Boeing Defence, Space & Security	Transport helicopter
Aérospatiale Alouette III	France	Sud Aviation	Light utility helicopter
HAL Prachand	India	Hindustan Aeronautics Limited	Attack helicopter
HAL Dhruv	India	Hindustan Aeronautics Limited	Utility helicopter
HAL Rudra	India	Hindustan Aeronautics Limited	Attack helicopter
HAL Light Utility Helicopter	India	Hindustan Aeronautics Limited	Utility helicopter

UAV (Unmanned Aerial Vehicles)

NAME	COUNTRY OF ORIGIN	MANUFACTURER	ROLE
IAI Heron (Machatz-1)	Israel	Israel Aerospace Industries	Unmanned surveillance and reconnaissance aerial vehicle
IAI Searcher	Israel	Israel Aerospace Industries	Reconnaissance UAV
ALS-50 (Suicide Drone)	India	Tata Advanced Systems Limited (TASL)	Loitering munition

OPERATIONS OF THE INDIAN AIR FORCE

NAME OF THE OPERATION	YEAR	IMPORTANT HIGHLIGHTS
Meghna Heli Bridge or Operation Cactus Lilly	1971	
Operation Meghdoot	1984	• Joint operation of Indian army and Air Force. • IAF airlifted Indian soldiers and dropped them to the peaks of Siachen Glacier.

NAME OF THE OPERATION	YEAR	IMPORTANT HIGHLIGHTS
Operation Poomalai or Eagle Mission 4	1987	• IAF airdropped supplies over Jaffna, Sri Lanka during the Sri Lankan civil war. • It involved airlifting and dropping essential supplies, including food packets, medicines, and relief materials, from transport aircraft.
Operation Cactus	1988	• India's successful tri-service military intervention in Maldives. • It aimed to prevent the military coup against the ruling Maldivian government headed by the then President Abdul Gayoom. • The coup was attempted by Abdul Luthufi, a Maldivian businessman, with the help of Sri Lankan separatist group People's Liberation Organisation of Tamil Eelam (PLOTE).
Operation Safed Sagar	1999	• It was conducted by IAF during the 1999 Kargil War. • In this, airstrike was launched against Pakistani intruder positions in the Kargil sector.
Operation Raahat	2015	• Evacuated Indian foreign nationals from Yemen during Yemeni Crisis.
Operation Maitri	2015	• Rescue and relief operations of IAF in Nepal after the 2015 earthquake.
Operation Sankat Mochan	2016	• Evacuate Indian citizens and other foreign nationals during South Sudanese Civil War.
Operation Insaniyat	2017	• Humanitarian assistance to Bangladesh due to large influx of refugees. • IAF provided relief materials consisting of rice, pulses, sugar, salt, cooking oil, tea, ready to eat noodles, biscuits, mosquito nets, etc.
Operation Bandar (Balakot air-strike)	2019	• Air strikes conducted by IAF against the major Jaish-e-Mohammed training facility at Balakot in Pakistan in response to the Pulwama terror attack which claimed the lives of 40 security personnel.

AIR FORCE EXERCISES

BILATERAL EXERCISES

NAME OF THE EXERCISE	COUNTRIES INVOLVED
Aviaindra	India and Russia
Cope India	India and United States

NAME OF THE EXERCISE	COUNTRIES INVOLVED
Desert Knight	India and France
Desert Warrior	India and Egypt
Garuda	India and France
Maitree Exercise	India and Thailand
Mitra Shakti	India and Sri Lanka
Sampriti	India and Bangladesh
Indradhanush	India and United Kingdom
Shinyuu Maitri	India and Japan
Siam Bharat	India and Thailand
Sindex	India and Singapore
Surya Kiran	India and Nepal
Veer Guardian	India and Japan
Yudh Abhyas	India and United States

Quick Facts

- The president of India conferred the rank of marshal of the Air Force to Arjan Singh on 26 January 2002. He is the first and only five-star rank officer in the Indian Air Force.
- Sachin Tendulkar was the first sportsperson and the first civilian without an aviation background to be awarded the honorary rank of group captain by the Indian Air Force.

INDIAN NAVY

Brief Introduction

The Indian Navy is the maritime branch of the Indian armed forces and was established as an independent entity on 2 January 1950. India became 'republic' in 1950 and the prefix 'Royal' was dropped from the erstwhile name of 'Royal Indian Navy' and rechristened as the Indian Navy.

On 22 April 1958, Vice Admiral R. D. Katari became the first Indian naval officer to take over as the Chief of the Naval Staff of the Indian Navy.

Headquarters: New Delhi

Navy Day: 4 December

Motto: Shaṁ No Varunaḥ ('May the Lord of Water be auspicious unto us')

March: Quick Jai Bharati ('Victory to India') and Slow: Anand Lok ('Realm of Joy')

Emblem of the Indian Navy: It has three main constituents, i.e., the national flag in the upper left canton adjacent to the staff, the state emblem underscribed with 'Satyamev Jayate' in golden colour on the upper right canton on the fly side, and a navy blue-gold octagon below the golden state emblem. The octagon has twin golden octagonal borders, encompassing the golden national emblem (lion capital of Ashoka – underscribed with 'Satyamev Jayate' in blue Devnagri script) resting atop an anchor; and superimposed on a shield. Below the shield, within the octagon, in a golden-bordered ribbon, on a navy blue background, is inscribed the motto of the Indian Navy 'Sham No Varunah' in golden Devnagri script.

Role of the Indian Navy

- Safeguard India's territorial waters, including its extensive coastline and island territories.

- Patrols India's Exclusive Economic Zone (EEZ) to prevent illegal activities such as poaching, smuggling, and unauthorized exploitation of marine resources.
- Defend India's maritime borders during conflicts and cut off enemy supply lines.
- Participate in international naval exercises, goodwill visits, and maritime collaborations to enhance India's diplomatic reach and influence.
- Provide immediate assistance and relief during natural disasters such as tsunamis, cyclones, and earthquakes.
- Conduct Search and Rescue (SAR) operations for distressed vessels and aircraft in the Indian Ocean and beyond.
- Ensure the security of vital sea routes crucial for international trade and energy supplies.
- Conduct and monitor maritime activities to gather intelligence and maintain situational awareness.
- Coordinate with the Indian Army and Air Force for joint operations, amphibious assaults, and integrated defence strategies.

ORGANIZATION & STRUCTURE OF THE INDIAN NAVY

- The Chief of the Naval Staff (CNS) is the head of the Indian Navy and is held by a four-star admiral. As of July 2024, the CNS is Dinesh K. Tripathi. The Vice Chief of the Naval Staff (VCNS) assists the CNS, and is responsible for coordinating and overseeing various functions of the navy.

Commands

The Indian Navy is divided into several operational and functional commands, each headed by a Flag Officer Commanding-in-Chief (FOC-in-C), who holds the rank of Vice Admiral.

- Western Naval Command, Mumbai, Maharashtra
- Eastern Naval Command, Visakhapatnam), Andhra Pradesh
- Southern Naval Command, Kochi, Kerala
- Andaman and Nicobar Command, Port Blair (sole tri-services command in the Indian armed forces, and is led by a Commander-in-Chief appointed on a rotational basis from the army, navy, and air force)

The Western and the Eastern Naval Commands are 'Operational Commands', and exercise control over operations in the Arabian Sea and the Bay of Bengal, respectively. The Southern Command is the Training Command.

Local Naval Defence for the Lakshadweep group of islands is overseen by the Naval Officer-in-Charge stationed in Lakshadweep.

Fleets

Indian Navy has two fleets, namely the Western Fleet, based at Mumbai, and the Eastern Fleet, based at Visakhapatnam. Each operational command has a Fleet Commander who oversees the deployment and operations of ships, submarines, and aircraft within their respective commands.

Operational and Training Establishments

- *Naval bases and stations:* Located strategically across India and abroad, these bases provide logistical support, maintenance facilities, and operational readiness.
- *Naval dockyards:* Major dockyards such as Naval Dockyard Mumbai and Naval Dockyard Visakhapatnam play a crucial role in shipbuilding, repairs, and maintenance.

- *Naval training establishments:* The seaman training is held at INS Chilika, Odisha. The officer training is conducted at the Indian Naval Academy (INA) in Ezhimala, Kerala.

Marine Commando Force (MCF)

MARCOS are marine commandos and elite special forces unit of the Indian Navy. They were founded in February 1987 and their headquarters are in INS Karna, Vishakapatnam. They are also known as 'Magarmach (Crocodile)' and 'Dadhiwala Fauj (The bearded army)'. They were formed in response to the need for a specialized force, capable of operating in varied and challenging maritime conditions. They specialize in conducting special operations such as counter-terrorism, direct action, reconnaissance, sabotage, hostage rescue, and unconventional warfare. MARCOS are equipped with advanced weapons, communication gear, night vision devices, and specialized equipment necessary for conducting clandestine operations.

Sagar Pawan

It is the aerobatic team of the Indian Navy's aviation arm. Its headquarters are in Dabolim Naval Air Station, Goa. The team specializes in paragliding techniques, safety protocols, and manoeuvres. They develop skills in launching, controlling, and landing paragliders in various weather conditions and terrains. It is one of the two naval aerobatic teams in the world. The other one is the Blue Angels, United States.

Sagar Pawan conducts demonstrations and displays of paragliding skills at naval events, air shows, and public exhibitions to showcase the capabilities of the navy.

Sagar Prahari Bal (SPB)

These are specialized units within the Indian Navy dedicated to coastal security and are responsible for patrolling in India's coastal water. SPB personnel are primarily responsible for safeguarding India's coastline, ports, and naval installations from maritime threats such as terrorism, smuggling, and unauthorized intrusions. They conduct regular patrols and surveillance along the coastline to detect and deter any suspicious activities.

INDIAN NAVY EQUIPMENT

All the active ships in the Indian Navy use the prefix INS, which stands for Indian Naval Ship or Indian Navy Station.

All the sailboats of the Indian Navy use the prefix INSV (Indian Naval Sailing Vessel).

NUCLEAR-POWERED BALLISTIC MISSILE SUBMARINES (SSBNs)

NAME	PENNANT NUMBER	CLASS	MANUFACTURER
INS Arihant	SSBN 80	Arihant	Shipbuilding Centre (SBC), Visakhapatnam, Andhra Pradesh
INS Arighat	SSBN 81	Arihant	Shipbuilding Centre (SBC), Visakhapatnam, Andhra Pradesh

CONVENTIONALLY POWERED SUBMARINES (SSK)

NAME	PENNANT NUMBER	CLASS	MOTTO	MANUFACTURER	ROLE
INS Kalvari	S21	Kalvari	Ever Onward	Mazagon Dock Limited, Mumbai	Attack submarine

NAME	PENNANT NUMBER	CLASS	MOTTO	MANUFACTURER	ROLE
INS Khanderi	S22	Kalvari	Akhand Abhedya Adrishya	Mazagon Dock Limited, Mumbai	Attack submarine
INS Karanj	S23	Kalvari	Nity Nirghosh Nirbheek	Mazagon Dock Limited, Mumbai	Attack submarine
INS Vela	S24	Kalvari	Vigilant, Valiant, Victorious	Mazagon Dock Limited, Mumbai	Attack submarine
INS Vagir	S25	Kalvari		Mazagon Dock Limited, Mumbai	Attack Submarine
INS Sindhughosh	S55	Sindhughosh		Russia	Attack submarine
INS Sindhuraj	S57	Sindhughosh		Russia	Attack submarine
INS Sindhuratna	S59	Sindhughosh		Russia	Attack submarine
INS Sindhukesari	S60	Sindhughosh		Russia	Attack submarine
INS Sindhukirti	S61	Sindhughosh		Russia	Attack submarine
INS Sindhuvijay	S62	Sindhughosh		Russia	Attack submarine
INS Sindhurashtra	S65	Sindhughosh		Russia	Attack submarine
INS Shishumar	S44	Shishumar		Howaldtswerke-Deutsche Werft, Kiel, Germany	Attack submarine
INS Shankush	S45	Shishumar		Howaldtswerke-Deutsche Werft, Kiel, Germany	Attack submarine
INS Shalki	S46	Shishumar		Howaldtswerke-Deutsche Werft, Kiel, Germany	Attack submarine
INS Shankul	S47	Shishumar		Howaldtswerke-Deutsche Werft, Kiel, Germany	Attack submarine

AIRCRAFT CARRIERS

NAME	PENNANT NUMBER	CLASS	MOTTO	MANUFACTURER
INS Vikramaditya	R33	Kiev	Strike Far, Strike Sure	Black Sea Shipyard, USSR, and Sevmash, Russia
INS Vikrant	R11	Vikrant	I defeat those who fight against me	Cochin Shipyard Limited

AMPHIBIOUS TRANSPORT DOCKS

NAME OF THE SHIP	PENNANT NUMBER	CLASS	ORIGIN	MOTTO	TYPE
INS Jalashwa	L41	Austin	United States	The fearless pioneers	Amphibious Transport Dock

LANDING SHIP TANK (LST)

NAME OF THE SHIP	PENNANT NUMBER	CLASS	ORIGIN	MOTTO	TYPE
INS Gharial	L23	Magar	India		Landing ship tank (LST)
INS Shradul	L16	Shradul	India	All for one, One for all	LST
INS Kesari	L15	Shradul	India		LST
INS Airavat	L24	Shradul	India		LST

LANDING CRAFT

NAME OF THE SHIP(S)	CLASS	ORIGIN	TYPE
INS LCU 51 INS LCU 52 INS LCU 53 INS LCU 54 INS LCU 55 INS LCU 56 INS LCU 57 INS LCU 58	Mk. IV LCU	India	Landing craft utility (LCU)

DESTROYERS

NAME OF THE SHIP	PENNANT NUMBER	CLASS	ORIGIN	MOTTO	TYPE
INS Visakhapatnam	D66	Visakhapatnam class	India	Attain Glory	Guided missile destroyer
INS Mormugao	D67	Visakhapatnam class	India	Destroyer in Sea	Guided missile destroyer
INS Imphal	D68	Visakhapatnam class	India		Guided missile destroyer
INS Kolkata	D63	Kolkata class	India	Always Prepared for Battle	Guided missile destroyer
INS Kochi	D64	Kolkata class	India	Oh mighty armed one, conquer the enemy	Guided missile destroyer
INS Chennai	D65	Kolkata class	India	Vanquisher of Enemies	Guided missile destroyer

NAME OF THE SHIP	PENNANT NUMBER	CLASS	ORIGIN	MOTTO	TYPE
INS Delhi	D61	Delhi class	India		Guided missile destroyer
INS Mysore	D60	Delhi class	India	Always Fearless	Guided missile destroyer
INS Mumbai	D62	Delhi class	India	I am Invincible	Guided missile destroyer
INS Rana	D52	Rajput class	Soviet Union		Guided missile destroyer
INS Ranvir	D54	Rajput class	Soviet Union		Guided missile destroyer
INS Ranvijay	D55	Rajput class	Soviet Union		Guided missile destroyer

CORVETTES

NAME OF THE SHIP	PENNANT NUMBER	CLASS	ORIGIN	TYPE
INS Kamorta	P28	Kamorta class	India	Anti-submarine warfare (ASW) corvette
INS Kadmatt	P29	Kamorta class	India	ASW corvette
INS Kiltan	P30	Kamorta class	India	ASW corvette
INS Kavaratti	P31	Kamorta class	India	Corvette
INS Kora	P61	Kora class	India	Corvette
INS Kirch	P62	Kora class	India	Corvette
INS Kulish	P63	Kora class	India	Corvette
INS Karmuk	P64	Kora class	India	Corvette
INS Kuthar	P46	Khukri class	India	Corvette
INS Khanjar	P47	Khukri class	India	Corvette
INS Vibhuti	K45	Veer class	India	Corvette
INS Vipul	K46	Veer class	India	Corvette
INS Vinash	K47	Veer class	India	Corvette
INS Vidyut	K48	Veer class	India	Corvette
INS Nashak	K83	Veer class	India	Corvette
INS Pralaya	K91	Veer class	India	Corvette
INS Prabal	K92	Veer class	India	Corvette
INS Abhay	P33	Abhay class	Soviet Union	ASW corvette

FRIGATES

NAME OF THE SHIP	PENNANT NUMBER	CLASS	ORIGIN	MOTTO	TYPE
INS Shivalik	F47	Shivalik class	India		Guided missile frigate
INS Satpura	F48	Shivalik class	India	Determination, Pride, Bravery	Guided missile frigate
INS Sahyadri	F49	Shivalik class	India		Guided missile frigate
INS Talwar	F40	Talwar class	India and Russia		Guided missile frigate
INS Trishul	F43	Talwar class	India and Russia		Guided missile frigate
INS Tabar	F44	Talwar class	India and Russia	Guts and Glory	Guided missile frigate
INS Teg	F45	Talwar class	India and Russia	Towards Eternal Glory	Guided missile frigate
INS Tarkash	F50	Talwar class	India and Russia		Guided missile frigate
INS Trikand	F51	Talwar class	India and Russia		Guided missile frigate
INS Brahmaputra	F31	Brahmaputra class	India		Guided missile frigate
INS Betwa	F39	Brahmaputra class	India		Guided missile frigate
INS Beas	F37	Brahmaputra class	India		Guided missile frigate
INS Tarasa	T94	Car Nicobar class	India	Patrol vessel	
INS Bangaram	T65	Bangaram class	India	Patrol vessel	
INS Bitra	T66	Bangaram class	India	Patrol vessel	
INS Batti Malv	T67	Bangaram class	India	Patrol vessel	
INS Baratang	T68	Bangaram class	India	Patrol vessel	
INS Trinkat	T61	Trinkat class	India	Patrol vessel	
INS Tarmugli	T62	Trinkat class	India	Patrol vessel	

OFFSHORE PATROL VESSELS

NAME OF THE SHIP	PENNANT NUMBER	CLASS	ORIGIN	TYPE
INS Saryu	P54	Saryu class	India	Offshore patrol vessel
INS Sunayna	P57	Saryu class	India	Offshore patrol vessel
INS Sumedha	P58	Saryu class	India	Offshore patrol vessel
INS Sumitra	P59	Saryu class	India	Offshore patrol vessel
INS Sukanya	P50	Sukanya class	South Korea and India	Offshore patrol vessel
INS Subhadra	P51	Sukanya class	South Korea and India	Offshore patrol vessel
INS Suvarna	P52	Sukanya class	South Korea and India	Offshore patrol vessel
INS Savitri	P53	Sukanya class	South Korea and India	Offshore patrol vessel
INS Sharda	P55	Sukanya class	South Korea and India	Offshore patrol vessel
INS Sujata	P56	Sukanya class	South Korea and India	Offshore patrol vessel

PATROL VESSELS

NAME OF THE SHIP	PENNANT NUMBER	CLASS	ORIGIN	TYPE
INS Car Nicobar	T69	Car Nicobar class	India	Patrol vessel
INS Chetlat	T70	Car Nicobar class	India	Patrol vessel
INS Cora Divh	T71	Car Nicobar class	India	Patrol vessel
INS Cheriyam	T72	Car Nicobar class	India	Patrol vessel
INS Cankaraso	T73	Car Nicobar class	India	Patrol vessel
INS Kondul	T74	Car Nicobar class	India	Patrol vessel
INS Kalpeni	T75	Car Nicobar class	India	Patrol vessel
INS Kabra	T76	Car Nicobar class	India	Patrol vessel
INS Koswarı	T77	Car Nicobar class	India	Patrol vessel
INS Karuva	T78	Car Nicobar class	India	Patrol vessel
INS Tillanchang	T92	Car Nicobar class	India	Patrol vessel
INS Tihayu	T93	Car Nicobar class	India	Patrol vessel
INS Tarasa	T94	Car Nicobar class	India	Patrol vessel
INS Bangaram	T65	Bangaram class	India	Patrol vessel
INS Bitra	T66	Bangaram class	India	Patrol vessel
INS Batti Malv	T67	Bangaram class	India	Patrol vessel

NAME OF THE SHIP	PENNANT NUMBER	CLASS	ORIGIN	TYPE
INS Baratang	T68	Bangaram class	India	Patrol vessel
INS Trinkat	T61	Trinkat class	India	Patrol vessel
INS Tarmugli	T62	Trinkat class	India	Patrol vessel

OPERATIONS OF THE INDIAN NAVY

NAME OF THE OPERATION	YEAR	IMPORTANT HIGHLIGHTS
Operation Vijay	December 1961	• Liberation of Goa and Daman and Diu from the Portuguese rule. • First integrated tri-service operation of India.
Operation Trident	December 1971	• Indian Navy's operation on Karachi port in Pakistan. • This was conducted during India-Pakistan war of 1971.
Operation Python	December 1971	• Follow-up of Operation Trident. • The navy again targeted Kemari Oil Refinery in Karachi to successfully create fuel crisis in Pakistan.
Operation Cactus	November 1988	• India's successful tri-service military intervention in Maldives. • It aimed to prevent the military coup against the ruling Maldivian government headed by the then President Abdul Gayoom. • The coup was attempted by Abdul Luthufi, a Maldivian businessman, with the help of Sri Lankan separatist group People's Liberation Organisation of Tamil Eelam (PLOTE).
Operation Talwar (Sword)	1999	Cut off the supply routes to Pakistani port during the Kargil War.
Operation Sukoon	August 2006	Evacuate Indian, Nepalese, and Sri Lankan nationals from the conflict zone of 2006 Lebanon War.
Operation Raahat	April 2015	Evacuate Indian citizens and foreign nationals from Yemen during the 2015 Yemini Crisis.
Operation Nistar	June 2018	Evacuate 38 stranded Indians around Socotra Island, which is located close to the Horn of Africa between the Gulf of Aden and the Arabian Sea. It was a Humanitarian and Disaster Relief Operation (HADR).
Operation Samudra Setu	May–July 2020	Repatriate Indian citizens from overseas during the COVID-19 pandemic.

BILATERAL NAVAL EXERCISES

NAME OF THE EXERCISE	COUNTRIES INVOLVED
AUSINDEX	India and Australia
Al-Mohed-Ai-Hindi	India and Saudi Arabia
BONGOSAGAR	India and Bangladesh
Ekatha	India and Maldives
Indra	India and Russia
JIMEX	India and Japan
Konkan	India and United Kingdom
Naseem-Al-Bahr	India and Oman
Samudra Shakti	India and Indonesia
SIMBEX	India and Singapore
SLINEX	India and Sri Lanka
Varuna	India and France
Zayed Talwar	India and UAE

MULTILATERAL

NAME OF THE EXERCISE	COUNTRIES INVOLVED
Malabar	Australia, Japan, India, and United States
Milan	Australia, Bangladesh, France, Indonesia, Iran, Japan, Malaysia, Mauritius, Myanmar, Russia, Seychelles, Sri Lanka, Thailand, United States, Vietnam (These are for 2024 edition. Participating countries keep on changing every year.)
Sea Dragon	Australia, India, Japan, South Korea, and United States

COORDINATED PATROLS (CORPATS)

NAME OF THE EXERCISE	COUNTRIES INVOLVED
IN-BN CORPAT	India and Bangladesh
IND-INDO CORPAT	India and Indonesia
INDO-THAI CORPAT	India and Thailand

CHIEF OF DEFENCE STAFF (CDS)

BRIEF INTRODUCTION

- CDS is the permanent chairman of the Chiefs of Staff Committee (CoSC) and principal military adviser to the defence minister on all matters related to the tri-services of the Indian armed forces.
- The post of CDS is occupied by a four-star and the senior most ranking officer of the Indian armed forces.
- CDS is the ex-officio secretary of the Department of Military Affairs making him accountable to the parliament on the armed forces.

- The Ministry of Defence recommends there is no fixed duration of the term of CDS, but it has an upper age limit of 65 years.
- General Bipin Rawat was appointed the country's first CDS on 31 December 2019. Lieutenant General Anil Chauhan is the current CDS of India.

HISTORY

- In 1999, the K. Subrahmanyam Committee, also known as the Kargil Review Committee recommended the comprehensive review of the national security framework for improved decision-making in defence matters.
- Based on this report, a group of ministers (GoM) recommended the creation of the Chief of Defence Staff (CDS) post in 2001.
- In May 2011, the Naresh Chandra Task Force recommended the creation of the permanent post of chairman of CoSC.
- In 2019, a committee of defence headed by Lt General D.B. Shekatkar recommended the creation of the post of CDS.
- Prime Minister Narendra Modi announced the creation of the post of CDS on 15 August 2019.
- On 24 December 2019, the Cabinet Committee on Security created the history post of CDS. As of July 2024, the CDS of India is Lieutenant General Anil Chauhan.

FUNCTIONS OF CDS

- Heads the Department of Military Affairs in the Ministry of Defence and serves as its secretary.
- Acts as the principal military advisor to the Union Defence Ministry on all tri-service matters.
- Participates as a member of the Defence Acquisition Council, chaired by the Union Defence Minister.
- Functions as the military advisor to the Nuclear Command Authority.
- Promotes jointness in operations, logistics, transport, training, support services, communications, and maintenance across the three services.
- Ensure optimal utilization and rationalization of infrastructure through joint efforts among the services.
- Implements the Five-Year Defence Capital Acquisition Plan and Two-Year Roll-on Annual Acquisition Plans, following the Integrated Capability Development Plan.
- Prioritizes inter-service capital acquisition proposals based on the anticipated budget.
- Introduces reforms in the three services to enhance combat capabilities and reduce wasteful expenditure.
- Facilitates the restructuring of military commands to optimize resource utilization by promoting joint operations, including the establishment of joint/theatre commands, as part of the Department of Military Affairs' mandate.

GALLANTRY AWARDS

- These awards are presented to military personnel as a formal recognition of their extraordinary bravery, service, and sacrifices for their nation. These gallantry awards are announced twice a year – on the occasion of the Republic Day and the Independence Day.
- The order of precedence of awards is the Param Vir Chakra, the Ashoka Chakra, the Mahavir Chakra, the Kirti Chakra, the Vir Chakra, and the Shaurya Chakra.

BRIEF HISTORY

- The first three gallantry awards instituted by the Government of India were Param Vir Chakra, Maha Vir Chakra, and Vir Chakra on 26 January 1950. However, these were deemed to have effect from 15 August 1947.
- On 4 January 1952, the Government of India instituted three gallantry awards: Ashoka Chakra Class-I, Ashoka Chakra Class-II, and Ashoka Chakra Class-III. These were deemed to have effect from 15 August 1947. Subsequently, these were named Ashoka Chakra, Kirti Chakra, and Shaurya Chakra respectively in January 1967.

SELECTION PROCESS

- The Ministry of Defence invited recommendations from the Armed Forces and the Union Home Ministry twice a year for the names of the awardees.
- The Central Honours & Awards Committee (CH&AC) considers these recommendations.
- The committee comprises the Union Defence Minister, three Service Chiefs, Defence Secretary.
- The Home Secretary is also a member of the cases recommended by the MHA.
- The recommendations are sent to the Prime Minister and President for approval.

WARTIME GALLANTRY AWARDS

- These are conferred for acts of bravery and valor during armed conflict or military operations against an enemy. The awards in this category are:

Param Vir Chakra

- It is the highest military decoration awarded for the most conspicuous bravery or some daring or pre-eminent act of valor or self-sacrifice, in the presence of the enemy, on land, at sea, or in the air.
- It was designed by Mrs Savitri Khanolkar, who drew inspiration from sage Dadhichi, a Vedic rishi.
- It is made of bronze and is circular.
- On the obverse side, the state emblem is embossed in the centre and is surrounded by four replicas of 'Indra's Vajra'.
- On the reverse side, it has 'PARAM VIR CHAKRA' embossed in both English and Hindi. It has two lotus flowers between the Hindi and the English inscriptions.
- The decoration is suspended from a straight swiveling suspension bar and is held by a 32-mm purple ribbon.
- It is conferred by the President to the awardees/Next-of-Kins (NoKs) on the occasion of the Republic Day Parade at the Rajpath.

Mahavir Chakra

- It is the second-highest military decoration awarded for acts of conspicuous gallantry in the presence of the enemy, whether on land, at sea, or in the air.
- It is circular and is made of standard silver. On the obverse side, there is a five-pointed heraldic star with the points of the star just touching the rim with the state emblem and motto embossed in the centre. The star is

polished and the centrepiece is in gold gilt and dorned.

- On the reverse side, 'Maha Vir Chakra' is embossed both in Hindi and English, and these two versions are separated by two lotus flowers.
- The fitting is swivel mounting. The ribbon is half-white and half-orange.

Vir Chakra

- It is the third-highest military decoration awarded for acts of conspicuous gallantry in the presence of the enemy, whether on land, at sea, or in the air.
- It is circular and is made of standard silver. On the obverse side, there is a five-pointed heraldic star with the points of the star just touching the rim, with the state emblem and motto embossed in the centre. The star is polished and the centrepiece is in gold gilt and domed.
- On the reverse side, 'Vir Chakra' is embossed both in Hindi and English, and these two versions are separated by two lotus flowers.
- The fitting is swivel mounting and the ribbon is half blue and half orange.

PEACETIME GALLANTRY AWARDS

These are conferred for acts of bravery during non-combat situations, such as counter-insurgency operations, rescue missions, and other acts of heroism in peacetime. The awards in this category are:

Ashoka Chakra

- It is the highest peacetime military decoration of India and is the peacetime equivalent of the Param Vir Chakra (PVC).
- It is circular and made of gold gilt. On the obverse side, it has an embossed replica of Ashoka's Chakra in the centre, surrounded by a lotus wreath. On its reverse, it has 'Ashoka Chakra' written in both English and Hindi, and these two versions are separated by two lotus flowers.
- It has a green colour ribbon divided into two equal segments by an orange vertical line.
- It is conferred by the President to the awardees/Next-of-Kins (NoKs) on the occasion of the Republic Day Parade at the Rajpath.

Kirti Chakra

- It is the second-highest peacetime military decoration in India.
- It is circular and made of standard silver. On the obverse side, it has an embossed replica of Ashoka Chakra in the centre, surrounded by a lotus wreath. On its reverse, it has 'Kirti Chakra' embossed in Hindi and English, and these two versions are separated by two lotus flowers.
- It has a green colour ribbon divided into three equal parts by two orange vertical lines.

Shaurya Chakra

- It is the third-highest peacetime military decoration in India.
- It is circular and made of bronze. On the obverse side, the medal has an embossed replica of Ashoka Chakra in the centre, surrounded by a lotus wreath. On the reverse side, it has 'Shaurya Chakra' written in both Hindi and English, and these two versions are separated by two lotus flowers.
- The green ribbon is divided into four equal parts by three vertical lines.

10 International Organizations and Indices

UNITED NATIONS

United Nations is an international organization that was established to maintain global peace and security. It was set up post the Second World War to cope with the aftermath of the world war and also prevent any future wars. However, in the last few years its scope has broadened and at present, the United Nations works on the following five main areas:

1. Maintain international peace and security
2. Protect human rights
3. Deliver humanitarian rights
4. Support sustainable development and climate action
5. Uphold international law

History of the United Nations

League of Nations was the predecessor of the United Nations. It was the first international organization that was created after the First World War to provide a forum for resolving international disputes and achieving peace and security. The Treaty of Versailles was the foundation stone of League of Nations and it was effective from 10 January 1920. However, the League of Nations ceased to exist on 20 April 1946, giving way to the United Nations.

MILESTONES IN THE HISTORY OF THE UNITED NATIONS

Preparatory Years-UN Charter History

1941: Inter-Allied Declaration: The Declaration of St. James Palace or the London Declaration

This was an important document signed during the Second World War by representatives of the Allied powers. It was signed on 5 January 1941, at St. James's Palace in London by the representatives of Great Britain, Canada, Australia, New Zealand, and the Union of South Africa and of the exiled governments of Belgium, Czechoslovakia, Greece, Luxembourg, the Netherlands, Norway, Poland, Yugoslavia, and of General de Gaulle of France. The key objectives of the declaration were to outline the shared principles and goals of the Allied powers in their fight against the Axis powers (Germany, Italy, and Japan). The declaration called for the establishment of a post-war international organization that would promote collective security and cooperation among nations. This was a precursor to the formation of the United Nations (UN) after the war.

1941: The Atlantic Charter

It was a joint declaration issued on 14 August 1941 by the United States and the United Kingdom during the Second World War. This was considered the origin of the Charter of the United Nations. It was signed by Franklin D. Roosevelt, the then president of the United States, and Winston Churchill, the then PM of the United Kingdom.

It was signed during a meeting on the ship H.M.S. Prince of Wales, 'somewhere at sea', thus came to be known as 'The Atlantic Charter'. The charter proposed a set of principles for international collaboration in maintaining peace and security.

1942: The Declaration by United Nations

It was for the first time that the term 'United Nations' was used in the document. The name 'United Nations' was coined by US President Franklin D. Roosevelt. The declaration was issued on 1 January 1942, during the Second World War, by representatives of 26 Allied nations. It marked the formation of a broad coalition of countries united in their commitment to defeat the Axis powers.

1943: Moscow and Teheran Conferences

During a conference held in Moscow from 18 October to 1 November 1943, a declaration was signed on 30 October 1943 by the governments of the Soviet Union, the United Kingdom, the United States, and China. The declaration emphasized for an early establishment of an international organization to maintain peace and security.

On 1 December 1943, the goal to establish an international organization was reaffirmed at the meeting of the leaders of the United States, the USSR, and the United Kingdom in Teheran.

1945: Dumbarton Oaks and Yalta

The representatives of the United States and the United Kingdom met separately with representatives of the USSR from (21 August–28 September) and of China (29 September–7 October) at Dumbarton Oaks in Washington DC. The first blueprint of the United Nations was prepared at this conference. The final outcome of the conference was issued on 9 October 1944. It was known as the 'Proposal for the Establishment of a General International Organization', which constituted the initial working document at the San Francisco Conference, in 1945.

On 11 February 1954 at the Yalta conference, US President Roosevelt, UK Prime Minister Churchill, and USSR's Premier Joseph Stalin declared their resolve to establish a general international organization to maintain peace and security. Thus, invites were sent out for the conference to be held in San Francisco in the United States on 25 April 1945. However, President Roosevelt died suddenly from a cerebral haemorrhage on 12 April 1945.

The San Francisco Conference

The invites for this conference were sent to 46 countries, including the four sponsors. These countries had subscribed to the United Nations charter and had declared war on Germany and Japan. The conference itself invited four other states – the Byelorussian Soviet Socialist Republic, the Ukrainian Soviet Socialist Republic, newly liberated Denmark, and Argentina.

The Charter of the United Nations was adopted unanimously along with the Statute of the International Court of Justice on 25 June 1945 at the San Francisco Opera House. Henceforth, the charter was signed at the San Francisco Conference on 26 June 1945.

However, the United Nations could come into existence only when the charter was approved by the congresses or parliaments of China, France, Great Britain, the Soviet Union, and the United States, and a majority of the other signatory states. The charter had to be ratified and deposited with the State Department of the United States. Thus, the United Nations charter came into effect on 24 October 1945, which is now observed as the official United Nations Day.

FACT FILE

Poland signed the United Nations charter on 15 October 1945 as an original signatory.

Facts about the United Nations

- Headquarters: New York, United States
- Original founding members: 51
- First Secretary-General: Trygve Halvdan Lie
- Total members: 193
- Observer states: 2 (Holy See and the state of Palestine)
- Official languages: 6 (Arabic, Chinese, English, French, Russian, and Spanish)
- United Nations Day: 24 October (Officially designated as the UN day by the General Assembly in the year 1947)
- Four pillars of the United Nations: peace and security, human rights, rule of law, and development
- Current Secretary-General: António Guterres

PRINCIPAL ORGANS OF THE UNITED NATIONS

UNITED NATIONS GENERAL ASSEMBLY (UNGA)

UNGA is the main policymaking organ and a single forum for multilateral discussions on international issues that are included in the Charter of the United Nations.

All UN member states are represented in the General Assembly and each member state has one vote. The decisions are taken by the two-thirds majority. The recommendations of UNGA are not binding on any of its member countries.

UNGA meets from September to December annually. At the beginning of each regular session, there is a general debate on the pressing international issues which is followed by a discussion on issues in one of the six main committees:

1. The Disarmament and International Security Committee (First Committee)
2. The Economic and Financial Committee (Second Committee)
3. The Social, Humanitarian and Cultural Committee (Third Committee)
4. The Special Political and Decolonization Committee (Fourth Committee)
5. The Administrative and Budgetary Committee (Fifth Committee)
6. The Legal Committee (Sixth Committee)

President of the UNGA

The presidency of the General Assembly rotates among the five regional groups, namely the Group of Asian States, the Group of Eastern European States, the Group of Latin American and Caribbean States, the Group of African States, the Western European and other States Group.

The president is elected by a simple majority vote of the UNGA and is elected at least three months before formally assuming office, usually in mid-June.

The president is the guardian of the GA Rules of Procedure but has no say in the actual decision-making of the GA. The president does not have a vote in the GA. Even on procedural matters, the PGA always remains under the authority of the GA.

PGA interacts and engages with the media, civil society, and the wider public. He/she can attend UN conferences and other international and regional intergovernmental meetings and visit member states.

Functions and Powers of UNGA

- To discuss issues related to international peace and security except those being discussed by the Security Council.
- To discuss and approve the UN budget.
- Election of
  - ➢ Non-permanent members of the Security Council.
  - ➢ The members of the Economic and Social Council (ECOSOC).

  - Judges of the International Court of Justice (jointly with the Security Council).
- To appoint the secretary-general on the recommendation of the Security Council.
- To discuss and make recommendations on the powers and functions of any organ of the UN.
- To request studies and make recommendations to promote international cooperation, the development of international law, the protection of human rights, and international collaboration on economic, social, cultural, educational, and health issues.
- To receive and discuss reports from the Security Council and other UN organs.

Quick Facts

First session of the UNGA: 10 January 1946, London

First president of the UNGA: Paul-Henri Spaak, foreign minister of Belgium

First woman to address UNGA: Frieda Dalen, Norway

First session of UNSC: 17 January 1946, London

UNITED NATIONS SECURITY COUNCIL (UNSC)

UNSC is a 15-member organ of the United Nations entrusted with the primary responsibility for maintaining international peace and security. UNSC is tasked with deploying peacekeeping operations to regions experiencing conflicts or threats to peace. It authorizes the use of force and takes actions to resolve disputes and maintain peace. It has the power to impose economic and diplomatic sanctions on countries or entities that violate international peace and security. It mediates and facilitates negotiations between parties to resolve disputes peacefully.

Structure of UNSC

In UNSC, there are 5 permanent and 10 non-permanent members. The five permanent members are the United States, China, France, Russia, and the United Kingdom. They are also known as P5. P5 have the Veto Power, which is the ability of a permanent member to stop a draft resolution from being adopted or to overturn a decision taken by the UNSC.

There are 10 non-permanent members, 5 of which are elected each year by the General Assembly for a two-year term.

Originally, there were 11 members of the Security Council: five permanent and six non-permanent members. It was in the year 1963 that an amendment was done in the UN charter to increase the membership of the Security Council.

Arria-Formula Meetings

These are informal and confidential meetings of Security Council. These are convened at the initiative of a member or members of the council. It provides interested council members an opportunity to engage in a direct dialogue with high representatives of governments and international organizations.

President of the UNSC

The presidency of the Security Council rotates monthly in the English alphabetical order of the names of the members of the council. If the country the president represents is directly involved in a dispute that is being considered by the Security Council, he/she may decide not to preside over the council during the period that this issue is being discussed. When this occurs, the representative of the member next in English alphabetical order temporarily assumes the presidency. The presidency of the Security Council is assigned to the state not the individual. As a result, any member of the government can preside over meetings during the month when their country has been assigned to the presidency of the council. In addition to presiding over meetings, the president also makes statements in his/her national capacity as a representative of the government.

ECONOMIC AND SOCIAL COUNCIL (ECOSOC)

ECOSOC coordinates the economic and social work of the United Nations and the UN family of organizations. It is a central forum for discussing international economic and social issues and for formulating policy recommendations. Also, it plays a key role in fostering international cooperation for development. It functions under the overall authority of the United Nations General Assembly and has 54 members that are elected by the General Assembly for a period of three-year terms.

It meets throughout the year; however, the major session is held in July.

It has five regional commissions that promote economic development and cooperation in their respective regions:

1. Economic Commission for Africa (ECA)
2. Economic Commission for Europe (ECE)
3. Economic Commission for Latin America and the Caribbean (ECLAC)
4. Economic and Social Commission for Asia and the Pacific (ESCAP)
5. Economic and Social Commission for Western Asia (ESCWA)

TRUSTEESHIP COUNCIL

The Trusteeship Council was established to supervise the administration of trust territories as they transitioned from colonies to sovereign nations.

Trust territories were basically once a part of the German and Ottoman Empires. At the end of the First World War, their control was passed over to the League of Nations. Once the UN Charter came into force in late 1945, these were renamed the United Nations Trust Territories.

There were 11 trust territories and the council suspended its activities in the year 1994 when Palau, the last trust territory, gained its independence.

However, the formal elimination of the Trusteeship Council would require the revision of the UN Charter.

INTERNATIONAL COURT OF JUSTICE (ICJ)

ICJ is the major judicial organ of the United Nations and was established in June 1945 by the Charter of the United Nations and began work in April 1946. It is also known as the World Court.

ICJ settles legal disputes among the member states in accordance with international law. It acts as an advisory body on legal questions referred to it by authorized United Nations organs and specialized agencies. It plays a crucial role in promoting the peaceful settlement of international disputes through legal means and diplomacy. Although the court's decisions are binding, enforcing them depends on the willingness of the parties involved to comply with the rulings.

ICJ has 15 Judges that are elected to nine-year terms of office by the United Nations General Assembly and the Security Council. Its headquarters are at Peace Palace, The Hague, Netherlands. It is the only main organ of the United Nations which is not located in New York, US.

Current President of ICJ: Nawaf Salam

SECRETARIAT

It is the executive arm of the United Nations and carries out the administrative work of the United Nations. It plays an important role in organizing international conferences, translating speeches and documents into UN's official languages, and setting agenda for the deliberative and decision-making bodies of the UN.

It functions under the administrative guidance of the secretary-general, who is appointed by the General Assembly on the recommendation of the Security Council for a period of five years.

Current Secretary-General: António Guterres

United Nations Flag and Emblem

The flag of the United Nations was approved by a United Nations General Assembly resolution on 20 October 1947 as the official emblem of the UN.

The original emblem of the United Nations was created by a team of designers headed by Oliver Lincoln Lundquist during the United Nations Conference on International Organization in 1945. The emblem of the United Nations was designed by Donal McLaughlin.

The flag consists of a white emblem on a blue background. Blue represents peace in opposition to red, for war. The UN emblem is a world map representing an azimuthal equidistant projection centred on the North Pole which is surrounded by two branches of the olive tree. The projection of the map extends to 60 degrees south latitude, and includes five concentric circles.

United Nations Sustainable Development Goals (UNSDGs)

SDGs basically provide a blueprint for a sustainable, prosperous, and peaceful future for the planet Earth. These were adopted in 2015 by all the member states of the United Nations General Assembly (UNGA). There are 17 SDGs that call for an urgent joint global initiative by developed and developing countries across the globe.

History of SDGs

- ***Earth Summit (June 1992, Rio de Janeiro, Brazil)***

  More than 178 countries adopted Agenda 21, which was a comprehensive plan that focussed on building a plan of action to build a global partnership for sustainable development to improve human lives and protect the environment.

- ***Millennium Summit (September 2000, UN Headquarters in New York, US)***

  All the members states adopted the Millennium Declaration that led to the elaboration of eight Millennium Development Goals (MDGs) to reduce extreme poverty by 2015.

- ***United Nations Conference on Sustainable Development (Rio+20) (June 2012, Rio de Janeiro, Brazil)***

  All the member states adopted the document 'The Future We Want'. As a part of this document, the member states focussed on launching the process to develop a set of SDGs to build upon the MDGs and to establish the UN High-level Political Forum on Sustainable Development (HLPF).

- ***2013: A 30-member Open Working Group to develop a proposal on the SDGs.***
- ***UN Sustainable Development Summit (September 2019, New York, US)***

  The UNGA adopted the 2030 Agenda for Sustainable Development which outlined 17 SDGs to be achieved by 2030.

Implementation of SDGs

- The Division for Sustainable Development Goals (DSDG) in the United Nations Department of Economic and Social Affairs (UNDESA) provides substantive support and capacity building for the SDGs and their related thematic issues.
- The annual HLPF serves as the central UN platform for the follow-up and review of the SDGs.
- The UN secretary-general presents an annual SDG Progress Report, which is developed in cooperation with the UN Statistical System, and is based on the global indicator framework and data produced by national statistical systems and information collected at the regional level.
- The Global Sustainable Development Report is produced once every four years to inform the quadrennial SDG review deliberations at the General Assembly. It is written by an Independent Group of Scientists appointed by the secretary-general.

THE SUSTAINABLE DEVELOPMENT GOALS

SDG 1: Extreme Poverty for All People Is Eradicated

SDG 2: There Is Zero Hunger

SDG 3: Equal Access to Healthcare

SDG 4: Quality Education

SDG 5: Gender Equality

SDG 6: Clean Water and Sanitation

SDG 7: Affordable and Renewable Energy

SDG 8: Economic Growth

SDG 9: Industry, Innovation, and Infrastructure

SDG 10: Reduced Inequalities

SDG 11: Sustainable Cities and Communities

SDG 12: Responsible Consumption and Production

SDG 13: Urgent Action to Combat Climate Change

SDG 14: Ocean and Sea Resources

SDG 15: Earth's Ecosystem

SDG 16: Peace, Justice, and Strong Institutions

SDG 17: Partnerships for the Goals

The United Nations System

PRINCIPAL ORGANS

GENERAL ASSEMBLY

Subsidiary Organs

- Disarmament Commission
- Human Rights Council
- International Law Commission
- Joint Inspection Unit (JIU)
- Main committees
- Standing committees and ad hoc bodies

Funds and Programm

UNDP United Nations Developr Programme

- **UNCDF** United Nations Capital Development Fun
- **UNV** United Nations Volu

UNEP[8] United Nations Environr Programme

UNFPA United Nations Populat

UN-HABITAT[8] United Nations Settlements Programme

UNICEF United Nations Childre

WFP World Food Programme (U

SECURITY COUNCIL

Subsidiary Organs

- Counter-Terrorism Committee
- International Residual Mech for Criminal Tribunals
- Military Staff Committee

ECONOMIC AND SOCIAL COUNCIL

Functional Commissions

- Crime Prevention and Criminal Justice
- Narcotic Drugs
- Population and Development
- Science and Technology for Development
- Social Development
- Statistics
- Status of Women
- United Nations Forum on Forests

Regional Commissio

ECA Economic Commission for

ECE Economic Commission for

ECLAC Economic Commission Latin America and the Caribb

ESCAP Economic and Social Commission for Asia and the

ESCWA Economic and Social Commission for Western As

SECRETARIAT

Departments and Offices[9]

EOSG Executive Office of the Secretary-General

DCO Development Coordination Office

DESA Department of Economic and Social Affairs

DGACM Department for General Assembly and Conference Management

DGC Department of Global Communications

DMSPC Department of Management Strategy, Policy and Compliance

DOS Department of Operational Support

DPO Department of Peace Operations

DPPA Department of Political and Peacebuilding Affairs

DSS Department of Safety and Security

OCHA Office for the Coordination of Humanitarian Affairs

OCT Office of Counter-Terrorism

ODA Office for Disarmament Af

OHCHR Office of the United Na High Commissioner for Huma

OIOS Office of Internal Oversight

OLA Office of Legal Affairs

OOSA Office for Outer Space Af

OSAA Office of the Special Adv Africa

SRSG/CAAC Office of the Spec Representative of the Secret General for Children and Arm Conflict

SRSG/SVC Office of the Specia Representative of the Secret General on Sexual Violence ir

SRSG/VAC Office of the Specia Representative of the Secret General on Violence Against

UNDRR United Nations Office fo Disaster Risk Reduction

INTERNATIONAL COURT OF JUSTICE

TRUSTEESHIP COUNCIL[6]

Published by the United Nations Department of Global Communications 23-00013 — July 2

esearch and Training

R United Nations Institute for armament Research

R United Nations Institute for ning and Research

C United Nations System Staff College

nited Nations University

ther Entities

ernational Trade Centre (UN/WTO)

AD[1,8] United Nations Conference on de and Development

R[1] Office of the United Nations h Commissioner for Refugees

S[1] United Nations Office for Project Services

A[1] United Nations Relief and Works ency for Palestine Refugees in the Near East

OMEN[1] United Nations Entity for Gender ality and the Empowerment of Women

acekeeping operations and political missions

ictions committees (ad hoc)

nding committees and ad hoc bodies

ther Bodies[10]

nmittee for Development Policy

nmittee of Experts on Public Administration

nmittee on Non-Governmental Organizations

manent Forum on Indigenous Issues

DS Joint United Nations Programme on /AIDS

GN United Nations Group of Experts on ographical Names

IM Committee of Experts on Global ospatial Information Management

esearch and Training

RI United Nations Interregional Crime and stice Research Institute

SD United Nations Research Institute for cial Development

C[1] United Nations Office on Drugs d Crime

United Nations Office at Geneva

HRLLS Office of the High Representative the Least Developed Countries, Landlocked veloping Countries and Small Island veloping States

United Nations Office at Nairobi

[2] United Nations Office for Partnerships

United Nations Office at Vienna

OUTH United Nations Youth Office

Related Organizations

CTBTO Preparatory Commission for the Comprehensive Nuclear-Test-Ban Treaty Organization

IAEA[1,3] International Atomic Energy Agency

ICC International Criminal Court

IOM[1] International Organization for Migration

ISA International Seabed Authority

ITLOS International Tribunal for the Law of the Sea

OPCW[3] Organization for the Prohibition of Chemical Weapons

WTO[1,4] World Trade Organization

Peacebuilding Commission

HLPF

High-level Political Forum on Sustainable Development

Specialized Agencies[1,5]

FAO Food and Agriculture Organization of the United Nations

ICAO International Civil Aviation Organization

IFAD International Fund for Agricultural Development

ILO International Labour Organization

IMF International Monetary Fund

IMO International Maritime Organization

ITU International Telecommunication Union

UNESCO United Nations Educational, Scientific and Cultural Organization

UNIDO United Nations Industrial Development Organization

UNWTO World Tourism Organization

UPU Universal Postal Union

WHO World Health Organization

WIPO World Intellectual Property Organization

WMO World Meteorological Organization

WORLD BANK GROUP[7]

- **IBRD** International Bank for Reconstruction and Development
- **IDA** International Development Association
- **IFC** International Finance Corporation

Notes:

1 Member of the United Nations System Chief Executives Board for Coordination (CEB).
2 The United Nations Office for Partnerships is the focal point vis-a-vis the United Nations Foundation, Inc.
3 IAEA and OPCW report to the Security Council and the General Assembly (GA).
4 WTO has no reporting obligation to the GA, but contributes on an ad hoc basis to GA and Economic and Social Council (ECOSOC) work on, inter alia, finance and development issues.
5 Specialized agencies are autonomous organizations whose work is coordinated through ECOSOC (intergovernmental level) and CEB (inter-secretariat level).
6 The Trusteeship Council suspended operations on 1 November 1994, as Palau, the last United Nations Trust Territory, became independent on 1 October 1994.
7 International Centre for Settlement of Investment Disputes (ICSID) and Multilateral Investment Guarantee Agency (MIGA) are not specialized agencies in accordance with Articles 57 and 63 of the Charter, but are part of the World Bank Group.
8 The secretariats of these organs are part of the United Nations Secretariat.
9 The Secretariat also includes the following offices: the Ethics Office, United Nations Ombudsman and Mediation Services, and the Office of Administration of Justice.
10 For a complete list of ECOSOC Subsidiary Bodies see un.org/ecosoc.

This Chart is a reflection of the functional organization of the United Nations System and for informational purposes only. It does not include all offices or entities of the United Nations System.

United Nations Sustainable Development Group (UNSDG)

UNSDG brings together various UN entities, agencies, funds, and programmes to work together in a coordinated manner to support countries in achieving the SDGs. UN entities within the UNSDG collaborate closely on various thematic areas to leverage their respective expertise and resources. The UNSDG reports on the progress of UN development activities and contributions to the SDGs to ensure transparency and accountability. It works on strengthening national statistical capacities for data collection, analysis, and monitoring of progress towards the SDGs. It was earlier known as the United Nations Development Group (UNDG).

UN SYSTEM – FUNDS AND PROGRAMMES

UNITED NATIONS DEVELOPMENT PROGRAMME (UNDP)

UNDP is an agency of the United Nations that supports and guides countries to eradicate poverty, reduce inequality, and promote sustainable growth. It works in collaboration with the governments, private sector, and civil society organizations to identify the gaps and provide technical expertise, policy advice, and financial support to help them develop and implement schemes, programmes, and projects that promote human development and sustainable economic growth. It empowers communities and governments to promote inclusive growth, gender equality, and protect human rights through all their activities.

UNDP is central to the UNSDG. The UNDP Administrator is the vice chair of the UNSDG, which unites about 37 entities of the UN system that are working together to achieve the United Nations SDG 2030.

UNITED NATIONS ENVIRONMENT PROGRAMME (UNEP)/UN ENVIRONMENT

UNEP is the leading environmental agency of the United Nations and a member of the UNSDG. It was established as the outcome of the first major global environmental conference held in Stockholm, Sweden, in 1972. It was set up to be a sort of 'world's parliament on the environment'.

Objectives and Functions of UNEP

- *Research and assessment of environmental issues:* It conducts research and assessments on global environmental issues to create a database and provide a scientific framework for the decision and policymaking at a higher level.
- *Environmental policies and advocacy:* UNEP works closely with key stakeholders such as governments, civil society, the private sector, and UN entities to develop environmental policies, strengthen environmental governance, and advocate for sustainable practices. It also advocates the integration and implementation of key international agreements and conventions in a country's policy in order to promote sustainable development.
- *Advisory, capacity building, and technical assistance:* It works in close collaboration with the governments and policymaking bodies of different countries to help them identify the key challenges concerning the environment and, develop and implement practical solutions. It also helps the institutes and countries in capacity building by providing the requisite training, resources, facilitating technology transfer, and knowledge sharing among the nations.

- *Sustainable Development Goals:* UNEP is the custodian for 25 SDG indicators – across SDG Goal 6, 8, 12, 14, 15, and 17. These indicators cover topics related to resource management and protection of water, marine and terrestrial ecosystems, circularity, and environmentally sound management of chemicals and waste.

About UN Environment Assembly (UNEA)

UNEA is the governing body of the UN Environment and is also the world's highest-level decision-making body on the environment. It was established in 2012 by the UNGA resolution as a result of the Rio+20 Conference on Sustainable Development. It replaced the Governing Council of the UNEP.

All the member countries of the UN are members of the UNEA. Besides the member countries, it allows and brings together different stakeholders such as high-level government representatives, environmental experts, scientists, and civil society organizations to discuss and make decisions on pressing environmental issues.

UNEA meets every two years at UNEP's headquarters to address critical environmental issues, set priorities for global environmental policies, and develop international environmental law. The resolutions adopted at UNEA might not be legally binding on the member countries.

UNITED NATIONS POPULATION FUND (UNFPA)

UNFPA is the United Nations agency that aims to improve the reproductive and maternal health of the population across the globe. It was established in the year 1969 as the United Nations Fund for Population Activities (UNFPA). It was brought under the ambit of the UNGA in 1971, and was renamed as United Nations Population Fund in 1987.

UNFPA is a subsidiary organ of the UNGA and receives overall policy guidance from ECOSOC. It reports to the UNDP/UNFPA Executive Board.

Objectives and Functions of UNFPA

UNFPA works on the premise that all human beings are entitled to equal rights and protections.

Its work is spread over the following areas:

- *Population data and research:* It supports census and surveys, conducts research, collects and analyses population data, and provides technical assistance for developing policies and programmes to help countries build demographic resilience.
- *Humanitarian response:* During the humanitarian crisis, it ensures access to sexual and reproductive health services, addresses gender-based violence, and provides essential supplies and support to affected populations, particularly women and girls.
- *Achieving universal sexual and reproductive health:* It promotes comprehensive sex education and supports access to sexual and reproductive health services, including family planning, maternal health care, prevention and treatment of sexually transmitted infections, and safe abortion services where legal.
- *Empowerment:* It partners with civil society, academic institutions, and the private sector; empowers individuals and governments by educating them about their human rights; and advocates for action.
- *Sustainable Development Goals:* UNFPA is the custodian of SDG Indicators 5.6.1 and 5.6.2. It is working with governments, partners, and other UN

agencies to directly tackle many of these goals – in particular Goal 3 on health, Goal 4 on education, and Goal 5 on gender equality.

Since 2018, the UNFPA is working towards achieving three transformative goals. These are also known as the three zeros and are to be fulfilled by 2030:

1. *Ending unmet need for family planning:* UNFPA provides access to voluntary family planning services and information. It is the world's single-largest provider of donated contraceptives to developing countries. It dismantles the barriers to these services and ensures that there's increased availability of contraceptives.
2. *Ending preventable maternal death:* UNFPA helps strengthen health systems, train and educate health workers and midwives, and improve access to a full range of reproductive health services. It also focusses on addressing the underlying social and economic factors that contribute to maternal mortality.
3. *Ending gender-based violence and harmful practices:* UNFPA works with policymakers, justice systems, and health systems. It engages men and boys to promote gender equality and women empowerment.

UNITED NATIONS HUMAN SETTLEMENTS PROGRAMME (UN-HABITAT)

UN-Habitat is the United Nations programme that works towards promoting the development of socially and environmentally sustainable towns and cities for human settlement and progress.

It collaborates with different governments, UN agencies, foundations, civil society organizations, academic institutions, and the private sector to build inclusive, safe, resilient, and sustainable cities and communities. As a part of the UN-Habitat's strategic plan 2014–19, it worked on seven focus areas:

1. Urban legislation, land, and governance
2. Urban planning and design
3. Urban economy
4. Urban basic services
5. Housing and slum upgrading
6. Risk reduction and rehabilitation
7. Research and capacity development

UN-Habitat Conferences

UN-Habitat was as an outcome of the UN Conference on Human Settlements and Sustainable Urban Development (Habitat I) held in Vancouver, Canada, 1977.

The mandate of the UN-Habitat was the outcome of the UN Conference on Human Settlements (Habitat II) held in Istanbul, Turkey, 1996.

The New Urban Agenda was adopted at the UN Conference on Housing and Sustainable Urban Development (Habitat III) held in Quito, Ecuador, 2016.

About New Urban Agenda (NUA)

The NUA lays down the basic guidelines and framework for urban development for the next 20 years. It has established a new global standard for sustainable urban development while building cities that can serve as engines of prosperity and centres of cultural and social well-being while protecting the environment. As a part of this agenda, the leaders have committed to:

- Provide basic services such as access to housing, safe drinking water and sanitation, nutritious food, healthcare and family planning, education, culture, and communication technologies for all citizens.

- Ensure that all citizens have access to equal opportunities and face no discrimination. The city authorities will take into account the needs of women, youth and children, people with disabilities, marginalized groups, older persons, indigenous people, among other groups.
- Promote measures that support cleaner cities, such as using renewable energy, providing better and greener public transport, and sustainably managing natural resources.
- Strengthen resilience in cities to reduce the risk and the impact of disasters by doing better urban planning, providing quality infrastructure, and improving local responses.
- Take action to address climate change by reducing their greenhouse gas emissions.
- Fully respect the rights of refugees, migrants, and internally displaced persons regardless of their migration status.
- Improve connectivity and support innovative and green initiatives by establishing partnerships with businesses and civil society to find sustainable solutions to urban challenges.
- Promote safe, accessible, and green public spaces where human interaction is facilitated.

UN-Habitat and SDGs

UN-Habitat is the custodian agency for 9 of the 15 indicators under SDG 11 and supports the monitoring and reporting of four indicators in other goals.

UNITED NATIONS CHILDREN'S FUND (UNICEF)

UNICEF is the United Nations agency working towards the protection, upliftment, and welfare of children and adolescents across the world. It supports child health and nutrition, safe water and sanitation, quality education and skill building, HIV prevention and treatment for mothers and babies, and the protection of children and adolescents from violence and exploitation.

UNICEF was established as the United Nations International Children's Emergency Fund to meet the emergency needs of children in post-war Europe and China.

UNICEF works on the following:

- *Child protection and inclusion:* It works in close association with different stakeholders across the world to protect and prevent children from any form of abuse, exploitation, trafficking, child labour, marriage, etc. It works with stakeholders and partners on developing and implementing policies and programmes that ensure that children grow up in a safe and inclusive environment without facing any sort of discrimination on the basis of gender, caste, creed, religion, nationality, or some disability.
- *Child survival:* UNICEF has helped to significantly reduce child mortality all over the world by working to reach the most vulnerable children, everywhere.
- *Education:* It advocates for and supports quality education for all children, with focus on ensuring access to primary education, particularly for marginalized and disadvantaged children.
- *Health and nutrition:* It works to ensure that children have access to basic health and nutrition.
- *Social inclusion:* It promotes social inclusion and advocates for the rights of children with disabilities, those living in poverty, and other vulnerable groups.

- *Emergencies:* It plays a critical role in providing emergency assistance to children and families affected by conflicts, natural disasters, and other humanitarian crises.
- *Research and data:* It conducts research and collects data on children's issues to form evidence-based policies and programmes.
- *Water, sanitation, and hygiene (WASH):* It promotes access to safe water, sanitation facilities, and hygiene practices to protect children's health and prevent diseases. It supports programmes that improve water and sanitation infrastructure in communities, schools, and health facilities.
- *Advocacy and policy development:* UNICEF advocates for policies and programmes that prioritize children's rights and well-being. It works to raise awareness, mobilize resources, and promote child-friendly policies and legislation at national and international levels.

UNICEF and SDG

UNICEF is the custodian for global monitoring of two indicators that measure progress towards Goal 16:

Indicator 16.2.1 Proportion of children aged 1–17 years who experienced any physical punishment and/or psychological aggression by caregivers in the past month; and

Indicator 16.2.3 Proportion of young women and men aged 18–29 years who experienced sexual violence by age 18.

It is also a co-custodian for global monitoring of:

Indicator 16.9.1 Proportion of children under five years of age whose births have been registered with a civil authority by age.

WORLD FOOD PROGRAMME (WFP)

WFP is the world's largest humanitarian organization that addresses hunger, provides food assistance, and promotes food security worldwide. It uses food assistance to build pathways to peace and stability for people recovering from conflict, disasters, and the impact of climate change. The first development programme was launched in Sudan in 1963.

It was awarded with the Nobel Peace Prize in 2020 for its efforts to provide food assistance in areas of conflict, and to prevent the use of food as a weapon of war and conflict.

The key focus areas of WFP are:

- *School feeding:* It works to prevent situations from deteriorating into famine by strengthening education, nutrition, livelihood resilience, and social protection systems such as school meals programmes.
- *Preventing and mitigating famine:* It uses technology to alert about the risk of famine and determine the most appropriate response.
- *Emergency response:* It provides immediate food assistance to people affected by crises such as armed conflicts, natural disasters, and refugee situations. It delivers food aid to ensure that those facing acute food shortages receive timely support.
- *Food security and resilience:* It supports initiatives that enhance food security and build resilience among communities vulnerable to food crises. This includes providing support for small-scale farmers and promoting sustainable agricultural practices.

- *Nutrition:* WFP focusses on combatting malnutrition, particularly among children, pregnant women, and breastfeeding mothers. The organization provides specialized nutritional support, such as therapeutic foods and nutritional supplements, to prevent and treat malnutrition in vulnerable populations.
- *Logistics and supply chain management:* It has extensive expertise in logistics and supply chain management. It ensures that there is timely and efficient delivery of food at the required places.
- *Policy and advocacy:* It advocates for policies and actions that address the root causes of hunger and promote food security. The organization raises awareness about global hunger issues, supports evidence-based policies, and works to mobilize resources and political commitment to fight hunger and malnutrition.

WFP and SDG

It focusses on fulfilment of SDG-2 of zero hunger by 2030.

S.NO.	NAME OF THE AGENCY	HEADQUARTERS	ESTABLISHED ON/YEAR	HEAD/CHIEF
1	United Nations Development Programme (UNDP)	New York, United States	22 November 1965	UNDP administrator: Achim Steiner
2	United Nations Environment Programme (UNEP)/UN Environment	Nairobi, Kenya	5 June 1972	Executive director: Inger Andersen
3	United Nations Population Fund (UNFPA)	New York, USA	1969	Executive director: Natalia Kanem
4	United Nations Human Settlements Programme (UN-Habitat)	Nairobi, Kenya	1977	Executive director: Maimunah Mohd Sharif
5	United Nations Children's Fund (UNICEF)	New York, US	11 December 1946	Executive director: Catherine M. Russell
6	World Food Programme (WFP)	Rome, Italy	19 December 1961	Executive director: Cindy McCain

UN SPECIALIZED AGENCIES

FOOD AND AGRICULTURE ORGANIZATION (FAO)

FAO is the specialized agency of the United Nations that leads international efforts to combat hunger, achieve food security for all, and promote sustainable development in the field of food and agriculture. The Motto of FAO is 'Let there be bread'.

Structure of FAO

The governing body of FAO is a conference of member nations, and it meets every two years to review the work carried out by FAO, and allocate future work and budget for a period of next two years. The conference elects the director-general and a council of 49 member states that acts as an interim governing body. This council serves three-year rotating terms.

It is composed of eight departments: Agriculture and Consumer Protection, Climate, Biodiversity, Land and Water Department, Economic and Social Development, Fisheries and Aquaculture, Forestry, Corporate Services and Technical Cooperation and Programme Management.

Objectives and Functions of FAO

- *Eradicating hunger:* It works towards eliminating hunger, food insecurity, and malnutrition. It supports countries in developing policies and programmes that prioritize food security and nutrition.
- *Enhancing agricultural productivity:* It provides technical expertise, assistance, requisite guidance, and capacity-building support to farmers to promote sustainable agricultural practices.
- *Sustainable management of natural resources:* It is a strong advocate of sustainable management of land, water, forests, and fisheries. It promotes conservation, biodiversity protection, and sustainable use of natural resources to safeguard ecosystems and support long-term food security and rural development.
- *Resilience building and disaster risk reduction:* It assists countries in building resilience to climate change, natural disasters, and other shocks that affect agriculture and food systems. It supports early warning systems, risk reduction measures, and emergency response mechanisms to protect livelihoods and food security in times of crisis.
- *Policy dialogue and knowledge sharing:* FAO is a knowledge organization and facilitates policy dialogue and knowledge exchange among governments, civil society organizations, researchers, and other stakeholders. It provides evidence-based analysis, technical expertise, and data to support informed decision-making and foster international cooperation on food and agriculture issues.
- *Improving livelihoods:* It aims to enhance rural livelihoods and reduce poverty through agricultural development. It supports initiatives that strengthen value chains, promote rural entrepreneurship, improve access to markets and finance, and foster sustainable and resilient agricultural systems.
- *Sustainable development goals:* FAO is the custodian UN agency for 21 indicators, for SDGs 2, 5, 6, 12, 14, and 15, and a contributing agency for a further five.

Food and Agriculture Organization of the United Nations (FAO) Statistical

FAOSTAT is an online database maintained by FAO that provides comprehensive and up-to-date statistical information on food and agriculture from countries all over the world. It is a comprehensive database that provides free access to agriculture and food data for 245 countries and territories from 1961 to the latest current data. It serves as a valuable resource for policymakers, researchers, analysts, and the public to access reliable and detailed data related to food production, trade, consumption, and other agricultural indicators.

INTERNATIONAL CIVIL AVIATION ORGANIZATION (ICAO)

The ICAO is a specialized agency of the United Nations that creates rules and regulations for safety, security, efficiency, and environmental protection in the aviation sector. ICAO is responsible for the establishment and maintenance of international Standards and Recommended Practices (SARPs), as well as Procedures for Air Navigation (PANS). The Chicago Convention of 1944 served as a starting point for the creation of the ICAO.

Objectives of ICAO

- *Safety:* ICAO works towards establishing and maintaining global standards and practices for providing safety in the aviation sector. It develops international regulations to ensure the safe operation of aircraft, airports, and aviation infrastructure. It releases Global Aviation Safety Plan (GASP) that outlines key activities for the triennium.

- *Air navigation Capacity and Efficiency:* ICAO releases Global Air Navigation Capacity and Efficiency Plan (Global Plan) that aims to increase the capacity and improve the efficiency of the global civil aviation system. It is focussed primarily on upgrading the air navigation and aerodrome infrastructure and developing new procedures to optimize aviation system performance.
- *Security and Facilitation:* ICAO has an important role in developing and promoting global standards and practices to protect civil aviation against acts of unlawful interference, such as terrorism. It provides training programmes and the implementation of security procedures at airports and throughout the aviation system.
- *Economic Development of Air Transport:* ICAO fosters the development of a sound and economically viable civil aviation system. It promotes fair competition, assists member states in developing air transport policies and regulations, and facilitates the negotiation of air services agreements between countries.
- *Environmental Protection:* ICAO works towards minimizing the adverse environmental effects of civil aviation activities. It encourages the development and implementation of alternative fuels and sustainable practices, and measures to reduce aircraft emissions, noise pollution, and the carbon footprint of the aviation industry.
- *Legal framework:* ICAO develops and maintains a framework of international agreements and conventions that govern civil aviation.

Structure of ICAO

- *Assembly:* It is the sovereign body of ICAO and is attended by all contracting states. It is conducted normally every three years. It elects the member states of the council, examines and takes appropriate action on the reports of the council, takes action on any matter reported to it by the council, and approves the budgets of the organization.
- *Council:* It is elected by the assembly every three years and it is composed of 36 states which are elected in three groups. It gives direction to the work of ICAO, and adopts Standards and Recommended Practices (SARPs).
- *Secretariat:* It works under the authority of the secretary-general and is divided into five main divisions: the Air Navigation Bureau (ANB), the Air Transport Bureau (ATB), the Technical Cooperation Bureau (TCB), the Legal Bureau (LB), and the Bureau of Administration and Services.

INTERNATIONAL FUND FOR AGRICULTURAL DEVELOPMENT (IFAD)

IFAD is an international financial institution and a specialized agency of the United Nations that focusses on eradicating poverty and addressing hunger in the rural areas of developing countries. IFAD is the only specialized global development organization exclusively focussed on and dedicated to transforming agriculture, rural economies, and food systems.

The World Food Conference of 1974 served as the starting point for the creation of IFAD.

Objectives of IFAD

- *Provide funds:* It provides loans, grants, and other forms of financial assistance to governments and rural development projects in developing countries. It invests in a wide range of initiatives, such as agricultural production, rural infrastructure development, market access, rural finance, and natural resource management.
- *Technical assistance:* It offers technical expertise, knowledge sharing, and capacity-building support to its partner countries. It works closely with governments, local communities, and other stakeholders to design and implement effective rural development programmes and projects.
- *Policy dialogue and advocacy:* It engages in policy dialogue and advocacy to promote pro-poor agricultural and rural development policies at the national and international levels. It works with governments, civil society organizations, and other partners to address the challenges facing rural communities and advocate for policies that prioritize poverty reduction and sustainable development.
- *Partnerships:* It collaborates with a wide range of partners, including governments, international organizations, non-governmental organizations, research institutions, and the private sector. It fosters partnerships to leverage resources, share knowledge and best practices, and coordinate efforts towards achieving common goals in rural development.

IFAD Strategic Framework 2016–25

It is the fifth strategic framework of IFAD and serves as an overarching policy guideline to provide direction to IFAD's work. It lists key development challenges and the larger global development architecture, and articulates IFAD's contribution to the 2030 Agenda for Sustainable Development (Agenda 2030). It has three strategic objectives:

1. Increasing the productive capacity of poor rural people
2. Increasing their benefits from market participation
3. Strengthening the environmental sustainability and climate resilience of their economic activities.

Structure of IFAD

- *Governing Council:* It is the main decision-making body and is open to all member states. The annual meeting and proceedings are the basis for IFAD's continued rural development efforts, along with its partners on the ground
- *Executive Board:* The Executive Board is responsible for overseeing the general operations of IFAD and for approving its programme of work. Membership on the Executive Board is determined by the Governing Council. The executive board members serve a three-year term of office.

INTERNATIONAL LABOUR ORGANIZATION (ILO)

ILO is the only tripartite agency of the United Nations in which governments, employers, and workers work together to set labour standards, develop policies, and devise programmes in order to promote decent work for all women and men. It is the first and oldest specialized agency of the United Nations and was established under the League of Nations.

It was awarded with the Nobel Peace Prize in 1969 for improving fraternity and peace among nations, pursuing decent work and justice for workers, and providing technical assistance to other developing nations.

Objectives of ILO

- *Establishing international labour standards:* It develops, establishes, and promotes standards and fundamental principles and rights at work in the form of conventions and recommendations on various topics concerning labour employment.
- *Promotes decent work:* ILO has been a strong advocate for the creation of decent and productive employment opportunities for both women and men. It addresses issues such as unemployment, child labour, slavery, etc. It encourages policies and programmes that promote fair wages, social protection, and skills development.
- *Provide technical assistance and capacity-building:* It provides technical assistance and training to governments, employers' organizations, and workers' organizations to support the development and implementation of effective labour policies and programmes. Also, it offers capacity-building programmes to the member countries for implementing labour standards and improving labour-related policies and practices.
- *Conduct research and analysis:* It conducts different studies and research to provide a data-based framework for its recommendations and policy formulation.
- *Facilitate social dialogues:* It promotes and encourages social dialogue as a means of addressing and negotiating labour issues and fostering cooperation among governments, employers, and workers.

ILO's Centenary Declaration

It is a landmark document adopted by the International Labour Organization (ILO) in June 2019 to mark the organization's 100th anniversary.

It is a short but crucial statement that looks at the major challenges and opportunities for the future of work, ranging from technology to climate change, from demographic shifts to the need for new skills. It provides guidance for dealing with these pressing issues and a platform for cooperation with other organizations in the international system.

Structure of ILO

The ILO accomplishes its work through three main bodies which comprise representatives of governments, employers, and workers:

- *International Labour Conference* sets the international labour standards and the broad policies of the ILO. It meets annually in Geneva. Often called an international parliament of labour, the conference is also a forum for discussion of key social and labour questions.
- *Governing Body* is the executive council of the ILO. It meets three times a year in Geneva. It takes decisions on ILO policy and establishes the programme and the budget, which it then submits to the conference for adoption.
- *International Labour Office* is the permanent secretariat of the International Labour Organization. It is the focal point for International Labour Organization's overall activities, which it prepares under the scrutiny of the Governing Body and under the leadership of the director-general.

INTERNATIONAL MARITIME ORGANIZATION (IMO)

IMO is the United Nations, specialized agency responsible for establishing international standards and regulatory framework for the safety and security of the international shipping industry and the prevention of marine and atmospheric pollution by ships.

In 1948, it was established as Inter-Governmental Maritime Consultative Organization, or IMCO, as a result of an international UN conference in Geneva. It was later renamed as International Maritime Organization in 1982. IMO's first task was to adopt a new version of the International Convention for the Safety of Life at Sea (SOLAS).

Objectives of IMO

- *Safety of shipping industry:* It develops and promotes international standards and regulations ensuring the safety of ships, crew, and passengers. It sets out comprehensive safety requirements for ships, which include ship design, construction, equipment, manning, etc. The IMO sets standards for ship design, construction, equipment, and operation to ensure the safety of seafarers and passengers on board ships.
- *Prevention of marine pollution:* It ensures that various aspects of marine pollution, including oil spills, air emissions, sewage, and garbage disposal from ships, are regulated. It is covered under the International Convention for the Prevention of Pollution from Ships (MARPOL).
- *Maritime security:* IMO has developed the International Ship and Port Facility Security (ISPS) code to enhance maritime security and counter maritime threats, such as piracy, terrorism, and smuggling. The code sets out measures to enhance the security of ships and port facilities.
- *Technical cooperation and capacity building:* It provides technical guidance and capacity-building support to the member countries to strengthen their maritime capabilities and ensure effective implementation of IMO standards and regulations. It is actively involved in maritime education, training, and infrastructure development.
- *Facilitate international trade and commerce:* It facilitates trade and commerce as shipping is the most efficient and cost-effective method of international transportation for most of the goods. It promotes measures to enhance the efficiency and effectiveness of shipping operations, such as the facilitation of maritime traffic, port operations, and electronic data exchange. It promotes efficient shipping practices, streamlining customs procedures, and facilitating electronic data exchange and communication in the maritime sector.
- *Legal framework and dispute resolution:* It develops, maintains, and adopts legal framework in the form of international conventions and protocols, which establish rights and obligations for member states and ship operators. Also, it provides a platform for resolving maritime disputes and supports the settlement of legal issues through its dispute resolution mechanisms.
- *Cyber security in shipping:* IMO has specific guidelines on maritime cyber risk management. It also provides high-level recommendations on how to mitigate against current and emerging cyber threats and vulnerabilities.

- *Regulation in fishing:* It is raising awareness around the Cape Town Agreement, which is a global treaty to ensure safety of fishing vessels. It will set minimum requirements on the design, construction, equipment, and inspection of fishing vessels of 24 m in length and over or equivalent in gross tons. Through these measures fishing vessels can be regulated and equipped to ensure efficient safety standards for fishers. It will also help in combatting illegal, unregulated, and unreported fishing, an authorized form of fishing practices which undermines national, regional, and global efforts to conserve and manage fish stocks.

Strategic Plan of IMO

The IMO Assembly, which meets every two years, adopts the strategic plan for the organization, which covers a six-year period.

Structure of IMO

IMO consists of an assembly, a council, five main committees, and a number of sub-committees to support the work of the main technical committees.

- *Assembly:* It is the highest governing body of IMO. It consists of all member states and it meets once every two years in regular sessions. It elects the council and is responsible for approving the work programme, voting the budget, and determining the financial arrangements of the organization.
- *Council:* It is the executive organ of IMO and is responsible, under the assembly, for supervising the work of the organization. It appoints secretary-general of IMO, coordinates the working of the organization, and works on the budget estimates of the organization. It is elected by the assembly for terms of two years.
- *IMO has five main committees:*
    1. Maritime Safety Committee (MSC)
    2. Marine Environment Protection Committee (MEPC)
    3. Legal Committee
    4. Technical Cooperation Committee
    5. Facilitation Committee

INTERNATIONAL TELECOMMUNICATION UNION (ITU)

ITU is the United Nations specialized agency for the growth and development of network, technology, and telecommunication services around the world. It was established as the International Telegraph Union on 17 May 1865 and was the first international organization. ITU entered into a formal agreement with the United Nations on 15 November 1947 to become a specialized agency of the United Nations from 1 January 1949.

Objectives of ITU

- *Global telecommunication regulation:* It sets global standards and regulations for the use of radio-frequency spectrum and satellite orbits to ensure efficient and interference-free use of telecommunications resources.
- *International telecommunication development:* It supports the development of telecommunications infrastructure and services in developing countries, bridging the digital divide and promoting digital inclusion.
- *Technical standardization:* It develops technical standards and protocols for telecommunications and ICT, enabling interoperability and seamless communication between different networks and devices.

- *Spectrum allocation:* It allocates radio-frequency spectrum and satellite orbits to different countries and operators to avoid interference and promote efficient use of spectrum resources.
- *Broadband development:* It advocates for the expansion of broadband access and promotes policies and initiatives to increase broadband connectivity worldwide.
- *Emergency telecommunications:* It provides emergency telecommunication assistance during disasters and humanitarian crises, facilitating communication for relief and recovery efforts.
- *Cybersecurity:* It works to enhance cybersecurity and promote the development of secure and resilient ICT networks and services.
- *Policy and advocacy:* It engages in policy discussions and advocacy efforts on telecommunications and ICT-related issues at the international level.

Structure of ITU

- *Plenipotentiary Conference:* It is the highest decision-making body of ITU. It is held every four years and brings together representatives from ITU member states to set the organization's general policies, strategic direction, and financial plans.
- *Council:* It is responsible for overseeing the implementation of decisions made by the Plenipotentiary Conference and conducting the administrative and financial affairs of the organization. It meets annually and consists of member states elected by the Plenipotentiary Conference.
- *Secretariat:* It is the administrative arm of the organization, responsible for managing day-to-day operations, providing support to ITU conferences and meetings, and implementing ITU programmes and activities. The secretary-general leads the Secretariat and is appointed by the Plenipotentiary Conference.
- *Sectors of ITU*
    - **Radiocommunication services (ITU-R):** It manages global radiocommunication services, including satellite communications, terrestrial broadcasting, and mobile communication systems. It allocates frequency bands and orbital slots, coordinates the use of these services, and ensures the efficient and reliable operation of global communication networks.
    - **Telecommunication standardization (ITU-T):** It is focussed on the standardization of telecommunication technologies and systems. This sector develops global standards and recommendations for a wide range of telecommunication services, including network protocols, data communication, optical networking, multimedia, and Internet technologies. ITU-T standards ensure interoperability and compatibility between different telecommunication systems and devices, enabling seamless communication and connectivity worldwide.
    - **Development (ITU-D):** It is dedicated to promoting the development and accessibility of telecommunication and ICT infrastructure and services in developing countries. This sector provides technical assistance, capacity building, and knowledge sharing to support the expansion and improvement of telecommunication networks and services in less-developed regions. ITU-D aims

to bridge the digital divide and promote digital inclusion by empowering countries to harness the potential of ICT for socio-economic development and improved quality of life.

UNITED NATIONS INDUSTRIAL DEVELOPMENT ORGANIZATION (UNIDO)

UNIDO is the specialized agency of the United Nations that focusses on promoting and accelerating industrial development in developing countries and economies in transition. Its primary mission is to help countries achieve inclusive and sustainable industrial growth, reduce poverty, and enhance economic competitiveness. It was established in 1966 and was incorporated as a specialized agency of the United Nations at Vienna in 1979.

The key functions and objectives of UNIDO are:

- *Industrial policy and capacity building:* UNIDO provides technical assistance and capacity-building support to governments and industries to develop effective industrial policies, strategies, and action plans that promote inclusive and sustainable industrial development.
- *Investment and technology promotion:* UNIDO facilitates investment in industrial projects and promotes the transfer and dissemination of technology to improve industrial productivity and competitiveness.
- *Sustainable industrialization:* UNIDO advocates for environmentally sustainable industrial practices and supports industries in adopting cleaner and more resource-efficient technologies to reduce their environmental footprint.
- *Small- and medium-sized enterprises (SMEs) development:* UNIDO focusses on empowering SMEs and entrepreneurs by providing them with training, technical assistance, and access to finance and markets to enhance their competitiveness and contribution to economic development.
- *Value chain development:* UNIDO works on enhancing the value chain in various industries, particularly in agribusiness and manufacturing sectors, to promote value addition, create employment opportunities, and foster economic growth.
- *Poverty reduction and inclusive growth:* UNIDO's initiatives aim to create decent jobs and improve living standards in developing countries, contributing to poverty reduction and inclusive economic growth.
- *Energy efficiency and renewable energy:* UNIDO promotes energy efficiency and the use of renewable energy sources in industrial processes to support the transition towards sustainable energy systems.
- *Gender equality and women's empowerment:* UNIDO integrates gender considerations in its projects and initiatives, advocating for women's economic empowerment and their inclusion in industrial development processes.

UNIDO and SDG

Its prime focus is on Sustainable Development Goal (SDG) 9: 'Build resilient infrastructure, promote inclusive and sustainable industrialization and foster innovation.'

Structure of UNIDO

- *General Conference:* The General Conference is the highest governing body of UNIDO. It meets every two years and consists of representatives from all member states. The General Conference sets the policies, approves budget, and provides overall guidance to the organization.

- *Industrial Development Board (IDB):* The IDB is a subsidiary body of the General Conference. It meets annually and is composed of representatives from a selected group of member states. The IDB reviews and recommends policies, programmes, and budgets to the General Conference.
- *Secretariat:* The UNIDO Secretariat is the administrative arm of the organization. It is responsible for managing the day-to-day operations of UNIDO, implementing programmes and projects, and providing support to member states. The director-general, who is appointed by the General Conference, leads the Secretariat.

UNITED NATIONS EDUCATIONAL, SCIENTIFIC AND CULTURAL ORGANIZATION (UNESCO)

UNESCO is the specialized agency of the UN that aims to build a culture of peace, eradicate poverty, and promote intercultural dialogue and sustainable development through education, science, culture, communication, and information. It collaborates with governments, international organizations, civil society, and other stakeholders to implement its programmes and initiatives. It was established as a successor to the League of Nations' International Committee on Intellectual Cooperation. The key objectives of UNESCO are

- *Education:* UNESCO promotes inclusive and quality education for all, advocating for access to education, improving the quality of education systems, and fostering lifelong learning opportunities. It supports educational policy development, teacher training, literacy programmes, and efforts to enhance educational access and equity.
- *Science:* UNESCO supports scientific research, cooperation, and the advancement of science for sustainable development. It promotes the use of scientific knowledge to address global challenges, including climate change and environmental sustainability.
- *Culture:* UNESCO works to safeguard and preserve cultural heritage, both tangible and intangible, as expressions of human creativity and diversity. It promotes cultural diversity and intercultural dialogue to foster mutual understanding and respect among different cultures.
- *Communication and information:* It is a strong advocate for freedom of expression, media freedom, and access to information. It promotes the use of communication and information technologies for sustainable development and the empowerment of individuals and communities.
- *Social and human science:* UNESCO continues to accomplish every day its fundamental humanist mission to support people in facing contemporary challenges, understanding each other, and working together to build lasting peace. UNESCO also helps to enable people to create and use knowledge for just, inclusive, resilient, and democratic societies.
- *World heritage sites:* It regularly identifies and protects cultural and natural heritage sites and promotes the conservation and preservation of these sites for future generations.

- *Gender equality:* It ensures that it promotes gender equality and women's empowerment in education, science, culture, and communication. It advocates for equal access to opportunities and resources for all genders.

Structure of UNESCO

- *General Conference:* The General Conference is the highest governing body of UNESCO. It meets every two years and consists of representatives from all member states. The General Conference sets the organization's policies, programmes, and budget, and it determines the strategic direction of UNESCO's work.
- *Executive Board:* The Executive Board is a subsidiary body of the General Conference. It meets twice a year and is composed of representatives from 58 member states. The Executive Board oversees the implementation of General Conference decisions, approves the budget, and provides recommendations on UNESCO's programmes and activities.
- *Secretariat:* The UNESCO Secretariat is the administrative arm of the organization, responsible for managing day-to-day operations and implementing UNESCO's programmes and projects. The director-general, appointed by the General Conference upon the recommendation of the Executive Board, leads the Secretariat.

WORLD HEALTH ORGANIZATION (WHO)

WHO is the specialized agency of the United Nations that partners with people, organizations, and governments across the world to promote the health and well-being of the people. The primary objective of WHO is to promote and protect global health, prevent the spread of diseases, and improve the overall well-being of people worldwide. WHO provides leadership in global health by setting health policies, priorities, and strategies. It coordinates and guides international efforts to address health challenges and promote health equity. The key functions and objectives of WHO are:

- *Health emergency response:* WHO plays a crucial role in responding to health emergencies, including disease outbreaks, natural disasters, and humanitarian crises. It mobilizes resources and expertise to support affected countries and communities.
- *Disease prevention and control:* WHO works to prevent and control communicable and non-communicable diseases. It conducts research, develops guidelines, and supports countries in implementing effective disease prevention and control measures.
- *Immunization and vaccination:* It promotes immunization as a critical public health intervention to protect people from vaccine-preventable diseases. It supports countries in strengthening their immunization programmes and ensuring equitable access to vaccines.
- *Health systems strengthening:* It advocates for strong and resilient health systems that can provide essential health services to all. It assists countries in developing and strengthening their healthcare infrastructure and workforce.
- *Maternal and child health:* It focusses on improving maternal and child health outcomes by supporting safe childbirth, promoting breastfeeding, and preventing childhood diseases and malnutrition.

- *Health information and research:* It collects and disseminates health information, statistics, and research findings to inform evidence-based health policies and programmes.
- *International Health Regulations (IHR):* It administers the International Health Regulations, which is a legal framework for preventing and responding to international public health emergencies, including disease outbreaks.
- *Collaboration and partnerships:* It collaborates with governments, international organizations, non-governmental organizations, and other stakeholders to advance global health goals and address health challenges collectively.
- *Health promotion and education:* It advocates for health promotion and education initiatives to raise awareness about healthy behaviours and lifestyle choices to improve public health outcomes.

Brief History of WHO

The representatives of Brazil and China had proposed the establishment of an international health organization in April 1945 at the United Nations (UN) meeting held in San Francisco. In 1946, a technical committee met in Paris and drew up proposals for the constitution of the International Health Organization which was presented at the International Health Conference in New York. On the basis of these proposals, the conference drafted and adopted the Constitution of the World Health Organization. An interim commission was also established until the Constitution of the World Health Organization came into force. The Constitution of the World Health Organization was signed on 22 July 1946 by representatives of 51 members of the UN and 10 other nations. However, for the constitution to come into force it had to be ratified by 26 signing countries. The constitution came into force on 7 April 1948. The first Health Assembly opened in Geneva on 24 June 1948 with delegations from 53 of the 55 member states. The Interim Commission ceased to exist at midnight on 31 August 1948, to be immediately succeeded by WHO.

Organizational Structure

- *World Health Assembly (WHA):* WHA is the highest decision-making body of WHO. It is composed of representatives from all member states and meets annually in Geneva, Switzerland. The WHA sets policies, approves the budget, and appoints the director-general.
- *Executive Board:* It is a subsidiary body of the WHA. It is composed of representatives from 34 member states who are elected for a three-year term. The Executive Board meets twice a year and implements the decisions and policies set by the WHA.
- *Director-general:* The director-general is the chief executive officer of WHO and is appointed by the World Health Assembly. The director-general provides leadership and direction to the organization and oversees its day-to-day operations.

Facts about WHO

- Headquarters: Geneva, Switzerland
- Regional offices: WHO has six regional offices that represent the organization's work in different regions of the world: Regional Office for Africa (AFRO), Regional Office for the Americas (AMRO/PAHO), Regional Office for the Eastern Mediterranean (EMRO), Regional Office for Europe (EURO), Regional Office for South-East Asia (SEARO), and Regional Office for the Western Pacific (WPRO).

- Total members: 194
- Parent organization: United Nations Economic and Social Council
- World Health Day: 7 April

WORLD INTELLECTUAL PROPERTY ORGANIZATION (WIPO)

WIPO is the specialized self-funded agency of the United Nations for Intellectual Property (IP) services, policy, information, and cooperation. It was established on 14 July 1967 as a result of WIPO convention or Convention Establishing the World Intellectual Property Organization. It aims to encourage innovation, creativity, and the use of intellectual property to foster economic, social, and cultural development. The key objectives of WIPO are:

- *Development of international IP treaties and standards:* It facilitates the development and harmonization of international treaties and agreements on Intellectual Property Rights (IPRs). These treaties provide a framework for the protection and enforcement of IP rights across different countries.
- *Administration of IP treaties:* It administers various international IP treaties, such as the Patent Cooperation Treaty (PCT), the Madrid System for the International Registration of Marks, and the Hague System for the International Registration of Industrial Designs.
- *Promotion of IP awareness and education:* WIPO works to raise awareness about the importance of intellectual property rights and their role in fostering innovation and creativity. It provides educational resources and training programmes on IP-related topics.
- *IP policy and advocacy:* WIPO conducts research and analysis on IP issues and provides policy advice to member states and stakeholders. It advocates for the recognition and protection of IP rights as a means to support economic growth and social development.
- *Dispute resolution:* It offers services for the resolution of intellectual property disputes through its Arbitration and Mediation Center. It provides a neutral and efficient platform for resolving IP-related disputes between parties.
- *Capacity building and technical assistance:* It provides technical assistance and capacity-building programmes to help countries develop effective IP systems and enforce IP laws. It supports the development of local expertise in IP matters.
- *IP Statistics and Information:* WIPO collects and publishes IP statistics and information to provide insights into global IP trends and developments. This data helps policymakers and stakeholders make informed decisions.

Services Offered by WIPO

- *Patent Cooperation Treaty (PCT):* PCT assists applicants in seeking patent protection internationally for their inventions, helps patent offices with their patent-granting decisions, and facilitates public access to a wealth of technical information related to those inventions. By filing one international patent application under the PCT, applicants can simultaneously seek protection for an invention in a large number of countries.
- *Madrid system - the international trademark system:* It is a treaty-based international system for the registration and management of trademarks in multiple countries and provides a convenient and cost-effective way for trademark owners to protect their marks in multiple jurisdictions with a single application.

- *Lisbon system:* Lisbon system for the International Registration of Appellations of Origin is a treaty-based international system that allows for the registration and protection of Appellations of Origin (AO) and Geographical Indications (GI) on an international scale. The system provides a convenient and effective means for producers of certain products with specific geographical origins to obtain international protection for their appellations.
- *WIPO Arbitration and Mediation Center:* The WIPO Arbitration and Mediation Center is a specialized institution that provides alternative dispute resolution (ADR) services for resolving commercial disputes, particularly those related to intellectual property (IP) and technology. It intends to facilitate the resolution of domestic and international commercial disputes in a time-efficient and cost-effective manner.
- *Hague system:* The Hague system for the International Registration of Industrial Designs is also known as the Hague Agreement. It is a treaty-based international system that allows for the centralized registration and management of industrial designs in multiple countries through a single application. It provides a practical business solution for registering up to 100 designs in 96 countries by filing a single international application.

UNITED NATIONS WORLD TOURISM ORGANIZATION (UNWTO)

UNWTO is the specialized agency of the United Nations that aims to promote tourism by identifying the opportunities in the sector and using them as a driver of economic growth, inclusive development, and environmental sustainability. The key objectives of UNWTO are:

- *Sustainable tourism development:* UNWTO supports sustainable tourism policies and practices to ensure optimal use of environmental resources, respect the socio-cultural authenticity of host communities, and provide socio-economic benefits for all.
- *Improving tourism competitiveness:* It improves UNWTO members' competitiveness through knowledge creation and exchange, human resources development, and the promotion of excellence in areas such as policy planning, statistics and market trends, sustainable tourism development, marketing and promotion, product development, and risk and crisis management.
- *Market research and statistics:* The UNWTO conducts research, collects data, and provides market intelligence on tourism trends, patterns, and impacts. It produces reports and publications that inform decision-makers, businesses, and other stakeholders about the state of the global tourism industry. The UNWTO promotes the use of evidence-based planning and decision-making in the tourism sector.
- *Tourism policy and governance:* The UNWTO provides guidance and support to governments in formulating effective tourism policies and governance frameworks. It offers technical assistance, capacity-building programmes, and policy recommendations to enhance the competitiveness and sustainability of the tourism sector.
- *Building partnerships:* Engaging with the private sector, regional and local

tourism organizations, academia and research institutions, civil society, and the UN system to build a more sustainable, responsible, and competitive tourism sector.

- *Tourism education and training:* The UNWTO fosters education and capacity building in the tourism sector. It develops educational programmes, training courses, and professional certifications to enhance the skills and knowledge of tourism professionals. The UNWTO supports initiatives that promote inclusive and quality tourism education and training.

Structure of UNWTO

- *General Assembly:* The General Assembly is the principal gathering of the World Tourism Organization. It meets every two years to approve the budget and programme of work and to debate topics of vital importance to the tourism sector. Every four years it elects a secretary-general.
- *Executive Council:* The Executive Council is UNWTO's governing board, responsible for ensuring that the organization carries out its work and adheres to its budget. It meets at least twice a year and is composed of members elected by the General Assembly in a ratio of one for every five full members.
- *Committees:* Specialized committees of UNWTO members advise on management and programme content. These include the Programme and Budget Committee, the Committee on Statistics and the Tourism Satellite Account, the Committee on Tourism and Competitiveness, the Committee on Tourism and Sustainability, the World Committee on Tourism Ethics, and the Committee for the Review of Applications for Affiliate Membership.
- *Secretariat:* The Secretariat is led by Secretary-General Zurab Pololikashvili from Georgia, who supervises 152 personnel at UNWTO's Madrid headquarters. These are responsible for implementing UNWTO's programme of work and serving the needs of members.

SDG Indicators

The UNWTO is custodian to two SDG indicators from the global indicator framework. These two indicators are:

1. *Indicator 8.9.1:* Tourism Direct Gross Domestic Product (download metadata)
2. *Indicator 12.b.1:* Implementation of standard accounting tools to monitor the economic and environmental aspects of tourism sustainability

UNIVERSAL POSTAL UNION (UPU)

UPU is the specialized agency of the United Nations that coordinates and regulates international postal services. UPU was established as a result of the signing of the Treaty of Bern in 1874. It has different key functions and objectives:

- *Facilitate communication:* It aims to develop efficient and accessible universal postal services of quality in order to facilitate communication between people, and organizations across the countries.
- *Standardization:* It establishes standards and regulations for the postal system in order to ensure quality uniformity and compatibility of the services being delivered across the countries.
- *Development of postal network:* It guides and facilitates the development and enhancement of postal infrastructure and networks in member countries. It also helps the countries in capacity building of the underserved areas and

modernization of the existing postal infrastructure.

- *Financial services:* It facilitates the provision of postal financial services, such as money transfers and international remittances. It facilitates the integration of postal networks into the global financial system and promotes financial inclusion, particularly in regions where traditional banking services are limited.
- *Technical assistance:* It provides technical assistance and support to member countries, particularly those with limited postal infrastructure or facing specific challenges. It offers guidance, training programmes, and financial assistance to help improve postal services and operations.

Postal Vision 2030

As a part of the Postal Vision 2030, the UPU aims to promote socio-economic development and contribute to the achievement of the UN-SDGs by 2030. It urges all key postal sector stakeholders to take action in four key areas:

1. *Decrease gaps in postal development:* Governments should decrease gaps through increased investments and focussed policies, and promote various ways to utilize the postal network for socio-economic development.
2. *Establish regulatory frameworks:* The different national level regulators of the sectors should work towards harmonizing and enhancing regulatory framework.
3. *Operational improvements:* Operators should seek to enhance their performance by implementing diversified strategies and operational improvements.
4. *Integration of different stakeholders:* Different stakeholders from the private sector and public institutions should pursue integration into the sector by engaging with traditional stakeholders, and vice versa. This means opening up the market, fostering partnerships, and enhancing the role of the UPU.

For the period 2021–25, UPU is following the Abidjan Postal Strategy and as a part of this strategy UPU as an organization aims to achieve the following by the end of the this period:

- Strengthen the UPU's mandate as the foremost forum for postal sector development.
- Reinforce the UPU's role as a provider of innovative and affordable technical solutions for postal sector stakeholders.
- Enable the UPU to become the prime information and knowledge centre of the postal sector.

Structure of UPU

The UPU consists of four bodies:

1. *The Congress:* It is the supreme decision-making body of UPU and meets every four years.
2. *The Council of Administration:* It ensures the continuity of the UPU's work between Congresses, supervises its activities, and studies regulatory, administrative, legislative, and legal issues.
3. *The Postal Operations Council:* The Postal Operations Council (POC) is the technical and operational mind of the UPU and consists of 48 member countries, elected during Congress.
4. *The International Bureau:* It provides logistical and technical support to the UPU's bodies.

WORLD METEOROLOGICAL ORGANIZATION (WMO)

WMO is an agency of the United Nations that promotes international cooperation and coordination in meteorology (weather and climate), operational hydrology, and related geophysical sciences. Prior to WMO, the International Meteorological Organization was the international NGO for the exchange of weather data and research. However, it was the World Meteorological Convention of 1947 that laid the foundation stone for the reforms of the IMO which ultimately led to the establishment of WMO. The key objectives of WMO are:

- *Weather forecasting and early warning systems:* The WMO works to improve weather forecasting capabilities and enhance early warning systems for natural hazards such as storms, hurricanes, floods, and droughts. It coordinates the collection and dissemination of meteorological data, ensuring timely and accurate forecasts to protect lives, property, and the environment.
- *Climate monitoring and prediction:* WMO supports the monitoring and understanding of climate variability and change. It promotes the development of climate observation networks, data analysis, and modelling to provide reliable climate predictions and assessments. The WMO assists member states in adapting to climate change impacts and mitigating greenhouse gas emissions.
- *Water resources management:* The WMO plays a key role in hydrological monitoring and the management of water resources. It provides guidance on water-related issues, such as the assessment of water availability, the monitoring of water quality, and the development of sustainable water management strategies. It supports countries in addressing water-related challenges, including water scarcity, floods, and droughts.
- *Capacity development and training:* The WMO assists member states in enhancing their meteorological and hydrological capabilities. It provides training, capacity-building programmes, and technical assistance to strengthen meteorological services, improve data collection and analysis, and enhance the application of weather and climate information in various sectors, such as agriculture, transportation, and disaster risk reduction.
- *International cooperation and partnerships:* It promotes international cooperation among its member states, regional organizations, and other stakeholders. It facilitates collaboration in the exchange of meteorological data and information, the development of common standards and practices, and the coordination of joint research and development projects. The WMO also works closely with other United Nations agencies and organizations involved in climate and sustainable development.

Structure of WMO

- *World Meteorological Congress (WMC):* WMC is the supreme body of the WMO and meets every four years. It sets the policies and overall direction of the organization, approves its budget, and elects the Executive Council and president.
- *Executive Council (EC):* EC is the governing body of the WMO and meets annually between sessions of the WMC. It is responsible for implementing the decisions of Congress, overseeing the activities of the WMO, and managing its affairs.

- *Secretariat:* The WMO Secretariat is responsible for the day-to-day administration and management of the organization. It supports the work of the WMC, Executive Council, technical commissions, and regional associations.
- *President:* The president of the WMO is elected by the WMC and serves as the head of the organization. The president represents the WMO in international forums and provides leadership and direction to the organization.
- *Regional associations:* The WMO is divided into six regional associations, namely:
  - African Meteorological Association (AMCOMET)
  - Asia-Pacific Region (WMO Regional Association II)
  - South America (WMO Regional Association III)
  - North America, Central America, and the Caribbean (WMO Regional Association IV)
  - Southwest Pacific (WMO Regional Association V)
  - Europe (WMO Regional Association VI)

WORLD BANK GROUP

The World Bank group is an international financial institution that provides financial and technical assistance to developing countries to support their economic development and reduce poverty.

It provides loans and grants to countries across the world. The World Bank's aim is to reduce poverty and promote sustainable development by providing financial resources, technical expertise, and knowledge sharing to its member countries. It collaborates with governments, private sector entities, civil society organizations, and other stakeholders to design and implement development projects that have a positive impact on people's lives and contribute to the achievement of the UNSDGs. The group consists of five institutions:

1. *International Bank for Reconstruction and Development (IBRD):* It provides loans, guarantees, risk management products, and advisory services to middle-income and creditworthy low-income countries, as well as by coordinating responses to regional and global challenges. Its primary focus is on development projects that aim to improve infrastructure, education, healthcare, and other key sectors in client countries.
2. *International Development Association (IDA):* It helps the world's poorest countries by providing credits and grants for programmes that boost economic growth, reduce inequalities, and improve people's living conditions. Credits are zero to low-interest loans. Its main goal is to implement projects and programmes that address issues of extreme poverty and promote sustainable development.

IBRD and IDA are collectively known as the World Bank.

3. *International Finance Cooperation (IFC):* It is the largest global development institution focussed on the private sector in developing countries. It provides investment and advisory services, and mobilizes private capital to address developmental challenges and promote economic growth.
4. *Multilateral Investment Guarantee Agency (MIGA):* It aims to promote Foreign Direct Investment (FDI) in developing countries by providing

guarantees to investors and lenders. By offering guarantees against non-commercial risks, MIGA helps encourage foreign investors to invest in projects and initiatives in these countries.

5. *International Centre for Settlement of Investment Disputes (ICSID):* It is an international arbitration institution for legal dispute resolution and settlement. It serves as a neutral platform for resolving investment-related conflicts and disputes in a fair and transparent manner.

Important Milestones of the World Bank Group

- The IBRD Articles of Agreement was drawn at the Bretton Woods Conference. This process was headed by John Maynard Keynes of the United Kingdom. The governing document of IBRD became effective on 27 December 1945.
- The IFC Articles of Agreement came into effect on 20 July 1956. IFC provided its first loan of US$2 million to Brazil for manufacturing electrical equipment in the year 1960.
- The Articles of Agreement of IDA came into effect on 24 September 1960.
- The MIGA Convention to establish MIGA came into force on 12 April 1988.
- The ICSID Convention was established by a multilateral agreement and entered into force on 14 October 1966.

Facts about the World Bank Group

- Parent organization: World Bank Group
- First annual meeting of World Bank: Savannah, Georgia in March 1946
- First president of the World Bank: Eugene Meyer
- First loan of World Bank: France, 1947
- First loan to a non-European country: Chile, 1948
- World Bank entered the bond market: 15 July 1947
- World bank's first loan to control environment pollution: Brazil, 1971

FACT FILE

The Bretton Woods Conference was officially known as the United Nations Monetary and Financial Conference. It was a gathering of delegates from 44 nations who met from 1 to 22 July 1944 in Bretton Woods, New Hampshire. They had met to agree upon a series of new rules for the post-Second World War international monetary system. The two major accomplishments of the conference were the creation of the International Monetary Fund (IMF) and the International Bank for Reconstruction and Development (IBRD).

INTERNATIONAL MONETARY FUND (IMF)

IMF is the international financial agency of the United Nations that works towards fostering international financial cooperation and stability. It provides financial assistance to member countries facing balance of payments problems or experiencing financial crises. This assistance comes in the form of financial programmes and policy advice tailored to the specific needs and circumstances of each country. It offers technical assistance and training to member countries to strengthen their economic institutions and policymaking capacity. This helps countries improve their economic management and governance practices. It conducts economic research and analysis on various issues, including global economic trends, financial stability, fiscal and monetary policies, and structural reforms. The research findings are published in reports, working papers, and other publications. It promotes international policy coordination to address global economic challenges and risks. It fosters cooperation among member countries to address issues such as exchange rate stability, capital flows, and financial regulation. The IMF works to promote debt sustainability in low-income countries and provides debt relief through the Heavily Indebted Poor Countries (HIPC) Initiative and the Catastrophe Containment and Relief Trust (CCRT) for countries affected by disasters.

The IMF was conceived in July 1944 when representatives of 44 countries agreed on a framework for international economic cooperation. These representatives met in the town of Bretton Woods, New Hemisphere, United States.

Facts about IMF

- First country to borrow loan: France (1947)
- Total members: 190
- Official language: English
- Parent organization: United Nations
- Total lending capacity: US$1 trillion
- Biggest contributors to the IMF: The United States, Japan, France, Germany, Italy, and the United Kingdom

Sources of Funds at IMF

There are mainly three sources of funds at IMF:

1. *Member quotas:* This is the major source of financing at the IMF. Each member of IMF has an assigned quota on the basis of its position in the world economy.
2. *New Arrangements to Borrow (NAB):* This is the second line of funding at the IMF. Under this, some member countries and institutions are ready to lend additional resources to meet the needs and address the challenges to the international financial system.
3. *Bilateral Borrowing Agreements (BBA):* This is the third line of funding at the IMF where the international organization enters into bilateral agreements in order to meet its members' financing needs.

Special Drawing Rights (SDRs)

It is an international reserve asset which was initially created as a supplementary asset in 1969.

However, it was redefined in 1973 as equivalent to the value of a basket of world currencies. Its value is based on a basket of five currencies – the US dollar, the euro, the Chinese renminbi, the Japanese yen, and the British pound sterling. It serves as the unit of account of the IMF.

Asset holders can exchange SDR for currency when needed as it serves as a unit of account of the IMF and other international organizations. The value of SDR in terms of US dollars is calculated on a daily basis, based on the spot exchange rates observed at around noon London time.

SDR basket is reviewed every five years and the Chinese currency 'renminbi' was the latest addition to this basket and was added in the year 2016.

It can be held by IMF's members and prescribed holders. Individuals and private entities cannot hold SDRs. The IMF distributes a general allocation to member countries in proportion to their quota shares at the IMF.

Bretton Wood's or Par Value System

The Par Value exchange system was followed at IMF until 1971. Under this system, the countries kept their exchange rates in terms of the US dollars, and the US dollar was valued in terms of gold. The difference in the rates could be adjusted only to correct a fundamental disequilibrium in the balance of payments, and only with the IMF's agreement. However, in the year 1971 US President Richard Nixon suspended the conversion of dollar into gold, leading to the end of this system. With the collapse of this system, the countries were free to choose their exchange arrangement according to their convenience.

RELATED ORGANIZATIONS OF THE UN

PREPARATORY COMMISSION ON COMPREHENSIVE NUCLEAR-TEST-BAN TREATY ORGANIZATION (CTBTO)

Preparatory Commission on CTBTO is an international organization established for the effective implementation of the Comprehensive Nuclear-Test-Ban Treaty (CTBT) and to put in place a global verification regime to monitor the compliance of the treaty.

CTBT bans all kinds of nuclear explosion whether military or peaceful. It is the cornerstone for the pursuit of nuclear disarmament globally.

S.NO.	NAME OF THE AGENCY	HEADQUARTERS	ESTABLISHMENT	HEAD(S)
1	Food and Agriculture Organization (FAO)	Rome, Italy	6 October 1945	Director-General: Qu Dongyu
2	International Civil Aviation Organization (ICAO)	Montreal, Quebec, Canada	4 April 1947	Secretary-General: Juan Carlos Salazar
3	International Fund for Agricultural Development (IFAD)	Rome, Italy	15 December 1977	President: Alvaro Lario
4	International Labour Organization (ILO)	Geneva, Switzerland	11 April 1919	Director-General: Gilbert Houngbo
5	International Maritime Organization (IMO)	London, United Kingdom	17 March 1948	Secretary-General: Arsenio Dominguez
6	International Telecommunication Union (ITU)	Geneva, Switzerland	17 May 1865	Secretary-General: Doreen Bogdan-Martin
7	United Nations Industrial Development Organization (UNIDO)	Vienna, Austria	17 November 1966	Director-General: Gerd Muller
8	United Nations Educational, Scientific and Cultural Organization (UNESCO)	Paris, France	16 November 1945	Director-General: Audrey Azoulay
9	World Health Organization (WHO)	Geneva, Switzerland		Director-General: Dr. Tedros Adhanom Ghebreyesus Chief Scientist: Dr. John Reeder

S.NO.	NAME OF THE AGENCY	HEADQUARTERS	ESTABLISHMENT	HEAD(S)
10	World Intellectual Property Organization (WIPO)	Geneva, Switzerland	Operational: 26 April 1970	Director-General: Daren Tang
11	United Nations World Tourism Organization (UNWTO)	Madrid, Spain	Established on: 1 November 1975	Secretary-General: Zurab Pololikashvili
12	Universal Postal Union (UPU)	Berne, Switzerland	Established on: 9 October 1874	Director-General: Masahiko Metoki
13	World Meteorological Organization (WMO)	Geneva, Switzerland	Established on: 23 March 1950	Secretary-General: Celeste Saulo
14	World Bank	Washington DC, United States		Current President: Ajay Banga MD & CFO: Anshula Kant Chief Economist: Indermit Gill
15	International Monetary Fund (IMF)	Washington DC, United States	Established on: 27 December 1945 Formal Operations: 1 March 1947	Managing Director: Kristalina Georgieva Chief Economist: Pierre-Oliver

CTBTO Preparatory Commission is an interim organization and would cease to function once CTBT enters into force. It will be replaced by CTBTO.

INTERNATIONAL ATOMIC ENERGY AGENCY (IAEA)

IAEA is an intergovernmental organization to promote safe, secure, and peaceful use of nuclear energy and technology at a global level. It is the international centre for cooperation in the field of nuclear energy.

Brief History

IAEA was created as a response to the strong concerns and fears arising from the discoveries and various applications of nuclear technology.

The agency's genesis was US President Eisenhower's 'Atoms for Peace' address to the UNGA on 8 December 1953. His speech helped shape IAEA's statute, which was approved by 81 countries unanimously in October 1956. However, it was the ratification of the statute by US President Eisenhower on 29 July 1957 that marked the official birth of the IAEA. The article II of IAEA's statute clearly lays down the dual objective of IAEA – promote and control the Atom.

IAEA Safeguards

These are the set of technical measures that ensure that the nuclear material and activities are used exclusively for peaceful purposes and not diverted for any unauthorized use.

They play a crucial role in the global security framework and assist the IAEA in verifying states' compliance with their legal obligations under safeguards agreements.

The Treaty on the Non-Proliferation of Nuclear Weapons (NPT) is the primary international treaty agreement that aims to prevent the proliferation of nuclear weapons. According to Article 3 of the Treaty, Non-Nuclear Weapon States are obligated to establish safeguards agreements with the IAEA as a means of upholding their commitments.

Objectives of IAEA

- *Promoting the peaceful use of nuclear energy:* It encourages the use of nuclear technology for various peaceful purposes, such as energy, climate change, environment, health, water, food and agriculture, electricity generation, agriculture, healthcare, and industry. It provides assistance to member states in developing nuclear energy programmes and ensuring their safe and secure operation.
- *Safeguards and verification:* IAEA Safeguards aim to prevent the diversion of nuclear materials and technologies from peaceful uses to nuclear weapons programmes. It verifies that states are fulfilling their obligations under the Treaty on the Non-Proliferation of Nuclear Weapons (NPT) and other relevant agreements.
- *Nuclear safety and security:* It works to enhance nuclear safety by establishing international safety standards, conducting safety reviews, and providing assistance to member states in strengthening their nuclear safety infrastructure. It also promotes nuclear security measures to prevent unauthorized access, theft, or illicit trafficking of nuclear materials.
- *Nuclear energy and technology:* The IAEA promotes the peaceful use of nuclear energy by facilitating knowledge sharing, providing information, conducting research, and fostering collaboration among member states. It supports nuclear power programmes, addresses nuclear waste management, and encourages innovation in nuclear technology.
- *Technical cooperation:* The IAEA provides technical assistance and support to member states in various areas, including nuclear power infrastructure development, radiation applications in healthcare and agriculture, nuclear safety and security, and capacity building. This assistance aims to promote sustainable development and enhance the peaceful use of nuclear technology.

Nobel Peace Prize 2005

IAEA and its Director-General Mohamed ElBaradei was awarded the Nobel Peace Prize in 2005 for their efforts to prevent nuclear energy from being used for military purposes and to ensure that nuclear energy for peaceful purposes is used in the safest possible way.

Structure of IAEA

- *General Conference:* It is the policy-making body at IAEA. It consists of representatives of the IAEA member states and they meet in a regular annual session. It elects a president and members of the General Committee at the beginning of each annual session. They hold office for the duration of the session. It finalizes the budget of the IAEA and also has discussions and provides recommendations on the requisite issues.
- *Board of Governors:* It is a policy-making body along with the annual General Conference of IAEA member states. It appoints the director-general of the IAEA with the approval of the General Conference. It examines and makes recommendations to the General Conference on the IAEA's financial statements, programme, and budget. It considers applications for membership, approves safeguards agreements, and the publication of the IAEA's safety standards.
- *Secretariat:* It is headed by the director-general and oversees the work of the following six departments: Nuclear Energy, Nuclear Safety and Security, Nuclear Sciences and Applications, Safeguards, Technical Cooperation, and Management.

Scientific Resources at IAEA

- *Nucleus:* It is IAEA's resource portal that provides access to over 100 scientific, technical, and regulatory resources, including databases, applications, publications, and training material. It can be used by IAEA counterparts in the government, industry, and scientific community.
- *International Nuclear Information System (INIS):* It is the world's largest collection of published information on the peaceful uses of nuclear science and technology. It helps the countries to build their nuclear information capacities. It was established in 1970.
- *Power Reactor Information System (PRIS):* It is a comprehensive database focusing on nuclear power plants worldwide. It is made available for registered users and the general public. The web-based PRIS-STATISTICS reporting system was developed in 2009 to make PRIS available globally.
- *Nuclear Data Services:* It provides the basic nuclear data for energy and non-energy applications, as well as atomic data for fusion energy research.

IAEA and SDGs

Many countries use nuclear science and technology to contribute to and meet their development objectives in areas, including energy, human health, food production, water management, and environmental protection. The use of these techniques contributes directly to 9 of the 17 SDGs.

The nine SDGs are:

1. Zero Hunger: SDG 2
2. Good Health and Well-being: SDG 3
3. Clean Water and Sanitation: SDG 6
4. Affordable and Clean Energy: SDG 7
5. Industry, Innovation and Infrastructure: SDG 9
6. Climate Action: SDG 13
7. Life below Water: SDG 14
8. Life on Land: SDG 15
9. Partnerships for the Goals: SDG 17

INTERNATIONAL CRIMINAL COURT (ICC)

ICC is the world's first and permanent independent international court which has the jurisdiction to prosecute individuals for the international crimes of genocide, crimes against humanity, war crimes, and the crime of aggression.

The legal basis for the creation of ICC was the adoption of the Rome Statute by 120 states on 17 July 1998. However, it came into force on 1 July 2002 after ratification by 60 countries.

Judges of the Court

ICC is composed of 18 judges, who are elected for terms of office of nine years by the Assembly of States Parties (ASP). The judges cannot be re-elected. They also elect, from among themselves, the ICC president and two vice presidents, who head the court. They are nominated by the respective member countries.

The Rome Statute System

Assembly of States Parties (ASP): It is the management oversight and legislative body of the ICC. Its role has been described in Article 112 of the Rome Statute. It is involved in managing, overseeing, and making legislative decisions for the court. Each country that has ratified or acceded to the Rome Statute has one vote in the ASP. The ASP is composed of representatives from different States Parties. They come together to establish the rules and regulations of the court and make important decisions regarding its management and oversight. These decisions include adopting normative texts, approving the budget, electing judges, the prosecutor, and deputy prosecutor(s), and addressing any issues related to non-cooperation. In addition, the ASP provides supervision over the presidency, registrar, and prosecutor of the court. It also has the authority to create subsidiary bodies, such as independent oversight mechanisms, to ensure effective functioning of the ICC.

Four organs of ICC:

1. *Presidency:* The Presidency of the International Criminal Court (ICC) consists of three judges: a president and two vice presidents. They are elected by a clear majority of 18 judges of the ICC and can serve a maximum of two terms, each lasting three years. The presidency is responsible for overseeing the overall administration of the court. They ensure that sentences imposed by the court are enforced and represent the court to the outside world.
2. *Chambers:* The chambers of the ICC are composed of 18 judges and are divided into three divisions: the pre-trial division, the trial division, and the appeals division. Each division has judges assigned to specific chambers. The pre-trial chambers handle issues that arise before the trial phase begins. The trial chambers are formed after the issuance of an arrest warrant and ensure fair trials are conducted. The appeals chambers handle appeals against the decisions of the trial chambers.
3. *Office of the Prosecutor:* The Office of the Prosecutor (OTP) is an independent organ of the ICC. It is responsible for receiving referrals and credible information about crimes falling under the jurisdiction of the court. The OTP examines these referrals and information, conducts investigations, and initiates prosecutions before the court.
4. *Registry:* The registry provides judicial and administrative support to all organs of the ICC. It is headed by the registrar. The registry assists the court in conducting fair, impartial, and public trials. It serves as the official communication channel for the court and is primarily responsible for the ICC's public information and outreach activities.

Trust Fund for Victims (TFV): The TFV was established in 2002 by the ASP to support and uphold the rights of victims and their families. Its main purpose is to provide reparations and assistance to victims. The TFV is governed by a board of directors and has a secretariat led by an executive director.

The TFV assists victims of crimes falling within the jurisdiction of the ICC. It provides general support such as physical and psychological rehabilitation, as well as material assistance to victims in need. Additionally, the TFV plays a crucial role in implementing reparations awarded by the court to victims as a result of convictions.

Legal process

- Preliminary examination: Before the ICC can investigate a case, the OTP must assess if there is enough evidence of serious crimes falling within the ICC's jurisdiction. They also consider if national proceedings are genuine and if opening an investigation would serve the interests of justice and the victims. If the requirements are not met or the situation is not under the ICC's jurisdiction, the ICC cannot investigate.

- Investigations: Once the prosecutor gathers evidence and identifies a suspect, they request ICC judges to issue an arrest warrant if they rely on countries to make arrests, or a summons to appear if the suspect can voluntarily appear. If the criteria for initiating an investigation are not met or the crimes fall outside the ICC's jurisdiction, the ICC's prosecution cannot proceed.
- Pre-trial stage: The suspect's initial appearance takes place before three pre-trial judges who confirm their identity and ensure they understand the charges. Confirmation of charges hearings follow, where judges decide, usually within 60 days, if there is enough evidence to proceed to trial after considering arguments from the prosecution, defence, and legal representative of victims. If the suspect is not arrested or does not appear, legal submissions can be made, but hearings cannot begin.
- Trial stage: The prosecution must prove the guilt of the accused beyond reasonable doubt before three trial judges. The judges consider all evidence and issue a verdict. If there is a guilty verdict, they also determine the sentence, which can be up to 30 years of imprisonment or, in exceptional circumstances, a life sentence. Verdicts can be appealed by the defence and the prosecutor, and judges can order reparations for victims. If there is insufficient evidence, the case is closed, and the accused is released. Acquittals are also subject to appeal.
- Appeals stage: Both the prosecutor and the defence have the right to appeal a trial chamber's decision on the verdict and sentence. Victims and the convicted person can appeal orders for reparations. Appeals are decided by five judges of the appeals chamber, who are different from those who gave the original verdict. The appeals chamber can uphold, amend, or reverse the appealed decision, which becomes the final judgment unless a retrial is ordered before the trial chamber.
- Enforcement of sentence: Sentences are served in countries that have agreed to enforce ICC sentences. If a guilty verdict is not upheld on appeal, the person may be released.

Jurisdiction

The court may exercise its jurisdiction in a situation where genocide, crimes against humanity, or war crimes were committed on or after 1 July 2002. It has no right to exercise its jurisdiction with respect to events which occurred before 1 July 2002.

ICC can use its jurisdiction if the crimes were committed by a citizen of a country that is a member of the UNSC through a resolution under Chapter VII of the UN Charter.

Also, the ICC has the power to prosecute individuals, not groups or states. The ICC does not replace national criminal justice systems; rather, it complements them.

Quick Facts

Headquarters: Hague, Netherlands

Official languages: English, French, Arabic, Chinese, Russian, and Spanish

Working languages: English and French

INTERNATIONAL ORGANIZATION FOR MIGRATION (IOM)

IOM is an international organization working closely with governmental, transpose intergoverntal, and non-governmental partners in order to promote humane and orderly migration.

IOM was preceded by the Provisional Intergovernmental Committee for the Movement of Migrants from Europe (PICMME), born in 1951 out of the chaos and displacement of Western Europe following the Second World War.

It started as an operational logistics agency, and had a series of name changes from PICMME to the Intergovernmental Committee for European Migration (ICEM) in 1952, to the Intergovernmental Committee for Migration (ICM) in 1980 to the current International Organization for Migration (IOM) in 1989, which reflects the organization's transition from being a logistics agency to a migration agency.

Objectives of IOM

- *Facilitating migration:* It works to ensure that migration happens in a safe and well-organized manner. They provide assistance and support to migrants, helping them with their journey, ensuring their rights are protected, and promote their well-being.
- *Migration policy development:* IOM helps countries develop policies and laws related to migration by providing advice and expertise to governments to create a fair and effective migration systems that benefit both the migrants and the countries involved.
- *Emergency response:* When there are crises or disasters, such as conflicts or natural disasters, IOM plays a crucial role in providing emergency assistance to affected migrants. They help with evacuation, shelter, and essential needs like food, water, and healthcare.
- *Combatting human trafficking:* IOM is actively involved in fighting against human trafficking, which is a serious crime that involves exploiting people for forced labour or other forms of exploitation. They work to prevent trafficking, protect victims, and assist in their rehabilitation and reintegration.
- *Migration and development:* IOM recognizes the positive contributions that migrants can make to the development of their home countries and the countries they move to. They promote programmes and initiatives that encourage the positive impact of migration on societies and economies, such as remittances and skills transfer.
- *Health and migration:* IOM pays special attention to the health needs of migrants, ensuring access to healthcare services and promoting awareness of health issues related to migration. They work to prevent the spread of diseases and provide assistance to migrants who may face health challenges during their journey.
- *Data and research:* It conducts and supports data production and research designed to guide and inform migration policy and practice. It helps to enhance IOM's programme delivery and contribute to a broader understanding of migration patterns and processes, as well as the links between migration research and migration policy and practice.

Organizational Structure

The director-general is the head of the IOM and is responsible for the overall management and administration of the organization. The director-general is appointed by the IOM's member states and serves as the chief executive officer.

ORGANIZATION FOR THE PROHIBITION OF CHEMICAL WEAPONS (OPCW)

The OPCW is an intergovernmental organization responsible for the successful implementation of the Chemical Weapons Convention, which entered into force on 29 April 1997. The CWC is the world's first multilateral disarmament agreement to provide for the elimination of an entire category of weapons of mass destruction within a fixed time frame. A chemical weapon is a chemical used to cause intentional death or harm through its toxic properties. It includes munitions, devices, and other equipment specifically designed to weaponize toxic chemicals.

The OPCW conducts inspections at declared chemical weapons facilities and other facilities that may be involved in activities related to the production, storage, or use of chemical weapons. The goal is to verify compliance with the CWC and ensure the complete elimination of chemical weapons. OPCW provides assistance and protection to member states in case of chemical incidents or emergencies. This includes support in dealing with chemical attacks, accidents, or threats. It provides technical assistance and capacity-building programmes to member states to enhance their ability to implement the provisions of the CWC effectively.

Structure of OPCW

- The Conference of the States Parties is the highest decision-making body of the OPCW. It meets annually to discuss and make decisions on matters related to the implementation and operation of the Chemical Weapons Convention.
- The Executive Council is responsible for conducting the day-to-day work of the OPCW and implementing the decisions of the Conference of the States Parties.
- The Technical Secretariat is the operational arm of the OPCW, responsible for carrying out inspections, verification activities, and technical assistance related to the elimination of chemical weapons. It is headed by the director-general.
- OPCW has a Scientific Advisory Board composed of independent experts who provide scientific advice and expertise on issues related to chemical weapons.

Nobel Peace Prize

OPCW was awarded the 2013 Nobel Peace Prize for its extensive efforts to eliminate chemical weapons.

WORLD TRADE ORGANIZATION (WTO)

WTO is the only international organization that deals with the global rules of trade between member countries. It negotiates trade rules and settles disputes among the member countries on the basis of WTO's agreements. It was established as an outcome of the Marrakesh Agreement which was signed by 123 countries on 15 April 1994. Prior to WTO, General Agreement on Tariffs and Trade (GATT) had established rules for international trade and commerce from 1948 to 1994.

However, GATT dealt with trade in goods, and WTO agreements include goods, services, and intellectual property. The key functions and roles of WTO are:

- *Trade agreements:* The WTO administers a series of trade agreements negotiated and signed by its member countries which cover a wide range of trade-related issues, including tariffs, non-tariff barriers, agriculture, services, intellectual property, and dispute settlement.
- *Multilateral trade negotiations:* It hosts negotiations among its member

countries to further liberalize trade and remove barriers. These negotiations aim to create a more open and predictable trading system.

- *Dispute settlement:* It has a dispute settlement mechanism that allows member countries to resolve trade disputes in a structured and rule-based manner. This helps prevent trade conflicts and promotes a fair and transparent resolution of trade disputes.
- *Trade policy review:* It conducts regular reviews of the trade policies and practices of its member countries. These reviews promote transparency and allow member countries to monitor each other's trade policies.
- *Technical assistance and training:* It provides technical assistance and training to developing countries to help them build capacity and better integrate into the global trading system.
- *Trade monitoring:* It monitors global trade flows and provides up-to-date trade statistics, helping member countries track and analyse trade developments.
- *Trade facilitation:* The WTO works to simplify and streamline customs procedures and other trade-related regulations to facilitate the movement of goods across borders.

Important Agreements of WTO

- *General Agreement on Tariffs and Trade (GATT):* GATT is the predecessor to the WTO and remains an integral part of the WTO agreements. It primarily deals with the reduction and elimination of tariffs on goods and the regulation of trade in goods among member countries.
- *Agreement on Agriculture (AoA):* This agreement aims to reform and liberalize global agricultural trade. It sets rules for reducing agricultural subsidies, improving market access for agricultural products, and addressing other issues related to agricultural trade.
- *Agreement on Technical Barriers to Trade (TBT Agreement):* The TBT Agreement aims to ensure that technical regulations, standards, and conformity assessment procedures do not create unnecessary obstacles to international trade. It encourages the use of international standards and promotes transparency in the development and application of technical regulations.
- *Agreement on Trade-Related Investment Measures (TRIMs Agreement):* This agreement seeks to eliminate trade-distorting investment measures and performance requirements imposed by countries on foreign investors. It promotes a non-discriminatory and transparent investment environment.
- *Agreement on Trade-Related Aspects of Intellectual Property Rights (TRIPS Agreement):* The TRIPS Agreement establishes minimum standards for the protection of intellectual property rights, including patents, trademarks, copyrights, and trade secrets. It aims to strike a balance between protecting intellectual property rights and promoting access to technology and knowledge.
- *Agreement on Trade in Services (GATS):* The GATS aims to liberalize trade in services among member countries. It sets rules for increasing market access and ensuring fair and transparent treatment for services trade.

Structure of WTO

- *Ministerial Conference:* It is the highest decision-making body of the WTO. It meets at least once every two years and is attended by trade ministers or representatives of all WTO member countries. The conference makes decisions on key trade-related issues and provides overall guidance to the organization.

- *General Council:* It is the principal body that oversees the functioning of the WTO in between ministerial conferences. It is composed of representatives from all WTO member countries and meets regularly to discuss and make decisions on various trade matters.
- *Secretariat:* It provides administrative and technical support to the various WTO bodies and member countries. It is headed by the director-general and is based at the WTO's headquarters in Geneva, Switzerland.

INTERNATIONAL TRADE CENTRE (ITC)

ITC is a joint agency of the World Trade Organization (WTO) and the United Nations (UN). It was established to promote international trade and support the sustainable development of small- and medium-sized enterprises (SMEs) in developing countries. The important functions and roles of ITC are:

- *Trade promotion:* ITC provides assistance to developing countries in enhancing their capacity to engage in international trade. It helps SMEs to connect with global markets, find buyers and suppliers, and access trade-related information and opportunities.
- *Export development:* It offers export development services and tools to support SMEs in developing countries in expanding their export activities. This includes market research, trade intelligence, and export training programmes.
- *Trade policy analysis:* It conducts research and analysis on trade policies and their impact on developing countries. It provides policymakers with evidence-based advice to support informed decision-making on trade-related issues.
- *Trade and market intelligence:* It collects and disseminates trade and market intelligence to assist businesses in identifying export opportunities, market trends, and potential buyers.
- *Capacity building:* It conducts capacity-building programmes and training workshops to enhance the skills and knowledge of entrepreneurs, trade support institutions, and policymakers in developing countries.
- *Gender and trade:* It promotes gender-inclusive trade policies and practices and supports women entrepreneurs in accessing international markets and participating in global value chains.
- *Sustainable and inclusive trade:* It emphasizes the importance of sustainable and inclusive trade practices that contribute to economic growth, poverty reduction, and environmental protection.
- *Trade and investment climate:* It works to improve the trade and investment climate in developing countries by addressing trade barriers, simplifying trade procedures, and enhancing trade-related infrastructure.
- *Market access and trade facilitation:* It assists developing countries in overcoming trade barriers and improving trade facilitation measures to enhance their competitiveness in international markets.
- *Business support services:* It provides business support services to SMEs, including training on export

management, product development, quality standards, and branding.

UNITED NATIONS PEACEKEEPING

UN peacekeeping is a joint effort between the Department of Peace Operations and the Department of Operational Support. It is composed of civilians, police, and military personnel. It helps countries torn by conflict to create conditions for promoting and maintaining law, order, and peace. It involves the deployment of military, police, and civilian personnel from various UN member countries to help stabilize volatile situations, support peace processes, protect civilians, and promote the rule of law. The primary goals of UN peacekeeping operations are to create a conducive environment for lasting peace, support the implementation of peace agreements, and protect vulnerable populations in areas of conflict.

However, UN peacekeeping operations can only be deployed with the consent of the parties involved in the conflict, including the host country's government and relevant non-state actors. Peacekeepers use force only in self-defence or defence of the mandate, and their primary role is to observe, monitor, and report on the situation. Peacekeeping missions are usually composed of personnel from various countries, forming a multinational force under the UN's command and control. They are also engaged in post-conflict stabilization efforts, including supporting the restoration of public services, promoting human rights, and facilitating the return of refugees and internally displaced persons.

S.NO.	NAME OF THE ORGANIZATION	ESTABLISHED	HEADQUARTERS	HEAD
1	Preparatory Commission on Comprehensive Nuclear-Test-Ban Treaty Organization (CTBTO)	19 November 1966	Vienna, Austria	Executive Secretary: Robert Floyd
2	International Atomic Energy Agency (IAEA)	29 July 1957	Vienna, Austria	Director-General: Rafael Grossi
3	International Criminal Court (ICC)		Hague, Netherlands	President: Piotr Hofmański
4	International Organization for Migration (IOM)		Geneva, Switzerland	Director-General: António Vitorino
5	Organization for the Prohibition of Chemical Weapons (OPCW)		Hague, Netherlands	Director-General: Fernando Arias
6	World Trade Organization (WTO)	1 January 1995	Geneva, Switzerland	Director-General: Ngozi Okonjo-Iweala
7	International Trade Centre (ITC)	1 January 1968	Geneva, Switzerland	Executive Director: Pamela Coke Hamilton
8	United Nations Peacekeeping			Secretary-General for peace operations: Jean-Pierre Lacroix

IMPORTANT INTERNATIONAL ORGANIZATIONS

ASIAN DEVELOPMENT BANK (ADB)

ADB is a multilateral regional development bank that provides grants, loans, technical assistance, and equity investments to promote social and economic development in the Asia and Pacific region. It was formed as a result of a resolution passed at the first Ministerial Conference on Asian Economic Cooperation held by the United Nations Economic Commission for Asia and the Far East in 1963.

Objectives of ADB

- *Regional cooperation and integration:* ADB supports and funds regional infrastructure projects and initiatives to enhance connectivity, trade, and investment within the region. It helps to foster economic integration and improve access to markets.
- *Poverty reduction and social development:* The prime focus of ADB is poverty reduction and social development in order to foster economic development in the region. It supports projects that are focussed on improving education, healthcare, clean water, and sanitation, as well as strengthening social safety nets and promoting gender equality.
- *Sustainable infrastructure development:* It invests in green infrastructure, renewable energy projects, climate change adaptation, and mitigation measures.
- *Knowledge sharing and capacity building:* It facilitates capacity building and knowledge sharing among the member countries. It conducts research, studies, and policy dialogues on various development issues. It offers training programmes, workshops, and seminars to enhance the skills and knowledge of government officials, professionals, and stakeholders.

Structure of ADB

Board of Governors: It is the highest policymaking body and comprises one representative from each member nation – 48 from the Asia-Pacific and 19 from outside the region.

- *Board of Directors:* The Board of Governors elect 12 members to form the Board of Directors, which performs its duties full time at the ADB headquarters. They supervise ADB's financial statements, approve its administrative budget, and review and approve all policy documents and all loan, equity, and technical assistance operations.
- *Management:* The president heads a management team comprising a managing director general and six vice presidents. The team supervises the work of ADB's operational, administrative, and knowledge departments.

Quick Facts

Number of founding members: 31

First President: Takeshi Watanabe

ASIAN INFRASTRUCTURE INVESTMENT BANK (AIIB)

AIIB is a multilateral financial institution established to provide financing for building Infrastructure for Tomorrow (i4t) in order to provide sustainable, economic and social development in Asia and beyond. On the environment front it addresses ecological impacts like water and air quality, biodiversity, pollution, and climate change. In terms of financial sustainability, it invests in projects with sound return on investment that raise economic growth and increase productivity. In terms of social sustainability, the projects should provide inclusive access. The bank is a brainchild of China and was first proposed in the year 2013.

AIIB was accorded permanent observer status at the United Nations in the year 2018.

Organizational Structure and Objectives of AIIB

- *Financing green infrastructure project:* AIIB invests in projects that deliver local environmental improvements and are dedicated to climate action. It provides a range of investments in renewable energy and low-carbon public transportation, as well as better water management and sanitation, pollution control, and enhancing ecosystem services. It has set an ambitious target of ensuring that 50 per cent of overall approved financing by 2025 will be directed towards climate finance.
- *Cross-border connectivity and regional cooperation:* AIIB supports projects that complement cross-border infrastructure connectivity by generating direct measurable benefits in enhancing regional trade, investment, digital and financial integration across Asian economies and beyond. By 2030, AIIB's target is for cross-border connectivity projects to represent 25–30 per cent of all financing approvals.
- *Technology-enabled infrastructure:* AIIB supports clients who transform their infrastructure sectors, including health and education infrastructure, by digital means and through technological applications.
- *Knowledge sharing and capacity building:* It promotes knowledge sharing, capacity building, and best practices in infrastructure development. It facilitates the exchange of experiences, lessons learned, and technical expertise among member countries and with other development partners. The AIIB supports research, training programmes, and partnerships to enhance the skills and knowledge of government officials, professionals, and stakeholders in infrastructure planning and implementation.
- *Facilitating private sector participation:* The AIIB encourages private sector participation in infrastructure development. It aims to mobilize private capital by co-financing projects with private sector entities and promoting public-private partnerships (PPPs).

Structure of AIIB

- *Board of Governors:* It is the highest decision-making body of AIIB. It consists of one governor and one alternate governor appointed by each member country.
- *Board of Directors:* It is responsible for the direction of the bank's general operations, exercising all powers delegated to it by the Board of Governors.
- *International Advisory Panel (IAP):* IAP supports the president and senior management on the bank's strategies, policies, and general operational issues. The panel meets at least twice a year (physically or virtually), including one meeting held alongside the bank's annual meeting of the Board of Governors.
- *Senior Management Team:* It is headed by the president elected for a period of five years and is eligible for re-election.

Quick Facts

Established on: 16 January 2016

Headquarters: Beijing, China

President of AIIB: Jin Liqn

NEW DEVELOPMENT BANK (NDB)

NDB is a multilateral bank established with the purpose of mobilizing resources for infrastructure and sustainable development projects in Emerging Markets and Developing Countries (EMDCs). It was formerly referred to as BRICS Development Bank and the idea to establish a BRICS bank was mooted by India at the fourth BRICS summit of 2012. The founding members of NDB are Brazil, Russia, India, People's Republic of China, and South Africa. The first president of BRICS banks was Mr. K. V. Kamath.

Focus Areas of NDB

- *Infrastructure development:* The NDB aims to support infrastructure development projects in its member countries. This includes investments in areas such as transportation, energy, water supply, and telecommunications, which are critical for economic growth and development.
- *Sustainable development:* It prioritizes financing projects that promote sustainable development and address environmental and social challenges. It supports initiatives related to renewable energy, climate change mitigation, clean water, and sustainable urban development.
- *Poverty reduction:* It seeks to finance projects that contribute to poverty reduction and inclusive growth. This involves supporting initiatives that enhance access to basic services, improve livelihoods, and promote social inclusion.
- *Innovation and technology:* It places emphasis on projects that foster innovation and technology advancements in its member countries. It supports initiatives that leverage technology to enhance economic productivity and social welfare.
- *Private sector development:* In addition to government-led projects, the NDB also promotes private sector development and encourages public-private partnerships (PPPs) to mobilize additional resources and expertise for development projects.
- *Financial inclusion:* The NDB aims to enhance financial inclusion by supporting projects that increase access to financial services for underserved populations and small- and medium-sized enterprises (SMEs).
- *Cross-border connectivity:* The NDB supports projects that enhance cross-border connectivity, trade, and economic cooperation among its member countries.
- *Disaster resilience:* The NDB recognizes the importance of building resilience to natural disasters and supports projects that enhance disaster preparedness and response capabilities.

Structure of NDB

- *Board of Governors:* The Board of Governors is the highest decision-making body of the NDB. It is composed of one governor from each member country, typically the country's finance minister or central bank governor. The board of governors sets the overall policies, strategies, and objectives of the NDB.
- *Board of Directors:* The Board of Directors is responsible for the day-to-day management and operations of the NDB. It is composed of one director from each member country. The Board of Directors makes decisions on project approvals, financing, budgeting, and other operational matters.

- *President:* The president is the chief executive officer of the NDB and is responsible for the overall management and administration of the institution. The president represents the NDB in its external relations and acts as the spokesperson for the bank.

Quick Facts

- Headquarters: Shanghai, China
- Current President: Dilma Vana Rousseff

ORGANIZATION FOR ECONOMIC COOPERATION AND DEVELOPMENT (OECD)

OECD is an international organization that advises governments on policies to support resilient, inclusive, and sustainable growth. It works in close collaboration with G7 and G20 to provide reforms and multilateral solutions to global challenges.

Brief History

OECD was established as the Organisation for European Economic Co-operation (OEEC) on 16 April 1948 to rebuild Europe after the Second World War with the American and Canadian aid, under the framework of Marshall plan. The convention to transform the OEEC into the OECD was signed at the Chateau de la Muette in Paris on 14 December 1960 and entered into force on 30 September 1961. This was done after the signing of Rome Treaty for launching European Economic Community in 1957.

The focus areas of OECD are:

- *Economic growth and productivity:* The OECD conducts research and analysis to promote sustainable economic growth and productivity improvements in member countries. It provides policy recommendations to enhance competitiveness and innovation, support small- and medium-sized enterprises (SMEs), and foster entrepreneurship.
- *Education and skills development:* The OECD focusses on improving education systems and developing skills to ensure that individuals have the necessary knowledge and abilities to thrive in the modern economy. It conducts comparative studies on education policies, assesses student performance, and promotes effective educational practices.
- *Innovation and technology:* The OECD works to foster innovation and technology advancements to drive economic growth and improve global competitiveness. It examines policies to support research and development, intellectual property rights, and the digital economy.
- *Employment and labour market Policies:* The OECD analyses labour market trends, policies, and challenges to promote inclusive and well-functioning labour markets. It provides recommendations on employment policies, workforce development, and social protection.
- *Trade and investment:* The OECD promotes open and transparent trade policies and reduces barriers to trade and investment among member countries. It conducts research on international trade trends and assesses the impact of trade and investment policies on economic growth.
- *Taxation and fiscal policy:* The OECD works on tax policy analysis and international cooperation to ensure fair and efficient taxation systems. It addresses tax-related challenges, including base erosion and profit shifting (BEPS) and digital taxation.

- *Environmental sustainability:* The OECD focusses on environmental policies to promote sustainable development, combat climate change, and protect natural resources. It supports efforts to transition to a low-carbon and environmentally friendly economy.
- *Social policy and inequality:* The OECD addresses social challenges, including income inequality, poverty, and social exclusion. It provides policy recommendations to enhance social cohesion, social protection systems, and the well-being of citizens.
- *Governance and public administration:* The OECD works on governance-related issues, including public sector reform, transparency, and anti-corruption measures. It promotes good governance practices to ensure effective public administration.
- *Development cooperation:* The OECD provides support to non-member countries through development cooperation initiatives. It assists in policy advice, technical assistance, and capacity building to foster sustainable development in partner countries.

Quick Facts

Total member countries: 38

Headquarters: Paris, France

Official languages: English and French

ORGANIZATION OF PETROLEUM EXPORTING COUNTRY (OPEC)

OPEC is an international organization of the leading oil-producing countries of the world that work to unify and coordinate petroleum policies among the member countries in order to secure fair and stable prices for petroleum in the international market. It was created at the Baghdad Conference in 1960 and the founding members of OPEC are Iran, Iraq, Kuwait, Saudi Arabia, and Venezuela.

OPEC+

OPEC+ refers to a cooperative arrangement between the member countries of OPEC and several non-OPEC oil-producing countries. It was established in 2016 to enhance oil market stability and manage global oil production levels through coordinated efforts.

The OPEC+ arrangement involves OPEC member countries, including countries like Saudi Arabia, Iraq, Iran, and Venezuela, working together with non-OPEC countries, notably Russia, Mexico, Kazakhstan, and others. The goal of OPEC+ is to collectively manage oil production levels to balance global oil supply and demand and maintain stable oil prices.

OPEC Fund

The OPEC Fund for International Development is a multilateral development finance institution established in 1976 by the OPEC member countries. The main objective of the OPEC Fund is to provide financial assistance to developing countries to support their socio-economic development projects and initiatives. It provides financial assistance through various financing instruments, including loans, grants, and technical assistance. Its financial support helps recipient countries implement development projects and build essential infrastructure. It funds projects in sectors that align with the development priorities of recipient countries. Projects are selected based on their potential to contribute to economic growth, poverty reduction, and sustainable development.

Quick Facts

- Headquarters: Vienna, Austria
- Current Secretary-General of OPEC: Haitham al-Ghais

NORTH ATLANTIC TREATY ORGANIZATION (NATO)

NATO is an intergovernmental military alliance which was established after the Second World War to secure peace in Europe and promote cooperation among its members and guard their freedom. The primary role of NATO is to protect peace and to guarantee the territorial integrity, political independence, and security of the member countries.

The founding treaty, North Atlantic Treaty was signed on 4 April 1949 in Washington DC by 12 European and North American countries. Article 5 of the Washington Treaty, which is NATO's founding document clearly mentions that attack or provocation on any of its member states is considered as an attack against all.

Operation Anchor Guard was the first mission of NATO and was launched in the year 1990 to survey the southern flank of NATO and to protect Turkish airspace after the Iraqi invasion of Kuwait.

Objectives of NATO

- *Collective defence:* The fundamental principle of NATO is collective defence. According to Article 5 of the NATO Treaty, an attack on one member country is considered an attack on all member countries, and they are committed to responding collectively to defend each other. This principle underscores the alliance's commitment to deterrence and the protection of its members.
- *Military cooperation and readiness:* NATO facilitates military cooperation and coordination among its member countries. It conducts joint military exercises, training programmes, and information sharing to enhance interoperability and readiness. NATO also maintains standing military forces and capabilities to respond to potential threats.
- *Political consultation and cooperation:* NATO serves as a platform for political consultation and cooperation among its member countries. It provides a forum for discussing security challenges, sharing information, and coordinating policies. Regular meetings and summits allow member countries to exchange views, discuss common interests, and make decisions on various security-related matters.
- *Crisis management and conflict resolution:* NATO engages in crisis management and conflict resolution efforts, both within its member countries and beyond. It has conducted peacekeeping operations, humanitarian interventions, and stabilization missions in different regions, working alongside other international actors. NATO's involvement aims to contribute to international security, stability, and the resolution of conflicts.
- *Partnerships and cooperation:* NATO maintains partnerships and cooperation programmes with countries outside the alliance. These partnerships aim to promote security, stability, and dialogue with partner countries, including through capacity-building initiatives, training programmes, and joint exercises. NATO also engages with other international organizations, such as the United Nations and the European Union, to enhance cooperation and coordination.

- *Defence spending and capability development:* NATO encourages its member countries to allocate a certain percentage of their GDP for defence spending and capability development. The alliance emphasizes the importance of maintaining modern military capabilities and ensuring fair burden-sharing among member countries.
- *Cyber defence and hybrid threats:* NATO recognizes the importance of addressing emerging security challenges, including cyber threats and hybrid warfare. It works to enhance cyber defence capabilities, information sharing, and cooperation among member countries to protect critical infrastructure and deter cyber attacks. NATO also addresses hybrid threats, which involve a combination of conventional and unconventional tactics, through a comprehensive approach.
- *Adaptation and partnerships:* NATO continuously adapts to the evolving security environment and the changing nature of threats. It has undergone strategic adaptations to address new challenges, such as terrorism, regional instability, and emerging technologies. NATO seeks to strengthen partnerships with like-minded countries and organizations to promote stability and security globally.

Structure of NATO

- *North Atlantic Council (NAC):* NAC is NATO's main political decision-making body. Each member state has a seat in the council. The council meets at various levels at least once a week or as required. It is chaired by the secretary-general, who assists the participants in reaching agreement on key issues.
- *Secretary-General:* The secretary-general is the head of the NATO international staff and serves as the organization's chief administrative officer. He or she is responsible for representing NATO externally, chairing meetings of NAC, and coordinating the work of various NATO bodies.
- *Military Committee:* The Military Committee is composed of the chiefs of defence of all member countries and is NATO's highest military authority. It provides military advice and recommendations to NAC and plays a crucial role in shaping NATO's military strategy and operations.
- *Integrated Military Command Structure:* NATO has an integrated military command structure that oversees the planning and conduct of NATO's military operations. It includes strategic commands, regional commands, and functional commands responsible for specific military areas and functions.

Key Facts

Total members: 31 countries and Iceland doesn't have an army of its own.

Official languages: English and French

First Secretary-General of NATO: Lord Ismay of the United Kingdom

Headquarters: Brussels, Belgium

Current Secretary-General of NATO: Jens Stoltenberg

Chair of NATO Military Committee: Robert Peter Bauer

ASSOCIATION OF SOUTH EAST ASIAN NATIONS (ASEAN)

ASEAN is a political and economic union of countries in South Asia to promote intergovernmental cooperation among its members by promoting cooperation at a political, economic, social, educational, and military level. It was established on 8

August 1967 in Bangkok, Thailand, with the signing of the ASEAN Declaration or the Bangkok Declaration.

The ASEAN Charter forms the foundation ground of working of ASEAN and it entered into force on 15 December 2008.

Objectives of ASEAN

- *Regional cooperation:* ASEAN aims to enhance regional cooperation and solidarity among its member countries. It seeks to create a sense of community and shared responsibility for the prosperity and security of the Southeast Asian region.
- *Political and security cooperation:* ASEAN members work together to promote political stability and conflict resolution in the region. The organization advocates for peaceful settlement of disputes and emphasizes the importance of dialogue and diplomatic solutions.
- *Economic integration:* ASEAN is committed to promoting economic growth and development in the region. It seeks to create a single market and production base, facilitate the free flow of goods, services, investment, and skilled labour, and enhance regional connectivity.
- *Social and cultural cooperation:* ASEAN aims to foster social progress and cultural development among its member countries. It promotes exchanges and cooperation in areas such as education, science and technology, culture, tourism, and health.
- *People-centred community:* ASEAN places importance on its people-centred approach, which emphasizes the well-being and welfare of the people in the region. It seeks to narrow the development gap among member countries and improve the quality of life for all citizens.
- *Dialogue partnerships:* ASEAN engages with various countries and international organizations through dialogue partnerships. It has established partnerships with major powers, regional neighbours, and international organizations to promote cooperation and collaboration.
- *Non-interference principle:* ASEAN adheres to the principle of non-interference in the internal affairs of member countries. It respects the sovereignty and independence of each member state and seeks to resolve regional issues through peaceful means.

Structure of ASEAN

- *ASEAN Summit* is the highest-level meeting of ASEAN leaders, held annually to discuss regional issues and set the organization's agenda. Various ministerial and working-level meetings are also conducted to address specific areas of cooperation.
- *ASEAN Secretariat* is the administrative body that supports the work of ASEAN. It is based in Jakarta, Indonesia, and serves as the central coordinating agency for ASEAN activities. The secretariat provides research, documentation, and logistical support to ASEAN meetings and initiatives.

Quick Facts

Founding members: Indonesia, Malaysia, Philippines, Singapore, and Thailand

Motto of ASEAN: One Vision, One Identity, One Community

First ASEAN Summit: Bali, Indonesia on 23–24 February 1976

ASEAN day: 8 August

As of 2023 there are 10 members Countries: Brunei, Cambodia, Indonesia, Laos, Malaysia, Myanmar, Philippines, Singapore, Thailand, and Vietnam

ASIA PACIFIC ECONOMIC COOPERATION (APEC)

APEC is a regional intergovernmental economic forum to promote balanced, inclusive, and sustainable economic trade and growth in the 21 economies of the Pacific rim region.

The idea of APEC was first mooted by the former prime minister of Australia Bob Hawke during a speech in Seoul, Korea, on 31 January 1989. APEC was established by 12 economies of Asia Pacific in the year 1989 at Canberra, Australia. The founding members of APEC are Australia, Brunei Darussalam, Canada, Indonesia, Japan, Korea, Malaysia, New Zealand, the Philippines, Singapore, Thailand, and the United States.

Focus Areas of APEC

- *Trade and investment liberalization and facilitation:* It aims to facilitate free and open trade and investment among its member economies. It seeks to reduce barriers to trade, promote economic integration, and strengthen regional economic linkages.
- *Regional economic integration:* APEC works towards enhancing economic integration in the Asia-Pacific region through initiatives such as the Free Trade Area of the Asia-Pacific (FTAAP) and the Bogor Goals, which aim for free and open trade and investment by 2020 for developed economies and 2025 for developing economies.
- *Connectivity*: APEC focusses on enhancing physical, institutional, and people-to-people connectivity in the region. It promotes infrastructure development, efficient transportation and logistics, and cooperation in areas such as telecommunications and digital technology.
- *Inclusive and sustainable growth:* APEC is committed to fostering inclusive and sustainable economic growth. It supports policies that promote social inclusion, reduce poverty, and protect the environment.
- *Food security:* APEC addresses food security challenges through initiatives that promote sustainable agriculture, enhance food supply chains, and address issues related to food trade and distribution.
- *Structural reform:* APEC encourages structural reforms in member economies to enhance economic efficiency, competitiveness, and productivity.
- *Women's economic empowerment:* APEC promotes gender equality and women's economic empowerment to ensure that women can fully participate in and benefit from economic activities.
- *Green growth:* APEC promotes sustainable development and green growth by addressing environmental challenges and promoting clean and renewable energy.

BAY OF BENGAL INITIATIVE FOR MULTI-SECTORAL TECHNICAL AND ECONOMIC COOPERATION (BIMSTEC)

BIMSTEC is a regional organization that focusses on technological and economic cooperation among the South Asian and Southeast Asian countries along the coast of the Bay of Bengal.

It was established with the signing of the Bangkok Declaration on 6 June 1997. It was initially known as BIST-EC (Bangladesh-India-Sri Lanka-Thailand Economic Cooperation).

However, with the entry of Myanmar in 1997, and Bhutan and Nepal in February 2004, it came to be known as BIMSTEC.

The charter of BIMSTEC was adopted on 30 March 2022 during the fifth BIMSTEC Summit.

Purpose of BIMSTEC

- Create a favourable environment for rapid economic development by identifying and implementing specific cooperative projects in agreed areas of collaboration and other areas as decided by the member countries. These areas of cooperation may be reviewed periodically.
- Speed up economic growth and social progress in the Bay of Bengal region through joint efforts based on equality and partnership.
- Promote active collaboration and mutual assistance in economic, social, technical, and scientific fields on matters of shared interest.
- Assistance through training and research facilities in education, professional, and technical spheres.
- Maintain peace and stability in the Bay of Bengal region through close collaboration in combatting international terrorism, transnational organized crime, natural disasters, climate change, and communicable diseases.
- Strive for poverty eradication in the Bay of Bengal region.
- Establishment of multidimensional connectivity and promotion of synergy among connectivity frameworks in the region for economic integration and shared prosperity.

Sectors of Cooperation

- Trade, Investment and Development; Sub-sectors: Blue Economy
- Environment and Climate Change; Sub-sectors: Mountain Economy
- Security; Sub-sectors: Counter-Terrorism and Transnational Crime; Disaster Management;
- Energy Agriculture and Food Security; Sub-sectors: Agriculture; Fisheries and Livestock
- People-to-People Contact; Sub-sectors: Culture; Tourism; Poverty Alleviation
- Science, Technology, and Innovation; Sub-sectors: Technology; Health; Human Resource Development
- Connectivity

Structure of BIMSTEC

- *Summit:* It is the highest policymaking body and comprises the heads of state or government of the member states.
- *Ministerial Meeting:* It comprises the foreign affairs ministers of the member states.
- *Sectoral Ministerial Meetings:* It comprises the ministers of line ministries responsible for carrying out the activities of the respective sectors

- *Senior Officials' Meeting:* It consists of the foreign secretaries/secretaries/appropriate Senior officials nominated by the BIMSTEC member states.
- *BIMSTEC Permanent Working Committee (BPCW):* It comprises senior officials of the respective National Focal Points (NFPs). NFPs are established within the foreign affairs ministries of the member states and serve as the point of contact for all the communication between BIMSTEC secretariat and member states.
- *BIMSTEC Secretariat:* It comprises the secretary-general, directors, and such other staff as may be required and approved by the member states. It is at Dhaka, Bangladesh.

Quick Facts

First Secretary-General of BIMSTEC: Sumith Nakandala from Sri Lanka

Official language: English

BRAZIL, RUSSIA, INDIA, CHINA, AND SOUTH AFRICA (BRICS)

BRICS is an informal group of the Federative Republic of Brazil, the Russian Federation, the Republic of India, the People's Republic of China, and the Republic of South Africa.

Initially, there were four members: Brazil, China, Russia, and India, and it was known as BRIC. However, with the addition of South Africa to the group in the year 2010, the name was changed to BRICS. The first BRICS ministerial meeting was held at the proposal of Russian President Vladimir Putin on the margins of a UN General Assembly Session in New York on 20 September 2006. The foreign ministers of Brazil, China, India, and Russia participated in this meeting. The first BRIC summit was hosted on 16 June 2009, in Yekaterinburg, Russia.

Objectives and Focus Areas of BRICS

- *Economic cooperation:* BRICS countries aim to promote economic cooperation and enhance trade and investment among member nations. They explore opportunities for economic growth and sustainable development.
- *Financial cooperation:* BRICS countries have established the New Development Bank (NDB) and the Contingent Reserve Arrangement (CRA) to provide financial support and stability during times of economic challenges.
- *Geopolitical dialogue:* BRICS facilitates regular dialogue among member nations to address global challenges and promote international peace and stability.
- *Development and infrastructure:* BRICS nations focus on infrastructure development and projects to support the growth and development of their economies.
- *Innovation and technology:* BRICS promotes cooperation in innovation, science, and technology to foster technological advancement and knowledge exchange.
- *Social and cultural exchange:* BRICS aims to enhance social and cultural exchange among member countries to strengthen people-to-people ties and understanding.
- *Advocacy for developing countries:* BRICS countries advocate for the interests and concerns of developing countries on international platforms.
- *Sustainable development:* BRICS emphasizes sustainable development and cooperation on environmental issues and climate change.

- *Collaboration in multilateral forums:* BRICS member countries collaborate in various multilateral forums and organizations to promote common interests and positions

GROUP OF FOUR (G4)

G4 is an informal group of Brazil, Germany, India, and Japan that support the reforms in the United Nations Security Council (UNSC). All these countries support each other's bid for a permanent candidature at the UNSC. All four countries meet on the sidelines of the annual high-level UN General Assembly session.

G7 (INTERNATIONAL GROUP OF SEVEN)

G7 is an informal intergovernmental forum of industrialized democracies comprising United States, Canada, France, Germany, Italy, Japan, and the United Kingdom.

Earlier, it was known as G8 with Russia being a part of it. However, Russia was expelled from this group in 2014 following the annexation of Ukraine Crimeia region. The G7 group meets annually to discuss important international issues such as global economic governance, international security, and energy policy.

G20 (GROUP OF TWENTY)

G20 is an intergovernmental forum of 19 countries and European Union for international economic cooperation. It represents around 85 per cent of the global GDP, over 75 per cent of the global trade, and about two-thirds of the world population. It was founded as an informal forum for the finance ministers and central bank governors to discuss global economic and financial issues in the wake of Asian financial crisis of 1997–98. However, in the wake of the 2007 economic crisis, the G20 was elevated to the level of heads of state/government and was designated the 'premier forum for international economic cooperation' in the year 2009. G20 summit is held annually and focusses on macroeconomic issues, trade, sustainable development, health, agriculture, energy, environment, climate change, and anti-corruption.

Members of G20: Argentina, Australia, Brazil, Canada, China, France, Germany, India, Indonesia, Italy, Japan, Republic of Korea, Mexico, Russia, Saudi Arabia, South Africa, Türkiye, United Kingdom, and United States, along with the European Union.

Objectives and Focus Areas

- *Economic cooperation:* It seeks to promote international economic cooperation and financial stability among its member countries. It addresses economic challenges and works towards sustainable and balanced economic growth.
- *Financial regulation:* It plays a significant role in coordinating financial regulation and policies to enhance the resilience of the global financial system and prevent financial crises.
- *Trade and investment:* G20 member countries work towards enhancing international trade and investment, reducing barriers, and promoting fair and open trade practices.
- *Employment and social inclusion:* It focusses on employment policies and social inclusion to ensure that economic growth benefits all segments of society.
- *Global development:* G20 members discuss and coordinate on global development issues, including poverty reduction, infrastructure development, and support for developing countries.

- *Climate change and sustainability:* The G20 addresses environmental challenges, including climate change, and promotes sustainable development and energy policies.
- *Innovation and digital economy:* G20 discussions include topics related to innovation, technology, and the digital economy to harness the potential of digital transformation for economic growth.
- *Women's empowerment:* The G20 emphasizes women's economic empowerment and gender equality as critical components of inclusive and sustainable growth.
- *Health and pandemic preparedness:* The G20 addresses global health challenges and pandemic preparedness, especially in light of the COVID-19 pandemic.

Quick Facts

- Host country of G20 summit 2023: India
- Theme: 'Vasudhaiva Kutumbakam' or 'One Earth · One Family · One Future'.

INDIAN OCEAN RIM ASSOCIATION (IORA)

IORA is an intergovernmental organization of 23 countries that border the Indian Ocean.

The vision for IORA was shared during South Africa's late President Nelson Mandela's visit to India in 1995. It was first established as the Indian Ocean Rim Initiative in Mauritius in the year 1995. However, it was formally established as Indian Ocean Rim Association for Regional Co-operation in March 1997 by signing of the Charter of the Indian Ocean Rim Association for Regional Co-operation.

Structure of IORA

- *Council of (Foreign) Ministers (COM):* It is the highest authority of IORA and meets annually to discuss the developments of IORA. It formulates policy, reviews progress on cooperation and makes decisions on new areas of cooperation. They elect a chair and a vice chair of the association, each for a period of two years.
- *Committee of Senior Officials (CSO):* It meets twice a year to review the progress IORA's agenda, implementation of the decisions taken by the COM, and considers recommendations by working groups.
- *Troika:* It consists of the chair, the vice chair and the previous chair and was established by the Council of Ministers. It reports to the COM and member states on matters such as pool y direction, the establishment of additional mechanisms, and the appointment, term of office, mandate and duties of the secretary-general.
- *Secretariat:* It is headed by the secretary-general and it manages, coordinates, services and monitors the implementation of policy decisions, work programmes and projects adopted by the COM. It is in Mauritius.

Priorities and Focus Areas of IORA

- *Maritime safety and security:* IORA aims to enhance maritime safety and security in the Indian Ocean region, including measures to combat piracy, maritime terrorism, and other transnational crimes. It promotes cooperation among member countries to ensure the safety of maritime trade and navigation.
- *Trade and investment facilitation:* IORA works towards promoting trade and investment facilitation among its member states. It aims to reduce

trade barriers, enhance economic connectivity, and foster greater economic cooperation and investment opportunities within the region.

- *Blue economy:* IORA focusses on harnessing the potential of the blue economy, which involves sustainable use and management of ocean resources. It encourages member countries to develop their marine sectors, including fisheries, aquaculture, renewable energy, and marine tourism.
- *Disaster risk management:* IORA prioritizes disaster risk management and resilience-building in the face of natural disasters and climate-related events. It facilitates information sharing, capacity building, and joint efforts to mitigate and respond to disasters in the region.
- *Women's economic empowerment:* IORA promotes women's economic empowerment and gender equality, recognizing the importance of women's participation in economic activities and decision-making processes.
- *Academic and scientific cooperation:* IORA fosters academic and scientific cooperation among member countries, encouraging collaboration in research, education, and knowledge sharing in areas relevant to the region's development.
- *Tourism promotion:* IORA supports tourism promotion and development as a means to enhance regional connectivity, cultural exchange, and economic growth.
- *Fisheries management:* IORA addresses issues related to sustainable fisheries management, including responsible fishing practices and conservation of marine resources.
- *Connectivity and infrastructure development:* IORA promotes regional connectivity and infrastructure development, including ports, roads, and digital connectivity, to facilitate economic integration and trade.
- *Cultural exchange and people-to-people connectivity:* IORA encourages cultural exchange and people-to-people connectivity among member countries, fostering greater understanding and mutual respect.

SHANGHAI COOPERATION ORGANISATION (SCO)

SCO is a permanent intergovernmental international organisation that aims to foster multilateral cooperation and enhance economic, political, defence, and international security relations among the member countries.

History of SCO

SCO is a successor to Shanghai Five, which comprised China, Kazakhstan, Kyrgyzstan, Russia, and Tajikistan. Shanghai Five was a political association based on the Agreement on Confidence-Building in the Military Field in the Border Area (Shanghai, 1996) and the Agreement on the Mutual Reduction of Armed Forces in the Border Area (Moscow, 1997). In 2001, Uzbekistan joined Shanghai Five, and the group was renamed as the SCO. The Charter of the Shanghai Cooperation Organisation was signed at the St. Petersburg Summit of the Heads of State of the SCO in June 2002 and entered into force on 19 September 2003.

Goals of SCO

- Enhance trust and foster amicable relations among the members.

- Facilitate collaboration in politics, trade and economy, science and technology, culture, education, energy, transportation, tourism, environmental protection, etc.
- Collaborate and work collectively in order to uphold and safeguard peace, security, and stability in the region, with the ultimate goal of establishing a new, democratic, equitable, and rational global political and economic order.

Structure of SCO

- *The Heads of State Council (HSC):* HSC is the highest decision-making body in the SCO. It meets once every year and takes decisions regarding important issues in terms of defining the priority areas of SCO, its interactions with other countries and international organizations.
- *The Heads of Government Council (HGC):* HGC meets once per year and approves the budget of SCO, consider and decide upon major issues related to particular, especially economic, spheres of interaction within the organization.
- *Council of Ministers of Foreign Affairs:* It looks into daily working of the organization, preparation of meetings of the HSC and has consultations on international problems within the SCO. They generally meet one month prior to a meeting of the Heads of State Council.
- *The Council of National Coordinators:* It coordinates and directs day-to-day activities of SCO. It makes the required preparation for the meetings of the HSC, HGC, and the Council of Ministers of Foreign Affairs. It hold its meetings at least three times a year.
- *Permanent bodies:* It has two permanent bodies:

1. *Regional Anti-Terrorist Structure (RATS):* It is a permanent SCO body established on 15 June 2001 with a mandate to promote cooperation among the member countries to combat terrorism, separatism, and extremism. It is headed by executive director and is headquartered in Tashkent, Uzbekistan.
2. *Secretariat:* It is the executive body of SCO and is headed by the secretary-general. It is situated in Beijing, China. It coordinates the daily activities of the SCO, implements the organizational decisions, declarations, and agendas of the SCO, carries out preliminary legal and financial assessments of draft treaties and regulations drawn up within the SCO framework, acts as the depositary of documents adopted within the SCO framework.

- *Non-governmental bodies:* It has two non-governmental bodies:

1. *SCO Interbank Consortium (SCO IBC):* It was established by the Council of Heads of Government with an aim to provide banking services and set up a mechanism for funding for investment projects sponsored by the governments of the SCO member states. The SCO IBC Council meets ad hoc upon the consensus of all of the parties at least once per year.
2. *SCO Business Council of the Shanghai Cooperation Organisation:* It is a non-governmental body which has members of highly influential business communities of the SCO member countries. It provides a platform for fostering the economic cooperation among the SCO member countries and establishing direct business and financial links among the members. It is headquartered in Moscow, Russia. The mandate of SCO includes education, science, new technology, healthcare

and agriculture, energy, transportation, telecommunications, credit and banking the Council.

SCO member states, observers, and partners are home to 207 UNESCO World Heritage Sites and in order to showcase this unique product of the region, SCO member countries have decided to designate one city as tourism and cultural capital every year under a rotating initiative. Kashi (Varanasi) is the first cultural capital of the SCO.

Full time members (as of 2023): China, India, Kazakhstan, Kyrgyzstan, Russia, Pakistan, Tajikistan, and Uzbekistan.

Official languages: Russian and Chinese

Chair of SCO 2023: India

Theme of SCO 2023: SECURE SCO

SOUTH ASIAN ASSOCIATION FOR REGIONAL COOPERATION (SAARC)

SAARC is a regional and intergovernmental geopolitical union of countries in South Asia which aims at holistic and sustainable development of the human resources and region. The SAARC charter was signed on 8 December 1985 in Dhaka, Bangladesh. At present, the members of SAARC are- Afghanistan, Bangladesh, Bhutan, India, Maldives, Nepal, Pakistan, and Sri Lanka. The official language is English.

Objectives of SAARC

- Enhance the standard of living leading to an improvised quality of life of the people of South Asia.
- Ensure that individuals of the region get adequate opportunities to live their life with dignity and at its full potential.
- Foster and expedite economic growth, social advancement, and cultural enrichment in the region.
- Foster and reinforce collective self-reliance among South Asian nations.
- Promote and enhance active collaboration and mutual support in various areas such as economics, social development, culture, technology, and science.
- Strengthen cooperation with other developing countries.
- Enhance collaboration among South Asian countries in international forums on matters of shared interests and collaborate with international and regional organizations pursuing similar goals and objectives.

Structure of SAARC

- *Summits:* It is the meeting of the heads of governments of the member countries and is the highest decision making authority under SAARC. The outcome of a summit is a declaration which is adopted by the heads at the concluding session of a summit.
- *Council of Ministers:* The Council of Ministers comprises the foreign ministers and it reviews the implementation of decisions taken by the summits. They have been meeting informally on the sidelines of the UNGA sessions in New York.
- *SAARC Secretariat:* It is headed by the secretary-general. It facilitates and oversees the execution of SAARC activities, provide support for its meetings, and serve as a channel for effective communication.
- *Standing Committee:* It comprises the foreign secretaries of the SAARC member states and reports to the Council of Ministers. It is responsible for overall execution and implementation of programme, identification of new areas of cooperation, and determination of inter-sectoral priorities.

- *Programming Committee:* It comprises heads of SAARC Divisions of Member State and meets before the meetings of standing committees. It looks into Calendar of Activities, Administrative and Financial Matters of the Secretariat and Regional Centres, Technical Committees, Working Groups, and Specialized Bodies.
- *Technical Committee:* It comprises representatives of member states who are responsible for the implementation, coordination, and monitoring of the programmes in their respective areas of cooperation.
- *Working Groups:* These formulate and oversee programmes and activities within the framework of SAARC to strengthen and promote regional cooperation in their respective areas.
- *Action Committee:* These are set up by the standing committee. It comprises member states concerned with the implementation of projects involving more than two but not all member states.

Principles of SAARC

- Uphold the principles of sovereign equality, territorial integrity, political independence, and non-interference in the internal affairs of other states, while promoting mutual benefit.
- This cooperation should not replace bilateral and multilateral cooperation but rather complement and support them.
- This cooperation should not contradict or conflict with existing bilateral and multilateral obligations.

Specialized Bodies of SAARC

- *SAARC Development Fund (SDF):* SDF provides financial support for collaborative projects in social sectors, including poverty alleviation and development. It operates under the governance of a board comprising representatives from the member states' Ministry of Finance.
- *South Asian University (SAU):* SAU is a globally recognized university situated in Delhi, India. SAU was established in 2010 and Prof. Gowher Rizvi from Bangladesh had prepared the Concept Paper for SAU. The university offers degrees in doctoral and master's programmes which are recognized by the University Grants Commission in India and by other SAARC countries.
- *South Asian Regional Standards Organization (SARSO):* SARSO was established to achieve and enhance coordination and cooperation among SAARC member states in the fields of standardization and conformity assessment. It aimed to develop harmonized standards for the region to facilitate intra-regional trade and to have access in the global market. Its secretariat is at Dhaka, Bangladesh.
- *SAARC Arbitration Council:* It is an intergovernmental body which provides legal framework and platform for dispute resolution and settlement among the member countries. Its headquarters are in Islamabad, Pakistan.

ORGANIZATION OF ISLAMIC COOPERATION (OIC)

OIC is an international organization of Islamic countries with 57 member countries that have come together to safeguard, protect, and promote the interests of Muslims across the world while maintaining and promoting international peace and harmony. It is the second largest organization in the world after the UN.

It was established on 25 September 1969 following the criminal arson of Al-Aqsa Mosque in Jerusalem. The OIC charter was adopted in 1972, and it sets out the objectives, principles, and fundamental objectives. The OIC programme is anchored in the provisions of its charter and focusses on 18 priority areas with 107 goals. The official languages of OIC are Arabic, English, and French.

Structure of OIC

- *Islamic Summit:* It is the highest authority of OIC and meets once every three years to deliberate and take policy decisions. It is composed of kings and heads of state and government of member states.
- *Council of Foreign Ministers:* It considers the means for the implementation of general policy of OIC and meets once a year.
- *General Secretariat:* It is the executive organ of OIC and is entrusted with the implementation of the decisions of the two preceding bodies. The secretary-general is the chief administrative officer of the organization and is elected by the Council of Foreign Ministers for a period of five years.

Focus Areas of OIC

- *Solidarity among the Islamic countries:* It aims to promote unity, solidarity, and cooperation among the member countries based on their shared Islamic heritage, values, and interests.
- *Promote science, technology, and innovation:* The member countries work together in areas such as research and development, knowledge sharing, capacity building, and the exchange of best practices. The OIC seeks to harness scientific and technological advancements for the benefit of its member states and the wider Muslim community.
- *Education and culture:* OIC focusses on promoting education, culture, and intercultural dialogue among member countries. It supports initiatives to improve access to quality education, enhance educational systems, and promote cultural diversity, heritage preservation, and cultural exchanges. The OIC aims to foster mutual understanding, tolerance, and respect among different cultures and civilizations.
- *Humanitarian assistance:* OIC provides support and assistance during times of crisis, such as natural disasters, conflicts, and refugee situations. The OIC coordinates humanitarian efforts, including relief operations, capacity building, and advocacy for the rights and well-being of affected populations.

WORLD ECONOMIC FORUM (WEF)

WEF is an international NGO that promotes private and public cooperation while providing a platform for businesses, industries, and governments to interact, engage, and work together. It engages the foremost political, business, cultural, and other leaders of society to shape global, regional, and industry agendas.

In 1971, it was established as the European Management Forum and drew business leaders from Europe, and beyond. However, in 1987, it was renamed as the World Economic Forum (WEF) and with the renaming it broadened its vision to become an international platform. In 2015, the forum was formally recognized as an international organization.

Focus Areas of WEF

- *Sustainable development and climate change:* WEF emphasizes the need for sustainable development and addressing climate change. It promotes discussions on sustainable economic models, renewable energy, resource efficiency, climate adaptation, and mitigation strategies. The WEF encourages public-private partnerships to advance sustainable development goals.

- *Technology and innovation:* WEF explores the impact of emerging technologies on societies and economies. It examines areas such as artificial intelligence, robotics, blockchain, digital transformation, cybersecurity, and data governance. The WEF promotes dialogue on responsible and ethical technological advancements and their implications for businesses and society.
- *Global economy and geopolitics:* The WEF analyses and provides insights into global economic trends, challenges, and opportunities. It convenes discussions on topics such as economic growth, trade, fiscal policies, financial stability, and geopolitical dynamics that shape the global economic landscape.
- *Health and well-being:* The WEF addresses global health challenges and promotes access to quality healthcare. It focusses on areas such as pandemic preparedness, healthcare delivery, innovation in healthcare systems, and addressing health inequities. The WEF engages public and private sector leaders to improve health outcomes worldwide.
- *Gender equality and social inclusion:* The WEF advocates for gender equality and social inclusion. It addresses issues related to gender gaps in the workforce, women's empowerment, diversity, and inclusion in leadership positions. The WEF promotes initiatives and partnerships to advance equality and inclusion across sectors.
- *Global governance and multilateralism:* The WEF supports multilateral cooperation and the strengthening of global governance systems. It facilitates discussions on international collaboration, sustainable development goals, trade policies, and geopolitical challenges. The WEF aims to foster dialogue and partnerships to address global issues collectively.

Meetings of WEF

The forum holds four major annual meetings:

1. *Annual meeting:* It is held in Davos-Klosters, Switzerland, and it shapes global, regional, and industry agendas at the beginning of the calendar year.
2. *Annual meeting of new champions:* It is held in China and is the annual meeting on innovation, science, and technology.
3. *Annual meeting of the global future councils:* It is held in the United Arab Emirates and brings together the world's leading knowledge community to share insights on the major challenges facing the world today.
4. *Industry strategy meeting:* It brings together industry strategy officers to shape industry agendas and explore how industries can shift from managing change to pioneering change.

NUCLEAR SUPPLIERS GROUP (NSG)

NSG is a multilateral export control regime (MECR) and an informal group of nuclear supplier countries that seeks to contribute to the non-proliferation of nuclear weapons through the implementation of two sets of guidelines for nuclear exports and nuclear-related exports. These guidelines are not legally binding on the member countries.

In addition to nuclear exports, the NSG also controls the export of certain nuclear-related dual-use items, technology, and equipment that could be used for nuclear weapons development or proliferation. The NSG operates on a voluntary basis, and countries can choose to join the group based on their commitment to non-proliferation objectives and adherence to the NSG guidelines.

Decisions within the NSG are made by consensus among member countries. Any country can object to a proposed nuclear transfer, and the objection leads to a halt in the transfer until the issue is resolved.

NSG Guidelines

These are the conditions of supply that are applicable for nuclear transfers for peaceful purposes.

- The first NSG guidelines were published by the International Atomic Energy Agency (IAEA) in the year 1978. These govern the export of items that are especially designed or prepared for nuclear use. These were applicable for the nuclear transfers to non-nuclear countries for peaceful purposes to help ensure that such transfers would not be diverted to unsafeguarded nuclear fuel cycle or nuclear explosive activities. It includes nuclear material, nuclear reactors, and equipment therefor; non-nuclear material for reactors, plants and equipment for the reprocessing, enrichment and conversion of nuclear material and for fuel fabrication and heavy water production; and technology (including software) associated with each of the above items. These items are known as Trigger List Items as the transfer of an item triggers safeguards.
- The second NSG guidelines were published by the IAEA in the year 1992. These govern the export of nuclear-related dual-use items and technologies, that is, items that can make a major contribution to an unsafeguarded nuclear fuel cycle or nuclear explosive activity; but that have non-nuclear uses as well, for example in industry. These items are known as Dual-Use Items.

WASSENAAR ARRANGEMENT

The Wassenaar Arrangement is a multilateral export control regime (MECR) that operates on the basis of voluntary information exchange among member countries concerning the transfer of conventional weapons and dual-use goods and technologies.

Under the arrangement, member states are obliged to provide reports on their arms transfers and transfers/denials of specific dual-use goods and technologies to destinations outside the agreement every six months.

The group regularly shares information related to both conventional and nuclear-capable technology that is either sold to or denied to countries beyond the arrangement. This information is maintained and updated through comprehensive lists of chemicals, technologies, processes, and products that hold significant military importance. The primary objective is to regulate the movement of technology, materials, or components to countries or entities that could potentially undermine international security and stability.

It was established in July 1996 and its secretariat is in Vienna, Austria.

The Wassenaar Arrangement Plenary is the decision-making body of the arrangement and meets annually. It is composed of representatives of all participating states.

AUSTRALIA GROUP

The Australia Group (AG) is an MECR and an informal group of countries that keep a check on the exports of Chemical and Biological Weapon (CBW) to prevent their proliferation. All the countries participating in the AG are parties to the Chemical Weapons Convention (CWC) and the Biological Weapons Convention (BWC). The licensing measures put in place for the member countries ensure that the exports of certain chemicals, biological agents, and dual-use chemical and biological manufacturing facilities and equipment do not contribute to the spread of CBW.

History

In the year 1984, the UN investigation team found violations of the 1925 Geneva Protocol in the Iran-Iraq war as there was the use of chemical weapons (CW) by Iraq. It had sourced the precursors of CW through legitimate trade channels. This led to the introduction of export control on certain chemicals that could be the processors of CWs. However, these controls lacked uniformity. Eventually, Australia proposed a meeting of the countries willing to have export controls in place. This led to the first meeting of AG in Brussels in June 1985. Since then, the annual meetings are held in Paris.

AG and Trade

As a part of this group, all the member countries have licensing measures over 89 chemical weapons precursors. AG group releases 'common control lists' in which participants also require licences for the exports of specific:

- Dual-use chemical manufacturing facilities, equipment, and related technology
- Plant pathogens
- Animal pathogens
- Biological agents
- Dual-use biological equipment and related technology

AG meets annually to discuss ways of increasing the effectiveness of participating countries' national export licensing measures to prevent would-be proliferators from obtaining materials for CBW programmes.

MISSILE TECHNOLOGY CONTROL REGIME (MTCR)

MTCR is a MECR that seeks to limit the proliferation of missiles and missile technology. Its focus is on rockets and unmanned aerial vehicles (UAVs) capable of delivering a payload of at least 500 kg to a range of at least 300 km, and on equipment, software, and technology for such systems.

MTCR is not a treaty and does not impose any legal binding on the member countries. It is an informal political understanding among the members. It was established by the G-7 (Canada, France, Germany, Italy, Japan, the United Kingdom, and the United States) industrialized countries in the year 1987. Initially, MTCR was established with a focus only on missiles for nuclear weapons delivery. However, the focus was expanded on the proliferation of missiles for the delivery of all types of weapons of mass destruction (WMD), i.e., nuclear, chemical, and biological weapons.

MTCR meets annually in a policy-level plenary meeting which is hosted by the country that is serving as the current chair. It has no formal secretariat. However, France serves as MTCR's point of contact (POC). The MTCR chair and partners undertake outreach activities with non-members in order to keep them updated about the group's activities and to provide practical assistance regarding efforts to prevent the proliferation of WMD delivery systems.

MTCR Guidelines and Annex

The MTCR guidelines are the common export control policy adhered by the member countries. These define the purpose of the MTCR and provide the overall structure and rules to guide the member countries. These do not distinguish between exports to partners and exports to non-partners.

The MTCR Annex is the MTCR's list of controlled items and is divided into two parts:

Category I: It includes complete rockets and UAVs, their major complete subsystems, related software and technology, and specially designed production facilities for these items. These items subject to an unconditional strong presumption of denial and are licensed for export only on rare occasions. The exports of production facilities for Category I items are prohibited absolutely.

Category II: It includes other less-sensitive and dual-use missile-related components. Their export is subject to licensing requirements taking into consideration the non-proliferation factors specified in the MTCR guidelines.

INTERNATIONAL CRIMINAL POLICE ORGANIZATION (INTERPOL)

INTERPOL is an intergovernmental organization that facilitates international cooperation between the police of member countries in order to reduce crime and make the world a safer place. It is a membership-based organization. The idea to establish INTERPOL was born at the first International Criminal Police Congress held in Monaco in April 1914. The International Criminal Police Commission (ICPC) was established on 7 September 1923. Post the Second World War in 1956, a new modernized Constitution was adopted and the ICPC became the International Criminal Police Organization (INTERPOL).

Objectives of INTERPOL

- *Exchange information and maintain database:* It is a platform to exchange information on crime and criminals such as names, fingerprints, stolen vehicles, passports, etc., and make it accessible in real-time to countries. These databases are helpful to enhance their investigative capabilities.
- *Connect police globally:* All the member countries are connected globally via each other and with the general secretariat via a communications system called I-24/7.
- *Issue notices:* INTERPOL doesn't have the authority to make arrests but it can facilitate cooperation among the member countries. It can issue red and yellow alerts. Red alert is an international alert for a wanted person and alerts police worldwide about internationally wanted fugitives. Yellow notice is a global police alert to help locate missing persons. It is published for victims of parental abductions, criminal abductions (kidnappings), or unexplained disappearances.
- *Combat crimes:* It provides expertise, investigative support, field operations, training, and networking to support a country's national efforts in combatting crimes in terrorism, cybercrime, and organized crime.
- *Investigative support:* It offers investigative support such as forensics, analysis, and assistance in locating fugitives around the world.
- *Policy development and guidance:* It keeps an eye on the future through research and development in

international crime and trends. It works on developing best practices, guidelines, and frameworks in areas such as cybersecurity, countering terrorism, combatting corruption, and protecting intellectual property rights.

Structure of INTERPOL

- *The General Assembly:* It is the supreme governing body at the INTERPOL which has members from each country. It gets together once a year and each member country has a single vote. It ensures INTERPOL's activities correspond to the needs of the member countries. Also, it elects the members of the Executive Committee.
- *Executive Committee:* It is a 13-member governing body which is responsible for supervising the execution of General Assembly's decisions. It administers the work of the General Secretariat and meets three times a year.
- *President:* He presides the meetings of General Assembly and Executive Committee. He is elected by the General Assembly for a period of four years.
- *The General Secretariat:* The General Secretariat is responsible for the coordination of the daily activities at INTERPOL. It is headed by the secretary-general. In each country, an INTERPOL National Central Bureau (NCB) provides the central point of contact for the General Secretariat and other NCBs. An NCB is run by national police officials and usually sits in the government ministry responsible for policing.

Strategic Framework 2022–25

The Strategic Framework 2022–25 is based on four strategic goals and 17 corresponding strategic objectives highlighting where INTERPOL intends to be in 2025. The member countries identified important strategic areas, possible risks, and lessons learned from the preceding strategic framework to come out with a more precise and inclusive framework. These are:

Strategic Goal 1: Trusted information for action

Strategic Goal 2: Enrich policing through partnerships

Strategic Goal 3: Advance and innovate policing

Strategic Goal 4: Enhance organizational performance and delivery

INTERNATIONAL UNION FOR CONSERVATION OF NATURE (IUCN)

IUCN is a membership union that brings together government, civil society organizations, NGOs, indigenous peoples' organizations, scientific and academic institutions, and business associations to create an international environmental network. It works towards sustainable development and conservation of nature and natural resources. It is a trusted policy and scientific advisor, and supports the implementation of the 2030 Agenda for Sustainable Development and the Sustainable Development Goals.

It was established as the International Union for the Protection of Nature (IUPN) in 1948 and was renamed as the International Union for the Conservation of Nature and Natural Resources (IUCN) in 1956. It was also known as the World Conservation Union from 1990 to 2008.

Objectives of IUCN

- *Conservation of biodiversity:* It plays an important role in conservation of biodiversity by promoting the protection and management of ecosystems, species, and habitats. It conducts research, provides guidance, and advocates for effective conservation policies and practices.

- *Sustainable utilization of natural resources:* It encourages the adoption of practices to ensure sustainable utilization of natural resources to reap the benefits derived from them.
- *Knowledge sharing and capacity building:* It acts as a facilitator for the exchange of knowledge and best practices among its members and the broader conservation community. It promotes capacity building, training programmes, and awareness-raising initiatives to enhance the understanding and implementation of conservation principles.
- *Policy and advocacy:* It plays a crucial role in influencing and shaping policies related to nature conservation and sustainable development. It provides expert advice, undertakes assessments, and advocates for sound environmental policies at national, regional, and international levels. Also, it ensures that policies are aligned with the UNSDGs for 2030.
- *Issue briefs and provide conservation tools:* IUCN's briefs are an accessible overview of the often complex issues related to nature conservation and sustainable development. The conservation tools are database, knowledge products, and important metrics that help organizations to design, monitor, and implement effective conservation.
- *Publications:* These are best practices, reports, analyses, standards, and periodicals that are prepared by IUCN's commissions.

Organizational Structure

IUCN has three components:

1. *Secretariat and Director-General:* The secretariat is led by the director-general and three deputy directors-general. The secretariat manages projects worldwide and coordinates support services to members and commissions. There are five centres working under the secretariat and these are focussed around environmental sustainability, economic feasibility and social equity, science and data, and international policy.
2. *Members:* It has over 1,400 member organizations which include states and government agencies at the national and subnational levels, NGOs large and small, indigenous peoples' organizations, scientific and academic institutions, and business associations. The state and government agency members make up approximately 14 per cent of IUCN's membership.
3. *Commissions:* These are broad and active networks of scientists and experts who provide IUCN and its members knowledge and policy advice to drive conservation and sustainable development. There are seven IUCN's commissions:

- Commission on Education and Communication
- Commission on Ecosystem Management
- Commission on Environmental, Economic and Social Policy
- Species Survival Commission
- World Commission on Environmental Law
- World Commission on Protected Areas
- Climate Crisis Commission

Red List of Threatened Species

It is a comprehensive inventory maintained by the International Union for Conservation of Nature (IUCN) for assessing the conservation status of various species of plants, animals, fungi, and other organisms worldwide. It helps in identifying species that require urgent conservation measures and attention. The IUCN Red List collects and analyses data from various sources, including scientific research, field surveys, and expert assessments, to provide accurate and up-to-date information about species' populations and trends. It is a critical indicator of the health of the world's biodiversity. It shows trends in overall extinction risk for species. Governments use the index to track their progress towards targets for reducing biodiversity loss. Species are classified into one of nine Red List categories: Extinct, Extinct in the Wild, Critically Endangered, Endangered, Vulnerable, Near Threatened, Least Concern, Data Deficient, and Not Evaluated. Vulnerable, Endangered, and Critically Endangered species are considered to be threatened with extinction. The IUCN Red List includes the IUCN Green Status of Species, which assesses the recovery of species' populations and measures their conservation success. There are eight Green Status Categories: Extinct in the Wild, Critically Depleted, Largely Depleted, Moderately Depleted, Slightly Depleted, Fully Recovered, Non-Depleted, and Indeterminate. A Green Status assessment looks at how conservation actions have affected the current Red List status.

Nature 2030 Programme

It was adopted at the IUCN World Conservation Congress in Marseille in 2021 and is an ambitious 10-year programme. This programme defines broad areas of work and sets aspirational targets as well as indicators to measure success for its five priority areas: people, land, water, ocean, and climate. It focusses to work on the priority areas through five pathways to transformative change: recognize, retain, restore, resource, and reconnect.

It will generate the science-based evidence and knowledge that decision-makers need, build trust and consensus among stakeholders, identify policy options and, critically, foster a culture of early and sustainable implementation. It is a global call to action to deliver clear and demonstrable contributions to the UNSDGs 2030.

FINANCIAL ACTION TASK FORCE (FATF)

FATF is the international global money laundering and terrorist financing watchdog. It establishes standards that act as the guidelines for the respective national authorities to frame their laws and regulations for illicit funds associated with drugs trafficking, arms trade, cyber fraud, and other serious crimes.

It was established in 1989 by the G7 countries to examine and develop measures to combat money laundering. Terror financing was added to FATF's mandate list in 2001.

Structure of FATF

- *FATF Plenary:* It is the highest decision-making and governing body of FATF that appoints FATF's president. It meets three times in a year and holds countries accountable if they do not comply with FATF's standards.
- *FATF Secretariat:* It is headed by FATF's executive secretary. The secretariat monitors money laundering, working

and funding of terrorist organizations, and developing best practices. It also assesses the action taken by the respective governments to implement the FATF standards effectively.

FATF's Recommendations and Mutual Evaluations

Recommendations are the framework of measures which countries should implement in order to combat money laundering, terrorist financing, and proliferation financing.

Mutual evaluations are peer reviews in which in-depth country reports and assessments are prepared to check the compliance of FATF's recommendations by the countries.

Methodology of FATF for Assessing Compliance of the Countries

It conducts mutual evaluations of its members' levels of implementation of the FATF recommendations on an ongoing basis. The assessment focusses on two areas:

1. *Effectiveness:* The countries need to demonstrate that it has an effective framework to protect its financial system from the illegal and illicit use of funds. The FATF's team evaluates countries on 11 key areas, or immediate outcomes, to determine the level of effectiveness of its efforts.
2. *Technical compliance:* The assessment ensures that countries meet all the technical requirements as per the FATF recommendations.

A mutual evaluation report is prepared. It provides an in-depth description and analysis of the country's financial system and also provides recommendations to the country to further strengthen its system.

FATF's Black and Grey Lists

The FATF identifies countries that have weak measures to combat money laundering and terrorist financing and these are issued three times a year. It issues two public documents or lists for the same.

1. *Black list:* The countries which are at high risk of money laundering and terror financing are included in this and they are designated as High-Risk Jurisdictions subject to a Call for Action. They are put under FATF's sanctions and are expected to apply countermeasures to protect the international financial system.
2. *Grey list:* The countries which are considered as the safe havens for supporting terror funding and money laundering are placed in this and they are designated as Jurisdictions under Increased Monitoring. The inclusion in the grey list serves as the warning to the countries that it may be put in the black list.

Quick Facts

Money laundering: It is the illegal process of hiding the origin of money in order to make it appear to have come from a legal source. Basically, the money is the outcome of illegal activities such as corruption, drug trafficking, and gambling.

Proliferation financing: It refers to the various financial activities conducted to develop, acquire, or transfer Weapons of Mass Destruction (WMD) and their delivery systems.

S.NO.	NAME OF THE AGENCY	HEADQUARTERS	ESTABLISHMENT	HEAD(S)
1	Asian Development Bank (ADB)	Mandaluyong, Philippines	19 December 1966	Current President: Masatsugu Asakawa
2	Asian Infrastructure Investment Bank (AIIB	Beijing, China	16 January 2016	President of AIIB: Jin Liqn
3	New Development Bank (NDB)	Shanghai, China		Current President: Dilma Vana Rousseff
4	Organization for Economic Co-operation and Development (OECD)	Paris, France		Current Secretary-General of OECD: Mathias Hubert Paul Cormann
5	North Atlantic Treaty Organization (NATO)	Brussels, Belgium		Current Secretary-General of NATO: Jens Stoltenberg Chair of NATO Military Committee: Robert Peter Bauer
6	Association of South East Asian Nations (ASEAN)	Jakarata, Indonesia	15 December 2008	Secretary-General: Kao Kim Hourn
7	Asia Pacific Economic Cooperation (APEC)	Singapore		Chairperson of APEC: Joe Biden, the president of the United States Executive Director: Rebecca Fatima Santa Maria
8	Bay of Bengal Initiative for Multi-Sectoral Technical and Economic Cooperation (BIMSTEC)	Secretariat: Dhaka, Bangladesh	6 June 1997	Current Secretary-General: Tenzin Lekphel
12	Brazil, Russia, India, China, and South Africa (BRICS)		2010	
13	G20 (Group of Twenty)		26 September 1999	Current Chairman: Narendra Modi, prime minister of India
14	Indian Ocean Rim Association (IORA)	Ebene, Mauritius	7 March 1997	
15	Shanghai Cooperation Organisation (SCO)	Beijing, China	15 June 2001	Secretary-General: Zhang Ming
16	South Asian Association for Regional Cooperation (SAARC)	Kathmandu, Nepal	8 December 1985	Secretary-General: Golam Sarwar
17	Nuclear Suppliers Group (NSG)		1974	Chair: Gustavo Ainchil (Argentina)
18	Organisation of Islamic Cooperation (OIC)	Jeddah, Saudi Arabia	25 September 1969	Secretary-General: Hissein Brahim Taha

S.NO.	NAME OF THE AGENCY	HEADQUARTERS	ESTABLISHMENT	HEAD(S)
19	World Economic Forum (WEF)	Cologny, Switzerland	24 January 1971	Founder: Klaus Schwab President: Borge Brende
20	Missile Technology Control Regime (MTCR)		1987	
21	International Criminal Police Organization (INTERPOL)	Lyon, France	7 September 1923	Secretary-General: Jurgen Stock
22	International Union for Conservation of Nature (IUCN)	Gland, Switzerland	5 October 1948	Director-General: Bruno Oberle President: Razan Al Mubarak
23	Financial Action Task Force (FATF)	Secretariat: Paris, France	1989	President: T. Raja Kumar

IMPORTANT INTERNATIONAL TREATIES AND AGREEMENTS

SENDAI FRAMEWORK FOR DISASTER RISK REDUCTION (2015–30)

- The Sendai framework on disaster reduction is an agreement that identifies four priority areas and seven global targets in order to prevent new and reduce existing disaster risks. These priority areas and global targets have been designed to prevent loss of lives, livelihoods, and health among the community. It covers technological hazards, in addition to natural hazards. Technological hazards include chemical/industrial hazards further to radiological, nuclear, biological, and others.
- The seven global targets and 38 global indicators will help to measure progress made by all countries on disaster risk reduction by the year 2030.
- Sendai Framework was a successor to Hyogo Framework for Action 2005–15: Building the resilience of nations and communities to disasters.
- The four areas are:
  1. Priority 1. Understanding disaster risk
  2. Priority 2. Strengthening disaster risk governance to manage disaster risk
  3. Priority 3. Investing in disaster risk reduction for resilience
  4. Priority 4. Enhancing disaster preparedness for effective response and to 'Build Back Better' in recovery, rehabilitation, and reconstruction
- Adopted at the Third UN World Conference on Disaster Risk Reduction in Sendai, Japan.
- Adopted on 18 March 2015.

ADDIS ABABA ACTION AGENDA ON FINANCING FOR DEVELOPMENT

- The Addis Ababa agenda is a global framework for financing sustainable development while aligning economic, social, and environmental priorities with the financing flows and policies.
- It was an outcome document of the Third International Conference on

Financing for Development held in Addis Ababa, Ethiopia.

- The document focusses on seven action areas, namely:
    1. Domestic public resources
    2. Domestic and international private business and finance
    3. International development cooperation
    4. International trade as an engine for development
    5. Debt and debt sustainability
    6. Addressing systemic issues
    7. Science, technology, innovation, and capacity building

PARIS AGREEMENT ON CLIMATE CHANGE OR PARIS ACCORD

- Paris Accord is a legally binding multilateral international treaty on climate change that was adopted by 196 parties at the UN Climate Change Conference (COP21) in Paris, France, on 12 December 2015.
- The agreement aims at substantial reduction of global greenhouse gas emissions in order to limit the increase in global temperature by 2°C above pre-industrial levels and pursue efforts to limit the temperature increase to 1.5°C above pre-industrial levels.
- As a part of this agreement, countries will be financed to mitigate climate change, provide technological support, and enhance their abilities to adapt to the impact of change in climate.
- The countries have to submit their Nationally Determined Contribution or NDC every five years. They need to communicate the actions taken by them to reduce their greenhouse gas emissions in order to fulfil the objectives of Paris Accord.
- The first global stocktake assessed the progress on Paris Agreement goals in 2023.
- Effective from: 4 November 2016.

RAMSAR CONVENTION ON WETLANDS

- The Ramsar Convention on Wetlands is an intergovernmental treaty that lays down the framework for national action on conservation and use of wetlands and their resources with international cooperation.
- The three pillars of Ramsar Convention are:
    1. Working towards the wise use of all the wetlands
    2. Designating suitable wetlands for the list of Wetlands International Importance and ensuring their effective management
    3. Cooperating internationally on transboundary wetlands, shared wetland systems, and shared species
- There are six international organization partners (IOPs) that work closely with Ramsar Convention. These are BirdLife International, International Union for Conservation of Nature (IUCN), International Water Management Institute (IWMI), Wetlands International, WWF International, and Wildfowl & Wetlands Trust (WWT).
- The Conference of the Contracting Parties (COP) is the policymaking organ that meets every three years to review the work done and provide recommendations for future.
- Signed on: 2 February 1971.
- Effective from: 21 December 1975.
- In India, the convention entered into force in India on 1 February 1982.

KYOTO PROTOCOL

- The Kyoto Protocol is an international treaty and the first operational measure under the United Nations Framework Convention on Climate Change (UNFCCC), which is an environmental treaty to limit and combat dangerous human interference with the climate system.
- As a part of Kyoto Protocol, industrialized countries and economies agree to limit and reduce their Green House Gases (GHG) emissions in accordance with their individually decided targets.
- A strict monitoring, review, and verification system, as well as a compliance system to ensure transparency has been established under this protocol.
- The first phase of Kyoto Protocol covered six categories of greenhouse gas (GHG) emissions: carbon dioxide (CO_2), methane (CH_4), nitrous oxide (N_2O), hydrofluorocarbons (HFCs), perfluorocarbons (PFCs), and sulphur hexafluoride (SF6). The 'Doha Amendment' established a second commitment period (2013–20) and nitrogen trifluoride (NF3) was added in the same.
- Signed on: 11 December 1997.
- Effective from: 16 February 2005.

MONTREAL PROTOCOL ON SUBSTANCES THAT DEPLETE THE OZONE LAYER

- Montreal Protocol is a multilateral environmental agreement that aims to protect the ozone layer by regulating the production and consumption of ozone-depleting substances (ODS).
- The ozone layer is present in Earth's stratosphere and is the protective shield that protects humans and the environment from harmful levels of ultraviolet radiation from the sun.
- It phases down the consumption and production of the different ODS in a step-wise manner, with different timetables for developed and developing countries.
- OzonAction is the implementing agency of Montreal Protocol. Most of the ODS mentioned in the protocol have either chlorine or bromine.
- Signed on: 16 September 1987.
- Effective from: 1 January 1989.

MINAMATA CONVENTION ON MERCURY

- Minamata Convention is an international multilateral environmental agreement that addresses the need of controlling anthropogenic release of mercury and its compound in the environment due to specific human activities.
- The convention is named after the city Minamata in Japan. There was a decade-long incidence of mercury poisoning after industrial wastewater containing methyl mercury was discharged into Minamata Bay. This water bioaccumulated in fish and shellfish in the bay and the local people who consumed seafood from Minamata Bay became very sick, and many died or were left severely disabled.
- Signed on: 10 October 2013.
- Effective from: 16 August 2017.

CONVENTION ON THE CONSERVATION OF MIGRATORY SPECIES OF WILD ANIMALS OR BONN CONVENTION

- Bonn Convention is an international agreement that aims to conserve and make sustainable use of migratory species and their habitats.

- It is the only global convention dealing with the conservation of migratory species and lays the legal foundation for internationally coordinated conservation measures throughout a migratory range.
- Signed on: 6 November 1979.
- Effective from: 1 November 1983.

UNITED NATIONS CONVENTION ON THE LAW OF THE SEA (UNCLOS) OR LAW OF THE SEA TREATY

- UNCLOS lays down a comprehensive regime for establishing the rules governing the sustainable use of the oceans and their resources. It also provides the framework for further development of specific areas of the law of the sea.
- Signed on: 10 December 1982.
- Effective from: 16 November 1994.

STOCKHOLM CONVENTION ON PERSISTENT ORGANIC POLLUTANTS

- It is an international treaty that aims to eliminate or restrict the production and use of persistent organic pollutants (POPs) to protect human health and the environment.
- POPs are toxic chemical substances that have the potential to accumulate in unhealthy quantities in humans and animals, persist in environment for long time, and are stable to natural breakdown.
- Signed on: 22 May 2001.
- Effective from: 17 May 2004.

GENEVA CONVENTIONS

- The Geneva conventions have four international treaties and three additional protocols that have rules limiting the barbarity of war. It is the foundation of modern international humanitarian law.

1. The First Geneva Convention protects wounded and sick soldiers on land during war.
2. The Second Geneva Convention protects wounded, sick, and shipwrecked military personnel at sea during war.
3. The Third Geneva Convention applies to prisoners of war.
4. The Fourth Geneva Convention protects civilians, including those in occupied territory.

- Effective from: 21 October 1950.
- The three additional protocols of Geneva conventions are:

1. Additional Protocol I: international conflicts
2. Additional Protocol II: non-international conflicts
3. Additional Protocol III: additional distinctive emblem

OPEN SKIES TREATY

- The Open Skies Treaty allows one country to conduct an unarmed aerial surveillance flight to collect data on military forces and activities over the other. It is possible only among the signatories of the treaty.
- The observing country needs to provide at least a 72 hours advance notice before conducting the surveillance. The host countries have 24 hours to acknowledge

the request and inform if the observing party may use its plane or the host will provide the plane. The host will have four hours to review the observing party's flight plan. There are specific points of entry, exit, and refuelling airfields. The complete process needs to be completed within 96 hours of the observing party's arrival unless otherwise agreed.

- The Open Skies Consultative Commission is the implementing body for the Treaty on Open Skies.
- Signed on: 24 March 1992.
- Effective from: 1 January 2002.

REGIONAL COMPREHENSIVE ECONOMIC PARTNERSHIP (RCEP)

- RCEP is a comprehensive free trade agreement between ASEAN members states and ASEAN's Free Trade Agreement (FTA) partners.
- ASEAN member states: Brunei Darussalam, Cambodia, Indonesia, Laos, Malaysia, Myanmar, Philippines, Singapore, Thailand, and Vietnam.
- ASEA's FTA partners: Australia, China, Japan, Korea, and New Zealand.
- Initially, India was a part of the RCEP. However, it later opted out on 4 November 2019.
- Signed on: 15 November 2020.
- Effective from: 1 January 2022.

COMPREHENSIVE AND PROGRESSIVE AGREEMENT FOR TRANS-PACIFIC PARTNERSHIP (CPTPP)

- CPTPP is a free trade agreement between Canada and 10 other countries in the Asia-Pacific. It covers virtually all sectors and aspects of trade between Canada and member countries to reduce trade barriers and facilitate trade.
- Ten countries are Australia, Brunei, Chile, Japan, Malaysia, Mexico, New Zealand, Peru, Singapore, and Vietnam.
- Signed on: 8 March 2018.
- Effective from: 30 December 2018.

CONVENTION ON THE PROHIBITION OF THE DEVELOPMENT, PRODUCTION, AND STOCKPILING OF BACTERIOLOGICAL (BIOLOGICAL) AND TOXIN WEAPONS (BTWC)

- BTWC is a disarmament treaty that mandates the elimination of existing biological weapons and prohibits developing, stockpiling, or using biological and toxin weapons.
- It was the first multilateral treaty categorically banning a class of weapon. There is no implementation body of BWC. However, a review meeting is held every five years to review its implementation, and establish confidence-building measures.
- Signed on: 10 April 1972.
- Effective from: 26 March 1975.

IMPORTANT INTERNATIONAL RANKING AND INDICES

CORRUPTION PERCEPTION INDEX (CPI)

- CPI ranks 180 countries around the world on their perceived level of public sector corruption with zero being highly corrupt and 100 being very clean.

- The CPI is based on data collected from 13 different surveys and assessments from 12 different institutions.
- It is released annually by Transparency International since 1995.
- Corruption Rank of India averaged 76.86 from 1995 until 2022. It was at an all-time high of 95.00 in 2011 and a record low of 35.00 in 1995.

EASE OF DOING BUSINESS (EoDB) INDEX

- The EoDB index is a ranking in which countries across the world are ranked on a scale from 0 to 100 by calculating an aggregate scores on the following 10 areas of business regulations: starting a business, dealing with construction permits, getting electricity, registering property, getting credit, protecting minority investors, paying taxes, trading across borders, enforcing contracts, and resolving insolvency.
- A lower numerical value is indicative of a high EoDB, and a high EoDB ranking means the regulatory environment is more conducive for starting and operating businesses.
- The index was created by Simeon Djankov, Michael Klein, and Caralee McLiesh.
- It is being released by the World Bank and the economies since 2003.
- India's rank in 2014 was 142 and it has shown a considerable improvement with a 63rd position in 2022.

GLOBAL ENERGY TRANSITION INDEX (ETI)

- ETI is released annually by the World Economic Forum. It benchmarks 115 countries on the performance of their current energy system and preparedness for the ongoing transition.
- The energy system is measured across economic development and growth, energy access and security, and environmental sustainability.
- It is quantified by 39 indicators used to rank countries on a scale of 0 to 100.
- In 2018, India was ranked at 78th position and it was ranked at 87th position in the ETI 2021.

GLOBAL GENDER GAP INDEX (GGI)

- The Gender Gap Index (GGI) measures gender equality based on the relative gaps between women and men across four key areas of health, education, economy, and politics.
- The sub metrics for the measurement of GGI are economic participation and opportunity, educational attainment, health and survival, and political empowerment for men and women.
- A score of zero (0) indicates complete inequality and a score of one (1) indicates complete equality.
- It is an annual index released by World Economic Forum (WEF) since 2006.
- India's global gender gap score has oscillated between 0.593 and 0.683 since the index was first compiled in 2006 to 2022.

GLOBAL PEACE INDEX (GPI)

- The Global Peace Index (GPI) is a composite index that measures the peacefulness of countries. It is made up of 23 qualitative and quantitative indicators, each of which is weighted on a scale of 1–5. The lower the score the more peaceful the country.
- It is an annual index released by the Institute for Economics and Peace (IEP) since 2007.
- India was at rank 123 in the year 2008

and has been ranked 135 in the year 2022.

GLOBAL INNOVATION INDEX (GII)

- The GII is an annual index that ranks countries on their capacity and innovation. It is developed jointly by Cornell University, INSEAD, and World Intellectual Property Organization (WIPO), and it is released by WIPO.
- It reveals the most innovative economies in the world, ranking the innovation performance of around 132 economies while highlighting innovation strengths and weaknesses. It is based on 80 indicators, compiled under 7 pillars.
- India climbed from the 81st spot in 2015 to the 40th spot in 2022 GII. India has shown remarkable improvement in this index.

GLOBAL LIVEABILITY INDEX

- The Global Liveability Index reviews and quantifies stability, healthcare, culture and environment, education, and infrastructure factors to determine liveability rankings for cities worldwide.
- It is an annual index released by the Economist Intelligence Unit (EIU).

GLOBAL TERRORISM INDEX (GTI)

- GTI is a comprehensive study that analyses the impact of terrorism on different countries of the world and ranks the countries on a scale from 0 to 10, where 0 represents no impact from terrorism and 10 represents the highest measurable impact of terrorism.
- It is released by the Institute for Economics & Peace (IEP) using data from Terrorism Tracker and other sources.
- Terrorism Index of India averaged 7.65 points from 2002 until 2021, reaching an all time high of 8.12 points in 2011 and a record low of 7.22 points in 2004.

GLOBAL HUNGER INDEX (GHI)

- GHI is a monitoring tool designed to comprehensively measure and track hunger at global, regional, and national levels.
- GHI is calculated on a formula that combines four indicators: undernourishment, child stunting, child wasting, and child mortality in order to capture the multidimensional aspect of hunger.
- It is a peer-reviewed annual report, jointly published by Concern Worldwide and Welthungerhilfe.
- GHI score for India has shown a slight worsening, with its GHI score increasing from 28.2 according to its 2014 GHI score to 29.1 according to its 2022 GHI score.

HENLEY'S PASSPORT INDEX

- The Henley Passport Index ranks the world's passports according to the number of destinations their holders can access without a prior visa. It is based on exclusive data from the International Air Transport Association (IATA).
- It compares the visa-free access of 199 different passports to 227 travel destinations.
- India's passport was ranked at 76th position in 2014 with a score of 52 and in 2023 it is at 85th position with a score of 59.

HUMAN DEVELOPMENT INDEX (HDI)

- The Human Development Index (HDI) is a summary measure of average achievement in key dimensions of human development: a long and healthy life, being knowledgeable and having a decent standard of living.
- The HDI is calculated as the geometric mean of normalized indices for each of the three dimensions.
- The health dimension is assessed by life expectancy at birth. The education dimension is measured by mean of years of schooling for adults aged 25 years and more and expected years of schooling for children of school entering age. The standard of living dimension is measured by gross national income per capita.
- It is released by the United Nations Development Programme (UNDP).
- In 2014 India's HDI value was 0.609 and in 2021 it was 0.633.

WORLD HAPPINESS REPORT

- The World Happiness Report ranks countries based on how happy their citizens perceive themselves to be. It is done by analysis of six variables: GDP per capita, social support, healthy life expectancy, freedom, generosity, and corruption.
- The evaluation is done on the basis of data collected from the Gallup World Poll.
- It is an annual report published by the United Nations Sustainable Development Solutions Network since 2012.
- India scored 4.77 in the year 2013 and it was at 4.04 in 2022. The average value for India from 2013 to 2022 was 4.21 points with a minimum of 3.78 points in 2021 and a maximum of 4.77 points in 2013.

WORLD ENERGY TRILEMMA INDEX

- It is the measurement of national energy system performances across each of the three trilemma dimensions: energy security, energy equity, and environmental sustainability based on national and international data.
- It is an annual index published by the World Energy Council in partnership with global consultancy Oliver Wyman, along with Marsh & McLennan Advantage of its parent Marsh & McLennan Companies.
- It includes recommended areas for improvements on policy coherence and integrated policy innovation, helping to develop well-calibrated energy system.
- In 2015, India was ranked at 107th position with a score of 2.99. India has been ranked 75th in the 2021 Index.

WORLD PRESS FREEDOM (WPF) INDEX

- WPF Index measures the degree of freedom available to journalists in 180 countries by pooling the responses of experts to a questionnaire on pluralism, media independence, media environment and self-censorship, legislative framework, transparency, and the quality of the infrastructure that supports the production of news and information. It is clubbed with quantitative data on abuses and acts of violence against journalists during the period of evaluation.
- This questionnaire is devised by Reporters without Borders or Reporters Sans Frontieres (RSF) and targeted media professionals, lawyers, and sociologists.

- It is an annual index that is being published every year since 2002 by RSF.
- In 2023, India was ranked at 161 position with a score of 36.62 and in 2014 India's was at 140 with a global score of 59.66.

GLOBAL MINORITY INDEX

- It is a comprehensive report of data compiled from 110 countries assessing how each country treated minority religions and the level of inclusivity it practised.
- It has been developed by Centre for Policy Analysis (CPA), Patna.
- It is the first international study to assign a grade to countries based on their treatment of respective religious minorities and is also the first study conducted by non-Western and Afro-Asian countries to index nations based on specific criteria.
- India has topped the Index followed by South Korea, Japan, Panama, and the United States.

11 Environment and Wildlife

INTRODUCTION TO THE ENVIRONMENT

The environment encompasses everything around us, including all living and non-living things. It includes natural elements such as air, water, and soil, as well as human-made structures and objects. The environment is essential for the survival and well-being of all living organisms, including humans.

COMPONENTS OF THE ENVIRONMENT

The environment is composed of biotic and abiotic components that interact and depend on each other.

BIOTIC COMPONENTS

- *Plants:* Provide oxygen, food, and habitats for various organisms.
- *Animals:* Play different roles in ecosystems, such as pollinators, predators, and prey.
- *Microorganisms:* Decompose organic matter and recycle nutrients in ecosystems.

ABIOTIC COMPONENTS

- *Air:* Contains gases essential for life, such as oxygen and carbon dioxide (CO_2).
- *Water:* Essential for all living organisms; found in rivers, lakes, oceans, and underground.
- *Soil:* Supports plant growth and is home to many organisms.
- *Sunlight:* Provides energy for photosynthesis and influences climate and weather patterns.

ECOSYSTEMS AND BIODIVERSITY

An ecosystem is a community of living organisms interacting with their physical environment. Ecosystems can be as large as a forest or as small as a pond. Biodiversity refers to the variety of life in a particular ecosystem or on Earth as a whole. High biodiversity is crucial for ecosystem stability and resilience.

IMPORTANCE OF BIODIVERSITY

Biodiversity is essential for the health and sustainability of ecosystems. It provides numerous benefits, including:

- *Ecosystem services:* Such as pollination, nutrient cycling, and water purification.
- *Resilience:* Diverse ecosystems are more resilient to environmental changes and disturbances.
- *Resources:* Biodiversity provides food, medicine, and raw materials for human use.

HUMAN IMPACT ON THE ENVIRONMENT

Human activities have a significant impact on the environment. These activities can lead to both positive and negative consequences.

POSITIVE IMPACTS

- *Conservation efforts:* Protecting endangered species and restoring habitats.
- *Sustainable practices:* Using resources in a way that meets present needs without compromising future generations.

NEGATIVE IMPACTS

- *Pollution:* Contamination of air, water, and soil by harmful substances.
- *Deforestation:* The removal of large areas of forests, leading to loss of biodiversity and disruption of ecosystems.
- *Climate change:* Global warming caused by the increase in greenhouse gases from activities like burning fossil fuels.
- *Overexploitation:* Unsustainable use of resources, such as overfishing and mining.

POLLUTION

Pollution is one of the most significant negative impacts of human activities. It affects the air we breathe, the water we drink, and the soil in which we grow our food. There are different types of pollution, including air pollution, water pollution, and soil pollution, each with its specific sources and harmful effects.

AIR POLLUTION

- *Sources:* Emissions from vehicles, industries, and the burning of fossil fuels.
- *Effects:* Respiratory problems, cardiovascular diseases, and climate change.
- *Solutions:* Using cleaner energy sources, promoting public transport, and implementing stricter emission regulations.

WATER POLLUTION

- *Sources:* Discharge of industrial waste, agricultural runoff, and plastic waste.
- *Effects:* Harm to aquatic life, contamination of drinking water, and disruption of ecosystems.
- *Solutions:* Treating industrial waste, reducing plastic use, and promoting sustainable farming practices.

SOIL POLLUTION

- *Sources:* Pesticides, industrial waste, and illegal dumping of hazardous materials.
- *Effects:* Loss of soil fertility, contamination of food crops, and harm to soil organisms.
- *Solutions:* Using organic farming methods, proper waste disposal, and soil remediation techniques.

DEFORESTATION

Deforestation is the large-scale removal of forests, which can lead to a variety of environmental problems. Forests play a crucial role in maintaining the ecological balance, supporting biodiversity, and regulating the climate.

- *Causes:* Logging, agricultural expansion, and urbanization.
- *Effects:* Loss of biodiversity, disruption of water cycles, and contribution to climate change.
- *Solutions:* Reforestation, promoting sustainable land use, and enforcing laws against illegal logging.

CLIMATE CHANGE

Climate change is a long-term alteration in the average weather patterns. It is primarily caused by the increase in greenhouse gases in the atmosphere due to human activities such as burning fossil fuels and deforestation.

- *Causes:* Emission of greenhouse gases from burning fossil fuels, deforestation, and industrial processes.
- *Effects:* Rising global temperatures, melting ice caps, sea-level rise, and extreme weather events.
- *Solutions:* Reducing greenhouse gas emissions, transitioning to renewable energy sources, and protecting forests.

INTERNATIONAL ENVIRONMENTAL AGREEMENTS

International agreements play a crucial role in addressing global environmental issues. Three important agreements are the Kyoto Protocol, the Vienna Convention, and the Paris Accord.

KYOTO PROTOCOL

The Kyoto Protocol is an international treaty aimed at reducing greenhouse gas emissions to combat climate change. It was adopted in Kyoto, Japan, in 1997 and came into force in 2005. The treaty set binding emission reduction targets for developed countries, recognizing their responsibility for the majority of historical emissions.

KEY FEATURES OF THE KYOTO PROTOCOL

Binding Emission Reduction Targets

- Developed countries, also known as Annex I countries, committed to reducing their greenhouse gas emissions by an average of 5.2 per cent below 1990 levels during the first commitment period (2008–12).

Flexible Mechanisms

- The Kyoto Protocol introduced three market-based mechanisms to help countries meet their emission targets:
- *Emissions trading:* Allows countries to buy and sell emission allowances.
- *Clean development mechanism (CDM):* Enables developed countries to invest in emission reduction projects in developing countries and earn carbon credits.
- *Joint implementation (JI):* Allows developed countries to earn emission reduction units by investing in projects in other developed countries.

Reporting and Verification

- Countries are required to monitor and report their greenhouse gas emissions and implement policies to achieve their targets. The protocol established a rigorous system for tracking and verifying emissions.

IMPACT OF THE KYOTO PROTOCOL

The Kyoto Protocol was a significant step in international climate policy. It encouraged countries to develop and implement policies for reducing greenhouse gas emissions and established the groundwork for future international climate agreements. However, the protocol faced several challenges:

- *Limited participation:* Some major emitters, such as the United States, did not ratify the protocol, reducing its overall effectiveness.
- *Emission reductions:* While some countries met their targets, global greenhouse gas emissions continued to rise, highlighting the need for more comprehensive and ambitious efforts.

VIENNA CONVENTION

The Vienna Convention for the Protection of the Ozone Layer is an international treaty aimed at protecting the ozone layer, which shields the Earth from harmful ultraviolet (UV) radiation. It was adopted in Vienna, Austria, in 1985 and entered into force in 1988.

KEY FEATURES OF THE VIENNA CONVENTION

Framework for International Cooperation

- The Vienna Convention provides a framework for countries to cooperate in research, monitoring, and information exchange on the ozone layer. It does not set binding targets but encourages collaborative efforts to protect the ozone layer.

Monitoring and Research

- Countries are encouraged to monitor the ozone layer and conduct research on substances that deplete it. The convention promotes the sharing of scientific data and research findings.

Public Awareness and Education

- The convention emphasizes the importance of raising public awareness about the importance of the ozone layer and the need to protect it.

IMPACT OF THE VIENNA CONVENTION

The Vienna Convention laid the foundation for the adoption of the Montreal Protocol, a more specific agreement targeting substances that deplete the ozone layer. The combined efforts of the Vienna Convention and the Montreal Protocol have been highly successful:

- *Reduction in ozone-depleting substances:* The production and use of ozone-depleting substances have been significantly reduced, leading to a gradual recovery of the ozone layer.
- *Global cooperation:* The convention fostered international cooperation and set a precedent for addressing other global environmental issues through collaborative efforts.

PARIS ACCORD

The Paris Accord, also known as the Paris Agreement, is an international treaty on climate change adopted in Paris, France, in 2015. It aims to limit global warming to well below 2°C above pre-industrial levels and pursue efforts to limit the temperature increase to 1.5°C.

KEY FEATURES OF THE PARIS ACCORD

Nationally Determined Contributions

- Under the Paris Accord, countries set their own emission reduction targets, known as Nationally Determined Contributions (NDCs). These targets are not legally binding but are subject to regular review and updating to enhance ambition over time.

Global Stocktake

- Every five years, countries gather to assess collective progress towards achieving the goals of the Paris Accord. This process, known as the global stocktake, aims to enhance transparency and accountability.

Support for Developing Countries

- The Paris Accord recognizes the need for financial, technological, and capacity-building support for developing countries to help them achieve their climate goals. Developed countries are encouraged to provide assistance through climate finance mechanisms.

Transparency and Accountability

- The accord establishes a robust transparency framework, requiring countries to report on their emissions and progress towards their NDCs. Independent experts review these reports to ensure accuracy and reliability.

IMPACT OF THE PARIS ACCORD

The Paris Accord is a landmark agreement that has garnered widespread support and commitment from countries around the world. It has several key impacts:

- *Global commitment:* The accord has encouraged countries to take ambitious climate action and set more stringent emission reduction targets.
- *Climate finance:* Developed countries have pledged financial support to help developing countries transition to low-carbon economies and adapt to the impacts of climate change.
- *Raising ambition:* The regular review process encourages countries to enhance their climate commitments and take stronger action to combat climate change.

ADDRESSING ENVIRONMENTAL ISSUES

To protect and preserve the environment, it is essential to address various environmental issues and implement effective solutions. Some of the major environmental issues include air pollution, water pollution, deforestation, and climate change.

AIR POLLUTION

Causes of Air Pollution

- *Vehicle emissions:* Exhaust from cars, trucks, and other vehicles release pollutants such as carbon monoxide, nitrogen oxides, and particulate matter into the air.
- *Industrial emissions:* Factories and power plants emit pollutants like sulphur dioxide, nitrogen oxides, and volatile organic compounds.
- *Burning fossil fuels:* The combustion of coal, oil, and natural gas for energy produces greenhouse gases and other pollutants.

EFFECTS OF AIR POLLUTION

- *Health problems:* Air pollution can cause respiratory diseases, cardiovascular problems, and other health issues.
- *Climate change:* Pollutants like (CO_2) and methane contribute to global warming and climate change.
- *Environmental damage:* Air pollution can harm ecosystems, damage crops, and degrade natural habitats.

SOLUTIONS TO AIR POLLUTION

- *Cleaner energy sources:* Transitioning to renewable energy sources like solar, wind, and hydroelectric power can reduce air pollution.

- *Public transport:* Promoting public transportation, carpooling, and electric vehicles can help reduce vehicle emissions.
- *Stricter regulations:* Implementing and enforcing regulations on industrial emissions and vehicle standards can help reduce pollution levels.

WATER POLLUTION

Causes of Water Pollution

- *Industrial waste:* Factories and industrial facilities discharge pollutants such as heavy metals, chemicals, and toxins into water bodies.
- *Agricultural runoff:* Pesticides, fertilizers, and animal waste from farms can contaminate rivers, lakes, and groundwater.
- *Plastic waste:* Improper disposal of plastic products leads to pollution of oceans, rivers, and other water bodies.

EFFECTS OF WATER POLLUTION

- *Harm to aquatic life:* Polluted water can harm fish, birds, and other aquatic organisms, disrupting ecosystems.
- *Human health risks:* Contaminated water can cause diseases and health problems to people who consume it.
- *Environmental degradation:* Water pollution can lead to the destruction of natural habitats and loss of biodiversity.

SOLUTIONS TO WATER POLLUTION

- *Treating industrial waste:* Proper treatment and disposal of industrial waste can prevent pollutants from entering water bodies.
- *Sustainable farming practices:* Reducing the use of pesticides and fertilizers, and implementing soil conservation techniques can minimize agricultural runoff.
- *Reducing plastic use:* Promoting the use of reusable products and recycling can help reduce plastic pollution.

DEFORESTATION

CAUSES OF DEFORESTATION

- *Logging:* The demand for timber and wood products leads to large-scale logging activities.
- *Agricultural expansion:* Clearing forests for agriculture, including livestock farming and plantation crops like palm oil and soybeans.
- *Urbanization:* Expanding cities and infrastructure projects often results in the clearing of forested areas.

EFFECTS OF DEFORESTATION

- *Loss of biodiversity:* Deforestation leads to the extinction of species and loss of habitats.
- *Climate change:* Forests act as carbon sinks, and their destruction releases stored (CO_2), contributing to global warming.
- *Disruption of water cycles:* Forests play a crucial role in maintaining the water cycle, and their removal can lead to changes in rainfall patterns and water availability.

SOLUTIONS TO DEFORESTATION

- *Reforestation:* Planting trees and restoring deforested areas can help recover lost forests and their benefits.
- *Sustainable land use:* Promoting sustainable agricultural practices and responsible land management can reduce the need for deforestation.

- *Enforcing laws:* Implementing and enforcing laws against illegal logging and deforestation can protect forested areas.

CLIMATE CHANGE

CAUSES OF CLIMATE CHANGE

- *Greenhouse gas emissions:* The burning of fossil fuels for energy and transportation releases greenhouse gases like (CO_2) and methane into the atmosphere.
- *Deforestation:* The removal of forests reduces the Earth's capacity to absorb (CO_2), exacerbating global warming.
- *Industrial processes:* Manufacturing and industrial activities release greenhouse gases and pollutants.

EFFECTS OF CLIMATE CHANGE

- *Rising temperatures:* Global temperatures are increasing, leading to heatwaves, melting ice caps, and rising sea levels.
- *Extreme weather events:* Climate change causes more frequent and severe weather events, such as hurricanes, droughts, and floods.
- *Impact on ecosystems:* Changing climate conditions affect ecosystems, leading to shifts in species distribution and biodiversity loss.

SOLUTIONS TO CLIMATE CHANGE

- *Reducing emissions:* Transitioning to renewable energy sources, improving energy efficiency, and reducing fossil fuel consumption can lower greenhouse gas emissions.
- *Protecting forests:* Conserving and restoring forests can enhance their role as carbon sinks and mitigate climate change.
- *Adapting to changes:* Implementing measures to adapt to the impacts of climate change, such as building resilient infrastructure and developing climate-smart agriculture.

THE ROLE OF INDIVIDUALS IN PROTECTING THE ENVIRONMENT

Everyone can contribute to environmental protection by adopting sustainable practices in their daily lives. Some simple actions include:

- *Reducing waste:* Recycling and composting, using reusable products, and minimizing single-use plastics.
- *Conserving energy:* Turning off lights and appliances when not in use, using energy-efficient devices, and supporting renewable energy.
- *Saving water:* Fixing leaks, taking shorter showers, and using water-saving appliances.
- *Supporting conservation efforts:* Participating in local environmental initiatives, supporting conservation organizations, and spreading awareness about environmental issues.

PRACTICAL STEPS FOR INDIVIDUALS

Reduce, Reuse, Recycle

Reducing waste is crucial for minimizing environmental impact. Individuals can start by reducing the amount of waste they produce. This includes avoiding single-use plastics, buying products with less packaging, and choosing reusable items.

Reusing items whenever possible, such as shopping bags and water bottles, also helps reduce waste. Recycling materials like paper, glass, and metal ensures they are processed and used again rather than ending up in landfills.

Energy Conservation

Energy conservation helps reduce greenhouse gas emissions and saves money. Simple actions like turning off lights and appliances when not in use, using energy-efficient light bulbs and appliances, and insulating homes can significantly reduce energy consumption. Supporting renewable energy sources such as solar and wind power also contributes to a cleaner environment.

Water Conservation

Water is a precious resource, and conserving it is essential. Fixing leaks, taking shorter showers, and using water-efficient fixtures can help reduce water waste. Additionally, using drought-resistant plants in gardens and landscaping can minimize the need for excessive watering.

Transportation Choices

Transportation is a significant source of greenhouse gas emissions. Opting for public transportation, carpooling, biking, or walking instead of driving alone can reduce emissions. For those who drive, maintaining vehicles for better fuel efficiency and considering electric or hybrid cars can make a difference.

Sustainable Consumption

Being mindful of consumption habits can positively impact the environment. Choosing products that are sustainably sourced, such as those with eco-friendly certifications, and supporting local and organic food producers can reduce environmental footprints. Reducing meat consumption and choosing plant-based diets can also lower greenhouse gas emissions associated with livestock production.

Advocacy and Education

Raising awareness about environmental issues and advocating for policies that protect the environment are crucial. Individuals can join or support environmental organizations, participate in community clean-up events, and engage in conversations about sustainability. Educating others about the importance of environmental protection and the steps they can take is vital for creating a collective impact.

THE 5Rs: EXPANDING ON WASTE MANAGEMENT

Traditionally, waste management has been guided by the 3Rs: reduce, reuse, recycle. However, recognizing the evolving needs of sustainable practices, the concept has expanded to include two additional principles: refuse and repurpose.

- *Refuse:* The first step is to refuse items that are not necessary or are environmentally harmful. By consciously avoiding products with excessive packaging or single-use items, we can significantly reduce waste.
- *Reduce:* The next principle is to minimize the amount of waste we generate. This involves choosing products with less packaging, using resources more efficiently, and cutting down on consumption.
- *Reuse:* Before disposing of items, consider if they can be used again. Reusing items or finding new purposes for them extends their lifecycle and reduces the demand for new products.

- *Repurpose:* Transforming an item from its original use to a new, valuable purpose is the essence of repurposing. This creative approach not only reduces waste but can also lead to innovative solutions and sustainable practices.
- *Recycle:* Finally, recycling involves processing used materials into new products to prevent waste. This step should be considered once the other Rs have been applied to minimize the need for virgin resources.

The inclusion of refuse and repurpose in the 5Rs reflects a more comprehensive approach to waste management, aiming to tackle waste more proactively and creatively.

GREEN ENERGY

Green energy refers to energy produced from renewable, sustainable sources that have minimal impact on the environment. These sources include:

- *Solar power:* Harnessing energy from the sun using photovoltaic cells or solar thermal systems.
- *Wind power:* Utilizing wind turbines to convert wind energy into electricity.
- *Hydroelectric power:* Generating electricity from the flow of water in rivers and dams.
- *Geothermal energy:* Exploiting the heat from the Earth's core to produce energy.
- *Biomass:* Using organic materials, such as plant and animal waste, to generate energy.

Green energy is pivotal in reducing greenhouse gas emissions, decreasing reliance on fossil fuels, and mitigating climate change. It promotes a cleaner, healthier environment and sustainable energy future.

GREEN ECONOMY

Green economy is an economic framework that seeks to improve human well-being and social equity while significantly reducing environmental risks and ecological scarcities. It encompasses several principles and goals:

- *Sustainability:* Ensuring that economic activities do not deplete natural resources or cause ecological harm.
- *Inclusivity:* Promoting social equity and reducing disparities by creating green jobs and ensuring fair distribution of economic benefits.
- *Efficiency:* Utilizing resources more efficiently and adopting technologies and practices that minimize waste and pollution.
- *Innovation:* Encouraging the development and adoption of green technologies and sustainable practices.

A green economy aims to balance economic growth with environmental sustainability, fostering an economy that is both prosperous and environmentally responsible. Key sectors include renewable energy, sustainable agriculture, green building, and waste management. This approach helps in achieving long-term ecological health and economic stability.

CARBON FOOTPRINT

Carbon footprint refers to the total amount of greenhouse gases, primarily CO_2, that are emitted directly or indirectly by human activities. These emissions are usually measured in equivalent tons of CO_2 over a specific period, often annually. The carbon footprint encompasses various sources of emissions, including:

- *Transportation:* Emissions from vehicles, aeroplanes, ships, and trains.

- *Energy use:* Emissions from electricity and heating, particularly from fossil fuel sources.
- *Industrial processes:* Emissions from manufacturing and industrial activities.
- *Agriculture:* Emissions from farming practices, livestock, and deforestation.
- *Waste:* Emissions from waste disposal and treatment, including methane emissions from landfills.

Reducing one's carbon footprint involves adopting practices that lower greenhouse gas emissions, such as using energy-efficient appliances, reducing car travel, consuming less meat, recycling, and supporting renewable energy sources. Understanding and minimizing carbon footprints are crucial for mitigating climate change and promoting sustainability.

BIOMIMICRY

Biomimicry is the practice of emulating nature's designs and processes to solve human problems and create sustainable innovations. By studying and mimicking the strategies found in nature, scientists, engineers, and designers develop technologies and systems that are more efficient, sustainable, and resilient.

EXAMPLES OF BIOMIMICRY

- *Velcro:* Inspired by the way burrs stick to animal fur, Swiss engineer George de Mestral invented Velcro in the 1940s.
- *Shinkansen bullet train:* The design of the train's nose was inspired by the kingfisher bird's beak, which allows it to dive into water with minimal splash, reducing noise and increasing efficiency.
- *Lotus effect:* The self-cleaning properties of the lotus leaf have inspired water-repellent and self-cleaning materials used in fabrics and paints.

BENEFITS OF BIOMIMICRY

- *Sustainability:* By leveraging nature's time-tested patterns and strategies, biomimicry promotes sustainable solutions that work in harmony with the environment.
- *Innovation:* Nature provides a rich source of inspiration for new technologies and products that can improve efficiency and performance.
- *Resilience:* Designs and systems inspired by nature tend to be more adaptable and resilient to changes, making them robust solutions in the face of environmental challenges.

FIELDS OF APPLICATION

- *Architecture:* Buildings designed to mimic natural ventilation and cooling processes, reducing energy consumption.
- *Medicine:* Developing medical adhesives inspired by the way mussels stick to rocks.
- *Agriculture:* Implementing farming practices that mimic natural ecosystems to improve soil health and crop resilience.

ETYMOLOGY AND COINAGE

- *Etymology:* The word 'biomimicry' comes from the Greek words 'bios', meaning life, and 'mimesis', meaning to imitate.
- *Coined by:* The term was popularized by Janine Benyus in her 1997 book *Biomimicry: Innovation Inspired by Nature.*

NET ZERO

Net zero refers to achieving a balance between the amount of greenhouse gases emitted into the atmosphere and the amount removed or offset. This concept is crucial for addressing climate change and limiting global warming to 1.5°C above pre-industrial levels, as per the Paris Agreement.

KEY CONCEPTS

- *Carbon neutrality:* Achieving net zero involves reducing carbon emissions as much as possible and offsetting the remaining emissions through various means.
- *Emissions reduction:* Implementing practices and technologies to significantly reduce greenhouse gas emissions from sources like transportation, industry, and energy production.
- *Carbon offsetting:* Compensating for emissions by investing in projects that absorb or reduce (CO_2), such as reforestation, renewable energy projects, or carbon capture and storage.

STRATEGIES TO ACHIEVE NET ZERO

- *Renewable energy:* Transitioning from fossil fuels to renewable energy sources like solar, wind, and hydroelectric power.
- *Energy efficiency:* Enhancing the efficiency of buildings, transportation, and industrial processes to reduce energy consumption.
- *Sustainable practices:* Adopting sustainable practices in agriculture, forestry, and waste management to minimize emissions.
- *Innovation and technology:* Developing and deploying new technologies that capture, store, or utilize carbon emissions effectively.
- *Policy and regulation:* Implementing policies and regulations that incentivize emissions reductions and support sustainable development.

EXAMPLES OF NET ZERO COMMITMENTS

- *Countries:* Many countries have pledged to achieve net zero emissions by mid-century, including the United Kingdom, Japan, and South Korea.
- *Companies:* Numerous corporations, such as Microsoft, Google, and Apple, have committed to becoming carbon neutral or achieving net zero emissions within specific timeframes.

IMPORTANCE OF NET ZERO

- *Climate mitigation:* Achieving net zero is vital for mitigating the impacts of climate change, such as extreme weather events, sea-level rise, and biodiversity loss.
- *Economic benefits:* Transitioning to a net zero economy can create new jobs, drive innovation, and reduce the economic costs associated with climate change.
- *Health and well-being:* Reducing emissions improves air quality, leading to better health outcomes and overall quality of life for communities.

CASE STUDIES OF INDIVIDUAL IMPACT IN FIGHT AGAINST CLIMATE CHANGE

GRETA THUNBERG

Greta Thunberg, a Swedish environmental activist, has inspired millions worldwide to take action against climate change. Starting with a solo protest outside the Swedish parliament in 2018, her 'Fridays for Future' movement has grown into a global youth-led campaign advocating for urgent climate action. Her efforts have raised awareness and influenced policymakers to address climate change more aggressively.

WANGARI MAATHAI

Wangari Maathai, a Kenyan environmentalist, founded the Green Belt Movement in 1977. The movement focuses on environmental conservation, community development, and women's empowerment. By planting millions of trees across Kenya, Maathai and her organization have contributed to reforestation, soil conservation, and improved livelihoods for communities.

CONCLUSION

Understanding our environment and the impact of our actions is crucial for ensuring a sustainable future. International agreements like the Kyoto Protocol, the Vienna Convention, and the Paris Accord play a vital role in addressing global environmental challenges. By taking responsibility for our actions and making informed choices, we can help protect and preserve the environment for ourselves and future generations.

SUMMARY

- *Environment:* Includes all living and non-living things, with biotic components (plants, animals, microorganisms) and abiotic components (air, water, soil, sunlight).
- *Human impact:* Includes positive impacts like conservation efforts and negative impacts like pollution, deforestation, and climate change.
- *International agreements:* Kyoto Protocol (reducing greenhouse gases), Vienna Convention (protecting the ozone layer), Paris Accord (limiting global warming).
- *Environmental issues and solutions:* Addressing air pollution, water pollution, deforestation, and climate change through various strategies.
- *Individual action:* Reducing waste, conserving energy and water, making sustainable consumption choices, and advocating for environmental protection.
- *Case studies:* Examples of individuals like Greta Thunberg and Wangari Maathai making a significant impact.

Indian Wildlife

INTRODUCTION

India is renowned for its rich and diverse wildlife, encompassing a wide range of ecosystems from the towering Himalayas to the arid Thar Desert, the lush Western Ghats to the vast Sundarbans. This incredible biodiversity includes a variety of flora and fauna, some of which are unique to the region. The country's commitment to wildlife conservation is reflected in its robust legal framework, numerous conservation projects, and international collaborations.

This chapter delves into the various aspects of Indian wildlife protection and conservation. It covers the Indian Wildlife Protection Act, laws related to forest, pollution, and environment, biodiversity and conservation efforts, the significance of the IUCN Red List, Ramsar sites, and the flagship Project Tiger initiative.

INDIAN WILDLIFE PROTECTION ACT

BACKGROUND AND ENACTMENT

The Indian Wildlife Protection Act (WPA) was enacted in 1972 in response to the alarming decline in wildlife populations across the country. The act was a significant legislative measure aimed at providing comprehensive protection to wildlife and their habitats. Prior to this, wildlife protection laws were fragmented and varied across different states, making effective conservation challenging.

KEY PROVISIONS

Protected Areas

The WPA provides for the establishment of protected areas such as national parks, wildlife sanctuaries, conservation reserves, and community reserves. These areas are critical for preserving habitats and ensuring the survival of various species.

- *National parks:* These are areas with a high degree of protection where human activities are highly restricted. National Parks focus on the conservation of biodiversity and the protection of ecological integrity.
- *Wildlife sanctuaries:* These are areas where certain rights of people living inside are permitted. Sanctuaries aim to protect specific species and their habitats while allowing regulated human activities.
- *Conservation reserves:* These areas act as buffer zones around national parks and wildlife sanctuaries, involving local communities in conservation efforts.
- *Community reserves:* These are areas where the community actively participates in conservation, providing a model for sustainable development and wildlife protection.

REGULATION OF HUNTING

The WPA categorizes wildlife into schedules based on their need for protection:

- *Schedule I:* Species that require absolute protection. Offences against these species attract the highest penalties.
- *Schedules II–IV:* Species that are also protected, but the penalties for offences are less severe than Schedule I.
- *Schedule V:* Species classified as vermin that can be hunted.
- *Schedule VI:* Plants that are protected from cultivation and destruction.

Hunting of animals listed under Schedules I–IV is strictly prohibited except for specific purposes such as education, research, or scientific management.

TRADE AND COMMERCE

The WPA regulates and restricts the trade and commerce of wildlife products. The act aims to curb illegal wildlife trade by implementing stringent checks and measures. It mandates the licensing of dealers and traders and sets severe penalties for violations.

PUNISHMENTS AND PENALTIES

The act outlines strict penalties for violations, including imprisonment and fines. For example, hunting or dealing with products of Schedule I animals can lead to imprisonment of up to seven years and fines. These stringent measures act as a deterrent against poaching and illegal trade in wildlife.

AMENDMENTS AND UPDATES

The WPA has been amended several times to address emerging challenges and incorporate new conservation strategies. Significant amendments include:

- *1991 Amendment:* Strengthened penalties and extended protection to more species.
- *2002 Amendment:* Introduced the concept of community reserves and increased penalties for wildlife offences.
- *2006 Amendment:* Established the National Tiger Conservation Authority (NTCA) and the Wildlife Crime Control Bureau (WCCB).

These amendments have made the WPA more robust, enabling it to address contemporary conservation challenges effectively.

LAWS RELATED TO FOREST, POLLUTION, AND ENVIRONMENT

India's legal framework for environmental protection is comprehensive, covering various aspects of forest conservation, pollution control, and overall environmental protection. These laws complement the WPA and collectively create a robust system for preserving the country's natural heritage.

FOREST CONSERVATION ACT, 1980

Objectives

The Forest Conservation Act (FCA) was enacted to regulate the diversion of forest land for non-forest purposes. The act aims to ensure that forest lands are not indiscriminately converted for developmental projects without adequate safeguards.

Key Provisions

- *Central government's approval:* The FCA mandates that any proposal for the diversion of forest land for non-forest purposes requires the prior approval of the central government.
- *Compensatory afforestation:* Proponents of projects involving forest land diversion must undertake compensatory afforestation to offset the loss of forest cover.

- *Penalties:* The act prescribes penalties for violations, including fines and imprisonment, to deter illegal deforestation and encroachments.

Impact

The FCA has played a crucial role in curbing deforestation and maintaining ecological balance. It has also promoted the concept of sustainable development by ensuring that developmental activities are carried out without compromising the integrity of forest ecosystems.

ENVIRONMENTAL PROTECTION ACT, 1986

Objectives

The Environmental Protection Act (EPA) is an umbrella legislation that provides a framework for the protection and improvement of the environment. The act empowers the central government to take all necessary measures to prevent environmental pollution and to address issues affecting the environment.

Key Provisions

- *Environmental standards:* The EPA authorizes the central government to set standards for emissions and discharges of pollutants into the environment.
- *Environmental impact assessment (EIA):* The act mandates EIA for certain projects to assess their potential environmental impacts before they are approved.
- *Penalties:* The EPA prescribes stringent penalties for non-compliance, including fines and imprisonment, to ensure adherence to environmental norms.

Impact

The EPA has been instrumental in regulating industrial pollution, ensuring sustainable development, and protecting natural resources. It has also provided a legal basis for public interest litigation (PIL) in environmental matters, empowering citizens to seek judicial intervention for environmental protection.

AIR (PREVENTION AND CONTROL OF POLLUTION) ACT, 1981

Objectives

The Air (Prevention and Control of Pollution) Act aims to combat air pollution by regulating the emissions of pollutants into the atmosphere. The act establishes Central and State Pollution Control Boards (CPCB and SPCBs) responsible for monitoring air quality and enforcing pollution control measures.

Key Provisions

- *Air quality standards:* The act mandates the establishment of air quality standards for different pollutants.
- *Regulation of industrial emissions:* The CPCB and SPCBs are empowered to regulate emissions from industrial sources and to ensure compliance with air quality standards.
- *Penalties:* The act prescribes penalties for violations, including fines and imprisonment, to deter non-compliance with air quality regulations.

Impact

The Air Act has significantly contributed to improving air quality in India by regulating industrial emissions and promoting cleaner technologies. It has also raised awareness about the importance of air quality and public health.

WATER (PREVENTION AND CONTROL OF POLLUTION) ACT, 1974

Objectives

The Water (Prevention and Control of Pollution) Act focuses on preventing and controlling water pollution. The act establishes Central and State Pollution Control Boards responsible for regulating water quality and preventing pollution of water bodies.

Key Provisions

- *Water quality standards:* The act mandates the establishment of water quality standards for different uses of water.
- *Regulation of effluents:* The CPCB and SPCBs are empowered to regulate the discharge of effluents from industrial sources into water bodies.
- *Penalties:* The act prescribes penalties for violations, including fines and imprisonment, to ensure compliance with water quality regulations.

Impact

The Water Act has played a crucial role in protecting India's water resources by regulating industrial discharges and promoting wastewater treatment. It has also helped in safeguarding public health by ensuring access to clean water.

BIODIVERSITY AND CONSERVATION

IMPORTANCE OF BIODIVERSITY

Biodiversity is the variety of life on Earth, encompassing the diversity of species, ecosystems, and genetic variations within species. It is crucial for maintaining ecological balance, providing ecosystem services, and supporting human livelihoods. India's biodiversity is among the richest in the world, making its conservation of paramount importance.

BIODIVERSITY HOTSPOTS IN INDIA

India is home to 4 of the world's 36 biodiversity hotspots, areas that are both rich in species and under significant threat from human activities. These hotspots are as follows:

- *The Western Ghats:* Known for its high levels of endemism and diverse ecosystems, the Western Ghats are home to numerous endemic species, including the Nilgiri tahr and the Malabar giant squirrel.
- *The Eastern Himalayas:* This region is characterized by its diverse habitats ranging from tropical rainforests to alpine meadows. It is home to species like the red panda and the snow leopard.
- *Indo-Burma:* Encompassing parts of Northeast India, this hotspot is rich in plant and animal diversity, including the Hoolock gibbon and the Asian elephant.
- *Sundaland (Nicobar Islands):* The Nicobar Islands are part of the Sundaland hotspot, known for their unique marine and terrestrial biodiversity.

CONSERVATION STRATEGIES

PROTECTED AREAS

India's network of protected areas, including National Parks, Wildlife Sanctuaries, and Biosphere Reserves, forms the backbone of its conservation strategy. These areas provide safe habitats for wildlife and help maintain ecological processes.

- *National parks and wildlife sanctuaries:* These areas focus on preserving habitats and protecting species from human disturbances. Some notable examples include Jim Corbett National Park, Kaziranga National Park, and Gir Wildlife Sanctuary.

- *Biosphere reserves:* Biosphere reserves are designated under the UNESCO Man and the Biosphere Programme. They aim to promote sustainable development while conserving biodiversity. Examples include the Nilgiri Biosphere Reserve and the Sunderban Biosphere Reserve.

COMMUNITY-BASED CONSERVATION

Involving local communities in conservation efforts is crucial for the success of conservation initiatives. Community-based conservation empowers local people to protect their natural resources and benefits them economically.

- *Community reserves:* The WPA provides for the establishment of community reserves, where local communities play a significant role in conservation and management.
- *Eco-sensitive zones:* These zones act as buffer areas around protected areas, promoting sustainable practices and involving local communities in conservation efforts.

SPECIES-SPECIFIC PROJECTS

Targeted conservation projects for key species address the specific needs of endangered species and their habitats. Some notable projects include:

- *Project Tiger:* Launched in 1973, Project Tiger aims to ensure a viable population of tigers in their natural habitats and to protect them from extinction.
- *Project Elephant:* Launched in 1992, Project Elephant focuses on conserving elephants and their habitats, addressing human–elephant conflict, and ensuring their welfare.
- *Crocodile Conservation Project:* Initiated in 1975, this project aims to protect and restore the population of crocodiles in India's rivers and wetlands.

BIODIVERSITY ACT, 2002

The Biological Diversity Act was enacted to preserve India's rich biodiversity, ensure the sustainable use of its components, and provide for the fair and equitable sharing of benefits arising from the use of biological resources.

- *Biodiversity Management Committees (BMCs):* The act mandates the establishment of BMCs at the local level to promote conservation and sustainable use of biological resources.
- *National Biodiversity Authority (NBA):* The NBA regulates access to biological resources and associated knowledge, ensuring that benefits are shared equitably.

CHALLENGES AND FUTURE DIRECTIONS

Despite significant progress, biodiversity conservation in India faces several challenges, including habitat fragmentation, human–wildlife conflict, climate change, and inadequate funding. Addressing these challenges requires:

- *Strengthening legal frameworks:* Enhancing the implementation and enforcement of existing laws and introducing new regulations where necessary.
- *Enhancing community participation:* Empowering local communities through education, capacity building, and economic incentives.

- *Promoting research and monitoring:* Investing in scientific research to understand biodiversity trends and develop effective conservation strategies.
- *International collaboration:* Engaging in global initiatives and partnerships to address transboundary conservation issues and share best practices.

IUCN RED LIST

OVERVIEW

The International Union for Conservation of Nature (IUCN) Red List is a comprehensive inventory of the global conservation status of plant and animal species. It serves as a critical tool for assessing the risk of extinction and guiding conservation actions.

CATEGORIES

The IUCN Red List classifies species into nine categories based on their extinction risk:

- *Extinct (EX):* No known individuals remaining.
- *Extinct in the wild (EW):* Known only to survive in captivity or as a naturalized population outside its historic range.
- *Critically endangered (CR):* Extremely high risk of extinction in the wild.
- *Endangered (EN):* High risk of extinction in the wild.
- *Vulnerable (VU):* High risk of endangerment in the wild.
- *Near threatened (NT):* Likely to become endangered in the near future.
- *Least concern (LC):* Lowest risk, widespread, and abundant.
- *Data deficient (DD):* Inadequate information to make a direct or indirect assessment of its risk of extinction.
- *Not evaluated (NE):* Has not yet been evaluated against the criteria.

INDIAN SPECIES ON THE RED LIST

India has numerous species listed on the IUCN Red List, highlighting the urgent need for conservation efforts. Some examples include:

- *Bengal tiger (Panthera tigris):* Listed as endangered, with habitat loss and poaching as major threats.
- *Asian elephant (Elephas maximus):* Listed as endangered, facing threats from habitat fragmentation and human–elephant conflict.
- *Indian rhinoceros (Rhinoceros unicornis):* Listed as vulnerable, primarily threatened by poaching for its horn.
- *Ganges river dolphin (Platanista gangetica):* Listed as endangered, affected by water pollution, habitat fragmentation, and fishing nets.
- *Great Indian bustard (Ardeotis nigriceps):* Listed as critically endangered, with habitat loss and hunting as major threats.

ROLE OF THE RED LIST

The IUCN Red List serves several important functions:

- *Awareness and education:* Raising awareness about the conservation status of species and the threats they face.

- *Policy and legislation:* Informing and guiding conservation policies and legislation at national and international levels.
- *Conservation planning:* Assisting in the prioritization of species and habitats for conservation action.
- *Research and monitoring:* Providing a basis for scientific research and long-term monitoring of species populations.

RAMSAR SITES

OVERVIEW

The Ramsar Convention, officially known as the Convention on Wetlands of International Importance, is an international treaty aimed at the conservation and sustainable use of wetlands. India is a signatory to the Ramsar Convention and has designated several wetlands as Ramsar sites.

SIGNIFICANCE OF RAMSAR SITES

Ramsar sites play a crucial role in maintaining ecological balance, supporting biodiversity, and providing ecosystem services. They are important for:

- *Water purification:* Wetlands act as natural filters, removing pollutants from water.
- *Flood control:* Wetlands absorb excess rainfall, reducing the risk of floods.
- *Biodiversity:* Wetlands provide habitat for a wide range of species, including many endangered and migratory birds.
- *Livelihoods:* Wetlands support the livelihoods of millions of people through activities such as fishing, agriculture, and tourism.

NOTABLE RAMSAR SITES IN INDIA

India has 49 Ramsar sites covering an area of over 1 million hectares. Some notable sites include:

- *Chilika Lake:* Asia's largest brackish water lagoon, located in Odisha. It is a critical habitat for migratory birds and supports a rich diversity of fish species.
- *Keoladeo National Park:* Located in Rajasthan, this UNESCO World Heritage Site is known for its avian diversity and is a key wintering ground for migratory birds.
- *Sundarbans Wetland:* Part of the world's largest mangrove forest, located in West Bengal. It is home to the Bengal tiger and numerous other species.
- *Loktak Lake:* Located in Manipur, it is known for its unique phumdis (floating islands) and rich biodiversity.
- *Nalsarovar Bird Sanctuary:* Located in Gujarat, it is an important wetland for migratory birds and supports a variety of aquatic plants and animals.

CONSERVATION AND MANAGEMENT

The designation of Ramsar sites brings international recognition and support for their conservation. Management plans for these sites focus on:

- *Habitat restoration:* Restoring degraded wetland habitats to enhance their ecological functions.
- *Sustainable use:* Promoting sustainable use of wetland resources to benefit local communities while ensuring conservation.

- *Monitoring and research:* Conducting scientific research and monitoring to inform management decisions and track the health of wetland ecosystems.
- *Community participation:* Involving local communities in the management and conservation of wetlands through awareness programmes and capacity building.

PROJECT TIGER

OVERVIEW

Project Tiger is one of the most successful and well-known wildlife conservation initiatives in India. Launched in 1973 by the Government of India, its primary goal is to ensure a viable population of tigers in their natural habitats and protect them from extinction.

OBJECTIVES

- *Habitat preservation:* Identifying and managing critical tiger habitats to ensure a safe and conducive environment for their survival.
- *Anti-poaching measures:* Implementing stringent anti-poaching measures and strengthening the legal framework to deter illegal activities.
- *Community involvement:* Engaging local communities in conservation efforts through awareness programmes and providing alternative livelihoods to reduce dependency on forest resources.
- *Scientific monitoring:* Using scientific methods and technology to monitor tiger populations and their habitats, ensuring effective management and timely interventions.

ACHIEVEMENTS

Project Tiger has been instrumental in increasing the tiger population in India. From a mere 1,827 tigers in 1973, the population has grown to approximately 2,967 in 2018, according to the All India Tiger Estimation report. The project has also led to the establishment of numerous tiger reserves across the country, providing safe havens for these magnificent big cats.

TIGER RESERVES

India currently has 50 tiger reserves spread across 18 states, covering an area of over 72,000 square kilometres. Some notable reserves include:

- *Jim Corbett Tiger Reserve:* Located in Uttarakhand, it is India's oldest and one of the most famous tiger reserves.
- *Ranthambore Tiger Reserve:* Located in Rajasthan, it is known for its thriving tiger population and historical ruins.
- *Bandhavgarh Tiger Reserve:* Located in Madhya Pradesh, it has one of the highest densities of tigers in India.
- *Kaziranga Tiger Reserve:* Located in Assam, it is also a UNESCO World Heritage Site known for its population of tigers, elephants, and the Indian one-horned rhinoceros.
- *Sundarbans Tiger Reserve:* Located in West Bengal, it is part of the largest mangrove forest in the world and home to the Bengal tiger.

CHALLENGES AND FUTURE DIRECTIONS

Despite its success, Project Tiger faces ongoing challenges such as habitat fragmentation and human–wildlife conflict.

The 2024 budget highlights the government's commitment to fostering a bio-economy, recognizing its potential to drive sustainable development and economic growth. The bio-economy encompasses various sectors such as agriculture, forestry, fisheries, food production, biotechnology, and bioenergy, all of which utilize biological resources and processes. By promoting innovation and investment in these areas, the budget aims to enhance resource efficiency, reduce environmental impact, and create new jobs.

BIO-ECONOMY

KEY INITIATIVES IN THE 2024 BUDGET FOR THE BIO-ECONOMY

- *Research and development:* Increased funding for research in biotechnology and bio-based industries to develop new products and technologies that can replace fossil-based materials.
- *Sustainable agriculture:* Support for farmers to adopt sustainable practices that increase productivity while preserving natural resources. This includes subsidies for organic farming, precision agriculture technologies, and bio-based fertilizers.
- *Renewable energy:* Investments in bioenergy projects, including biofuels and biogas, to reduce dependence on fossil fuels and lower greenhouse gas emissions.
- *Circular economy:* Promotion of circular economy principles in the bio-economy, encouraging recycling and the use of bio-based materials in various industries to minimize waste.
- *Public–private partnerships:* Encouragement of collaborations between the public sector, private companies, and research institutions to accelerate the commercialization of bio-based innovations.
- *Regulatory support:* Streamlining regulatory processes to facilitate the development and approval of new bio-based products and technologies, ensuring they reach the market more efficiently.

By prioritizing the bio-economy, the 2024 budget aims to create a resilient and sustainable economic model that leverages biological resources for long-term prosperity and environmental stewardship.

GEOPARK

A Geopark is a designated area that promotes the protection and sustainable use of geological heritage while also fostering economic development, primarily through geotourism. These parks are part of the Global Geoparks Network, supported by UNESCO, and are recognized for their unique geological features, which can include rock formations, fossils, and landscapes of significant scientific importance.

KEY FEATURES OF A GEOPARK

- *Geological heritage:* Geoparks protect areas with significant geological features, which can range from unique rock formations and fossils to notable landscapes that provide insights into the Earth's history.
- *Education:* They serve as outdoor classrooms, offering educational programmes and activities that help the public and students to understand

geological processes and the importance of conserving Earth's heritage.

- *Sustainable tourism:* Geoparks promote sustainable tourism by encouraging visitors to explore and appreciate geological sites in ways that do not harm the environment. This includes developing infrastructure like trails, interpretive centres, and guided tours that highlight the geological significance of the area.
- *Local development:* By attracting tourists, Geoparks contribute to the local economy. They create jobs, support local businesses, and can lead to the development of new enterprises centred around geotourism.
- *Community involvement:* Successful Geoparks involve local communities in their development and management, ensuring that the benefits of tourism and conservation efforts are shared and that local cultures and traditions are respected.
- *Conservation:* Beyond just geological features, Geoparks often include efforts to conserve biodiversity, cultural heritage, and scenic landscapes within their boundaries.

Examples of Activities and Attractions in Geoparks

- *Hiking and trekking:* Trails that take visitors through areas of geological interest.
- *Museums and visitor centres:* Facilities that provide educational exhibits and resources about the geological features of the park.
- *Workshops and events:* Educational workshops, lectures, and community events that focus on geology, conservation, and sustainable practices.
- *Interactive exhibits:* Hands-on displays and activities that allow visitors to engage with geological concepts in a fun and informative way.

BIOME

A biome is a large ecological area on the Earth's surface with distinct climate, plants, and animals. Each biome consists of multiple ecosystems that share similar environmental conditions and life forms. Biomes are defined by factors such as temperature, precipitation, and the types of organisms that inhabit them. They can be found across continents and include both terrestrial and aquatic regions.

MAJOR TYPES OF BIOMES

Tropical Rainforest

- *Climate:* Warm and wet year-round, with high humidity.
- *Flora:* Dense, multi-layered forests with a high diversity of plants, including tall trees, vines, and epiphytes.
- *Fauna:* Diverse animal life, including insects, birds, mammals, and reptiles.

Savanna

- *Climate:* Warm with seasonal rainfall.
- *Flora:* Grasses dominate, with scattered trees and shrubs.
- *Fauna:* Large herbivores like elephants, giraffes, and zebras, and predators like lions and cheetahs.

Desert

- *Climate:* Very dry, with extreme temperature variations between day and night.
- *Flora:* Sparse vegetation, including cacti and succulents.
- *Fauna:* Animals adapted to dry conditions, such as reptiles, insects, and nocturnal mammals.

Temperate Forest

- *Climate:* Moderate temperatures with distinct seasons.
- *Flora:* Deciduous trees (like oak and maple) and evergreen trees (like pine and fir).

- *Fauna:* Diverse species including deer, bears, birds, and insects.

Grassland (Prairie/Steppe)

- *Climate:* Moderate with seasonal precipitation.
- *Flora:* Dominated by grasses and few trees.
- *Fauna:* Grazing animals like bison and antelope, and predators like wolves and coyotes.

Taiga (Boreal Forest)

- *Climate:* Cold with long winters and short summers.
- *Flora:* Coniferous trees like spruce and pine.
- *Fauna:* Animals adapted to cold, such as moose, lynxes, and bears.

Tundra

- *Climate:* Very cold with short, cool summers and long, harsh winters.
- *Flora:* Low-growing plants like mosses, lichens, and dwarf shrubs.
- *Fauna:* Animals with adaptations to cold, such as caribou, arctic foxes, and migratory birds.

Aquatic Biomes

- *Freshwater:* Includes rivers, lakes, and wetlands. Home to fish, amphibians, and aquatic plants.
- *Marine:* Includes oceans, coral reefs, and estuaries. Diverse life forms including fish, marine mammals, and invertebrates.

IMPORTANCE OF BIOMES

- *Biodiversity:* Biomes support diverse plant and animal species, each adapted to their specific environment.
- *Climate regulation:* Different biomes play a role in regulating the Earth's climate by influencing weather patterns and storing carbon.
- *Ecosystem services:* Biomes provide essential services such as clean water, air, and fertile soil.
- *Cultural significance:* Many biomes have cultural importance to human societies, offering resources and recreation.

THREATS TO BIOMES

- *Climate change:* Alterations in temperature and precipitation patterns can disrupt the delicate balance of biomes.
- *Deforestation:* Clearing forests for agriculture or development reduces habitat for many species.
- *Pollution:* Contaminants can degrade ecosystems and harm wildlife.
- *Overexploitation:* Overfishing, hunting, and harvesting of resources can lead to population declines and extinction.

CONSERVATION EFFORTS

- *Protected areas:* Establishing national parks and reserves to safeguard biodiversity.
- *Sustainable practices:* Promoting agriculture, forestry, and fishing practices that do not deplete natural resources.
- *Restoration projects:* Rehabilitating degraded ecosystems to restore their functions and biodiversity.
- *Education and awareness:* Raising public awareness about the importance of biomes and how to protect them.

BIOMASS PERIOD

A biomass pyramid is a graphical representation that shows the distribution of biomass among different trophic levels in an ecosystem. Biomass refers to the total mass of living organisms in a given area or volume. The pyramid typically consists of several levels, each representing a different group of organisms, from producers at the base to top predators at the apex.

ONE-LINE DEFINITIONS, ETYMOLOGY, AND COINERS OF KEY ECOLOGICAL TERMS

Ecosystem

- *Definition:* A community of living organisms interacting with their physical environment.
- *Etymology:* From Greek 'oikos' (house) and 'systema' (system).
- *Coined by:* Arthur Tansley in 1935.

Ecology

- *Definition:* The branch of biology that deals with the relations of organisms to one another and to their physical surroundings.
- *Etymology:* From Greek 'oikos' (house) and 'logos' (study).
- *Coined by:* Ernst Haeckel in 1866.

Biodiversity

- *Definition:* The variety of life in the world or in a particular habitat or ecosystem.
- *Etymology:* From Greek 'bios' (life) and Latin 'diversitas' (variety).
- *Coined by:* Walter G. Rosen in 1985 during the planning of the National Forum on Biodiversity.

Environment

- *Definition:* The surroundings or conditions in which a person, animal, or plant lives or operates.
- *Etymology:* From French 'environ' (around, surrounding).
- *Coined by:* The term has been in use since the mid-fourteenth century and does not have a single coinage attribution.

Conservation

- *Definition:* The preservation, protection, or restoration of the natural environment and wildlife.
- *Etymology:* From Latin 'conservare' (to keep, guard, observe).
- *Coined by:* The term has been in use since the late fourteenth century in the context of preserving resources and does not have a single coinage attribution.

12 Arts and Culture

INTRODUCTION

What do we look for when we read about the art and culture of any place? There are many facets in the answer to this question. Let's take a look.

Art and culture represent the rich tapestry of human civilization, interweaving the delicate, intricate textures of life in every country of the world.

When we study the art and culture of a particular period in time, whether ancient or the modern era, noticeable elements are evident in style and influence.

Let's put them into separate categories for better understanding.

We will notice there are three major sections: visual, literary, and performing arts.

SECTION 1

VISUAL ARTS

Have you looked at a painting and marvelled at its extraordinary beauty?

What made it so striking that you wanted to stop and study it better?

The art of painting rose exponentially between the 1300s and 1600s, when an enormous eruption of brilliant art was created in Europe, especially in Italy, France, and Spain.

Even today, in the twenty-first century, we stand in awe and marvel at the treasure trove of stunning paintings that were created during this era. Let us look deeper.

Renaissance Period – 1350 – 1620 AD

The French word 'renaissance' literally means 'rebirth'.

Art, painting, sculpture, music, architecture and literature during the fourteenth, fifteenth, and sixteenth centuries in Europe blossomed with growing awareness of nature, along with the revival of classical learning and enhanced individualistic thought.

This period is renowned for the extraordinary output in creative work, particularly in Italy, which became the centre of glorious artwork.

However, historical sources indicate that interest in humanistic learning, individualism, and nature had been present even during earlier times but grew exponentially in the fifteenth and sixteenth century with contemporary social and economic changes.

Let's know about some remarkable artists of that glorious time.

Leonardo da Vinci (1452–1519)

Da Vinci is arguably a genius par excellence, be it in the Renaissance era or modern day innovation.

He was an Italian sculptor, painter, draftsman, engineer, whose skill and intelligence epitomizes the Renaissance humanist ideal.

His drawing of the Vitruvian Man clearly depicts how the adult human male body is divided into separate equal parts. The drawing shows the man with his arms and legs wide apart while a superimposed drawing shows the inside with a circle and a square. It creates a three-dimensional perspective and remains a globally recognized concept of ideal body proportions.

Da Vinci's phenomenal paintings are among the most well-known and authoritative of this celebrated era. His minutely detailed notebooks reveal a scientific inquiry and mechanical inventive genius centuries ahead of his time.

Painted by Da Vinci around 1495, 'The Last Supper' depicts the dramatic incident in which Jesus declares one of the Apostles will betray him. Leonardo's painting realistically expresses the posture and gesture of each of the 12 disciples, as per his character. It is a brilliant presentation of diverse human emotions rendered in stunning artistic composition.

Undoubtedly, the world's most prized and popular artwork, the 'Mona Lisa' by Da Vinci draws thousands of visitors to the Louvre Museum in Paris each day where it is on display, drawn by her mysterious gaze and enigmatic smile.

Michelangelo (1475–1564)

A brilliant artist of the Italian Renaissance, he was sculptor, painter, architect, and was commissioned to sculpt the marble statue of David for the cathedral of Florence. Michelangelo reused a block left unfinished for decades.

The stunning minute details on the marble figure are exceptional. The veins are sharply visible on the hands, while taut muscles and an astonishing skin texture add to incredible reality.

His works in painting, sculpture, and architecture remain the most celebrated, even in the twenty-first century.

The frescoes on the Sistine Chapel ceiling are a testament to his brilliance. 'The Creation of Adam', a monumental artwork, is among the best known of his works.

Titian (1488–1576)

Renowned Italian Renaissance painter of the Venetian school of art, he was recognized when he was fairly young as a supremely gifted painter. In his painting 'The Rape of Europa', Europa is depicted being carried off, arms and legs flying, on the back of Jupiter depicted as a garlanded white bull.

Raphael (1483–1520)

Master painter and architect of the Italian High Renaissance, he is recognized for his striking Madonnas. His artwork is highly esteemed for the clarity of form, lucid composition, and visual grandeur.

Peter Paul Rubens (1577–1640)

Rubens was a Flemish painter and a brilliant exponent of Baroque style of dynamism, vitality, and sensuous exuberance. Though his masterpieces are portraits and landscapes, Rubens is best recognized for religious and mythological compositions.

Rembrandt (1606–69)

Rembrandt was a Dutch Baroque painter and printmaker. He had the extraordinary ability to depict people in their many moods and striking attire.

Rembrandt is renowned as a painter of light and shade, an artist who preferred candid reality, so much so that some would attribute his preference for 'ugliness to beauty'.

From early in his career, Rembrandt painted mainly portraits. The majority of his paintings and sketches comprise studies of faces, some of the self-portraits.

However, the centre of Rembrandt's body of art consists mainly of biblical, and some historical, mythological, and allegorical studies, which he did in pen and ink or chalk.

His mastery of composition, along with his portrayal of space and light, shows exceptional skill. The way he shapes contours, forms, and uses colour, combined with his expressive brushstrokes, radiates creativity and brilliance.

Johannes Vermeer (1632–75)

A Dutch artist, his realistic paintings are highly esteemed in the history of art, with 36 of them remaining. His career began in the early 1650s with large-scale biblical, mythological scenes.

Vermeer's later paintings, for which he is most celebrated, are primarily of his subjects in interior settings. Remarkable for their pristine light and form, these paintings exude a serene, timeless sense of dignity.

Vermeer also painted landscapes and allegorical scenes.

Sandro Botticelli (1445–1510)

A brilliant painter of the Florentine Renaissance, his iconic paintings *The Birth of Venus* and *La Primavera* represent the spirit of the Renaissance for their spectacular depictions of the mythological characters.

Jan van Eyck (1395–1441)

A Dutch painter, he mastered the innovative technique of oil painting, focusing primarily on naturalistic portraits and religious themes. Van Eyck often incorporated hidden religious symbols in his work. His most renowned masterpiece, *The Adoration of the Mystic Lamb*, can be found at the altar of the cathedral in Ghent.

Pierre-Auguste Renoir (1841–1919)

Pierre-Auguste Renoir was a French painter and originally associated with the Impressionist movement. His early works are typical Impressionist scenes of real life, filled with vibrant colour and light.

In the mid-1880s, Renoir broke off from the movement for a more disciplined, formal technique of portraits and figure paintings, particularly of women.

His masterpieces from this period include *La Loge, Dance at Le Moulin de la Galette, Luncheon of the Boating Party*, and *Madame Charpentier and Her Children.*

Vincent van Gogh (1853–90)

Vincent van Gogh was a Dutch painter and among the greatest of the post-Impressionists. His use of vibrant colours, forceful brushwork, and contoured forms greatly influenced modern art.

Though living in impoverished circumstances, van Gogh's paintings became astoundingly popular after his death, especially in the late twentieth century when his art sold for record-breaking sums at auctions around the world.

Henri de Toulouse-Lautrec (1864–1901)

Henri de Toulouse-Lautrec was a French artist whose paintings reveal his outstanding insight. They depict diverse facets of Parisian nightlife and the contemporary world of entertainment.

His brilliant works include *In the Circus Fernando: The Ringmaster*. Rejecting the traditional medium of oil on canvas, Toulouse-Lautrec made his first poster, *Moulin Rouge: La Goulue*, earning great fame.

Claude Monet (1840–1926)

Claude Monet, a French painter and leading figure of the Impressionist movement, pioneered a technique of painting the same subject in a series, capturing different lighting and atmospheric conditions. He would switch canvases as the light or his focus changed. These series, such as his depictions of haystacks and the Rouen Cathedral, were often exhibited together.

At Giverny, Monet created the water-lily pond that served as an inspiration for his final series of paintings. His popularity rose exponentially in the second half of the twentieth century when his works displayed in museums across the world drew enormous crowds.

Édouard Manet (1832–83)

Manet was a French painter who broke traditional techniques of representation by choosing subjects from contemporary events. His *Le Déjeuner sur l'herbe* (Luncheon on the Grass) provoked hostile critics but enthused young painters who later formed the nucleus of the Impressionist group. His other notable works include *Olympia* and *A Bar at the Folies-Bergère*.

Edgar Degas (1834–1917)

Degas was a French painter, sculptor, and print-maker and was celebrated in the Impressionist group. He is widely acknowledged for his images of Parisian life. His principal subject was the female figure and his works ranged from sombre portraits in his early years to compositions of laundresses, cabaret singers, and milliners of his time.

Notably, Degas made several works of ballet dancers and their signature movements.

Paul Cézanne (1839–1906)

Cezanne was a French painter and a pioneer of modern painting. Originally closely associated with the Impressionists, he focused more on the structure of objects than on the effects of light. His compositions were built around cubic forms, bold patches of colour, and strong architectural lines.

In the 1870s, he broke off from the Impressionists, exploring his own radically new way of simultaneously depicting deep space and flat design, often classified as post-Impressionist.

Pablo Picasso (1881–1973)

Picasso was a Spanish expatriate painter, sculptor, printmaker, ceramicist, and stage designer. One of the greatest and most-influential artists of the twentieth century and the creator of Cubism, with Georges Braque.

This technique signified the 're-presentation' of the form of objects and their position in space instead of duplicating them and the process of subdividing objects, of space, light and shadow, and even colour.

Inconsistencies such as different perspectives of view, contrary axes, and various light sources find place, all in the same picture. Including abstract and representational elements on the same picture plane added to the signature compositions.

Paul Gauguin (1848–1903)

Paul Gauguin was a French painter, printmaker, and sculptor who wanted to express a 'primitive' expression of spiritual and emotional states in his artworks.

He shared a unique bond with Vincent van Gogh and is recognized for his self-imposed exile in Tahiti, French Polynesia. His innovative artistic experiments had a profound impact on various avant-garde movements that emerged in the early twentieth century.

Frida Kahlo (1907–54)

Frida Kahlo was a Mexican painter best known for her candid, vibrant self-portraits on subjects like death, identity, and the human body.

In 1925, Kahlo met with a serious accident and went through 30 operations on her body. She taught herself to paint while recovering and began studying the Old Masters.

One of her striking early paintings was *Self-Portrait Wearing a Velvet Dress* and the well-known *The Two Fridas*. The dramatic portions of her life, from the serious injury to a turbulent marriage, many love affairs and alcoholic bouts inspired several books and movies after her death.

Henri Matisse (1869–1954)

Henri Matisse was considered the most important French painter of the twentieth century. He pioneered the Fauvist movement and his subjects were largely domestic or figurative with a defined Mediterranean spirit.

Edvard Munch (1863–1944)

Munch was a Norwegian painter and printmaker, and his unique usage of mental themes based on the tenets of late nineteenth-century symbolism created substantial German Expressionism in the early twentieth century.

His painting *The Scream* is perceived as a symbol of modern spiritual anguish.

Andy Warhol (1928–87)

An American artist and filmmaker, Warhol was a key figure and pioneer of the Pop Art movement in the 1960s, known for transforming everyday commercial culture into celebrated art.

A master of self-promotion, he crafted an image of the artist as a detached, almost empty persona, yet one who achieved fame, success, and influence as both a celebrity and businessman.

Salvador Dalí (1904–89)

Dalí was a Spanish Surrealist painter. Surrealism essentially meant works of 'anti-art that deliberately defied reason'. But here, Surrealism's emphasis was on positive expression. It provided a major alternative to the contemporary, highly formalist Cubist movement.

Known for his exploration of subconscious imagery, Dalí was highly influential in the art world. As a student, he absorbed a wide range of artistic styles and demonstrated remarkable technical skill as a painter, developing a distinct and surreal approach to his work.

To bring up images from his subconscious mind, Dalí began to induce hallucinatory states in himself. His striking painting *The Persistence of Memory* depicting limp melting watches is a brilliant example of this.

Banksy (Born 1974)

He is an anonymous British graffiti artist known for his critical and rebellious art, mostly done in public places.

His artworks often feature multilayered stencils combined with various media, incorporating existing objects on his chosen 'canvas', such as street signs or fire hydrants. This approach transforms his pieces into captivating street art installations that blend seamlessly with their urban surroundings.

Banksy's art often appears unexpectedly, and expectedly causes considerable media attention.

Marc Chagall (1887–1985)

Chagall was a French painter, printmaker, and designer who composed his images based on emotional and poetic associations, rather than on rules of pictorial logic.

Before the advent of Surrealism, his early works were among the first expressions of psychic reality in modern art.

His works in various media include sets for plays and ballets, etchings illustrating the Bible, and stained-glass windows.

ART IN INDIA

Do you want to know about the Indian artists who have left an indelible imprint on the art scenario? Each had their own individualistic style and came from diverse parts of the country. Let's check them out.

Jamini Roy (1887–1972)

From West Bengal, the artist was one of the best-known Indian painters of the twentieth century. He rejected his academic training in late 1920s and early 1930s and developed his singular style with its unique linears and earthy colours. He realized that he needed to draw inspiration from his own culture and traditions and not from Western ideas. He followed this with the decision to look at tribal art and rural folk for his work. The large oval eyes of his subjects are his signature style and remain a highlight of his art.

Most of his paintings were based on Bengali folk traditions and represented the transition of modern Indian art from traditional European leanings to a renewed inclination for conventional iconography and abstract forms.

His subject matter ranged from Indian mythology to musicians (tribal drum players) to Christ and portraits of contemporary figures like Mahatma Gandhi.

Raja Ravi Varma (1848–1906)

Ravi Varma was an Indian painter whose works reveal the merging of European academic art with complete Indian sensibility and iconography. He became well-known for producing affordable lithographs of his paintings, making his work accessible to a wider audience. This not only expanded his influence as a painter but also elevated his status as a public figure.

His lithographs helped bring fine arts to the general public, shaping popular artistic tastes. His portrayals of Hindu deities and scenes from Indian epic poetry and the *Puranas* gained widespread acclaim, making his work a cultural touchstone for many.

The artist was closely related to the royal family of Travancore of Kerala in India. Despite the criticism of his paintings as 'Calendar Art', his work *The Begum's Bath* sold for a record price.

His elaborate and ornate paintings *Shakuntala* and *The Milkmaid* are examples that exude a special beauty.

Amrita Sher-Gil (1913–41)

Sher-Gil was one of the pioneers of the modern movement in Indian art; her father was Indian and mother Hungarian. Since childhood, she displayed a striking inclination for painting and was encouraged to pursue this passion.

Inspired by Paul Cézanne, Amedeo Modigliani, and Paul Gauguin, Sher-Gil went to École des Beaux-Arts in Paris to study art. She returned to India later and continued her work.

Sher-Gil was able to prove to Western societies that Indians were capable of creating fine art. Her work is regarded with high esteem and the Indian government has stipulated that her art, when sold in India, must remain in the country.

Sher-Gil's paintings are among the most expensive by Indian women painters today. However, unfortunately, not many acknowledged her work when she was alive.

Abanindranath Tagore (1871–1951)

He was the creator and principal artist of the Indian Society of Oriental Art and founded the Bengal School of Art, which was instrumental in the importance of modern Indian painting. A noted writer, he wrote for children under an affectionate name 'Aban Thakur'. His well-known books *Rajkahini, Nalak,* and *Khirer Putul* remain gems in Bengali literature for children.

Abanindranath Tagore was a visionary artist dedicated to revitalizing traditional Indian painting styles by incorporating modern influences. His creations *Bharat Mata, Radha and Krishna,* and *The Passing of Shah Jahan* are apt examples of his skill in syncing the old with the new, and showcasing India's rich heritage

Nandalal Bose (1882–1966)

Nandalal Bose's nationalist and patriotic paintings resonate with a deep love for his homeland. His artwork *Bapuji* is a tribute to Mahatma Gandhi, while *Santals* and *Saraswati* exude the rich cultural depths of India, truly representing the nation's ideology.

M. F. Husain (1915–2011)

Maqbool Fida Husain was a prolific and controversial artist. He began his career as a billboard painter and is known to have painted some of the posters of the

Hindi film industry early in his career. His dynamic paintings of horses brought huge attention and his art began to sell for astronomical sums of money.

Tyeb Mehta (1925–2009)

Tyeb Mehta's abstract art transcended traditional boundaries, using bold colours and striking shapes to express deep emotions. Works like *Mahishasura*, *Falling Bird*, and *Kali* invite viewers into a captivating interplay of colour and form, encouraging them to delve into the infinite possibilities of abstraction.

S. H. Raza (1922–2016)

S. H. Raza, the French-Indian artist, utilized geometric shapes and vibrant colours to express a sense of unity that goes beyond the visual realm. His works, such as *Bindu*, *Saurashtra*, and *La Terre*, encourage viewers to reflect on the mystical dimensions of his art.

Vasudeo S. Gaitonde (1924–2001)

Vasudeo S. Gaitonde's abstract paintings delve into the exploration of the inner self and the metaphysical. The use of muted colours and an atmospheric quality in his work evokes a profound sense of serenity, inviting viewers to introspect and forge a deeper connection with their inner selves.

TRADITIONAL INDIAN ART

Just like conventional methods of painting, for instance, watercolour, oil, or charcoal, there are also various modes of painting.

Let's look at the significant ones prevalent in India.

Tanjore Painting

Tanjore (or Thanjavur) painting is a unique style of South India from the town of Thanjavur (or Tanjore) in Tamil Nadu. The art form originates from around 1600 AD, when the rulers of Thanjavur encouraged art, classical dance, music, literature, in Telugu and Tamil, and painting of primarily Hindu religious subjects in temples.

These paintings are characterized by rich and vivid colours, clear iconic composition, glittering gold foil covering delicate, intricate work with an abundant inlay of precious and semi-precious gems. The subjects of most paintings are Hindu gods, goddesses, and saints.

Episodes from Hindu *Puranas* and other religious texts were visualized, sketched, and painted, with the main figure in the centre of the artwork, surrounded by subsidiary figures, themes, and subjects.

There are also several instances when Jain, Sikh, Muslim, and other religious subjects have been featured in Tanjore paintings.

Kalamkari

Kalamkari has its origins centuries ago in Telangana and Andhra Pradesh, India, and is an integral part of traditional Indian art. The paintings depict scenes from Hindu religious scriptures. They were used as decorations on temple walls with legends of deities depicted in beautiful art form.

Kalamkari is derived from the word 'kalam', or pen, and is an elaborate method of painting with great details on cloth. It picturizes legends and mythology into art on cloth and is distinctive in its style.

Kalamkari painting has two styles: Srikalahasti (freehand drawing) and Machilipatnam (using block-printing technique).

The signature motif of 'Tree of Life' is an especially popular Kalamkari theme, recurring often in paintings. Animals and birds like peacocks, tigers, and deer are also frequently used as popular motifs.

Like many other traditional Indian crafts, Kalamkari uses only natural materials and vegetable dyes, and includes cotton cloth, dried unripe fruit and milk, charcoal sticks, alum, and natural pigments in red, indigo, and yellow.

Rajasthani Miniature

Rajasthani painting is a distinctive style of miniature art that flourished in the independent Hindu states of Rajasthan from the seventeenth to the nineteenth century.

It was patronized by the Rajputs, who were dominant at that time.

Among notable ones, the Mewar school of painting and Marwar school of painting were prominent during the eighteenth century. This type of painting was influenced by Western illustrations, while the Mughal style also played a part in the later years of its development. The subjects mainly depicted are based on the mythology of the Hindu god Krishna and his consort Radha.

There are also some paintings of the principal Hindu epics and spiritual texts. In the eighteenth century, court portraits and court scenes, as well as hunting scenes, became more common.

Patachitra

Patachitra refers to traditional cloth-based scroll painting found primarily in the eastern Indian states of Odisha and West Bengal. This art form is celebrated for its intricate details and vibrant depictions of mythological narratives and folktales. Raghurajpur, in Odisha, is noted for this art form and the artists showcase tremendous skill in their work. Their artwork consists of stories from Hindu mythology and about Lord Jagannath, the presiding deity of Puri.

Patachitra paintings are made on a special canvas where cotton cloth is layered with a tamarind paste and then coated with clay powder.

The artisans are so prolific and masters of this craft that when the cloth is dried and stable, the colours are filled in directly without initial drawings.

The colours are all natural, derived from natural sources like lamp soot and powdered conch shells. Each painting can take up to weeks or months to be completed.

Madhubani

Madhubani art is a type of painting practised in the Mithila region of India and is named after the Madhubani district of Bihar in India, where it originated.

Artists make these paintings in diverse mediums using their fingers, twigs, brushes, and matchsticks. The paint is made from natural dyes and pigments. The paintings showcase striking patterns created with geometric patterns.

Traditionally, Patachitra paintings were created on freshly plastered mud walls and floors of huts. However, they are now also produced on cloth, handmade paper, and canvas, expanding their accessibility and appeal.

Madhubani paintings are made from the paste of powdered rice. This art form has remained largely confined to a certain geographical area and the skill has passed down the centuries. Also, content and style have remained unaltered.

Batik

Although Batik is prolific at present in India, there is no historical record on when or from where this form of art originated, though it is held in greater importance in Southeast Asia and Indonesia.

Batik is created by applying wax to fabric using either a spouted tool to draw dots and lines or a copper stamp for printing. This process allows for intricate designs and patterns to be formed on the fabric. The applied wax is dye proof, and so the artisan can selectively colour by soaking the cloth in one colour, removing the wax with boiling water, and repeating if more colours are needed.

The most ancient evidence of Batik in India is found in the beautiful murals and paintings of the Ajanta and Ellora Caves in Maharashtra, where the graceful figures are depicted in fabrics with motifs similar to batik.

Manjusha Painting

This is another traditional Indian art form that belongs to the Bhagalpur region of Bihar. It is characterized by the intricate motifs and patterns, many with snakes which have symbolic value. The paint is made from natural dyes.

Kangra Painting

The Kangra Valley of Himachal Pradesh is renowned for its signature style of painting, known as Kangra. This style showcases delicate lines, soft muted colours and is based on the divine love between Radha and Lord Krishna.

Warli Painting

This is a tribal art form belonging to Maharashtra and is characterized by the dark monochrome stick-like figures. These are basically scenes from daily life and are created with white pigment on dark backgrounds. Nature too finds place in these paintings.

Where It All Began...

When you stop to admire a beautiful painting or an exquisite artwork, you may be amazed that the journey of art in its nascent form began aeons ago.

Cave paintings located in diverse regions of the world are proof of the quest for art in civilizations that dates back to centuries ago.

The primitive cave paintings are the first known recorded proof of humans expressing art in its very basic structure.

Archaeological sites have discovered ancient cave paintings, some of them are located in India.

CAVE PAINTINGS IN INDIA

Bhimbetka

The earliest evidence of art in South Asia, prehistoric cave paintings, was discovered in the Bhimbetka rock shelters of Raisen district in Madhya Pradesh.

This is a UNESCO World Heritage Site of seven hills with more than 750 rock shelters distributed over 10 km and are said to be more than 30,000 years old.

Ajanta

A UNESCO World Heritage Site, the Ajanta Caves situated in Aurangabad, Maharashtra, are notably Buddhist religious art and include enthralling paintings and rock-cut sculptures, describing the many moods and gestures of the Buddha and his disciples.

These are among the finest surviving pieces of ancient Indian art and were carved and painted in two phases, the first around the second century BCE and the latter from 400 to 650 CE.

Murals

What Is a Mural?

The history of Indian murals began in early medieval times, from the second century BC to the eighth–tenth century AD.

Approximately 20 locations in India feature murals from this period, primarily found in natural caves and rock-cut chambers. Notable sites include the Ajanta Caves, Bagh Caves, Sittanavasal Caves, and Armamalai Cave in Tamil Nadu, as well as the Kailasanatha temple in the Ellora Caves, along with sites in Ramgarh and Sitabinji.

Murals from this period primarily portray religious themes related to Buddhism, Jainism, and Hinduism, although some locations feature secular paintings as well. Among these is the Jogimara Cave in Chhattisgarh, the oldest known painted cave, along with the Sitabinji Caves, both dated between the third and first centuries BCE.

ROCK CARVED TEMPLES

Konark Sun Temple

The Konark Sun Temple, dedicated to Surya, the Hindu Sun God, is a thirteenth-century CE Hindu Sun temple at Konark, near Puri, a city in Odisha. The temple was built by King Narasingha Deva around 1250.

The temple complex is fairly large and is dominated by a stone carved 100-ft-high chariot with enormous wheels and horses. Spectacular in appearance, much of the main temple, that was about 200 ft high, has now turned into ruins with time.

Mahabalipuram

Mamallapuram, also known as Mahabalipuram, is located in Tamil Nadu, in South India. It is renowned for the UNESCO World Heritage Site of seventh-to eight-century rock-cut temples at Mahabalipuram. The ancient structure draws thousands of tourists. The temples are 'rathas' or chariots, mandapas (sanctuaries), and a giant rock relief on the outside which depicts the 'Descent of the Ganges'. There are also ancient *rock-cut* shore temples, most of which are now under the sea.

Elephanta Caves

The Elephanta Caves are situated on Elephanta Island, also known as Gharapuri Island, and feature two hillocks divided by a narrow valley. These rock-cut caves were built around the mid-fifth to sixth centuries AD, with Cave 1 being the most significant, measuring 39 m in length. Dominating the entrance to Cave 1 is the impressive 7-m-high sculpture of 'Sadashiva', which depicts the three aspects of Shiva: Creator, Preserver, and Destroyer.

SECTION 2

LITERARY ARTS

How Did Humans First Begin to Write?

Papyrus

Papyrus refers both to the writing material used in ancient times and to the plant from which it was made, known as *Cyperus papyrus*, commonly called the paper plant.

The papyrus plant was grown in the Nile Delta region of Egypt, where its stalks were harvested. The central pith of the stalk was cut into thin strips, pressed together, and dried to create a smooth, thin writing surface.

Paper made from papyrus was the chief writing material in ancient Egypt, was adopted by the Greeks, and was used extensively in the Roman Empire.

Parchment

Parchment, the processed skins of certain animals – chiefly sheep, goats, and calves – that were prepared for the purpose of writing on them.

Palm leaf manuscripts

Palm leaf manuscripts are, as the name suggests, made out of dried palm leaves. These were used as writing materials in India and Southeast Asia as far back as fifth century BC. They began to be used in other regions subsequently as texts on dried leaves of the Palmyra palm. Their use declined with the advent of the printing press in the nineteenth century when they were replaced by handwritten manuscripts.

A Sanskrit Shaivism text from the ninth century discovered in Nepal is among the oldest surviving palm leaf manuscripts.

Johannes Gutenberg

Johannes Gutenberg was a fourteenth-century German inventor, who invented printing from movable type. It was historic, since information through books and texts could now be made more accessible and available to ordinary people.

The Gutenberg Bible was the first complete book and the earliest printed from movable type, named the Gutenberg printer after its creator, in Germany. The three-volume work, presented in Latin text, was printed in 42-line columns and notably lacked a title page and page numbers.

LITERARY ARTS

What Is Literature?

Literature is often looked upon as a textual reflection of society. With time, it evolves and the characteristics also undergo change. What is predominantly active in society takes precedence and finds popularity with the people of that respective era. Across the world, we find this evident in the literature of any country.

Greek Literature

Homer (ninth or eight century BCE) was ancient Greek poet. Though almost nothing is known of his life, it is generally understood that Homer was blind. The ancient Greeks attributed the great epic poems 'The Iliad' and 'The Odyssey' to him.

'The Iliad', set against the backdrop of the Trojan War, narrates the story of Achilles' wrath, while 'The Odyssey' follows Odysseus's journey home after the war. Together, these two epics formed the foundation of Greek education and culture during the Classical era and continue to be among the most important works in the European literary tradition.

Russian Literature

The nineteenth century is one of the most fruitful periods in world literature and enjoyed as much importance and esteem in Russia as in the West.

Fyodor Dostoevsky (1821–81)

Dostoevsky was a Russian novelist and short-story writer known for his profound psychological insights and unsettling explorations of the human mind. His works, which navigate the darkest aspects of human nature alongside moments of enlightenment, had a significant influence on twentieth-century literature.

When imprisoned in Siberia for his political involvement, Dostoevsky wrote *Notes from the Underground*. In *Crime and Punishment*, a philosophical and a darkly psychological account of a murder, Dostoevsky reveals the mindset of the intelligentsia who thought themselves to be superior to ordinary people.

Leo Tolstoy (1828–1910)

Tolstoy is regarded among the greatest novelists in world literature.

His novels showcase his point that no theory is enough on its own to reveal the complexities of life, and which does not follow any pattern. He denied the existence of historical laws and insisted that ethics is a matter not of rules but of supreme sensitivity to the particular. His brilliant novels *War and Peace* and *Anna Karenina* are brilliant examples of his unique view of life.

Anton Pavlovich Chekhov (1860–1904)

He was a Russian playwright and a short-story writer. He wrote *Three Sisters* and *The Cherry Orchard* apart from other plays and stories. His plays are performed even today to a well-received audience.

Maxim Gorky (1868–1936)

Gorky was a Russian and Soviet writer and a proponent of Socialism, nominated five times for the Nobel Prize in Literature.

Gorky's most famous works are his early short stories, which include *Twenty Six Men and a Girl* and *The Lower Depths*. Gorky himself judged the novel Mother as among his works of failure. However, his *The Life of Klim Samgin* is considered a masterpiece by many critics.

Boris Pasternak (1890–1960)

Pasternak was a Russian poet who wrote the novel *Doctor Zhivago* and which brought him the Nobel Prize in Literature in 1958. However, it triggered so much antagonism in the Soviet Union that he had to decline the honour.

It is a remarkable story set in the unsettling times of the Russian Revolution with the merciless treatment of innocent victims. It combines incredible romance, poetic insight and is also a defining spiritual journey. It soon turned into a global sensation and was circulated secretly in his own country.

THE NOBEL PRIZE

Alfred Nobel (1833–96)

Alfred Nobel was a Swedish chemist, engineer, and industrialist best known for inventing dynamite and other powerful explosives. He also established the Nobel Prizes to recognize outstanding contributions to humanity in various fields.

The Nobel Prizes (five till 1969, when a sixth was added) are awarded annually from a fund bequeathed for that purpose by the Swedish inventor and industrialist Alfred Nobel.

In the will he wrote in 1895, Nobel directed that the majority of his fortune be allocated to a fund for awarding five annual prizes 'to those who, during the preceding year, shall have conferred the greatest benefit on mankind'.

The prizes may be withheld or not awarded if no deserving candidate, as defined by Nobel's will, can be identified, or if global circumstances hinder the collection of necessary information for making a decision, as occurred during the First and Second World Wars.

The prizes are accessible to everyone, regardless of nationality, race, creed, or ideology.

A recipient can receive the award multiple times. The ceremonial presentations for the prizes in physics, chemistry, physiology or medicine, literature, and economics occur in Stockholm, while the peace prize is awarded in Oslo, all on 10 December, the anniversary of Nobel's death. Laureates typically receive their prizes in person and are required to deliver a lecture during the award ceremonies.

The laureates usually receive their prizes in person, and each recipient delivers a lecture in connection with the award ceremonies.

The prizes are widely regarded as the most prestigious awards given for cerebral achievement in the world.

The Nobel Prize in Literature is awarded, as stipulated in the will of Alfred Bernhard Nobel, 'to those who, during the preceding year, shall have conferred the greatest benefit on mankind' in the realm of literature. The award is presented by the Swedish Academy in Stockholm.

Winners of the Nobel Prize in Literature with the Year They Were Awarded

- Rudyard Kipling 1907
- Rabindranath Tagore 1913
- George Bernard Shaw 1925
- Eugene O'Neill 1936
- Pearl Buck 1938
- T. S. Elliot 1948
- Boris Pasternak 1958 (Declined)
- Ernest Hemingway 1954
- Hermann Hesse 1946
- William Faulkner 1947
- Bertrand Russell 1950
- Albert Camus 1957
- John Steinbeck 1962
- Jean-Paul Sartre 1964
- Gabriel Garcia Marquez 1982
- Pablo Neruda 1971
- Orhan Pamuk 2006
- Kazuo Ishiguro 2017
- Peter Handke 2019
- Louise Gluck 2020
- Abdulrazak Gurnah 2021
- Arnie Ernaux 2022
- Jon Foss 2023

IMPACTFUL NOVELS

Every reader has their personal favourite novel or writer. Someone can be swept away by a searing story of a family drama, while someone else will be deeply moved by the harsh reality of war. Or, the novel could be about the Holocaust with its chilling horrors of torture and massacre, and then again, it could be based primarily on passion and romance.

Have you read any of these books that received global critical acclaim with their impressive story and striking characters?

Here are some novels chosen for their deep revelations of humankind, in love and war, in diverse situations and predicaments.

To Kill a Mockingbird by Harper Lee

Harper Lee's classic novel *To Kill a Mockingbird* (1960) won a Pulitzer Prize in 1961 and was made into an Academy Award-winning film the next year.

Harper Lee, regarded as one of the most influential authors, published only a single novel (until its controversial sequel was published in 2015 just before she passed away).

The novel explores racism in the American South through the innocent yet perceptive eyes of a clever young girl named Jean Louise (Scout) Finch. Its iconic characters, particularly the compassionate and fair-minded lawyer Atticus Finch, served as role models and helped shift perspectives in the United States during a period of intense racial tension.

To Kill a Mockingbird won the Pulitzer Prize for Fiction in 1961 and was made into an Academy Award-winning film in 1962.

Gone with the Wind by Margaret Mitchell

Gone with the Wind is a novel by American author Margaret Mitchell, first published in 1936. Set in Georgia during the American Civil War and the Reconstruction Era, the story follows the struggles of Scarlett O'Hara, a pampered daughter of a wealthy plantation owner.

This historical novel features a coming-of-age story and became a top American bestseller in 1937.

Mitchell received the Pulitzer Prize for the book in 1937. It has been a controversial subject for its reference to the South, both black and white.

It was adapted into a film with the same name in 1939. This film won the Academy Award for Best Picture at the twelfth annual Academy Awards ceremony.

Atlas Shrugged by Ayn Rand

Ayn Rand was a Russian-born American author known for her strong convictions. She developed a philosophical system called Objectivism. Born in Russia, she immigrated to the United States in 1926.

Her novel *Atlas Shrugged*, published in 1957, is her longest work and the fourth and final novel released during her lifetime. Rand referred to it as her 'magnum opus' in fiction, describing its theme as the 'role of man's mind in existence'. The novel incorporates elements of science fiction, mystery, and romance.

The novel explores philosophical themes of Objectivism. It dealt with reason, property rights, individualism, libertarianism, and capitalism; depicts what Rand saw as the failures of governmental coercion; and contains her most extensive statement of her philosophical system. The book describes a dystopian United States in which publicly traded companies suffer under increasingly burdensome laws and regulations. The novel was not received well when it was released but became increasingly popular later. It was instrumental in influencing the mindset of politicians and thinkers.

Anna Karenina by Leo Tolstoy

Anna Karenina is a novel by the Russian author Leo Tolstoy published in book form in 1878. Considered to be one of the greatest works of literature ever written, Tolstoy himself called it his first true novel.

The novel deals with themes of betrayal, faith, family, marriage, Imperial Russian society, desire, and the differences between rural and urban life. The story is about an extramarital affair between Anna and cavalry officer Count Alexei Kirillovich Vronsky that shocks the conservative society of St. Petersburg. The novel is set against the backdrop of the liberal reforms introduced by Emperor Alexander II of Russia and the swift societal changes that ensued. It has been adapted into various forms of media, including theatre, opera, film, television, ballet, figure skating, and radio drama.

The Great Gatsby by F. Scott Fitzgerald

F. Scott Fitzgerald's *The Gatsby* is singular as one of the most important novels for studying literature students. The novel is told from the perspective of a young man named Nick Carraway who has recently moved to New York City and is befriended by his eccentric nouveau riche neighbour with mysterious origins, Jay Gatsby.

The novel provides an insider's look into the Jazz Age of the 1920s in U.S. history and also critiquing the idea of the 'American Dream'.

One Hundred Years of Solitude by Gabriel Garcia Marquez

The late Colombian author Gabriel García Márquez published his most renowned work, *One Hundred Years of Solitude*, in 1967. The novel chronicles the story of seven generations of the Buendía family, tracing the founding of their town, Macondo, until its eventual destruction along with the last descendants of the family.

One Hundred Years of Solitude delves into the genre of magic realism, highlighting the extraordinary aspects of everyday life while presenting mystical elements as commonplace. Márquez underscores the significance and influence of myth and folklore in conveying history and reflecting Latin American culture.

The novel earned numerous awards for Márquez, ultimately leading to his receipt of the Nobel Prize in Literature in 1982, recognizing his entire body of work, with *One Hundred Years of Solitude* often regarded as his most celebrated achievement.

A Passage to India by E. M. Forster

E. M. Forster wrote his novel *A Passage to India* after several trips to India during his early life, and it was published in 1924. The story revolves around Dr. Aziz, a Muslim Indian, and his interactions with Cyril Fielding, an English professor, and Adela Quested, a visiting English schoolteacher.

When Adela comes to believe that Aziz has assaulted her during a trip to the Marabar Caves in the fictional city of Chandrapore, tensions between the Indian community and the British colonialists escalate. The novel explores the potential for friendship and connection between English and Indian individuals, despite the cultural differences and imperial tensions that exist between them.

Don Quixote by Miguel Cervantes

Miguel de Cervantes's *Don Quixote*, arguably the most famous work of Spanish literature, was published in full in 1615. The novel follows a man who adopts the name 'Don Quixote de la Mancha' and embarks on a quest driven by his obsession with romantic novels about chivalry, aiming to revive the tradition and become a hero himself.

The character of Don Quixote has become an iconic figure and an archetype, significantly influencing various major works of art, music, and literature since its publication. The impact of the text was so profound that the term 'quixotic' was coined, referring to someone who is 'foolishly impractical, especially in the pursuit of ideals; particularly characterized by rash, lofty romantic ideas or extravagantly chivalrous actions'.

Beloved by Toni Morrison

Toni Morrison's 1987 haunting novel *Beloved* is about Sethe, a slave who flees to Cincinnati, Ohio, in 1873. The novel looks deeply into the misery and despair of slavery even after becoming free.

The trauma suffered by Sethe and her emotional pain when she has to kill her own child, Beloved, from becoming a slave for life is described with searing effect.

The novel was praised for its exploration of the psychological effects of slavery and the significance of family and community in the healing process. *Beloved* received the Pulitzer Prize for Fiction in 1988.

Fahrenheit 451 by Ray Bradbury

Fahrenheit 451 is a dystopian novel by American writer Ray Bradbury, published in 1953. It depicts a future American society where books are banned, and 'firemen' are tasked with burning any that are discovered. The story is told from the perspective of Guy Montag, a fireman who becomes disillusioned with his role in censoring literature and destroying knowledge. He eventually resigns from his job and dedicates himself to preserving literary and cultural works.

Bradbury wrote *Fahrenheit 451* during the Second Red Scare and the McCarthy era, drawing inspiration from the book burnings in Nazi Germany and ideological repression in the Soviet Union. His stated motivation for writing the novel has evolved over the years. In a 1956 radio interview, he mentioned that his concern about the potential for book burnings in the United States prompted him to write the book.

Later, he characterized the novel as a commentary on how mass media diminishes interest in reading literature. Bradbury also connected the themes of censorship in the book to political correctness, calling it 'the real enemy these days' and labelling it as a form of 'thought control and freedom of speech control'.

Jane Eyre by Charlotte Bronte

Charlotte Brontë's *Jane Eyre* was first published in 1847 under the pseudonym Currer Bell to conceal the author's identity as a woman. Fortunately, perceptions have shifted significantly since then, and Brontë is now recognized for her contribution to one of the most groundbreaking novels about women in history.

At a time when female authors often felt compelled to hide their identities, *Jane Eyre* presents a narrative of women's empowerment and individualism. The titular character evolves from an orphaned, impoverished girl into a successful and independent woman. This novel combines elements of Gothic and Victorian literature, revolutionizing the genre by emphasizing Jane's personal growth and determination.

INDIAN LITERATURE

From the Beginning...

The earliest Indian literature took the form of the sacred texts of Hinduism, known as the *Vedas*, which were composed in Sanskrit. This was followed by prose commentaries on the *Brahmanas* and the *Upanishads*. Sanskrit literature thrived from around 1500 BCE to about 1000 CE, reaching its peak development between the first and seventh centuries CE. Since Sanskrit was closely associated with the Brahmanical religion of the *Vedas*, other religious traditions like Buddhism and Jainism adopted different literary languages, such as Pali and Ardhamagadhi. These languages, along with other related dialects, eventually contributed to the formation of modern languages in northern India.

Indian literature was heavily influenced by two major Sanskrit epic poems: the *Mahabharata* and the *Ramayana*, as well as the *Bhagavata Purana* and other *Puranas*.

The South Indian language of Tamil is an exception to this pattern of Sanskrit influence because it has a classical tradition of its own.

Beginning in the nineteenth century, particularly during the height of British control over the subcontinent, Western literary models influenced Indian literature, mostly on the use of vernacular prose on a major scale. Literary forms like the novel and short story were adopted by Indian writers, along with realism and raising social questions and psychological descriptions.

Kalidasa

Kalidasa, a renowned Sanskrit poet and dramatist from the fifth century CE, is often considered one of the greatest Indian writers across all time periods. His remarkable works include the dramas *Shakuntala*, *Meghaduta*, and *Kumarasambhava*, among others.

Little is known about Kalidasa's personal life, and while his poems provide some hints, they do not explicitly confirm his background as a Brahman. He appears to embody a blend of liberal thought while remaining committed to traditional Hindu beliefs. His name, which translates to 'Servant of Kali', suggests that he was a Shaivite, a follower of Lord Shiva (whose consort is Kali). However, he also pays homage to other deities, particularly Vishnu, in his works.

Kabir (1440–1518)

Kabir was an Indian poet and mystic, revered as a poet-saint by Hindus, Muslims, and Sikhs. His birth is shrouded in mystery and it is also uncertain who his parents were. According to one legend, his mother, who was an unwed Brahman, abandoned Kabir. He was found and adopted by a Muslim weaver. He was later strongly influenced by a Hindu ascetic. Thus, he was transformed by both religions.

Kabir is considered as impartial to community biases and as one who integrates both Hindu and Muslim beliefs into his work. Yet, he was also critical of both in equal measure, seeing them as parallel in their erroneous ways. He believed in complete faith in the main truth of life, and Kabir's rhythmic couplets found many followers for their impactful wisdom.

Surdas

Surdas was a sixteenth-century blind Hindu devotional poet and singer renowned for his poetry dedicated to Lord Krishna. His compositions predominantly used the Braj language, though he also wrote in other medieval Hindi dialects, such as Awadhi. Surdas's works express deep devotion and love for Krishna, capturing the essence of bhakti (devotional) literature in India.

Tulsidas (1511–1623)

Tulsidas was a revered Hindu saint and poet known for his deep devotion to Lord Rama. He composed works in various languages, including Sanskrit, Awadhi, and Braj Bhasha, but he is most famous for the *Hanuman Chalisa* and the epic *Ramcharitmanas*, which is a vernacular retelling of the Sanskrit *Ramayana* that narrates the life of Rama in Awadhi.

Tulsidas spent a significant portion of his life in Banaras (Varanasi) and Ayodhya, and the Tulsi Ghat along the Ganges in Varanasi is named in his honour. He also initiated the

Ramlila drama, a folk-theatre adaptation of the *Ramayana*, which continues to be performed in various forms today.

Vidyapati (1352–1448)

Vidyapati was a renowned poet and saint from the Maithili tradition, celebrated for his contributions as a playwright, composer, biographer, philosopher, and royal priest. He wrote in multiple languages, including Sanskrit, Prakrit, Apabhramsha, and Maithili. His literary influence extended beyond Maithili and Sanskrit, impacting various eastern Indian literary traditions. Vidyapati is particularly known for his devotional poetry dedicated to Lord Shiva and his romantic verses that explore themes of love and longing, solidifying his place as a pivotal figure in Indian literature.

THE INDIAN EPICS

Ramayana

The *Ramayana* was composed in Sanskrit by the poet Valmiki around 300 BCE and in its present form consists of about 24,000 couplets divided into seven volumes. The poem describes the birth of Lord Rama in the kingdom of Ayodhya, the training received by him from sage Vishwamitra, and the bow-and-arrow contest in which he won Sita as his bride. When Rama is banished as heir from the kingdom, he is accompanied by Lakshman, his brother, to spend 14 years in exile.

In the forest, when Rama and Lakshman are tricked into hunting a deer, Ravana, the demon king of Lanka, abducts Sita. Rama and Lakshman set out to rescue her.

The epic is about this journey and its conflicts and trials. Sugriva, a monkey god with an enormous team, assists Rama in the thrilling rescue of Sita. However, she has to face a trial by fire to prove her fidelity. The people of Ayodhya question the queen's chastity and Rama banishes her to the forest where she meets the sage Valmiki (who wrote the *Ramayana*) and gives birth to Rama's sons. Rama and Sita are reunited when the sons come of age, but still being looked upon with doubt, Sita is embraced and swallowed by Earth, her mother.

Mahabharata

The *Mahabharata* is an epic written around 400 BCE and is regarded by Hindus as a religious text about 'dharma' and is a record of events of that era. It is centric to the theme of the struggle for sovereignty between two groups of cousins, the Kauravas (sons of Dhritarashtra, descendant of Kuru) and the Pandavas (sons of Pandu). The poem is made up of almost 100,000 couplets, divided into 18 sections. Traditionally, it has been ascribed to the sage Ved Vyasa.

The story is about the rivalry and battles, with many twists and turns, between the two groups. The feud culminates in a series of great battles on the field of Kurukshetra when the Kauravas are completely destroyed while only the five Pandava brothers and Krishna survive.

What Is Indian Literature?

Indian Literature includes writings in the country in a variety of vernacular languages that include Sanskrit, Prakrit, Pali, Bengali, Bihari, Gujarati, Hindi, Kannada, Kashmiri, Malayalam, Oriya, Punjabi, Rajasthani, Tamil, Telugu, Urdu, Lahnda, Saraiki, and Sindhi, among others, as well as English. Initially, the texts were basically religious and were then followed by writings in Science, Maths, Astronomy, Poetry, and Drama.

ANCIENT INDIAN LITERATURE

The earliest Indian literature consisted of the sacred texts of Hinduism known as the

Vedas, which were composed in Sanskrit. These texts were supplemented by prose commentaries, including the *Brahmanas* and the *Upanishads*. Sanskrit literature flourished from around 1500 BCE to approximately 1000 CE, reaching its peak between the first and seventh centuries CE.

In addition to sacred and philosophical works, the literary landscape expanded to include various genres such as devotional poetry, court poetry, plays, and narrative folktales. Since Sanskrit was closely linked to the Brahmanical traditions of the *Vedas*, other religions, like Buddhism and Jainism, adopted different literary languages – Pali and Ardhamagadhi, respectively. These developments contributed to the emergence of modern languages in northern India.

The literature of those languages depended largely on ancient Indian background, which includes two Sanskrit epic poems, the *Mahabharata* and the *Ramayana*, as well as the *Bhagavata Purana* and the other *Puranas*.

Additionally, the Sanskrit philosophies were the source of philosophical writing in later literature, and the Sanskrit schools of rhetoric were of great importance for the development of court poetry in much of the modern literature.

Tamil

The South Indian language of Tamil is an exception to this pattern of Sanskrit influence because it has a classical tradition of its own. It is a Dravidian language native to the Tamil people of South Asia. Tamil is the official language of the Indian state of Tamil Nadu and union territory of Puducherry, and is also spoken by a significant population in Kerala, Karnataka, Andhra Pradesh, Telangana, and the Andaman and Nicobar Islands. One of 22 scheduled languages in the Constitution of India, Tamil was the first to be classified as a classical language of India.

Tamil is one of the longest-surviving classical languages in the world, renowned for its rich literary tradition. The variety and quality of classical Tamil literature have earned it a place among the great classical traditions and literatures of the world.

Recorded Tamil literature has a history spanning over 2,000 years, with the earliest period dated from 300 BCE to 300 CE. The oldest epigraphic records, found on rock edicts and 'hero stones', date back to around the third century BCE. This extensive literary heritage reflects the cultural and historical significance of the Tamil language and its literature.

HINDI LITERATURE

Hindi literature began to emerge in the seventh century AD, achieving a consistent form by the tenth century. Most of the earlier literary works were composed in verse and used dialects other than Khari Boli, which forms the basis for modern Hindi and Urdu. Khari Boli did not gain prominence as a literary language until the late seventeenth century. Meanwhile, Braj continued to be a popular medium for poetry until the late nineteenth century, after which Khari Boli became the dominant form. This shift highlights the anomaly that the language of modern Hindi literature differs significantly from that of earlier periods.

Munshi Premchand (1880–1936)

Premchand was an Indian writer famous for his modern Hindi literature. He was a pioneer of Hindi and Urdu social fiction and was one of the first authors to write about caste hierarchies and the plights of women and labourers prevalent in the society of the late 1880s. His works include *Godaan*, *Karmabhoomi*, *Gaban*, *Mansarovar*, and

Idgah. He wrote more than 12 novels, 300 short stories, and many essays, and translated many foreign works into Hindi.

Amrita Pritam (1919–2005)

Amrita Pritam was an Indian novelist, essayist, and poet, who wrote in Punjabi and Hindi. She is a renowned writer in Punjabi literature and has written around 100 books of poetry, essays, Punjabi folk songs, which have been translated into several Indian and foreign languages. Her most famous work was *Pinjer* in 1950, in which she wrote about violence against women. It was adapted into a film with the same name.

After the Partition, Pritam migrated from Lahore to India. She won the Sahitya Akademi Award in 1956, and is the sole woman to have been awarded for a work in Punjabi. She received the Jnanpith Award, one of India's highest literary awards in 1982, and was also awarded the Padma Shri in 1969 and the Padma Vibhushan in 2004. In that same year she was honoured with India's highest literary award, the Sahitya Akademi Fellowship, for lifetime achievement.

Bhisham Sahni (1915–2003)

Bhisham Sahni was an acclaimed Indian writer, playwright, and actor, best known for his novel and television screenplay *Tamas*, which offers a poignant and powerful depiction of the Partition of India. In recognition of his contributions to literature, he was awarded the Padma Bhushan in 1998 and the Sahitya Akademi Fellowship in 2002. Sahni was actively involved in various literary and cultural organizations, further enriching India's literary landscape.

Geetanjali Shree (Born 1957)

Geetanjali Shree is an Indian Hindi-language novelist and short-story writer based in New Delhi, India. She is the author of several short stories and five novels. In 2022, her novel *Ret Samadhi* (2018), translated into English as *Tomb of Sand* by Daisy Rockwell, won the International Booker Prize.

Apart from those mentioned, there are other eminent writers in Hindi literature that include Mahadevi Verma, Harivansh Rai Bachchan, Jaishankar Prasad, Suryakant Tripathi 'Nirala', Ramdhari Singh Dinkar, Dharamveer Bharti, and Krishna Sobti.

BENGALI LITERATURE

Bibhutibhushan Bandyopadhyay (1894–1950)

Bibhutibhushan Bandyopadhyay was a Bengali writer whose best-known works include *Pather Panchali*, *Chander Pahar*, and along with other eminent ones such as *Adarsha Hindu Hotel* and *Ichamati*. *Pather Panchali* brought the writer immense prestige in Bengali literature. *Pather Panchali* and its sequels, *Aparajito* and *Apur Sansar*, were made into films by Satyajit Ray to form the renowned *Apu trilogy*.

Bankim Chandra Chatterjee (1838–94)

Bankim Chandra Chatterjee was a prominent Indian novelist and poet, renowned for his 1882 Bengali novel *Anandamath*, which is considered a landmark in modern Bengali and Indian literature. He is also celebrated for composing 'Vande Mataram', a poem in Sanskrit that personifies India as a Mother Goddess and inspired many during the Indian independence movement. In addition to his novels, Chatterjee wrote several critical treatises in Bengali, significantly contributing to the literary and cultural landscape of India.

Sarat Chandra Chatterjee (1876–1938)

Sarat Chandra Chatterjee was a Bengali novelist and short-story writer of the early twentieth century and wrote in simple lucid language about the lives of ordinary people in cities and villages. His sharp skill in observing people and their behaviour, the joys and despair, reveals his excellent understanding of human nature.

Ishwar Chandra Vidyasagar (1820–91)

Ishwar Chandra Vidyasagar was an Indian educator and social reformer of the nineteenth century and made immense contributions to modernize Bengali prose. He simplified the Bengali alphabet by structuring it in a simple and interesting way and is a landmark in Bengali literature. He was a strong campaigner for Hindu widow remarriage and also against child marriage.

Mahasweta Devi (1926–2016)

Mahasweta Devi was a renowned Bengali writer and activist, celebrated for her impactful literary contributions in Bengali. Among her notable works are *Hajar Churashir Maa*, *Rudali*, and *Aranyer Adhikar*. She dedicated her efforts to advocating for the rights and empowerment of tribal communities across West Bengal, Bihar, Madhya Pradesh, and Chhattisgarh. In recognition of her significant contributions to literature and social activism, she received several prestigious awards, including the Sahitya Akademi Award (in Bengali), the Jnanpith Award, and the Ramon Magsaysay Award, as well as India's esteemed civilian honours, the Padma Shri and Padma Vibhushan.

INDIAN AWARDS FOR LITERATURE

The Jnanpith Award is the oldest and highest award in literature that was instituted in 1961 and is awarded to the best creative literary writing by writers in any of the 22 languages and English, recognized in the Constitution. The award is presented annually.

The Sahitya Akademi Award is the second-highest literary award and was instituted in 1954. It is awarded to those who have achieved literary merit through their works in poetry and prose, in any of the 24 major languages recognized by the Akademi.

INDIAN REFORMERS AND GLOBAL ICONS

Raja Ram Mohan Roy (1772–1833)

Raja Ram Mohan Roy was an Indian reformer and one of the founders of the Brahmo Sabha in 1828, the precursor of the Brahmo Samaj, a social-religious reform movement in the Indian subcontinent. His remarkable influence was apparent in the fields of politics, public administration, education, and religion. He is renowned for his efforts to abolish the malpractices of sati and child marriage.

The Brahmo Samaj was one of the most influential religious movements in India and was instrumental in the development of modern India. Ram Mohan Roy's impact on modern Indian history was his revival of the pure and ethical principles of the Vedanta school of philosophy as found in the *Upanishads*. He preached the unity of God, made early translations of Vedic scriptures into English.

The Brahmo Samaj played a major role in reforming and modernizing Indian society. He successfully campaigned against sati, the practice of burning widows. He established a number of schools to popularize a modern system of education in India and thus is considered the 'Father of the Indian Renaissance' by many historians.

Swaml Vivekanand (1863–1902)

Born Narendranath Datta, Swami Vivekananda was a Hindu monk, philosopher, religious teacher, and the chief disciple of Shree Ramakrishna, the mystic. He was a key figure in the introduction of Vedanta and Yoga to the Western world. The father of modern Indian nationalism, he is credited with raising interfaith awareness and bringing Hinduism to the status of a major world religion. Vivekananda was inclined from a young age toward religion and spirituality. He later found his guru Ramakrishna and became a monk.

After the death of Ramakrishna, Vivekananda extensively toured the country to acquire first-hand knowledge of the living conditions of Indian people of that time, in British-ruled India. Moved by their plight, he travelled to the United States at the 1893 Parliament of Religions in Chicago, where he delivered his distinguished speech beginning with 'Sisters and brothers of America ...' while introducing Hinduism to Americans. Vivekananda delivered many lectures across the United States, England, and Europe, disseminating the core tenets of Hindu philosophy.

In India, Vivekananda founded the Ramakrishna Math, which provides spiritual training for monastics and householder devotees, and the Ramakrishna Mission, which provides charity and social work. He was also a major force in contemporary Hindu reform movements and contributed to the concept of nationalism in colonial India. He is now widely regarded as one of the most influential people of modern India and a patriotic saint.

INDIANS WRITING IN ENGLISH

Beginning in the nineteenth century, particularly during the height of British control over the subcontinent, Western literary models had an impact on Indian literature, the most striking result being the introduction of the use of vernacular prose on a major scale. Such forms as the novel and short story started to be adopted by Indian writers, as did realism and an interest in social questions and psychological description. A tradition of literature in English was also established in the subcontinent.

Vikram Seth (Born 1952)

Seth is an Indian novelist and poet. He has won prestigious awards such as Padma Shri,

Sahitya Akademi Award, and more. Seth has published books on poetry and some novels. In 1980, he wrote *Mappings*, his first book of poetry. The publication of *A Suitable Boy*, a 1,349-page long novel, turned Seth into a literary sensation. It was adapted into a television drama series later. His novel, *An Equal Music*, deals with the troubled love-life of a violinist.

His poetry book *The Golden Gate* became a hit with readers in India and abroad.

Salman Rushdie (Born 1947)

Salman Rushdie is an Indian-born British-American novelist. His work is a mixture of vivid imagery and fiction based on history. Rushdie's novel, *Midnight's Children* (1981), won the Booker Prize in 1981. After the publication of his novel, *The Satanic Verses*, Rushdie became the target of fanatic conservatives and a fatwa calling for his death was issued by Ayatollah Ruhollah Khomeini, a religious leader of Iran. In 2022, a man stabbed Rushdie after rushing onto the stage where the novelist was scheduled to deliver a lecture in Chautauqua, New York. He subsequently published a novel *Knife* based on this shocking incident.

V. S. Naipaul (1932–2018)

Sir Vidiadhar Surajprasad Naipaul, or V. S. Naipaul, was an Indian origin Trinidad-born writer of works of fiction and nonfiction in English. He wrote in prose that was widely admired, but his views sometimes also aroused controversy. Naipaul's breakthrough novel *A House for Mr Biswas* was published in 1961. Naipaul won the Booker Prize in 1971 for his novel *In a Free State* and was awarded the Nobel Prize in Literature in 2001.

R. K. Narayan (1906–2001)

R. K. Narayan was an Indian writer and novelist known for his work set in the fictional South Indian town of Malgudi. Narayan wrote the very popular semi-autobiographical trilogy of *Swami and Friends, The Bachelor of Arts,* and *The English Teacher*. The fictional town of Malgudi was first introduced in *Swami and Friends* and then made into a highly popular and successful television series. His novel *The Guide* was made into a film with the same name which won a Filmfare Award for Best Film.

Narayan wrote on the social context and everyday life of his characters by mixing the content with humour and wit. He received many awards, including the Padma Vibhushan and the Padma Bhushan, India's second- and third-highest civilian awards, and the Sahitya Akademi Fellowship, the highest honour of India's National Academy of Letters.

Mulk Raj Anand (1905–2004)

Mulk Raj Anand was an Indian writer in English, recognized for his depiction of the lives of the poorer castes in traditional Indian society. One of the pioneers of Indo-Anglian literature, he was one of the first India-based writers in English to gain a global readership. Anand is admired for his novels and short stories, noted for their perceptive insight into the lives of the oppressed and for their analysis of impoverishment, exploitation, and misfortune. His novel *Untouchable* focused on the inhuman conditions borne by lower castes and their ostracizing from society. He was awarded the Padma Bhushan.

Arundhati Roy (Born 1961)

Arundhati Roy is an acclaimed Indian writer, recognized primarily for her debut novel, *The God of Small Things*, published in 1997. This remarkable work won the Booker Prize for Fiction that same year and went on to become the best-selling book by a non-expatriate Indian author. In addition to her literary achievements,

Roy is a dedicated political activist, actively engaged in various human rights and environmental issues.

Aravind Adiga (Born 1974)

Aravind Adiga is an Indian writer and journalist. His debut novel, *The White Tiger*, won the 2008 Man Booker Prize, the fourth Indian-born author to win the prize. The book received critical acclaim and was made into a film.

Amitav Ghosh (Born 1956)

Amitav Ghosh is a prominent Indian author who received the prestigious Jnanpith Award in 2018, recognized as India's highest literary honour. Ghosh's intricate novels employ sophisticated narrative techniques to explore the complexities of both national and personal identities, particularly within the context of India and South Asia. His body of work includes historical fiction and nonfiction that addresses significant themes such as colonialism and climate change. Notably, his *Ibis Trilogy* delves into the events surrounding the First Opium War and its far-reaching consequences. Ghosh has been honoured with two Lifetime Achievement Awards, four honorary doctorates, and was conferred the Padma Shri in 2007.

Jhumpa Lahiri (Born 1967)

Jhumpa Lahiri is an Indian-origin British-American author known for her short stories, novels, and essays in English and, more recently, in Italian. Her debut collection of short stories, *Interpreter of Maladies* (1999), won the Pulitzer Prize for Fiction and her first novel, *The Namesake* (2003), was adapted into the popular film of the same name. She has also translated some of her own writings and those of other authors from Italian into English.

ENGLISH LITERATURE

William Shakespeare (1564–1616)

William Shakespeare was a poet and dramatist and considered by many to be the greatest dramatist of all time. Shakespeare's plays, written in the late sixteenth and early seventeenth centuries for a small local theatre, are now performed and read more often and in more countries than ever before.

His enormous body of work consists of 39 plays, 154 sonnets, and three long narrative poems apart from some collaborative writings. His plays have been translated into every major language and he remains without a doubt the most influential writer in the English language, while his works continue to be studied and reinterpreted.

Shakespeare produced most of his well-known works between 1589 and 1613. His early plays were primarily comedies and histories and are regarded as some of the best works produced in these genres. He then wrote mainly tragedies until 1608, among them *Romeo and Juliet*, *Hamlet*, *Othello*, *King Lear*, and *Macbeth*. In the last phase of his life, he wrote tragicomedies like *The Winter's Tale* and *The Tempest.*

Christopher Marlowe (1564–93)

Marlowe was an English playwright, poet of the Elizabethan era, and was the first to achieve critical acclaim for his use of 'blank Verse', which became the standard for the era. His plays are distinguished by their heroes.

Jane Austen (1775–1817)

Jane Austen was an English novelist known primarily for her six novels placed at the end of the eighteenth century. Austen's plots often explore the dependence of women on marriage for the pursuit of favourable social standing and economic security. Her deft use of social commentary, realism, and biting irony have earned her acclaim among critics and scholars. Her novels *Sense and Sensibility*, *Pride and Prejudice*, *Mansfield Park*, and *Emma* are her critique of society and its predetermined consensus on women and the way of life. She wrote two other novels, *Northanger Abbey* and *Persuasion* apart from other writings and an unfinished novel.

George Eliot (1819–80)

Mary Ann Evans is known by her pen name George Eliot. Since women writers were not favoured or encouraged at that time, she wrote under a male name. She was an English novelist, poet, journalist, translator, and one of the leading writers of her time. She wrote seven novels, including the well-known *The Mill on the Floss.*

The Brontë Sisters

Charlotte (1816–55), **Emily** (1818–48), and **Anne Brontë** (1820–49) were renowned poets and novelists who made significant contributions to literature. Like many of their female contemporaries, they chose to publish their works under male pseudonyms. Their writings garnered immediate attention for their passionate themes and originality. Charlotte's *Jane Eyre* was the first to achieve notable success, while Emily's *Wuthering Heights* and Anne's *The Tenant of Wildfell Hall*, along with other works, were later celebrated as masterpieces of literature, gaining recognition after their deaths.

Sir Arthur Conan Doyle (1859–1930)

Arthur Conan Doyle was a British author and physician, best known for introducing the iconic character Sherlock Holmes in *A Study in Scarlet*, published in 1887. This work marked the beginning of a series that includes four novels and 56 short stories featuring Holmes and Dr. Watson, which have become landmarks in the crime fiction genre.

Doyle was a prolific writer whose literary contributions extended beyond the Sherlock Holmes series. He wrote in various genres, including fantasy, science fiction, humour, plays, romances, poetry, nonfiction, and historical novels.

Virginia Woolf (1882–1941)

Woolf is considered one of the most important modern twentieth-century authors. She pioneered the 'stream of consciousness' method as a narrative form.

Woolf began writing professionally in 1900. Her best-known works include the novels *Mrs Dalloway* (1925) and *To the Lighthouse* (1927). She is also known for her essays such as "A Room of One's Own" (1929). Her works, translated into more than 50 languages, have attracted attention and widespread commentary for inspiring feminism.

A very unconventional novel, *Mrs Dalloway* describes exactly one day in the life of British socialite, Clarissa Dalloway. Using a combination of third-person narration and thoughts of various characters, the novel uses a stream-of-consciousness style. The result is a deeply personal and revealing look into the characters' minds, relying on them rather than a plot to tell its story. The thoughts of the characters include constant regrets and thoughts of the past, struggles with mental illness and post-traumatic stress from the First World War, and the effect of social pressures.

ENGLISH POETRY

Romantic Poets

John Keats (1795–1821)

John Keats was an English Romantic lyric poet whose poetry was marked by vivid imagery and sensuous appeal and, at the same, expanding on philosophy using classical legends. His classic odes define poetic supremacy. They are essentially lyrical meditations on an object or quality that compel the poet to reflect upon his own longings and their connections to the world outside. This was forced upon Keats when his brother passed away and his own failing health. His struggle for self-awareness and certainty through the liberating powers of his imagination are vividly portrayed in his odes. These poems, with their rich, exquisitely sensuous detail and deep meditative thoughts, are gems in Romantic poetry.

Lord Byron (1788–1824)

George Gordon Byron was a British Romantic poet and satirist whose poetry and personality captured the imagination of Europe. Renowned as the 'gloomy egoist' of his autobiographical poem 'Childe Harold's Pilgrimage' in the nineteenth century, he is now more attributed for the satiric realism of Don Juan. Byron's writings are more patently autobiographical than even those of his fellow self-revealing Romantics. He became aware of reality's imperfections, but the scepticism and cynicism bred of his disillusionment coexisted with a lifelong propensity to seek ideal perfection in all of life's experiences.

Percy Bysshe Shelley (1792–1822)

Percy Bysshe Shelley was an English writer who is considered as one of the major English Romantic poets but did not achieve fame during his lifetime. Recognition came his way only after his death, and he became an important influence on subsequent generations of poets. His poetic imagery, mastery of genres and verse forms, and the stirring visuals thrown up in his choice of words are par excellence. Shelley also wrote fiction and several essays on political, social, and philosophical issues. His famous line 'O wind, if winter comes, can spring be far behind?' conjure in the mind of the reader a picture of a thousand words.

William Wordsworth (1770–1850)

William Wordsworth was an English poet and the primary representative of the English Romantic revolution in poetry. His contribution to it was threefold – he formulated, in his poems and his essays, a new attitude toward nature. He also probed deeply into his own sensibility about the 'growth of a poet's mind' in *The Prelude*. It was the first long autobiographical poem. Third, he placed poetry at the centre of human experience, 'it is as immortal as the heart of man'. 'The Daffodils' is a stirring lyrical poem on the beauty of nature and the deep pleasure that a field of daffodil flowers arouses in the poet.

Lord Alfred Tennyson (1809–92)

Tennyson was an English poet whose composition 'Timbuktu' was among his first poems. He also wrote short lyrics such as 'Break, Break, Break', and 'The Charge of the Light Brigade', among others. Much of his verse was based on classical myths such as 'Ulysses'. Tennyson also wrote notable blank verse 'Tithonus' and 'Idylls of the King'. Though he attempted drama, his plays enjoyed little success.

Samuel Taylor Coleridge (1772–1834)

Coleridge was an English poet, literary critic, philosopher, and theologian who was a founder of the Romantic movement in England. He was also a member of the Lake Poets. He wrote 'The Rime of the Ancient Mariner' and 'Kubla Khan' and coined many words and phrases like 'suspension of disbelief'.

LEGENDARY AMERICAN WRITERS

John Steinbeck (1902–68)

Steinbeck was an American writer who won the Nobel Prize in Literature in 1962 for his realistic and imaginative writings. He wrote 33 books, including 16 novels, six nonfiction books, and two collections of short stories. His novels *Cannery Row, East of Eden,* and *Of Mice and Men* are well known. *His Grapes of Wrath* won him the Pulitzer Prize in 1939. Most of Steinbeck's work is set in the Salinas Valley of California.

Arthur Miller (1915–2005)

Miller was an American playwright, essayist, and screenwriter. His most popular plays include *All My Sons* (1947), *Death of a Salesman* (1949), *The Crucible* (1953), and *A View from the Bridge* (1955). He wrote several screenplays, including *The Misfits* (1961). Miller received the Pulitzer Prize for Drama for the drama *Death of a Salesman* which is considered one of the best American plays of the twentieth century.

Eugene O'Neill (1888–1953)

Eugene O'Neill, an American playwright, wrote plays that were among the first to introduce drama techniques of realism. He was awarded the Nobel Prize in Literature in1936. O'Neill is also the only playwright to win four Pulitzer Prize for Drama. O'Neill's plays were among the first to include speeches in American English vernacular and involve characters on the fringes of society.

AMERICAN POETS

Maya Angelou (1928–2014)

Angelou was an American poet, and civil rights activist. She received several awards and more than 50 honorary degrees. Angelou's series of seven autobiographies focuses on her childhood and early adult experiences. The first, *I Know Why the Caged Bird Sings* (1969) brought her international recognition and acclaim. She then publicly discussed aspects of her personal life. She was respected as a spokesperson for Black people and women, and her works are widely used in schools and universities worldwide.

Emily Dickinson (1830–86)

Dickinson was an American poet who was lesser known in her lifetime and gained importance later. Though a prolific writer her only publications during her lifetime were 10 of her nearly 1,800 poems and on letter. Her poems were unique for her era: they had short lines, typically lacking title Many of her poems deal with themes of death and immortality.

Thomas Stearns Eliot (1888–1965)

Thomas Stearns Eliot was a poet, essayist, and a playwright. He is considered among the greatest poets of the twentieth century and also a key persona in Modernist English poetry. His language, writing style, and verse structure brought new life to English poetry. He is also noted for his critical essays, which re-looked at long-held cultural traditions.

Eliot first attracted widespread attention for his poem 'The Love Song of J Alfred Prufrock' which was followed by 'The Waste Land', 'The Hollow Men', and 'Ash Wednesday'. He wrote seven plays which included *Murder in the Cathedral* and *The Cocktail Party*. He was awarded the Nobel Prize in Literature in 1948.

Several women were awarded the Nobel Prize in Literature.

Among them are...

Pearl S. Buck

Nelly Sachs

Nadine Gordimer

Toni Morrison

Doris Lessing

Alice Munro

Svetlana Alexievich

Olga Tokarczuk

Louise Glück

Annie Ernaux

EMINENT INDIANS

Mahatma Gandhi (1869–1948)

Mohandas Karamchand Gandhi was an Indian lawyer, strongly against colonial rule, a devoted patriot and political activist using nonviolence as an effective means to fight for India's independence from British rule. He inspired movements for civil rights and freedom across the world. The honorific Mahatma was bestowed on him for his extraordinary contribution to India's struggle for independence. Gandhi's birthday, 2 October, is commemorated in India as Gandhi Jayanti, a national holiday.

Gandhi was one of the greatest national and civil rights leaders of the twentieth century and is internationally esteemed for his nonviolent protest (satyagraha) to achieve political success. This model of nonviolent protest has inspired civil rights leaders across the world, such as Martin Luther King, Jr. and Nelson Mandela.

Rabindranath Tagore (1861–1941)

Tagore was a Bengali poet, writer, playwright, composer, philosopher, social reformer, and painter. He was instrumental in reshaping Bengali literature, music, and art in the late nineteenth and early twentieth centuries. He wrote *Gitanjali*, an offering of lyrical poems, and was awarded the Nobel Prize in Literature in 1913. He was the first non-European to win the Nobel in Literature.

In 1901, he founded the 'Shantiniketan' (Abode of Peace) in Bolpur, West Bengal, where the unique concept of a distinctive blend of the best of Indian and Western traditions would be amalgamated and taught to the students. It became Viswa-Bharati University subsequently. Tagore began experimenting with painting in his late sixties and his paintings captured the essence of nature and the human form in their purest forms. They embody his spiritual connection with nature and the world around him.

Tagore modernized Bengali literature with his stirring novels, lyrical poems, melodious songs, enchanting dance dramas, and lucid, enlightening essays. He wrote on pertinent topics that were predominant in society: caste system, political bias, women's empowerment, patriotism, and more.

He composed India's national anthem 'Jana Gana Mana' and Bangladesh's 'Amar Shonar Bangla' while Sri Lanka's national anthem is inspired by Tagore. His song 'Banglar Mati, Banglar Jal' is now the state anthem of West Bengal.

Sarojini Naidu (1879–1949)

Naidu was a political activist, feminist, poet, and the first Indian woman to be president of the Indian National Congress and to be appointed an Indian state governor. She was called 'the Nightingale of India'. Sarojini Naidu also led an active literary life and attracted notable Indian intellectuals to her famous salon in Bombay (now Mumbai). Her first volume of poetry, *The Golden Threshold* (1905), was followed by *The Bird of Time* (1912), and in 1914 she was elected a fellow of the Royal Society of Literature.

SECTION 3

PERFORMING ARTS

Classical Dances of India

Dance is an ancient and celebrated cultural tradition in India.

Each state, each region has its own individual dance form; some are based on classical tradition, yet others follow a folk-driven style.

Folk dances are found in most rural districts, each drawing big crowds of its followers. Yet again, dance that is incorporated into Indian cinema, Hindi films in particular, has its own mix-and-match formula of blending classical dance with modern dance, and this form of dance has its own devoted fans. These are so popular that they are played at weddings, festivals, clubs, and parties.

Here are the most significant classical dance forms of India.

Bharatanatyam

Bharatanatyam is a dance of Tamil Nadu, in southern India. It traces its origins to *Natyashastra*, an ancient treatise on theatre written by the priest Bharata. Originally a temple dance for women, Bharatanatyam expresses Hindu religious stories and its devotion. Its popularity increased in the twentieth century when more people began to perform on the stage. The characteristic stance is the bent knees posture while the feet keep the continuous rhythm of dance movements. Facial expressions and hand gestures convey the emotion and enact the story.

Kathakali

Kathakali is from the state of Kerala, in southwestern India. Similar to

Bharatanatyam, Kathakali is also a religious dance and draws expression from the *Ramayana* and stories from Shaiva folklore. Kathakali is traditionally performed by male dancers, who even take the female roles. The costumes are very heavy and the makeup especially elaborate, which often takes hours to create. The faces are painted like vivid coloured masks with enormous headdresses.

Kathak

Kathak is a dance of northern India and performed by both men and women. The movements include intricate footwork, with heavy bells worn around the ankles, and characteristic gestures and fast twirling of the body with the rhythm of the music. It was mainly performed in the courts of rulers and nawabs.

Its origins are said to be 'kathakars', professional storytellers or wandering bards of North India who used a mixture of dance, song, and drama.

Manipuri

This dance form is from Manipur in northeastern India and thus the name, with its roots in local folk traditions and rituals. The performers enact scenes from the life of Lord Krishna. It has softness and grace in the rhythmic movements.

Female dancers display infinite fluidity in the arms and hands while male dancers have forceful movements. The dance is often accompanied by narrative chanting and chorus songs.

Kuchipudi

Unlike the other styles, Kuchipudi requires strong skills in dancing and singing. From the state of Andhra Pradesh, this dance form follows strict rules and rituals with a dedicated introduction, sprinkling of holy water, burning of incense, with invocation of deities. Traditionally, the dance was performed by men, even the female roles, although now it is also performed by women.

Odissi

This dance form is native to Odisha, in eastern India. Predominantly for women, it incorporates postures found in temple sculptures. Based on archaeological findings, Odissi is considered as the oldest of the surviving Indian classical dances. It is a highly complex and expressive dance, with many mudras (symbolic hand gestures), and sensuous body movements and expressive facial displays.

Mohiniattam

Mohiniattam is a semi-classical dance form belonging to Kerala, in South India. The dance is performed by women to pay tribute to the Hindu God Vishnu in his avatar as the beguiling Mohini. According to Hindu mythology, Vishnu took the form of Mohini to distract the demon Bhasmasura while the gods drank the elixir of immortality by churning the celestial oceans and saved the universe from destruction. This legend is the basis of any performance of this dance form.

Mohiniattam showcases the essence of feminine grace, through delicate dance footing, swaying body movements, and emotive facial expressions.

DO YOU KNOW?

Nataraja and Hindu Mythology

Nataraja, the Hindu god Shiva in his form as the cosmic dancer, is represented in metal or stone in many Shaivite temples, particularly in South India. In the most common type of image, Shiva is depicted with four arms and flying locks dancing on the figure of a dwarf, who is sometimes identified as Apasmara (a symbol of human ignorance). Shiva's back right hand holds the damaru (a special shaped drum); the front right hand displays the 'abhaya' mudra (without fear); the back left hand carries Agni (fire) in a vessel or in the palm of the hand; and the front left hand is held across his chest in the 'gajahasta' pose (elephant-trunk) with the wrist limp and fingers pointed down to the uplifted left foot. The locks of Shiva's hair stand out in several strands interspersed with flowers, a skull, a crescent moon, and the figure of Ganga (where Ganges is personified as a goddess). His figure is encircled by a ring of flames, the 'Prabhamandala'. In classic Sanskrit treatises on dance, this form, the most common representation of Nataraja, is called the 'Bhujanga Trasa'.

MUDRAS

Mudras are hand gestures that are used extensively in Indian classical dance forms and are essential components of Abhinaya. Each mudra holds a specific meaning and is used to complement facial expressions and body movements during performances. They also serve to represent various ideas ranging from divine attributes to natural elements or emotions. For instance, Abhayamudra, which shows an open palm raised upwards, symbolizes protection or reassurance; similarly, Abhishekamudra resembles sprinkling water from one's hand and is used to signify purification rituals found within Buddhist imagery as well as classical dances on divine themes. Mastery over mudras requires rigorous training as they must be executed with precision in both the hand gesture itself and in its synchronization with rhythmical body movements.

RASAS

Rasa translates to 'emotion' or 'essence'. It plays a prominent role in shaping performances across various dance forms by evoking specific sentiments among audiences through carefully crafted narratives. These are rooted in emotionally charged experiences known collectively as navarasa, the nine primary categories of human feelings—love (Shringara), humor (Hasya), fear (Bhaya), compassion (Karuna), anger (Rudra), heroism (Vira), peace (Shanta), wonder (Adbhuta), and disgust (Bhibatsa). Understanding rasas and gaining the ability to convey them is highly essential for classical dancers in order to be able to engage viewers emotionally.

UNESCO WORLD HERITAGE SITES IN INDIA

The 1972 Convention concerning the protection of the World Cultural and Natural Heritage declared a list for the preservation of both natural and cultural heritage sites.

There are over 40 World Heritage sites in India listed since 1983, and over 30 Cultural Heritage sites and 7 Natural World Heritage Sites.

Assam

Manas Wildlife Sanctuary

Kaziranga National Park

Bihar

Mahabodhi Temple Complex

Archaeological site of Nalanda Mahavira at Nalanda

Chandigarh

Architectural work of Le Corbusier

Delhi

Red Fort Complex

Humayun's Tomb

Qutub Minar and its monuments

Goa

Churches and Convents of Goa

Gujarat

Champaner-Pavagadh Archaeological Park

Rani Ki Vav (the Queen's stepwell)

Historic city of Ahmedabad

Dholavira – a Harappan city

Himachal Pradesh

Great Himalayan National Park Conservation Area

Mountain Railways of India

Karnataka

Group of Monuments at Hampi

Group of Monuments at Pattadakal

Madhya Pradesh

Khajuraho Group of Monuments

Buddhist Monuments at Sanchi

Rock shelters of Bhimbetka

Maharashtra

Ajanta Caves

Ellora Caves

Elephanta Caves

Chhatrapati Shivaji Terminus (earlier Victoria terminus Mumbai)

Victorian – Gothic and Art Deco Ensembles of Mumbai

Odisha

Sun Temple, Konark

Rajasthan

Jantar Mantar

Hill Forts of Rajasthan

Jaipur City

Keoladeo National Park

Sikkim

Khangchendzonga National Park

Tamil Nadu

Group of Monuments at Mahabalipuram

Great Chola temples

Mountain Railway of India (Nilgiri)

Telangana

Kakatiya Rudreshwara Ramappa Temple

Uttarakhand

Nanda Devi and Valley of Flowers National Park

Uttar Pradesh

Taj Mahal

Agra Fort

Fatehpur Sikri

West Bengal

Sundarbans National Park

Mountain Railways of India (Darjeeling Himalayan Railways)

UNESCO WORLD HERITAGE SITES ACROSS THE WORLD

(Excluding India)

- Taos Pueblo (Indian Village, New Mexico)
- Machu Picchu, ancient city in Peru
- Socotra Island, Yemen in recognition of its distinct plant and animal life
- Baku, the capital city of Azerbaijan
- Lighthouse of Alexandria, Egypt

- Marrakech, Morocco
- Petra, ancient city in Jordan
- Great Wall of China, China
- Victoria Falls, Zambia and Zimbabwe
- Pyramids of Giza, Egypt
- Ha Long Bay, Vietnam
- Hanging Gardens of Babylon, Mesopotamia
- Haein Temple Complex, South Korea
- Christ the Redeemer statue, Brazil
- Sigiriya, Sri Lanka
- Chichen Itza, ancient city, Mexico
- Copan, ancient city , Honduras
- Cocos Island, Costa Rica

Old Seven Wonders of the World

- Colossus of Rhodes
- Great Pyramid of Giza
- Hanging Gardens of Babylon
- Statue of Zeus at Olympia
- Temple of Artemis at Ephesus
- Mausoleum at Halicarnassus
- Lighthouse of Alexandria

Of these, four were destroyed by earthquake, two were destroyed by fire, and only one is still standing.

Music in India

Hindustani music, one of the two primary kinds of Indian classical music, is located in the northern part of the country. The other principal one, Carnatic music, is in the southern part. Islamic conquests and resulting influences introduced Arab and Persian styles that merged with Hindustani music traditions. However, Muslim culture did not influence Carnatic music.

Both Northern and Southern India share the use of ragas (traditional frameworks for composition), apart from the rhythm or 'taal'. Although vocal music plays an important role, instrumental music receives more prominence in Hindustani music than in Carnatic music.

MUSICAL INSTRUMENTS

Musical instruments are believed to have originated in the Indian subcontinent as early as during the Vedic period. These instruments were initially used to accompany the recitation of the Vedas as music played an integral role in Hindu cultural practices. The significance of musical instruments in Indian performing arts is further emphasized in the Natya Shastra, which also includes a comprehensive classification and analysis of various instruments. Bharata Muni categorized musical instruments into the following four main types:

Avanaddha Vadya: Skin-covered percussion instruments (e.g. drums).

Tata Vadya: Stringed instruments, which can be Bowed (e.g. sarangi, violin) and Plucked (e.g. veena, sitar).

Sushira Vadya: Wind instruments played using the breath (e.g. flute, shehnai).

Ghana Vadya: Solid instruments made from hard materials such as wood or metal (e.g. gongs, cymbals, bells).

GHARANAS

Gharanas are distinct schools of Hindustani classical music, each characterized by unique styles, traditions, and pedagogical approaches. The term 'gharana' signifies a lineage or family of musicians who have preserved and passed on their musical heritage through generations. Musicians from a gharana, referred to as gharanedaar, are known for their specific techniques and interpretations associated with their school.

Each gharana has its own repertoire of compositions, known as gharaneedar bandish, which reflect the stylistic nuances of that particular tradition. Notable gharanas include the Gwalior gharana, one of the oldest that is known for its Khayal singing; the Agra gharana, linked to Tansen's descendants; and the Kirana gharana, recognized for its emotive depth. The Patiala gharana, an offshoot of Gwalior gharana, is celebrated for its complex vocal techniques and improvisational style. Other prominent gharanas include Bhendi Bazar, Rampur, Sham Chaurasi, and Indore. These schools have undergone considerable adaptation and innovation within their specific frameworks, thus ensuring that they retain their relevance over the years.

Agra Gharana: Agra Gharana is a notable school of Hindustani music linked to the descendants of Tansen's daughter, Saraswati. Renowned for its rich vocal tradition, this gharana has produced eminent musicians, including Ustad Ghulam Abbas Khan and Ustad Faiyyaz Khan.

Bhendi Bazar Gharana: Founded by three brothers from Bijnor—Chajju Khan, Nazir Khan, and Khadim Hussain Khan—the Bhendi Bazar gharana is known for its songs composed to praise Lord Shiva. Prominent figures from this gharana include Anjani Bai Malpekar and Shiv Kumar Shukla.

Gwalior Gharana: As one of the oldest gharanas in Hindustani music, Gwalior gharana traces its lineage to Nathan Peerbaksh. It has influenced numerous other styles and boasts notable artists like Vishnu Digamber Paluskar and Rehmat Khan Bawle.

Indore Gharana: The Indore gharana descends from Chhange Khan and his son Shahmir Khan. Influenced by both Bhendi Bazar and Kirana styles, it features prominent musicians such as Ustad Amir Khan and Pandit Amarnath.

Kirana Gharana: Originating from Kirana near Saharanpur in Uttar Pradesh, this gharana is celebrated for its emotional expressiveness. Key figures include Abdul Wahid Khan and Sawai Gandharva, who have significantly shaped its current form.

Patiala Gharana: The Patiala gharana emerged from a family of musicians serving at the court of Patiala in Punjab. Notable artist from this gharana who are renowned for their vocal prowess include Bade Ghulam Ali Khan and Fateh Ali Khan.

Rampur Gharana: An offshoot of the Gwalior gharana, Rampur gharana has produced illustrious musicians such as Allauddin Khan and Ravi Shankar.

Sham Chaurasi Gharana: Sham Chaurasi gharana hails from a small town near Hoshiarpur in Punjab. Though its members are now diminished in number, it has produced significant musicians such as Sain Karim and continues to influence other gharanas such as Patiala.

Pandit Ravi Shankar (1920–2012)

Ravi Shankar was an illustrious Indian musician, primarily a sitar player, and also a brilliant composer. He was instrumental in generating western appreciation for Indian classical music.

Shankar spent most of his youth studying music and dance and touring extensively in India and Europe with his brother Uday's dance troupe. At 18, he gave up dancing and for the next seven years studied the sitar under the noted musician Ustad Allauddin Khan.

In the course of his long career, Shankar became the world's best-known exponent of Hindustani (North Indian) classical music, performing with India's most-distinguished percussionists and making dozens of successful recordings. Shankar composed the film scores for the Indian director Satyajit Ray's famous *Apu* trilogy (1955–59).

Alla Rakha (1919–2000)

Alla Rakha was an Indian tabla player, widely acknowledged in his day as one of the finest in India. As a regular accompanist of Indian sitar virtuoso Ravi Shankar in the 1960s and '70s, he was largely responsible for developing interest in the tabla among non-Indian audiences.

Alla Rakha began to learn tabla when he was just 12 years old. Later he joined All India Radio at Lahore and was transferred to Bombay (now Mumbai) as a senior percussionist. Initially he had a difficult time proving himself, but soon his command of the tabla impressed connoisseurs and laypersons alike.

In 1943, Alla Rakha left All India Radio to work in film music. By 1958 he had become disenchanted with the film industry and left that arena to focus on classical music. He toured globally with Ravi Shankar, and they developed a musical partnership that lasted three decades. As Shankar's counterpart, Alla Rakha played a key role in raising international awareness of the tabla as well as Indian classical music. Alla Rakha also teamed with other virtuosic musicians, such as sarod master Ali Akbar Khan, to perform artful competitive duets known as 'Jugalbandis'.

Ali Akbar Khan (1922–2009)

Ali Akbar Khan was a renowned Indian Hindustani Classical sarod player of the Maihar gharana, known for his virtuosity when playing the instrument. Trained as a classical musician and instrumentalist by his father, Baba Allauddin Khan, he also composed numerous classical 'ragas' and music for film. He established a music school in Calcutta in 1956, and the Ali Akbar College of Music which moved with him to California in the United States. He often performed and recorded in the West, frequently in collaboration with his brother-in-law, the composer and sitarist Ravi Shankar.

As a composer, Khan is known for his film scores, such as in Satyajit Ray's Devi (1960) and the Ismail Merchant–James Ivory production *The Householder* (1963), and as the creator of many ragas. Khan was instrumental in popularizing Indian classical music in the West, both as a performer and as a teacher. Khan was accorded India's second-highest civilian honour, the Padma Vibhushan, in 1989 and was nominated five times for the Grammy Award.

Bismillah Khan (1916–2006)

Bismillah Khan, often referred to by the title Ustad, was a musician who popularized the Shehnai, a reeded woodwind instrument. He played it with such brilliance and perfection that his name became inextricably linked with it. Shehnai is often played during Indian marriages for its evocative melody. Khan was a devout Muslim but performed at both Hindu and Muslim ceremonies and was considered a symbol of religious harmony.

Bismillah Khan was awarded India's highest civilian honour, the Bharat Ratna, in 2001.

Amjad Ali Khan (Born 1945)

Amjad Ali Khan is an Indian classical sarod player and is renowned for his clear 'taans'. Khan was born into a classical musical family and has performed internationally since the 1960s. He was awarded India's second-highest civilian honour, Padma Vibhushan, in 2001; India's third-highest civilian honour, Padma Bhushan, in 1991; and Padma Shree in 1975. Khan was awarded the 21st Rajiv Gandhi National Sadbhavna Award. He was awarded the Sangeet Natak Akademi Award in 1989 and the Sangeet Natak Akademi Fellowship in 2011.

Pandit Shivkumar Sharma (1938–2022)

An Indian classical musician, Pandit Shivkumar Sharma, the santoor player, is credited with adapting the santoor for Indian classical music. As a music composer, he collaborated with Indian flautist Hariprasad Chaurasia under the collaborative name Shiv–Hari and composed music for such hit Indian films as *Faasle* (1985), *Chandni* (1989), and *Lamhe* (1991).

Sharma was awarded the Sangeet Natak Akademi Award in 1986, and the Padma Shri and Padma Vibhushan (India's fourth- and second-highest civilian awards) in 1991 and 2001, respectively.

Hariprasad Chaurasia (Born 1938)

An Indian music director and classical flautist, he plays the bansuri in the Hindustani classical tradition. Chaurasia started learning vocal music from his neighbour, Rajaram, at the age of 15. Later, he switched to playing the flute under the tutelage of Bholanath Prasanna of Varanasi for eight years. He joined the All India Radio, Cuttack, Odisha in 1957 and worked as a composer and performer. He was awarded the Padma Vibhushan in 2000.

A. R. Rahman (Born 1966)

Rahman is an Indian composer whose extensive body of work for film and stage has earned him accolades across the world. Rahman redefined contemporary Indian music and his work is notable for integrating Eastern classical music with electronic music sounds, world music genres, and traditional orchestral arrangements.

Rahman has won two Academy Awards, two Grammy Awards, a BAFTA (British Academy Film and Television Award), in addition to numerous Filmfare and other awards. The noted musician has been honoured with the Padma Bhushan, one of the highest civilian awards of the Government of India.

HINDUSTANI CLASSICAL MUSIC

Hindustani classical music, also known as 'Bhartiya Shastriya Sangeet', is the classical music tradition of northern India. Played on traditional instruments like the veena, sitar, and sarod, it traces its origins to the twelfth century CE, when it branched off from Carnatic music, the classical style of South India. Unlike Carnatic music, which features compositions in Sanskrit, Kannada, Telugu, Tamil, and Malayalam, Hindustani music often uses Hindi, Braj, Avadhi, Rajasthani, Urdu, and Punjabi.

Hindustani classical music is typically taught through a system of schools known as 'gharanas' and is deeply embedded in Indian culture, with performances held both nationally and internationally.

Pandit Bhimsen Joshi (1922–2011)

He was one of the greatest Indian vocalists from Karnataka, in the Hindustani classical tradition. Is renowned for his '*khayal*' style of singing, as well as for his popular renditions of devotional music like Bhajans. Joshi was from the Kirana gharana of Hindustani classical music.

In 1998, he was awarded the Sangeet Natak Akademi Fellowship, the highest honour conferred by Sangeet Natak Akademi, India's national academy of music, dance and drama. Later, he was awarded the Bharat Ratna, India's highest civilian honour, in 2009.

Kishori Amonkar (1932–2017)

Amonkar was an Indian classical vocalist from the Jaipur gharana with its distinctive style. She is considered to be one of the foremost classical singers in India. She was a performer of the classical genre 'khyal' and the light classical genres 'thumri' and 'bhajan'.

Jasraj (1930–2020)

Pandit Jasraj was an iconic Indian classical vocalist, associated with the Mewati gharana. His illustrious musical career spanned over 75 years, during which he earned immense national and international recognition. Renowned for his soulful renditions, he was celebrated for blending classical depth with emotional expression. His contributions to Indian classical music earned him numerous prestigious awards and accolades, solidifying his legacy as one of the most revered figures in Indian music history.

Rashid Khan (1968–2024)

Ustad Rashid Khan was an Indian classical musician in the Hindustani tradition. He belonged to the Rampur-Sahaswan gharana, and was the great-grandson of this gharana's founder Inayat Hussain Khan.

Kumar Gandharva (1924–92)

Pandit Kumar Gandharva, born as Shivaputra Siddharamayya Komkalimath, was a renowned Indian classical singer celebrated for his distinctive vocal style. Unlike many classical musicians, he chose not to adhere strictly to the tradition of any particular gharana, instead forging his own innovative path. His music was marked by creativity and a willingness to experiment with the classical form, making him a singular figure in Indian classical music.

CARNATIC CLASSICAL MUSIC

M. S. Subbulakshmi (1916–2004)

An Indian Carnatic singer, she was the first musician to be awarded the Bharat Ratna, India's highest civilian honour. She was also the first Indian musician to receive the prestigious Ramon Magsaysay award and the first Indian to perform at the United Nations General Assembly in 1966.

VOCALIST AND MUSIC COMPOSER

Hemanta Mukhopadhyay (1920–89)

Hemanta Mukherjee, professionally known as Hemant Kumar, was an iconic Indian music director and playback singer who made significant contributions to Bengali and Hindi music. He also performed in various other Indian languages, including Marathi, Gujarati, Odia, Assamese, Tamil,

Punjabi, Bhojpuri, Konkani, Sanskrit, and Urdu.

Hemanta was particularly revered for his work in Bengali and Hindi film music, as well as his renditions of Rabindra Sangeet. He won two National Awards for Best Male Playback Singer. In addition to his success as a playback singer, he established himself as a talented composer, solidifying his prominence in the Indian music industry by the mid-1950s.

In Bengali, he was one of the primary exponents of Rabindra Sangeet along with being the most sought-after singer. Hemanta composed music for his directorial film *Ananda Math* in Hindi. Simultaneously, he attained huge popularity in Bombay as a playback singer. He was nominated for the Padma Bhushan in 1987, which he declined politely, having turned down a Padma Shri earlier.

Lata Mangeshkar (1929–2022)

Lata Mangeshkar was a legendary Indian playback singer noted for her distinctive voice and a vocal range that extended over more than three octaves. Her career spanned eight decades, and she recorded songs for the soundtracks of more than 2,000 Indian films. Mangeshkar recorded songs in over 36 Indian languages apart from some foreign languages. Primarily she sang in Hindi, Bengali, Nepali, and Marathi.

She received several accolades and honours throughout her career. In 1989, the Dadasaheb Phalke Award was bestowed on her by the Government of India, and in 2001 she was awarded the Bharat Ratna, India's highest civilian honour.

Asha Bhosle (Born 1933)

Asha Bhosle is a legendary Indian playback singer renowned for her remarkable versatility across various genres in Indian cinema. She is often regarded as one of the most influential and iconic singers in Hindi cinema. Over a career spanning more than eight decades, Asha has recorded songs for films and albums in numerous Indian languages, earning widespread acclaim.

Her extensive list of accolades includes two National Film Awards, nine Filmfare Awards – seven of which were for Best Female Playback Singer – and a Lifetime Achievement Award. Additionally, she received two Grammy nominations. In 2000, she was awarded the prestigious Dadasaheb Phalke Award, and in 2008, she received the Padma Vibhushan, India's second-highest civilian honour.

In 2011, the *Guinness Book of World Records* recognized Asha Bhosle as the most recorded artist in music history, further cementing her legacy in the global music industry.

Kishore Kumar (1929–87)

Kishore Kumar was an Indian playback singer, musician, and actor. He was one of the most popular singers in the country, noted for his yodelling and ability to sing songs in different voices and very contrasting pitches. Apart from Hindi, he also sang in Bengali, Marathi, Assamese, Gujarati, Kannada, Bhojpuri, Malayalam, Odia, and Urdu.

Kumar was also a very talented actor, especially in comic roles. He won eight Filmfare Awards for Best Male Playback Singer out of 28 nominations and holds the record for winning and being nominated for the most Filmfare Awards in that category.

K. L. Saigal (1904–47)

Kundan Lal Saigal, or K. L. Saigal, was an Indian actor and playback singer who worked in Hindi cinema, then located in Calcutta (now Kolkata). His unique voice, with a slight nasal undertone, was a mixture of deep baritone and light tenor, which became his signature tone. In his career, Saigal acted in around 36 feature films, of which 28 are in Hindi, 7 in Bengali, and 1 in Tamil.

Mohammed Rafi (1924–80)

Mohammed Rafi was an Indian playback singer and is one of the greatest and most influential singers of India. His incredible versatility and range in octaves brought him enormous popularity. Equally adept at singing ghazals and classical songs, to bhajans and foot-tapping popular numbers to sad romantic melodies, he could blend and mould his voice to the persona of the actor in the film.

He received six Filmfare Awards and one National Film Award. In 1967, he was honoured with the Padma Shri by the Government of India. Rafi recorded over 1,000 songs for Hindi films and many other Indian languages. He recorded as many as 7,000 songs throughout his career, spanning several languages and dialects.

Manna Dey (1919–2013)

Manna Dey (Prabodh Chandra Dey) was a renowned and an illustrious Indian playback singer, music director, and musician. He was trained in classical music and is widely recognized among the most versatile and celebrated vocalists in the Hindi film industry and acknowledged for his distinct contributions in integrating Indian classical music with Hindi commercial films.

Through his career of over five decades, Dey recorded more than 3,000 songs. While the majority of his songs were in Bengali and Hindi, he showcased his prowess in many other Indian languages, including Bhojpuri, Punjabi, Assamese, Gujarati, Kannada, Malayalam, and Chhattisgarhi.

He was honoured with the Padma Shri in 1971, followed by the Padma Bhushan in 2005 and the Dadasaheb Phalke Award in 2007 for his outstanding contribution to Indian music from the Government of India.

Mukesh (1923–76)

Mukesh was an eminent Indian playback singer of the Hindi film industry. He won the National Best Playback Award in 1973. He was also popular as being the voice of Raj Kapoor, Manoj Kumar, and other actors in the Hindi film industry.

Talat Mahmood (1924–98)

Talat Mahmood, an Indian playback singer, is considered among the most popular male Indian film song and ghazal singers. He did not succeed as an actor but found a considerable amount of success as a playback singer.

He was presented the Padma Bhushan award in 1992, for his brilliant contributions in cinema music. His signature stirring voice was extremely popular, and romantic songs were his forte.

Geeta Dutt (1930–72)

Geeta Dutt was an Indian classical and playback singer and became a prominent voice in Hindi cinema and Bengali cinema. She also sang modern Bengali songs in the non-film genre. Her signature lilting voice with its subtle toes gave it added sweetness and allure.

CURRENT POPULAR SINGERS IN HINDI FILMS

Arijit Singh (Born 1987)

Arijit Singh is an extremely talented Indian playback singer and music composer and the recipient of several laurels including a National Film Award and seven Filmfare Awards. He has recorded songs in several Indian languages, predominantly Hindi and Bengali and is noted for his ability of performing songs in diverse music genres. At present, he is one of the top playback singers in the Hindi film industry.

Shreya Ghoshal (Born 1984)

Shreya Ghoshal is an Indian singer noted for her wide vocal range and versatility. One of the most prolific and talented singers, she has recorded songs for films and albums in different Indian and foreign languages. Among her many accolades are five National Film Awards, and seven Filmfare Awards, apart from Kerala State Film Awards and Tamil Nadu State Awards.

Sonu Nigam (Born 1973)

Sonu Nigam is an extremely talented Indian playback singer and music director. He is a recipient of Padma Shri, India's fourth-highest civilian award. In his teens, Nigam began his career as a participant in a reality show, after which he began conducting the popular music reality show *Sa Re Ga Ma* and other programmes on television.

Nigam sings primarily in Hindi but has also sung in Bengali, Marathi, Telugu, Tamil, Odia, Bhojpuri, Gujarati, Malayalam, Nepali, Tulu, Chhattisgarhi, Meitei, and other Indian languages.

MODERN GLOBAL MUSIC

Jazz

Jazz is a music genre that originated in the African-American communities of New Orleans, Louisiana, in the late nineteenth and early twentieth centuries, with its roots in blues, ragtime, European harmony, and African rhythmic rituals.

Since the 1920s, jazz has been recognized as a major form of musical expression in traditional and popular music. Jazz is characterized by swing and blue notes, complex chords, polyrhythms, and improvisation.

Any attempt to arrive at a precise, all-encompassing definition of jazz is probably futile. Jazz has been, from its very beginnings at the turn of the twentieth century, a constantly evolving, expanding, changing music, passing through several distinctive phases of development.

As jazz spread around the world, it drew on national, regional, and local musical cultures, which gave rise to different styles. New Orleans jazz began in the early 1910s, combining earlier brass band marches, French quadrilles, biguine, ragtime, and blues with collective polyphony improvisation. Cool jazz developed near the end of the 1940s, introducing calmer, smoother sounds and long, linear melodic lines.

Bebop

Bebop took the harmonies of the old jazz and superimposed on them additional 'substituted' chords. It also broke up the metronomic regularity of the drummer's rhythmic pulse and produced solos played in double time with several bars packed with sixteenth notes. The result was complicated improvisation.

The movement originated during the early 1940s in the playing of trumpeter Dizzy Gillespie, with Charlie Christian, Thelonious Monk, Kenny Clarke, and Charlie 'Bird' Parker.

Rap

Rap, which originated in African-American communities in New York City, is a musical style in which rhythmic and/or rhyming speech is chanted ('rapped') to musical accompaniment. This backing music, which can include digital sampling (music and sounds extracted from other recordings), is also called hip-hop, the name used to refer to a broader cultural movement that includes rap, DJ-ing (turntable manipulation), graffiti painting, and break dancing.

Hip-hop

Hip-hop is a cultural movement that attained widespread popularity in the 1980s and '90s. It was also the backing music for rap, the musical style incorporating rhythmic and/or rhyming speech, that became its most lasting and influential art form.

The term hip-hop refers to four major elements: deejaying, rapping, graffiti painting, and B-boying, which encompasses hip-hop dance, style, and attitude, along with expressive body language.

Hip-hop originated in the predominantly African-American economically depressed South Bronx section of New York City in the late 1970s and gained huge popularity in the 1980s and '90s. It became the backing music for rap, the musical style incorporating rhyming speech that was the movement's most lasting form.

Symphony

Symphony, a lengthy form of musical composition for orchestra, normally consisting of several large sections, or movements, at least one of which usually employs sonata form, also called first-movement form.

Symphonies were first composed around 1740–1820. During the nineteenth century, symphonies grew longer, and late in the century grew so much that reaction set in; hence, composers began using new techniques to achieve dynamic coherence. Economic considerations forced a reduction in the size of orchestras and amount of rehearsal time available to mid-twentieth-century composers, further justifying a return to less extravagant symphonic thinking.

Opera

Opera is a form of staged drama that is entirely set to music, consisting of vocal performances accompanied by instrumental music. These performances often feature orchestral overtures and interludes. In some operas, the music flows continuously throughout an act, while in others, the performance is divided into distinct musical segments or 'numbers'. These numbers may be separated by recitative, a style of singing that closely resembles spoken dialogue, or by actual spoken lines, enhancing the dramatic storytelling.

Popular Music

Popular music is any commercially oriented music primarily intended to be received and appreciated by a wide audience, generally in literate, technologically advanced societies dominated by urban culture. Unlike traditional folk music, popular music is written by known individuals, usually professionals, and does not evolve through the process of oral transmission.

Rock

Rock is a style of popular music that emerged in the 1950s and by the end of the twentieth century it became the world's dominant form of popular music. Originating in the United States in the 1950s, it spread to other English-speaking countries and across Europe in the '60s, and by the '90s its impact went global.

Rock's commercial importance was also reflected in the mushrooming multinational recording industry, in the sales racks of international record retailers, and in the playlists of music radio and television anchors.

Ballad

Ballad is a short narrative folk song, whose distinctive style became established in Europe in the late Middle Ages and is present where communities follow the habit of folk singing. The term 'ballad' also applies to any narrative composition suitable for singing. France, Denmark, Germany, Russia, Greece, and Spain, as well as England and Scotland, possess impressive ballad collections.

Funk

Funk is a rhythm-heavy musical genre that gained popularity in the 1970s and early 1980s, serving as a bridge between soul and later African-American musical styles. Originating from the African-American oral tradition, the term 'funk' lacks a precise literal meaning but refers to a distinctive, energetic form of urban dance music. It is characterized by hard, syncopated bass lines and drumbeats, with various instruments contributing to a rhythmic counterplay that creates the signature 'groove' of funk music.

WESTERN CLASSICAL MUSIC COMPOSERS

Of all the many Western classical composers, the three that consistently appear in the top spots are Beethoven, Bach, and Mozart. They differed in style, skill, innovation, and popularity, and are often regarded as some of the most significant.

Ludwig van Beethoven (1770–1827)

Ludwig van Beethoven, a German composer and pianist, is considered one of the greatest composers in history. He built upon the classical traditions of his mentors, Joseph Haydn and Wolfgang Amadeus Mozart, while introducing personal emotional depth into his compositions. This innovation significantly influenced the Romantic composers that followed him. Despite gradually losing his hearing, Beethoven continued to compose some of his most renowned works during the last decade of his life, including *Symphony No. 9 in D Minor*, *Symphony No. 5 in C Minor*, *Moonlight Sonata*, and *Für Elise*.

Johann Sebastian Bach (1685–1750)

Johann Sebastian Bach was a German composer and organist of the Baroque period. His contemporaries admired him for his talent as a musician but thought his compositions were old-fashioned. A rediscovery of his work in the early nineteenth century led to the so-called Bach revival, in which he came to be seen as one of the greatest composers of all time. His most-celebrated compositions include *Brandenburg Concertos, The Well-Tempered Clavier, Suites for Unaccompanied Cello*, to name a few.

Wolfgang Amadeus Mozart (1756–91)

An Austrian composer of the Classical period, Wolfgang Amadeus Mozart is widely recognized as one of the greatest composers of Western music. He is the only composer to write and excel in all of the musical genres of his time. He began his career as a child prodigy. Notable compositions include *The Marriage of Figaro, Elvira Madigan*, and *Clarinet Quintet in A Major.*

Johannes Brahms (1833–97)

Johannes Brahms was a German composer and pianist of the Romantic era, though he remained deeply rooted in the classical tradition. His compositions spanned a wide range of genres, including symphonies, concertos, chamber music, piano pieces, and choral works, often reflecting the influence of folk music. Among his most celebrated works are *Symphony No. 3 in F Major* and the *Hungarian Dances*. Brahms' music is known for its emotional depth, structural complexity, and melodic beauty.

Richard Wagner (1813–83)

German composer and theorist Richard Wagner profoundly transformed Western music and extended the opera tradition. He is renowned for his innovative use of *leitmotifs* – recurring musical themes that represent characters, places, or events – which he intricately developed throughout his compositions. Wagner's major works include operas like *The Flying Dutchman, Tristan and Isolde*, and the monumental four-opera cycle *The Ring of the Nibelung.* His work revolutionized the structure and emotional depth of opera, leaving a lasting impact on music and drama.

Claude Debussy (1862–1918)

French composer Claude Debussy developed new and complex harmonies and musical structures and his major works include *Clair de lune, La Mer, Prelude to the Afternoon of a Faun, and the Opera Pelléas et Mélisande.*

Pyotr Ilyich Tchaikovsky (1840–93)

Pyotr Ilyich Tchaikovsky is celebrated as one of the most popular Russian composers in history. Educated in the Western European musical tradition, he blended elements from French, Italian, and German music into a distinctive personal style that retained a strong Russian character. Tchaikovsky is particularly renowned for his compositions for ballet, with some of his most famous works being *Swan Lake*, *The Sleeping Beauty*, and *The Nutcracker*. His ability to evoke deep emotion through music has made his works timeless classics in the world of classical music.

Frédéric Chopin (1810–49)

Frédéric Chopin was a Polish French composer and pianist of the Romantic period. He was one of few composers to devote himself to a single instrument, and his sensitive approach to the keyboard allowed him to exploit all the resources of the piano, including innovations in fingering and pedalling. He is thus primarily known for writing music for the piano, notably *Nocturne, Op. 9 No. 2 in E-flat Major, Nocturne in C-sharp Minor, B. 49,* and *Heroic Polonaise.*

Joseph Haydn (1732–1809)

Joseph Haydn was an Austrian composer who played a pivotal role in shaping the classical style of music in the eighteenth century. He was instrumental in establishing the forms and styles of both the string quartet and the symphony. A prolific composer, Haydn created numerous celebrated works, including *Symphony No. 92 in G Major*, the *Emperor Quartet*, and *Cello Concerto No. 2 in D Major*. His compositions are often noted for their lightness, wit, and elegance, showcasing his mastery of musical structure and expression.

Antonio Vivaldi (1678–1741)

Antonio Vivaldi was an Italian composer and violinist from the Baroque period, renowned for his contributions to various musical forms, including operas, solo instruments, and small ensembles. He is particularly celebrated for his concertos, which feature virtuosic solo passages interspersed with sections for the entire orchestra. Vivaldi composed around 500 concertos, with his most famous work being *The Four Seasons*, a set of four violin concertos that vividly depict the characteristics of each season.

Sergei Vasilyevich Rachmaninoff (1873–1943)

Rachmaninoff was a Russian composer, virtuoso pianist, and conductor. He is widely considered one of the finest pianists of his day and, as a composer, one of the last great representatives of Romanticism in Russian classical music. His compositions exude song-like melodicism, expressiveness, dense contrasting textures, and rich orchestral melody.

DANCE

ICONS OF INDIA

Uday Shankar (1900–77)

Uday Shankar was an influential Indian dancer and choreographer renowned for developing a unique fusion style of dance that blended Indian classical, folk, and tribal elements with European theatrical techniques. His innovative approach helped popularize modern dance in India and abroad during the 1920s and 1930s. As a pioneer in this field, Shankar played a significant role in transforming and elevating Indian dance on the global stage.

Exposed to both Indian classical dance and folk dance while growing and also to ballet during his stay in Europe, Shankar created a new dance style by bringing elements of both styles together. In 1931, he founded Europe's first Indian dance company. He is credited for ushering in a new era for traditional Indian temple dances, which until then had been known for their strict interpretations. In 1938, he established the 'Uday Shankar India Cultural Centre' in Uttarakhand and invited maestros of their respective art to teach. These included Sankaran Namboodiri for Kathakali, Kandappa Pillai for Bharaṭanatyam, Ambi Singh for Manipuri, and Ustad Allauddin Khan for music. Several artists and dancers became part of this unit. In 1962, he received the Sangeet Natak Akademi Fellowship for lifetime achievement, the highest award given by Sangeet Natak Akademi, and in 1971, he received the Padma Vibhushan, India's second-highest civilian award.

Pandit Birju Maharaj (1938–2022)

Birju Maharaj was an illustrious dancer, composer, singer, and exponent of the Lucknow 'gharana' of Kathak dance in India. He was a descendant of the Maharaj family of Kathak dancers, his father and guru was Acchan Maharaj. He was also an accomplished Hindustani classical music vocalist, and became the head of Kathak Kendra in New Delhi until his retirement in 1998, when he started his own dance institute 'Kalashram' in Delhi. Birju Maharaj was a recipient of the Padma Vibhushan, India's second-highest civilian honour, in 1986. He also spread the knowledge of Hindustani classical music and percussion instruments. His Kathak performances, in addition to mythological stories, had contemporary elements including stories from daily life and social issues, which were communicated through his dance performance.

INDIAN CLASSICAL THEATRE

Classical Sanskrit theatre in India flourished during the first nine centuries CE. Principles on acting appear in the writings of Panini, the Sanskrit grammarian of the fifth century BCE, and references to actors, dancers, mummers, theatrical companies, and academies are found in Kautilya's book on statesmanship, the *Arthashastra*.

IMPORTANT FORMS AND CONCEPTS IN INDIAN THEATRE

Bharatamuni is credited as the author of the Natya Shastra, an encyclopedic work on dramaturgy that has profoundly influenced Indian theatre.

Bhavai is a folk dramatic form from Gujarat that integrates music and dance into its performances.

Chhau is a traditional dance drama form found in three eastern Indian states, namely, Mayurbhanj (Orissa), Purulia (West Bengal), and Seraikella (Bihar). Each regional variant showcases unique characteristics and themes, with performances typically centered around mythology and everyday life.

Jatra is a popular theatrical art form from Bengal that evolved from Vaishnava musical plays centered around Krishna, which were introduced by saint Chaitanya Mahaprabhu in the 16th century.

Khyal is a popular folk theatre from Rajasthan that evolved from earlier poetic compositions into a musical dramatic style. Initially rooted in folk traditions, Khyal can be considered an amalgamation of various regional influences, although it retains its operatic essence.

Kudiyattam is a traditional form of Sanskrit theatre practiced in Kerala, primarily performed by the Chakyar and Nambiar communities within temple precincts. This ancient art form, which dates back to the 9th century, incorporates elaborate staging and intricate performances.

The **Natyashastra** is an encyclopedic treatise on dramaturgy attributed to Bharata Muni and composed between the 2nd century BCE and 2nd century CE. This seminal work encompasses 36 chapters and approximately 6,000 verses, covering a wide array of topics related to theater.

Ramlila is a popular theatrical spectacle originating in North India that dramatizes episodes from the Ramayana, particularly those translated into Hindi by poet Tulsidas in the 17th century. This tradition began in Varanasi where Tulsidas presented portions of his Ramcharitmanas over several nights at various locations throughout the city.

The term **Sutradhar**, literally meaning 'string-holder', has its roots in both puppet theatre and drama. Some scholars believe it evolved from the term Suta, referring to ancient ballad singers who narrated epics and Puranas.

Vidushaka is a stock character in Sanskrit theatre, often portrayed as a dwarf with distinct physical traits such as baldness and protruding teeth. He serves as a jester and confidant to the hero, typically a king, providing comic relief while also playing a crucial role in advancing the plot.

Yakshagana is a vibrant open-air dance–drama form from Karnataka that blends elements of folk traditions with classical music and ritualistic performances. Evolving during the 15th to 16th centuries, Yakshagana draws its themes from mythological literature, epics, and Puranas.

THEATRE IN INDIA

The National School of Drama (NSD) in New Delhi was founded in 1959 for the study of theatre and providing training in acting, stagecraft, and related subjects. It is considered the foremost school of its kind in India and was established under the aegis of the Sangeet Natak Akademi (India's national academy of music, dance and drama). Under the direction of Ebrahim Alkazi (1962–77), the school emerged as India's premier theatre-training institute. It became autonomous in 1975, although it continued to be fully funded by the Indian government.

Ebrahim Alkazi (1925–2020)

Alkazi was an Indian theatre director and drama teacher. A rigid disciplinarian, he instilled in his acting students an awe and reverence that they still carry with them, with several of them having had the privilege of continuing the practice and training in the NSD Repertory Company. He was also the Director of National School of Drama, New Delhi from 1962 to 1977 .

He staged over 50 plays in his lifetime. His designs for the open-air venues were acclaimed for their visual nature and for the original spins he put on each stage production. He won the BBC Broadcasting Award in 1950.

Badal Sircar (1925–2011)

Badal Sircar was an Indian dramatist and theatre director, known for his anti-establishment plays during the Naxalite movement in the 1970s. He brought theatre out of the proscenium into the public arena when he transformed his own theatre company, Shatabdi, as a third theatre group. He wrote more than 50 plays of which *Ebong Indrajit*, *Basi Khabar*, and *Saari Raat* are renowned pieces.

He remains one of the most translated among Indian playwrights. He was awarded the Padma Shri in 1972, Sangeet Natak Akademi Award in 1968, and the Sangeet Natak Akademi Fellowship, the highest honour in the performing arts, in 1997.

Vijay Tendulkar (1928–2008)

Vijay Tendulkar was a leading Marathi playwright, movie and television writer, literary essayist, political journalist, and social commentator. He is best known for his plays *Shantata! Court Chalu Aahe, Ghashiram Kotwal*, and *Sakharam Binder*. Many of Tendulkar's plays derived inspiration from real-life incidents or social upheavals, which focussed on harsh realities. Tendulkar was a dramatist and theatre personality in Maharashtra for over five decades.

Utpal Dutt (1929–93)

Utpal Dutt was a prominent figure in Bengali theatre, who initially started his career in English theatre. In the 1940s, he founded 'The Shakespeareans', captivating audiences with his powerful productions. Dutt's impact extended beyond the stage; he was instrumental in the Group Theatre movement and delved into 'Epic Theatre', drawing inspiration from Bertolt Brecht. His legacy continues through the Little Theatre Group and his significant contributions to both Bengali and Hindi cinema. Dutt portrayed iconic characters in numerous dramas and films, including a notable role in the Hindi film *Bhuvan Shome*.

Girish Karnad (1938–2019)

Girish Karnad was an Indian actor, film director, Kannada writer, playwright who mainly worked in Kannada, Hindi, Tamil, Telugu, Malayalam, and Marathi films. His rise as a playwright in the 1960s marked the coming of age of modern Indian playwriting in Kannada and received the 1998 Jnanpith Award, the highest literary honour conferred in India.

Karnad composed plays, often using history and mythology to tackle contemporary issues for over four decades. He played an active part in the world of Indian cinema working as an actor, director, and screenwriter, in Hindi and Kannada cinema.

Karnad was conferred Padma Shri and Padma Bhushan by the Government of India and won four Filmfare Awards, of which three are Filmfare Award for Best Director, Kannada and the fourth for Filmfare Best Screenplay.

Theatre in England

Theatre is probably the performing art for which England is best known. Theatrical performance that emerged during the Middle Ages borrowed elements from wandering entertainers, traditional and ancient folk agricultural rituals, and dances such as the Morris dance. England remains one of the foremost contributors to world theatre and this is evident in its iconic theatrical institutions, like the Royal Shakespeare Company, the Royal National Theatre, and the numerous theatres that flourish in London's celebrated West End district.

In the twentieth century, works of English playwrights were much acclaimed, from John Osborne to Harold Pinter and Tom Stoppard, and the musical extravaganzas of Andrew Lloyd Webber.

PUPPETRY

Evidence of puppetry in India traces back to the Indus Valley Civilization, where archaeological finds uncovered toys that could be operated with strings. Puppet references can also be found in classical literature, such as the epic Mahabharata, which compares human life to a puppet governed by the strings of fate.

The existence of puppetry in ancient Indian culture is highlighted further in Buddhist texts, including the Therigatha, which references both string and shadow puppetry.

Currently, all four primary kinds of puppets—string, shadow, glove, and rod—continue to be well-liked throughout India. Every area presents its distinct styles and methods, mirroring local customs in music, dance, painting, and folklore. Regions such as Rajasthan, Orissa, Karnataka, Tamil Nadu, Andhra Pradesh, and West Bengal are especially famous for their vibrant puppetry tradition. These regional differences not only amuse but also function as crucial storytelling channels that communicate moral teachings and cultural stories, making certain that this age-old art form remains relevant in modern society.

Bommalattam, Gombeyatta, Kathputli, Kundhei, glove puppets, rod puppets, etc. are examples of puppetry forms from various regions in India.

CINEMA IN INDIA

Dada Saheb Phalke Award

The Dadasaheb Phalke Award is India's highest award in the field of cinema. It is presented annually at the National Film Awards ceremony by the Directorate of Film Festivals, an organization set up by the Ministry of Information and Broadcasting.

The recipient is honoured for their 'great and outstanding contribution to the growth and development of Indian cinema' and is selected by a committee consisting of eminent personalities from the Indian film industry.

The award comprises a Swarna Kamal (Golden Lotus) medallion, a shawl, and a cash prize of ₹10,00,000 (US$12,000). The first recipient of the award was actress Devika Rani, who was honoured at the seventeenth National Film Awards. Till 2023, 53 awardees were presented this award. The most recent recipient is veteran actress Waheeda Rehman who was honoured at the 69th National Film Awards ceremony.

The National Film Awards is the most prominent film award ceremony in India. Established in 1954, it has been administered, along with the International Film Festival of India and the Indian Panorama, by the Indian government's Directorate of Film Festivals since 1973.

Every year, a national panel appointed by the government selects the winning entry, and the award ceremony is held in New Delhi where the President of India presents the awards. This is followed by the inauguration of the National Film Festival, where award-winning films are screened for the public. Declared for films produced in the previous year across the country, they hold the distinction of awarding merit to the best of Indian cinema as well as presenting awards for the best films in each region and language of the country.

INDIAN CINEMA FILM DIRECTORS

Dadasaheb Phalke (1870–1944)

Dadasaheb Phalke was an Indian Film producer, director, screenwriter, and was known as the 'Father of Indian Cinema'. His debut film, *Raja Harishchandra*, was the first Indian movie released in 1913, and is now known as India's first full-length feature film. He made 95 feature-length films and 27 short films in his career, spanning over 19 years, until 1937, including his most noted works: *Mohini Bhasmasur* (1913), *Satyavan Savitri* (1914), *Lanka Dahan* (1917), *Shri Krishna Janma* (1918), and *Kaliya Mardan* (1919). In his honour, the Dadasaheb Phalke Award was instituted as the highest honorary award under the National Film Awards by the Government of India and was first presented in 1969.

Shyam Benegal (Born 1934)

He is a leading Indian director of 'parallel' cinema and has directed films dealing with various social issues of Indian society. Notable ones include *Ankur, Nishant, Mandi, Bhumika, Trikaal, Bose the Forgotten hero*, among many others. He is a pioneer of the movement for realistic cinema.

Govind Nihalani (Born 1940)

Govind Nihalani is an Indian film director, cinematographer, screenwriter, and producer, known for his work in the movement of parallel Hindi cinema. He is the recipient of six National Film Awards and five Filmfare Awards. Some films directed by him include *Ardh Satya*, *Aakrosh*, *Hazaar Chaurasi ki Maa*, and *Tamas*.

Bimal Roy (1909–66)

Bimal Roy was an eminent Indian Film director and is renowned for his sensitive and touching films that include *Do Bigha Zamin*, *Devdas*, *Bandini*, *Madhumati*, *Sujata*, among others. He won a number of awards in his career, including 11 Filmfare Awards and 2 National Film Awards. He is an eminent director and held in high regard even today.

Hrishikesh Mukherjee (1922–2006)

Hrishikesh Mukherjee was an Indian film director, editor, and writer. He is regarded as one of the most iconic filmmakers of Indian cinema. He directed over 40 films in his career spanning over four decades. Renowned for the social awareness themes in his films, they also depicted the life of the quintessential middle-class people and their trials and tribulations. His major successful films include *Satyakam*, *Anupama*, *Anand*, *Abhimaan*, *Namak Haram*, among others. He was awarded the Dadasaheb Phalke Award in 1999 and the Padma Vibhushan in 2001.

Mani Ratnam (Born 1956)

Mani Ratnam is an acclaimed Indian filmmaker known for his influential work in both Tamil and Hindi cinema. He made his directorial debut with *Pallavi Anu Pallavi* in 1983. However, it was the success of *Mouna Ragam* that established him as a prominent director in Tamil-language cinema. Ratnam's artistic style is significantly shaped by Hollywood conventions and music videos, evident in his film *Nayakan* (1987), which is a reimagining of Francis Ford Coppola's *The Godfather*, inspired by the life of Mumbai underworld don Varadarajan Mudaliar.

V. Shantaram (1901–90)

Shantaram was an Indian film director, film producer, screenwriter, and actor known for his work in Hindi and Marathi films. His best-known films include *Dr Kotnis Ki Amar Kahani*, *Do Aankhen Barah Haath*, *Navrang*, and several more. His illustrious career extended almost seven decades and he used the film medium to advocate for humanism and expose bigotry and injustice as well. He was awarded the Dadasaheb Phalke Award in 1985 and the Padma Vibhushan in 1992 posthumously.

Guru Dutt (1925–64)

Guru Dutt was an Indian film actor, director, producer, choreographer, and writer and is regarded as among the greatest filmmakers of Indian cinema.

He directed many Hindi films; several of these films gained a cult following internationally – *Pyaasa* (1957), *Kaagaz Ke Phool* (1959), *Chaudhvin Ka Chand* (1960), and *Sahib Bibi Aur Ghulam* (1962). All of these films have attained cult status in Hindi cinema.

Adoor Gopalakrishnan (Born 1941)

Adoor Gopalakrishnan is an Indian film director, script writer, and producer, and is regarded as one of the most notable and renowned filmmakers in India. With the release of his first feature film *Swayamvaram*, Gopalakrishnan pioneered the new wave in Malayalam cinema during the 1970s.

ICONIC ACTORS IN HINDI CINEMA

Dilip Kumar (1922–2021)

Dilip Kumar (born Muhammad Yusuf Khan) was an iconic and talented Indian actor who worked in Hindi cinema. He dominated the Indian cinema from late 1940s through the 60s, and holds the record for winning the most number of Filmfare Awards for Best Actor and was also the inaugural recipient of the award. He is credited with the highest number of box-office records in Hindi cinema. In a career spanning over five decades, Kumar worked in around 60 films in a variety of roles.

For his contributions to film, the Government of India awarded him with the Padma Bhushan in 1991 and the Padma Vibhushan in 2015, the country's third- and second-highest civilian awards, respectively. He was also awarded India's highest accolade in the field of cinema, the Dadasaheb Phalke Award, in 1994.

Ashok Kumar (1911–2001)

Ashok Kumar (born Kumudlal Ganguly) was an Indian actor who attained legendary status in Indian cinema. He was considered the first big star of Hindi cinema as well as the first lead actor to play an anti-hero. He also became the first star to reinvent himself, enjoying a long and hugely successful career as a character actor. He was honoured in 1988 with the Dadasaheb Phalke Award, the highest national award for cinema artists by the Government of India. He also received the Padma Bhushan in 1999 for his contributions to Indian cinema.

Devika Rani (1908–94)

Devika Rani was the first recipient of the Dadasaheb Phalke Award. She was regarded as the First Lady of Indian Cinema for her successful career that spanned 10 years, from the 1930s to the 1940s. She was also awarded the Padma Shri. In 1934, her husband Himanshu Rai established a studio, Bombay Talkies, which produced several successful films over the next 5–6 years. During that time, Devika Rani played the lead role in many films, and her on-screen pairing with Ashok Kumar became popular in India. After Rai's death in 1940, Devika Rani took control of the studio and produced some more films. In 1945, she retired from films, married the Russian painter Svetoslav Roerich and moved to his estate near Bangalore.

Pramathesh Chandra Barua (1903–51)

P. C. Barua was an Indian actor, director, and screenwriter of Indian films in the pre-independence era from Assam. Barua's breakthrough with New Theatres came with *Devdas* in 1935 when the film was first made in Bengali, with Barua himself playing the title role.

Prithviraj Kapoor (1906–72)

Prithviraj Kapoor, an Indian actor, is also considered as one of the founding figures of Hindi cinema. He founded the Prithvi Theatres in 1944 as a travelling theatre company based in Bombay. Patriarch of the Kapoor family of Hindi films, of which four generations have played active roles in the Hindi film industry and continues to this day.

With his son Shashi Kapoor's marriage to Jennifer Kendal, Prithvi Theatre merged with the Indian Shakespeare theatre company, Shakespeareana, and the company got a permanent home in Mumbai in 1978. His three sons, Raj Kapoor, Shammi Kapoor, and Shashi Kapoor, continued the tradition of working in films. In 1954, he was awarded the Sangeet Natak Akademi Fellowship, and in 1969, the Padma Bhushan by the Government of India. He was posthumously awarded the Dadasaheb Phalke Award for the year 1971, the highest accolade in Indian cinema.

Madhubala (1933–69)

Madhubala was an Indian actress of the Hindi film industry. In a career spanning over 20 years, the actor had appeared in more than 60 films.

Madhubala's portrayal of Anarkali in the historical epic drama *Mughal-e-Azam*, 1960, which was the highest grossing film in India of that time, brought her enormous acclaim and the sole nomination for the Filmfare Award for Best Actress. Critics have described it as one of the finest in Indian cinematic history.

Meena Kumari (1933–72)

Meena Kumari was an Indian actress and poet, who worked in Hindi films. Popularly called the Tragedy Queen, she is among the most highly regarded and is held in high esteem in the history of Indian cinema. In a career spanning over 33 years, from child actress to adult, Kumari starred in over 90 films. The actor won four Filmfare Awards in the Best Actress category and created history at the 10th Filmfare Awards, in 1963, by receiving all the three Best Actress nominations and also won the honour for her spectacular performance in *Sahib Bibi aur Ghulam*. In the 13th Filmfare Awards, 1966, she won her last Best Actress award for *Kaajal*. She was also a poet and a playback singer, and brought out an album, 'I Write, I Recite' of her poems.

Om Puri (1950–2017)

Om Puri, a multifaceted film persona whose diverse career spread across drama, Bollywood and Hollywood. He appeared in mainstream commercial Hindi films as well as Urdu, Malayalam, Bengali, Kannada, English, Punjabi, Gujarati, Telugu, and Marathi films, as well as independent and art films and also starred in several international cinema.

A product of the National School of Drama, Puri's impact on Indian art films and mainstream cinema is palpable. He is best known for his roles in *Aakrosh*, *Arohan*, *Ardh Satya*, and television films like *Sadgati* and *Tamas*. He is widely regarded as one of the finest actors in world cinema. Puri won two National Film Awards for Best Actor, two Filmfare Awards, and India's fourth-highest civilian award Padma Shri in 1990.

Amitabh Bachchan (Born 1942)

Bachchan is an Indian actor who works primarily in Hindi films. With a cinematic career spanning over five decades, he has played pivotal roles in over more than 200 films. He has won numerous accolades in his career, including a record number of National Film Awards in Best Actor category and many awards at international film festivals and award ceremonies.

He has won 16 Filmfare Awards and is the most nominated performer in any major acting category at Filmfare with 34 nominations in Best Actor and 42 nominations overall.

The Government of India honoured him with the Padma Shri in 1984, the Padma Bhushan in 2001, the Padma Vibhushan in 2015, and India's highest award in the field of cinema, the Dadasaheb Phalke Award in 2018 for his contributions to the film world. Bachchan also has worked in several noted Hollywood films.

Waheeda Rehman (Born 1938)

Regarded as one of Hindi cinema's most accomplished actresses, she has worked in more than 90 feature films, in a career spanning over five decades. An accomplished dancer as well as an evocative actress, Rehman has played several heart-winning characters and given iconic sterling performances. Her accolades include a National Film Award and three Filmfare Awards. She was honoured with India's civilian awards: the Padma Shri in 1972 and the Padma Bhushan in 2011. In 2021, she was honoured with the Dadasaheb Phalke Award, India's highest award in the field of cinema.

TAMIL CINEMA

Gemini Ganesan (1920–2005)

Gemini Ganesan was one of the stalwarts of Tamil cinema, who acted in a variety of roles but is especially noted as a romantic lead, which earned him the title of Kadhal Mannan ('King of Romance') among his fans. Together with his contemporaries Sivaji Ganesan and M. G. Ramachandran (MGR), Gemini Ganesan was one of the three best-known actors of the twentieth-century Tamil cinema.

Sivaji Ganesan (1928–2001)

Sivaji Ganesan was a versatile star of Tamil cinema. When Annadurai formed the Dravida Munnetra Kazhagam (DMK) political party in 1949, Ganesan joined and made his film debut with the classic DMK film *Parasakthi*. By the mid-1950s Ganesan had begun to move away from the DMK and its atheistic policies. He soon attained fame by appearing in several mythological films, *Veerapandiya Kattaborman* (1960), which is probably his best-known work.

Rajinikanth (Born 1950)

Rajinikanth is an incredibly talented and successful Indian actor who works predominantly in Tamil cinema. His career spans over five decades and the actor has done over 170 films in Tamil, Hindi, Telugu, Kannada, Bengali, and Malayalam.

He is undoubtedly one of the most successful and popular actors in the history of Indian cinema. He is renowned for his unique dialogues and has an enormous fan base internationally with a cult following. He was honoured with Padma Bhushan by the Government of India in 2000, Padma Vibhushan in 2016, India's third- and second-highest civilian honours, and the highest award in the field of cinema Dadasaheb Phalke Award in 2019 for his contributions to Indian cinema.

Rajinikanth has won a National Film Award, seven Tamil Nadu State Film Awards, and one Filmfare Award.

INDIAN FILM STUDIOS

Bombay Talkies

After early Indian experiments in silent film, Bombay Talkies, launched by Himansu Rai in 1934, spearheaded the growth of Indian cinema. Over the years, several classic genres emerged from Bollywood: the historical epic, notably *Mughal-e-Azam* (1960), *Sholay* (1975), *Pakeezah* (1972), and mythological movie *Jai Santoshi Maa* (1975).

Mehboob Studio

It is an Indian film and recording studio in Mumbai, founded in 1954 by director and producer Mehboob Khan and is most known for films like *Mother India* (1957), which won the Filmfare Awards for Best Film and Best Director. It is spread over 4.2 acres of land and includes five stages for film shooting.

Gemini Studio

This was an Indian film studio based in Madras, now Chennai. It was launched when S. S. Vasan, a businessman, bought Motion Picture Producers' Combines and renamed it. The studio re-opened under the name Gemini. The new facade had a statue of 'The Gemini Twins', blowing the bugle. Gemini Studio was the place where many artists and technicians made a name and found success in the South Indian Film industry.

New Theatres

This film studio was founded in Calcutta in 1931 by producer B. N. Sircar, recipient of Dadasaheb Phalke Award in 1970. Sircar built a processing laboratory and gathered a talented group to run the show. Under his guidance, New Theatres became a symbol of Bengali cinema's aesthetic quality and technical brilliance.

INDIAN FILM DIRECTORS

Satyajit Ray (1921–92)

Satyajit Ray was a Bengali motion-picture director, writer, and illustrator who brought the Indian cinema to world recognition with *Pather Panchali* (1955; The Song of the Road) and its two sequels, as the *Apu* trilogy. As a director, Ray was noted for his humanism, versatility, and detailed control over his films and their music. He was one of the greatest filmmakers of the twentieth century.

Some of Ray's finest films were based on novels or other works by Rabindranath Tagore, who was the principal creative influence on the director. His iconic works include *Charulata* (1964), *Teen Kanya* (1961), and *Ghare Baire* (1984).

Most of Ray's works focussed on the city of Calcutta (now Kolkata) and its people. *Mahanagar* (1963), *Pratidwandi* (1970), *Seemabaddha* (1971), and *Jana Aranya* (1975) are about middle-class people and their struggle to survive in a commercial, materialistic world and also look at Maoist-inspired violence, government repression, and mushrooming corruption.

Mrinal Sen (1923–2018)

Sen was an Indian filmmaker from Calcutta who explored the social and political realities of his city in his films. Several of his films of the 1960s, such as *Akash Kusum* (1965), showcased his attempt to move away from the boundaries of commercial cinema. *Bhuvan Shome* (1969) starred renowned Indian actor Utpal Dutt in an iconic role and Sen used cryptic humour amidst the stark background of an Indian village to depict the message. It was a landmark in Indian cinema for its unconventional treatment of the subject as well as characters depicted.

In his Calcutta trilogy *Interview* (1971), *Calcutta 71* (1972), and *Padatik* (1973), Sen studied the unrest and violence of the city under Naxalite movement. Middle-class morality is showcased in *Ek Din*

Pratidin (1979) and *Kharij* (1982). Sen directed several other renowned films.

Ritwik Ghatak (1925–76)

Ritwik Ghatak was a noted Indian film director, screenwriter, and playwright. His cinema is primarily remembered for its meticulous depiction of unjust social norms, harsh reality, Bengal's partition. He won the National Film Award 'Rajat Kamal Award' for Best Story in 1974 for *Jukti Takko Aar Gappo* and Best Director's Award from Bangladesh Cine Journalist's Association for *Titash Ekti Nadir Naam*. The Government of India honoured him with the Padma Shri for Arts in 1970.

INTERNATIONAL CINEMA

THE OSCARS

The Oscar is an Academy Award, presented annually by the Academy of Motion Picture Arts and Sciences located in Beverly Hills, California, U.S., to recognize achievements in the film industry.

The awards were first presented in 1929, and winners are presented with a gold-plated statuette commonly called Oscar.

Winners are chosen from the following 24 categories: Best Picture, Actor, Actress, Supporting Actor, Supporting Actress, Direction, Original Screenplay, Adapted Screenplay, Cinematography, Production Design, Editing, Original Score, Original Song, Costume Design, Make-up and Hairstyle, Sound Mixing, Sound Editing, Visual Effects, Foreign Language Film, Animated Feature Film, Live-Action Short, Documentary Feature, Actor, Actress, Supporting Actor, Supporting Actress, Directing, Original Screenplay, Adapted Screenplay, Cinematography, Production Design, Editing, Original Score, Original Song, Costume Design, Makeup And Hairstyling, Sound Mixing, Sound Editing, Visual Effects, Foreign-Language Film, Animated Feature Film, Animated Short, Live-Action Short, Documentary Feature, and Documentary Short.

Only members of the Academy of Motion Picture Arts and Sciences may nominate and vote for candidates for the award.

Several Indian individuals and films have received or been nominated for the Academy Awards (also known as the Oscars) in different categories.

As many as 20 Indians have been nominated and 10 have won Oscars, including in the scientific and technical category.

Bhanu Athaiya became the first Indian to win an Academy Award for designing the costumes for Richard Attenborough's *Gandhi* (1982).

Satyajit Ray was presented an Honorary Academy Award in 1992; he was the sole Indian to receive this honour.

Resul Pookutty and **A. R. Rahman** won the Academy Award for Best Sound Mixing and Best Original Score, respectively, for the 2008 British film *Slumdog Millionaire*. Rahman also was awarded for Best Original Song alongside lyricist Gulzar for the song 'Jai Ho' from the same film, becoming the first Indian to have won more than one Academy Award.

At the 95th Academy Awards, three Indian productions garnered nominations, with *RRR* winning for Best Original Song and *The Elephant Whisperers* taking home the award for Best Documentary Short Film. This marked a historic moment, as *RRR* became the first Indian feature film to win an Oscar, while *The Elephant Whisperers* was recognized as the first Indian documentary short film to achieve this honour.

NOVELS IN ENGLISH ADAPTED FOR THE SCREEN AND WHICH WON OSCARS

Gone with the Wind

The classic American romance starring Clark Gable and Vivien Leigh in their unforgettable performance as Rhett Butler and Scarlett O'Hara was adapted from Margaret Mitchell's only published novel with the same name. Not only was the book a success, winning Mitchell her 1937 Pulitzer Prize for Fiction, but the 1939 film adaptation became a resounding sensation, winning a record number of 10 Academy Awards in 1939, including Best Picture, Best Adapted Screenplay, and Best Director.

To Kill a Mockingbird

The globally renowned novel by Harper Lee was adapted into the 1962 Oscar-winning film adaptation of the same name by Robert Mulligan. Starring Gregory Peck as Atticus Finch and Mary Bedham as Scout, the book adaptation was favourably received by audiences, who enjoyed watching the Pulitzer-winning novel on screen enacted by the renowned actors. The film was a commercial and critical success, as it went on to win three Academy Awards in 1962, including Best Adapted Screenplay, Best Actor (Male), and Best Art Direction.

A Beautiful Mind

The 2001 Academy Award winner for Best Picture, *A Beautiful Mind*, was inspired by the 1998 Pulitzer-winning bestseller *A Beautiful Mind: The Life of Mathematical Genius and Nobel Laureate John Nash* by Sylvia Nasar. Starring Russell Crowe as the brilliant mathematician, the film received widespread acclaim for its sensitive portrayal of mental illness and Crowe's outstanding performance. *A Beautiful Mind* won a total of three Academy Awards in 2001, including Best Picture and Best Adapted Screenplay.

Schindler's List

Thomas Keneally's 1982 historical novel *Schindler's Ark*, based on Holocaust saviour Oskar Schindler, was adapted to Spielberg's award-winning 1993 historical drama film *Schindler's List*. Starring Liam

Neeson as the eponymous hero alongside Ben Kingsley and Ralph Fiennes, the film was globally acclaimed as one of the greatest films of all time and went on to dominate the 66th Academy Awards, winning seven awards including Best Picture, Best Adapted Screenplay, and Best Director.

Forrest Gump

Winston Groom's 1986 *Forrest Gump* is brought to life by Tom Hanks, with his convincing portrayal of the eponymous endearing young character as he navigates through his eventful life, the imaginative film adaptation adding to the novel's popularity after its release. The film went on to win five Academy Awards in 1995, including Best Picture, Best Adapted Screenplay, and Best Actor in a Leading Role, among others.

TRIVIA

Did you know these classics too were adapted for the screen?

- *Jane Eyre*
- *Les Miserables*
- *The Great Gatsby*
- *Wuthering Heights*
- *Anna Karenina*
- *The Importance of being Earnest*
- *Pride and Prejudice*
- *Moby Dick*
- *A Farewell to Arms*
- *For Whom the Bell Tolls*
- *Of Mice and Men*
- *War and Peace*
- *The Brothers Karamazov*
- *Crime and Punishment*
- *Oliver Twist*
- *East of Eden*
- *The Grapes of Wrath*
- *Cannery Row*
- *Treasure Island*
- *Lord of the Flies*
- *Howard's End*
- *All Quiet on the Western Front*
- *Gulliver's Travels*
- *A Christmas Carol*
- *David Copperfield*
- *Doctor Zhivago*
- *Far from the Madding Crowd*

13 Sports

Sports are organized physical activities that involve competition, skill, and physical effort. They can be individual or team-based, indoor or outdoor.

They are important to maintain the overall health of a being. Sports foster the spirit of teamwork and instil a sense of discipline, time management, and perseverance among the participants.

IMPORTANT INTERNATIONAL SPORTS EVENTS

OLYMPIC GAMES

- The Olympic Games are a major international multi-sport event in which athletes from all over the world participate.
- These are held every four years. Since 1994, the Olympic Games have alternated between the Summer and Winter editions every two years within each four-year Olympiad cycle.
- The Youth Olympic Games are for athletes who fall in the age group of 15–18 years.
- The first edition of the modern Olympic Games was held in Athens, Greece, in 1896. The first Winter edition was held in Chamonix, France, in 1924.
- The symbol of the Olympic games is the Olympic rings. These are five intertwined rings that represent five inhabited continents of the world–Europe, Asia, Oceania, Africa, and the Americas. The rings are blue, yellow, black, green, and red and are placed over a white flag. The Olympic flag was flown for the first time in the 1920 Summer Olympics held in Antwerp, Belgium.

- The official motto of the Olympic Games is 'Citius, Altius, Fortius', which means 'Faster, Higher, Stronger'.
- The Olympic flame is lit at Olympia, Greece, several months before the Olympic Games. During the Olympic torch relay, the flame is carried from Olympia to the place where the Olympic Games will be held. During the opening ceremony of the Olympic Games, the Olympic cauldron is lit and the flame continues to burn in the cauldron until it is extinguished at the closing ceremony. The Olympics flame was used for the first time in the 1928 Summer Olympics held in Amsterdam, Netherlands.
- The International Olympic Committee organizes the Olympic Games. It is a non-governmental sports organization headquartered in Lausanne, Switzerland. It funds the games and chooses the host city for the Olympics.

Paris 2024 (Games of the XXXIII Olympiad or 2024 Summer Olympics)

- The 2024 Summer Olympics were held in Paris, France, with the motto 'Ouvrons grand les Jeux' which means 'Games wide open'.
- These were held from 26 July to 11 August 2024, and saw a participation of 10,714 athletes in 32 sporting events.
- The sporting events were primarily held in Paris, along with the neighbouring cities of Saint-Denis, Le Bourget, Nanterre, Versailles, and Vaires-sur-Marne.
- The United States (126) won the maximum number of medals followed by China (91) and Japan (45) at second and third positions, respectively.

India at Paris 2024

- There were 117 athletes in the Indian contingent to compete in 16 sports disciplines. The contingent comprised 70 men and 47 women competing in 69 events for 95 medals.
- The 16 sports disciplines were archery, athletics, badminton, boxing, equestrian, golf, hockey, judo, rowing, sailing, shooting, swimming, table tennis, and tennis.
- Gagan Narang was appointed the chef de mission (head of mission) and Shiva Keshavan was his deputy.
- P. V. Sindhu and Sharath Kamal were the designated flag-bearers for the opening ceremony.
- Tennis star Rohan Bopanna, at 44, is the oldest athlete to represent India at Paris 2024, while swimmer Dhinidhi Desinghu, at 14, is the youngest competitor.
- Athletics was the largest contributor to the Indian contingent with 29 players. Javelin thrower Neeraj Chopra led the athletics team.
- Indian shooters secured a quota in every Olympic shooting category for the first time. India sent a 21-member shooting contingent, the biggest shooting team in India's Olympic history.
- Race walkers Priyanka Goswami and Akshdeep Singh were the first Indians to qualify for athletics events at Paris 2024.

Medals at Olympics 2024

- In total, India won six medals – one silver and five bronze medals.
- Manu Bhaker won the first medal for India at the Paris 2024 Olympics. She bagged a bronze and became the first Indian woman to win an Olympic shooting medal.
- Manu Bhaker and Sarabjot Singh won the bronze medal in a mixed team 10-m air pistol shooting. With this, Manu Bhaker became the first Indian to win two medals in a single edition of the Olympics.
- Swapnil Kusale won a bronze medal at the men's 50-m rifle three positions event.
- Indian men's hockey team won the bronze medal under the captaincy of Harmanpreet Singh. It defeated Spain to win this medal.
- Neeraj Chopra became the most successful individual Olympian after he won a silver medal in the javelin throw.
- Aman Sehrawat became India's youngest Olympic medalist by winning a bronze in wrestling.

Paralympics

- The Paralympics are international multisport events for athletes with disabilities. These are held almost immediately following the respective Olympic Games. They follow the same pattern as the Olympic Summer and Winter Paralympic Games.

These are governed by the International Paralympic Committee (IPC).

- IPC was founded in 1989 and is headquartered in Bonn, Germany.
- The first Paralympic Summer Games were held in the Summer Olympics in Seoul, South Korea, in 1988.

Paralympics 2024 (XVII Paralympic Games)

- The 2024 Paralympic Games were the 17th Summer Paralympic Games held from 28 August to 8 September 2024 in Paris, France.
- The motto was 'Ouvrons grand les Jeux', which means 'Games wide open'.
- China (221) won the maximum number of medals followed by Great Britain (124) and the United States (105).
- India won a total of 29 medals in its most successful Paralympic campaign ever. It finished at the 18th place in the overall medal tally. In total, India won 7 gold, 9 silver, and 13 bronze medals.

NAME OF THE ATHLETE	SPORTS	MEDALS
Harvinder Singh	Archery	Gold
Sumit Antil	Athletics	Gold
Dharambir	Athletics	Gold
Praveen Kumar	Athletics	Gold
Navdeep Singh	Athletics	Gold
Nitish Kumar	Badminton	Gold
Avani Lekhara	Shooting	Gold
Nishad Kumar	Athletics	Silver
Yogesh Kathunia	Athletics	Silver
Sachin Khilari	Athletics	Silver
Parnav Soorma	Athletics	Silver
Thulasimathi Murugesan	Badminton	Silver
Suhas Yathiraj	Badminton	Silver
Manish Narwal	Shooting	Silver
Rakesh Kumar and Sheetal Devi	Shooting	Bronze
Preethi Pal	Athletics	Bronze (2)
Deepthi Jeevanji	Athletics	Bronze
Mariyappan Thangavelu	Athletics	Bronze
Sundar Singh Gurjar	Athletics	Bronze
Hokato Hotozhe Sema	Athletics	Bronze
Simran	Athletics	Bronze
Manisha Ramadass	Badminton	Bronze
Nithya Sresivan	Badminton	Bronze
Kapil Parmar	Judo	Bronze
Mona Agarwal	Shooting	Bronze
Rubina Francis	Shooting	Bronze

COMMONWEALTH GAMES

- The Commonwealth Games (CWG) is an international multi-sport event that features athletes from the Commonwealth of Nations. The Commonwealth of Nations is an international association of 56 countries or member states, which are former territories of the British Empire from which it developed.
- These are held every four years and have undergone several name changes from the British Empire Games in 1930–50, the British Empire and Commonwealth Games in 1954–66, the British Commonwealth Games in 1970–74, and finally, the Commonwealth Games (since 1978).
- It features a range of sports, including athletics, table tennis, swimming, shooting, boxing, weightlifting, and netball, among others.
- They were held for the first time in 1930 in Hamilton, Canada. It saw 59 events with participation from 400 athletes from 11 countries. It had six sports: athletics, boxing, lawn bowls, rowing, swimming and diving, and wrestling.
- The Commonwealth Games Federation (CGF) manages the CWG and selects the host cities. The headquarters of CGF are in London, England.
- The 2022 CWG, officially known as the XXII CWG and commonly known as Birmingham 2022 were organized in Birmingham, England. Their motto was 'Games for Everyone'.

Commonwealth Youth Games

- These are international multi-sport events for athletes in the age group of 14–18 years.
- The first edition was held in Edinburgh, Scotland, in 2010. These are held in the year before the CWG are held.
- These are organized and managed by the CGF.

ASIAN GAMES (ASIAD)

- It is a multi-sport event that sees the participation of athletes from the continent of Asia. It is held every four years, and the first Asian Games were held in New Delhi in 1951.
- These are organized by the Olympic Council of Asia (OCA) and are considered the second largest multi-sport event after the Olympic Games. OCA is headquartered in Kuwait.
- The 2022 Asian Games were rescheduled to be held in September–October 2023 in Hangzhou, Zhejiang, China.

CRICKET WORLD CUP

International Cricket Council Men's Cricket World Cup

- It is the international cricketing championship of One Day International (ODI) cricket in which 50-over matches are played. It was organized for the first time in June 1975 in England.
- The World Cup is held every four years. India hosted the 2023 ODI World Cup. Australia won the 2023 edition by defeating India.

Women's Cricket World Cup

- It is the oldest and most prestigious international tournament of women's cricket. The first match in this tournament was held in 1973, in England.
- It is organized by International Cricket Council (ICC) and in this tournament, 50-over matches are played between the participating teams. Since 2005, the World Cup has been played every four years.

- Australia won the 2022 Women's World Cup. India will host the 2025 World Cup.

ICC Men's Twenty20 World Cup

- It is an international cricketing tournament in which there are 20-over matches between the participating teams.
- It is a biennial tournament organized by the ICC. India won the 2024 Men's Twenty20 (T20) World Cup.

ICC Champions Trophy

- It is a ODI tournament organized by the ICC and was held for the first time in the year 1988 in Bangladesh.
- It is also known as the 'Mini World Cup'.
- Pakistan won the 2017 ICC Champions Trophy after defeating India. The 2025 ICC Champions Trophy will be held in Pakistan.

FOOTBALL

FIFA (Fédération Internationale de Football Association) World Cup

- It is an international football tournament organized by **FIFA (Fédération Internationale de Football Association)** every four years. The World Cup sees the participation of 32 teams.
- The first FIFA World Cup was held in 1930 in Uruguay.
- FIFA is an international governing body of football and is headquartered in Zurich, Switzerland.
- Brazil has the maximum number of World Cup wins, making it the most successful team.
- Argentina won the 2022 FIFA World Cup. The 2026 FIFA World Cup will be hosted by Mexico, Canada, and the United States.
- The FIFA U-20 World Cup is an international football tournament for men under the age of 20 years. The inaugural tournament was hosted by Tunisia in 1977. Uruguay won the 2023 World Cup. The 2025 FIFA U-20 World Cup will be held in Chile.
- The FIFA U-17 World Cup is an annual international football tournament for men under the age of 17 years. Germany won the 2023 FIFA U-17 World Cup.

TENNIS

- Grand Slams are the four major prestigious international tennis championships and these are:

Australian Open (The Happy Slam)

- It is an annual tennis tournament held in Melbourne, Victoria, Australia.
- It is played on a hard court and features men's and women's singles, men's, women's, and mixed doubles, juniors' championships, and wheelchair, legends, and exhibition events.
- It was held for the first time in 2005.

French Open (Roland-Garros)

- It is an annual tennis tournament held in Paris, France. It is played on the clay court and is the only Grand Slam tournament to be played on this surface.
- It is played in five major categories; men's singles, women's singles, men's doubles, women's doubles, and mixed doubles.
- It was opened as an international tournament for the first time in 1925.

Wimbledon

- Wimbledon is the oldest and most prestigious tennis tournament in the world. In 1877, the championship was played for the first time.
- It is held on the grass court in London, United Kingdom. It has a strict all-white

dress code for competitors and royal patronage. It also has a tradition of consuming strawberries and cream.

- It is played in the following categories: men's singles, women's singles, men's doubles, women's doubles, mixed doubles, and junior and wheelchair events.

US Open

- It is an annual hardcourt tennis tournament held in Queens, New York. It is the fourth and final Grand Slam tournament.
- It was held for the first time in 1881.
- It consists of five primary championships: men's and women's singles, men's and women's doubles, and mixed doubles. The tournament also includes events for senior, junior, and wheelchair players.

IMPORTANT INDIAN SPORTS EVENTS

KHELO INDIA (NATIONAL PROGRAMME FOR DEVELOPMENT OF SPORTS)

- The government of India launched the Khelo India Programme in 2017–18 to revive and improve the sports culture in India at its grassroots level.
- It focusses on identifying and nurturing young sporting talent across various disciplines. Under this programme, the government aims to offer quality coaching, infrastructure, and financial support for the players to make them fit to represent India at various international tournaments.
- It has 12 verticals:
  1. Play field development
  2. Physical fitness of school going children
  3. State-level Khelo India centres
  4. Sports for peace and development
  5. Talent search and development
  6. Annual sports competitions
  7. Support to national/regional/state sports academies
  8. Promotion of sports among persons with disabilities
  9. Community coaching development
  10. Utilization and creation/ upgradation of sports infrastructure
  11. Sports for women
  12. Promotion of rural and indigenous/ tribal games
- The Khelo India Youth Games (KIYG) takes place annually in two categories: KIYG-U17 which focusses on athletes from schools below the age of 17 years. KIYG-21 focusses on the college students under the age of 21 years. All the athletes compete with each other in different sporting disciplines.
- The Khelo India University Games is for university-level athletes and provides them with opportunities to compete and develop.
- The Khelo India Winter Games specifically focusses on winter sports such as skiing, ice hockey, snow baseball, mountaineering, and snowboarding.
- As a part of the Khelo India Programme, the Ministry of Youth Affairs & Sports partnered with the states to create a world-class sporting infrastructure named Khelo India State Centre of Excellence.

- The government also provides scholarships to eligible athletes to help them prepare for international sporting events.

KIRTI (KHELO INDIA RISING TALENT IDENTIFICATION)

- KIRTI has been launched under the umbrella of the Khelo India mission. It is an athlete-focussed programme that will use Information Communication & Technology and Data Analytics to predict the sporting acumen of an aspiring athlete.
- A target of 20 lakhs annual assessment in FY 2024–25 has been set to identify the talent under this project.
- In this, a district will be treated as a unit of assessment where physical education teachers and experts will be hunting and identifying the talent.
- In the first phase, archery, athletics, boxing, football, hockey, kabaddi, kho-kho, volleyball, weightlifting, and wrestling have been identified as the 10 Khelo India disciplines.

INDIAN PREMIER LEAGUE (IPL)/TATA IPL

- IPL is an annual professional T20 cricket league in India. The Board of Control for Cricket in India (BCCI) founded it in 2008.
- As of 2024, it has 10 franchise teams: Chennai Super Kings, Delhi Capitals, Gujarat Titans, Kolkata Knight Riders, Lucknow Super Giants, Mumbai Indians, Punjab Kings, Rajasthan Royals, Royal Challengers Bengaluru, and Sunrisers Hyderabad.
- Both national and international cricketers participate in IPL, and they are selected through an auction.
- Orange cup is awarded to the highest run-scorer at the end of each season. A purple cap is awarded the highest wicket-taker at the end of each season.
- Kolkata Knight Riders won the 2024 IPL.

WOMEN'S PREMIER LEAGUE (WPL)/TATA WPL

- WPL is an annual professional T20 women's cricket league in India. Its first season was played in March 2023.
- As of 2024, there are five franchise teams: Delhi Capitals, Gujarat Giants, Mumbai Indians, Royal Challengers Bengaluru, and UP Warriorz.
- The Royal Challengers Bengaluru won the Tata WPL 2024.

INDIAN SUPER LEAGUE (ISL)

- ISL is the professional football league of men in India. IMG–Reliance, Star Sports, and the All India Football Federation (AIFF) launched ISL in 2013. However, the first season of ISL was kicked off in 2014.
- As of 2024, ISL has 13 clubs: Bengaluru, Chennaiyin, East Bengal, Goa, Hyderabad, Jamshedpur, Kerala Blasters, Mohammedan, Mohun Bagan SG, Mumbai City, NorthEast United, Odisha, and Punjab.
- Mohun Bagan SG won the 2023 ISL.

HOCKEY INDIA LEAGUE (HIL)/COAL INDIA HOCKEY LEAGUE

- It is a professional field hockey league organized by Hockey India (HI), the governing body for field hockey in India.
- It was formed in 2013 and the last tournament was held in 2017. It was stopped after the 2017 edition due to financial issues. However, it is expected to restart in 2024.
- It has six teams: Dabang Mumbai, Kalinga Lancers, Delhi Waveriders, Punjab Warriors, Uttar Pradesh Wizards, and Ranchi Rays.

PRO-KABADDI LEAGUE (PKL)

- PKL is a professional kabaddi league for Indian men. It was launched in 2015 and has made kabaddi popular throughout the world.
- It is an initiative by Mashal Sports Pvt. Ltd. and Disney Star. It has both national and international players who are selected through auctions.
- As of 2024, the teams of PKL are Bengal Warriors, Bengaluru Bulls, Dabang Delhi KC, Gujarat Giants, Haryana Steelers, Jaipur Pink Panthers, Patna Pirates, Puneri Paltan, Chennai Thalaivas, Telangana Titans, Mumbai Mavericks, and UP Yoddhas.
- Puneri Paltan won the 2023–24 Pro Kabaddi League.

NATIONAL SPORTS AWARDS

These awards recognize and honour the excellence and exemplary performances of sportsmen and women in their respective fields at national and international events. These are awarded annually by the Ministry of Youth Affairs and Sports.

MAJOR DHYAN CHAND KHEL RATNA AWARD

- It is the highest sporting honour in India. It was established in 1991–92 and is named after the hockey wizard, Major Dhyan Chand.
- The award comprises a medallion, certificate, and a cash prize. It is given to the sportsmen who have consistently performed outstandingly for four years.
- The first awardee of this award was Vishwanathan Anand, India's first world chess champion.
- Abhinav Bindra is the youngest player honoured with the Khel Ratna Award. He is a sports shooter and an Olympic gold medallist.
- Karnam Malleswari was the first Indian woman to receive the Khel Ratna. She is an Olympic bronze medal-winning weightlifter.

ARJUNA AWARD

- This is the second-highest sporting honour in India. It is named after Arjuna from the ancient Indian epic *Mahabharata*.
- The winners are awarded for their consistently good performance over four years.
- The winners will receive a statuette of Arjuna, a certificate, and a cash prize.
- This award was given for the first time in 1961. The first woman Arjuna Award winner was Anna Lumsden, a hockey player.

DRONACHARYA AWARD

- It is India's highest sporting honour for the coaches. Dronacharya was Arjuna's guru in the *Mahabharata*, and this award is named after him.

- It is awarded to individuals who coach sportsmen to win medals at international events.
- It was given for the first time in 1985 to three recipients: Bhalchandra Bhaskar Bhagwat (boxing), Om Prakash Bharadwaj (boxing), and O. M. Nambiar (athletics).
- Renu Kohli was the first woman coach to win the award in 2002.

MAJOR DHYAN CHAND AWARD FOR LIFETIME ACHIEVEMENT IN SPORTS & GAMES

- This is the lifetime achievement in sports conferred on the sportsmen who have had a significant career and also contributed towards promoting their sports during their lifetime.
- It was awarded for the first time in 2002 to three recipients: Shahuraj Birajdar (boxing), Ashok Diwan (hockey), and Aparna Ghosh (basketball).

MAULANA ABUL KALAM AZAD (MAKA) ROLLING TROPHY

- It is the oldest national award for the best-performing university or educational institution in sports.
- It is named in honour of India's first education minister Shri Abul Kalam Azad, who was also a freedom fighter.
- The reward comprises a rolling MAKA Trophy that gets passed on to the winner each year and a cash prize.
- The first recipient of this award was Bombay University for the year 1956–57.

RASHTRIYA KHEL PROTSAHAN PURASKAR

- This award rewards public and private organizations that have played an important role in the promotion and development of sports over the last three years.
- The award takes into account the following four segments: identification and nurturing of budding and young talent, encouragement of sports through corporate social responsibility, employment of sportspersons and sports welfare measures, and sports for development.
- The winners are honoured with a citation and a trophy.

IMPORTANT SPORTS

ARCHERY

- Archery involves shooting arrows to a specific target using a bow. Conventionally, it was practised as a means to hunt food. However, in modern times, it has evolved into a competitive sport.
- There are three types of bows used in archery: recurve, compound, and barebow.
- Archery can be categorized into the following: target, indoor, and field.
- In target archery, the archers shoot at stationary circular targets set at specific distances. There are five colour target zones: gold, red, blue, black, and white rings. The outermost zone has the lowest score and the innermost has the highest.
- In indoor archery, the archers shoot inside a building at stationary circular targets over approximately short distances of 18 m.
- The field archery happens around a natural terrain where the archers shoot at stationary circular targets of various sizes set at different distances, heights, and angles.

- The Archery Association of India is the national governing body of archery in India.
- Globally, the World Archery Federation is the governing body of archery.

Indian Archers

Deepika Kumari, Dola Banerjee, Rajat Chauhan, Jyothi Surekha Vennam, Rahul Banerjee, Limba Ram, Abhishek Verma, and Prathamesh Samadhan Jawkar

International Archers

Mike Schloesser (Netherlands), Darrell Pace (United States), Jozef Bosansky (Slovakia), Mathias Fullerton (Denmark), Nico Wiener (Austria), Ella Gibson (Great Britain), Sara Lopez (Colombia), Alexis Ruiz (United States), Tanja Gellenthien (Denmark), and Kim Soo-Nyung (South Korea)

ATHLETICS (TRACK AND FIELD)

- Athletics is a group of track and field events which involve various disciplines in running, walking, jumping, and throwing.
- The governing body of the world's athletics is World Athletics. It defines athletics in six disciplines: track and field, road running, race walking, cross-country running, mountain running, and trail running.
- Usain Bolt is a Jamaican sprinter and is known as the fastest man on Earth. He is an eight-time Olympic gold medalist and the world record holder in the 100, 200, and 4 × 100 m relay.
- P. T. Usha is a retired 'track and field Indian athlete'. She is also known as the 'Golden Girl' and 'Payyoli Express'. She has won four gold medals and seven silver medals in the Asian Games.

DISCIPLINE	EVENTS
Sprints	100, 200, 400 m
Middle/long	800, 1,500, 3,000, 5,000, 10,000 m steeplechase
Hurdles	100, 110, 400 m hurdles
Road running	Half marathon, marathon
Jumps	High jump, pole vault, long jump, triple jump
Throws	Shot put, discus throw, hammer throw, javelin throw
Combined events	Heptathlon, decathlon
Race walks	20-km, 35-km race walk
Relays	4 × 100 relay, 4 × 400 relay
Cross country	Cross country
Mountain running	Mountain running
Ultra running	Ultra running
Trail running	Trail running

BADMINTON

- Badminton is a racquet sport in which the racquets are used to hit a shuttlecock across the net. It involves two players (singles) and four players (doubles).
- The net is placed in the centre of the rectangular court which stands at a height of 1.55 m at the edges and 1.524 m at the centre.
- For singles match, the width of the court is 5.18 m but for doubles, it is 6.1 m. The full length of the court is 13.4 m.
- A shuttlecock is conical-shaped and has a base of cork with feathers or synthetic material making up for the rest. The rackets are lightweight and typically made of materials such as carbon fibre and solid steel.
- It was played for the first time in the Olympics in 1992.
- The governing body for badminton in India is the Badminton Association of India and at the international level it is Badminton World Federation (BWF).

NATIONAL			
NAME	**STATE**	**FACTS**	**AWARDS**
Prakash Padukone	Karnataka	• Ranked World No. 1 in 1980. • First Indian to win the All England Open Badminton Championships	• Arjuna Award • Padma Shri
Srikanth Kidambi	Andhra Pradesh	First Indian to reach the World Championship final in the men's singles discipline.	• Arjuna Award • Padma Shri
Satwiksairaj Rankireddy	Andhra Pradesh	• Fastest hit in badminton by a male player, with his smash reaching a speed of 565 km/h. • Rankireddy and Chirag Shetty are the only doubles pair from India to become World No. 1. • Rankireddy and Chirag Shetty are the first Indians to win a gold at the Asian Games in badminton.	• Arjuna Award • Major Dhyan Chand Khel Ratna
Chirag Shetty	Maharashtra	• Rankireddy and Chirag Shetty are the only doubles pair from India to become World No. 1. • Rankireddy and Chirag Shetty are the first Indians to win a gold at the Asian Games in badminton.	• Arjuna Award • Major Dhyan Chand Khel Ratna
Pullela Gopichand	Andhra Pradesh	• Chief National Coach for the India national badminton team. • Only Indian coach to win the 'Honorable Mention' by the International Olympic Committee at the 2019 Coaches Lifetime Achievement Awards.	• Arjuna Award • Major Dhyan Chand Khel Ratna • Padma Shri • Dronacharya Award • Padma Bhushan • Rashtriya Khel Protsahan Puruskar
Parupalli Kashyap	Telangana	First male player from India to reach the quarter-finals of men's singles at the 2012 London Olympics	Arjuna Award
P. V. Sindhu	Andhra Pradesh	• First and only Indian to become the badminton world champion. • First Indian woman to win consecutive Olympics medals.	• Arjuna Award • Padma Shri • Major Dhyan Chand Khel Ratna • Padma Bhushan
Ashwini Ponnappa	Karnataka	• First medal in doubles – women. • First gold medallist – mixed – team.	Arjuna Award
Jwala Gutta	Maharashtra	Played a total of 316 matches: maximum by any Indian in both mixed and women's doubles.	Arjuna Award

NATIONAL			
NAME	STATE	FACTS	AWARDS
Saina Nehwal	Telangana	• First Indian badminton player to have won an Olympic medal. • Only Indian to have won at least one medal in every BWF major individual event.	• Arjuna Award • Padma Shri • Major Dhyan Chand Khel Ratna • Padma Bhushan

Some of the international badminton players are as follows:

- *Male*: Shi Yuqi (P.R. China), Viktor Axelsen (Denmark), Jonatan Christie (Indonesia), Anders Antonsen (Denmark), Li Shifeng (P.R. China), Naraoka Kodai (Japan), Lee Zii Jia (Malaysia), Kunlavut Vitidsarn (Thailand), Anthony Sinisuka Ginting (Indonesia), and Nishimoto Kenta (Japan).
- *Female:* An Seyoung (Republic of Korea), Chen Yufei (P.R. China), Tai Tzu-Ying (Chinese Taipei), Carolina Marín (Spain), Yamaguchi Akane (Japan), Wang Zhiyi (P.R. China), Han Yue (P.R. China), He Bingjiao (P.R. China), Gregoria Mariska Tunjung (Indonesia), and Ohori Aya (Japan).

BOXING

- Boxing is a combat sport where two participants are involved in a contest of speed, reflexes, strength, and endurance. Both of them are wearing protective gloves.
- Participants use hand wraps, mouth guards, and headgear as protective gear.
- Boxing is performed in a square ring measuring 16–24 ft on each side. It is of two types: amateur and professional boxing.
- Boxing was included in the Olympics in 1904 and women's boxing was introduced in the Olympics 2012.
- Vijendra Singh became the first Indian boxer to win a bronze medal at the Olympics in the men's middleweight (75 kg) category.
- Mary Kom won the second Olympic medal (bronze) in the flyweight (51 kg) category.
- Lovlina Borgohain won the third Olympic medal (bronze) in the welterweight (69 kg) category.

FOOTBALL

- Football is also known as soccer in some countries. It is played between two teams of 11 players.
- It is played on a rectangular grass or artificial turf which is 100–110 m long and 64–75 m wide. The goalpost is located at both ends.
- The match is played for 90 minutes with two 45-minute halves. The football has a circumference of 68–70 cm.
- The equipment includes a jersey, shorts, socks, shin guards, and cleats. Goalkeepers also wear gloves for better grip and protection.
- Some of the important skills required while playing football are defending, goalkeeping, shooting, passing, and dribbling.
- FIFA governs the international football. The All India Football Federation (AIFF) is the governing body of football, futsal, and beach soccer in India.
- Sunil Chhetri is regarded as one of the best Indian footballers of all

time. Bhaichung Bhutia, also known as 'Sikkimese Sniper' is a former professional footballer in India.

- Some of the international footballers are Lionel Andrés Messi (Argentina), Cristiano Ronaldo (Portugal), and Neymar da Silva Santos Júnior (Brazil).

CRICKET

- Cricket is a bat-and-ball game played between two teams. Each team consists of 11 players, including batsmen, bowlers, and all-rounders.
- It is played in different formats: test cricket, ODI, T20, etc.
- Cricket is played on an oval or circular field. At its centre, there is a rectangular flat surface called *pitch* –3 m wide and 22 yards long. Both ends of the pitch have a wicket made up of three vertical stumps with two horizontal bails placed on their top.
- The protective gear includes pads, gloves, a helmet, and a box (protective cup) for batsmen and close-in fielders.
- The ICC is the governing body of international cricket and organizes the World Cup. It is headquartered in Dubai, United Arab Emirates.
- The BCCI is the governing body of cricket in India. It is headquartered in Mumbai, Maharashtra.
- Some of the renowned Indian cricketers are Sachin Tendulkar, M. S. Dhoni, Virat Kohli, Rohit Sharma, Hardik Pandya, Jaspreet Bumrah, and Surya Kumar Yadav.
- Some of the renowned international cricketers are Sir Don Bradman (Australia), Sir Garfield Sobers (West Indies), Shane Warne (Australia), Sir Viv Richards (West Indies), Steve Waugh (Australia), and Ricky Ponting (Australia).

FIELD HOCKEY (HOCKEY)

- Hockey is a team sport in which two teams play using a hockey stick and a hockey ball. Each team consists of 11 players – 10 field players and a goalkeeper. There are defenders, midfielders, and forwards.
- The matches are played on grass or artificial turf. The protective gear used in the games is shin guards, mouthguards, helmets, chest protectors, padded gloves, and leg guards.
- The pitch is a 91.4 m × 55 m rectangular field. There are goals at both ends of the field and each goal is 2.14 m high and 3.66 m wide. The shooting circle is 15 m baseline.
- The members of the 2024 Indian National Hockey team (Men) are P. R. Sreejesh, Krishan Bahadur Pathak, Harmanpreet Singh (vice captain), Gurinder Singh, Amit Rohidas, Surender Kumar, Jarmanpreet Singh, Rupinder Pal Singh, Manpreet Singh (captain), Vivek Sagar Prasad, Chinglensana Singh, Raj Kumar Pal, Dilpreet Singh, Hardik Singh, Ramandeep Singh, Lalit Kumar Upadhyay, Mandeep Singh, Shamsher Singh, Gursahibjit Singh, Kothajit Singh Kadangbam, Birendra Lakra, Nilakanta Sharma, Gurjant Singh, and S. V. Sunil.
- The members of the 2024 Indian National Hockey team (women) are Savita (captain), Bichu Devi Kharibam, Nikki Pradhan, Udita, Ishika Chaudhary, Gurjit Kaur, Vaishnavi Vitthal Phalke, P. Sushila Chanu, Nisha, Salima Tete, Monika, Neha, Sonika, Baljeet Kaur, Lalremsiami, Navneet Kaur (vice captain), Vandana Katariya, Sangita Kumari, Beauty Dungdung, Rani, Reena Khokhar, and Sharmila Devi.

- Major Dhyan Chand is one of the best hockey players in the world. He is widely known as 'the Wizard' and 'the magician'.
- Dhanraj Pillay is a former Indian field hockey player and former captain of the Indian hockey team.
- The International Hockey Federation (FIH) is the international governing body of field hockey and indoor field hockey. Hockey India governs and conducts activities for both men's and women's hockey in India.

KABADDI

- Kabaddi is a contact sport played between two teams of seven players each. This sport is believed to have originated in India.
- The playing area is a rectangular court, measuring 13 m × 10 m for men and 12 m × 8 m for women.
- The game requires agility, speed, and the ability to hold breath while chanting. It involves strategic thinking to tag defenders and avoid tackles.
- Amateur Kabaddi Federation of India regulates all forms of kabaddi, that is, national, indoor, beach, and circle style.

BASEBALL

- It is a bat-and-ball team sport played between two teams of nine players each.
- Each of the teams takes turns to either be the 'batting' team or the 'fielding' team. The batting team tries to hit the ball that the pitcher (from the other team) throws. If they hit it, they try to run around the bases. There are four bases: first, second, third, and home plate. These are arranged in diamond shape.
- The goal is to run around all the bases and get back to home plate to score a run. The fielding team tries to stop the player.
- Major League Baseball is the professional league of baseball in the United States and Canada.
- Some famous players are Ty Cobb, Walter Johnson, Hank Aaron, Roger Clemens, Barry Bonds, etc.

BASKETBALL

- It is a team sport in which two teams having five players each, play against each other. The teams have to score runs by shooting the ball through the opposing team's hoops.
- It is played on a rectangular court in which there are two hoops at the opposite ends. The hoop is placed at a 10 ft height from the ground and its diameter is 46 cm. The diameter of the basketball is 24 cm.
- A basketball game is divided into four quarters, each lasting 10–12 minutes.
- The National Basketball Association is the professional basketball league in the United States and Canada.
- Some famous players are Michael Jordan, Stephen Curry, Larry Bird, Kevin Durant, etc.

SWIMMING

- Swimming is a sport that involves individuals navigating and moving through water using different parts of their body. It can be an individual or team sport.
- Generally, competitive swimming is done in a swimming pool. However, there can be open water swimming as well in which swimmers swim through lakes, rivers, and seas oceans.
- The four major styles of swimming are freestyle (front crawl), breaststroke, backstroke, and butterfly.

- An Olympic-style pool is 50 m in length and 25 m in width. It has 8–10 lanes which are 2.5 m wide. It is typically 2 m deep.
- The basic equipment required by a swimmer is swimsuit, swim cap, goggles, swim fins, drag suit, hand paddles, kick board, pull buoy, ankle bands, and snorkel.
- World Aquatics is the international governing body for all water sports. It was formerly known as FINA (Fédération internationale de natation).
- The Swimming Federation of India is the national governing body for aquatic sports in India.
- Some famous Indian swimmers are S. Pradeep Kumar, Sharath Gayakwad, Nihar Ameen, Sandeep Sejwal, Virdhal Khade, Prasanta Karmakar, Srihari Nataraj, Shikha Tandon, Dhinidhi Desinghu, and Arati Saha.
- Some famous international swimmers are Michael Phelps, Mark Spitz, Aleksandr Popov, Pan Zhanle, Bobby Finke, Gretchen Walsh, Mollie O'Callaghan, Katie Ledecky, and Summer McIntosh.

CHESS

- Chess is a board game involving two players and is played on a chessboard with 64 squares. These squares are arranged in an 8 × 8 grid that alternates between light and dark colours.
- Each player controls 16 pieces: 1 king, 1 queen, 2 rooks, 2 knights, 2 bishops, and 8 pawns. All the pieces are arranged in two rows, where the pawns are arranged in the second row and the remaining ones are arranged in the first row.
- The game of chess involves check and checkmate. Of the two players, either of them has to attack the opponent. Check is when the king of the opponent is under immediate threat/attack. Checkmate happens when the king has no possible escape and the opponent checks it.
- The World Chess Federation (Fédération Internationale des Échecs [FIDE]) is the governing body of the World Chess Championship. Grandmaster is the highest achievable title by a chess player. It is awarded by FIDE and is held for a lifetime.
- Vishwanathan Anand was the first grandmaster from India. Koneru Humpy was the first Indian Indian woman to become a grandmaster. She is also the youngest woman to become the grandmaster in the world. Some other grandmasters are Vaishali Rameshbabu, P. Shyaamnikhil, Gukesh D., Aditya Samant, P. Karthikeyan, Rameshbabu Praggnanandhaa, Sayantan Das, Vignesh N. R., Aditya Mittal, and Divya Deshmukh.
- Some international grandmasters are Garry Kasparov, Magnus Carlsen, Ding Liren, Zhu Jiner, Olga Girya, and Aleksandra Goryachkina.

TENNIS

- Tennis is a racket sport in which two players (singles) or four players (doubles) players use the tennis racket to strike a ball across the net.
- The tennis court is rectangular. It measures 23.77 m in length, 8.23 m in width for singles matches and 10.97 m for doubles. The court is divided by 0.914 m wide net. The diameter of the ball should be 65.41–68.58 mm and the ball must weigh 56.0 and 59.4 gm.
- The modern tennis court was designed by Major Walter Clopton Wingfield.

- The International Tennis Federation is the world governing body of tennis.
- The All India Tennis Association is the governing body of tennis in India.

NATIONAL			
NAME	STATE	FACTS	AWARDS
Mahesh Bhupathi	Tamil Nadu	First Indian tennis player to win a Grand Slam.	Padma Shri
Leander Paes	Maharashtra	Record for the most doubles wins in the Davis Cup.	• Major Dhyan Chand Khel Ratna Award • Arjuna Award • Padma Shri • Padma Bhushan
Vijay Amritraj	Madras	Inducted into the International Tennis Hall of Fame in Newport, Rhode Island.	Padma Shri
Prajnesh Gunneswaran	Tamil Nadu	• Winner of 2 ATP titles. • Winner of 8 ITF titles in singles.	Arjuna Award
Sumit Nagal	Haryana	Sixth Indian player to win a junior Grand Slam title.	
Rohan Bopanna	Karnataka	• Oldest first-time No. 1 at the age of 43. • Partnership with Aisam-ul-Haq Qureshi of Pakistan, and both of them were known as IndoPak Express.	• Arjuna Award • Padma Shri
Sania Mirza	Telangana	Highest-ranked Indian female player ever.	• Arjuna Award • Padma Bhushan • Padma Shri
Ankita Raina	Maharashtra	Winner of 11 ITF singles titles.	Arjuna Award

INTERNATIONAL		
NAME	COUNTRY	FACTS
Novak Djokovic	Serbia	Ranked No. 1 for a record total of 428 weeks in a record 13 different years by the Association of Tennis Professionals (ATP), and finished as the year-end No. 1 a record eight times.
Roger Federer	Switzerland	Ranked world No. 1 in singles by the ATP for 310 weeks, including a record 237 consecutive weeks, and finished as the year-end No. 1 five times.
Rafael Nadal	Spain	Ranked world No. 1 in singles by the ATP for 209 weeks, and has finished as the year-end No. 1 five times.
Carlos Alcaraz Garfia	Spain	Youngest year-end No. 1 in ATP ranking history.
Martina Hingis	Switzerland	First Swiss player to win a major title and to attain a world No. 1 ranking.
Dinara Safina	Russia	
Victoria Azarenka	Belarus	

TABLE TENNIS

- Table tennis is a racket sport played by two or four players who hit a lightweight ball back and forth across a table using small rackets.
- A rectangular table of 2.74 m long, 1.525 m wide, and 76 cm high divided by a net. A polymer ball of 40 mm diameter is used. The racket is usually laminated and made of wood with rubber on either/both sides.
- It was included for the first time in the 1988 Olympics.
- The International Table Tennis Federation (ITTF) is the governing body of table tennis.
- The Table Tennis Federation of India is the governing body for table tennis in India.

NATIONAL PLAYERS			
NAME	STATE	FACTS	AWARDS
Manika Batra	Delhi	First Indian woman to bag a commonwealth table tennis individual gold medal in CWG 2018.	• Major Dhyan Chand Khel Ratna Award • Arjuna Award
Mouma Das	West Bengal		• Arjuna Award • Padma Shri
Sathiyan Gnanasekaran	Tamil Nadu	• First Indian paddler to sign a contract with Okayama Rivets for the Japanese T-league. • Won gold in the ITTF Challenge –Spanish Open, in Almeria (2017) in the men's singles category and created history by becoming the first Indian table tennis player ever to win two ITTF pro tour titles.	Arjuna Award

NAME	STATE	FACTS	AWARDS
Sharath Kamal	Tamil Nadu	First Indian table tennis player ever to become 10-time Senior National Champion.	• Arjuna Award • Padma Shri • Khel Ratna Award
Manav Thakkar	Gujarat	Holds the first position in ITTF World Under-21 Men Singles Rankings.	
Kamlesh Mehta	Maharashtra	• First Indian to receive Fair Play Trophy at the Commonwealth Championships in 1989. • National observer for table tennis.	Arjuna Award

INTERNATIONAL PLAYERS	
NAME	COUNTRY
Wang Chuqin	China
Hugi Calderano	Brazil
Felix Lebrun	France
Sun Yingsha	China
Chen Meng	China
Hina Hayta	Japan

WRESTLING

- Wrestling is a combat sport that involves grappling techniques such as throws, joint locks, pins, and other holds to overpower an opponent.
- The different types of wrestling are sumo, sambo, freestyle, folkstyle, Greco-Roman, joint-locks professional wrestling, etc.
- The World Wrestling Championships are organized by United World Wrestling.

NATIONAL WRESTLERS			
NAME	STATE	FACTS	AWARDS
Khashaba Dadasaheb Jadhav	Maharashtra	India's first individual Olympic medallist at the 1952 Helsinki Olympics.	Arjuna Award (posthumously)
Udey Chand	Haryana	First individual world championship medal winner.	First Arjuna Award
Sushil Kumar	Delhi	First and only Indian to win a gold medal at World Wrestling Championships.	• Arjuna Award, 2005 • Major Dhyan Chand Khel Ratna award • Padma Shri
Yogeshwar Dutt	Haryana	Bronze medal at 2012 Olympics	Major Dhyan Chand Khel Ratna Award

NAME	STATE	FACTS	AWARDS
Ravi Kumar Dahiya	Haryana	• Silver medal at 2020 Tokyo Olympics. • Gold medal at 2022 Commonwealth Games.	Major Dhyan Chand Khel Ratna Award
Aman Sehrawat	Haryana	Gold medal at the Asian Wrestling Championships.	
Sakshi Malik	Haryana	• First Indian woman's wrestler to win a medal at Olympic Games. • First Indian wrestler to feature in *Time* magazine's list of the 100 most influential people in the world.	• Padma Shri • Major Dhyan Chand Khel Ratna Award
Alka Tomar	Uttar Pradesh	First Indian woman to win a gold medal at the wrestling world championships.	Arjuna Award
Geeta Phogat	Haryana	First Indian woman to win a gold medal at the Commonwealth Games in 2010.	Arjuna Award
Babita Phogat	Haryana	Gold medal at the 2014 Commonwealth Games in Glasgow.	Dronacharya Award
Vinesh Phogat	Haryana	First Indian woman to win two medals at the World Wrestling Championships.	• Major Dhyan Chand Khel Ratna • Arjuna Award • Padma Shri
Ritu Phogat	Haryana	Gold medal at the 2016 Commonwealth Wrestling Championship.	
Antim Panghal	Haryana	India's first-ever U-20 world wrestling champion.	Arjuna Award
Anshu Malik	Haryana	First Indian wrestler to win a silver medal at the World Championships in the women's division.	Arjuna Award
Nisha Dahiya	Haryana	Silver medal at the 2023 Asian Wrestling Championships.	
Reetika Hooda	Haryana	Silver medal at the 2024 Wrestling Ranking Series.	

MALE INTERNATIONAL WRESTLERS	
NAME	COUNTRY
Aleksandr Karelin	Russia
Buvaisar Hamidovich Saitiev	Russia
Aleksandr Vasilyevich Medved	Soviet Union
Mavlet Alavdinovich Batirov	Russia
Mijain Lopez	Cuba
Roman Vlasov	Russia
Sharif Sharifov	Azerbaijan
Elbrus Tedeyev	Ukraine
Vladimir Khinchegashvili	Georgia
Kim Hyeon Woo	South Korea
Artur Aleksanyan	United States
FEMALE INTERNATIONAL WRESTLERS	
Patricia Anne Stratigeas	Canada
Mercedes Justine Kaestner-Varnado	United States
Amy Christine Dumas	United States
Mickie Laree James	United States
Alexis Cabrera	United States

14 National Insignia

NATIONAL EMBLEM

- The emblem is used on official documents, currency, and government properties to symbolize the authority of the Indian state.
- It is an adaptation of the Lion Capital of Ashoka from the ancient city of Sarnath, near Varanasi, Uttar Pradesh. It has four lions with one lion hidden from view. The four lions are standing back-to-back, symbolizing power, courage, pride, and confidence.
- The lions rest on a circular abacus that has four smaller animals. These are the guardians of the four directions: the lion of the north, the elephant of the east, the horse of the south, and the bull of the west. The abacus rests on a lotus in full bloom, exemplifying the fountainhead of life and creative inspiration.
- Below the emblem is a motto 'Satyameva Jayate', inscribed in Devanagari script, which means 'Truth Alone Triumphs'.

NATIONAL FLAG (TIRANGA)

- The national flag of India is a tricolour with three horizontal bands. The ratio of the width of the flag to its length is two to three.
- The topmost saffron colour symbolizes the strength and courage of the country. The middle white band represents peace and truth. The white band has a 24-spoke Ashoka Chakra adopted from the Sarnath Lion Capital. It is a navy-blue wheel representing law, dharma, and motion. The green colour symbolizes the fertility, growth, and auspiciousness of land.
- On 22 July 1947, it was adopted by the Constituent Assembly of India and it became India's official flag on 15 August 1947.

NATIONAL ANTHEM

- The national anthem of India is, Jana Gana Mana, and Rabindranath Tagore composed it.
- It was originally composed in Bangla and was adopted in its Hindi version by the Constituent Assembly as the National Anthem of India on 24 January 1950.
- The full version of the national anthem is

Jana-gana-mana-adhinayaka jaya he

Bharata-bhagya-vidhata

Punjaba-Sindhu-Gujarata-Maratha

Dravida-Utkala-Banga

Vindhya-Himachala-Yamuna-Ganga

uchchala-jaladhi-taranga

Tava Shubha name jage,
tava shubha asisa mage,

gahe tava jaya-gatha.

Jana-gana-mangala-dayaka jaya he

Bharata-bhagya-vidhata.

Jaya he, Jaya he, Jaya he,

jaya jaya jaya, jaya he.

Rabindranath Tagore

NATIONAL SONG

- The national song of India is 'Vande Mataram' and was composed in Sanskrit by Bankim Chandra Chatterjee. It was a part of Bankim Chandra's most famous novel *Anand Math* (1882).
- It was sung for the first time in the Indian National Congress's 1896 session.
- It was a source of inspiration to the people in their struggle for freedom.
- The song was adopted as the national song of India on 24 January 1950.

Postal stamp commemorating Bankim Chandra Chatterjee

NATIONAL ANIMAL

- The national animal of India is the royal Bengal tiger (*Panthera tigris*). It has a thick yellow coat of fur with dark stripes.
- It represents strength, agility, and enormous power. In 1973, the government of India started 'Project Tiger' to conserve its population.

NATIONAL BIRD

- The national bird of India is the Indian peafowl (*Pavo cristatus*)/peacocks.
- It is a colourful, swan-sized bird, with a fan-shaped crest of feathers.
- It has a white patch under the eye and a long and slender neck.

NATIONAL FLOWER

- The national flower of India is lotus *(Nelumbo nucifera)*. It is an aquatic plant with broad floating leaves and bright, fragrant flowers that grow only in shallow waters.
- It symbolizes purity, knowledge, and spirituality, rising unstained from the muddy waters.

NATIONAL TREE

- The national tree of India is the banyan tree (*Ficus benghalensis*).
- The tree represents stability, strength, and unity, as well as acts as a sheltering figure in Indian villages. It represents eternal life due to its seemingly ever-expanding branches.

NATIONAL FRUIT

- The national fruit of India is mango (*Mangifera indica*). It is also known as the 'king of fruits'.

NATIONAL AQUATIC ANIMAL

The national aquatic animal of India is the Ganges river dolphin (*Platanista gangetica*). It is primarily found in the Ganges and Brahmaputra rivers.

WORLD'S FIRSTS FROM INDIA – A SELECTED LIST

Category	Details
First tandoor ovens	Remnants of clay ovens or tandoors have been found at the sites of the Indus Valley Civilization, dating back to 2600 BCE
First drainage system	The Indus Valley Civilization had a sophisticated drainage system around 2600 BCE
First pappadams	As per scriptures of Hinduism, pappadams existed about 2500 years ago
First veterinary hospital	In the reign of Ashoka the Great (r. 268–232 BCE), the first veterinary hospital was established in India to work on the tenets of the *Shalihotra Samhita*, one of the earliest treatise on veterinary medicine
First listing of protected species	Ashoka is believed to have built a list of protected species as part of the legislation. The oldest such list is found in the Fifth Pillar Edict from 242 BCE, which was also probably a revised list
First stupas	The earliest stupas have existed in India from around fifth century BCE. The construction of Buddhist stupas began on a large scale during the reign of Ashoka
First to espouse 'money is everything' philosophy	The *Arthashastra*, composed between third century BCE and third century CE mentioned three pursuits of life – wealth, charity, and desire. It also emphasized that money was the way to achieve the other two pursuits as well
First laws against cruelty	The *Arthashastra* mentioned fines for people who inflicted pain on quadrupeds
First casinos	The idea of casinos was first mentioned in *Arthashastra*, where the operation was defined as being undertaken and supervised by the superintendent of gambling who was responsible for providing equipment and accommodation and could levy 5 per cent of the winnings as revenue

First social stratification based on 'caste'	*Manusmriti* dated back to the first to third century CE is a part of scriptures and *Dharmsastras* of Hinduism. It acknowledges and justifies the caste system that divides Hindus into four castes based on their 'Karma' and 'Dharma': Bhramins, Kshatriyas, Vaishyas, and Shudras. The caste system was legally abolished in 1950
First sex manual	The *Kama Sutra* set in the second to third century CE is believed to be the earliest sex manual in the world
First to give the atomic theory of time	The Jain sect of philosophers in Northern India conceptualized time as a string of countless
First general theory of quantum physics	The first general theory of quantum physics was applied to all material phenomena by Jain philosophers around 400–500 BCE
First practice of yoga	Believed to have originated around 400 CE, yoga was a spiritual Hindu practice to detangle the spirit from the entanglements of the lived human experience. Patanjali's *Yoga Sutras* is believed to be the first text on yoga
First to refine sugar	Sugar plantations was established by around 1000 BCE. Refinement of sugar is believed to have taken place during the Gupta Empire, although *Arthashastra* also contains the description of a sugar mill
First merry-go-round	Prince Bhoja of Malwa describes a rotating mechanical amusement ride called *Rathadota*
First parachute	The Indian text *Prabhavakacavita* mentions two brothers who jumped off a tall tower and landed safely with the help of two special 'umbrellas'
First ice cream	Dairy-based ice desserts were first developed by the Mughals in the 1500s
First kulfi	The Mughals were the ones to invent kulfi – a sweet dairy-based dessert prevalent in India
First rust-proof iron	The Iron Pillar at the Qutub Minar complex in Delhi was constructed around 400 CE. The pillar has since then stood in the open and has not shown any sign of rust

EDUCATION TIMELINE

EARLY PERIOD

- 5000 BCE – Gurukuls were the ancient traditional system of education
- 1500–600 BCE – The *Vedas* such as the *Rig Veda* are believed to be written. Early education involved teaching and learning the tenets taught in the *Vedas* and the *Upanishads*
- 600–200 BCE – The *Dharmasutras* and *Brahmanas* form the basis of teaching and learning
- 500 BCE – The *Upanishads* encouraged the teacher and the student to be explorers in the search of knowledge
- 2nd century BCE–3rd century CE – *Arthashastra* by Chanakya is placed in this era
- 2nd century BCE–2nd century CE – The *Charaka Samhita*, a compendium of Indian Ayurveda is believed to have been written. It formed the base for early medical education along with the *Sushruta Samhita* that covered more on medicine and surgery
- 6th–13th century CE – The Nalanda Mahavihara is established in the Gupta Empire
- 12th–13th century CE – Temple Schools were established such as the Nataraja Temple in Chidambaram
- 945 CE – Rashtrakuta dynasty established buildings with Royal patronage with arrangements for educators and scholars
- 1542 – Jesuits introduced India to European learning and the printing of books
- 1820s – Establishment of missionary schools
- 1835 – Madras Medical College is established; English Education Act is passed
- 1854 – The Wood's Despatch stipulated reforms in the education system
- 1857 – Earliest universities are set up

20TH CENTURY

- 1951 – First IIT is established
- 1961 – National Council for Education Research and Training (NCERT) is formed
- 1995 – Mid-day meal scheme is launched
- 1956 – University Grants Commission is set up under the UGC Act
- 1968 – First National Educational Policy is announced

21ST CENTURY

- 2001 – Sarva Shiksa Abhiyaan launched
- 2009 – Right to Education Act is passed; Rashtriya Madhyamik Shiksha Abhiyan is launched
- 2020 – New National Educational Policy is introduced

TRANSPORT TIMELINE

EARLY PERIOD

- 2300 BCE – The first tidal dock is believed to have been established at Lothal (present-day Gujarat)
- 16th century – The existing Grand Trunk Road is rebuilt by the Sur Empire, Mughal Empire, and the British Empire
- 1850s – The work on the Grand Trunk Road nears completion
- 1853 – First Railway line established and first railway service began
- 1873 – The first horse-drawn tramway operates in India

20TH CENTURY

- 1911 – Aviation begins in India
- 1932 – The civil aviation sector takes off in India
- 1934 – Indian Roads Congress is formulated
- 1942 – Department of War Transport is established to look after the demands of transport in war time
- 1943 – The first road development plan (the Nagpur Plan) is worked out
- 1972 – International Airports Authority of India (IAAI) is established
- 1986 – National Airport Authority is established; six national waterways are established by the Inland Waterways Authority of India; computerized ticketing and reservation services are introduced in Indian Railways at Delhi
- 1987 – The Bureau of National Civil Aviation Security is formed after the first tragic crash in India (Air India Flight 182)
- 1988 – The National Highways Authority of India (NHAI) is established under the NHAI Act
- 1999 – The Mountain Railways of India are designated as UNESCO World Heritage Site

21ST CENTURY

- 2004 – Chhatrapati Shivaji Maharaj Terminus is declared a UNESCO World Heritage Site
- 2009 – Ministry of Road Transport, Shipping and Highways is bifurcated into Ministry of Shipping and Ministry of Road Transport and Highways
- 2019 – The Vande Bharat Express is flagged off
- 2020 – Delhi metro's magenta line becomes completely driverless
- 2022 – First surety bond insurance for infrastructure products is launched
- 2023 – First dual-way elevated taxiway of the country inaugurated in Delhi

BUSINESS AND ECONOMY TIMELINE

EARLY PERIOD

- 500 BCE – The Mahajanapadas issue punch-marked silver coins
- 2nd century BCE–3rd century CE – The *Arthashastra* by Chanakya is written
- 1st millennium BCE – Silk Road trade in India
- 14th century CE – Maritime trade is carried out between South India and Southeast and West Asia
- 1640 – First mint is set up in India by the East India Company
- 1813 – The Charter Act of 1813 removed restrictions of international trade
- 1875 – First stock exchange established

20TH CENTURY

- 1947 – First union budget announced
- 1950 – Planning commission is set up to oversee planning, allocation of resources and implementation, and appraisal of the five-year plans
- 1950s–1991 – Nationalization of various companies across sectors
- 1955 – The Indian insurance sector is nationalized; LIC is established; the Essential Commodities Act is passed
- 1957 – Mundhra scandal, the first big financial scam of Independent India
- 1964 – Unit Trust of India (UTI) is established
- 1966 – Devaluation of the Indian rupee; the Amul 'Utterly Butterly' topical ad campaign begins
- 1969 – 14 private banks are nationalized
- 1981–82 – India borrows from the International Monetary Fund (IMF)
- 1988 – Securities and Exchange Board of India (SEBI) is established
- 1991 – Economic Liberalization announced by the then PM Narasimha Rao
- 1992 – Infamous securities scam takes place
- 1998 – Amartya Sen becomes the first Indian to win Nobel Prize in Economics

21ST CENTURY

- 2000 – Conception of Special Economic Zones
- 2016 – Demonetization of '500' and '1,000' notes is announced
- 2017 – Goods and Services Tax (GST) launched
- 2018 – Nirav Modi scam is brought to light
- 2019 – Abhijit Banerjee wins the Nobel Prize in Economics with wife Esther Duflo and American economist Michael Kremer

SCIENCE, TECHNOLOGY AND SPACE TIMELINE

EARLY PERIOD

- 900 BCE – Earliest Indian astronomical text, *Vedanga Jyotisa* is believed to have originated
- 800 BCE – The *Shulba Sutras* believed to be written by Baudhayana are from this time
- 6th–2nd century BCE – Earliest atomistic theory is brought forward by Kanada in the *Vaisheshika Sutra*
- 3rd–2nd century BCE – Pingala described the system of binary numbers in his book, *Chandahsastra*
- 5th century CE – Aryabhata uses trigonometric functions of sine and versine
- 15th century CE – The Kerala School of Astronomy and Mathematics worked on the expansion of trigonometric functions
- 448 CE – Inscriptions found from the Gupta Empire indicate the usage of decimals
- 598–668 CE – Bhramagupta was one of the first mathematicians to treat 'zero' as a number

20TH CENTURY

- 1930 – C. V. Raman wins the Nobel Prize in Physics
- 1954 – Homi J. Bhabha sets up Trombay, the atomic energy establishment
- 1963 – Vikram Sarabhai establishes the country's first rocket launching station at Thumba
- 1969 – Indian Space Research Organization (ISRO) is established
- 1972 – The Space Commission and Department of Space is set up
- 1974 – First nuclear test is conducted
- 1975 – First satellite, Aryabhata, is launched
- 1981 – Indian Antarctic Programme is kickstarted
- 1984 – First Indian man in space, Rakesh Sharma spends seven days in space as part of the Intercosmos programme
- 1988 – Centre for Cellular and Molecular Biology sets up DNA fingerprinting technology
- 1991 – PARAM, the first indigenous supercomputer is developed

21ST CENTURY

- 2009 – Venkatraman Ramakrishnan wins the Nobel Prize in Chemistry
- 2013 – Mars Orbiter Mission launched
- 2023 – Chandrayaan-3 lands near the lunar South Pole; Aditya L1 launched

CINEMA AND PHOTOGRAPHY TIMELINE

20TH CENTURY

- 1913 – First indigenous feature film, *Raja Harishchandra* is released
- 1918 – Indian Cinematograph Act 1918
- 1931 – The sound era begins with *Alam Ara*, the first talkie
- 1950s–60s – Touted as the 'Golden Era' of Indian Cinema, it saw the rise of actors such as Guru Dutt, Meena Kumari, and Dilip Kumar
- 1955 – *Pather Panchali*, part of the first film trilogy, releases
- 1961 – The Film Institute of India is established along with the Film Finance Commission
- 1964 – National Film Archives are formed
- 1970s – The era of the Bollywood 'Masala' movies which saw actors like Hema Malini, Dharmendra, and Rajesh Khanna among others; this also saw the rise of Amitabh Bachchan and the 'angry young man' persona; Yash Raj Films is incorporated
- 1970 – The term 'Bollywood' is coined for the Hindi-language cinema
- 1975 – *Sholay*, regarded as one of the most iconic films, releases
- 1979 – Dharma Productions is established by Yash Johar
- 1982 – Bhanu Athiya wins India's first oscar
- 1983 – *Jaane Bhi Do Yaaro*, a cult classic, directed by Kundan Shah is released
- 1986 – India becomes the largest producer of films
- 1987 – *Mr India*, a breakthrough sci-fi superhero film, releases
- 1990s – This era saw the rise of the three Khans – Shahrukh, Aamir, and Salman.
- 1995 – *Dilwale Dulhaniya Le Jayenge* releases and eventually becomes the longest-running film in Indian history

21ST CENTURY

- 2001 – *Dil Chahta Hai*, a modern classic, releases
- 2008 – *Ghajini* becomes the first Indian movie to gross ₹100 crore
- 2009 – *3 Idiots* becomes the first film to gross ₹200 crore
- 2014 – *PK* grosses ₹300 crore
- 2015 – *Bahubali* becomes the first film to gross ₹500 crore
- 2016 – *Dangal* crosses the ₹1,000 and eventually the ₹2,000 crore mark
- 2020 – Films begin to release on OTT platforms amid the COVID-19 pandemic
- 2023 – *Adipurush* with an estimated budget of ₹700 crore becomes the most expensive film produced

THE ARTS TIMELINE

EARLY PERIOD

- 9000–7000 BCE – Rock paintings at Bhimbetka capture the life of the ancient man
- 2500 BCE – Warli artform flourishes, showcasing the life of the people of the Warli tribe
- 2350–2000 BCE – The Pashhupati seal from Mohenjo daro depicts a possibly three-headed figure seated and surrounded by animals.
- 2300–1750 BCE – The Dancing Girl bronze statue is dated back to this period
- 322–185 BCE – The Pillars of Ashoka show distinct style of craft
- 500 BCE–500 CE – The *Natyashastra* is believed to belong to this period
- 500 BCE – Panini's grammar treatise in Sanskrit, *Ashtadhyayi* is attributed to this period
- 2nd century BCE – The temple art and rock paintings of the Indus Valley Civilization; Khadagiri Caves are one of the earliest examples of theatre architecture in India
- 1st century BCE – Bhasa, one of the earliest playwrights of India is believed to belong to this period
- 1st century CE – The sculptures and paintings brought about new artistic expressions
- 5th century CE – The Ajanta and Ellora Caves showcase the rock-cut art
- 14–15th century CE – Standardization of Carnatic music by Purandara Dasa
- 16th century – Miniature painting with heavy Persian influences flourishes; the Tanjore painting style emerges in the Thanjavur district of Tamil Nadu
- 1562 – Tansen, a famous musician and composer is believed to join Akbar's court around this time
- 1870s – Raja Ravi Varma's realistic artworks gain traction

20TH CENTURY

- 1913 – Rabindranath Tagore wins the Nobel Prize For Literature
- 1953 – Sangeet Natak Akademi established
- 1954 – Sahitya Akademi, Lalit Kala Akademi, National Gallery of Modern Art (New Delhi) established
- 1965 – The Jnanpith Award instituted
- 1966 – M. S. Subbulakshmi performs at the UN General Assembly
- 1972 – First book fair conducted in New Delhi
- 1975 – Gopal Sharman's *The Ramayana* showcased on Broadway and West End
- 1995 – Contemporary Indian paintings are auctioned abroad for the first time

MEDIA AND COMMUNICATIONS TIMELINE

EARLY PERIOD

- 321–297 BCE – Earliest evidence of a formalized postal service was evidenced in the reign of Chandragupta Maurya
- 1556 – First printing press comes to India
- 1780s – Print media begins in India
- 1846–1904 – Evidences of a regular postal system using bullocks
- 1852 – First stamp called the Scinde Dawk is released

20TH CENTURY

- 1921 – First amateur radio is licensed
- 1927 – Beginning of radio broadcasting
- 1931 – First pigeongram
- 1936 – All India Radio is established
- 1959 – Doordarshan is launched
- 1966 – Press Council of India is formed
- 1982 – Colour TVs are introduced
- 1986 – Mahanagar Telephone Nigam Limited (MTNL), is established
- 1987 – Ramanand Sagar's *Ramayan* launched on television
- 1990s – Emergence of satellite television
- 1993 – Experiments with privatizing radio broadcasting
- 1995 – First mobile call made between Jyoti Basu and Sukh Ram; Videsh Sanchar Nigam Limited (VSNL) becomes the first provider of internet services
- 1997 – Telecom Regulatory Authority of India (TRAI) is established

21ST CENTURY

- 2000 – Bharat Sanchar Nigam Limited (BSNL) is formed; arrival of cable internet; first net fax service begins
- 2003 – Private and direct-to-home (DTH) services begin in India
- 2005 – Orkut, a social media site launched in India
- 2010 – 3G spectrum is auctioned by the government
- 2012 – 4G services are offered
- 2013 – The last telegram is sent
- 2015 – Over-the-top (OTT) services gain popularity
- 2019 – Merger of MTNL and BSNL announced
- 2020 – India crosses 500 million internet users
- 2022 – 5G services launched

SPORTS TIMELINE

EARLY PERIOD

- 3rd millennium BCE – Dholavira, Gujarat shows traces of a stadium with terraced stands
- 4th century BCE – Origins of Kabaddi are attributed to this period
- 13th century – Indigenous forms of wrestling exist such as Malla-Yuddha which later developed into 'Dangals' and eventually modern-day wrestling in India
- 19th century – Snooker originates in India among the British Army officers stationed here; modern polo evolved from existing games such as *Kanjei-bazee* or *Pulu* that was played in Assam

20TH CENTURY

- 1900 – Norman Pritchard represents India in the Paris Olympics and wins two silver medals
- 1920 – India sends an official contingent to the 1920 Antwerp Olympics
- 1924 – The National Games of India are held for the first time
- 1927 – Indian Olympic association is formed
- 1928 – India wins its first gold medal at the Olympics (Hockey); the Board of Control for Cricket in India (BCCI) is formed
- 1934 – India makes its debut at the Commonwealth Games
- 1951 – The first ever Asian Games are held in New Delhi
- 1958 – Milkha Singh, the 'Flying Sikh' (Athletics) wins three gold medals at the Asian Games
- 1968 – India makes its debut at the Olympic Paralympic Games
- 1981 – India participates in the inaugural World Games
- 1983 – India wins its first Cricket World Cup under the captaincy of Kapil Dev
- 1984 – India participates in the South Asian Games
- 1986 – P. T. Usha (Athletics) wins four gold medals at the Asian Games

21ST CENTURY

- 2008 – Abhinav Bindra (Shooting) wins the first individual gold medal at the Olympics
- 2010 – India hosts the Commonwealth Games
- 2011 – India wins the Cricket World Cup under the captaincy of Mahendra Singh Dhoni
- 2019 – P. V. Sindhu becomes the first Badminton World Champion; Mary Kom becomes the first boxer in the world to win eight World Championship medals
- 2020 – Neeraj Chopra wins the first gold medal in Athletics at the Olympics; Motera Stadium, the largest in the world, is completed
- 2023 – India crossed the 100-medal mark at the Asian Games

IMAGE COPYRIGHT INFORMATION

All images used inside the book (except for the ones mentioned below) have been taken from Shutterstock.com.

The images/graphics used on page numbers 187, 308, 311, 325, 331, 337, 349, 637 have been designed using assets from Freepik.com.

Quick and Concise Series

Quick and Concise is a series of beginners guides to various subjects of enduring relevance - covering history, economics, literature, philosophy, mathematics, and the arts, among others. This easy-to-understand series strikes a balance between in-depth information and accessibility. An effortless read, quick and concise is a crisp compendium for readers.

QC makes learning addictive!

Chambers Fact Series

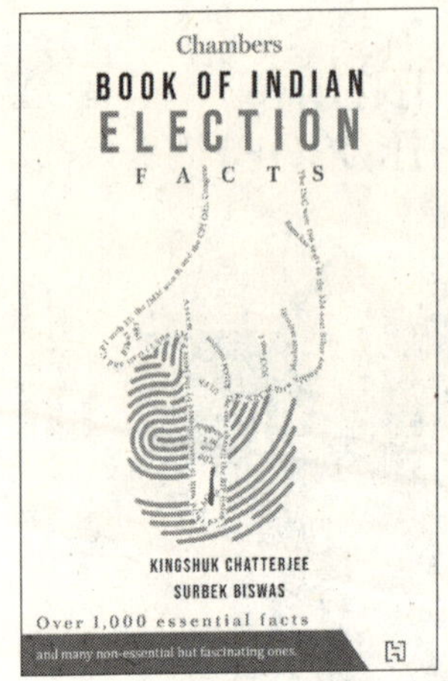

The series covers various subjects that are of professional, academic and general interest. These comprehensive factbooks provide essential facts along with fun-to-read trivia. First time ever here is a set of fact-based books that not only can be your dependable subject references but also are lively and often witty, enough to be your pleasure reading.

Chambers Facts - where facts breathe and even leap at you!

Chambers Dictionaries and Vocabulary

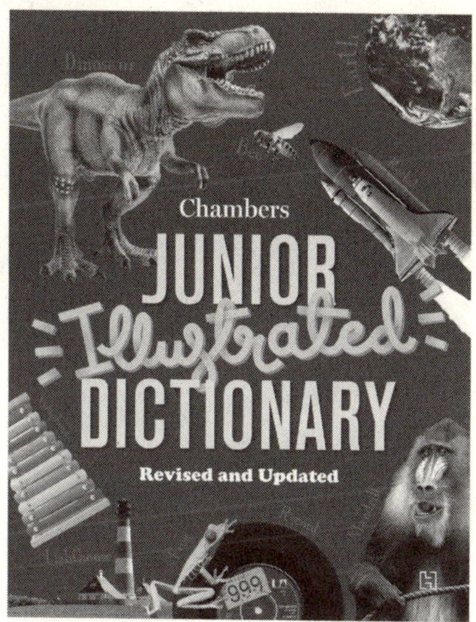